Maker Innovations Series

Jump start your path to discovery with the Apress Maker Innovations series! From the basics of electricity and components through to the most advanced options in robotics, Machine Learning, and even the metaverse, you'll forge a path to building ingenious hardware and controlling it with cutting-edge software. All while gaining new skills and experience with common toolsets you can take to new projects or even into a whole new career.

The Apress Maker Innovations series offers project-based learning with a strong foundation in theory and best practices. So you get hands-on experience while also learning the key concepts, terminology, and creative processes that professionals such as entrepreneurs, inventors, and engineers, use when developing and executing hardware projects. You can learn to design circuits, program AI, create IoT systems for your home or even city, or build immersive environments for the Metaverse. Each book provides the building blocks to bring your ideas to life, and so much more!

Whether you're a beginning hobbyist or a seasoned entrepreneur working out of your basement or garage, you'll scale up your skillset to become a hardware design and engineering pro. And often using low-cost and open-source software such as Raspberry Pi, Arduino, PIC microcontroller, and Robot Operating System (ROS). Programmers and software engineers will also find opportunities to expand their skills, as many projects use popular languages and operating systems like Python and Linux.

If you want to build a robot, set up a smart home, assemble a weather-ready meteorology system, create a brand-new circuit using breadboards and design software, or even build anything with LEGO, this series has all that and more! Written by creative and seasoned Makers, every book tackles both tested and leading-edge approaches and technologies, for bringing your visions and projects to life.

More information about this series at https://link.springer.com/bookseries/17311.

Practical PLC Programming for Beginners

A Hands-On Guide to Learning PLC Programming with CODESYS

Dariusz Wrebiak

Apress®

Practical PLC Programming for Beginners: A Hands-On Guide to Learning PLC Programming with CODESYS

Dariusz Wrebiak
Karlsruhe, Germany

ISBN-13 (pbk): 979-8-8688-2429-6   ISBN-13 (electronic): 979-8-8688-2430-2
https://doi.org/10.1007/979-8-8688-2430-2

Managing Director, Apress Media LLC: Welmoed Spahr
Acquisitions Editor: Miriam Haidara
Desk Editor: James Markham
Editorial Project Manager: Marina Engler

Cover designed by eStudioCalamar

Distributed to the book trade worldwide by Springer Science+Business Media New York, 1 New York Plaza, New York, NY 10004. Phone 1-800-SPRINGER, fax (201) 348-4505, e-mail orders-ny@ springer-sbm.com, or visit www.springeronline.com. Apress Media, LLC is a Delaware LLC and the sole member (owner) is Springer Science + Business Media Finance Inc (SSBM Finance Inc). SSBM Finance Inc is a **Delaware** corporation.

For information on translations, please e-mail booktranslations@springernature.com; for reprint, paperback, or audio rights, please e-mail bookpermissions@springernature.com.

Apress titles may be purchased in bulk for academic, corporate, or promotional use. eBook versions and licenses are also available for most titles. For more information, reference our Print and eBook Bulk Sales web page at http://www.apress.com/bulk-sales.

Any source code or other supplementary material referenced by the author in this book is available to readers on GitHub. For more detailed information, please visit https://www.apress. com/gp/services/source-code.

If disposing of this product, please recycle the paper

Dedicated to everyone who wants to understand industrial automation and PLC programming – this book is my contribution to you, from someone who has already walked this path.

Table of Contents

Chapter 9: Conveyor Control and Product Quality Assurance 371

Chapter 11: Practical Tips and Best Practices 515

About the Author

 **Dariusz Wrebiak** is an experienced industrial automation specialist with over 20 years of professional expertise spanning both the IT and OT industries. His career in PLC programming began in 2008, focusing on SIEMENS S7-300 and S7-400 controllers. Since then, he has specialized in PLC programming, automation system implementation, and industrial process control.

After more than 16 years of hands-on experience as a PLC programmer, working with SIEMENS (Simatic Manager, TIA Portal, PCS7), B&R, Rockwell Automation, and CODESYS platforms, he took on a new challenge by joining SIEMENS AG, contributing to the development of PLC firmware for the SIMATIC PCS neo system. Having begun his automation journey as a PLC programmer working with SIEMENS controllers, he now contributes to the development of the very PLC technology he once worked with as a user.

He was inspired to write this book based on his own journey as a self-taught PLC programmer. Over the years, he realized that many available materials focus heavily on theory but lack practical, step-by-step guidance. His goal is to bridge this gap by providing a comprehensive, real-world guide to PLC programming that helps both beginners and professionals master automation concepts effectively.

About the Technical Reviewer

 **Massimo Nardone** has more than 27 years of experience in security, web/mobile development, and cloud and IT architecture. His true IT passions are security and Android. He has been programming and teaching how to program with Android, Perl, PHP, Java, VB, Python, C/C++, and MySQL for more than 27 years. He holds a Master of Science degree in Computing Science from the University of Salerno, Italy. He has worked as chief information security officer (CISO), software engineer, chief security architect, security executive, and OT/IoT/IIoT security leader and architect for many years.

Acknowledgments

I would like to begin by expressing my deepest gratitude to my family for their patience, understanding, and unwavering support throughout the writing of this book. Much of this work was done in my free time, outside of work, during moments that would normally belong to them. Their encouragement and tolerance made it possible for me to stay focused and bring this project to completion.

I would also like to thank CODESYS GmbH for granting permission to use the CODESYS platform in this book. Their support made it possible to create a realistic, hands-on project and allowed this book to be based on tools and workflows used in real industrial automation. Without this approval, the practical foundation of this book would not have been possible.

Finally, I would like to thank the team at Apress for believing in this project and giving me the opportunity to turn an idea into a published book. I sincerely appreciate their professional guidance, structured editorial process, and assistance in refining and preparing the manuscript for publication.

Preface

At the outset, I would like to briefly describe why I decided to write this book. Upon assuming the position of *Head of Electrical and Software Engineering*, one of my responsibilities was to recruit new team members in our company. During the job interviews, I realized that young engineers, especially fresh graduates, did not fully understand what it means to work as a PLC programmer. Despite their well-developed academic knowledge, they lacked practical experience. While this may seem normal – to seek candidates with practical skills, you need to look for candidates with experience – it turned out that this approach was flawed. I had the opportunity to hire someone with five years of experience, but after two years, it became clear that this job was neither desirable nor performed successfully by the candidate. It is worth emphasizing that not everyone has the predisposition for this profession, despite all declarations regarding equality and equal opportunities.

The idea of writing this book arose two years after assuming the aforementioned position. My goal is to support young people who would like to find out what the job of a PLC programmer really entails. During conversations with other people, the question about my daily duties often arose. When I mentioned that I am a PLC programmer, I was often mistakenly associated with the IT industry. In reality, most of my work involves sitting in front of a computer and programming, which may lead to such conclusions, but this is just the tip of the iceberg. I often had to reject candidates in job interviews because they simply did not fit the position. In such situations, I always wondered what motivated them to apply.

I began to consider my beginnings in this job and recall how it all started. As a self-taught practitioner, I immediately started programming PLCs on projects under the guidance of my senior colleague at work, who introduced me to the world of PLC controllers. Together, we visited various facilities, started up installations, and completed projects. He was incredibly helpful, answered my questions, and constantly challenged me. His approach to the profession significantly shaped me because he was my authority and mentor in this field. His support and guidance played a crucial role in my professional development. Among the *Star Wars* fans in our company, due to this relationship, I began to be called his Padawan.

In the meantime, I turned to books, searched the internet, and participated in various thematic forums. Starting my journey with SIEMENS controllers, I naturally came across a forum for products of this manufacturer. However, during my career, I did not come across any book that presented a practical approach to this profession or even just programming. Although there are many publications on this topic, when I reached for subsequent titles describing the construction of PLC controllers or discussing input/output modules, practical guidelines on configuration and programming in a real engineering environment were often lacking. It was precisely this gap that prompted me to decide to write this book.

Throughout my career, I had the opportunity to cooperate with leading players in the industry, such as SIEMENS or Rockwell Automation, as well as with medium-sized companies, such as B&R or WAGO. However, I also gained significant experience working with smaller but dynamically developing manufacturers, including SABO. Initially, I considered uploading projects to real PLC hardware, but I concluded that this was not the main goal of this book. I want to focus on programming itself and introduce readers to what working with PLCs really entails. Additionally, using real hardware would increase costs and the risk of errors during application startup. I want to show what this job is about while minimizing financial outlays. My goal is to give young people, who are facing the choice of a career path, the opportunity to try and test whether working with PLCs meets their expectations.

Before starting to write this book, I had to decide which programming environment to choose. There are many different options on the market, but not all of them are free and easily accessible. In this context, I would like to thank CODESYS for granting me official permission to use their software to write this book. I chose this environment because of its freeness and functionality, which makes it a valuable tool. CODESYS does not financially support this project; this is my personal opinion, and I can recommend it with a clear conscience to both people learning PLC programming and professionals working in this field. It is also important to emphasize that all rights to CODESYS are owned by CODESYS GmbH, and their logo is protected by trademark law.

While writing this book, I will also refer to other programming environments such as TIA Portal (SIEMENS) or Automation Studio (B&R), but all programs and examples included in this book will be possible to compile in the CODESYS environment. I decided not to use real PLC hardware, which raises the question of how we will test our applications. The answer is simple: using a simulator, also provided by CODESYS. All tools can be downloaded free of charge from the CODESYS Store; under no circumstances should other sources be used. All steps leading through this process will be described in this book.

In summary, it should be noted that in the OT industry, there is an important fact: if you master one tool for programming PLCs, you can quickly learn to use other platforms. This is a key aspect that emphasizes the flexibility and versatility of this field. This is particularly important because the current job market clearly favors employees, and the lack of experts in this field is clearly noticeable. Therefore, I want to share with you the knowledge and experience gained over the past 16 years in this field. I invite you to this journey, which will take you from theory to practice and allow you to explore deeper the fascinating world of PLC programming.

Introduction

Learning PLC programming can seem overwhelming at first. Many available resources focus heavily on technical theory, leaving beginners unsure how to move from abstract concepts to practical implementation. This book was created to bridge that gap by offering a hands-on, project-based approach to learning PLC programming with CODESYS. My goal is to guide you step by step, helping you build real-world skills while working through practical examples that mirror what engineers encounter in industrial automation.

This book is intended for anyone interested in learning PLC programming, whether you are a high school or university student, a technician, or an aspiring engineer. No prior knowledge of PLCs or industrial automation is required. The only prerequisites are basic computer skills and familiarity with the Windows operating system. Even if you already have some experience, you may find the structured, hands-on approach useful for reinforcing core automation concepts and gaining confidence in applying them.

The book is organized around a continuous, project-based storyline. Each chapter builds on the previous one, gradually guiding you from basic concepts to more advanced automation tasks. You will start by understanding the fundamentals of PLCs, their role in industrial systems, and how they interact with the physical world. From there, you will implement digital and analog control, create visualization interfaces, manage process sequences, and integrate quality assurance checks into an automated production line. By working through these projects, you will understand PLC programming and industrial automation workflows.

Throughout the book, emphasis is placed on practical learning. Every example and project is designed to be hands-on, allowing you to experiment, simulate, and test your solutions. The exercises are built around the CODESYS platform, using Ladder Logic (LAD), Function Block Diagram (FBD), and Sequential Function Chart (SFC) languages to provide a realistic and industry-relevant experience.

By the end of this book, you will have acquired both the theoretical knowledge and practical skills necessary to program PLC controllers. You will be able to design, implement, and troubleshoot automated systems, and you will gain insight into real-world industrial automation practices. My hope is that this book not only teaches you the technical skills but also inspires you to explore, experiment, and continue learning in the exciting field of industrial automation.

CHAPTER 1

Initiating Your Journey

Our journey in exploring the world of PLC controllers will begin with setting up an engineering station where we will create our PLC programs. The first step will be to download the CODESYS environment from the CODESYS Store. To do this, it will be necessary to create an account on the CODESYS Store. Registration is free, and I will guide you through the process step by step. I would like to emphasize once again, as I mentioned in the foreword, that the CODESYS Store is the only place from which the installation file should be downloaded.

Downloading the CODESYS Environment from the CODESYS Store

We go to the *store.codesys.com* page through a web browser. Upon reaching the main CODESYS Store page, pay attention to two download options: *"Download 32 Bit"* and *"Download 64 Bit"*. Choose the appropriate option according to your computer's operating system. For example, if you are using a 64-bit version of Windows 10,

click the *"Download 64 Bit"* button (Figure 1-1).

© Dariusz Wrebiak 2026
D. Wrebiak, *Practical PLC Programming for Beginners*, Maker Innovations Series,
https://doi.org/10.1007/979-8-8688-2430-2_1

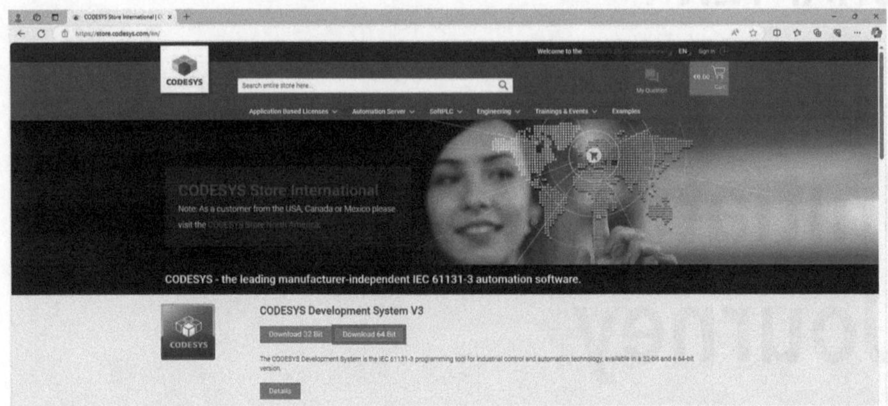

Figure 1-1. *View of the CODESYS Store page, with the "Download 64 Bit" button*

Upon clicking, a window will appear with the option to create a new account or log in to the CODESYS Store. Assuming not all readers of this book have a company account in the CODESYS Store, I will also create an individual account during the writing of this book and describe the process. Click the *"Create Account"* button (Figure 1-2).

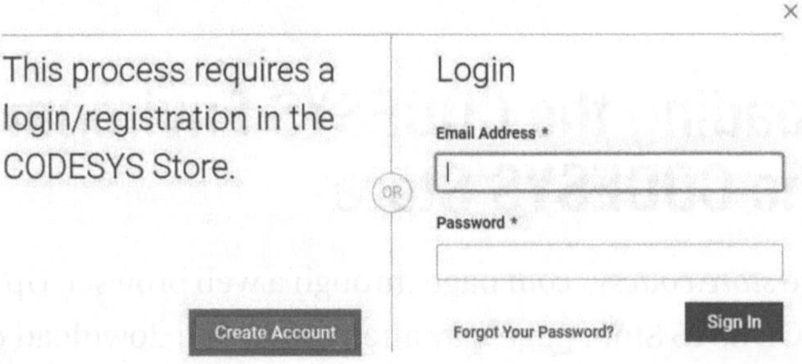

Figure 1-2. *Registration or login window for the CODESYS Store*

As mentioned earlier, we have the option to create two types of accounts in the CODESYS Store: a company account and an individual account. In the case of this book, an individual account provides all the necessary features to continue our journey into the world of PLC controllers. So, click the *"Create Individual Customer Account"* button (Figure 1-3).

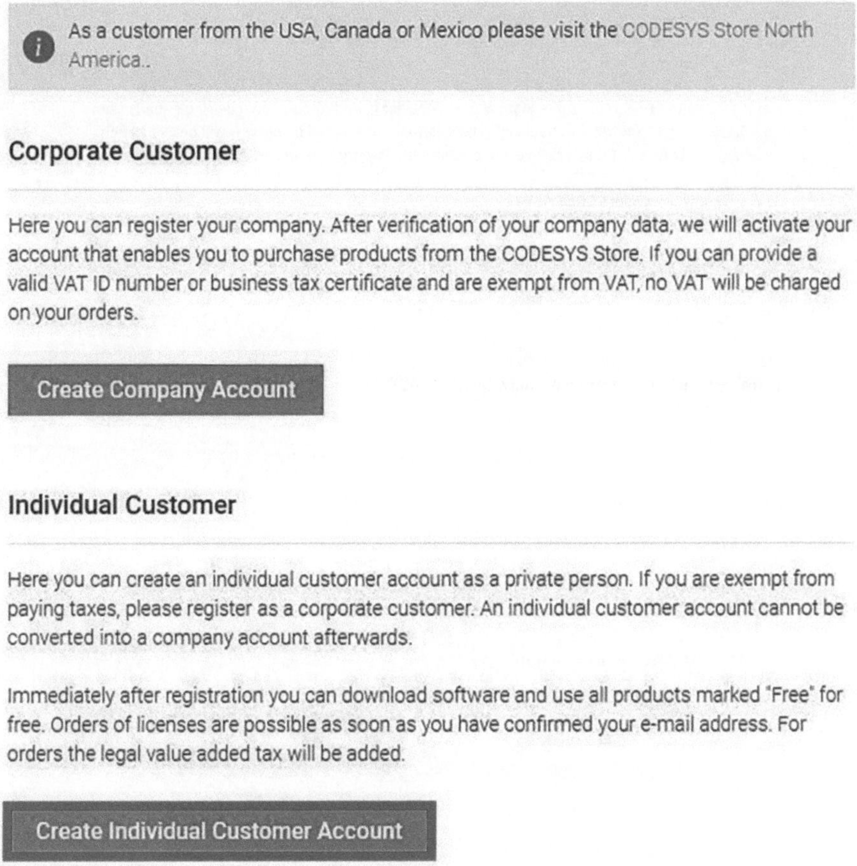

As a customer from the USA, Canada or Mexico please visit the CODESYS Store North America..
Corporate Customer
Here you can register your company. After verification of your company data, we will activate your account that enables you to purchase products from the CODESYS Store. If you can provide a valid VAT ID number or business tax certificate and are exempt from VAT, no VAT will be charged on your orders.
Create Company Account
Individual Customer
Here you can create an individual customer account as a private person. If you are exempt from paying taxes, please register as a corporate customer. An individual customer account cannot be converted into a company account afterwards.
Immediately after registration you can download software and use all products marked "Free" for free. Orders of licenses are possible as soon as you have confirmed your e-mail address. For orders the legal value added tax will be added.
Create Individual Customer Account

Figure 1-3. *Selection of account type (company or individual) during the registration process in the CODESYS Store*

The next step is to fill out the registration form. It is not necessary to fill in all the fields; just fill in those marked with a red asterisk. After filling in the required fields, click the *"Create Individual Customer Account"* button at the bottom of the form (Figure 1-4).

Create New Customer Account
Personal Information

Salutation   First Name *   Last Name *   Title

☐ CODESYS Newsletter
Yes, I would like to be informed by e-mail about new products and product updates as well as
events related to CODESYS. I agree that my user behavior is evaluated when receiving e-mails from
the CODESYS Group (newsletter tracking). The information obtained in this way will be used when
designing future newsletters exclusively to optimize the information offered to me.

Do you already work with CODESYS V3?

Do you already work with CODESYS V2.3?

If "Yes": From which company have you acquired CODESYS?

Address Information

Company

Phone number (Required for shipment) *

Street *

Figure 1-4. *Registration form in the CODESYS Store*

If everything went smoothly, an email will be sent to the email address
provided in the registration form with a link to confirm your email address.
Simply click the *"Confirm Your Account"* button. After completing this step,
you will receive another email confirming the successful registration in the
CODESYS Store.

Next, go back to the *store.codesys.com* page, and click the *"Download 64 Bit"* button again. This time, in the login window, enter the email address and password you entered in the registration form, then click the *"Sign In"* button. If you have successfully logged in to the CODESYS Store, click the *"Download 64 Bit"* button again.

After completing these steps, the *"License Agreement"* window will appear, which we accept by clicking the *"Accept"* button (Figure 1-5).

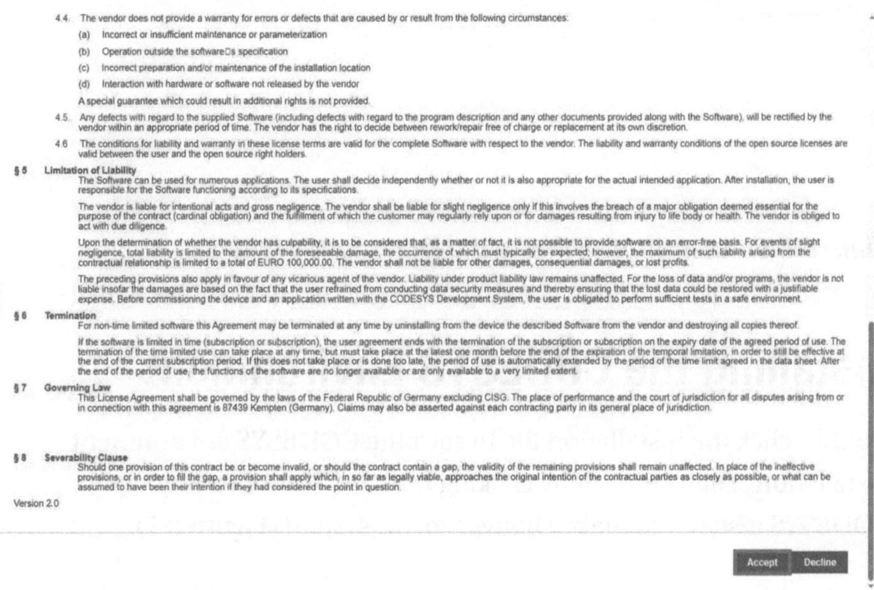

4.4.   The vendor does not provide a warranty for errors or defects that are caused by or result from the following circumstances:

(a)   Incorrect or insufficient maintenance or parameterization

(b)   Operation outside the software□s specification

(c)   Incorrect preparation and/or maintenance of the installation location

(d)   Interaction with hardware or software not released by the vendor

A special guarantee which could result in additional rights is not provided.

4.5.   Any defects with regard to the supplied Software (including defects with regard to the program description and any other documents provided along with the Software), will be rectified by the vendor within an appropriate period of time. The vendor has the right to decide between rework/repair free of charge or replacement at its own discretion.

4.6   The conditions for liability and warranty in these license terms are valid for the complete Software with respect to the vendor. The liability and warranty conditions of the open source licenses are valid between the user and the open source right holders.

§ 5   **Limitation of Liability**

The Software can be used for numerous applications. The user shall decide independently whether or not it is also appropriate for the actual intended application. After installation, the user is responsible for the Software functioning according to its specifications.

The vendor is liable for intentional acts and gross negligence. The vendor shall be liable for slight negligence only if this involves the breach of a major obligation deemed essential for the purpose of the contract (cardinal obligation) and the fulfilment of which the customer may regularly rely upon or for damages resulting from injury to life body or health. The vendor is obliged to act with due diligence.

Upon the determination of whether the vendor has culpability, it is to be considered that, as a matter of fact, it is not possible to provide software on an error-free basis. For events of slight negligence, total liability is limited to the amount of the foreseeable damage, the occurrence of which must typically be expected; however, the maximum of such liability arising from the contractual relationship is limited to a total of EURO 100,000.00. The vendor shall not be liable for other damages, consequential damages, or lost profits.

The preceding provisions also apply in favour of any vicarious agent of the vendor. Liability under product liability law remains unaffected. For the loss of data and/or programs, the vendor is not liable insofar the damages are based on the fact that the user refrained from conducting data security measures and thereby ensuring that the lost data could be restored with a justifiable expense. Before commissioning the device and an application written with the CODESYS Development System, the user is obligated to perform sufficient tests in a safe environment.

§ 6   **Termination**

For non-time limited software this Agreement may be terminated at any time by uninstalling from the device the described Software from the vendor and destroying all copies thereof.

If the software is limited in time (subscription or subscription), the user agreement ends with the termination of the subscription or subscription on the expiry date of the agreed period of use. The termination of the time limited use can take place at any time, but must take place at the latest one month before the end of the expiration of the temporal limitation, in order to still be effective at the end of the current subscription period. If this does not take place or is done too late, the period of use is automatically extended by the period of the time limit agreed in the data sheet. After the end of the period of use, the functions of the software are no longer available or are only available to a very limited extent.

§ 7   **Governing Law**

This License Agreement shall be governed by the laws of the Federal Republic of Germany excluding CISG. The place of performance and the court of jurisdiction for all disputes arising from or in connection with this agreement is 87439 Kempten (Germany). Claims may also be asserted against each contracting party in its general place of jurisdiction.

§ 8   **Severability Clause**

Should one provision of this contract be or become invalid, or should the contract contain a gap, the validity of the remaining provisions shall remain unaffected. In place of the ineffective provisions, or in order to fill the gap, a provision shall apply which, in so far as legally viable, approaches the original intention of the contractual parties as closely as possible, or what can be assumed to have been their intention if they had considered the point in question.

Version 2.0

Figure 1-5. *Window with the "License Agreement", with the "Accept" button*

At this point, we will start downloading the CODESYS installation file. At the time of writing, this is the latest version, released just a few days ago, namely, version V3.5 + Service Pack 20. After the download is complete, close your browser and go to the *"Downloads"* folder on your hard drive, where you should find the *"CODESYS 64 3.5.20.0.exe"* file (Figure 1-6).

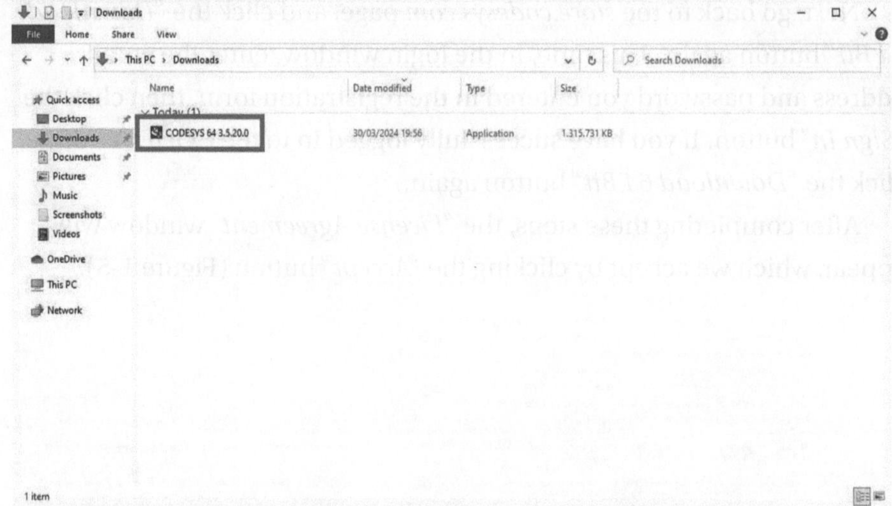

Figure 1-6. *Installation file in the Downloads folder*

Installing the CODESYS Environment

Double-click the installation file to start the CODESYS environment
installation. Then confirm by clicking the *"Yes"* button, allowing the
CODESYS installer to make changes to our system (Figure 1-7).

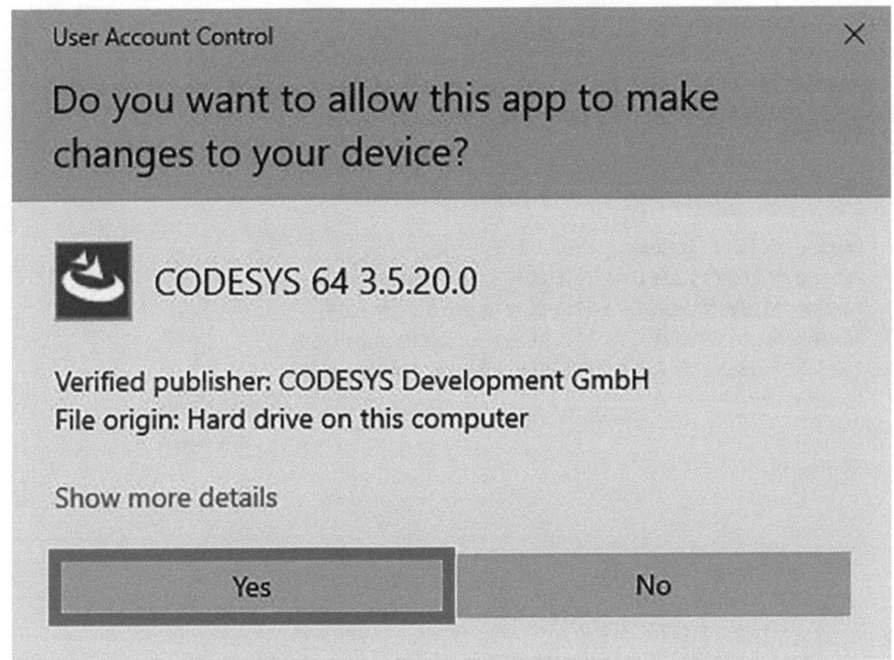

Figure 1-7. *CODESYS environment installation process, with the "Yes" button to confirm system changes*

In the next step, click the *"Install"* button to install the necessary tools needed for CODESYS to function properly (Figure 1-8).

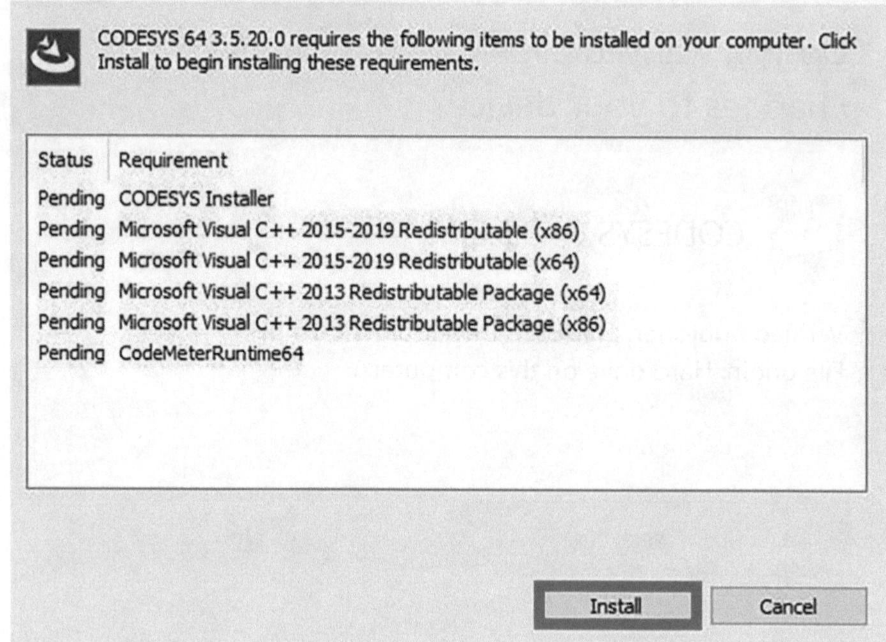

Figure 1-8. *Additional tools installation screen, with the "Install" button highlighted to continue the installation process*

After successfully installing the necessary components, the CODESYS environment installation process will begin (Figure 1-9).

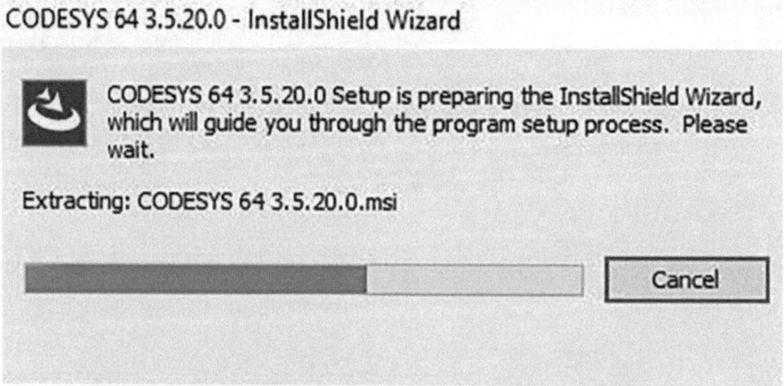

Figure 1-9. *CODESYS environment installation process*

Next, click the *"Next"* button to proceed to the next installation step (Figure 1-10).

Figure 1-10. *CODESYS environment installation process, with the "Next" button highlighted to proceed to the next step*

Then we must agree to the license terms. Click the *"I accept the terms in the license agreement"* radio button, and click the *"Next"* button to proceed to the next step (Figure 1-11).

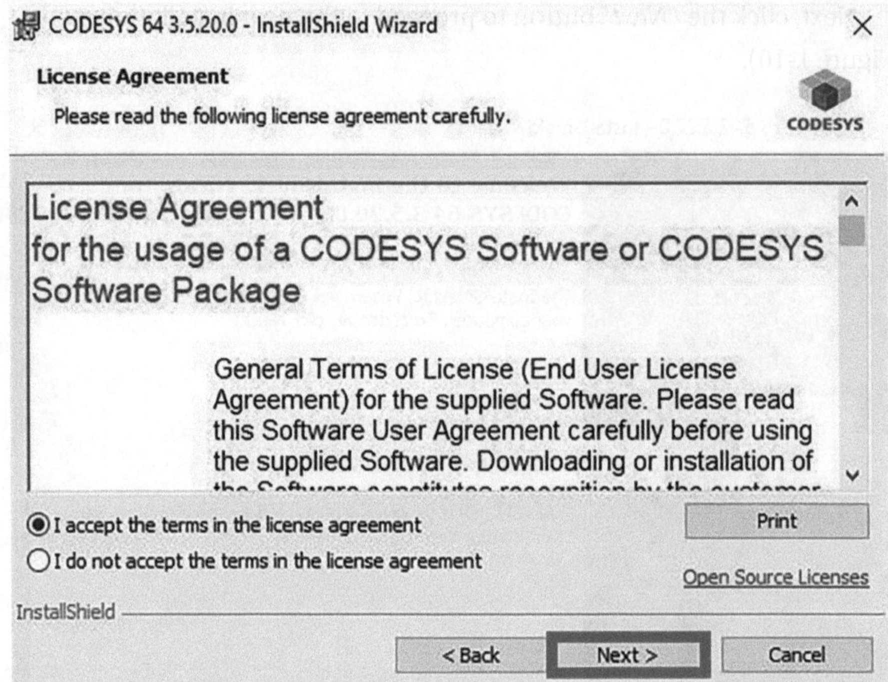

Figure 1-11. *CODESYS license agreement acceptance window*

In the next step, click the *"I have read the information"* radio button, indicating that we have read the information about the *"Release Notes"*, and then click the *"Next"* button to proceed to the next step (Figure 1-12).

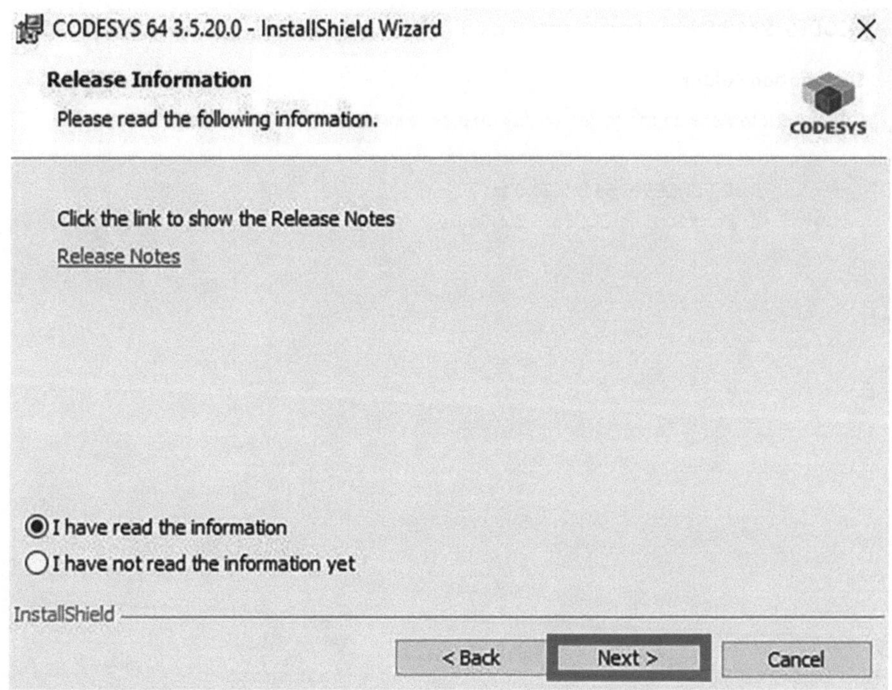

Figure 1-12. *Confirmation window after reviewing the "Release Notes", with the "Next" button highlighted*

In the next step, you can choose the destination folder where CODESYS will be installed. I left the default folder and did not change these settings. I simply clicked the *"Next"* button (Figure 1-13).

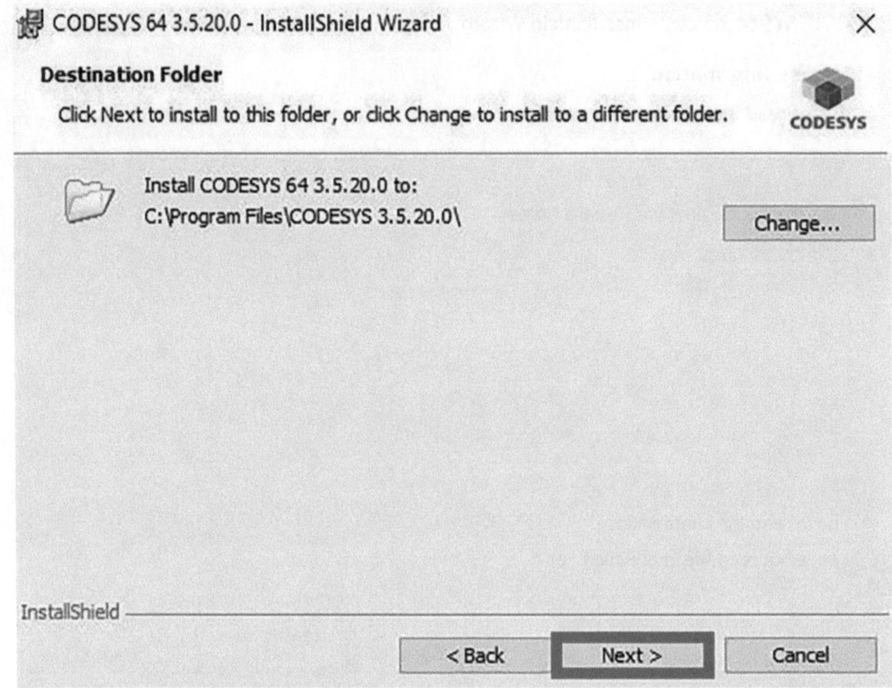

Figure 1-13. *Selection of the target installation folder for CODESYS*

Next, you have the option to choose the type of installation: *"Complete"* or *"Custom"*. In this case, I opted for a complete installation by clicking the *"Next"* button (Figure 1-14).

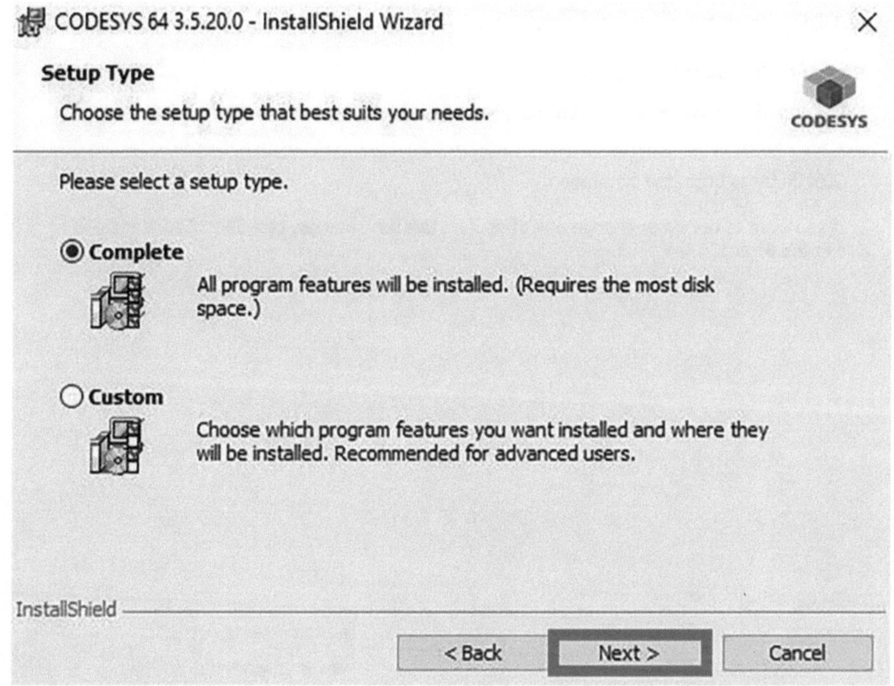

Figure 1-14. *Selection of installation type (complete or custom) for CODESYS*

After configuring the installation, click the *"Install"* button to install CODESYS according to our settings (Figure 1-15).

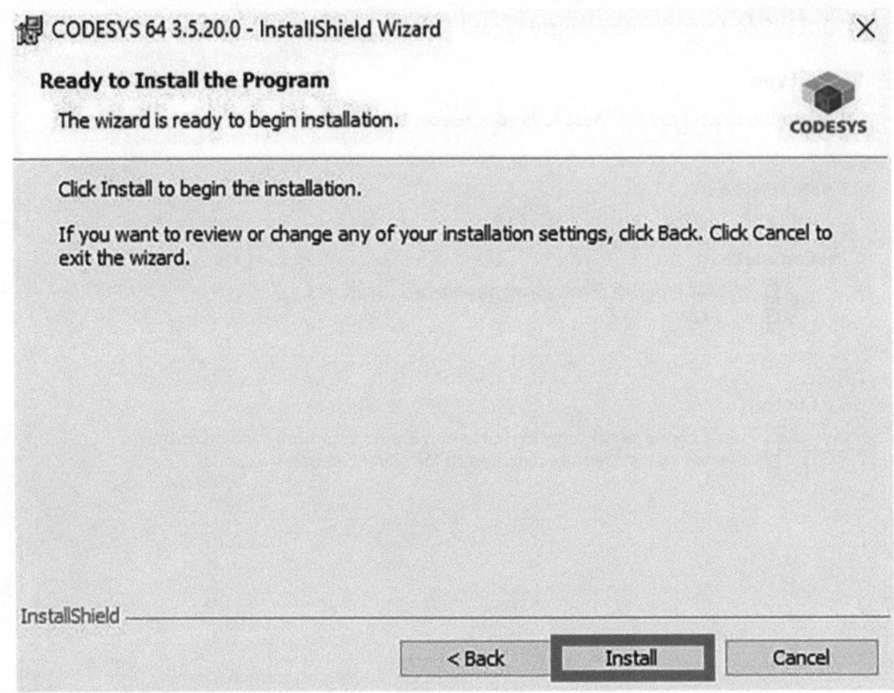

Figure 1-15. *Confirmation of CODESYS installation configuration*

At this point, the CODESYS installation will begin, so a little patience will be needed (Figure 1-16).

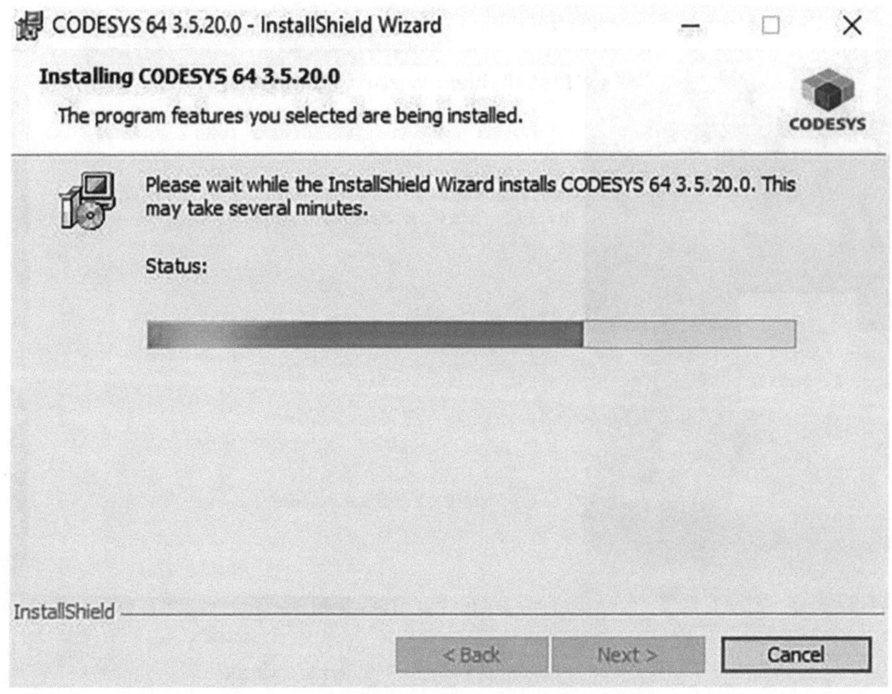

Figure 1-16. *CODESYS installation process screen, showing installation progress information*

After the installation is complete, click the *"Finish"* button to complete the process (Figure 1-17).

Figure 1-17. *Finish of the CODESYS installation process*

A shortcut to the newly installed CODESYS will be created on your computer's desktop (Figure 1-18).

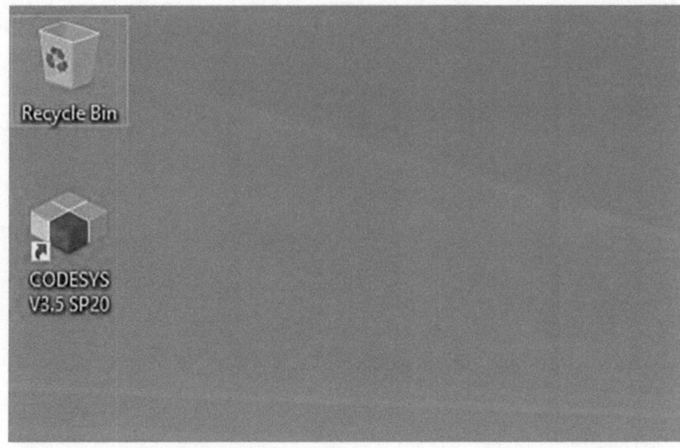

Figure 1-18. *Computer desktop with a shortcut to CODESYS*

Creating the First PLC Project

It's time to create our first PLC program and test it in the simulator. To launch the CODESYS environment, double-click the shortcut created on the desktop during installation. The CODESYS environment will start up (Figure 1-19).

Figure 1-19. *CODESYS startup window*

After launching the CODESYS environment, the startup page will open
automatically. By default, this page is always displayed every time a new
instance of CODESYS is launched. You can turn this off by unchecking the
"Show page on startup" check box in the lower left corner. Personally, I
uncheck this box because I don't like it when this page appears every time
I start up. Additionally, when I work offline, the page won't load anyway.
So, I leave the *"Close page after project load"* check box checked and the
"Show page on startup" check box unchecked (Figure 1-20).

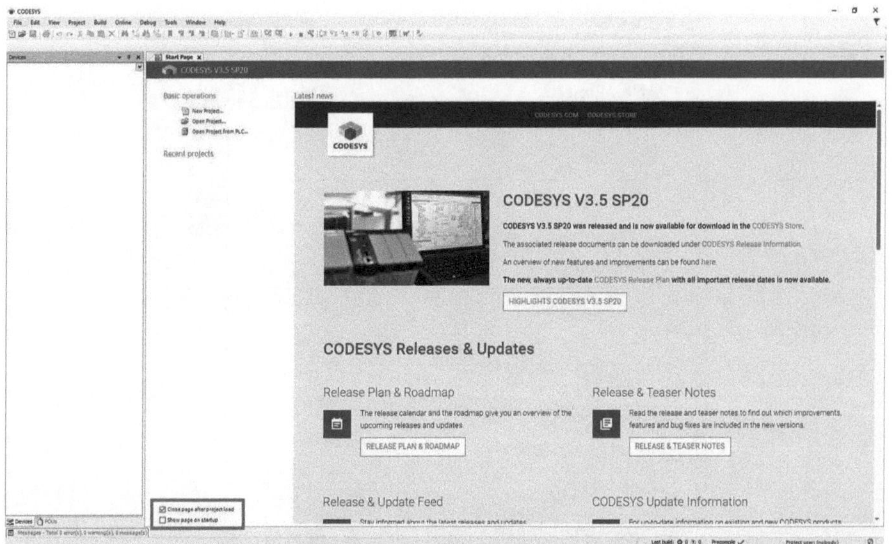

Figure 1-20. *CODESYS after startup with the option to disable automatic display of the startup page*

To create a new project, select *"File ➤ New Project..."* from the menu (Figure 1-21).

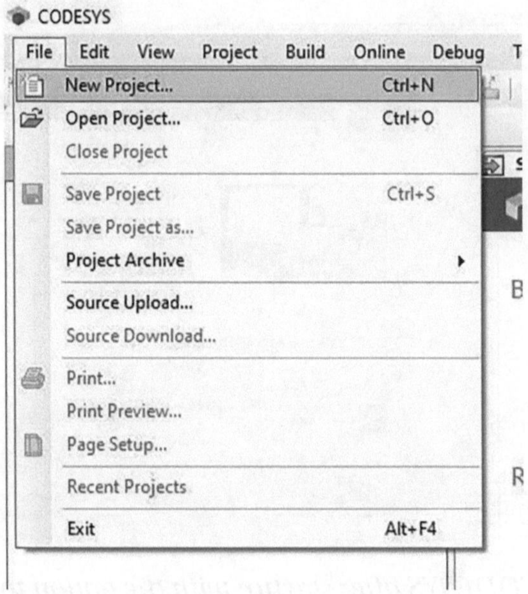

Figure 1-21. *"File ➤ New Project..." menu*

In the new project creation window, we have several options to choose from. In the *"Categories"* list, select *"Projects"*, and from the *"Templates"* list, select *"Standard project"*. I named our project *"HelloWorld"*. On drive C, I created a folder named *"PLC"*, inside which there is a folder named *"Chapter_01"*, and that's where we'll save our first program. Click the *"OK"* button to create our project (Figure 1-22).

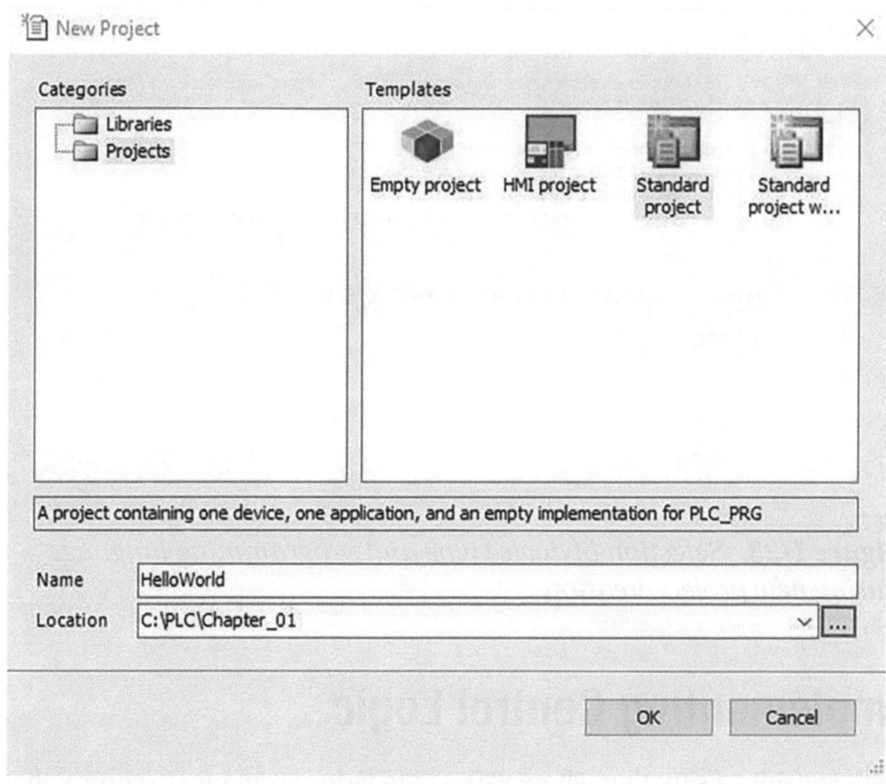

Figure 1-22. *New project creation window*

Next, you will be asked about the type of device, i.e., PLC controller,
to which we will load our program. In our case, we will work with the
SoftPLC CODESYS Control Win SL simulator, not with physical hardware,
so we need to select *"CODESYS Control RTE V3 (CODESYS)"* from the
list in the *"Device"* field. In the *"PLC_PRG in"* field, we need to specify the
programming language we will use to implement our control logic. In this
case, we will choose *"Ladder (LD2)"* (Figure 1-23).

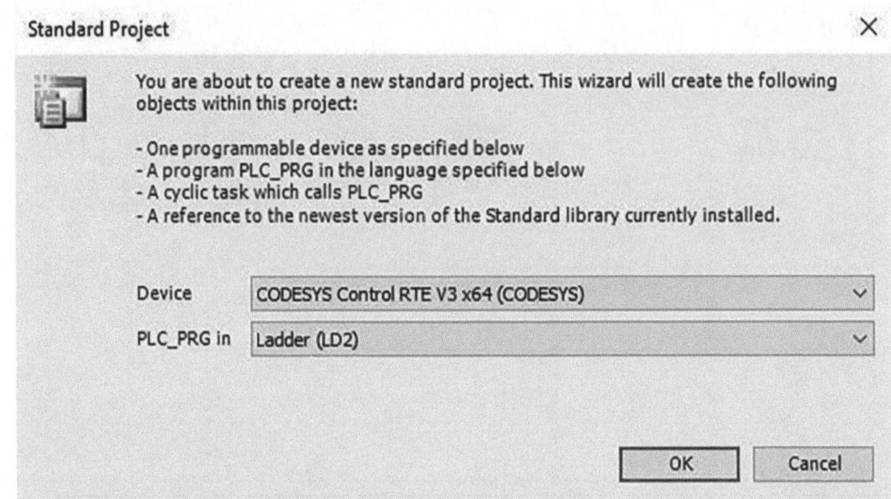

Figure 1-23. *Selection of device type and programming language during new project creation*

Implementing Control Logic

Let's consider a situation where we want to write a program to control the lighting in a room. When the light switch is in the on position, the room light will be on. The light will remain on as long as the switch remains in that position. When the switch is turned off, the light will go off.

Currently, I will skip the detailed discussion of the project structure, focusing on starting our engineering station. If something seems unclear at this point, don't worry – everything will become clearer as you progress through the reading.

The place where we will create our first control logic is the *"PLC_PRG (PRG)"* module located in the *"Devices"* window on the left side. The access path is: *"Hello World ➤ Device (CODESYS Control RTE V3 x64) ➤ PLC Logic ➤ Application"* (Figure 1-24).

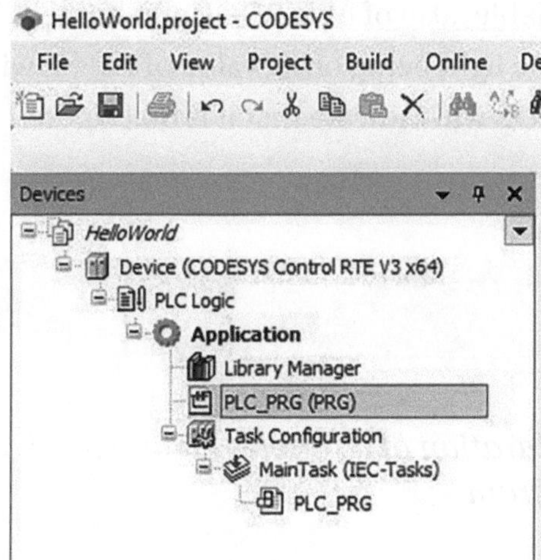

Figure 1-24. *Project structure view*

Double-clicking the *"PLC_PRG (PRG)"* module will open the editor divided into two spaces. In the upper part, we will declare variables that we will use in our program, and in the lower part, we will implement the control logic (Figure 1-25).

Figure 1-25. *PLC_PRG program editor window, with areas for variable declaration and control logic implementation*

To implement the control logic, we need two variables. The first one, of type BOOL, will represent the state of the light switch as *"Light_Switch"*. It will take on the value FALSE when the switch is off and TRUE when it is on.

The second variable, also of type BOOL and named *"Light_On"*, will reflect the state of the light being on. A value of FALSE will indicate that the light is off, while TRUE will indicate that it is on (Figure 1-26).

Figure 1-26. *Declaration of variables Light_Switch and Light_On in the PLC_PRG program*

Listing 1-1. Listing 1-1 shows the declaration of variables Light_Switch and Light_On in the PLC_PRG program

```
PROGRAM PLC_PRG
VAR
    Light_Switch : BOOL; // FALSE = Light switch is
                    off;↵  TRUE = Light switch is on.
    Light_On : BOOL; // FALSE = Light is off; TRUE =
                    Light↵  is on.
END_VAR
```

Now that we have declared our variables, it's time to implement the control logic. To edit the PLC program, click the left mouse button on the first network in the lower part of the editor. The editing field will then be highlighted in pink (Figure 1-27).

Figure 1-27. *Selection of the first network in the lower space of the PLC_PRG program*

Next, we need to implement a simple condition: if the light switch is on, i.e., the variable *"Light_Switch"* is TRUE, then the light must be on, so we also set the variable *"Light_On"* to TRUE. The simplest way to do this is to set the *"Light_On"* variable to TRUE as soon as the *"Light_Switch"* variable is set to TRUE. Similarly, if the *"Light_Switch"* variable is set to FALSE, then the *"Light_On"* variable must also be set to FALSE. To implement this control logic, select the open contact from the *"Ladder ➤ Insert Contact"* menu (Figure 1-28).

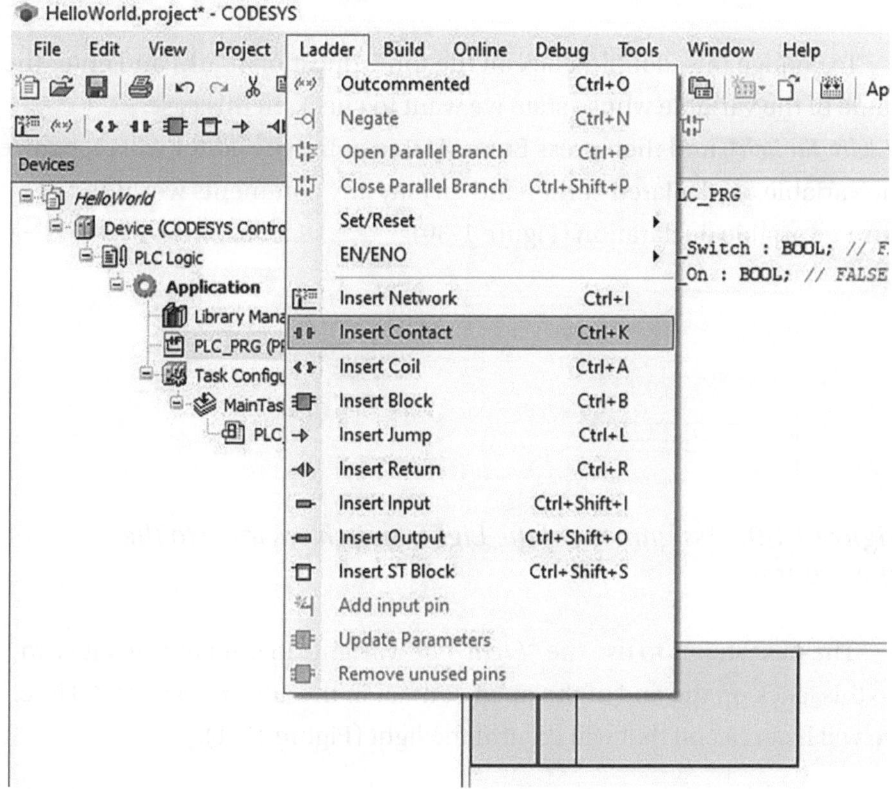

Figure 1-28. *Insertion of an open contact into the editor*

When inserting the open contact into the editor, you will notice that none of the variables are assigned to it, as indicated by the three question marks (Figure 1-29).

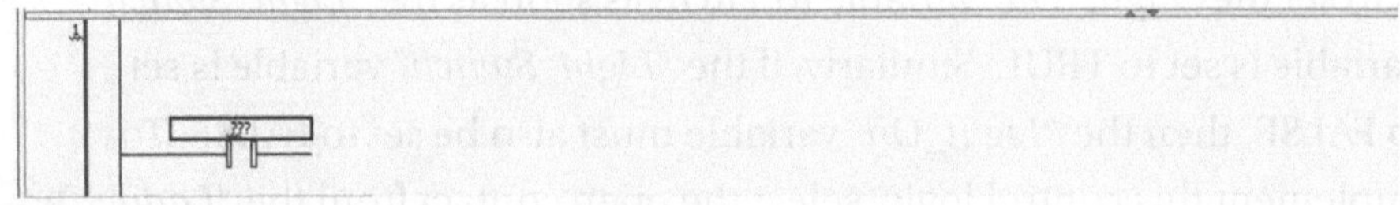

Figure 1-29. *Editor window with the symbol of three question marks visible*

To change this, double-click on the three question marks and enter the name of the variable whose state we want to check, in this case, *"Light_Switch"*, and then press Enter. At this point, the editor will recognize the variable we declared earlier and display any comments we added during variable declaration (Figure 1-30).

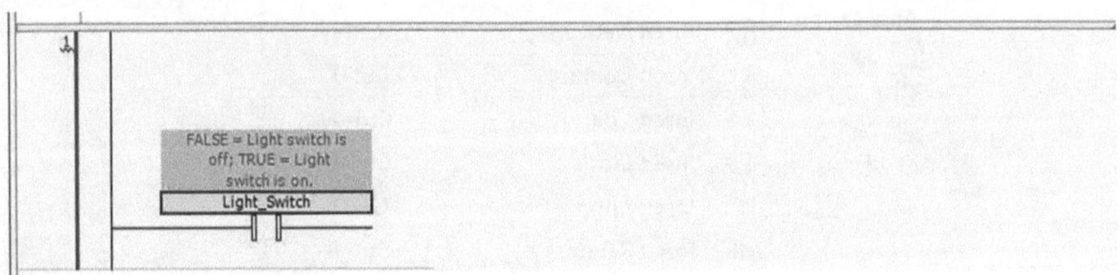

Figure 1-30. *Assignment of the Light_Switch variable to the open contact*

The next step is to use the *"Light_On"* variable in our control logic. To do this, click on the end of the open contact in the editor to select it. Here, we will insert a coil that will control the light (Figure 1-31).

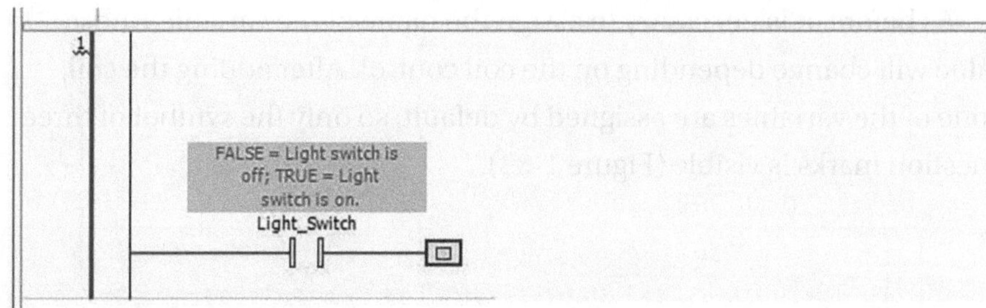

Figure 1-31. *Highlighted end of the open contact to which the coil will be connected*

To add a coil to our program, select the *"Ladder ➤ Insert Coil"* option from the menu (Figure 1-32).

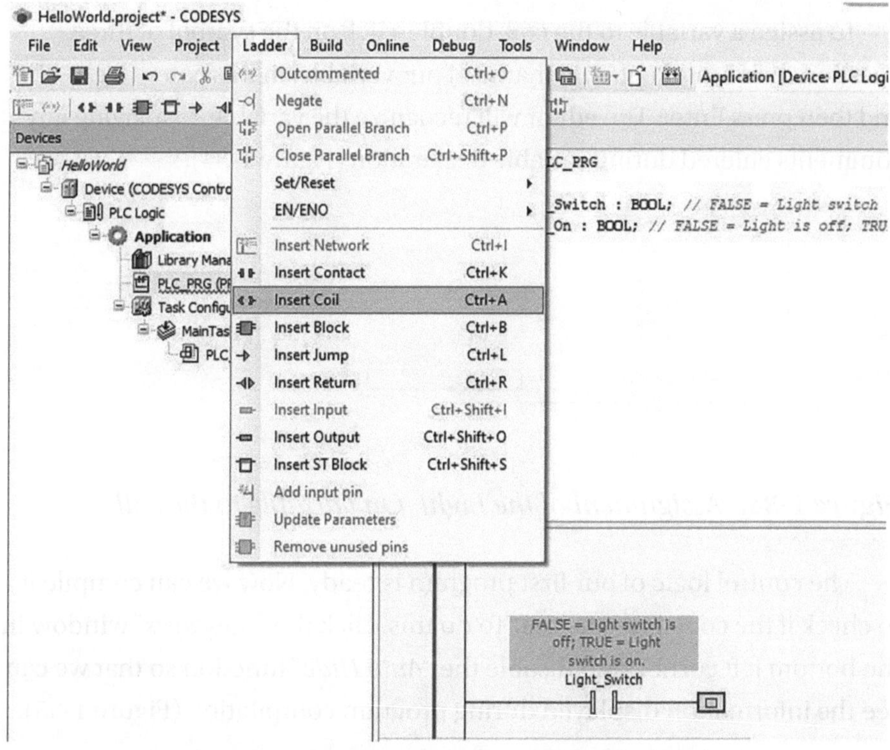

Figure 1-32. *Insertion of a coil into the control logic*

As before, it is necessary to assign the name of the variable whose value will change depending on the coil control. After adding the coil, none of the variables are assigned by default, so only the symbol of three question marks is visible (Figure 1-33).

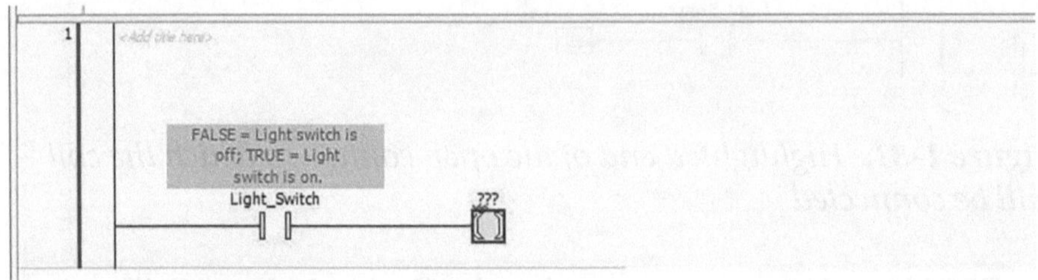

Figure 1-33. *Editor window after inserting the coil*

To assign a variable to the coil, double-click on the symbol of three question marks, and enter the name of our variable, in this case, *"Light_On"*, and then press Enter. The editor will recognize the variable, displaying any comments entered during variable declaration (Figure 1-34).

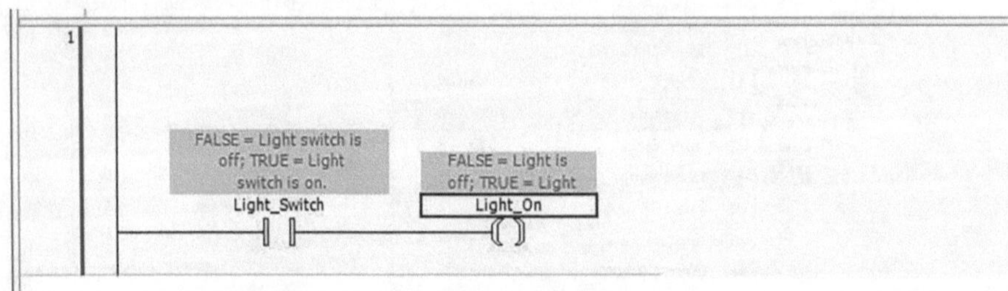

Figure 1-34. *Assignment of the Light_On variable to the coil*

The control logic of our first program is ready. Now we can compile it to check if the code is error-free. To do this, click the *"Messages"* window in the bottom left corner, and disable the *"Auto Hide"* function so that we can see the information displayed during program compilation (Figure 1-35).

Figure 1-35. *"Messages" window, where compilation code information will be displayed*

Next, compile our program by selecting *"Build ➤ Generate Code"* from the menu (Figure 1-36).

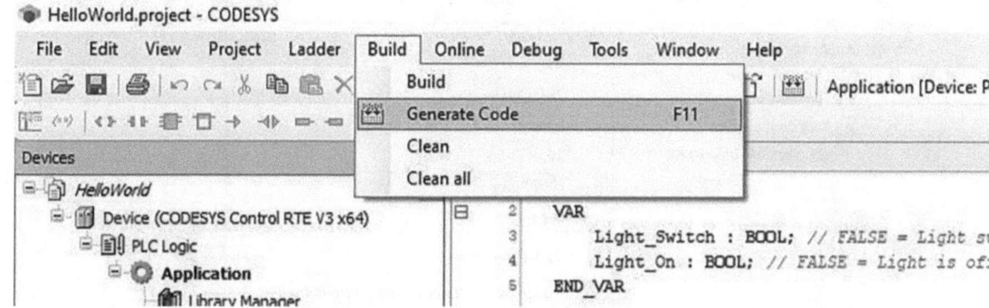

Figure 1-36. *PLC program code generation in CODESYS*

If the compilation is successful, we should see a message indicating no errors or warnings regarding the compilation and the readiness of our program for download (Figure 1-37).

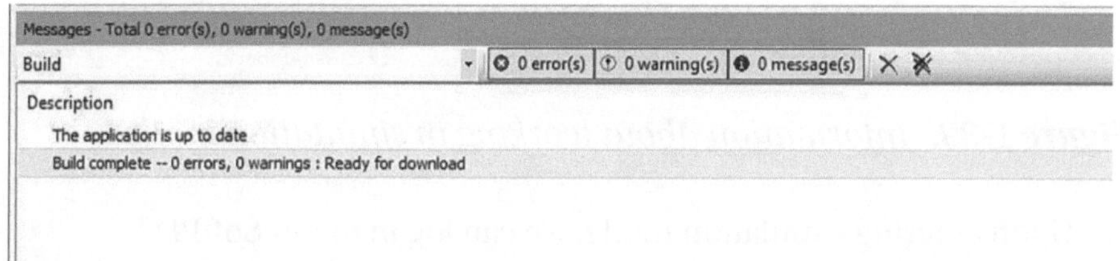

Figure 1-37. *Message about successful code compilation in CODESYS, with readiness to load the program to the controller*

Running the Simulator

At this point, we need to run the simulator since, as we know, in this book, we won't be working with real hardware. To run the simulator, select *"Online ➤ Simulation"* from the main menu (Figure 1-38).

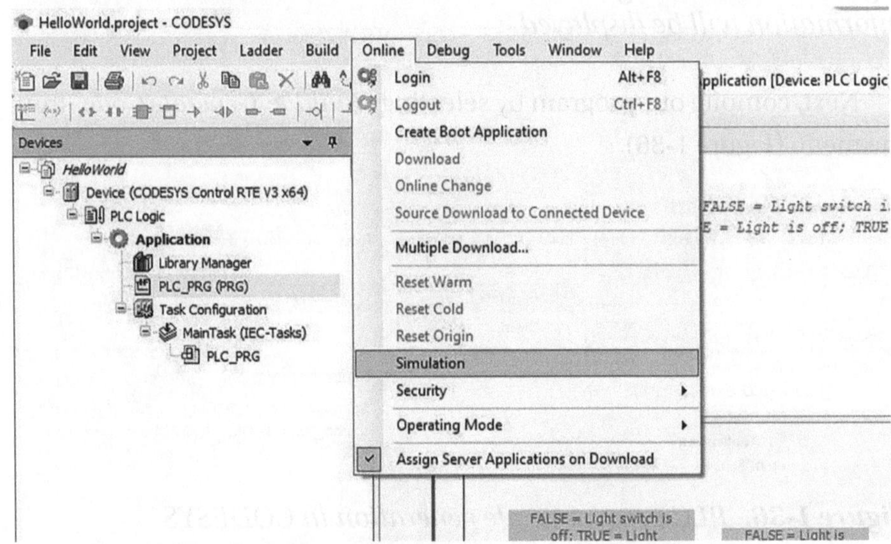

Figure 1-38. *"Online ➤ Simulation" menu in CODESYS*

The status bar will display information indicating that we are working in simulation mode (Figure 1-39).

Figure 1-39. *Information about working in simulation mode*

Upon entering simulation mode, we can log in to our SoftPLC controller by selecting *"Online ➤ Login"* from the main menu (Figure 1-40).

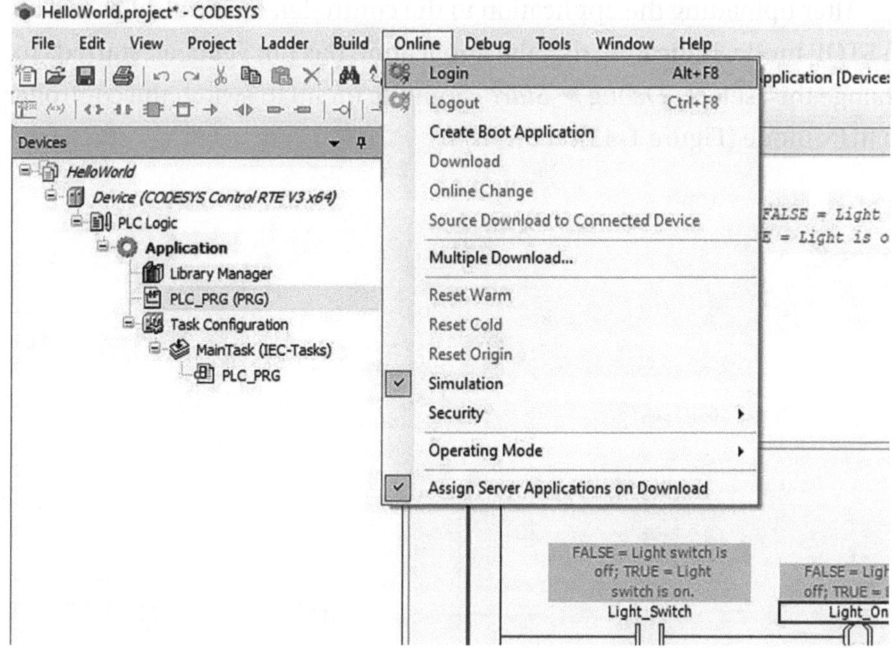

Figure 1-40. *Login window to the SoftPLC controller in CODESYS*

At this point, a window will appear with a message indicating that the application does not yet exist in our SoftPLC controller, along with a question asking if we want to download it. Click the *"Yes"* button to continue (Figure 1-41).

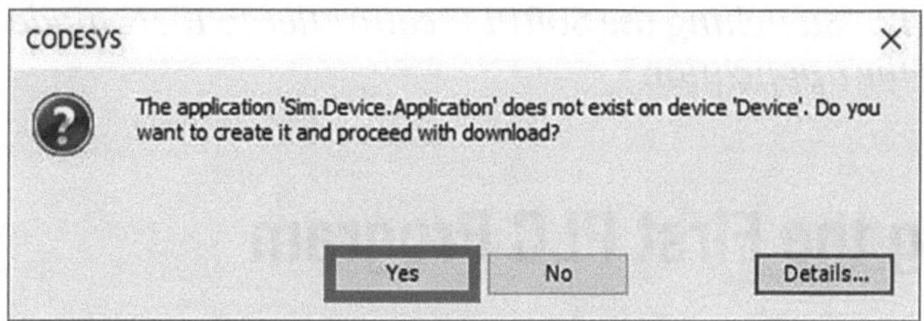

Figure 1-41. *Confirmation of application installation on the SoftPLC controller*

After uploading the application to the controller, our controller will be in STOP mode, indicating that the application has not yet been started. To change this, select *"Debug ➤ Start"* from the menu to switch the controller to RUN mode (Figure 1-42).

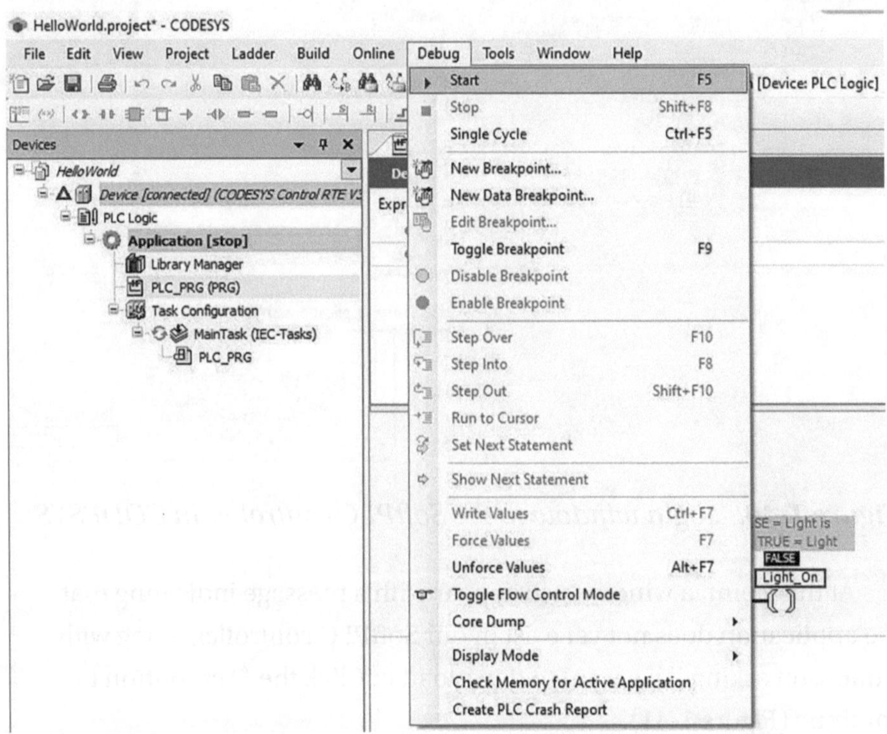

Figure 1-42. *Switching the SoftPLC controller to RUN mode after installing the application*

Testing the First PLC Program

From this moment, our controller is in RUN mode, and our application is running. We see that both variables are set to FALSE, which basically means that the light switch is off, and thus the light is not illuminated. So far, everything is as expected; our control logic is working as designed (Figure 1-43).

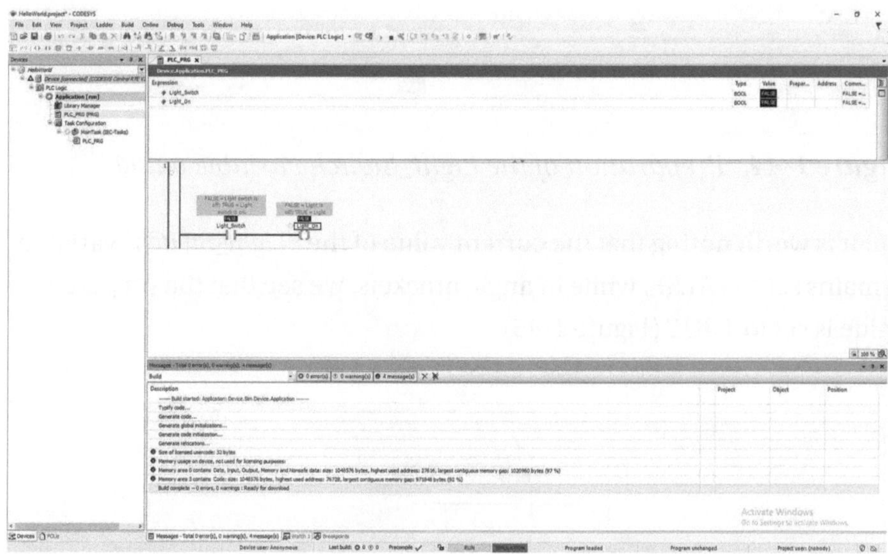

Figure 1-43. *SoftPLC controller in RUN mode after launching the application in the simulator*

Now we want to check if switching the light switch will turn on our light. To do this, we will manipulate the value of the *"Light_Switch"* variable. In a real-world scenario, the *"Light_Switch"* variable would be mapped to a digital input, where a real light switch would be connected, and the variable would read FALSE when the switch is off and TRUE when the light switch is on. However, in this case, we will manipulate the value of the *"Light_Switch"* variable and observe how the value of the *"Light_On"* variable, which controls the light, changes.

To do this, during the operation of our application, in the area where we declared our variables, we have a table showing our variables and their values. In addition, we have an additional field called *"Prepared value"*. We can click the left mouse button in this field for the *"Light_Switch"* variable to prepare a value. In this case, the value of this field will be set to TRUE (Figure 1-44).

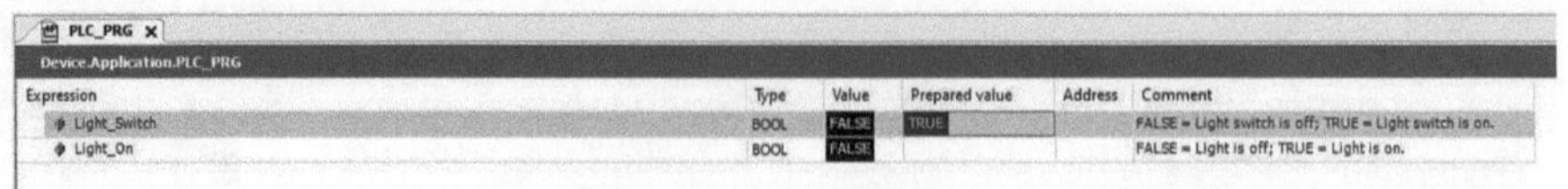

Figure 1-44. *Preparation of the Light_Switch variable value*

It is worth noting that the current value of the *"Light_Switch"* variable remains set to FALSE, while in angle brackets, we see that the prepared value is set to TRUE (Figure 1-45).

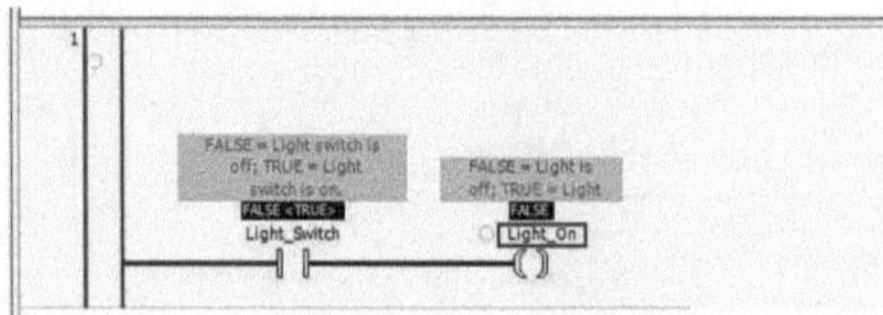

Figure 1-45. *Current value and prepared value of the Light_Switch variable*

To rewrite the values from the *"Prepared value"* field to the variable, right-click, and select *"Write All Values of 'Device.Application'"* from the menu (Figure 1-46).

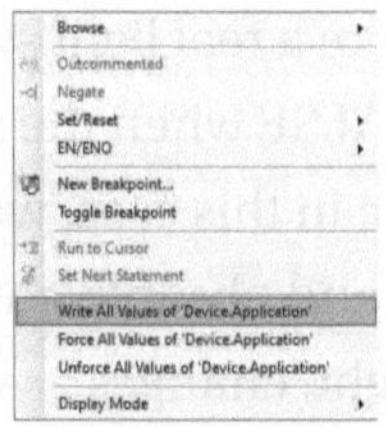

Figure 1-46. *Writing all values in Device.Application*

When the value of the *"Light_Switch"* variable changes to TRUE, the control logic sets the *"Light_On"* variable to TRUE, thus turning on the light (Figure 1-47).

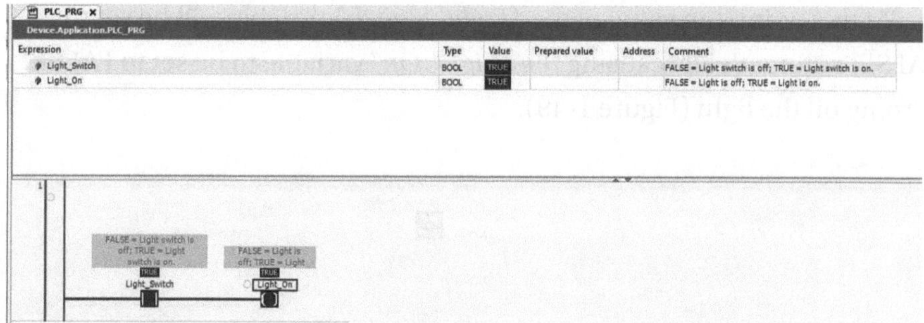

Figure 1-47. *Turning on the light after changing the Light_Switch variable value*

Turning off the light is done by setting the *"Light_Switch"* variable to FALSE. To do this, click the *"Prepared value"* field to prepare the value to FALSE (Figure 1-48).

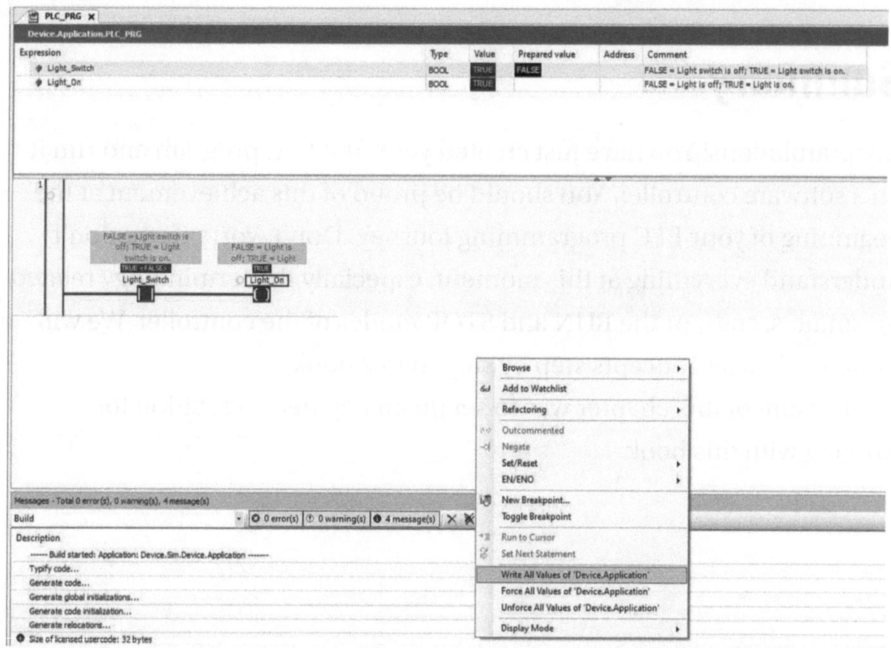

Figure 1-48. *Preparation of the Light_Switch variable value and saving all values*

At this point, the value of the *"Light_Switch"* variable will be set to FALSE, automatically causing the *"Light_On"* variable to be set to FALSE, turning off the light (Figure 1-49).

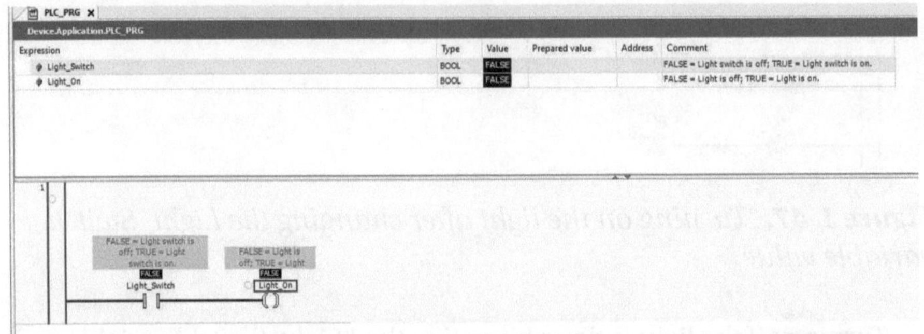

Figure 1-49. *Turning off the light after changing the Light_Switch variable value*

Summary

Congratulations! You have just created your first PLC program and run it on a software controller. You should be proud of this achievement at the beginning of your PLC programming journey. Don't worry if you don't understand everything at this moment, especially the terminology related to contacts, coils, or the RUN and STOP modes of the controller. We will explain all these concepts step by step in this book.

The aim of this chapter was to set up an engineering station for working with this book.

CHAPTER 2

Exploring PLC Fundamentals

In this chapter, we will take a detailed look at the PLC (Programmable Logic Controller), a key component in the field of industrial automation. The PLC is an advanced device that plays a central role in controlling and monitoring various processes in industry. Its main task is to control machines, devices, and production processes by executing specific sequences of operations in a programmable manner.

Throughout this reading, we will not only familiarize ourselves with the structure and operation of the PLC but also with its key functions in the control system. We will learn about the benefits of using PLCs in various industries and how widely they are utilized in practice.

Furthermore, we will discuss how the PLC communicates with the external world, including its interaction with sensors and actuators.

Applications of PLC in Daily Life

PLC controllers are an integral part of many aspects of our daily lives and industrial economy. Their versatility and reliability make them indispensable in various fields. Here are a few examples:

© Dariusz Wrebiak 2026
D. Wrebiak, *Practical PLC Programming for Beginners*, Maker Innovations Series,
https://doi.org/10.1007/979-8-8688-2430-2_2

- Traffic Lights

  An example of PLC controller usage in everyday life is the control of traffic lights on streets. These systems are programmed to ensure smooth traffic flow, minimizing congestion, and ensuring pedestrian and driver safety. PLC controllers are responsible for changing the light colors according to specific road conditions and signals from sensors.

- Industrial Manufacturing

  In the industrial sector, PLC controllers are used to control and monitor various production processes. For example, in car factories, these devices control robots, machinery, and assembly lines, ensuring optimal performance and product quality. In the food industry, PLC controllers are used to control packaging, labeling, and sorting processes.

- Building Automation

  In the construction sector, PLC controllers are used to automate various building systems such as air conditioning, lighting, security systems, and energy consumption monitoring. They enable greater energy efficiency and user convenience.

- Transportation Systems

  In transportation systems, PLC controllers are used to control the movement of trains, trams, elevators, conveyor belts, and other transportation devices. They ensure travel safety, optimize travel time, and minimize the risk of failures.

These examples only partially illustrate the scope of PLC controller applications in various aspects of everyday life. Their versatility and reliability make them key components in today's technological world.

Manufacturers

The German company SIEMENS is one of the most well-known manufacturers of PLC controllers worldwide. Their latest line, SIMATIC S7, includes models such as the S7-1200 (Figure 2-1, Figure 2-2, Figure 2-3) and S7-1500 (Figure 2-4, Figure 2-5, Figure 2-6), which are highly versatile and efficient. Programming these controllers is done using software known as TIA Portal.

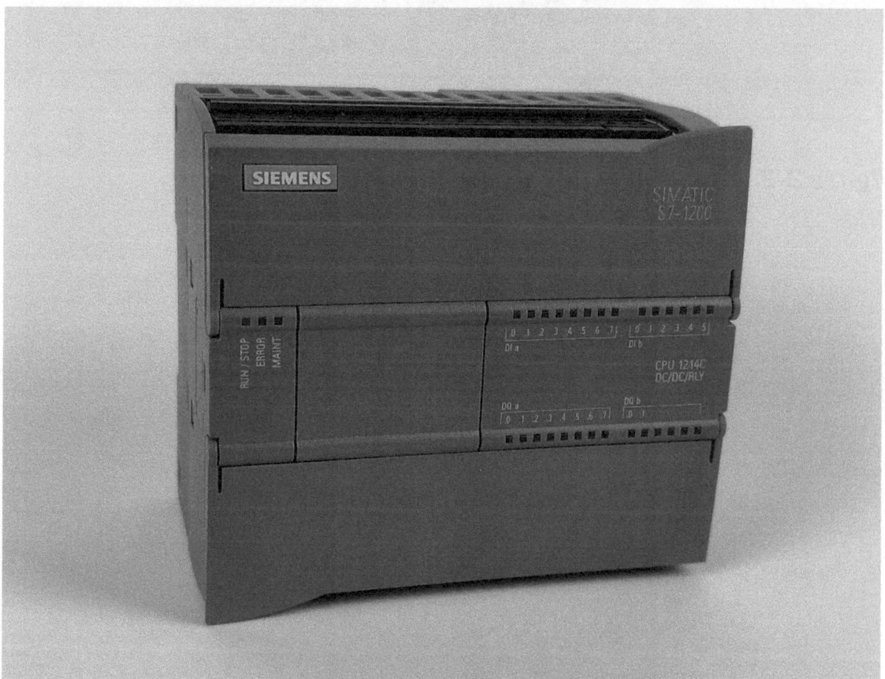

Figure 2-1. *PLC controller SIEMENS S7-1200*

Figure 2-2. *PLC controller SIEMENS S7-1200*

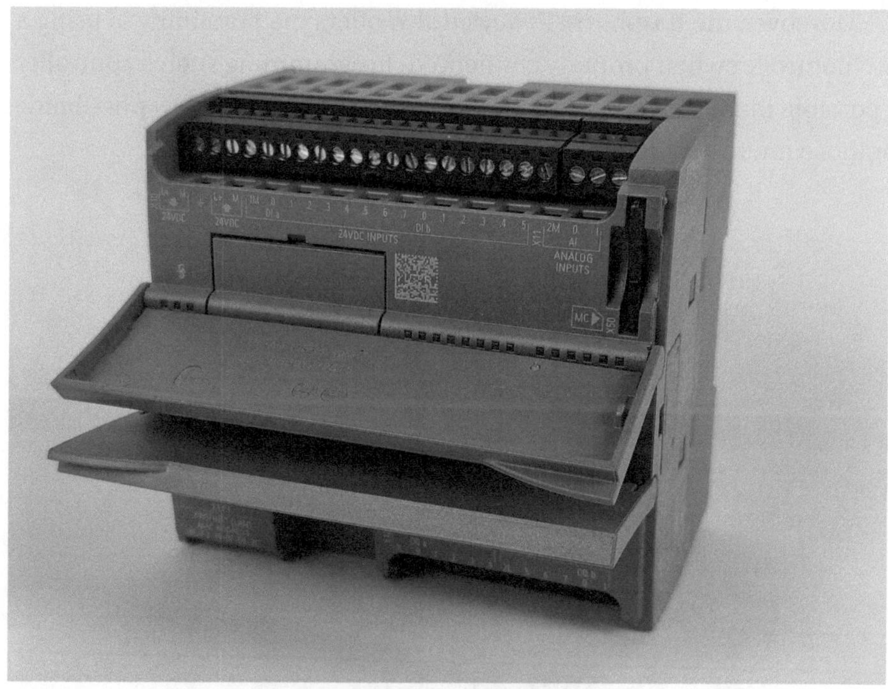

Figure 2-3. *PLC controller SIEMENS S7-1200*

Another competitive player in the market is the American company Rockwell Automation, formerly known as Allen-Bradley. Their latest controllers are programmed using software called STUDIO 500.

Despite the dominance of SIEMENS and Rockwell Automation in the market, it's also worth noting smaller manufacturers like the Austrian company B&R, which is now part of the ABB group. Their products offer competitive prices and high quality. The software needed to program B&R controllers is called Automation Studio.

Additionally, emerging innovations are changing the landscape of PLC controllers. The Autonomy project (`www.autonomylogic.com`) has spread knowledge about how these devices work and has made them more accessible to enthusiasts and hobbyists.

Moreover, the Raspberry Pi device also offers the possibility of using a PLC controller when properly configured. Programming such a controller is possible thanks to tools like CODESYS, which opens up new possibilities for those interested in the subject.

Figure 2-4. *PLC controller SIEMENS S7-1500*

Figure 2-5. *PLC controller SIEMENS S7-1500*

Figure 2-6. *PLC controller SIEMENS S7-1500*

Description of PLC Structure and Operation

What exactly is a PLC (Programmable Logic Controller)? It's a specially designed computer for industrial applications. It includes a processor, memory (ROM, RAM, FLASH), and programming capability (Figure 2-7). Newer models of PLCs often come equipped with displays for monitoring the device's status. However, it differs from the typical computer we use every day, such as our laptops or desktop PCs. The first difference is that a PLC is a real-time system. This means that the program executed by the PLC runs cyclically, in an endless loop. In PLCs, applications are typically executed, also known as control logic, which are responsible for controlling technological processes, for example, testing the durability of springs used in car chassis production. Therefore, we don't run typical applications like WhatsApp for chatting with friends on PLCs, but rather implement control logic responsible for industrial processes. This is the classical approach to PLCs, although some manufacturers introduce new models that can run various applications. However, in this book, we will focus on traditional PLCs as real-time devices that control industrial processes.

Processor
Memory (ROM, RAM, FLASH)
Bus

Figure 2-7. *Block diagram of the control unit structure*

PLC Controller   A computerized electronic system used to control industrial processes, which performs specific operations or tasks in response to input signals.

Real-Time System   It is a computer system that ensures data processing and execution of operations within specified time frames. In such systems, it is crucial that responses to events occur within a defined time, which is essential in applications requiring quick reactions to changes in the environment.

An important aspect is configuring the cyclic call of applications. This can be done through the Task Manager, where we precisely set the frequency of calling the Task class, for example, every 200 ms. We can treat the Task class as a container in which we place all the applications that are to be called at a specific frequency. We can configure several such Task classes, depending on our needs regarding the frequency of calling programs (Figure 2-8, Figure 2-9).

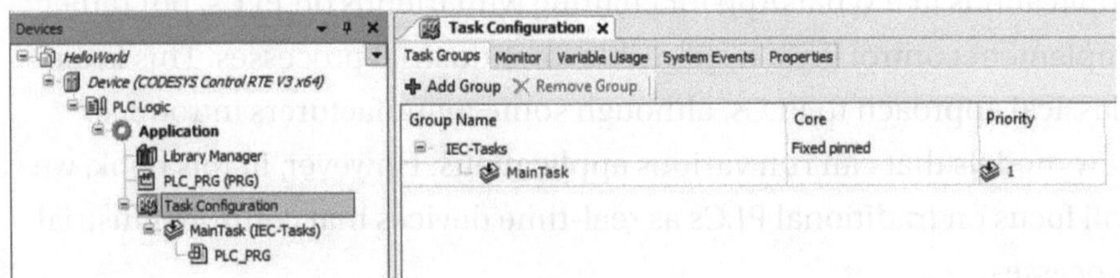

Figure 2-8. *Task Manager (Task Configuration) in CODESYS*

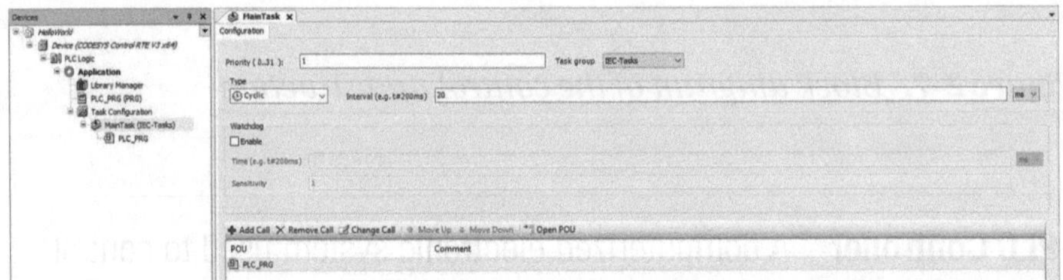

Figure 2-9. *Task class (MainTask) in CODESYS*

In such a device, the application operates cyclically, meaning the program runs from start to finish and then starts again, uninterrupted, unless manually interrupted. The execution of the program can be halted by changing the device state from RUN mode to STOP mode. Conversely, by changing from STOP mode to RUN mode, the program will resume, and the cycle will begin again (Figure 2-10).

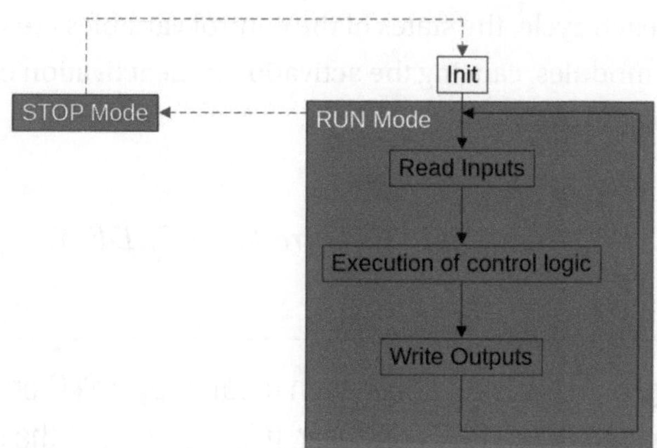

Figure 2-10. *Block diagram describing the operation of a PLC controller*

We distinguish between two basic modes: RUN and STOP. If the controller is in STOP mode (Figure 2-11), no application is active, meaning no program assigned to the Task class is executed. Typically, the control system is configured so that in STOP mode, all outputs are set to FALSE to prevent accidental activation of devices. This is a safety measure; however, there are situations where certain devices should remain activated even when the controller is in STOP mode. It is possible to configure the controller in such a way that specific outputs remain active in STOP mode, despite the control logic being inactive.

Figure 2-11. *STOP mode of PLC controller in CODESYS*

If the controller is in RUN mode (Figure 2-12), it means that the application assigned to the Task class is cyclically called. After the program execution is complete, the cycle starts again. During each cycle of the program, the states of digital and analog inputs are read, and then the control logic checks these states and controls the devices based on them.

At the end of each cycle, the states of the control variables are written
to the output modules, causing the activation or deactivation of the
corresponding devices.

Figure 2-12. *RUN mode of PLC controller in CODESYS*

Control Logic   This is an application created by a PLC programmer
and downloaded to the PLC controller. It is the heart of the control
process, which processes input signals in real time, generating
appropriate output signals. This application allows for defining the
system's behavior based on input conditions and enables easy
editing and modification using dedicated software provided by the
manufacturer of the PLC controller.

The Communication with the External World

We've mentioned that our application communicates with the external
world to control the technological process. So, how does our controller
gather information from the external world and execute actions? Every
controller, besides the processor and memory, is equipped with input and
output modules, to which various sensors and actuators are connected.

Sensor   It is a device connected to the input modules of a PLC
controller, used to gather information about the controlled object.
Sensors transmit digital or analog signals.

Actuator   It is a device connected to the output modules of a PLC controller, used to control a process. An actuator can be, for example, an electric motor, valve, or pump. Actuators convert control signals from the PLC into physical actions in the controlled process.

Input and output modules are divided into digital and analog types. Digital modules can accept one of two values: TRUE or FALSE, which are used by PLC programmers. It's worth noting that these values correspond to electrical voltage – TRUE represents 24V DC, while FALSE represents 0V DC. In the automation industry, this standard voltage level is commonly used, so nearly every PLC manufacturer operates at this voltage. In other words, with digital modules, we work with two values: TRUE (24V DC) or FALSE (0V DC) (Figure 2-13).

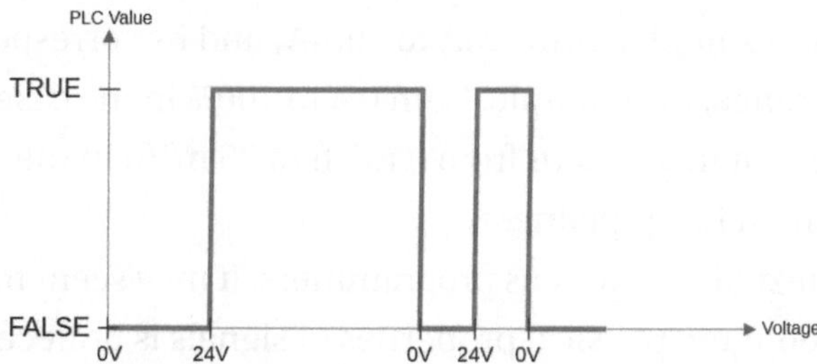

Figure 2-13. *Graphic representation of a digital signal*

Digital Signal   It is an electrical signal that takes one of two values, such as TRUE or FALSE, representing logical states.

In the context of analog modules (Figure 2-16, Figure 2-17, Figure 2-18), the situation becomes more complex. In this case, we deal with various configuration possibilities. Let's take a closer look at how such a module operates. Unlike digital modules, where we have a simple on/off state, analog modules allow working with various parameters such as voltage, current, or resistance. One of the commonly used methods for measurement or control is the utilization of a current signal ranging from 4mA to 20mA.

Let's consider a scenario where we want to monitor the water level in a tank using a sensor connected to an analog input. The signal transmitted to this input varies in the range from 4mA to 20mA. We can interpret this as follows: when the tank is completely empty, the current signal is 4mA, corresponding to 0% water level. When the tank is filled to 25%, the current signal changes to 8mA. Similarly, 50% water level corresponds to 12mA, which is exactly halfway through the measurement range. If the tank is filled to 100%, the current signal reaches the maximum value of 20mA, representing the upper limit of the measurement range.

The characteristic of this type of measurement is linear. The manufacturer of each sensor typically provides on the nameplate the signal range, for example, from 4mA to 20mA, and its corresponding measurement range, for example, from 0% to 100% in the case of water level measurement in a tank or from 0 m³/h to 25 m³/h in the case of liquid flow measurement in a pipeline.

In the context of our work as programmers, it may seem that detailed information about the physical properties of signals is unnecessary. However, to properly program a PLC controller, we need to understand how sensors and other external devices work. Often, signals are not transmitted directly as voltage or current, but they may be converted into other values. Our task is to properly configure the hardware modules, although in reality, our code operates on numbers rather than physical units such as voltage or current. Ultimately, it is the analog-to-digital converter that converts the signal into numbers, but it is up to us to appropriately adjust the module configuration.

An interesting fact is the possibility of connecting a sensor with a measurement range from 4mA to 20mA to an analog channel with a range from 0mA to 20mA. In such a case, it will be necessary to apply a certain programming trick. However, in this book, we assume that we are using sensors operating in the range from 4mA to 20mA, and these signals will be scaled to engineering units used in our measurements.

In addition to measurement channels operating in the range from 4mA to 20mA, a less common method is voltage measurement, for example, in the range from 0V to 10V or from -10V to 10V. Current signals are more preferred in the industry due to their greater resistance to external interference and energy losses in cables compared to voltage signals. When designing any control system, it is worth remembering this.

In the case of digital signals, we have access to one of two values: TRUE or FALSE. However, what does it look like for analog signals? Here, much depends on the manufacturer of the PLC. For example, in SIEMENS controllers from the S7 series, current or voltage is scaled to numerical values ranging from 0 to 27648. The value 0 corresponds to 4mA, while the value 27648 corresponds to 20mA when the analog channel is configured in this range. The same applies to voltage measurement from 0V to 10V.

In this book, we use CODESYS as our main engineering environment. This gives us access to a wide range of controllers that we can program. This is crucial because a proper understanding of the specifications of a given module is essential for efficient design and implementation of solutions.

For the purposes of this book, I assume that our analog signals operate in the range from 4mA to 20mA, corresponding to numerical values in the range from 0 to 32767. Let's take pressure measurement as an example. Suppose we have a sensor providing an analog signal in the range from 0 to 6 bars (Table 2-1).

Table 2-1. *Interpretation of numerical values*

Current (Sensor)	PLC Value (CODESYS)	Pressure
4mA	0	0 bar
8mA	13107	1.5 bar
12mA	19660	3 bar
16mA	26214	4.5 bar
20mA	32767	6 bar

Since we are working with a simulator rather than physical equipment, our analog values will be stored or read in variables of type UINT, which in reality would be mapped to analog inputs or outputs (Figure 2-14).

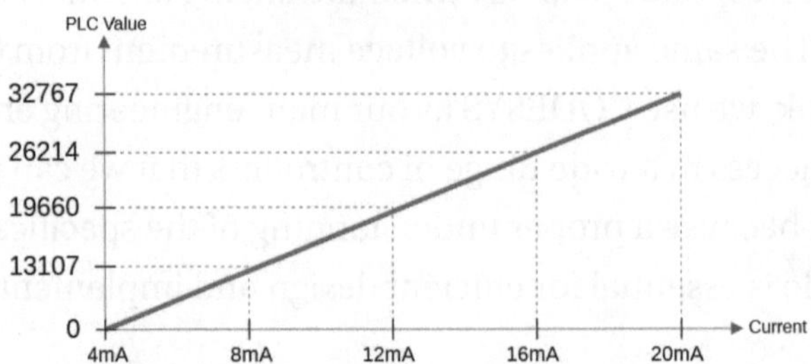

Figure 2-14. *Graphic representation of an analog signal*

Analog Signal   This is an electrical signal that can take infinitely many different values within a specified range, typically representing continuous changes over time.

So, we already know that the PLC communicates with the external world through digital and analog input and output modules. Sensors, connected to the input channels, gather signals from the environment, which are then passed to the control unit, i.e., our PLC. Inside the PLC, these signals are processed and interpreted when the application (control logic) is executed. At the end of the cycle, output signals are produced, which are transmitted to the output modules. Through the actuators connected to the output modules, interaction with the external world occurs, for example, by turning on or off a motor (Figure 2-15).

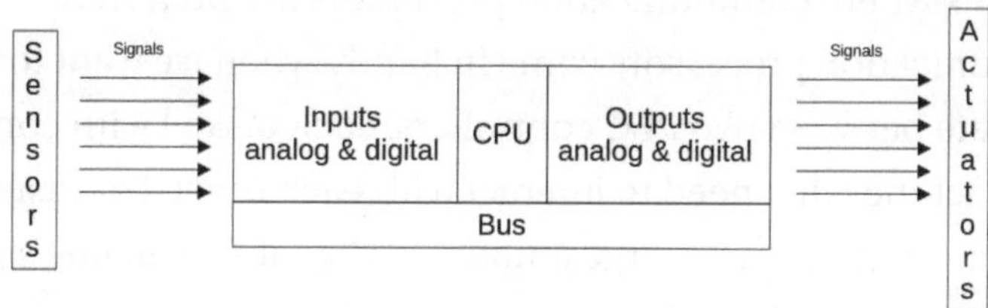

Figure 2-15. *Diagram of connections between the PLC and various external devices, such as sensors, valves, motors, etc*

Input/Output Module   This is a component of a PLC used for gathering data from the environment (inputs) and controlling external devices (outputs).

Besides standard input and output modules, the PLC can be equipped with so-called technological modules. These are devices designed to perform special tasks, such as fast pulse counting. Why not connect such pulses to a normal digital input? In this case, the pulse frequency is so high that a standard digital input would not be able to recognize them. Technological modules enable more precise and efficient data processing than standard input/output modules. Among them are, for example, temperature measurement modules, which allow direct connection of temperature sensors PT100 or PT1000, depending on the input channel configuration. Another example is a module enabling the handling of PWM signals, a function impossible to achieve using standard digital outputs.

The next modules that can be equipped with our PLC controller are communication processors. These are very useful modules that handle various communication protocols. But why use such processors when sensors and actuators can be connected directly to digital input or output modules, for example? It's true that this is one possible solution, but there are situations where communication processors are preferred.

Communication processors come in handy when we want to communicate between two PLC controllers, each tasked with controlling separate machines that need to interact with each other. For instance, when we need to transmit a large amount of digital and analog signals between these controllers. Using conventional input and output modules could significantly increase project costs, including electrical work and wiring expenses.

Imagine that we need to transfer 50 digital signals and 20 analog signals between these controllers. In such a scenario, a communication processor comes into play, enabling efficient and reliable data exchange between the devices, minimizing costs, and simplifying installation.

There are many communication protocols used in industry. In such cases, manufacturers of two machines implement support for a specific communication protocol, which can be compared to using a certain language through which the machine is able to communicate with another. With such a solution, as hardware, we only need one communication processor in each of the controllers and one communication cable connecting these two machines. The remaining part of the work is solely about implementing the protocol in the PLC application. Therefore, this task is reserved for the programmer.

Figures 2-16, 2-17, and 2-18 show different views of the analog output module.

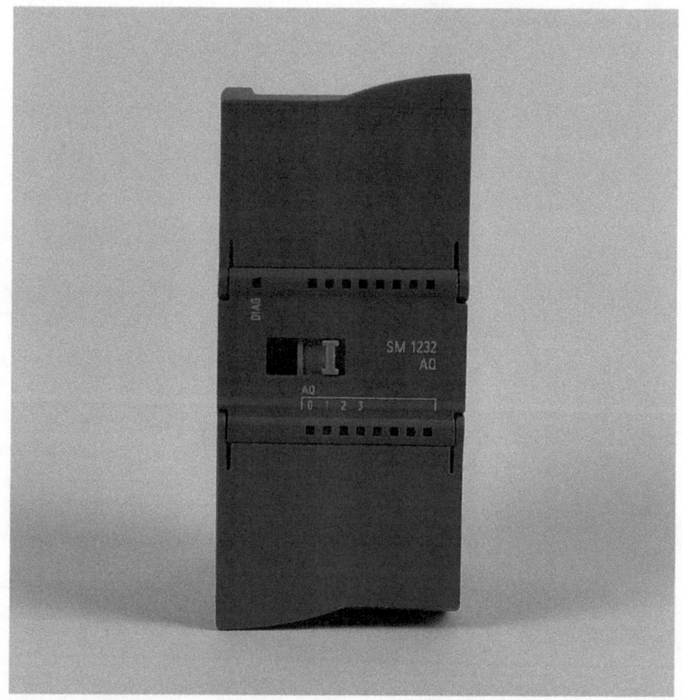

Figure 2-16. *Analog output module compatible with the SIEMENS S7-1200 PLC controller*

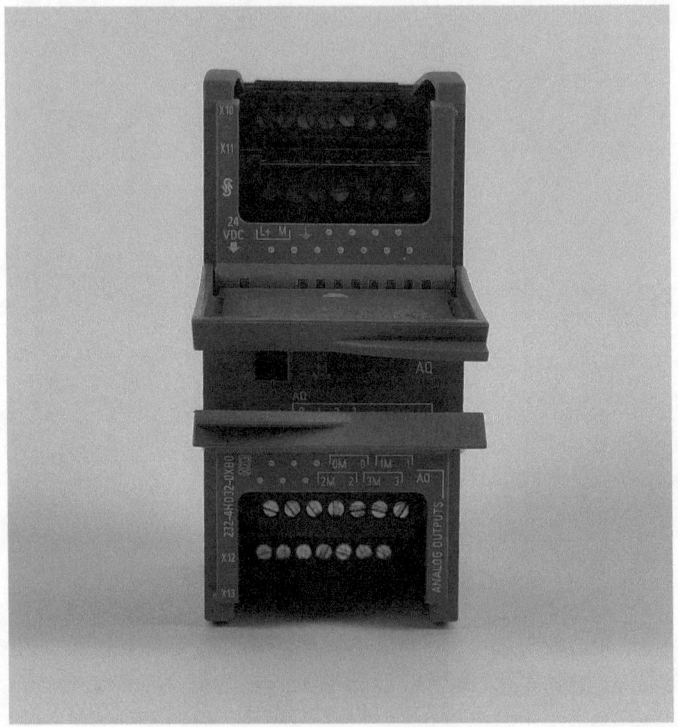

Figure 2-17. *Analog output module compatible with the SIEMENS S7-1200 PLC controller*

Figure 2-18. *Analog output module compatible with the SIEMENS S7-1200 PLC controller*

Summary

In this chapter, we delved into the main aspects of communication between a PLC controller and the external world. We learned the differences between digital and analog input and output modules, understood why current signals are preferred in the industry, and discussed the role of technological modules and communication processors. We also learned about the importance of communication protocols in machine integration and the role they play in the control process. With this understanding, we are ready to move on to more advanced topics related to PLC programming.

CHAPTER 3

Understanding the Automation Pyramid

In today's world, where industry is becoming increasingly automated and complex, understanding the structure of automation systems is crucial for the effective design, programming, and maintenance of industrial installations. The automation pyramid is a concept that allows us to view these systems from the perspective of different levels, starting from basic sensors and actuators, all the way up to enterprise-wide management systems.

In this chapter, I will discuss the automation pyramid and provide practical examples related to each level of this structure. The lowest level of the automation pyramid is the *"Field Level"*, where directly controlled devices such as sensors and actuators are located.

Next, I will move on to the *"Control Level"*, where PLC controllers take control of industrial processes, executing control logic.

The next stage will be to discuss the *"Supervisory Level"*, where visualization systems such as HMI and SCADA play a crucial role in monitoring and controlling industrial processes. Through practical anecdotes from my experience, I will illustrate the significance of visualization systems for effective management of industrial installations.

Next, I will present the *"Planning Level"* and *"Management Level"*, illustrating their tasks and how they influence the functioning of the entire enterprise. In the final part of this chapter, I will present the complete

© Dariusz Wrebiak 2026
D. Wrebiak, *Practical PLC Programming for Beginners*, Maker Innovations Series,
https://doi.org/10.1007/979-8-8688-2430-2_3

graphic of the automation pyramid, summarizing the discussed concepts and laying the groundwork for the practical aspects of PLC programming, which will be the main focus of the next stage of our journey through automation systems.

Get ready to delve into the intricacies of the automation pyramid and discover how understanding its structure can benefit the design and programming of industrial systems. Ready? Let's begin our journey through automation systems.

Levels "Field Level" and "Control Level"

In essence, the first two levels of the automation pyramid were already discussed in the previous chapter, where I covered the structure of the PLC and its role in industrial processes. We analyzed the structure of sensors and actuators, which form the foundation of every automated installation.

Now, let's examine how these elements fit into the broader context of industrial automation systems. The automation pyramid, also known as the ISA-95 pyramid, serves as a useful model for understanding the various levels of control and management in an industrial environment.

At the bottom of the pyramid lies the *"Field Level"*, where operations are conducted at the level of sensors and actuators. Here, data regarding the process state, temperature, pressure, and other production-related parameters are collected (Figure 3-1).

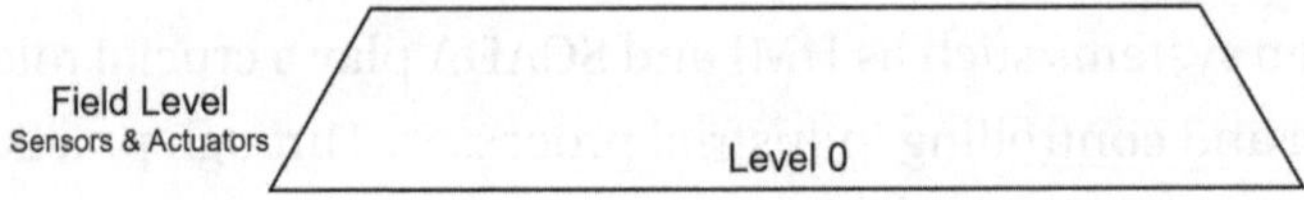

Figure 3-1. *Level 0 "Field Level" of the automation pyramid*

The next level is the *"Control Level"*, which sits above the *"Field Level"*. Here, PLC controllers, hardware PID controllers, and DCS (Distributed Control System) systems are located. They process data from sensors and make appropriate control decisions (Figure 3-2).

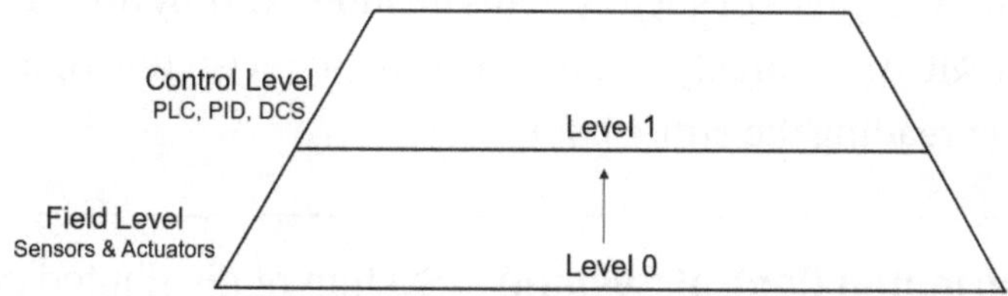

Figure 3-2. *Level 1 "Control Level" of the automation pyramid*

Now, let's examine how the first two levels fit into the structure of the automation pyramid. Although I've already discussed the construction of PLC controllers in the previous chapter, it's worth briefly touching on the topic of PID controllers and DCS systems, as they also belong to the *"Control level"*.

At an early stage of writing this book, I initially intended to include more advanced topics – such as a detailed discussion and custom implementation of a PID controller. However, as the manuscript grew and I focused on building a solid foundation in PLC programming, I realized that covering everything I had in mind would be unrealistic within a single volume. Rather than trying to fit too much into a limited space, I decided to concentrate on the essentials and make this book a practical starting point for those new to PLC programming and industrial automation.

Distributed Control Systems (DCS) are advanced control systems that integrate monitoring, control, and management functions for industrial processes. They are characterized by a distributed architecture, where individual control modules are located in various locations within the industrial plant. DCS enable the collection of data from multiple process points, their processing, and real-time decision-making. They are widely used in industries such as chemical manufacturing, petrochemicals, energy, and food processing, where comprehensive control of production processes is required.

I understand that if you're just starting your journey with PLCs, you might not be familiar with DCS systems. However, don't worry – DCS systems are beyond the scope of this book. Nevertheless, I want to provide a comprehensive overview of automation systems, which is why I mention DCS systems. Examples of such systems include PCS7 by SIEMENS or APROL by B&R. Additionally, I encourage you to revisit the topic of DCS systems after reading the entire book.

DCS (Distributed Control System)   System of distributed control coordinating and managing industrial processes at various levels.

Level "Supervisory Level"

In today's world, when we think about visualizing industrial processes, we immediately envision advanced HMI (Human–Machine Interface) and SCADA (Supervisory Control and Data Acquisition) systems. However, before these digital solutions emerged, operators had to manage in a different way.

Before the third industrial revolution, the visualization of processes in power plants or factories looked completely different. It often consisted of a simple board with hand-drawn schematics and indicator lights and manual input devices such as push buttons (Figure 3-6, Figure 3-7, Figure 3-8), position switches (Figure 3-9, Figure 3-10, Figure 3-11), key switches (Figure 3-12, Figure 3-13, Figure 3-14). Today, I would like to share with you a story that perfectly illustrates this approach.

During one of the upgrades of a power plant, I came across an old but still functional visualization board. It was a simple construction with bulbs and analog pointers. Operators were so attached to it that even during the control system overhaul, they insisted on keeping it.

Figure 3-3. *The LED used in automation systems*

Figure 3-4. The LED used in automation systems

Figure 3-5. *The LED used in automation systems*

During the modernization, we decided to update this board by replacing the bulbs with LED lights (Figure 3-3, Figure 3-4, Figure 3-5), which changed color depending on the status of the devices. Even when the main control system was turned off, thanks to the UPS power supply, operators could monitor the operation of the main circulation pumps, which supplied hot water to approximately 45,000 city residents.

This anecdote demonstrates that even in the digital age, there are simple yet effective ways of visualizing industrial processes. It's a perfect example of how simplicity can sometimes be the key to efficient industrial process management.

It's also worth mentioning a particular anecdote that illustrates the significant role visualization systems play in the context of an entire control system. The project involved desalinating seawater for a village in South

America and was the result of collaboration among several companies from different industries. Each company contributed to the project pro bono, working for the cause and supporting the initiative.

One of the companies provided the PLC controller, but due to a lack of resources, it wasn't possible to implement a visualization system. The idea was to conduct diagnostics using a laptop and engineering software. As part of the project, another company supplied solar panels to power the entire control system, making the installation completely energy self-sufficient. Yet another company involved in the project provided essential equipment such as pumps, tanks, sensors, and valves.

Figure 3-6 to Figure 3-8 show push buttons.

Figure 3-6. *Push button used in automation systems*

Figure 3-7. *Push button used in automation systems*

Figure 3-8. *Push button used in automation systems*

The entire installation, aimed at carrying out the reverse osmosis process, relied on a simple visualization system consisting of four LED lights and two buttons for controlling and monitoring the process. The lack of an elaborate visualization system made diagnosis and maintenance of the installation difficult, and the need to use a VPN tunnel for interventions further complicated the situation. Additionally, the personnel operating the installation lacked proper training.

Figure 3-9 to Figure 3-11 show position switches.

Figure 3-9. *Two-position switch*

Figure 3-10. *Two-position switch*

Figure 3-11. *Two-position switch*

The whole situation illustrates the significance of properly designing a visualization system that enables quick diagnosis and response to failures. The lack of this functionality not only caused stress and anxiety related to repairs but also had a negative impact on personal life, taking away time meant for family. This is an important example that underscores the importance of visualization systems in the entire control system and the necessity of carefully selecting the right solution for a given project.

Figure 3-12 to Figure 3-14 show key switches.

Figure 3-12. *Key switch*

Figure 3-13. *Key switch*

Figure 3-14. *Key switch*

After sharing several anecdotes related to visualization systems, it's worth moving on to presenting the various options available when building a control system. We'll focus on modern control systems, which also include modern visualization systems. One of the simplest devices that can be used for visualizing a technological process is an HMI panel. HMI stands for Human–Machine Interface. So, it can be said to be a kind of intermediary between the machine and the human who will operate the machine or installation. Various messages about the current state of the machine or installation are displayed on such a screen. In addition, there is almost always the possibility of interacting with the machine or installation. The simplest example would be starting or stopping an application implemented in the PLC controller.

Visualization   Graphic representation of data and information in a user-friendly format.

As we can see, visualization systems fulfill a very important function, which is the ability to run applications that are located in the PLC controller, without the knowledge and skills of PLC programming. This is a very significant advantage provided by visualization systems.

HMI (Human–Machine Interface)

HMI (Human–Machine Interface)   User interface enabling control and monitoring of industrial devices.

HMI, which stands for Human–Machine Interface, is a user interface used to operate and monitor individual devices or machines in a factory. It is a local tool that enables interaction between humans and machines at a local level. HMIs are often built into touch panels (Figure 3-15, Figure 3-16, Figure 3-17), which display various messages about the current state of the machine or installation. In addition, they also allow interaction with the device, such as starting or stopping an application implemented in the PLC controller.

Benefits of Using HMI

- *Ease of use*: Thanks to the graphical user interface, HMI provides intuitive operation of industrial machines and equipment, allowing operators to manage production processes quickly and effectively.

- *Fast response*: HMI enables quick response to changes in production processes by immediately displaying information about failures, alarms, or other important events.

- *Local control capability*: HMI allows local control over machines and devices, enabling operators to perform simple control operations without the need to rely on the central SCADA system.

- *Easy customization*: HMI interfaces are often configurable, allowing for easy adaptation to specific applications or operator preferences.

Figure 3-15. *HMI panel*

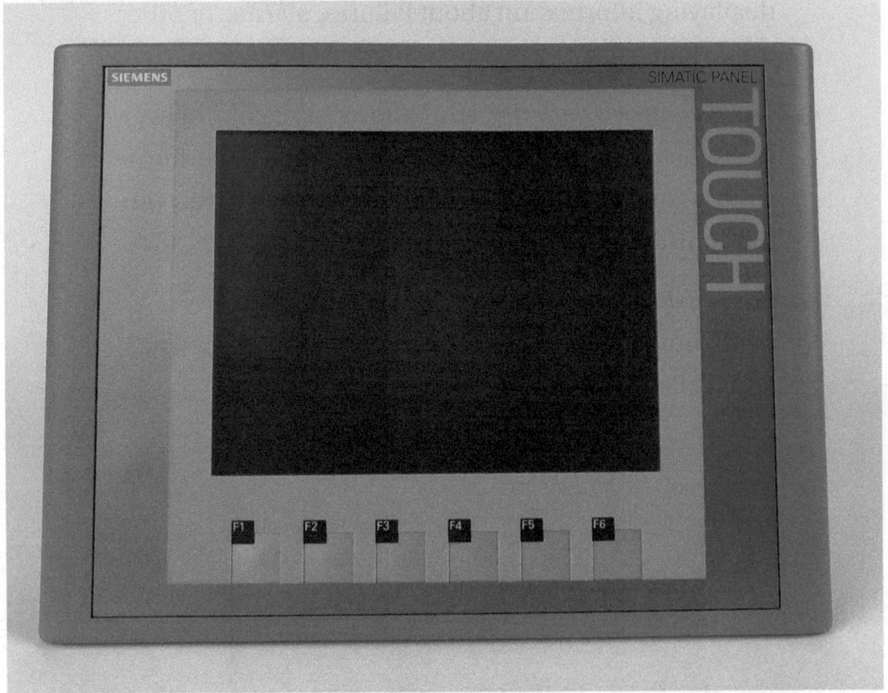

Figure 3-16. *HMI panel*

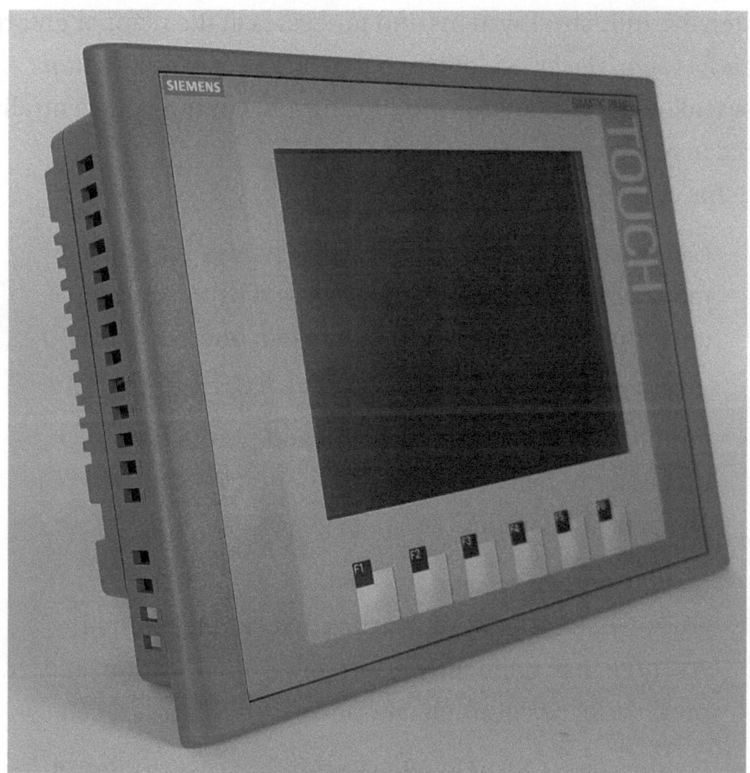

Figure 3-17. *HMI panel*

SCADA (Supervisory Control and Data Acquisition)

SCADA (Supervisory Control and Data Acquisition)   Advanced system for monitoring, controlling, and collecting data from industrial processes at the plant or enterprise level.

SCADA, which stands for Supervisory Control and Data Acquisition, is an advanced system that enables monitoring, control, and data collection from extensive industrial systems and processes at the plant or enterprise level. It is a system designed for managing large-scale production processes, allowing continuous monitoring and control of decentralized industrial installations.

Benefits of Using SCADA

- *Centralized management*: SCADA enables centralized management of production processes by integrating data from multiple control points into one system.

- *Real-time monitoring*: With SCADA, operators can monitor the status of equipment and production processes in real time, allowing for quick response to changes and failures.

- *Intelligent resource management*: SCADA offers advanced data analysis features that enable optimal resource management, performance optimization, and production cost minimization.

- *Remote access*: SCADA allows remote access to control and monitoring systems, enabling operators to monitor production processes from anywhere and at any time.

Both HMI and SCADA systems play a crucial role in industrial processes, providing operators with intuitive tools for monitoring, controlling, and optimizing production. Their use enables increased efficiency, cost reduction, and improved quality of manufactured products.

In summary, HMI serves as a local user interface for controlling individual machines or devices, while SCADA is an advanced system for managing and monitoring extensive industrial processes on a large scale.

Both HMI and SCADA systems feature alarm collection and triggering functions, as well as notifications about the status of installations or machinery. Additionally, both systems allow for data collection from analog measurements and other parameters, enabling trend creation.

However, it's not just real-time monitoring but also the capability to gather this data that is significant. And thus, we have arrived at another element of the visualization system, which is the Historian.

Historian   System enabling the collection, archiving, and analysis of historical data from industrial processes.

The Historian is an integral component in both SCADA and HMI systems, playing a crucial role in data collection and analysis. It's a system that enables real-time data collection and archives it for long-term analysis and monitoring of industrial processes.

Benefits of Using Historian

- *Improved diagnostics*: By collecting and analyzing historical data, Historian enables quick detection of anomalies in the control system, allowing for swift response and problem elimination.

- *Process optimization*: Analysis of data gathered by Historian identifies areas where improvements or optimizations can be made, leading to increased efficiency and reduced production costs.

- *Report generation*: Historian allows for the generation of detailed reports on process performance, trends, alarms, and other important parameters, facilitating reporting and decision-making at the management level.

- *Ensuring compliance with regulations*: By archiving data according to specified industry standards and regulations, Historian helps companies maintain compliance with legal and regulatory requirements as well as audits.

Functions of Historian

- *Real-time data collection*: Historian is capable of continuously collecting data from multiple points in the process, providing up-to-date information on the status of installations or machinery.

- *Data archiving*: Data gathered by Historian is archived in a structured and secure manner, enabling later analysis and utilization.

- *Data analysis*: Historian offers tools for data analysis, including generating charts, reports, as well as advanced trend analysis and forecasting techniques.

- *Integration with other systems*: Historian can be integrated with other management systems, such as ERP or MES systems, allowing for full integration of data and production processes.

Practical Applications of Historian

- *Production performance monitoring*: By collecting data on machine performance and production processes, Historian enables continuous monitoring of performance and identification of areas requiring improvement.

- *Fault diagnostics*: Analysis of historical data allows for quick diagnosis and repair of faults and disturbances in the control system, contributing to minimizing production downtime.

- *Reporting processes*: Historian facilitates the generation of reports regarding performance, trends, alarms, and other relevant parameters of production processes, allowing for ongoing monitoring and analysis of plant activities.

Historian thus forms an integral part of visualization systems, providing not only the ability to collect data but also to analyze and utilize it to optimize production processes and ensure compliance with regulatory requirements.

After discussing the theoretical aspects of visualization and automation systems, it's worth looking at practical examples of their application. One such story is an anecdote related to the modernization and digitization of a control system in one of the factories, which I had the opportunity to conduct.

The management of the factory decided to fully automate the temperature control process in one of the production stages. Previously, operators monitored and adjusted the temperature manually, requiring constant supervision. When the proposal to introduce a new automated control system emerged, many operators feared for their professional future. They were afraid that their jobs would be automated, and they would become redundant.

After the system upgrade, the temperature control was taken over by the logic of the PLC controller, and the entire process became automated. The new visualization system allowed operators to switch between manual mode, where they made decisions about opening or closing valves, and automatic mode, where the PLC controller made decisions based on measured temperature values. Factory workers, although initially skeptical about the new system, quickly realized its benefits.

During the personnel training on operating the new control system, it became evident that one of the key issues is educating employees about changes in their roles. Although automation meant less manual work, there was still a need for monitoring the system and making decisions based on data gathered through visualization.

As the person responsible for implementing the system, I had the pleasure of training personnel from various cultural backgrounds, visiting different parts of the world. While traveling, I witnessed the diversity of people and their approaches to work. I noticed that regardless of culture or nationality, all factory workers had the same concerns and hopes regarding the introduction of the new system.

This anecdote illustrates how technology can change the way work is done and how processes are managed in the industry, emphasizing the importance of proper training for personnel to operate new automation systems. Moreover, it shows that being a PLC programmer is not just about sitting in front of a computer but also involves interacting with people and traveling the world to implement new technologies.

After discussing concepts such as HMI, SCADA, and Historian, we now move on to placing these key elements at the *"Supervisory Level"*. Here, they focus on enabling monitoring, control, and management of industrial processes on a broader scale. Visualization systems, such as Human–Machine Interface (HMI) and Supervisory Control and Data Acquisition (SCADA), play a crucial role here, integrating with Historian to provide comprehensive analysis, monitoring, and optimization of production activities (Figure 3-18).

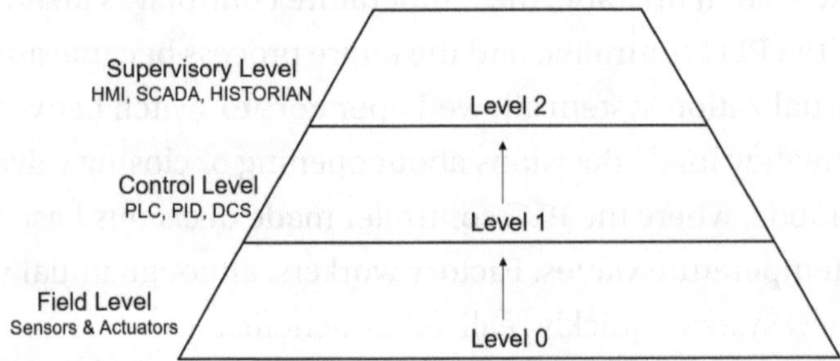

Figure 3-18. *Level 2 "Supervisory Level" of the automation pyramid*

After discussing the *"Field Level"*, *"Control Level"*, and *"Supervisory Level"*, let's now delve into the new concept of the *"Operational Technology Layer"*, which integrates these three levels into a cohesive structure. This layer encompasses key elements enabling monitoring, control, and management of industrial processes on a broader scale. It's the point where data collected by sensors at the *"Field Level"* is transmitted to PLC controllers at the *"Control Level"* and then utilized by visualization systems at the *"Supervisory Level"* for process control and monitoring.

In this context, the *"Operational Technology Layer"* serves as a crucial element facilitating the monitoring, control, and management of industrial processes (Figure 3-19).

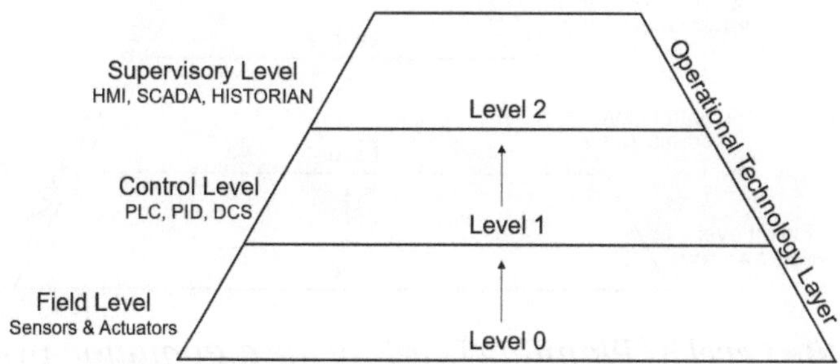

Figure 3-19. *"Operational Technology Layer" of the automation pyramid*

OT Layer   Layer of systems and technologies related to production operations and process control.

Level "Planning Level"

When we cross the boundaries of control and supervision levels, we reach the area called the *"Planning Level"*, which resides in the *"Crossover Layer"*. Here, the focus is on MES (Manufacturing Execution System), APS (Advanced Planning and Scheduling), and OEE (Overall Equipment Effectiveness) systems (Figure 3-20).

Crossover Layer   Layer connecting systems and technologies from industrial areas with information technology systems.

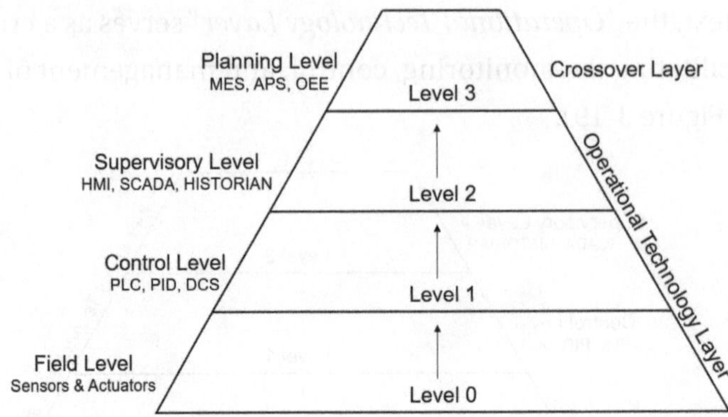

Figure 3-20. *Level 3 "Planning Level" of the automation pyramid*

The Manufacturing Execution System (MES) is software designed for monitoring, managing, and reporting production activities in real time. MES integrates production processes on the assembly line, providing visibility and control over manufacturing operations. In practice, MES is responsible for scheduling production tasks, managing materials and resources, quality control, and monitoring production performance. It is an essential tool for optimizing production processes and improving operational efficiency.

The Advanced Planning and Scheduling (APS) system is a tool used for planning and scheduling production tasks in a more advanced manner than traditional planning methods. APS enables the optimization of production schedules, taking into account various factors such as resource availability, production constraints, order fulfillment deadlines, and customer preferences. By using APS, it is possible to better utilize resources, reduce downtime on the production line, and increase production flexibility.

Overall Equipment Effectiveness (OEE) is a measure of the total efficiency of equipment, which assesses how machines are utilized in the production process compared to their maximum potential. OEE takes into account three key components: equipment availability, performance, and quality of production. By monitoring OEE, areas where the production process can be optimized to achieve higher efficiency and profitability can be identified.

MES, APS, and OEE systems work together to ensure efficient planning, management, and optimization of production processes at the Planning Level. Their integration enables better resource utilization, increased production efficiency and flexibility, and improved product quality.

MES (Manufacturing Execution System)   Production management system integrating manufacturing processes on the assembly line.

APS (Advanced Planning and Scheduling)   Advanced tool for planning and scheduling production tasks.

OEE (Overall Equipment Effectiveness)   Indicator of overall equipment performance, measuring their effective utilization in production.

Level "Management Level"

The final but crucial level of the automation pyramid is the *"Management Level"*, whose main objective is to manage the entire production process and gather, process, and analyze data at a strategic level. This level is an integral part of the *"Information Technology Layer"*, which is responsible for managing information technology systems within the organization (Figure 3-21).

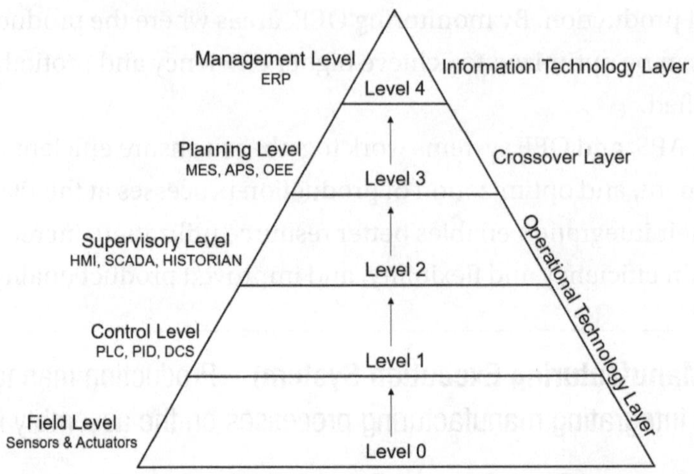

Figure 3-21. Level 4 "Management Level" of the automation pyramid

At the "Management Level", Enterprise Resource Planning (ERP) systems play a crucial role. These systems integrate various areas of a company's operations, such as production, finance, sales, logistics, and human resources management. As a result, they provide a unified source of data and enable effective resource management across all levels of the organizational hierarchy.

In the context of industrial automation, ERP systems play a crucial role in optimizing production processes by ensuring efficient resource management and production scheduling. They enable order planning, inventory monitoring, supplier order management, and production cost tracking.

ERP (Enterprise Resource Planning)   System integrating various areas of enterprise activity for efficient resource and process management.

Moreover, ERP systems integrate with other systems used at lower levels of the automation pyramid, such as MES (Manufacturing Execution System) or APS (Advanced Planning and Scheduling), enabling comprehensive control over production processes at all stages. This allows managers and decision-makers access to reliable data and comprehensive analyses, facilitating informed business decision-making.

Absolutely, ERP systems are indeed an integral part of an enterprise's IT infrastructure, and their effective utilization is crucial for gaining a competitive edge in the market.

IT Layer   Layer encompassing information technology systems and technologies processing data at the organizational level.

Summary

We've reached the pinnacle of the pyramid. This pyramid is what we call the automation pyramid. We've discussed the general concepts and definitions that make up the different levels. After reading the first part of the book, we have an understanding of how automation systems are structured. Now that we're familiar with the theory, it's time to delve into the practical aspects of programming PLC controllers.

The aim of the first part was to present the subject from a theoretical perspective. Now, we will move on to the practical part, which involves delving into the intricacies of programming PLC controllers. In the upcoming chapters, we will navigate within the *"OT Layer"* between the *"Control level"* and *"Supervisory Level"*. The main focus will be on programming control logic for the PLC controller, but we will also implement visualizations.

As readers, we are ready to take on this challenge. We have realized the importance of understanding theory, but now it's time for practice. Programming PLC controllers opens the door to the fascinating world of industrial automation, where our knowledge and skills have a real impact on the operation and efficiency of control systems.

As we can see, the discussed theoretical aspects of the automation pyramid are the foundation for our further learning. Now that we have solid groundwork, we can eagerly continue our journey into the world of PLC programming. We have to start somewhere, and we are ready for this challenge!

CHAPTER 4

Digital IO for Lighting Control

In this chapter, we will implement our first control logic and create a simple visualization. Let's imagine a scenario where a factory has decided to automate the quality control process of their product, and for this purpose, a new hall has been constructed where this quality control will take place. However, before anything can be automated, the first thing that needs to be done in the newly built hall is to turn on the lighting so that the hall can be expanded with various automation components without any issues.

This will be our first task as PLC programmers. Before starting any programming work, we always receive contact information for the person or group of people who designed and conceived the system. They can provide a precise description of what the control system should do. In practice, this is often one person, known as the process technologist. The process technologist provides technical specifications, functional requirements, and test scenarios that programmers must consider in their work. Sometimes, as programmers, we participate in meetings and discussions about the system's operation. As I mentioned in previous chapters, the work of a PLC programmer is not just about sitting in front of a computer.

© Dariusz Wrebiak 2026
D. Wrebiak, *Practical PLC Programming for Beginners*, Maker Innovations Series,
https://doi.org/10.1007/979-8-8688-2430-2_4

Application Scenario

Let's take a detailed look at the application scenario provided by the process technologist.

Application Scenario: Lighting control in the quality control hall.

Technological Description: A lighting system has been installed in the quality control hall, controlled by a PLC. This system allows both manual control of the lighting via switches installed on the walls and automatic responses to various environmental factors, such as detecting the movement of employees in the hall.

Application Functions

1. *Manual operation*: Employees in the hall can manually turn the lighting on and off using switches placed on the hall walls.

2. *Automatic operation*: The system automatically responds to employee movement in the hall using motion sensors, turning the lighting on and off depending on the presence of people.

3. *Emergency lighting*: In the event of a detected threat, such as fire or smoke, the system automatically turns on the emergency lighting. In such a case, the regular lighting should not be active.

Additional Elements

- *Hall sector division*: By dividing the hall into sectors, lighting can be independently controlled in different areas, allowing better adaptation of the lighting to the

needs of each sector. The hall is divided into sectors
because each area will perform specific functions
during the quality control process.

In addition to the technological process description, a very important document that a PLC programmer works with is the electrical schematic of the entire control system. The design of the electrical schematics is the responsibility of the electrical engineer, with whom the programmer often collaborates in case of any doubts or questions regarding the control system.

From the electrical schematic, we can learn exactly what we are controlling and, most importantly, prepare a complete list of input and output signals that we will need to use during the implementation of the PLC program (Table 4-1).

Table 4-1. *List of signals that we will use in our lighting control program for the quality control hall*

Type of Signal	Name	Description
Digital input	Lighting all areas	Hand request to switch on the lighting in all areas
Digital input	Lighting area I	Hand request to switch on the lighting in the 1st area
Digital input	Lighting area II	Hand request to switch on the lighting in the 2nd area
Digital input	Lighting area III	Hand request to switch on the lighting in the 3rd area
Digital input	Motion area I	Motion detected in the 1st area

(continued)

Table 4-2. (*continued*)

Type of Signal	Name	Description
Digital input	Motion area II	Motion detected in the 2nd area
Digital input	Motion area III	Motion detected in the 3rd area
Digital input	No emergency	Request to switch off the emergency lighting
Digital output	Lighting area I	Switch on/off the lighting in the 1st area
Digital output	Lighting area II	Switch on/off the lighting in the 2nd area
Digital output	Lighting area III	Switch on/off the lighting in the 3rd area
Digital output	Emergency lighting	Request to switch on the emergency lighting

Since we have defined the list of input and output signals and have knowledge about how our application should work, we can proceed to the implementation of the program.

Application Implementation

Creating a New Project

We launch CODESYS and create a new project by selecting *File* ➤ *New Project* from the menu (Figure 4-1).

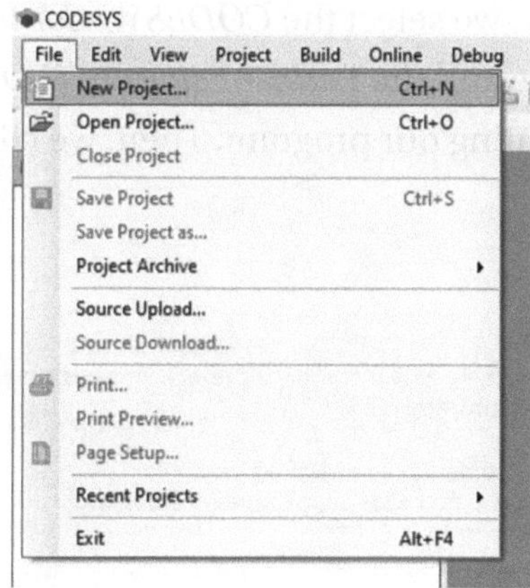

Figure 4-1. *File ➤ New Project*

Categories is *Projects,* and the Templates is *Standard project.* We name the project *LightingControl* and specify the location where we want to save our project. I will save my project in *C:\PLC\Chapter_04* (Figure 4-2).

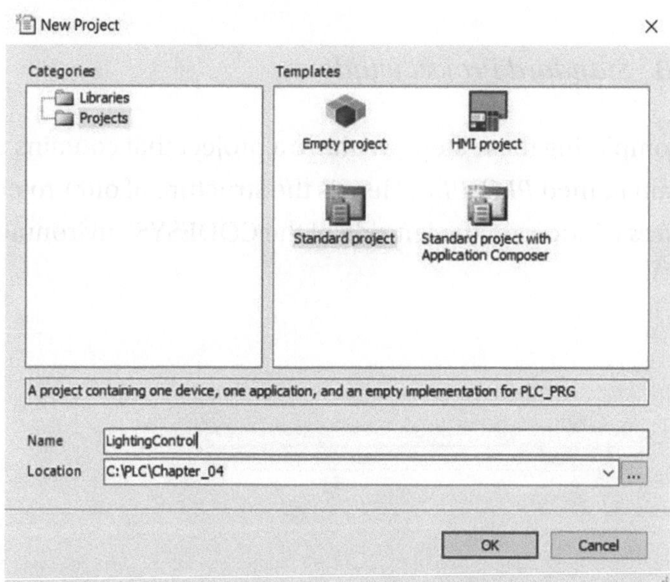

Figure 4-2. *New Project window*

In the next window, we select the *CODESYS Control RTE V3 x64 (CODESYS)* device type and the *Ladder Diagram (LD2)* programming language for implementing our program. Then, we click the *OK* button (Figure 4-3).

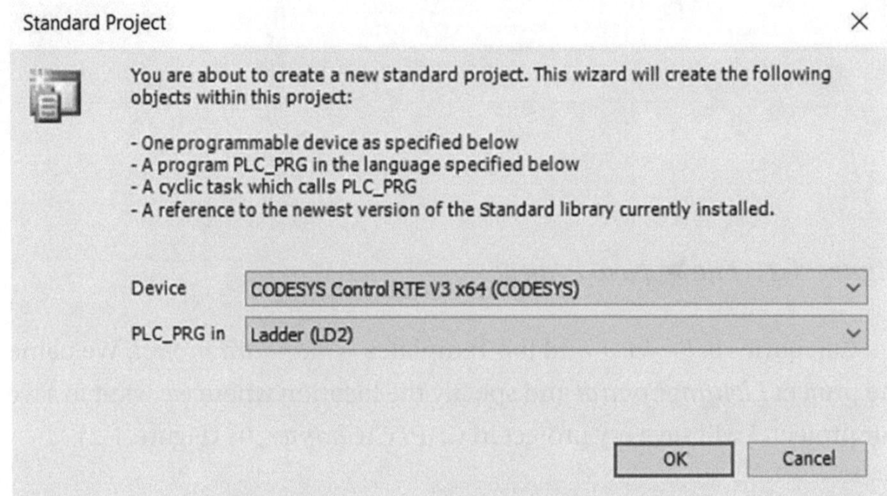

Figure 4-3. Standard Project window

After completing these steps, we have a project that contains an empty PLC program named *PLC_PRG*. Here is the structure of our project, visible in the *Devices* window on the left side of the CODESYS environment (Figure 4-4).

Figure 4-4. *Project structure in the Devices window*

Adding Global Variables

The next step will be to add a new object to our project, specifically a global variable list, where we will declare variables. These variables will represent digital inputs and outputs.

To begin, right-click the *Application* in the *Devices* window, then select *Add Object* ➤ *Global Variable List…* (Figure 4-5).

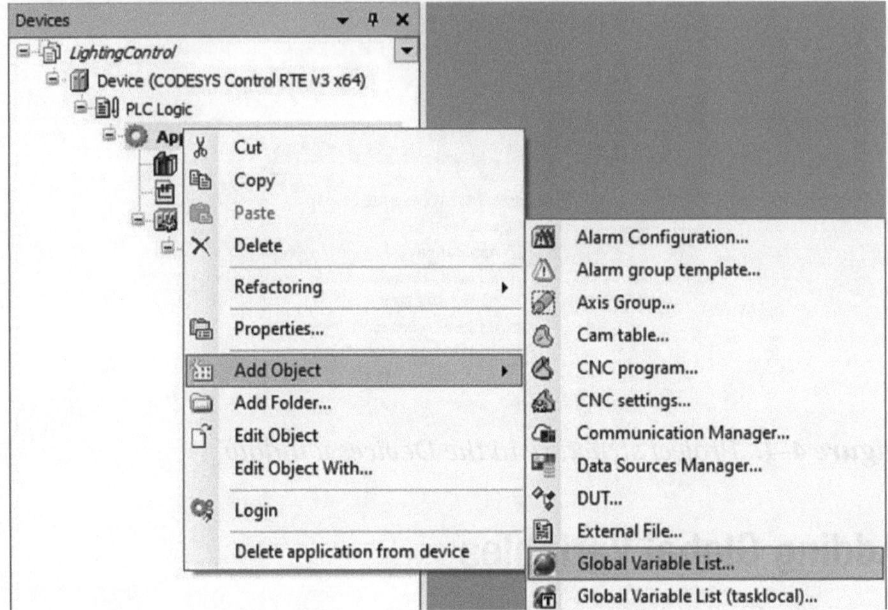

Figure 4-5. *Application ➤ Add Object ➤ Global Variable List...*

Name the new variable list as *GVL_InputsOutputs*, where we will store all variables related to inputs and outputs in the PLC program. Click the *Add* button (Figure 4-6).

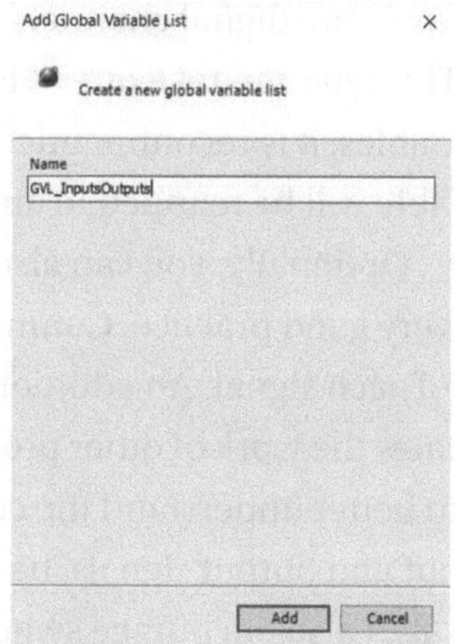

Figure 4-6. *Add Global Variable List window*

After adding the new object, the editor for *GVL_InputsOutputs* will open (Figure 4-7). Initially, the list is empty, but we will soon add our required variables. The editor allows switching between two views: Textual View and Tabular View, using the buttons on the right side.

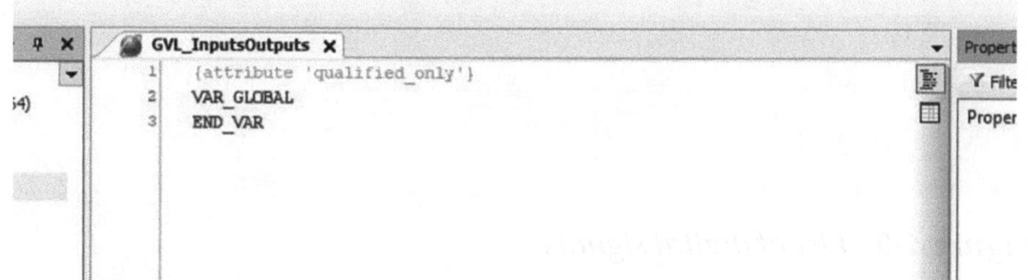

Figure 4-7. *Global variables editor*

Listing 4-1. Listing 4-1 shows the syntax for declaring variables in textual mode.

```
Name_of_Variable : Type_of_Variable;
```

All our inputs and outputs are digital channels; therefore, the type of all variables is BOOL. This type can take one of two values: TRUE or FALSE. When naming variables, it is recommended to use prefixes that indicate whether the variable will be mapped to an input channel DI_ or an output channel DO_. Optionally, you can also add a comment to each variable, which is a very good practice. Comments help quickly understand the function of each signal. An additional advantage of writing comments is that it facilitates the work of other programmers on our project, as it helps them to better understand the code. Here's how I would declare a list of digital input and output signals, based on the electrical schematic table (Figure 4-8). I also encourage switching to the tabular view to see the differences compared to the textual view.

```
GVL_InputsOutputs
 1    {attribute 'qualified_only'}
 2    VAR_GLOBAL
 3        // Digital Inputs
 4        DI_HAND_LIGHTING_ALL_AREAS : BOOL;      // Hand request to switch on the lighting in all areas
 5        DI_HAND_LIGHTING_AREA_I : BOOL;         // Hand request to switch on the lighting in 1st area
 6        DI_HAND_LIGHTING_AREA_II : BOOL;        // Hand request to switch on the lighting in 2nd area
 7        DI_HAND_LIGHTING_AREA_III : BOOL;       // Hand request to switch on the lighting in 3rd area
 8        DI_MOTION_DETECTED_AREA_I : BOOL;       // Motion detected in 1st area
 9        DI_MOTION_DETECTED_AREA_II : BOOL;      // Motion detected in 2nd area
10        DI_MOTION_DETECTED_AREA_III : BOOL;     // Motion detected in 3rd area
11        DI_NO_EMERGENCY : BOOL;                 // Request to switch on the emergency lighting
12
13        // Digital Outputs
14        DO_LIGHTING_AREA_I : BOOL;              // Switch on/off lighting in 1st area
15        DO_LIGHTING_AREA_II : BOOL;             // Switch on/off lighting in 2nd area
16        DO_LIGHTING_AREA_III : BOOL;            // Switch on/off lighting in 3rd area
17        DO_EMERGENCY_LIGHTING : BOOL;           // Switch on/off emergency lighting
18    END_VAR
```

Figure 4-8. *List of digital signals*

After declaring the variables, save the project by clicking *File* ➤ *Save Project* (Figure 4-9) and then compile the project by selecting *Build* ➤ *Generate Code* (Figure 4-10). Remember to compile the project after every change made to it.

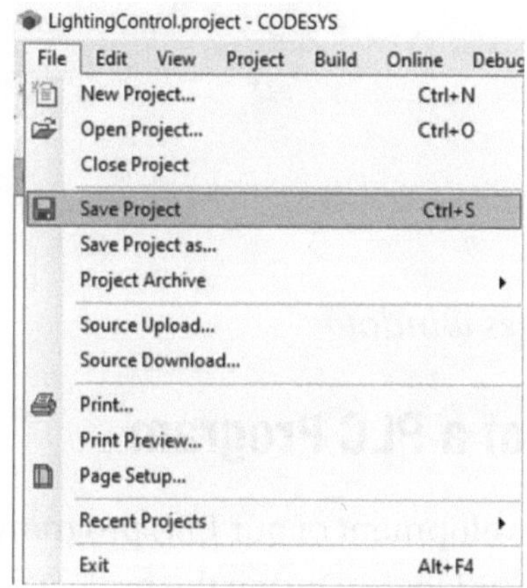

Figure 4-9. *File* ➤ *Save Project*

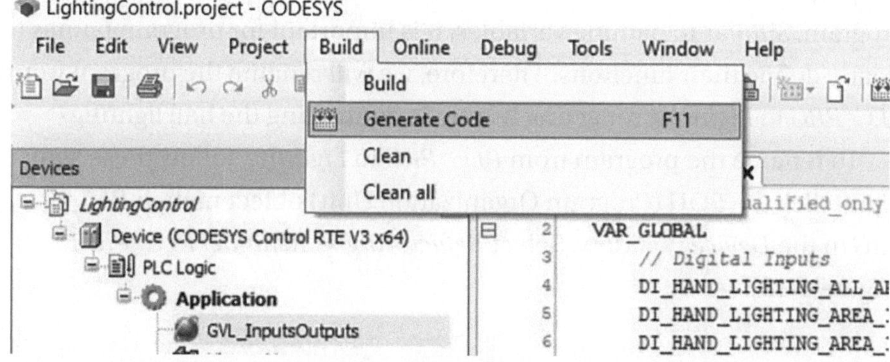

Figure 4-10. *Build* ➤ *Generate Code*

After successfully declaring the variables, in the *Messages* window, you should see information confirming that the application has been compiled successfully (Figure 4-11).

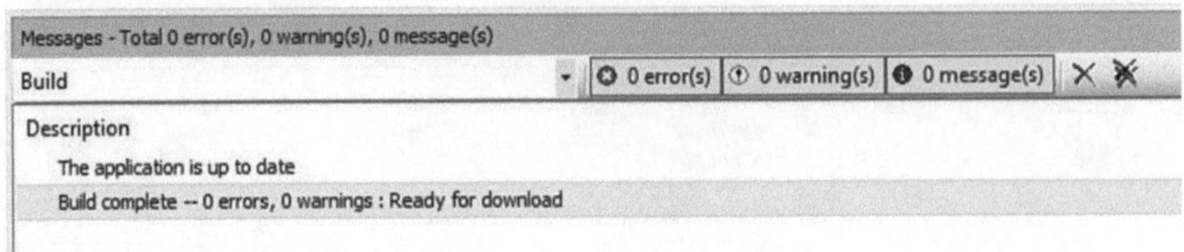

Figure 4-11. *Messages window*

Implementation of a PLC Program

The next step in the development of our PLC program will be the
implementation of control logic. During the project setup, we chose
the Ladder programming language (LD2) for our main program, which
was originally named *PLC_PRG*. Currently, this is the only program in
our project responsible for control. We will now proceed to rename this
program. Similar to naming variables, it is important for program names to
clearly define their functions. Therefore, we will rename the program from
PLC_PRG to *Lighting*, reflecting its role in controlling the hall lighting.

To rename the program from *PLC_PRG* to *Lighting*, follow these steps:
Right-click the POU (Program Organization Unit) object named *PLC_
PRG* in the *Devices* window. Select *Refactoring* ➤ *Rename 'PLC_PRG'...*
(Figure 4-12).

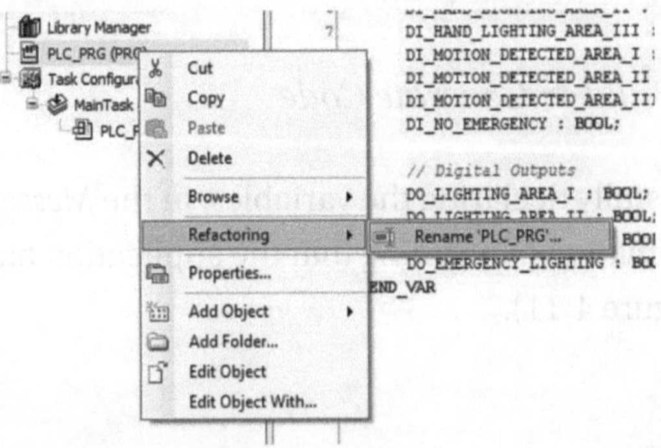

Figure 4-12. *Refactoring PLC_PRG*

In the *Rename* window, enter the new program name, which is *Lighting*, and then click the *OK* button (Figure 4-13).

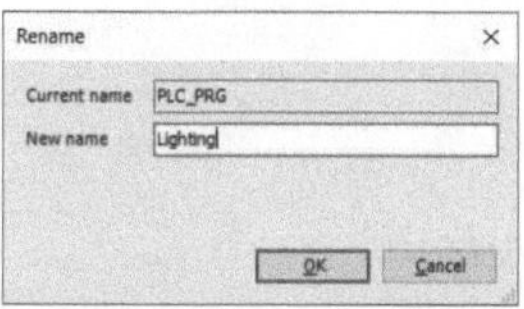

Figure 4-13. *Rename window*

By clicking the *OK* button, we confirm the changes in the *Refactoring* window, which informs us which elements will be modified (Figure 4-14).

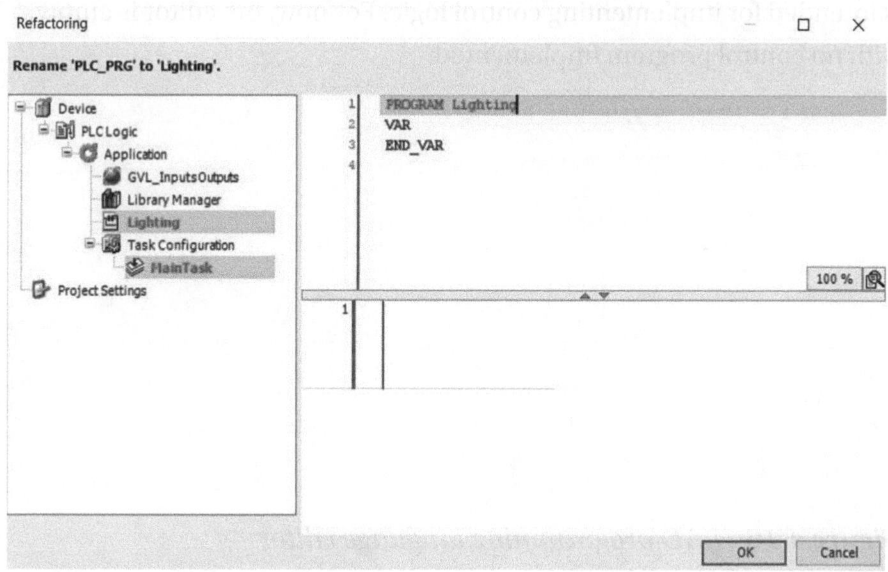

Figure 4-14. *Refactoring window*

After completing this process, we will see in the *Devices* window that all references to *PLC_PRG* have been updated to *Lighting* (Figure 4-15).

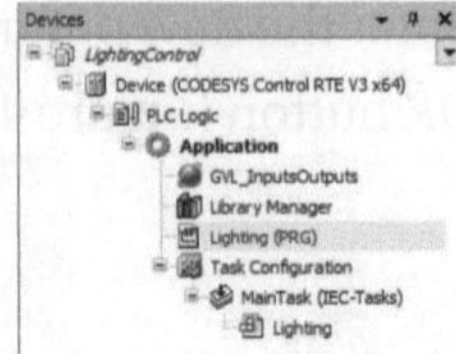

Figure 4-15. *Devices window*

Double-click the *Lighting* program in the *Devices* window on the left to open the PLC programming editor (Figure 4-16). The editor is divided into two parts: the upper part is used for declaring local variables, where we can switch between textual and tabular views. The lower part of the editor is intended for implementing control logic. For now, the editor is empty, with no control program implemented.

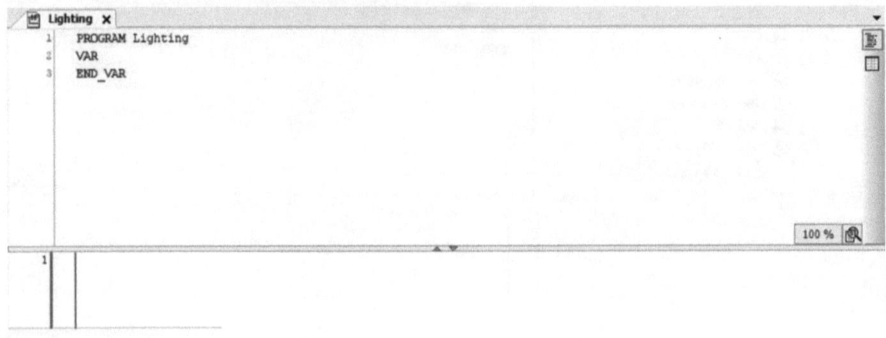

Figure 4-16. *LAD programming language editor*

Emergency Lighting

We begin the implementation of control logic by programming the emergency lighting. Let's assume that when the input signal *DI_NO_EMERGENCY* is in a high state (TRUE), it indicates the absence of any threat that would require the emergency lighting to be turned on. However, when the PLC reads this signal as a low state (FALSE), it indicates the detection of a threat, in which case the emergency lighting should be turned on.

To implement this control logic, select the first network in the editor, which was automatically created after adding the program file to our project (Figure 4-17).

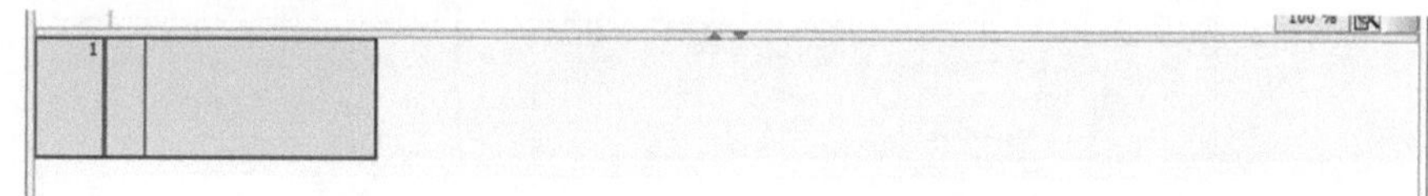

Figure 4-17. *The highlighted first network in the editor*

From the menu, select *Ladder ➤ Insert Contact* to add a contact to our program (Figure 4-18). The Normally Open Contact will be inserted (Figure 4-19).

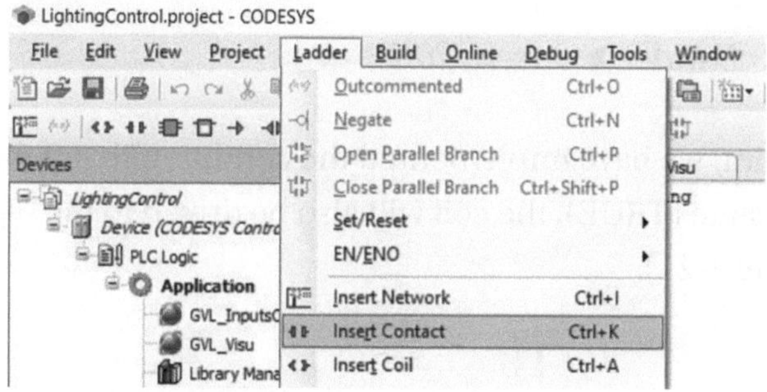

Figure 4-18. *Ladder ➤ Insert Contact*

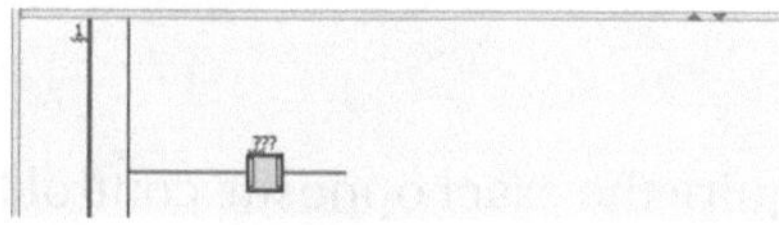

Figure 4-19. *Inserted NO contact*

Next, click on the endpoint of the added contact to select it, then from the menu, choose *Ladder* ➤ *Insert Coil* to insert a coil into our program (Figure 4-20).

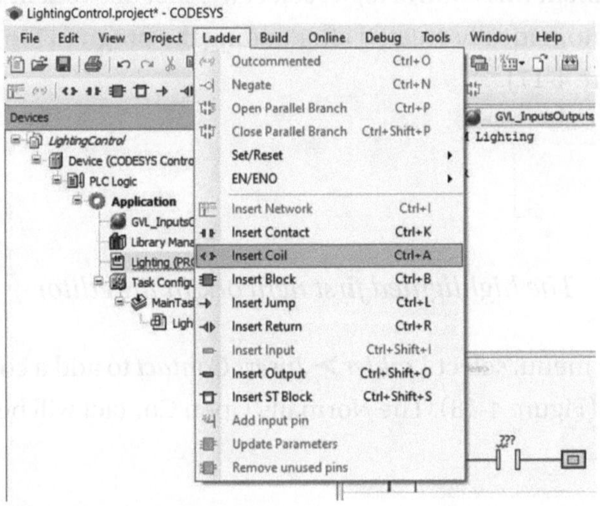

Figure 4-20. *Ladder* ➤ *Insert Coil*

At this point, we have implemented the condition that if the contact is in the high state (TRUE), the coil will also be driven to the high state (TRUE) (Figure 4-21).

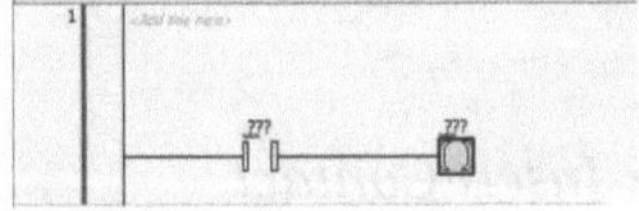

Figure 4-21. *The control logic sets the coil to TRUE when the contact is set to TRUE.*

In our case, we require the exact opposite control logic because the input signal *DI_NO_EMERGENCY* informs us of the absence of danger when it is in the high state (TRUE). Therefore, we need to change our normally open (NO) contact to a normally closed (NC) contact. To do this, click on the NO contact symbol and choose *Ladder* ➤ *Negate* from the menu (Figure 4-22). The negated NO contact changes its symbol to an NC contact (Figure 4-23).

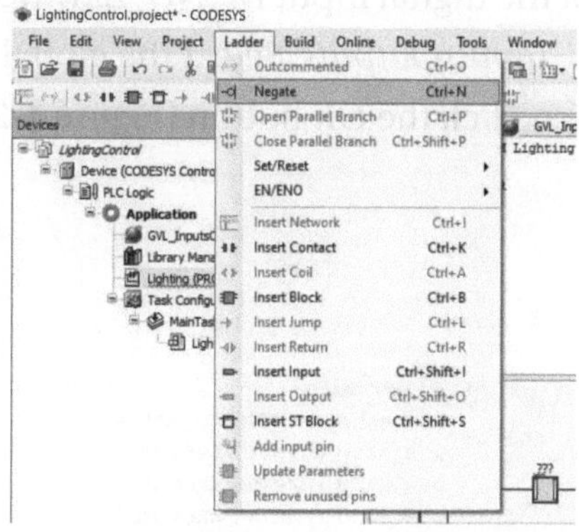

Figure 4-22. *Ladder* ➤ *Negate*

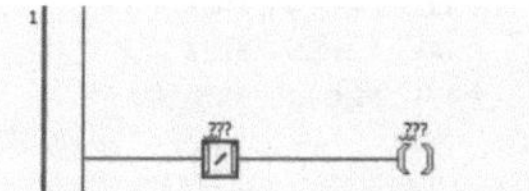

Figure 4-23. *The negated NO contact changes its symbol to an NC contact.*

The next step after implementing the control logic is to assign the appropriate variables to our NC contact and coil. To do this, double-click on the symbol with three question marks that is visible above the NC contact symbol. On the right side, a small button will appear, which you should click (Figure 4-24).

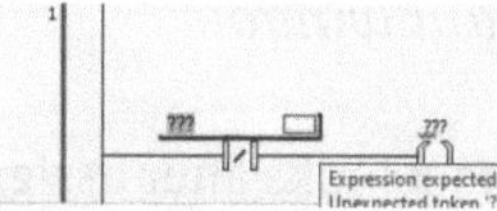

Figure 4-24. *Assigning a variable to the contact*

After clicking the button on the right side, the *Input Assistant* window
will open. Here, you need to specify the variable name that should be
assigned to the NC contact used in the control logic. In this case, we want
to monitor the state of the digital input *DI_NO_EMERGENCY*, located
at *Application* ➤ *GVL_InputsOutputs*. Select the global variable *DI_NO_
EMERGENCY*, and then click the *OK* button (Figure 4-25).

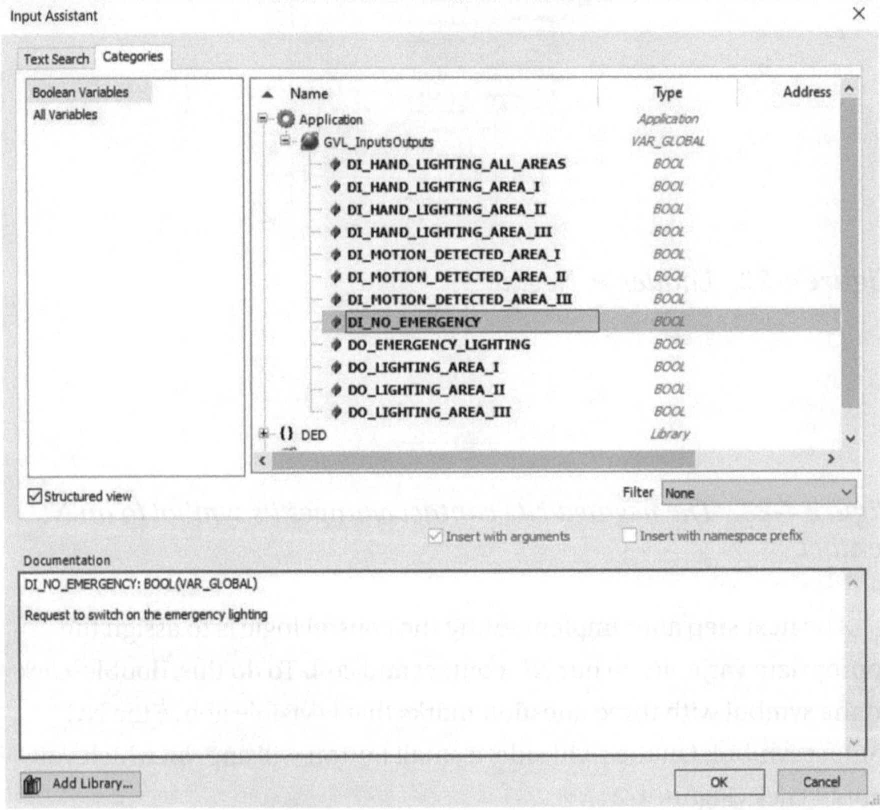

Figure 4-25. *Input Assistant window*

Here is how the NC contact looks after assigning the digital input *DI_
NO_EMERGENCY* to it (Figure 4-26).

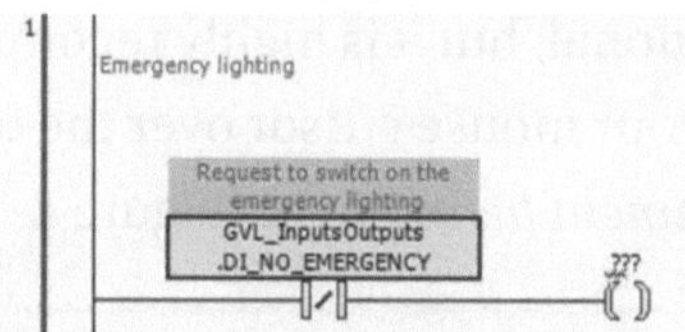

Figure 4-26. *NC contact with the variable assigned to it*

Then we need to assign a digital output to the coil that will control the emergency lighting. We can do this similarly to how we assigned the NC contact, but this time we'll use a different option.

Click on the symbol with three question marks above the coil. Then, on the keyboard, type the prefix *"do_"* and press *Ctrl + Space*. This will open a window containing all variables with the prefix *"do_"* that have been declared as global variables. It's worth noting that case sensitivity doesn't matter in this case. I often use this method instead of selecting variables through the *Input Assistant* window (Figure 4-27).

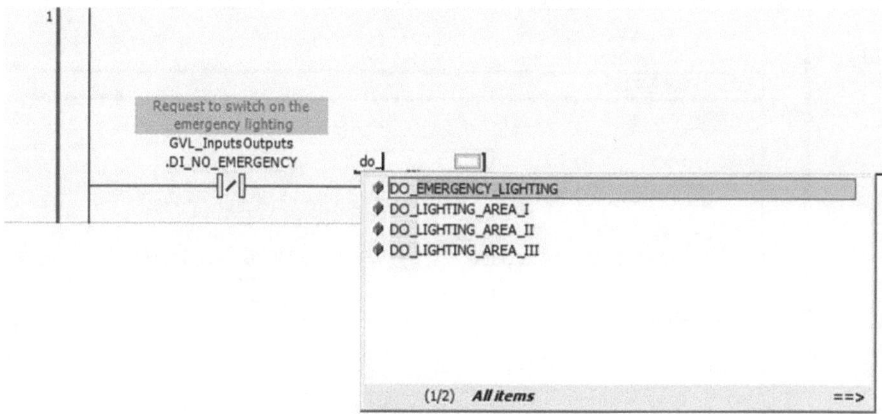

Figure 4-27. *List of variables matching the prefix "do_"*

From the list, select the digital output *DO_EMERGENCY_LIGHTING*, and confirm your selection by pressing Enter. The final step we should take is to add a comment to our network to maintain code clarity.

Adding comments is optional, but it is highly recommended practice. To add a comment, hover your mouse cursor over the top part of the network and click the *"<Add comment here>"* field (Figure 4-28).

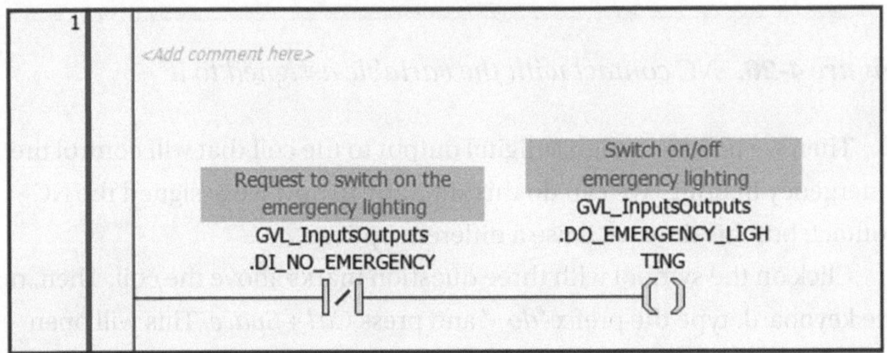

Figure 4-28. *Adding a comment to the network*

Next, let's enter the comment *Emergency lighting* for our network. This is how our emergency lighting control logic looks (Figure 4-29).

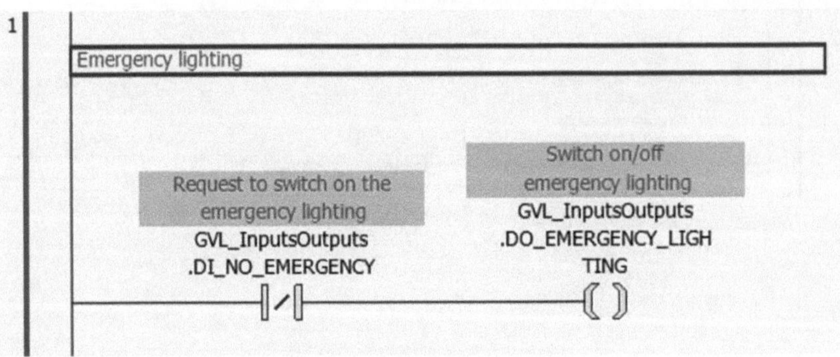

Figure 4-29. *Network Emergency lighting*

Normally Open Contact   A normally open (NO) contact is a logical element in PLC programming that allows current to flow only when it is activated. In its inactive state, the circuit is open, meaning there is no current flow.

Normally Closed Contact   A normally closed (NC) contact is a logical element in PLC programming that allows current to flow in its inactive state. When it is activated, the circuit opens, interrupting the current flow.

Coil   In PLC programming, a coil is an executive element that controls the outputs of the system. When the program logic requires the coil to be energized, it becomes active, which can start the device or output assigned to that coil.

Testing PLC Program in the Simulator

Let's test our PLC program in the simulator. To do this, start the simulator by navigating to *Online* ➤ *Simulation* in the menu (Figure 4-30).

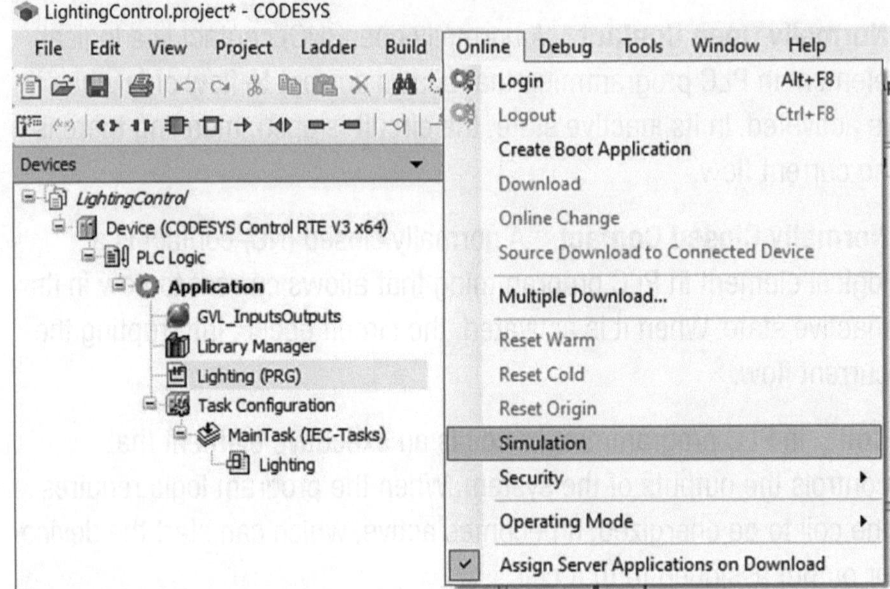

Figure 4-30. *Online ➤ Simulation*

Next, select *Online ➤ Login* from the menu to log in to the PLC controller (Figure 4-31).

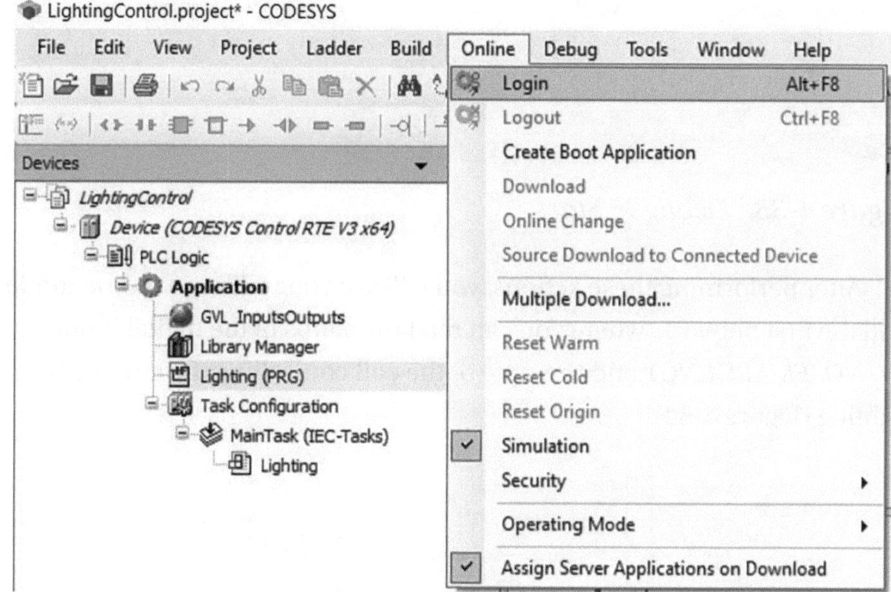

Figure 4-31. *Online ➤ Login*

On the screen, you will see a window informing you that the application does not exist in the controller. To proceed, click the *Yes* button. This message will always appear after restarting the simulator (Figure 4-32).

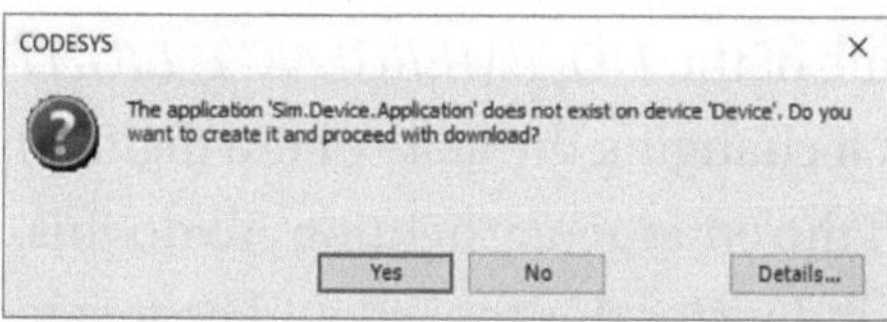

Figure 4-32. *Information about the application not existing*

Next, switch the controller from STOP mode to RUN mode by selecting *Debug ➤ Start* from the menu (Figure 4-33).

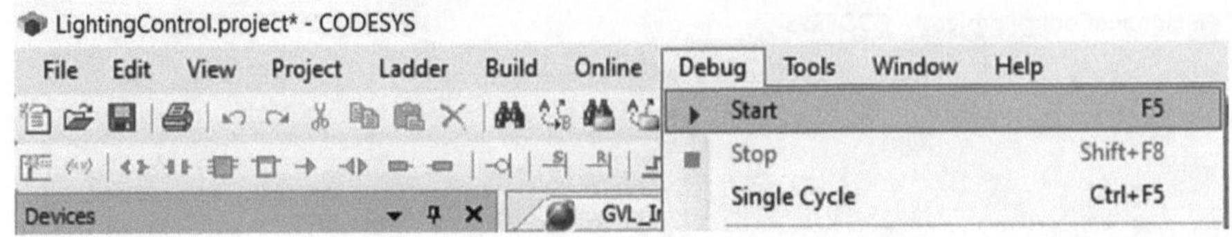

Figure 4-33. *Debug ➤ Start*

After performing these actions, you will see your editor in online mode and the first network, where you can read the status of the digital input *DI_NO_EMERGENCY* and the state of the coil controlling the emergency lighting (Figure 4-34).

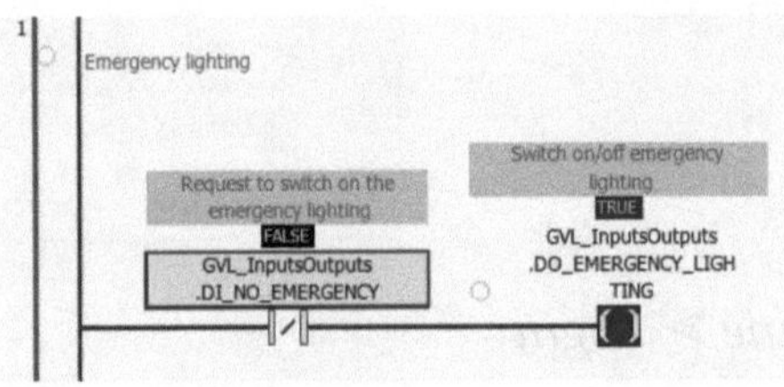

Figure 4-34. *Emergency lighting network in online mode*

According to the application scenario, when the digital input is in the low state (FALSE), it indicates that there has been a malfunction in the hall. In such a situation, the emergency lighting should be turned on, which is confirmed by the state of the *DO_EMERGENCY_LIGHT* coil set to TRUE.

Now, let's check if changing the state of the digital input from FALSE to TRUE will turn off the emergency lighting. To do this, we will use a tool called *Watch*. The window for this tool should be located in the lower part of the CODESYS environment (Figure 4-35). If it's not visible, you can open it by selecting *View ➤ Watch ➤ Watch 1* from the menu.

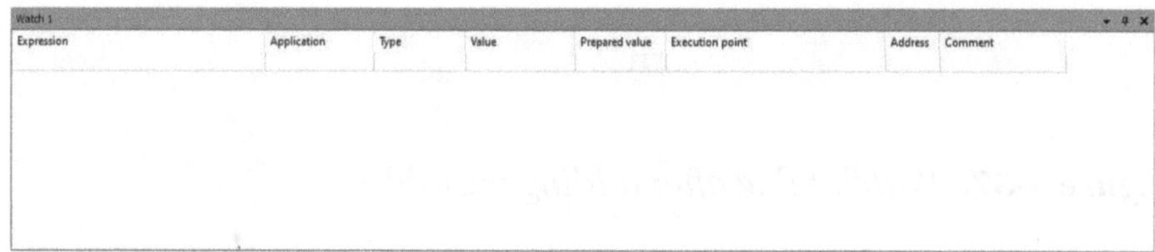

Figure 4-35. *Watch window*

In the *Watch* window, in the *Expression* column, we can select
variables that we want to monitor and change their values. Let's add
the variable representing the digital input *DI_NO_EMERGENCY* to the
Watch table (Figure 4-36). We have two options to do this: either select the
variable using the *Input Assistant* window or add it using the keyboard. We
learned both methods when assigning variables to control logic.

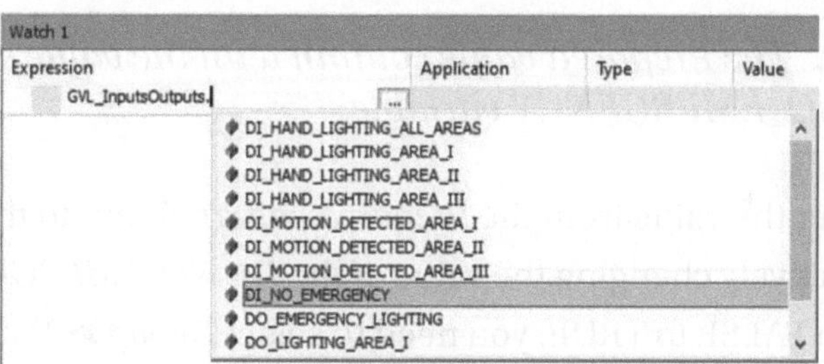

Figure 4-36. *Adding a variable to the Watch table*

After adding a variable to the *Watch* table, we can obtain more
information about the variable, such as its type or any comments we
added during declaration. However, the most important columns will be
Value and *Prepared value*. As part of the exercise, let's add another variable
representing the digital output *DO_EMERGENCY_LIGHTING* to the Watch
table. In the *Value* column, we can see the current state of the variables
(Figure 4-37).

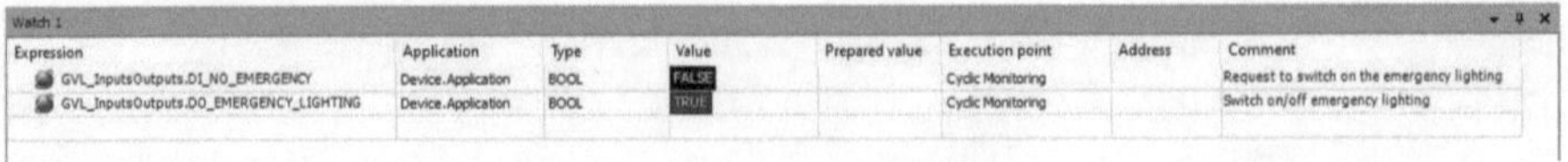

Figure 4-37. *Watch table after adding variables*

To change the value of the variable representing the digital input, left-click on the empty cell under the *Prepared value* column for the *DI_EMERGENCY_LIGHTING* variable. The CODESYS environment will automatically set the value in the column to TRUE, which is opposite to the current value of the variable (Figure 4-38).

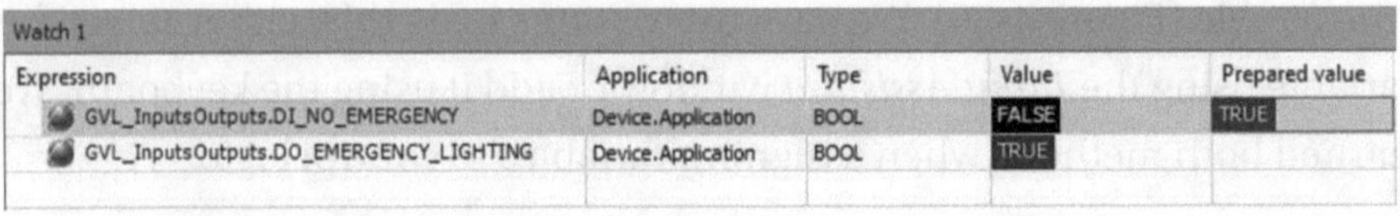

Figure 4-38. *The Prepared value column with the value set to TRUE for the DI_NO_EMERGENCY variable*

To transfer the value from the *Prepared value* column to the *Value* column, effectively changing the value of the *DI_NO_EMERGENCY* variable from FALSE to TRUE, you need to select *Debug* ➤ *Write Values* from the menu (Figure 4-39).

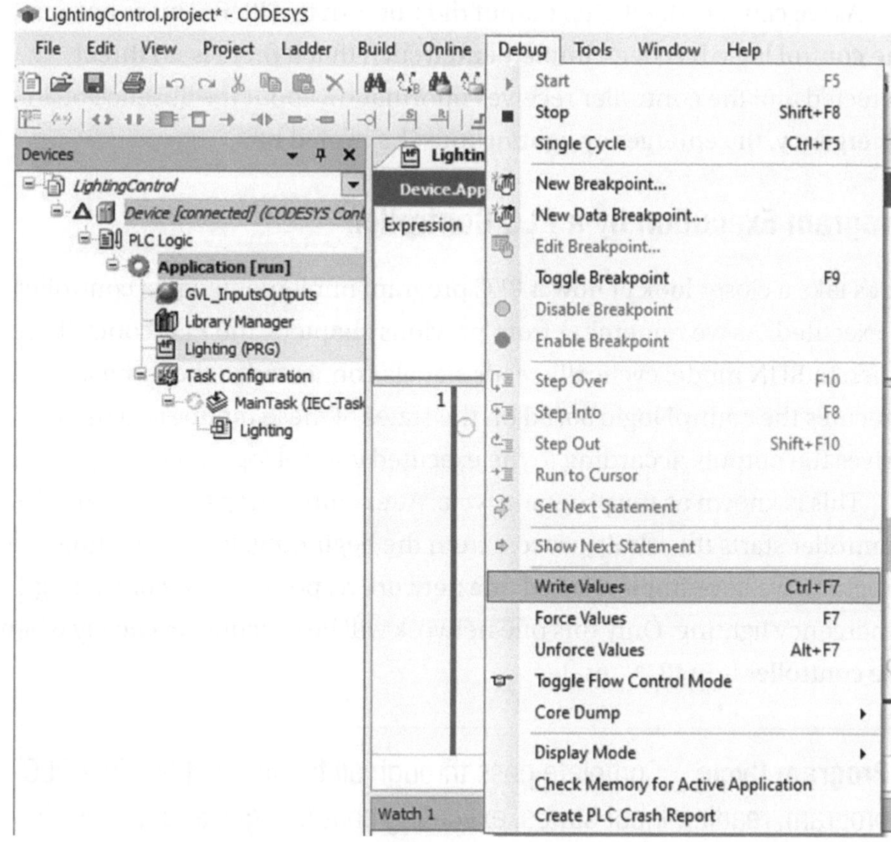

Figure 4-39. *Debug ➤ Write Values*

When the digital input state changes to TRUE, the state of the digital output changes to FALSE. This means that the PLC controller has been informed that the emergency situation has ended, so the emergency lighting has been turned off.

Now, let's do a small exercise: let's set the digital output to TRUE even though the digital input also has a TRUE value. In other words, let's try to turn on the emergency lighting even though the controller indicates there is no emergency. For the variable *DO_EMERGENCY_LIGHTING*, set the value in the *Prepared Value* column to TRUE, and then select *Debug ➤ Write Values* from the menu.

As we can see, the digital output did not turn to TRUE. This is because the control logic has been implemented such that if there is no threat detected and the controller receives information about the absence of an emergency, the emergency lighting must be turned off.

Program Execution by a PLC Controller

Let's take a closer look at how a PLC program implemented in a controller is executed. As we remember from previous chapters, the PLC controller, when in RUN mode, cyclically reads signals connected to the inputs, executes the control logic based on the states of these inputs, and then drives the outputs according to the executed control logic code.

This is known as the program cycle. After completing the cycle, the controller starts the whole process from the beginning. In our Lighting program, we have implemented one network responsible for controlling emergency lighting. Only this one network will be executed cyclically when the controller is in RUN mode.

Program Cycle   Complete pass through all the instructions in a PLC program, reading input states, executing control logic, and driving the outputs. After completing one cycle, the controller immediately starts the next cycle. This process repeats continuously while the controller is in RUN mode.

The LAD programming language is highly valued by electricians because programs written in this language resemble electrical schematics. It is often said that program code written in LAD is simply an interactive electrical circuit.

LAD (Ladder Diagram) Language   Graphical programming language used in PLC controllers that resembles ladder-like electrical circuit diagrams. Programs in LAD consist of vertical power rails and horizontal "rungs" representing control logic. This language is intuitive for electrical engineers, allowing for easy creation and reading of control programs.

The program code written in the LAD language is always executed from top to bottom and from left to right (Figure 4-40). If we look at the code of our program, it is easy to agree with this statement. The left side of the program represents the power supply of the entire control system, for example, 24V DC, and the right side represents the ground (GND). When current flows from the left side to the right, we have a closed electrical circuit, which allows for the switching on or off of various devices and actuators, represented in the LAD program by the coil symbol. The conditions for closing the circuit are defined by the use of NO or NC contacts and other function blocks.

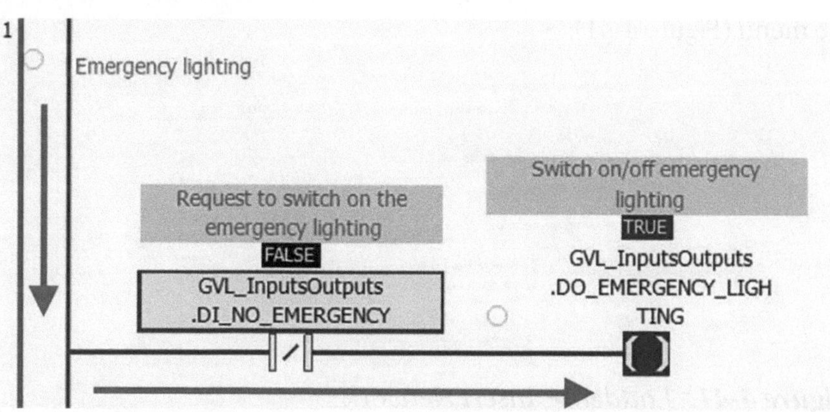

Figure 4-40. Execution of a PLC program from top to bottom and from left to right

If we had implemented multiple networks, after completing the control logic in the first network, the PLC controller would proceed to the second network and execute its control logic. This process would continue until the last network, after which the entire cycle would start anew, beginning with the execution of the control logic in the first network.

Lighting for Area I

Now that we understand how a PLC controller executes a program written in LAD, let's proceed to the implementation of the hall lighting control logic. The scenario assumes that the hall is divided into three sectors that can be illuminated separately. Additionally, the lighting can only be turned on when the emergency lighting is not activated, meaning there are no emergencies in the building. Lighting control can be automatic, using motion sensors installed in the hall, or manual, using light switches on the building walls.

We will begin by implementing the condition to turn on the lighting for the first sector when the hall lighting switch is turned on. To do this, let's add another network to our program. Click *Ladder* ➤ *Insert Network* from the menu (Figure 4-41).

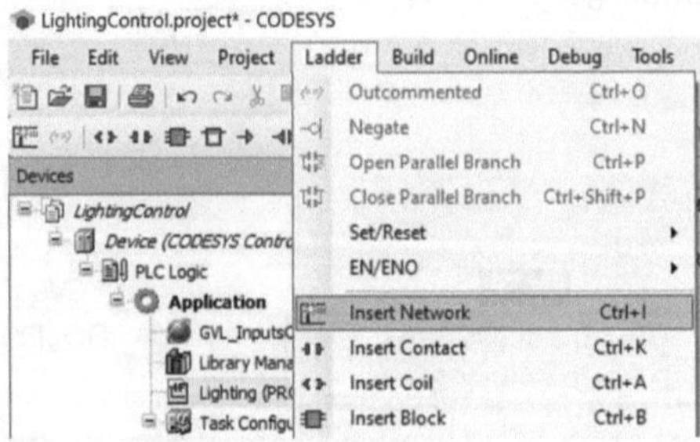

Figure 4-41. *Ladder* ➤ *Insert Network*

An empty network has been added to our control program. Now we can implement the control logic for turning on the lighting in Area I. We will read the state of the digital input *DI_HAND_LIGHTING_AREA_I*. If this input is high (TRUE), it means that the switch on the hall building wall is turned on. In this case, we will activate the digital output *DO_LIGHTING_AREA_I*, which turns on the lighting in Area I. Remember that the hall lighting can only be activated when there are no emergencies (Figure 4-42).

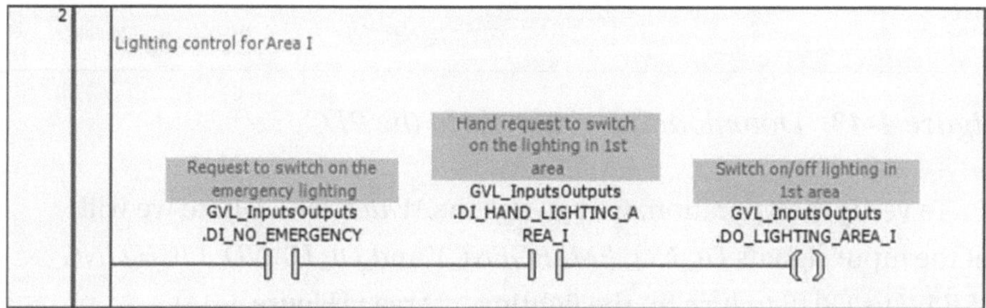

Figure 4-42. *Network Lighting control for Area I*

Next, you need to save the project and download the changes to the controller. The procedure is similar to downloading the first network. However, this time, CODESYS will notify us that there is already an application in the controller and display a dialog box where we will need to make a decision. Choose the option *"Login with online change"* and click *OK* (Figure 4-43).

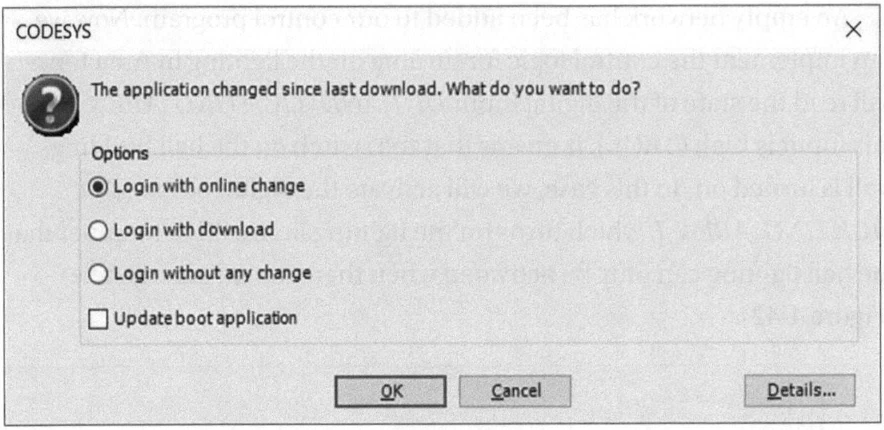

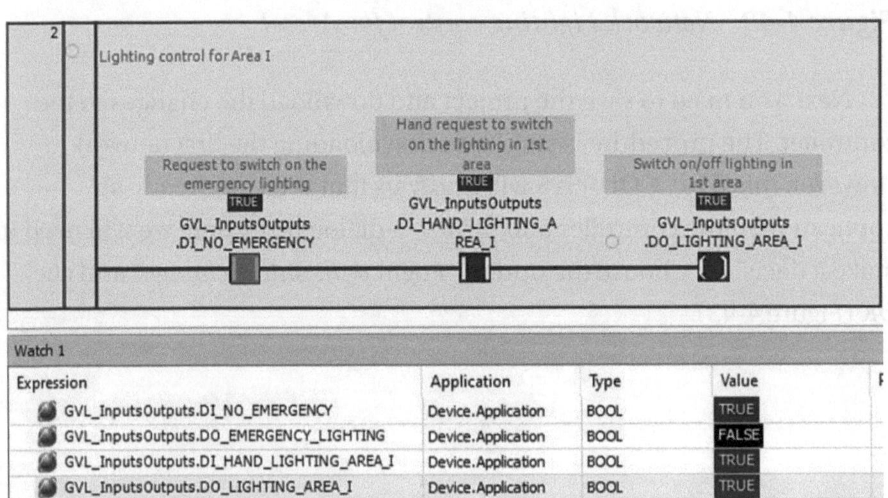

Figure 4-43. *Downloading program to the PLC*

To verify the operation, we can use the *Watch* tool, where we will set the input signals *DI_NO_EMERGENCY* and *DI_HAND_LIGHTING_ AREA_I* to TRUE to turn on the lighting in Area I (Figure 4-44).

Figure 4-44. *Lighting on in Area I*

I encourage you to conduct tests using the *Watch* tool to verify and test the conditions under which the lighting in Area I will be turned on or off.

The control system scenario also assumes that a lighting switch will be installed on the walls of the hall building, which will turn on the lighting in all three sectors simultaneously. The signal referred to is *DI_HAND_LIGHTING_ALL_AREAS*. Let's add a condition to our control logic that states if the lighting switch for Area I or the lighting switch for all sectors is activated, set the output *DO_LIGHTING_AREA_I* to high (TRUE).

To implement this, we need to add a branching before reading the input *DI_HAND_LIGHTING_AREA_I*. Click on the triangle symbol that appears when hovering over the bottom part of the second network, between the inputs *DI_NO_EMERGENCY* and *DI_HAND_LIGHTING_AREA_I* (Figure 4-45).

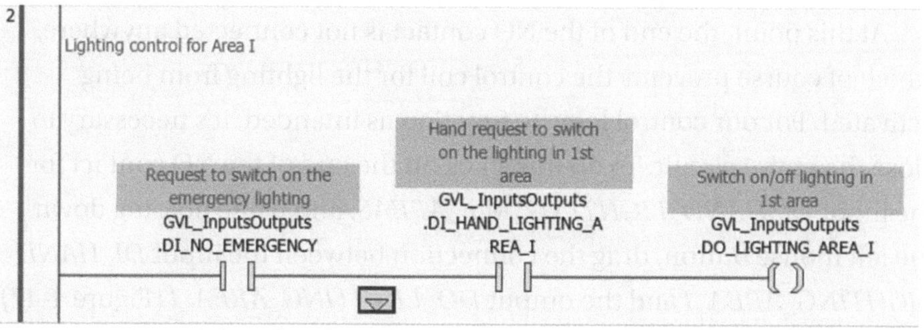

Figure 4-45. *Adding a branch*

Next, let's select *Ladder* ➤ *Insert Contact* from the menu and assign the digital input *DI_HAND_LIGHTING_ALL_AREAS* to the newly inserted NO contact (Figure 4-46).

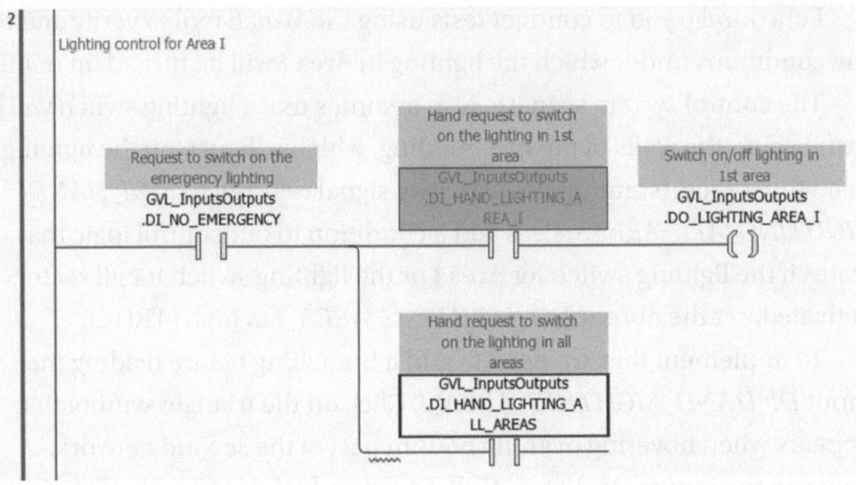

Figure 4-46. *Adding an NO contact with assigned input*

At this point, the end of the NO contact is not connected anywhere, which of course prevents the control coil for the lighting from being activated. For our control logic to function as intended, it's necessary to close the entire circuit. To do this, click on the end of the NO contact for the input *DI_HAND_LIGHTING_ALL_AREAS*, and while holding down the left mouse button, drag the connection between the input *DI_HAND_LIGHTING_AREA_I* and the output *DO_LIGHTING_AREA_I* (Figure 4-47).

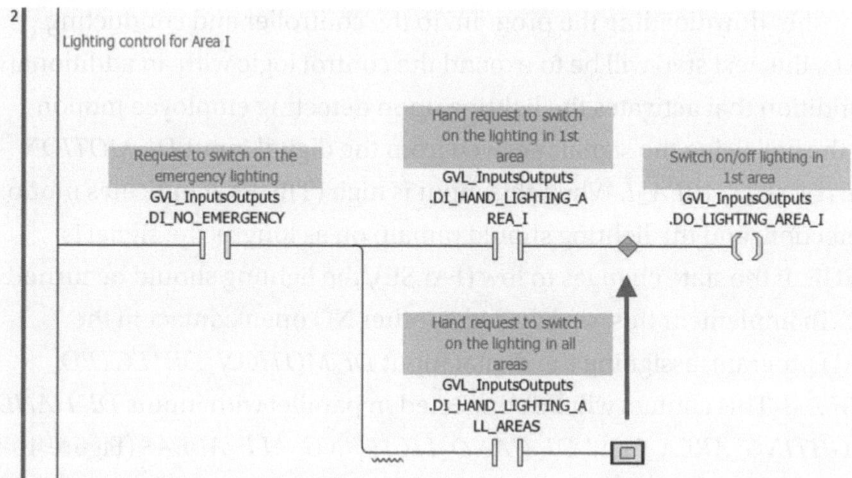

Figure 4-47. *Closing the circuit*

After completing these steps, we have implemented control logic that ensures the lighting in Area I will be activated only when there are no emergencies in the hall building, and either the lighting switch in Area I or the lighting switch for all sectors is turned on (Figure 4-48).

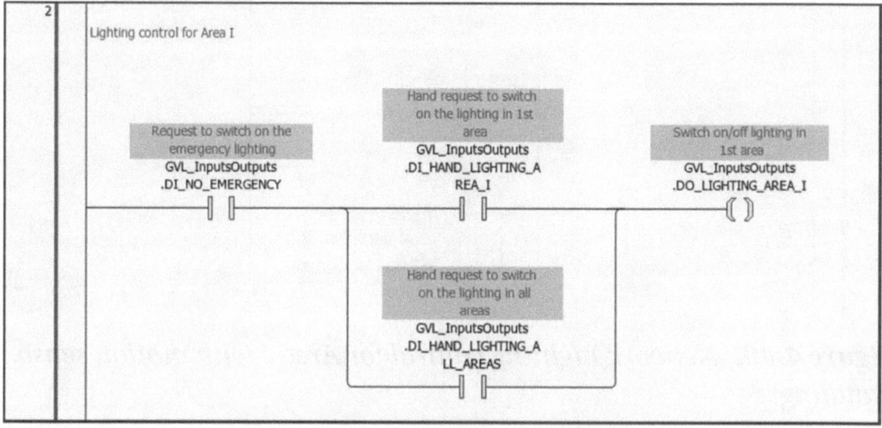

Figure 4-48. *Network Lighting control for Area I*

After downloading the program to the controller and conducting tests, the next step will be to expand the control logic with an additional condition that activates the lighting upon detecting employee motion in the hall using the signal received from the digital input *DI_MOTION_ DETECTED_AREA_I*. When this input is high (TRUE), it indicates motion detection, and the lighting should remain on as long as the signal is TRUE. If the state changes to low (FALSE), the lighting should be turned off. To implement this, simply add another NO open contact in the LAD program, assigning the digital input *DI_MOTION_DETECTED_ AREA_I*. This contact will be connected in parallel with inputs *DI_HAND_ LIGHTING_AREA_I* and *DI_HAND_LIGHTING_ALL_AREAS* (Figure 4-49).

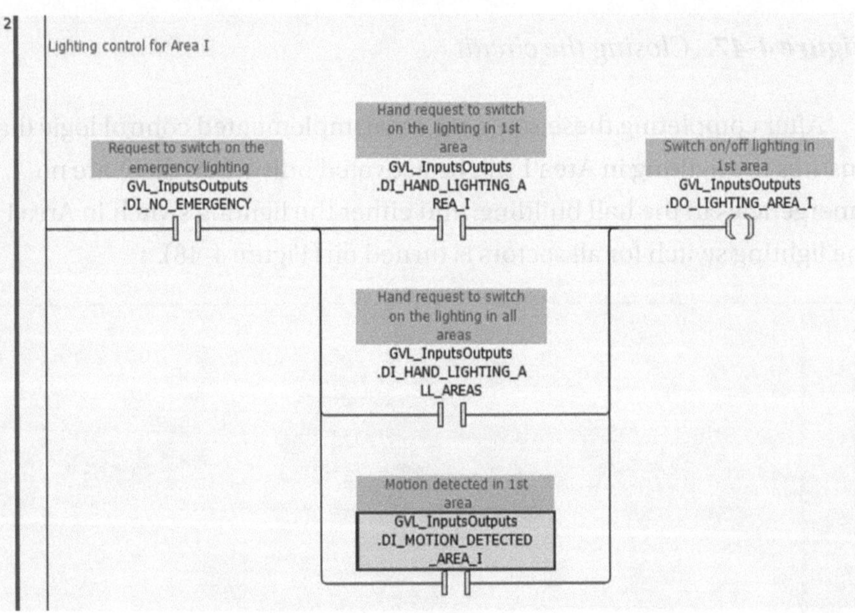

Figure 4-49. *Network Lighting control for Area I with motion sensor handling*

During tests with the *Watch* tool, we will quickly notice that if the controller receives information indicating no emergencies, regardless of which digital inputs are activated, the lighting in Area I will remain on.

However, the application includes two modes for controlling hall lighting: manual through switches on the walls and automatic, which responds to signals from motion sensors.

Before we proceed to expand the control logic to incorporate this functionality, let's focus on two types of component connections in the LAD program that were used in our control logic: series connection and parallel connection.

Series Connection   In LAD programming, a series connection refers to a configuration where logical elements are placed one after another in a line. All elements must be active for current to flow through the circuit.

Parallel Connection   In LAD programming, a parallel connection refers to a configuration where logical elements are connected in parallel to each other. It is sufficient for one of the elements to be active for current to flow through the circuit.

Automatic Mode

Let's now expand the control logic to include both manual and automatic modes. Information about the lighting mode will be selected by employees through the visualization system. Therefore, we need to add new global variables to our project, which will act as a bridge between the PLC program and the visualization system. However, these variables will not be declared in the global variables list *GVL_InputsOutputs*, as this list is intended only for the declaration of control system inputs and outputs. Of course, there's nothing stopping us from declaring the visualization system variables in this list, and our project would compile without any issues. However, for the sake of project clarity, I encourage separating these two concerns.

Similarly to the *GVL_InputsOutputs* list, we add a new list to the project named *GVL_Visu*. Upon opening this list, we declare two variables, *HANDMODE* and *AUTOMODE*, of type BOOL, which will be responsible for selecting the control mode. I will make these declarations in the tabular view, rather than the textual view, as previously (Figure 4-50).

	Scope	Name	Address	Data type	Initialization	Comment	Attributes
1	VAR_GLOBAL	**HANDMODE**		BOOL			
2	VAR_GLOBAL	**AUTOMODE**		BOOL			

Figure 4-50. *Declaration of global variables in the GVL_Visu list*

The implementation of the automatic mode is straightforward. Before the digital input *DI_MOTION_DETECTED_AREA_I*, a NO (normally open) contact should be connected in series. To do this, click the left mouse button on the symbol of the two triangles (Figure 4-51), and from the menu, select *Ladder* ➤ *Insert Contact*.

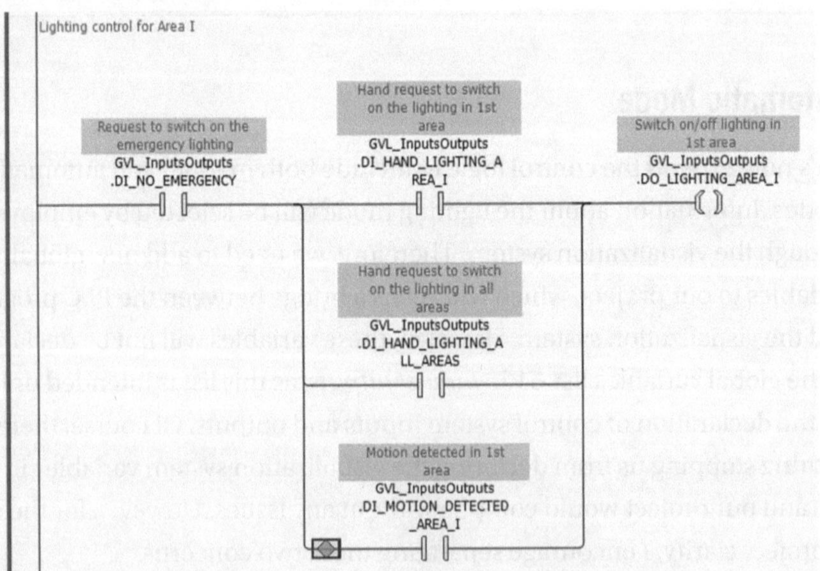

Figure 4-51. *Adding automatic mode to control logic*

Assign the *AUTOMODE* variable, which we declared in the *GVL_Visu* global variables list, to the newly inserted NO contact (Figure 4-52). This way, the lighting will only turn on when both variables are in a high state (TRUE). If the motion sensor is activated, but the control system is not in automatic mode, the lighting will not turn on. I encourage you to test this scenario using the *Watch* tool.

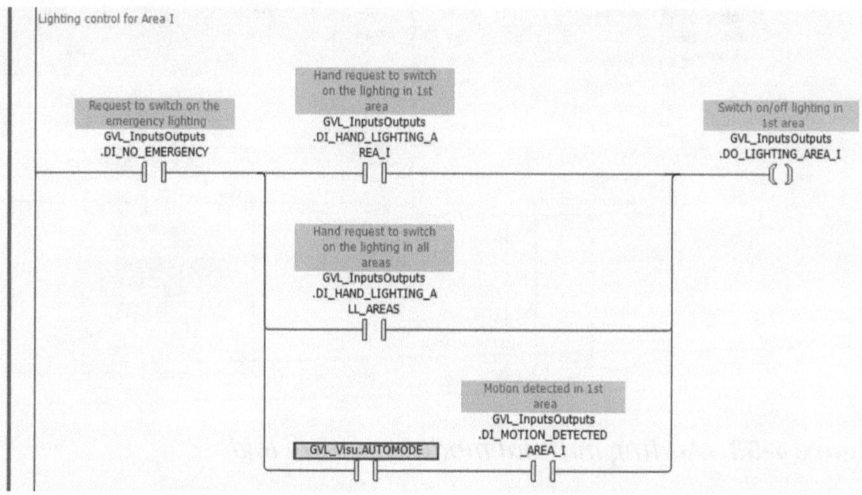

Figure 4-52. *Automatic mode*

Hand Mode

The next step will be the implementation of the manual mode. This will be a bit more complex because we need to slightly change the structure of our control logic. Let's start by placing a NO (normally open) contact in the program, which will be connected in series to the digital input *DI_HAND_LIGHTING_AREA_I*. To do this, click the left mouse button before this input, select the symbol of the two triangles, and then from the menu, choose *Ladder* ➤ *Insert Contact* (Figure 4-53).

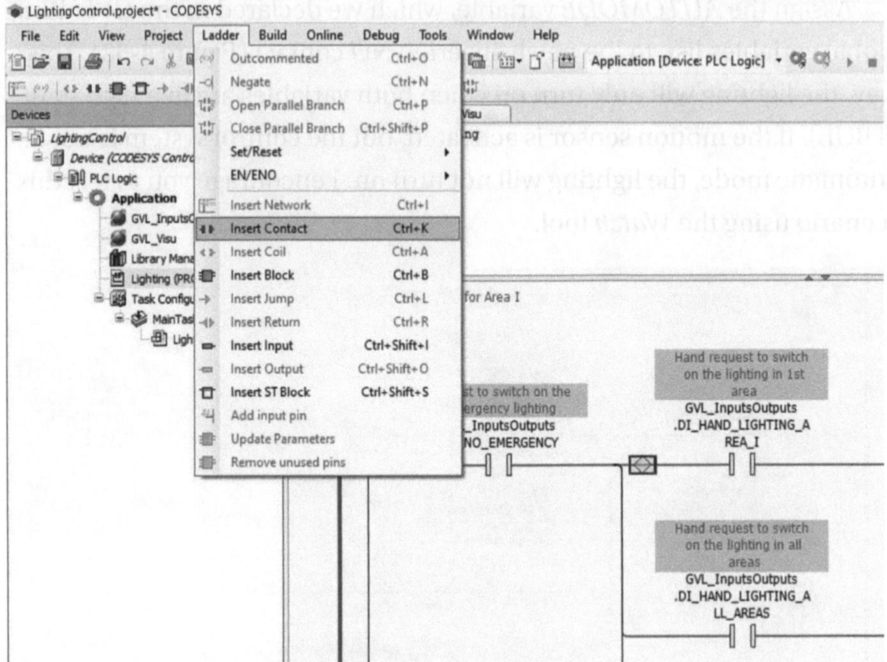

Figure 4-53. *Adding manual mode to control logic*

Assign the *HANDMODE* variable to the newly inserted NO contact (Figure 4-54).

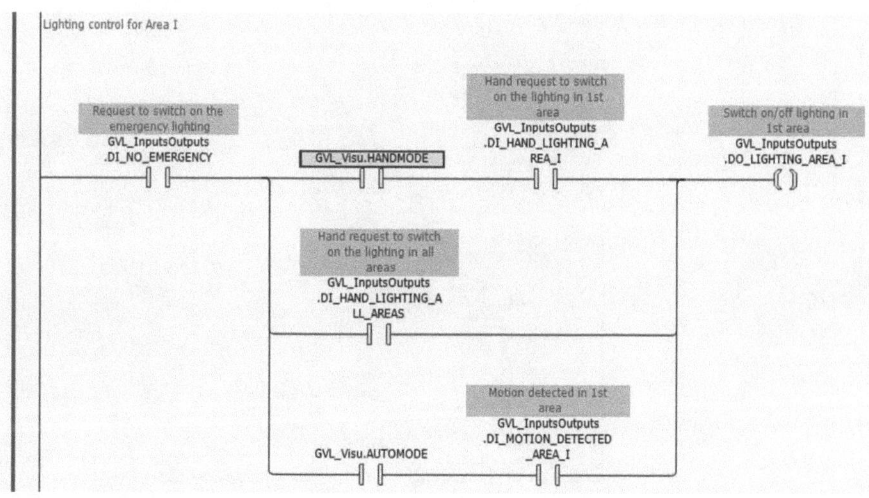

Figure 4-54. *Hand mode*

In this case, the lighting switch for the first sector depends on the state
of manual control. However, we still need to make the lighting switch for
all areas dependent. If we were to leave our control logic as it currently
stands, regardless of the control mode chosen, if the switch for all areas is
on, the lighting in the first area would still turn on.

Let's modify our control logic so that the input *DI_HAND_LIGHTING_
ALL_AREAS* is also connected in series with the *HANDMODE* variable.
To do this, click on the NO contact that we want to modify. In this case,
it's the input *DI_HAND_LIGHTING_ALL_AREAS*. We want the input of
this contact to be connected in series with the output of the *HANDMODE*
contact and in parallel with the contact *DI_HAND_LIGHTING_
AREA_I*. Therefore, while holding down the left mouse button, drag the
connection to the triangle symbol between the *HANDMODE* contact and
the *DI_HAND_LIGHTING_AREA_I* contact (Figure 4-55).

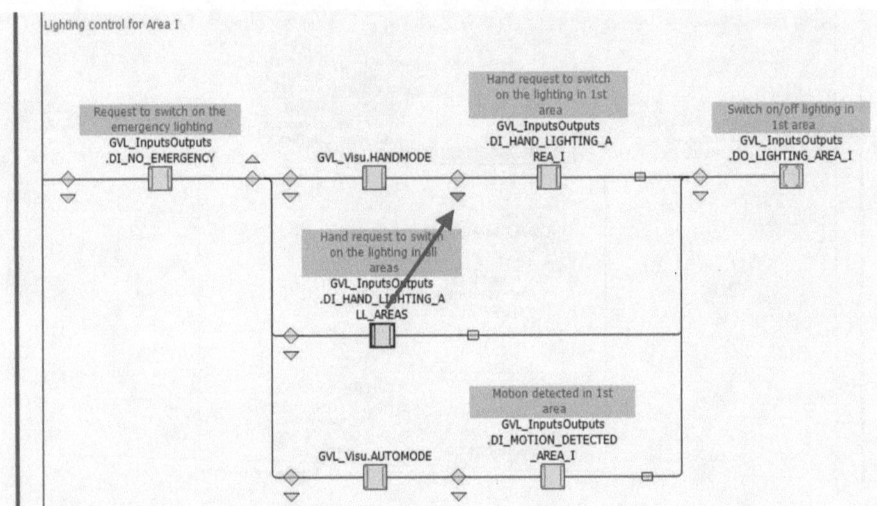

Figure 4-55. *Changing the contact connection*

The final step remaining is to connect the output of the *DI_HAND_ LIGHTING_ALL_AREAS* contact to the coil *DO_LIGHTING_AREA_I* to close the control circuit (Figure 4-56).

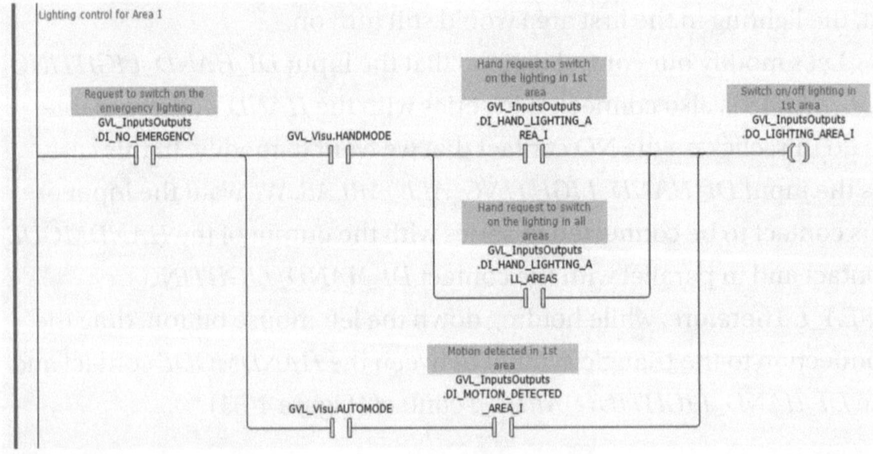

Figure 4-56. *Hand mode*

In this way, we have completed the implementation of the control logic for the lighting in the first area. Now we can download our program to the controller and test it using the *Watch* tool.

After testing the control logic for the first area, we are ready to implement the control logic for the next two areas. The only difference will be in changing the respective inputs and outputs. This is a common practice during PLC program implementation. Once we have a program ready for one segment of the installation, most of the time is spent on implementing that part. Subsequent segments of the installation usually involve copying the code with minor adjustments. I even had the opportunity to implement three identical installations built side by side, where operators used them interchangeably. When one installation underwent maintenance, the other two could still be used, avoiding the need to stop the entire production line. In reality, most of my time was spent implementing the control logic for the first installation. The other two were minor adjustments, such as correctly assigning input and output variables and adjusting the visualization system, such as valve names, pumps, and sensors.

I encourage you to now test with the LAD editor to practice using the editor's capabilities. This should be the entire program that controls the lighting in the quality control hall for all three sectors, including emergency lighting (Figure 4-57, Figure 4-58, Figure 4-59, Figure 4-60). If you encounter any issues with implementation, all example applications can be downloaded from my GitHub repository. Here's the link to the repository: *https://github.com/DWrebiak/practical-plc-programming-for-beginners*.

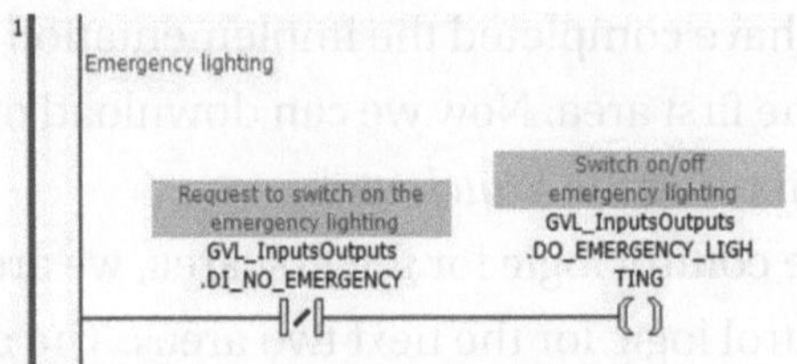

Figure 4-57. *Network 1: Emergency lighting*

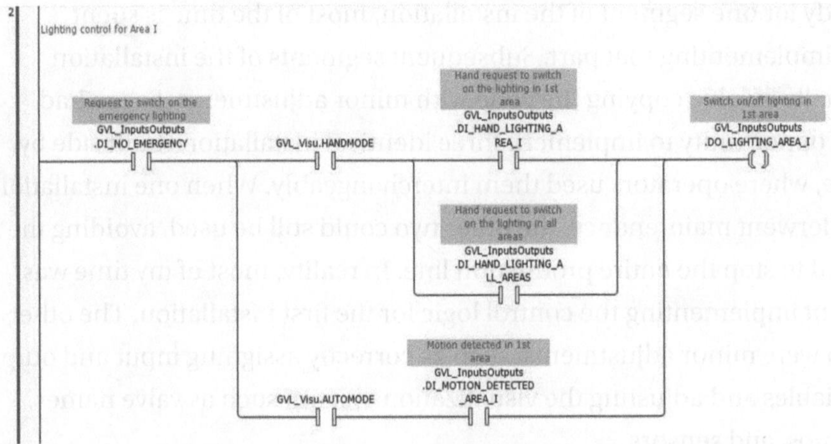

Figure 4-58. *Network 2: Lighting control for Area I*

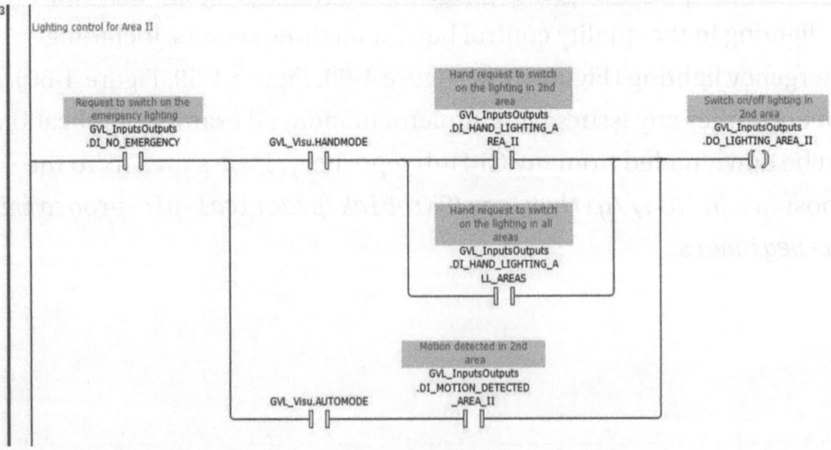

Figure 4-59. *Network 3: Lighting control for Area II*

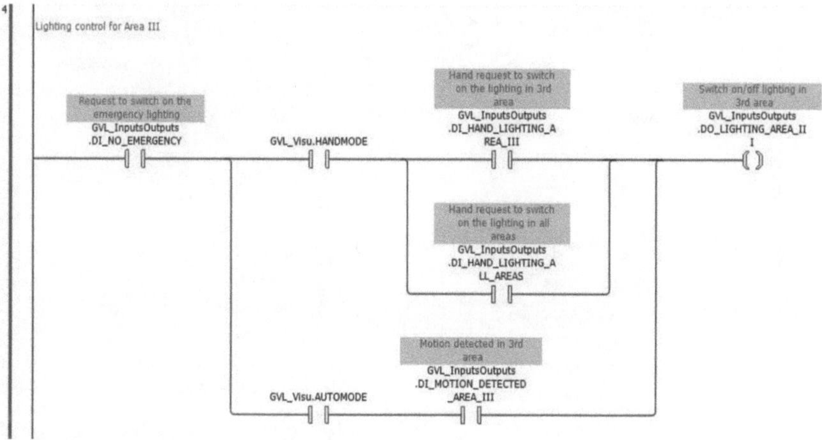

Figure 4-60. *Network 4: Lighting control for Area III*

And so we have reached the end of implementing the control logic responsible for emergency lighting and the lighting in the product quality control hall. Now it's time to implement visualization for our PLC program. As mentioned earlier, industrial installations are operated by personnel who may not have knowledge of CODESYS or other engineering environments. However, they still need to operate production lines, machines, or other industrial installations. This is where visualization comes into play.

Implementation of Visualization

Our goal is to create a visualization that allows switching between manual and automatic modes without the need to use the *Watch* tool in CODESYS.

To accomplish this, we need to add a new *Visualization* object to our project. In the project structure, select *Application* and right-click. Then choose *Add Object* ➤ *Visualization...* (Figure 4-61).

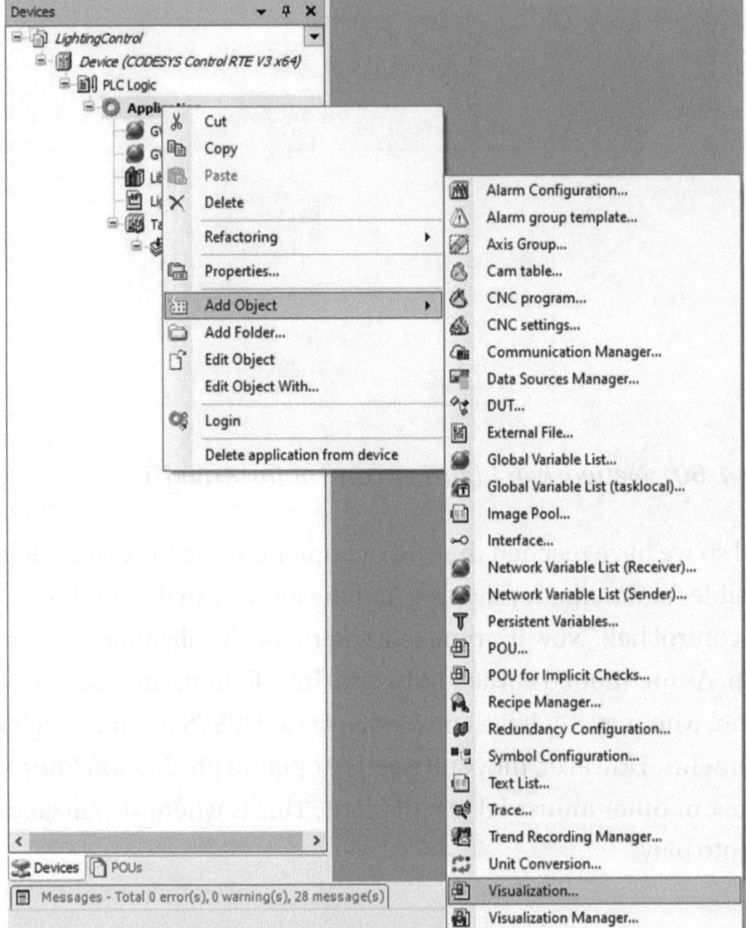

Figure 4-61. *Application ➤ Add Object ➤ Visualization*

In the open window, we can change the name of our visualization and optionally activate the symbol library. In this case, we leave all settings at their defaults and click the *Add* button (Figure 4-62).

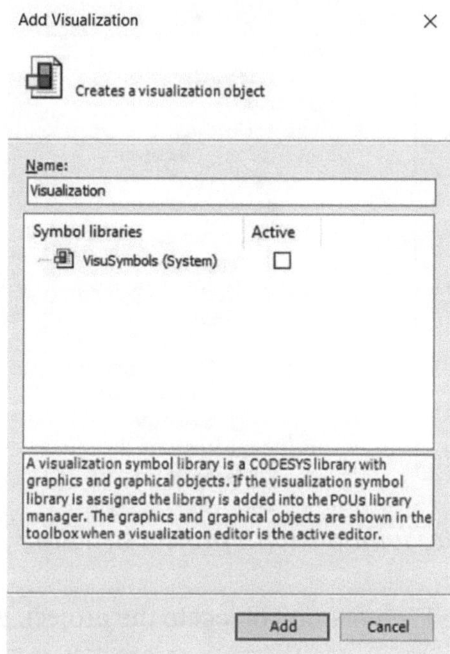

Figure 4-62. *Add Visualization window*

This is how the structure of our project should look after adding the *Visualization* object (Figure 4-63).

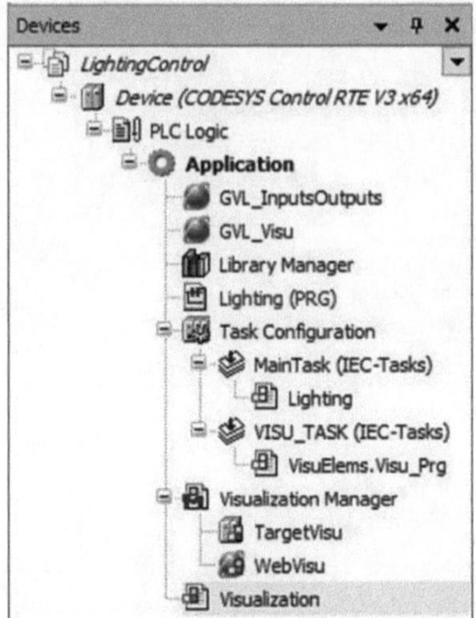

Figure 4-63. *Device window with project structure*

After adding the *Visualization* object to the project, the visualization editor should open automatically (Figure 4-64). If it didn't, double-click the *Visualization* component in the *Devices* window to open the editor.

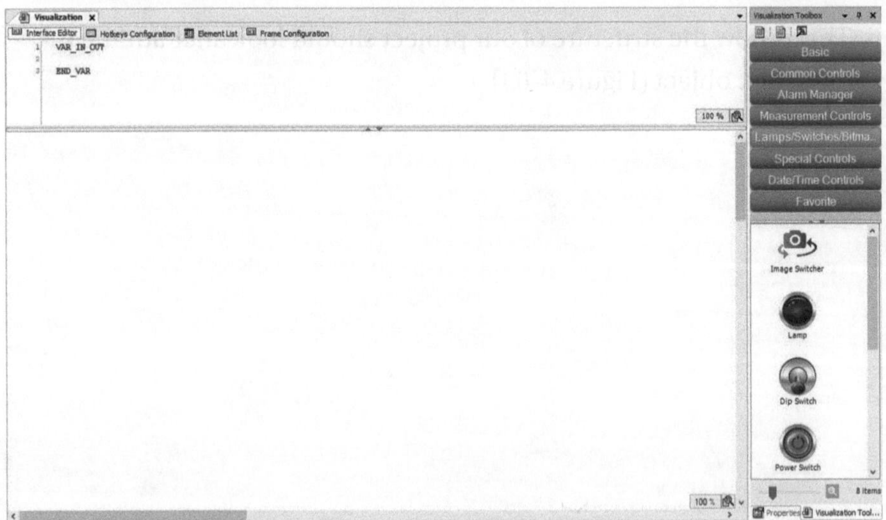

Figure 4-64. *Visualization editor window*

Status

In our visualization application, we will present the current status of the lighting. The operator will be able to easily check whether emergency lighting is on or off and monitor the status of lighting in the individual areas of the quality control hall.

We will start by adding a *Label* control, which will serve as the title for our visualization. In the *Visualization Toolbox* on the right side, choose *Common Control* ➤ *Label* (Figure 4-65).

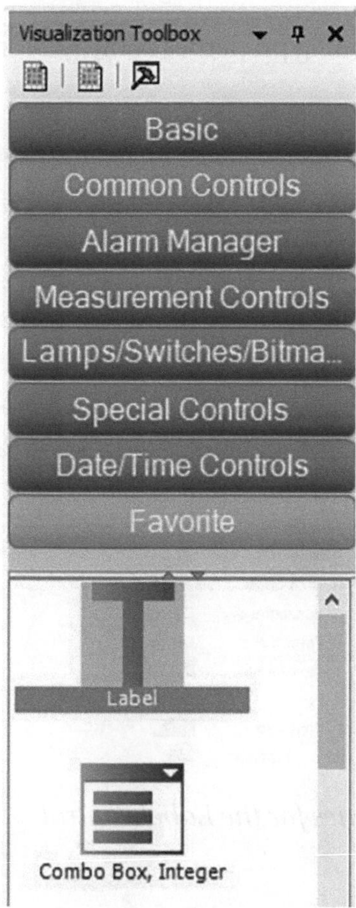

Figure 4-65. *Common Control* ➤ *Label*

Next, we drag the *Label* control into the visualization editor using the Drag and Drop function. After adding it, the *Properties* window for the *Label* control will appear on the right side. We change the following settings:

- Texts → Text: *Lighting*

- Position → X: *265*

- Position → Y: *5*

- Text properties → Font: *Large Headline*

We leave the remaining properties of the *Label* control unchanged (Figure 4-66).

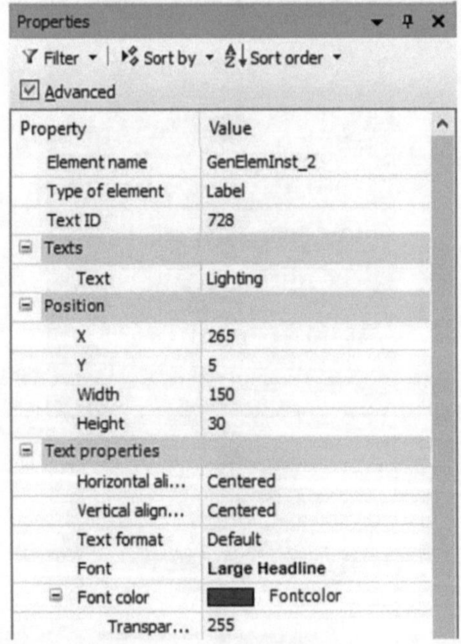

Figure 4-66. *Properties for the Label control*

Now we will add controls to our visualization that will indicate the status of emergency lighting in the quality control hall. Let's start by adding two *Label* controls and configuring their properties:

- Texts → Text: *Status*

- Position → X: *88*

- Position → Y: *65*

- Text properties → Font: *Headline*

and

- Texts → Text: *Emergency*

- Position → X: *11*

- Position → Y: *105*

This is how the visualization mask should look in the editor (Figure 4-67).

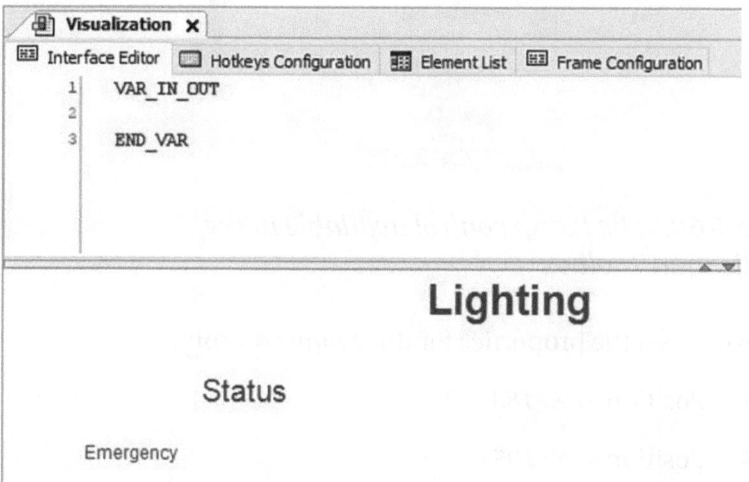

Figure 4-67. *Visualization editor with Label controls*

Next, we will add a *Lamp* control to the visualization, which can be found in the *Lamps/Switches/Bitmaps* controls set (Figure 4-68).

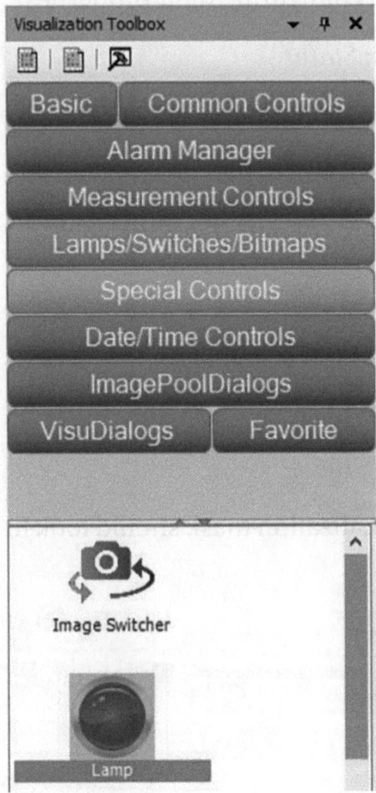

Figure 4-68. *The Lamp control available in the Visualization Toolbox*

Next, we set the properties for this *Lamp* control:

- Position → X: *183*

- Position → Y: *105*

- Position → Width: *30*

- Position → Height: *30*

The next step will be to make this control dynamic. This means that if the emergency lighting is activated, the lamp should glow yellow as a warning. If the emergency lighting is not activated, the lamp should remain unlit.

To achieve this, we need to bind the *Variable* property to the digital output *DO_EMERGENCY_LIGHTING* (Figure 4-69). This way, the lamp control will automatically respond to changes in the digital output state.

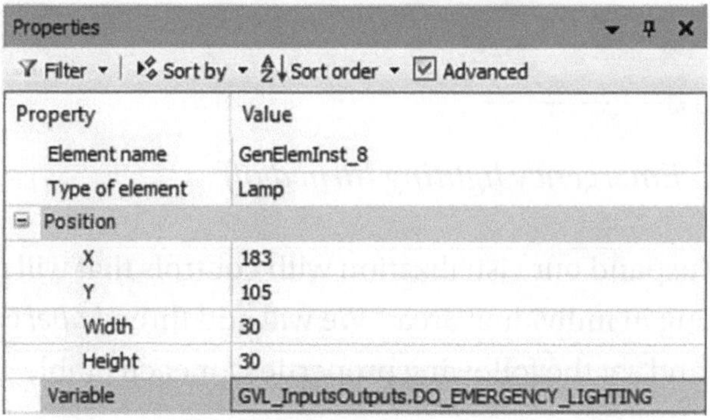

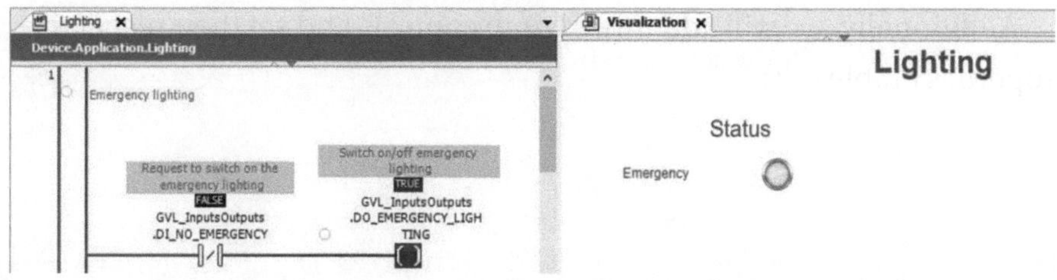

Figure 4-69. *Properties of the Lamp control*

After downloading the modified program to the controller, we notice that the Emergency lamp is glowing yellow, indicating the activation of the digital output responsible for emergency lighting (high state TRUE). On the left side is the emergency lighting control logic, and on the right side is the visualization of this logic (Figure 4-70).

Figure 4-70. *Emergency lighting activated*

Now let's set the digital input *DI_NO_EMERGENCY* to TRUE, signaling to the PLC controller that there is no emergency. As a result, the PLC controller will turn off the emergency lighting, which will be reflected in the visualization (Figure 4-71).

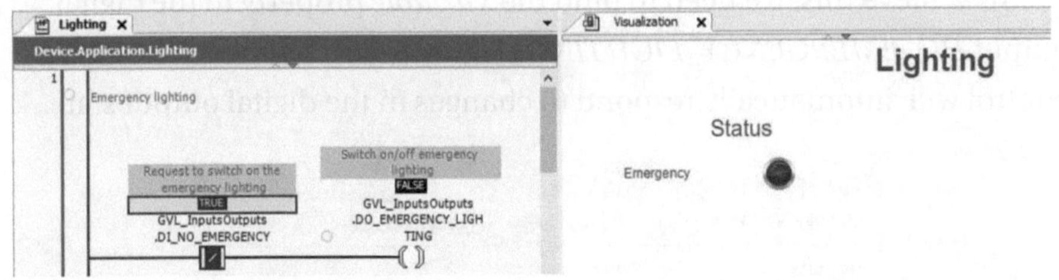

Figure 4-71. *Emergency lighting turned off*

Let's now expand our visualization with controls that will represent the status of lighting in individual areas. We will add three *Label* controls to the visualization and set the following properties for each (Table 4-2).

Table 4-2. *Properties of Label controls*

Properties	1st Label	2nd Label	3rd Label
Texts → Texts	Area I	Area II	Area III
Position → X	11	11	11
Position → Y	145	185	225

Additionally, we will add three *Lamp* controls and set their respective properties (Table 4-3).

Table 4-3. *Properties of Lamp controls*

Properties	1st Lamp	2nd Lamp	3rd Lamp
Position → X	183	183	183
Position → Y	145	185	225
Position → Width	30	30	30
Position → Height	30	30	30
Variable	GVL_InputsOutputs. DO_LIGHTING_ AREA_I	GVL_InputsOutputs. DO_LIGHTING_AREA_ II	GVL_InputsOutputs. DO_LIGHTING_AREA_ III
Background → Image	Green	Green	Green

This is how the layout of our visualization should look (Figure 4-72).

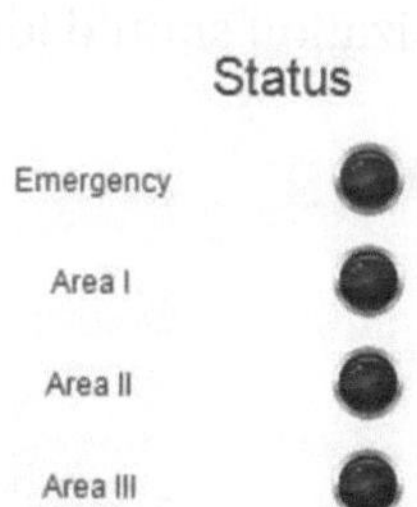

Figure 4-72. *Visualization layout: Status*

I encourage you to test the visualization by setting different inputs that control the lighting in individual areas. This way, we can thoroughly test our application.

Operational Mode

We still need to set the variables responsible for the manual or automatic control mode from CODESYS. It's time to implement this functionality in the visualization.

Let's start by adding three controls to the visualization: one *Label* control and two *Button* controls. The *Button* control can be found in the same set as the *Label* control, which is *Common Controls*. Next, we set the properties of each control according to the table below (Table 4-4).

Table 4-4. *Properties of Label control and Button controls*

Properties	Label	1st Button	2nd Button
Texts → Texts	Operational mode	HAND	AUTO
Position → X	437	442	442
Position → Y	65	105	145
Position → Width	160	150	150
Text properties → Font	Headline	Default	Default

Here is how the layout of our visualization should look (Figure 4-73).

Figure 4-73. *Visualization layout: Operational mode*

Now, our goal is to program the *HAND* and *AUTO* buttons in such a way that pressing them sets or resets the *HANDMODE* and *AUTOMODE* variables, which we use in the lighting control logic.

Click the *HAND* button and assign the global variable *GVL_Visu. HANDMODE* to the property *Input configuration* ➤ *Toggle* ➤ *Variable*. Make sure that the *Advanced* check box at the top of the *Properties* window is checked (Figure 4-74).

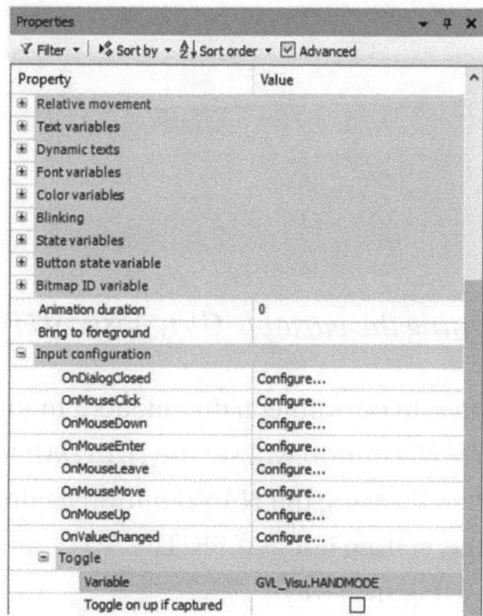

Figure 4-74. *Assigning the variable GVL_Visu.HANDMODE*

Similarly, proceed with the *AUTO* button, but this time assign the global variable *GVL_Visu.AUTOMODE* to the property *Input configuration* ➤ *Toggle* ➤ *Variable* (Figure 4-75).

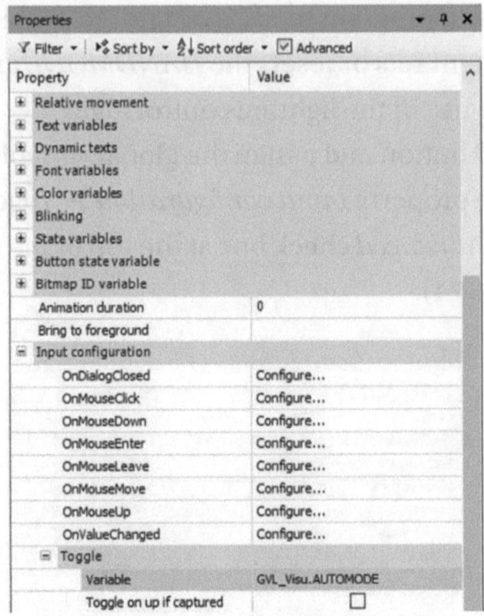

Figure 4-75. *Assigning the variable GVL_Visu.AUTOMODE*

We save all changes to our project, download it to the controller, and test it. Pressing the *HAND* button will set the *HANDMODE* variable to TRUE in the controller. Pressing the *HAND* button again will reset the *HANDMODE* variable, setting it to FALSE. The AUTO button will behave in exactly the same way (Figure 4-76).

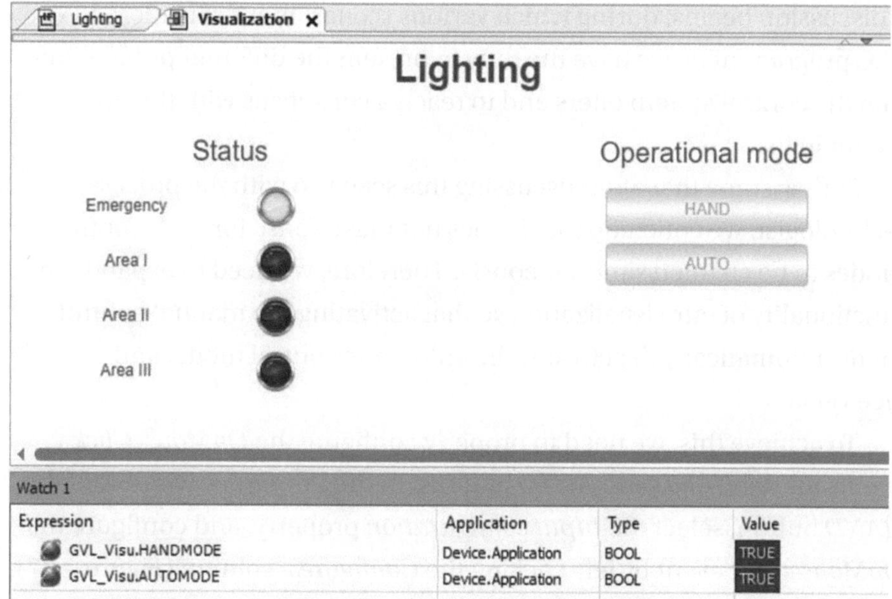

Figure 4-76. *Two operating modes HAND and AUTO activated simultaneously*

However, during testing of our application, we will quickly realize that from the visualization level, we can set both operating modes simultaneously, which results in the lighting being turned on if the switch on the hall wall is activated or the motion sensor is triggered.

Is this good or bad? In the case of our application, it is not clearly defined whether both operating modes (manual and automatic) can be activated simultaneously. This is a common situation in the daily life of a PLC programmer. We implement certain functionality and reach a point where we are unsure how the control system should behave in a given situation. In such cases, it is always worth consulting with the process technologist. Furthermore, sometimes the process technologist might also be uncertain and may require further consultations. In such cases, a discussion begins, during which various scenarios are considered. As PLC programmers, we have the duty to present the different possibilities that the control system offers and to reach a consensus with the process technologist.

Let's assume that after discussing this scenario with the process technologist, we conclude that it does not make sense for both control modes to be enabled simultaneously. Therefore, we need to expand the functionality of our visualization so that activating the manual control mode automatically deactivates the automatic control mode, and vice versa.

To achieve this, we need to properly configure the *OnMouseClick* events for the *HAND* and *AUTO* buttons. In the Properties window of the *HAND* button, select the *Input configuration* property, and configure the *OnMouseClick* event by left-clicking the *Configure...* column (Figure 4-77).

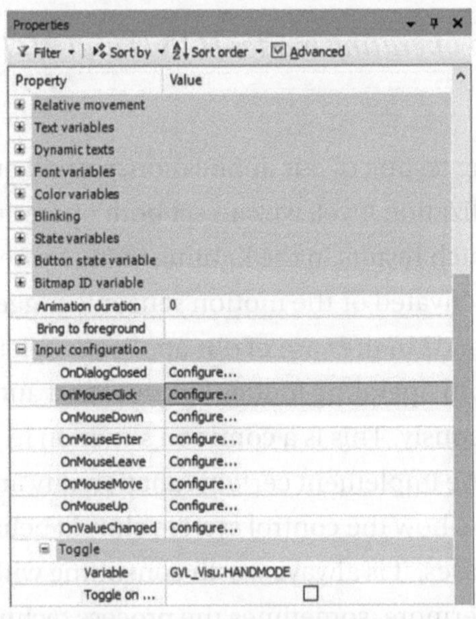

Figure 4-77. *Configuring the OnMouseClick event for the HAND button*

After clicking the *Configure...* column, the *Input Configuration* window will appear. In this window, on the left side, select *Execute ST-Code* and click the right arrow to move this function to the central part of the *Input Configuration* window. In the ST code editor, enter the code that will reset the global variable *AUTOMODE* (Figure 4-78).

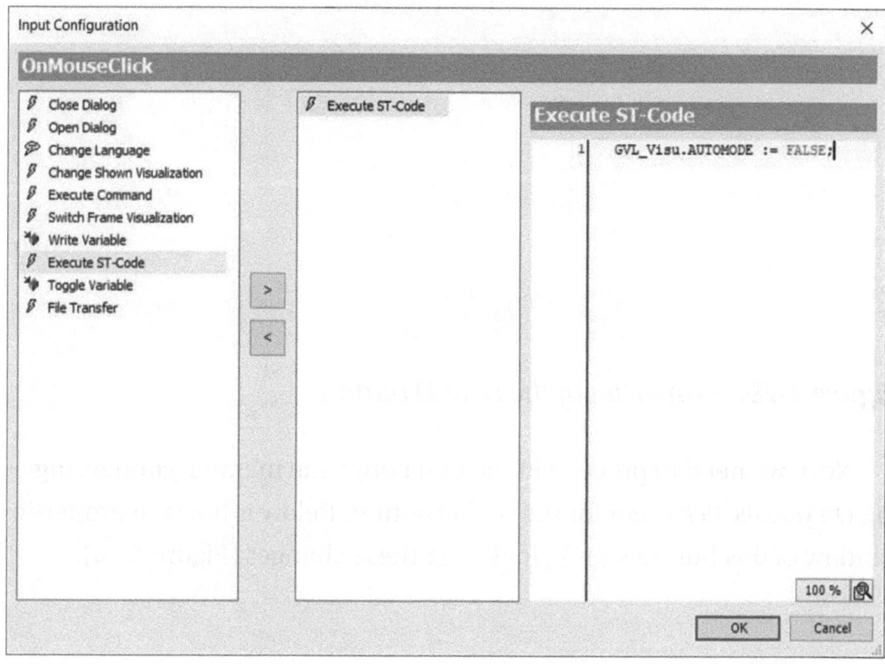

Figure 4-78. *Input Configuration window*

After these changes, the *HAND* button will have two functions. Whenever it is clicked, we will set the global variable *AUTOMODE* to FALSE and toggle the value of the *HANDMODE* variable. Here is how the Properties window of the *HAND* button should look after these changes (Figure 4-79).

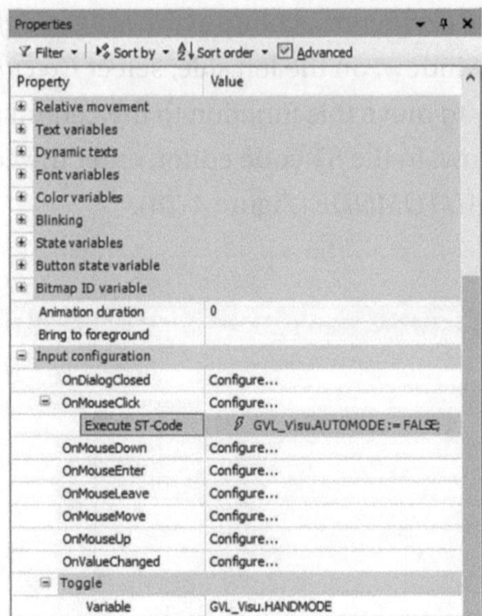

Figure 4-79. *Properties of the HAND button*

Next, we need to proceed in the exact opposite manner, configuring the *OnMouseClick* event for the *AUTO* button. Below is how the Properties window of this button should look after these changes (Figure 4-80).

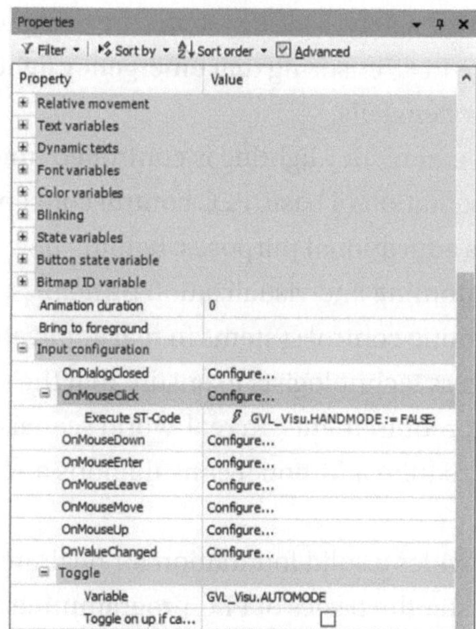

Figure 4-80. *Properties of the AUTO button*

After making all the changes, we save the project, download it to the controller, and conduct tests. At this point, the operator using the visualization system cannot set both manual and automatic modes simultaneously. However, as PLC programmers, we have this capability using the *Watch* tool provided by CODESYS.

Summary

In this chapter, I have presented the process of creating a lighting control system using CODESYS, which includes programming control logic and creating visualization.

My key emphasis regarding emergency lighting is essential to remember. Under normal conditions, emergency lighting is not directly controlled by the PLC. Typically, external fire alarm panels are responsible for its control, ensuring safety. These systems are designed to operate independently of the PLC, ensuring that emergency lighting functions even if the control system fails.

In our example, emergency lighting is controlled from the PLC, simplifying the presentation of basic PLC control concepts for beginners. This scenario serves educational purposes, helping new users grasp fundamental programming and visualization principles.

When implementing control systems in real applications, it is crucial to consult with process technologists to ensure that the system meets safety and efficiency requirements. In real-world scenarios, certain functionalities may require additional consultations and testing to ensure reliable operation.

This chapter provides a solid foundation for beginners looking to understand and master the basics of PLC programming and visualization in CODESYS. I encourage further experimentation and deeper learning in the subsequent chapters of the book.

Basic Gate Control in the Production Facility

The next task we will undertake after implementing the automation for the hall lighting control is the automation of gates and entrance doors. As we already know, the quality control hall has been divided into three areas. Each sector will have a separate gate or entrance. The gates will allow access for larger vehicles, such as forklifts or delivery trucks, while the entrances will serve as entry and exit points for employees.

Having already familiarized ourselves with basic PLC program components, such as NO and NC contacts and coils, in this chapter, we will explore additional elements that will enable us to develop control logic further. We will learn about a new graphical programming language called FBD (Function Block Diagram), used to create control logic. We will introduce the RS flip-flop and new tools available in the CODESYS environment, such as *Task Configuration* and *Library Manager*.

Let's continue our journey through the world of PLC controllers.

© Dariusz Wrebiak 2026
D. Wrebiak, *Practical PLC Programming for Beginners*, Maker Innovations Series,
https://doi.org/10.1007/979-8-8688-2430-2_5

Application Scenario

To Area I, there must be an entrance through an external door and a gate leading outside the building. Various devices used for building the quality control line will be brought in through this gate.

To Area II, there will be doors leading to office spaces.

To Area III, there will be only a gate through which forklifts will enter to collect products from the quality control hall.

Each gate and door will be equipped with the following sensors and actuators:

- Limit switch indicating the gate is fully closed

- Limit switch indicating the gate is fully open

- Photoelectric sensor indicating the presence of people or objects in the gate's operational area

- Motion sensor or button for opening the gate

- Motor for opening and closing the gate

All doors and the gate in Area I can be opened by pressing a button. The gate in Area III will be opened using a motion sensor. In Area III, the gate will be used exclusively by forklifts picking up finished products from the quality control hall. Thanks to the motion sensor, the operator will not have to dismount the forklift to open the gate – it will open automatically upon detecting movement.

It is worth noting that the entrance and gate in Area I lead to the outside of the building. To open this gate, simply press a button, which activates the control system. In such facilities, additional authorization devices, such as RFID cards or other identification keys, are often installed. Upon using them, if the card has the appropriate access, the gate will open automatically. If the authorization system denies access, the gate will not open, preventing unauthorized individuals from entering the factory or installation premises.

In our scenario, we assume that there is no additional authorization system and that every person on the factory premises has undergone appropriate safety training. The mere fact that someone is on the factory grounds indicates that they have access to that specific part of the installation.

It is important to remember that, in reality, before a PLC programmer begins any work on-site, various formalities must be completed. This process can often take up to two days to ensure all conditions for safe work are met. Large companies have made significant progress in this area, and today, it is often possible to complete safety training online before arriving on-site to commission the system.

Project Organization

Before we expand our PLC program and visualization, it is essential to understand how industrial buildings, which house various factories, installations, and machines consisting of sensors and actuators, are structured. You may recall this division from the chapter on the automation pyramid. By familiarizing ourselves with this brief theoretical introduction, we will find it easier to grasp the practical aspects of building a PLC program structure.

First, it's important to note that there is no single universal standard for the naming of buildings and installations in the industry that applies worldwide. However, there are certain widely used practices and industry standards that aid in the identification and classification of different types of industrial installations. Here are a few of them:

- *Acronyms and abbreviations*: Many industries use acronyms to simplify identification and communication. For example, WWT stands for "Waste Water Treatment."

- *ISO standards*: The International Organization for Standardization (ISO) publishes various standards that can include aspects of naming and classification of industrial installations. An example is ISO 14001 for environmental management systems, which may specify certain principles for the identification and documentation of installations.

- *Industry codes and standards*: Specific sectors such as chemical, energy, or pharmaceutical industries have particular standards and codes that might include naming conventions. For instance, in the energy industry, acronyms like CHP for "Combined Heat and Power" or PV for "Photovoltaic" are common.

- *Local and regional regulations*: Different countries may have specific legal requirements and regulations regarding the classification and naming of buildings and industrial installations.

- *Corporate internal standards*: Large corporations often have their own internal naming standards applied across various branches and locations. These standards help maintain consistency and facilitate resource management and internal communication.

- *Industry standards*: Trade organizations often publish guidelines and recommendations for best practices, including naming conventions. For example, the American Petroleum Institute (API) or the International Electrotechnical Commission (IEC) may issue such guidelines for their respective sectors.

Although there is no single worldwide standard, these various sources help create consistent and understandable naming systems across different industries. As PLC programmers, we do not need to invent names for buildings, installations, sensors, or actuators ourselves. This is done by the people who plan the entire installation, and we receive ready-made plans. These plans always include electrical schematics and often a P&ID (Piping and Instrumentation Diagram), which shows all the sensors and actuators we will control. Such plans also include all the equipment, not just the control system components. For example, there may be ball valves that are operated manually. The purpose of the P&ID is to provide a comprehensive view of the installation.

Since we now understand that there is no universal standard, we will assume the following scenario for our case. Industrial installations or segments of production lines where the final product quality is checked are usually named according to their function and industry specifics. We have received information that the newly built quality control hall is named QCS, which stands for "Quality Control Station." This station is where products undergo various tests and inspections to ensure they meet specified quality standards. As mentioned, each installation includes various sensors and actuators. Therefore, using the abbreviation QCS (Quality Control Station) as a prefix for the entire quality control line, and then applying this prefix to individual sensors or actuators, is a very professional and logical approach. This naming system has several advantages:

- *Consistency*: All quality control-related elements will have a uniform prefix, facilitating the identification and management of these devices.

- *Clarity*: The prefix QCS clearly indicates that a particular element is part of the quality control system, which can be helpful for both employees and service technicians.

- *Organization*: Such a naming system helps maintain order in technical documentation and resource management systems.

Here are a few possible examples that are common engineering practices from everyday life:

- *QCS-LIC1*: Quality Control Station – Level Indicator Controller 1

- *QCS-V1*: Quality Control Station – Valve 1

- *QCS-TIC1*: Quality Control Station – Temperature Indicator Controller 1

- *QCS-PIC1*: Quality Control Station – Pressure Indicator Controller 1

- *QCS-M1*: Quality Control Station – Motor 1

- *QCS-S1*: Quality Control Station – Sensor 1

Such naming conventions not only facilitate device identification and maintenance but can also contribute to improving operational efficiency through faster issue resolution and better communication among team members. Implementing a naming system based on prefixes and numbering that reflects the function and location of devices is a good engineering practice.

Now that we have the theoretical introduction behind us, we can move on to the practical part. We'll start by organizing the structure of our project. Let's copy our current project, *LightingControl.project*, from the directory *C:\PLC\Chapter_04* to the directory *C:\PLC\Chapter_05*, and rename it to *QCS.project*. In the CODESYS environment, after opening the project, we'll notice that the main project branch starts with the name *QCS*, reflecting our Quality Control Station installation (Figure 5-1).

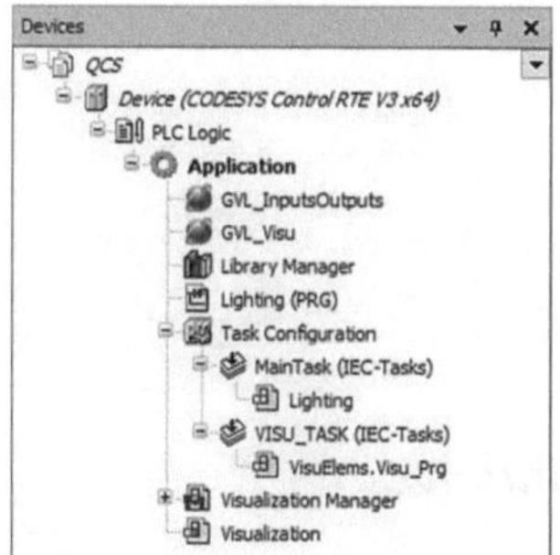

Figure 5-1. *Devices window*

As we know, QCS is the prefix for our installation that we'll be controlling. This prefix will be added to the name of every component belonging to the installation, including sensors and actuators. This also applies to our PLC control system. Now, let's name our PLC controller and add numbering to it. In the *Devices* window, right-click on our PLC controller, currently named *Device*, and then select *Refactoring* ➤ *Rename 'Device'...* (Figure 5-2).

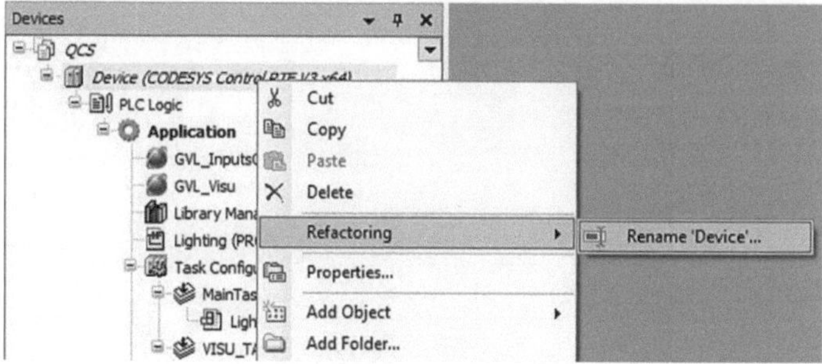

Figure 5-2. *Device* ➤ *Refactoring* ➤ *Rename 'Device'...*

In the *Rename* window, enter the new name for our controller; let it be *PLC1* (Figure 5-3).

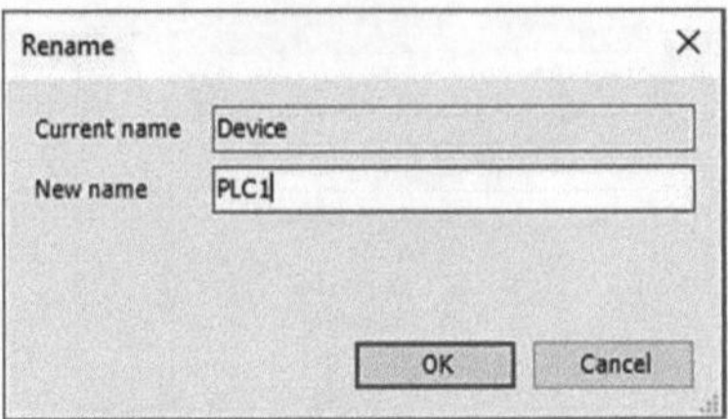

Figure 5-3. *Rename window*

Next, in the *Refactoring* window, we confirm all the changes by clicking
the *OK* button (Figure 5-4).

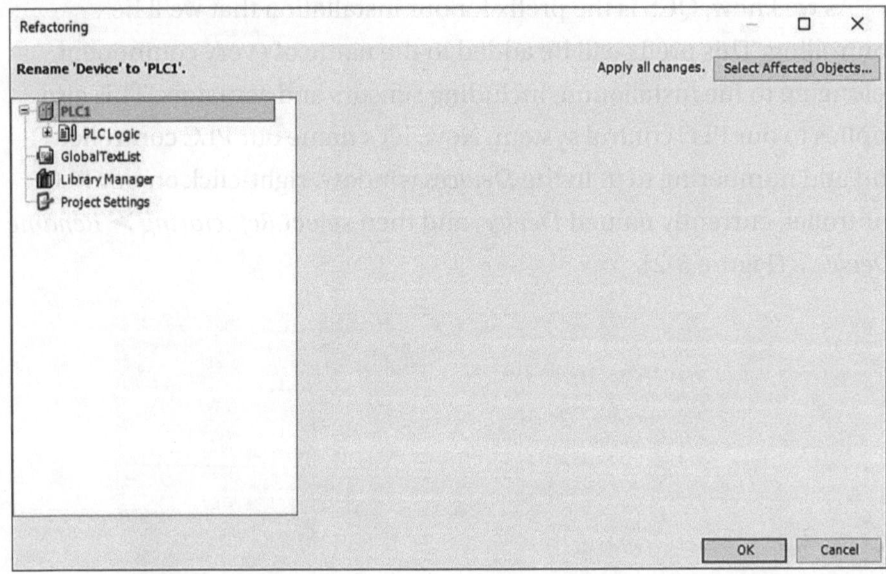

Figure 5-4. *Refactoring window*

The next good practice that will facilitate organization for future work
on the project is adding some information about the project itself. We
can do this by selecting *Project ➤ Project Information...* from the menu
(Figure 5-5).

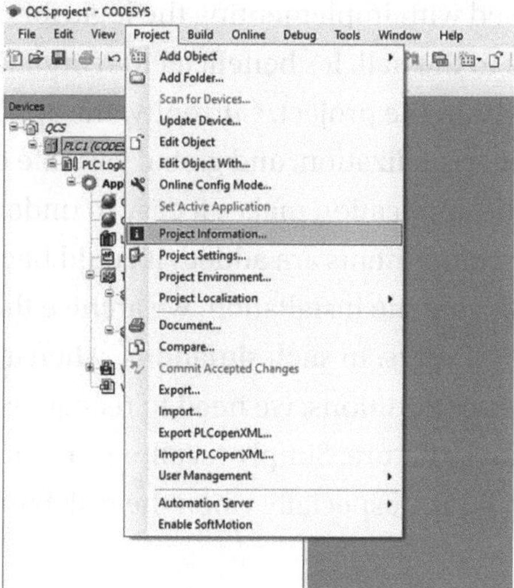

Figure 5-5. *Project ➤ Project Information...*

In the *Summary* tab, we enter basic information about our project, and then confirm by clicking the *OK* button (Figure 5-6).

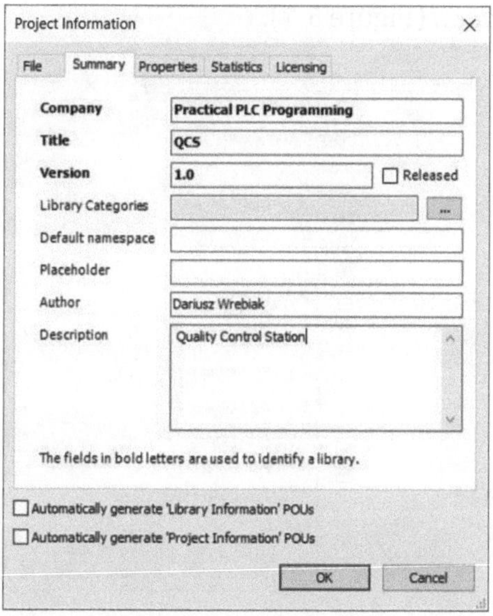

Figure 5-6. *Project Information window*

Before we proceed with implementing the logic for controlling the
gates and entrances to the hall, it's beneficial to reorganize the structure
of our application within the project. Currently, the application consists of
lighting control logic, visualization, and global variable declarations. While
the current size of the application makes it easy to understand its structure,
as it grows and new components are added, it could become confusing.

Often, after deploying the installation, we archive the project and may
not revisit it for several years. In such situations, when a client returns with
a request for changes or additions, we need to reacquaint ourselves with
the entire application structure. Simply recalling which component does
what can take many hours, especially when the task falls to a different
programmer.

To avoid such problems from the very beginning, it's important to
maintain an organized project structure. I always strive to separate the
components responsible for PLC control logic from the visualization. In
our project, we can add various elements, including new folders. I suggest
adding a folder named *PLC*. To do this, right-click *Application*, and select
the option *Add Folder...* (Figure 5-7).

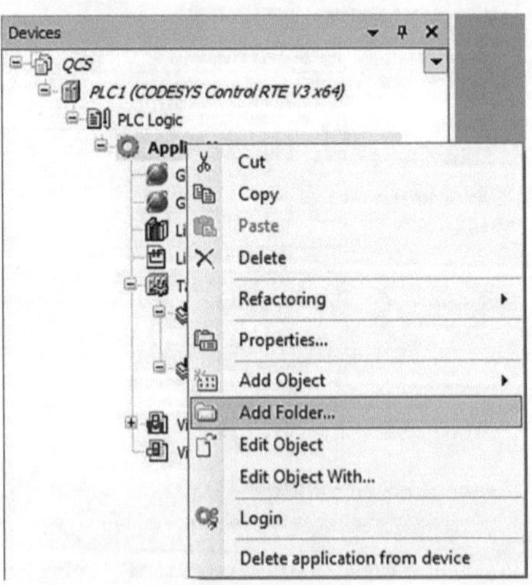

Figure 5-7. *Application ➤ Add Folder...*

In the *Add Folder* window, enter the name *PLC* and click the *OK* button (Figure 5-8).

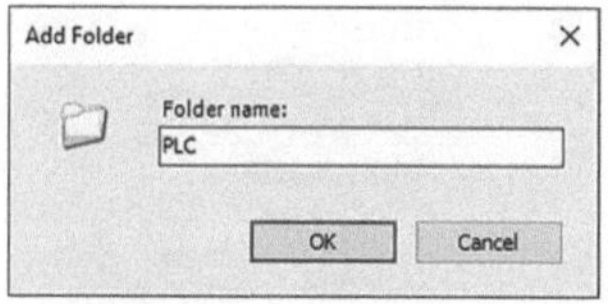

Figure 5-8. *Add Folder window*

Next, in the *Devices* window, let's drag and drop the global variables *GVL_InputsOutputs* into the newly created *PLC* folder. Additionally, let's add a folder named *ControlLogic* to the *PLC* folder and move the *Lighting* program into it.

In the same manner, let's add a folder named *Visualization* to the project. Within the *Visualization* folder, create a subfolder named *Pages*. Move the *Visualization Manager* object and the global variables *GVL_Visu* into the *Visualization* folder. Then, move the *Visualization* object into the *Pages* folder.

These minor changes will save us a lot of time in the future when we need to locate specific elements in our application. This logical organization effectively separates the PLC program from the visualization. Here is how the structure of our program should look now (Figure 5-9).

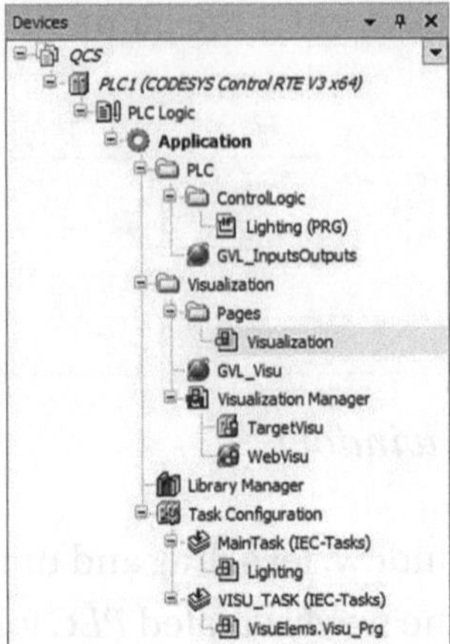

Figure 5-9. *Devices window*

PLC Program Implementation
Global Variables Declaration

Now that we have clarity on what needs to be controlled, it's time to gather all signals from the electrical diagram that we will use to create the control logic (Table 5-1).

Table 5-1. *Necessary signals that will enable us to accomplish the task*

Type of Signal	Name	Description
Digital input	QCS-DLS1	Down Limit Switch for Gate 1 (Area I)
Digital input	QCS-ULS1	Up Limit Switch for Gate 1 (Area I)
Digital input	QCS-PE1	Photoelectric Sensor for Gate 1 (Area I)
Digital input	QCS-PB1	Push Button for Gate 1 (Area I)

(continued)

Table 5-1. (*continued*)

Type of Signal	Name	Description
Digital input	QCS-DLS2	Down Limit Switch for Entrance 1 (Area I)
Digital input	QCS-ULS2	Up Limit Switch for Entrance 1 (Area I)
Digital input	QCS-PE2	Photoelectric Sensor for Entrance 1 (Area I)
Digital input	QCS-PB2	Push Button for Entrance 1 (Area I)
Digital input	QCS-DLS3	Down Limit Switch for Entrance 2 (Area II)
Digital input	QCS-ULS3	Up Limit Switch for Entrance 2 (Area II)
Digital input	QCS-PE3	Photoelectric Sensor for Entrance 2 (Area II)
Digital input	QCS-PB3	Push Button for Entrance 2 (Area II)
Digital input	QCS-DLS4	Down Limit Switch for Gate 2 (Area III)
Digital input	QCS-ULS4	Up Limit Switch for Gate 2 (Area III)
Digital input	QCS-PE4	Photoelectric Sensor for Gate 2 (Area III)
Digital input	QCS-MS1	Motion Sensor for Gate 2 (Area III)
Digital output	QCS-M1-OPEN	Motor M1 – signal to open Gate 1 (Area I)
Digital output	QCS-M1-CLOSE	Motor M1 – signal to close Gate 1 (Area I)
Digital output	QCS-M2-OPEN	Motor M2 – signal to open Entrance 1 (Area I)
Digital output	QCS-M2-CLOSE	Motor M2 – signal to close Entrance 1 (Area I)
Digital output	QCS-M3-OPEN	Motor M3 – signal to open Entrance 2 (Area II)
Digital output	QCS-M3-CLOSE	Motor M3 – signal to close Entrance 2 (Area II)
Digital output	QCS-M4-OPEN	Motor M4 – signal to open Gate 2 (Area III)
Digital output	QCS-M4-CLOSE	Motor M4 – signal to close Gate 2 (Area III)

The table shows that each signal has a unique name starting with a prefix indicating the installation, followed by a function designation and numbering. At first glance, this might seem intricate: why do all sensors for *Gate1* have number 1, whereas for *Gate2*, the limit switches and photoelectric sensor have number 4, and the motion sensor has number 1? What is the logic behind this, and how were these specific signals assigned to each gate?

Explanation needed here. As mentioned earlier, PLC programmers often work based on electrical schematics and P&ID diagrams, from which they gather this information. In an installation or machine, there are no two signals with identical names. In the example provided, the situation was intentionally complicated to demonstrate that designing a system does not always prioritize logical ordering of numbering and device names, but rather focuses on the uniqueness of signal names and actuators. While this scenario is realistic, it is unlikely. Typically, those planning installations strive for logically connected names.

The attentive reader might notice a certain inconsistency: for *Gate2*, there is a motion sensor that controls the gate, but there are also motion sensors throughout the hall that control the lighting! Why then weren't the lighting motion sensors named, but the gate sensor was? The reason is straightforward. I did this intentionally to highlight the way variables are named. The variable name *DI_MOTION_DETECTED_AREA_I* is descriptive, whereas *DI_MS1* conveys no information, especially to someone unfamiliar with the installation. This demonstrates how important it is to add comments to variables, particularly where the name alone isn't sufficient for full understanding. In real-world scenarios, all motion sensors in the lighting installation would also have unique names.

Now that we have clarity on naming variables, it's time to declare them in the *GVL_InputsOutputs* list (Figure 5-10).

```
(* Gates and entrances *)
// Digital Inputs
DI_DLS1 : BOOL;                    // QCS-DLS1: Down Limit Switch for Gate 1 (Area I)
DI_ULS1 : BOOL;                    // QCS-ULS1: Up Limit Switch for Gate 1 (Area I)
DI_PE1 : BOOL;                     // QCS-PE1: Photoelectric Sensor for Gate 1 (Area I)
DI_PB1 : BOOL;                     // QCS-PB1: Push Button for Gate 1 (Area I)
DI_DLS2 : BOOL;                    // QCS-DLS2: Down Limit Switch for Entrance 1 (Area I)
DI_ULS2 : BOOL;                    // QCS-ULS2: Up Limit Switch for Entrance 1 (Area I)
DI_PE2 : BOOL;                     // QCS-PE2: Photoelectric Sensor for Entrance 1 (Area I)
DI_PB2 : BOOL;                     // QCS-PB2: Push Button for Entrance 1 (Area I)
DI_DLS3 : BOOL;                    // QCS-DLS3: Down Limit Switch for Entrance 2 (Area II)
DI_ULS3 : BOOL;                    // QCS-ULS3: Up Limit Switch for Entrance 2 (Area II)
DI_PE3 : BOOL;                     // QCS-PE3: Photoelectric Sensor for Entrance 2 (Area II)
DI_PB3 : BOOL;                     // QCS-PB3: Push Button for Entrance 2 (Area II)
DI_DLS4 : BOOL;                    // QCS-DLS4: Down Limit Switch for Gate 2 (Area III)
DI_ULS4 : BOOL;                    // QCS-ULS4: Up Limit Switch for Gate 2 (Area III)
DI_PE4 : BOOL;                     // QCS-PE4: Photoelectric Sensor for Gate 2 (Area III)
DI_MS1 : BOOL;                     // QCS-MS1: Motion Sensor for Gate 2 (Area III)

// Digital Outputs
DO_M1_OPEN : BOOL;                 // Motor M1: signal to open Gate 1 (Area I)
DO_M1_CLOSE : BOOL;                // Motor M1: signal to close Gate 1 (Area I)
DO_M2_OPEN : BOOL;                 // Motor M2: signal to open Entrance 1 (Area I)
DO_M2_CLOSE : BOOL;                // Motor M2: signal to close Entrance 1 (Area I)
DO_M3_OPEN : BOOL;                 // Motor M3: signal to open Entrance 2 (Area II)
DO_M3_CLOSE : BOOL;                // Motor M3: signal to close Entrance 2 (Area II)
DO_M4_OPEN : BOOL;                 // Motor M4: signal to open Gate 2 (Area III)
DO_M4_CLOSE : BOOL;                // Motor M4: signal to close Gate 2 (Area III)
```

Figure 5-10. *Inputs and outputs for gates and entrances*

Programming Language FBD

After declaring the input and output variables for controlling the gates and entrances to the hall, let's proceed to implement the control logic for *Gate1* located in Area I.

In this application scenario, however, we do not have a detailed description of how we are supposed to control our gate. This is a common scenario encountered in everyday life. The technical description provides a very general outline, and the rest we must figure out ourselves.

Let's start with a brief summary of what we know from the electrical schematic and P&ID diagram. The gate has a lower limit switch that signals when the gate is fully closed (QCS-DLS1). It also has an upper limit switch that signals when the gate is fully open (QCS-ULS1). Additionally, the gate is equipped with a photoelectric sensor (QCS-PE1) that detects the absence of people or objects in its area of operation. The gate can be opened by pressing a button mounted on both sides (external and internal) of the gate (QCS-PB1). In this case, the controller receives only one signal, regardless of which button is pressed. This method of control is sufficient. It could certainly be split into two separate signals, but that would increase the project costs because each button would require a separate digital input in the controller, necessitating additional hardware modules. The gate is operated by the QCS-M1 motor, which allows for operation in two directions: opening and closing. This is how the P&ID diagram presents *Gate1* (Figure 5-11).

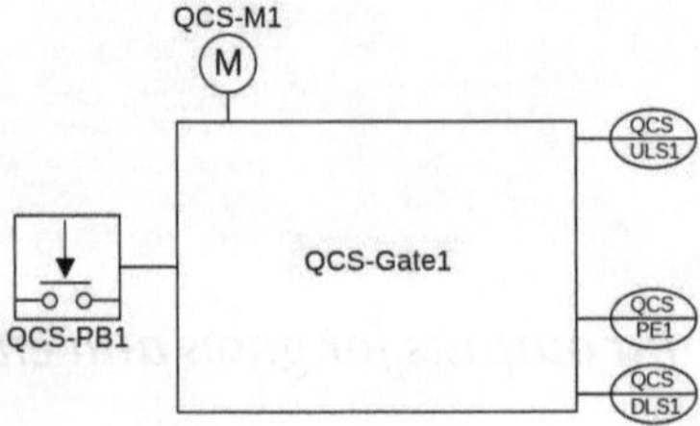

Figure 5-11. *P&ID diagram for Gate1*

Since we have now gathered all the necessary signals for *Gate1*, we can proceed to implement the control logic based on the knowledge we have acquired in previous sections. Our goal is to program *Gate1* so that when the QCS-PB1 button is pressed, it opens completely, achieving full opening based on the signal from the QCS-USL1 limit switch.

Let's start by adding a new program to our project in the *ControlLogic* folder. Let's name this program *GatesAndEntrances* and select the *Function Block Diagram (FBD)* programming language (Figure 5-12).

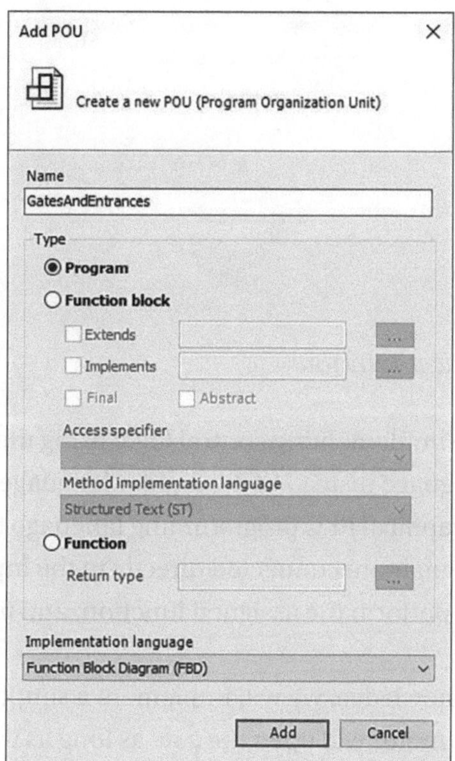

Figure 5-12. *Add POU window*

After adding the new program to the project, the PLC program editor
will open automatically. Meanwhile, the *Devices* window displays the
structure of our project (Figure 5-13).

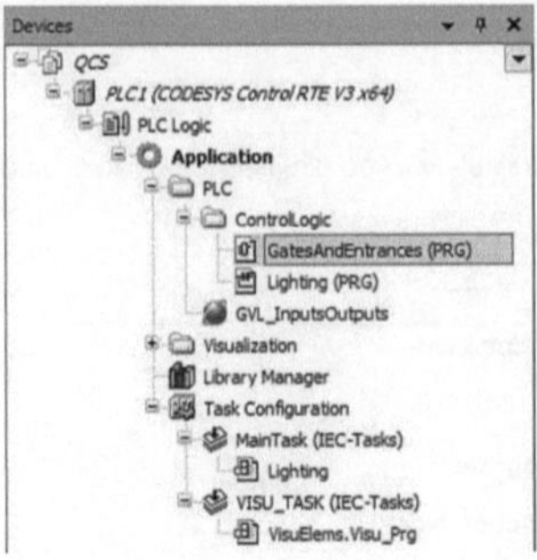

Figure 5-13. *Devices window*

This time we're implementing control logic using the Function Block Diagram (FBD) language instead of the Ladder language used previously. FBD is a popular graphical PLC programming language that does not use contacts or coils; signals are connected directly to the inputs of function blocks, which then perform the assigned function, and finally set the outputs.

Based on this knowledge, we will implement a simple control logic where the QCS-M1 motor will open the gate as long as the QCS-PB1 button is pressed and the upper limit switch QCS-ULS1 has not been reached. In the editor, let's select *Network 1*, and from the *FBD/LD/IL* menu, choose *Insert Empty Box* (Figure 5-14).

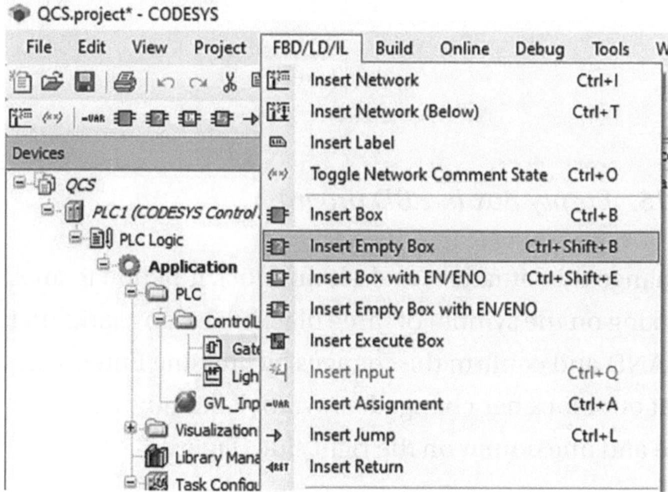

Figure 5-14. *FBD/LD/IL ➤ Insert Empty Box*

Function Block Diagram (FBD)   A graphical programming language used to create programs for PLC controllers. In FBD, programs are built using function blocks that represent various logical and mathematical functions. These blocks are interconnected by lines that depict the flow of signals. Unlike Ladder Diagram (LD), in FBD, input signals are connected directly to the inputs of function blocks, which execute assigned operations and generate corresponding output signals. FBD is particularly useful for designing complex control systems where the logic can be visualized and modified easily.

To clarify, the empty function block that has been added to our program currently features two inputs and one output. However, no input or output signals have been assigned to this block, nor does it currently possess any specific function or name (Figure 5-15).

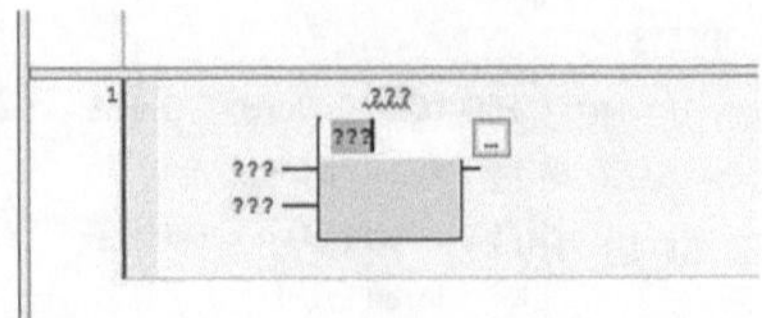

Figure 5-15. *Empty Box in FBD program*

Let's change this situation, and set the block function to an AND logic gate by clicking on the symbol of three black question marks on the block. Then type AND and confirm the changes by pressing Enter. This way, we will see that our block has changed its symbol and now has two inputs on the left side and one output on the right side (Figure 5-16).

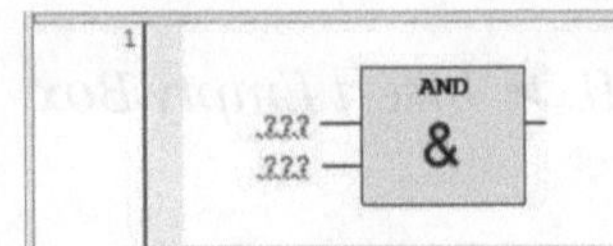

Figure 5-16. *Logic gate AND in the FBD program*

AND Logic Gate   A fundamental element in digital logic and PLC programming, which performs the logical AND operation. The AND gate has two or more inputs and one output. The output of the AND gate is high (TRUE) only when all of its inputs are high (TRUE). Otherwise, the output is low (FALSE). The AND gate is commonly used to implement conditions where all criteria must be met simultaneously.

Let's now set the parameters for the AND block, using inputs *DI_PB1* and *DI_ULS1* on the left side. Replace the question marks with variables that reflect the states of the digital inputs (Figure 5-17).

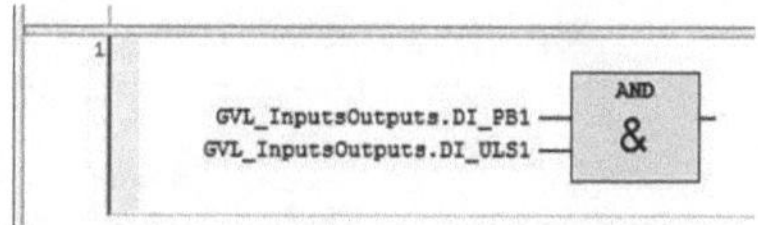

Figure 5-17. *Block AND with assigned inputs*

At this point, however, the output of the AND block will be set to high (TRUE) when both inputs are high, meaning when the gate opening button is pressed and when the gate reaches the fully open position. However, our goal is to set the digital output that controls the gate opening to high (TRUE) only when the button is pressed and the gate has not reached the fully open position. Therefore, we need to negate the input *DI_ULS1* of the AND block. To do this, click on the input of the AND block associated with the variable *DI_ULS1*, and from the menu, select *FBD/LD/IL* ➤ *Negation* (Figure 5-18).

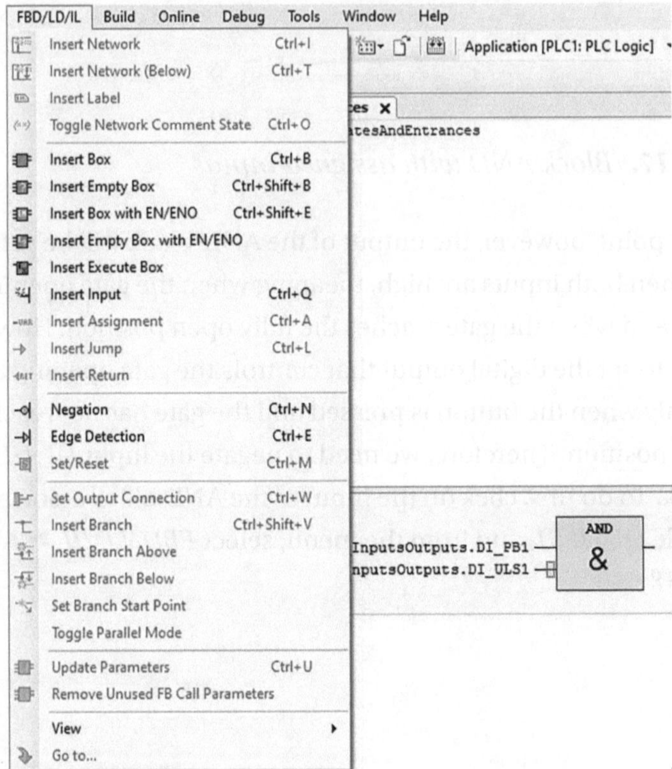

Figure 5-18. *FBD/LD/IL ➤ Negation*

With the AND block implemented in this way, the output will always be set to high (TRUE) when the button is pressed and the gate has not reached the fully open position (Figure 5-19).

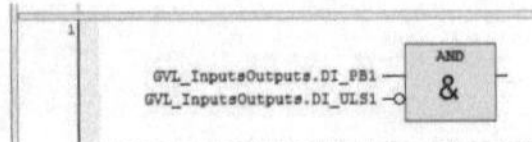

Figure 5-19. *Inputs of the AND block*

The next step will be assigning the output of the AND block, which controls the gate opening, to the output *DO_M1_OPEN*. To do this, select the output of the AND block and choose *FBD/LD/IL ➤ Insert Assignment* from the menu (Figure 5-20).

176

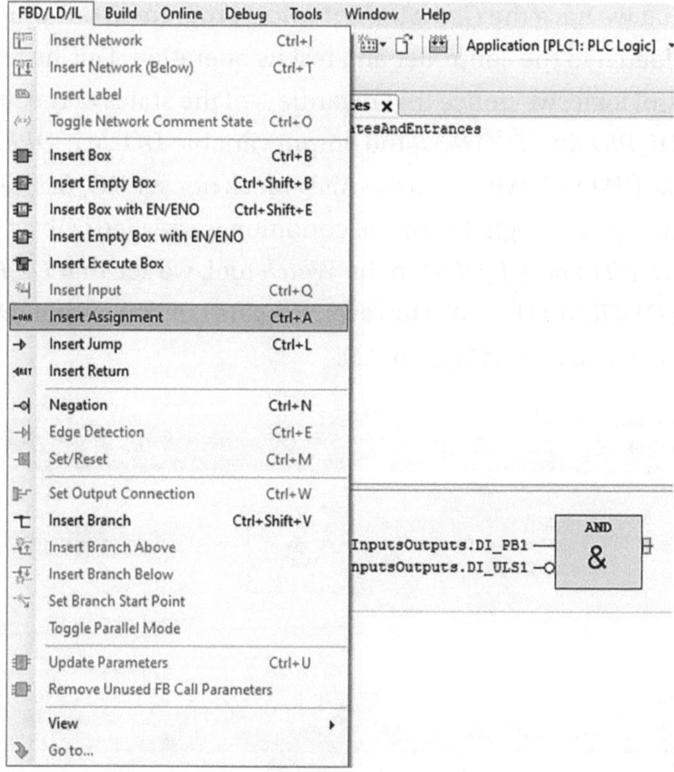

Figure 5-20. *FBD/LD/IL ➤ Insert Assignment*

Next, replace the three question marks with the variable associated with the digital output *DO_M1_OPEN* (Figure 5-21).

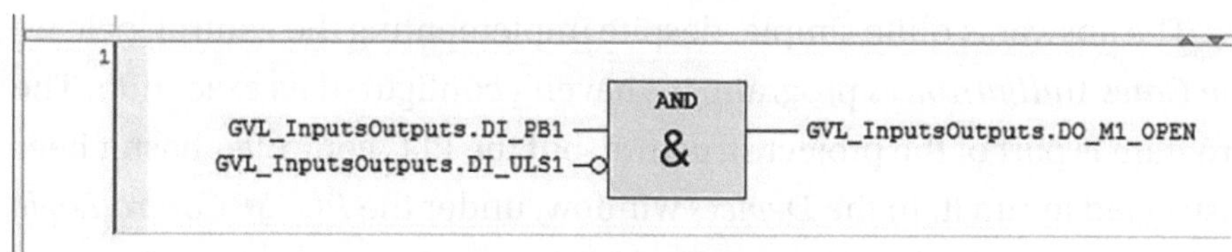

Figure 5-21. *Network 1 with an AND block*

Now that we have the *GatesAndEntrances* program in our project, it's time to upload it to the controller and test its operation. During testing of the control logic, we notice that regardless of the states of the input variables *DI_PB1* and *DI_ULS1*, the output variable *DO_M1_OPEN* always remains low (FALSE). Why does the AND block not set *DO_M1_OPEN* to high (TRUE) even though the logical condition is satisfied? Observing the values of *DI_PB1* and *DI_ULS1* in the *Watch* tool, we see that *DI_PB1* is TRUE and *DI_ULS1* is FALSE. However, the gate control output, *DO_M1_OPEN*, remains inactive (Figure 5-22).

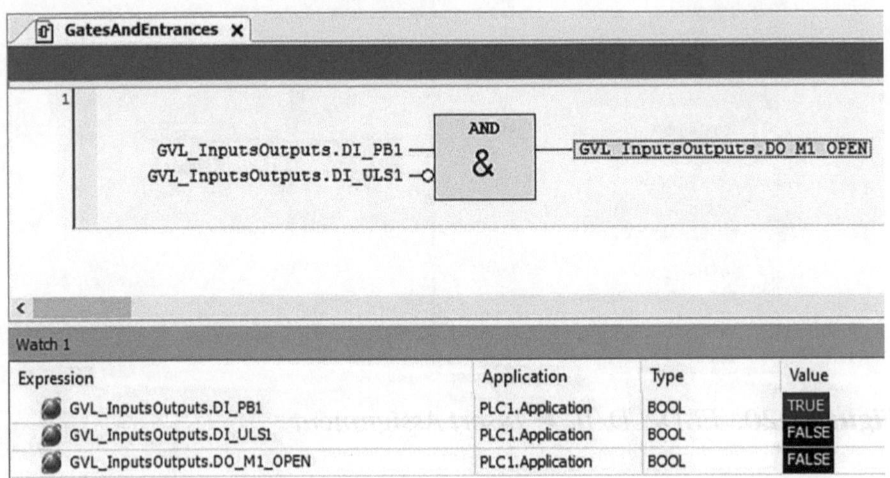

Figure 5-22. *Network 1 and the Watch tool*

The answer is quite simple: despite implementing the control logic in the *GatesAndEntrances* program, we haven't configured its execution. The program is part of the project structure, but the PLC controller hasn't been instructed to run it. In the *Devices* window, under the *PLC ➤ ControlLogic* folder, you can see that the *GatesAndEntrances* program is marked in gray, indicating it's inactive (Figure 5-23). It's time to familiarize ourselves with what *Task Configuration* entails.

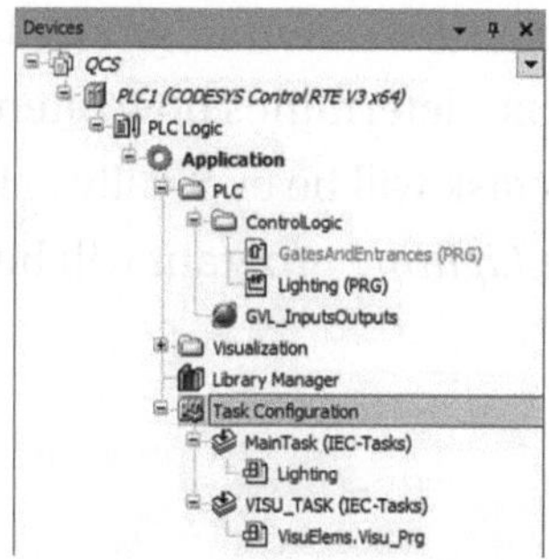

Figure 5-23. *Devices window*

Task Configuration

Let's now briefly discuss what *Task Configuration* is and how to use it. In the *Devices* window, we see two configured tasks: *MainTask*, which executes the *Lighting* control program, and *VISU_TASK*, responsible for visualization. Double-click *Task Configuration* in the *Devices* window to open the configuration panel (Figure 5-24).

Group Name		Core	Priority
IEC-Tasks		Fixed pinned	
	MainTask		1
	VISU_TASK		31

Figure 5-24. *Task Configuration*

We see that we have defined two tasks: *MainTask* and *VISU_TASK*, which belong to the *IEC-Tasks* group. In this window, we also have the option to add a new group if necessary. Now let's proceed to configure the *MainTask*. To view the configuration panel more closely, double-click *MainTask (IEC-Tasks)* in the *Devices* window. Here, we can change the call priority and assign the task to another group if needed. An important parameter is *Interval,* which determines how often in milliseconds the programs assigned to this task will be cyclically called. In our case, setting it to 20 ms means that the *Lighting* program will be called exactly every 20 ms (Figure 5-25).

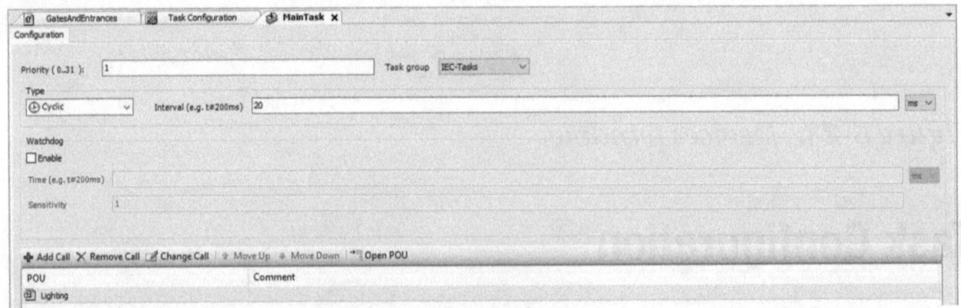

Figure 5-25. *MainTask configure window*

To add a call to the *GatesAndEntrances* program to the *MainTask,* click *Add Call* in the configuration window. Then, in the *Input Assistant* window, select the path to the *GatesAndEntrances* program and confirm your choice by clicking *OK* (Figure 5-26).

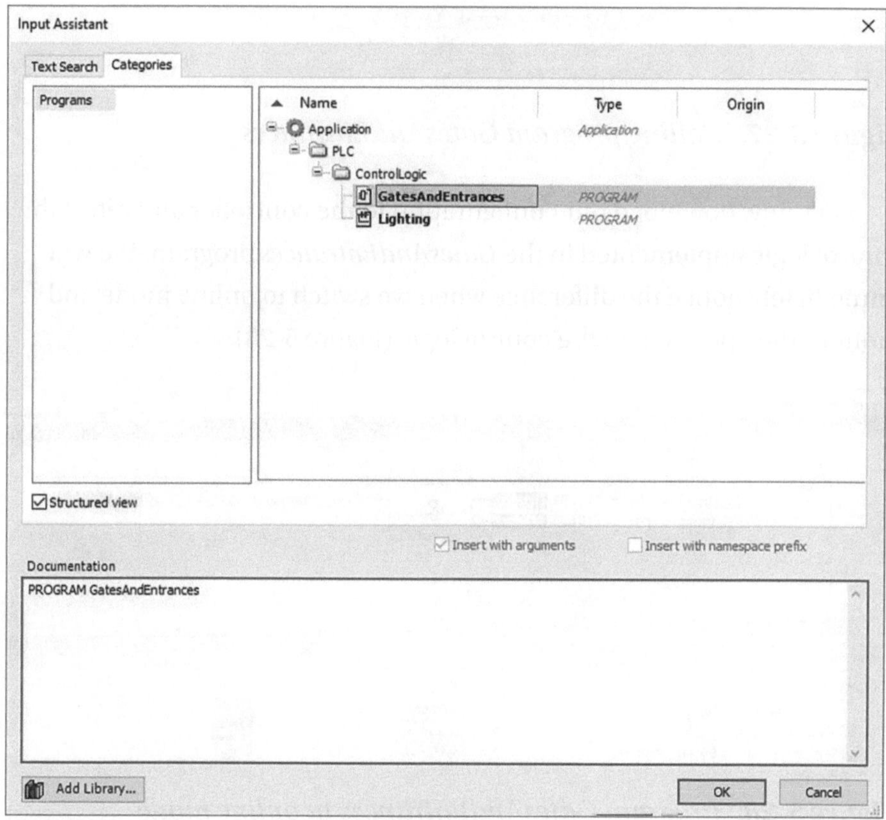

Figure 5-26. *Input Assistant window*

At this point, we can see that after executing the *Lighting* program, the PLC controller will proceed to call the *GatesAndEntrances* program (Figure 5-27). Here, we also have the option to reconfigure the order of program calls. For example, if we want the *GatesAndEntrances* program to be executed before the *Lighting* program, we should select the *GatesAndEntrances* program and then click the *Move Up* button in the configuration menu.

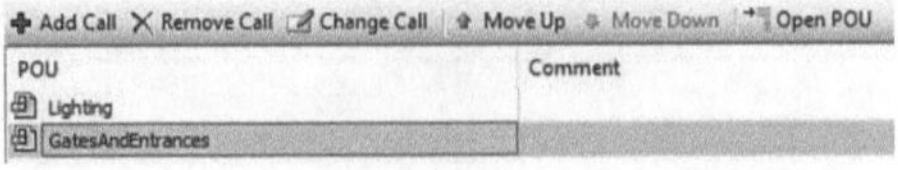

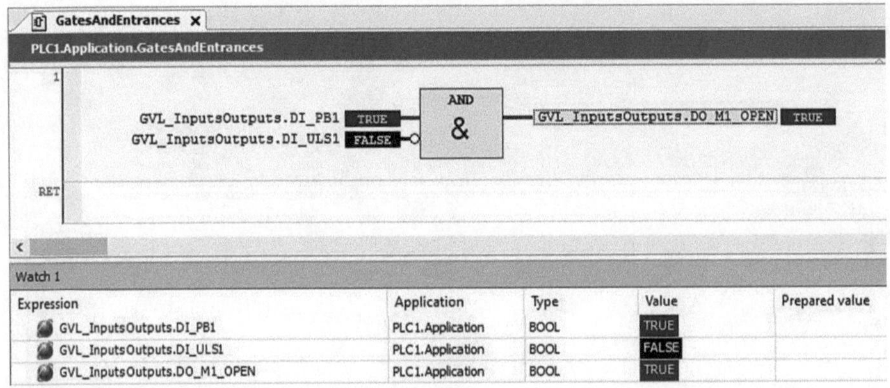

Figure 5-27. *Calling program GatesAndEntrances*

Let's now download our configuration to the controller and retest the control logic implemented in the *GatesAndEntrances* program. We will immediately notice the difference when we switch to online mode and monitor the operation of the control logic (Figure 5-28).

Figure 5-28. *Program GatesAndEntrances in online mode*

Gate1 Opening Control Logic

We have created a simple program that opens the gate to its full open position when the button is pressed. However, this is not the solution we would expect. We would prefer that after a single press of the button, the gate opens automatically to its full position, and once the full open position is reached, the controller automatically sets the digital output controlling the gate to a low state (FALSE).

To achieve this, we need to use a block that implements such a function. Change the name of the AND block to RS, and confirm it by pressing Enter. This is how Network 1 should look after the changes (Figure 5-29).

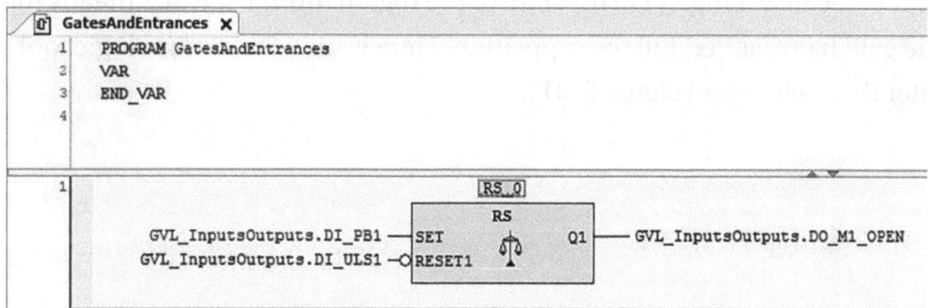

Figure 5-29. *RS block in control logic*

We see a small difference compared to the AND block; namely, above the RS block, there is a field where CODESYS automatically assigned the block name to *RS_0*. If we compiled our project now, we would get an error message that *RS_0* is not defined. This is a requirement of the RS block, which specifies that a name must be assigned to the block.

Let's declare a variable of type RS as a local variable for the *GatesAndEntrances* program named *Gate1_RS_Open* and assign it to the RS block in the control logic. This is how our program should look after the changes (Figure 5-30).

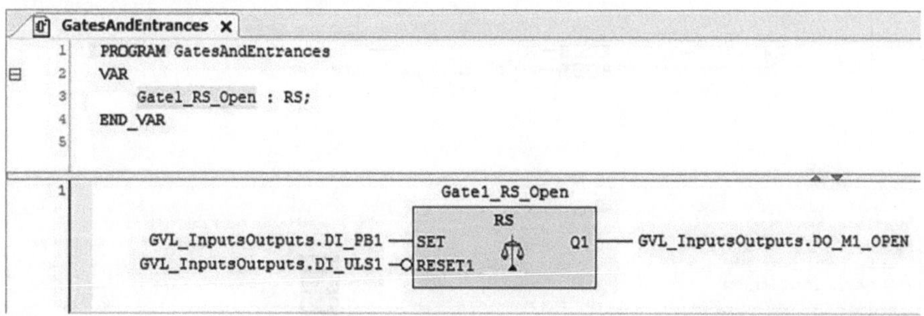

Figure 5-30. *RS block with assigned name*

The RS block works as follows: when the SET input is set to high (TRUE), the Q1 output will also be set to high (TRUE) and will remain in this state until the RESET input is set to high (TRUE). Therefore, we need to make one more change to our control logic, namely, to negate the RESET input, because a high (TRUE) state of the digital input *DI_USL1* means that the gate has reached full open position. Here is how the control logic looks after these changes (Figure 5-31).

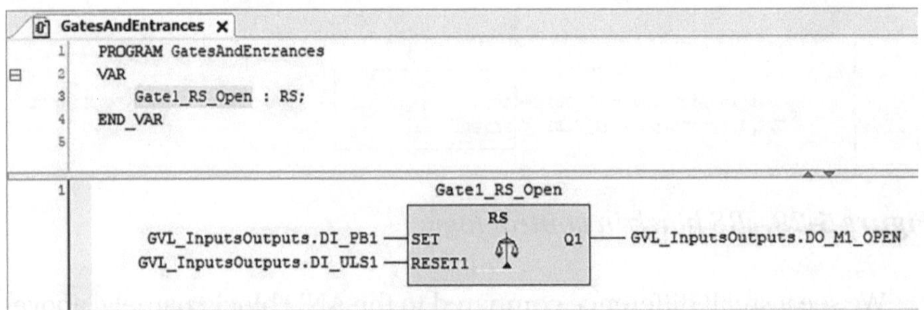

Figure 5-31. *RS block controlling the gate*

Let's download this program to the controller and test its functionality. Let's start from the moment when the button is not pressed and the gate has not reached the upper limit switch. In this case, the output *DO_M1_OPEN* is in a low state (FALSE) (Figure 5-32).

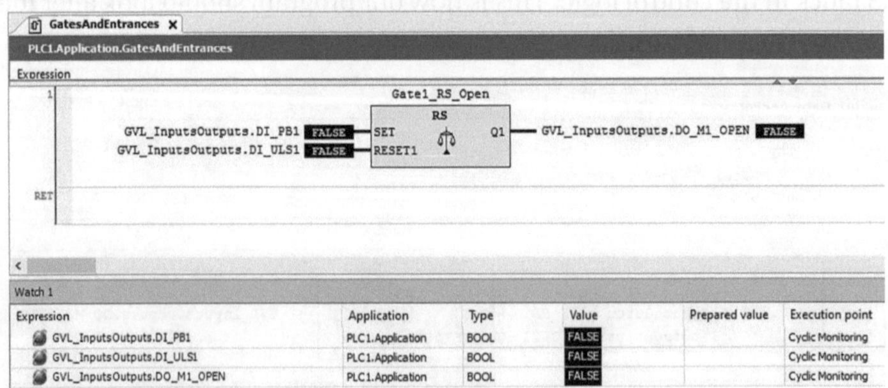

Figure 5-32. *DO_M1_OPEN is FALSE*

Next, press the gate opening button, setting the *DI_PB1* input to TRUE. At this moment, the *DO_M1_OPEN* output will be set to a high state (TRUE), which will cause the gate to open (Figure 5-33).

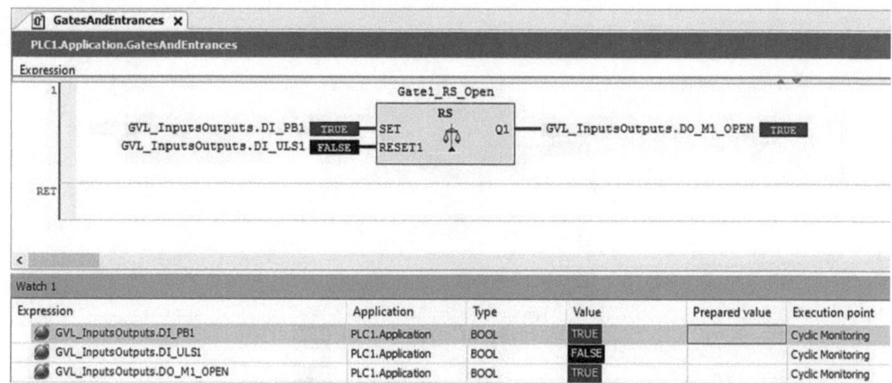

Figure 5-33. *DO_M1_OPEN is TRUE*

Next, set the *DI_PB1* variable to FALSE, indicating that the button is no longer pressed. As we will observe, even though the button is not pressed, the *DO_M1_OPEN* output remains in a high state (TRUE) (Figure 5-34).

Figure 5-34. *DO_M1_OPEN is TRUE, while DI_PB1 is FALSE*

The gate will continue to open until the upper limit switch informs the PLC that the gate is fully open. In practice, this means setting the *DI_ULS1* variable to high (TRUE). At this point, the *DO_M1_OPEN* output will immediately be set to low (FALSE), which means the gate will stop opening and remain in the fully open position (Figure 5-35).

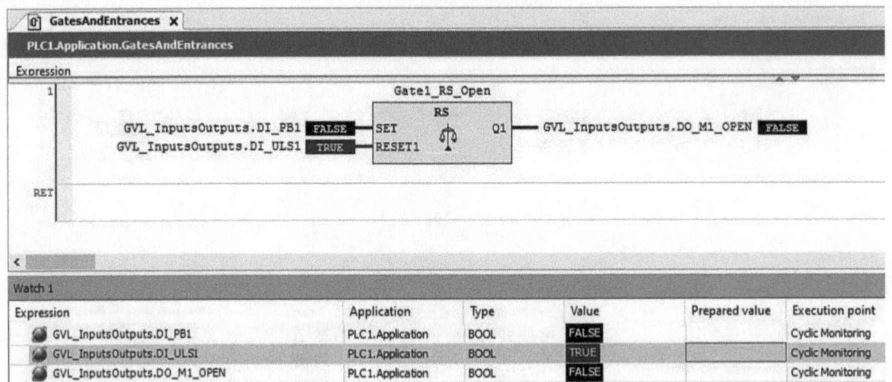

Figure 5-35.   *DO_M1_OPEN is FALSE and DI_ULS1 is TRUE*

Let's now check what happens if we press the gate-opening button while the gate is in the fully open position. Set the digital input *DI_PB1* to TRUE while keeping the input *DI_ULS1* also set to TRUE (Figure 5-36).

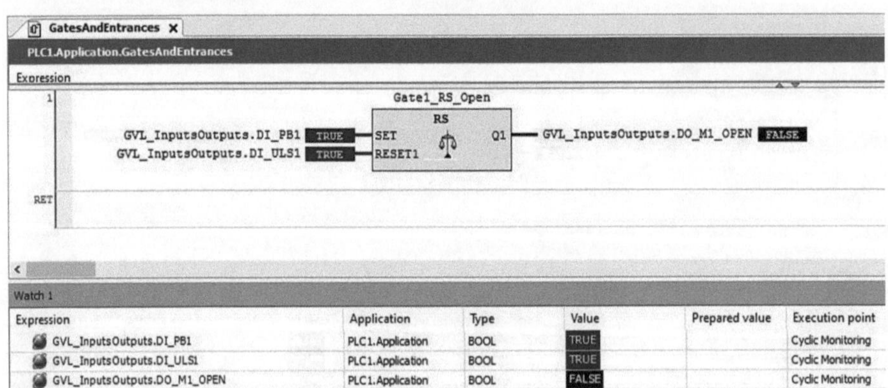

Figure 5-36.   *DI_PB1 is TRUE and DI_ULS1 is TRUE*

We see that in this case, the gate-opening control output has not been set to TRUE. Despite attempting to open the gate by pressing the button, the gate control output remains in the low state (FALSE). Why does this happen? This is due to the use of the RS block, where the RESET input takes precedence over the SET input, hence the name RESET1. When both inputs are simultaneously in the high state (TRUE), the Q1 output will not be set to TRUE because the RESET1 input dominates the SET input.

This feature of the RS block is crucial and must be considered when designing control logic. For a gate that has reached the fully open state, we do not want the motor to continue running even if the button is pressed. Therefore, the upper limit switch takes precedence over the request to open the gate by pressing the button.

RS Flip-Flop   A fundamental memory element in digital logic and PLC programming, capable of storing a single bit of information. It has two inputs, Set (S) and Reset (R), and one output Q. When the Set input (S) is activated (TRUE) and the Reset input (R) is inactive (FALSE), the output Q is set to high (TRUE). When the Reset input (R) is activated (TRUE), the output Q is reset to low (FALSE), regardless of the state of the Set input (S). In this configuration, the RS flip-flop has a dominant RESET, meaning that if both inputs are simultaneously high (TRUE), the output Q will be reset to low (FALSE). The RS flip-flop is used for storing state or implementing bistable functions in control applications.

Gate1 Closing Control Logic

Since we can now open the gate fully, let's now devise a way to implement the control logic for closing it. The gate has two additional sensors that we haven't used yet: a sensor for the fully closed gate position and a photoelectric sensor that detects the absence of objects in the gate's operating area. In practice, such a set of sensors is sufficient. If we observe how automatic gates work, we notice that they are opened using a button. Then the gate opens fully, and subsequently, when the photoelectric sensor informs the controller about the absence of objects in the gate's area, which may prevent it from closing, the gate should be closed until fully closed.

Now let's proceed to implement this control logic in *Network 2*, which will control the *DO_M1_CLOSE* output. In the *GatesAndEntrances* program, let's add a local variable of type RS named *Gate1_RS_Close*, and in *Network 2*, let's implement the following control logic (Figure 5-37).

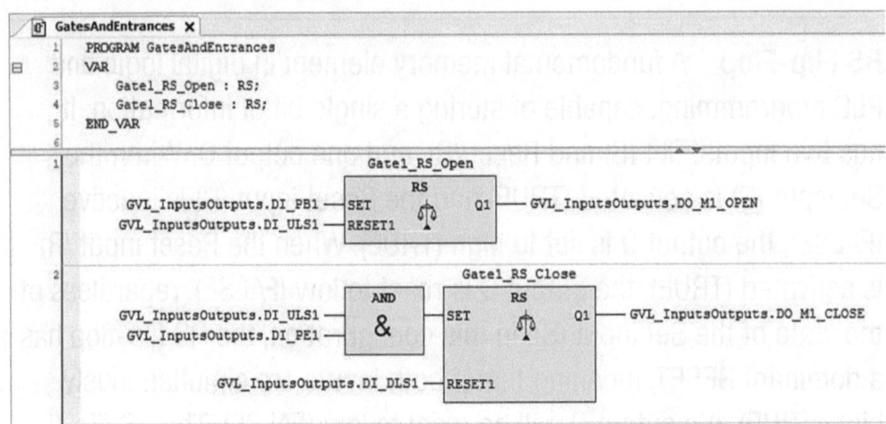

Figure 5-37. *Network 2*

In this case, the gate is fully open, indicated by the digital input *DI_ULS1* set to high (TRUE). Additionally, the gate will not close due to the low state (FALSE) of the photoelectric sensor, indicating the presence of obstacles in the gate's operating area (Figure 5-38). These obstacles could include people passing through the gate or objects such as boxes.

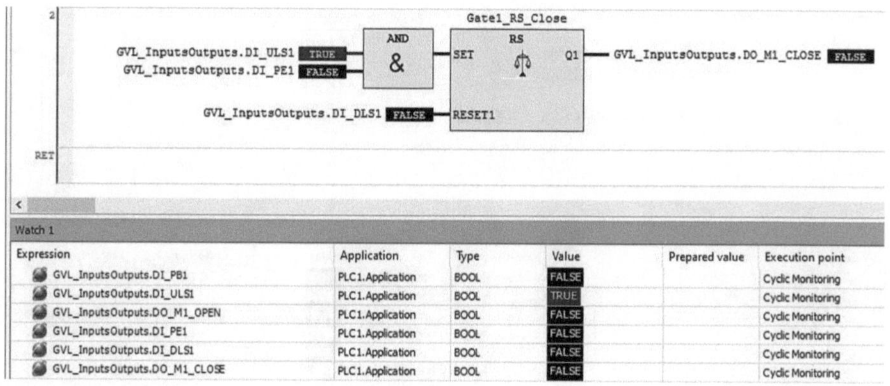

Figure 5-38. *DI_ULS1 is TRUE and DI_PE1 is FALSE*

Let's set the variable *DI_PE1* to TRUE now to start the gate closing process (Figure 5-39).

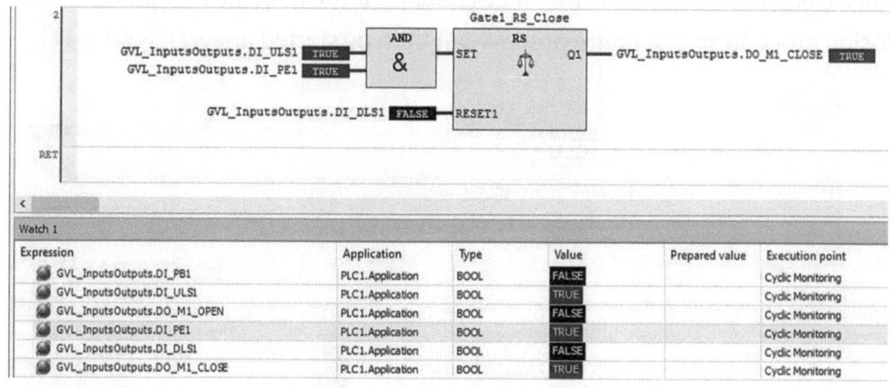

Figure 5-39. *DI_ULS1 is TRUE and DI_PE1 is TRUE*

The next step will be to set the upper limit switch to FALSE because the gate is in the process of closing. We can see that the output *DO_M1_CLOSE* remains in the high state (TRUE) (Figure 5-40).

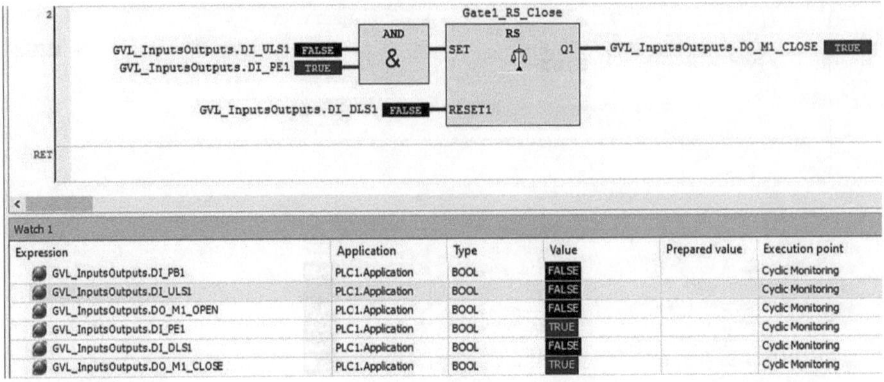

Figure 5-40. *DI_ULS1 is FALSE, DI_PE1 is TRUE, and DO_M1_CLOSE is TRUE*

When the gate reaches the lower limit switch, the output controlling the gate closing will be set to the low state (FALSE), indicating the completion of the closing procedure. The entire process can then be started anew (Figure 5-41).

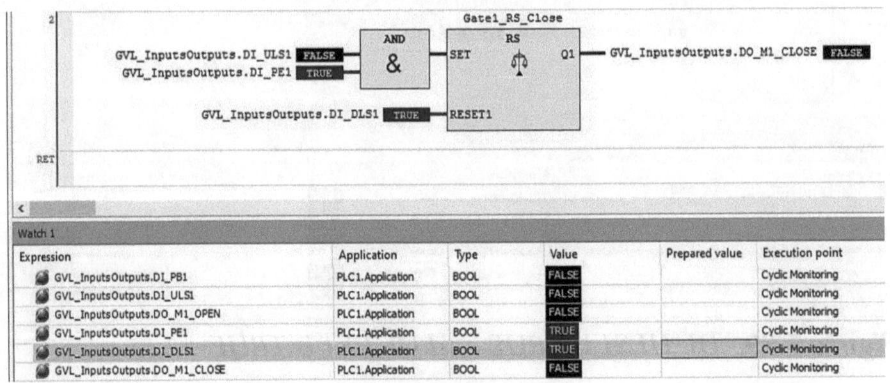

Figure 5-41. *DI_DLS1 is TRUE and DO_M1_CLOSE is FALSE*

Alright, great! We've already implemented the logic for opening and closing the gate. We can celebrate that. But is everything really perfect? Let's analyze a scenario where the gate is in the process of closing, meaning it has descended from the upper limit switch but hasn't reached the lower limit switch yet. The gate is in the middle position (Figure 5-42).

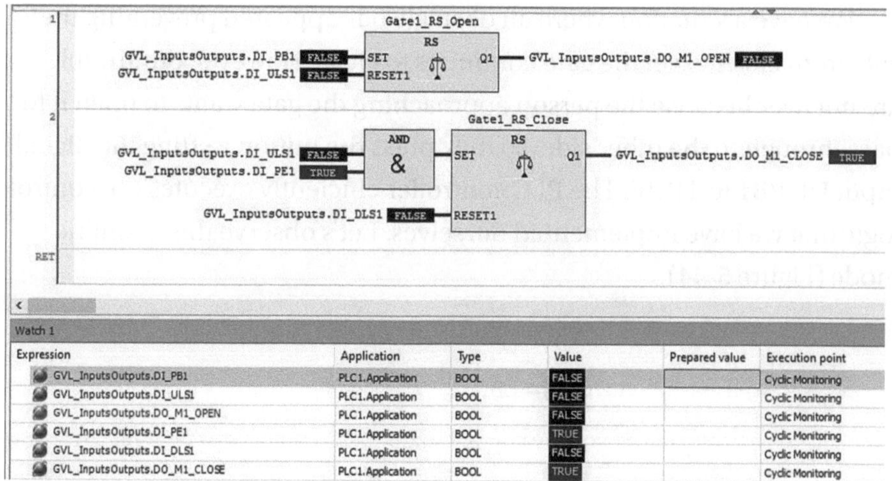

Figure 5-42. *The gate is in the process of closing*

We have a situation where the gate is halfway open and someone approaches it, causing the photoelectric sensor to signal to the controller with a low state (FALSE) that an object has appeared, preventing the gate from closing. Despite this, the controller continues to close the gate because the control logic dictates that the closing operation should only end when the gate reaches the fully closed position (Figure 5-43).

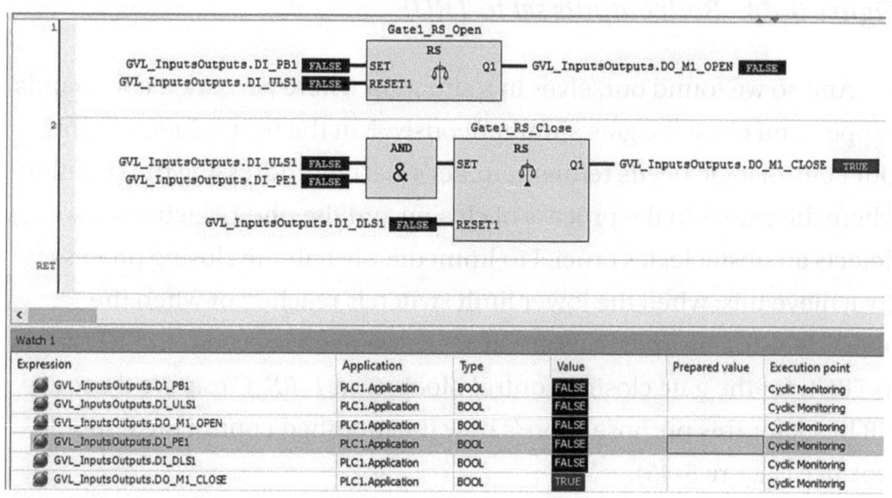

Figure 5-43. *The gate is still in the process of closing*

We have a situation where an obstacle has appeared preventing the gate from closing, yet the gate continues to close. However, our troubles are not over because the person approaching the gate wants to open it to pass through to the other side, so they press the button, setting the digital input DI_PB1 to TRUE. The PLC controller efficiently executes the control logic that we have implemented ourselves. Let's observe this in online mode (Figure 5-44).

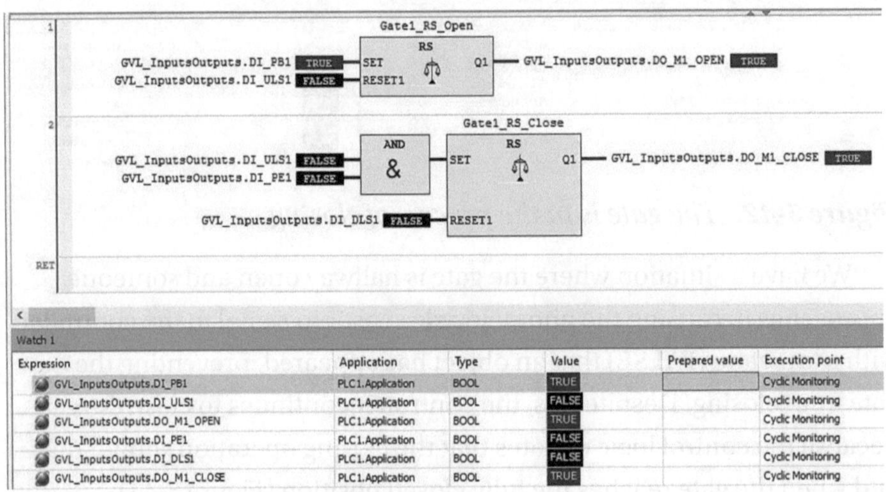

Figure 5-44. *Both outputs set to TRUE*

And so we found ourselves in a situation where we issued commands to open and close the gate simultaneously. Not the best solution, right? Our control logic needs refinement.Let's start by addressing the situation where the gate is in the process of closing and the photoelectric sensor detects an obstacle. It's crucial to immediately halt the closing process. To achieve this, when the lower limit switch is reached or when the photoelectric sensor detects an obstacle, we need to set the RESET1 input to TRUE for the gate closing control block, *Gate1_RS_Close*. We'll use an OR block for this purpose. Here's how the modified control logic should look like (Figure 5-45).

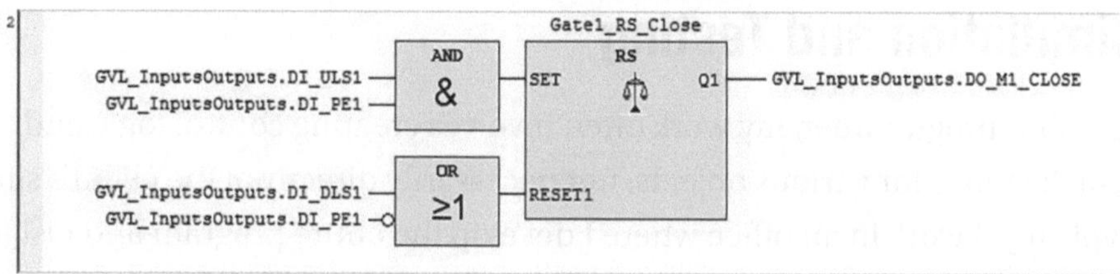

Figure 5-45. *Network 2*

OR Logic Gate   A fundamental element in digital logic and PLC programming, which performs the logical operation of OR. The OR gate has two or more inputs and one output. The output of an OR gate is high (TRUE) if at least one of its inputs is high (TRUE). If all inputs are low (FALSE), the output is also low (FALSE). The OR gate is used to implement conditions where at least one criterion must be satisfied.

After testing, we noticed that the gate immediately interrupts the closing process as soon as the photoelectric sensor signals a low state (FALSE), indicating a lack of permission for the gate to close.

We observe that we only have four inputs and two outputs, totaling six digital signals. However, the number of scenarios we need to test to ensure the correctness of the entire gate opening and closing procedure is significant. Dealing with four inputs still allows for clear state switching in the *Watch* table. However, in the case of a machine with, for example, two hundred signals, manual application testing would be impossible.

How then should we handle such cases to ensure that our application is both functional and safe?

Simulation and Testing

As a PLC programmer, my work often involves creating control logic and visualizations for various objects, not necessarily directly at the client's site. Typically, I work in an office where I develop the entire program and test it on a simulator. Visits to the client usually occur during installation startup. At this stage, I've already tested about 90% to 95% of the entire installation. The remaining 5% to 10% usually involves optimizing controllers and adjusting timings to achieve the best operational parameters. These final tasks are most efficiently performed on-site, with the physical object under control.

For my work, I typically deploy a simulator that substitutes the physical object, allowing me to conduct most tests in the office before going on-site. When on-site, I am prepared to optimize the process and make minor adjustments to control logic if the client has specific requirements.

At this stage of our development as PLC programmers, we're not yet capable of creating our own simulators. However, let's imagine we have access to a function block that simulates the opening and closing of a gate. Our task will be to use this ready-made function block, parameterize it, and integrate it into the PLC program. In the repository we downloaded from my GitHub, in the *Chapter_05* folder, there is a compiled library named *Simulator.compiled-library*. We will need to install this library in our environment and utilize the function block provided by this library.

Let's open the *Library Manager* by double-clicking on it on the left side of the *Devices* window (Figure 5-46).

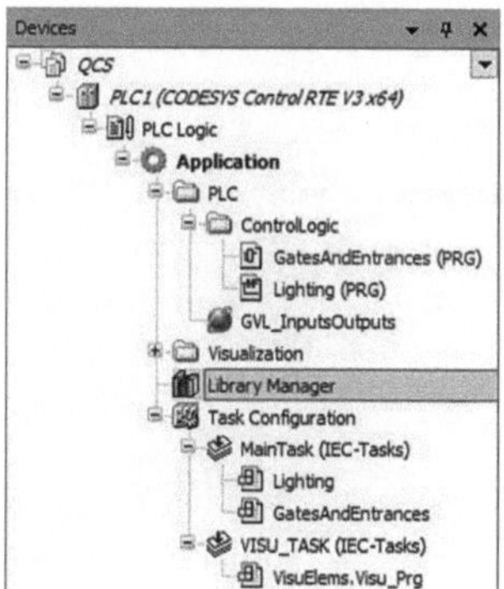

Figure 5-46. *Devices window*

In this window, you will see a set of all libraries used in the *PLC1. Application* (Figure 5-47).

Figure 5-47. *Library Manager*

To install the *Simulator* library in our local library repository, go to the top menu of the *Library Manager* and click the *Library Repository* tab. In the opened *Library Repository* window, click the *Install...* button located on the right side of the window (Figure 5-48).

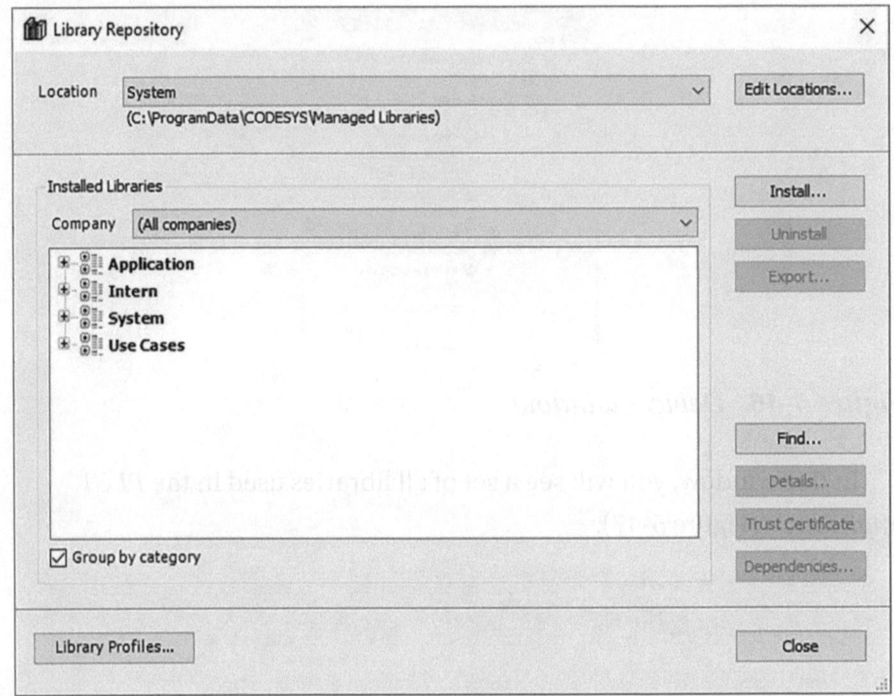

Figure 5-48. *Library Repository*

Next, in the dialog window, you need to select the library you want
to install in the repository. In my case, this file is located at *C:\PLC\
Chapter_05\Simulator.compiled-library* (Figure 5-49).

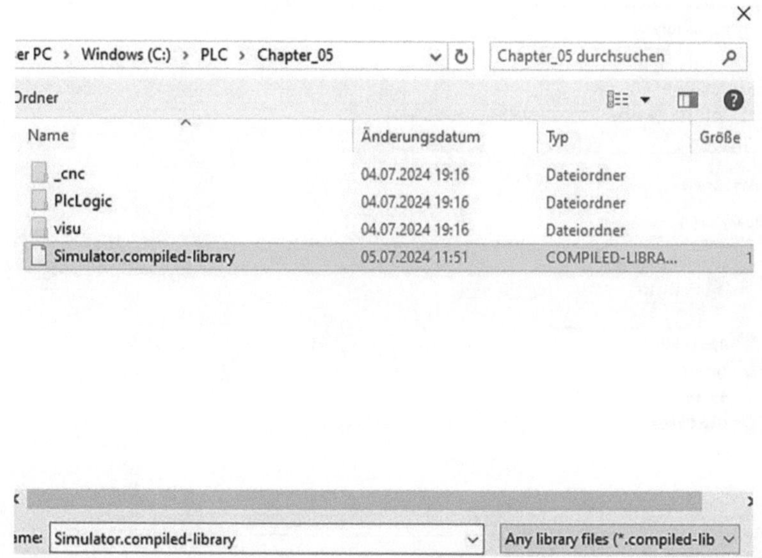

Figure 5-49. *Dialog window*

After successfully installing the library, an additional list *(Miscellaneous)* containing the library named *Simulator* will appear in the repository. Next, click the *Close* button to close the *Library Repository* window (Figure 5-50).

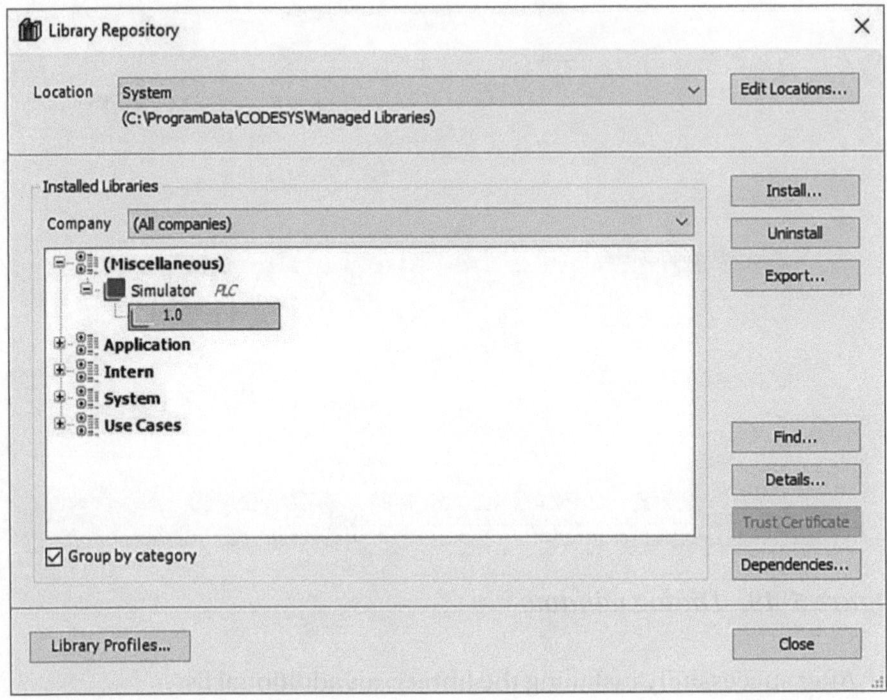

Figure 5-50. *Library Repository*

After installing the *Simulator* library in our repository, it's time to add it to our project. In the *Library Manager* window, click *Add Library*, then select *Miscellaneous* ➤ *Simulator*, and confirm the selection by clicking *OK* (Figure 5-51).

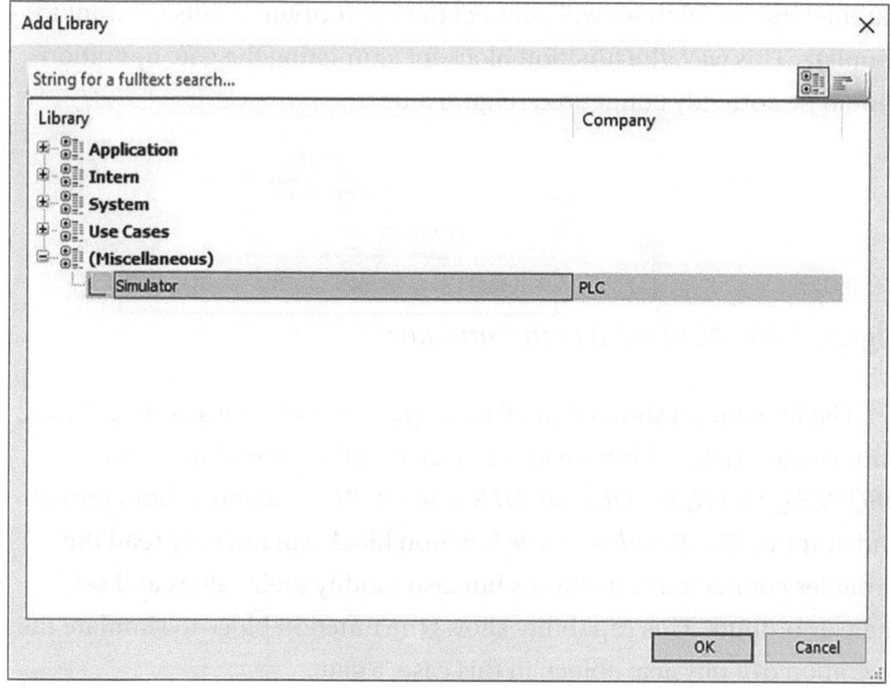

Figure 5-51. *Add Library*

Now it's time to use a function block from the simulator in our
GatesAndEntrances program. Let's declare a new function block named
Gate1_Sim, which will be of type *Simulator.Gate* (Figure 5-52).

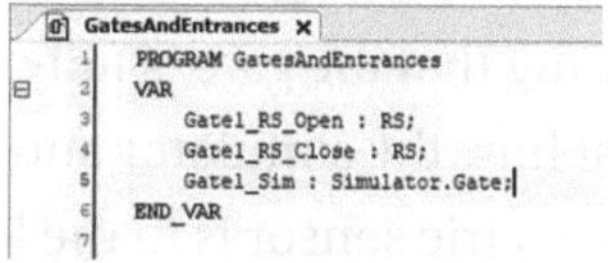

Figure 5-52. *Declaration of variables in the
GatesAndEntrances program*

Next, let's add Network 3 to our program and place an *Empty Box* block
within it. Set its parameters so that the type is set to *Simulator.Gate*, and
name the function block *Gate1_Sim*. The function block accepts four input

parameters, to which we will connect the appropriate inputs we want to simulate. This way, the function block for simulating the gate operation should be correctly configured (Figure 5-53).

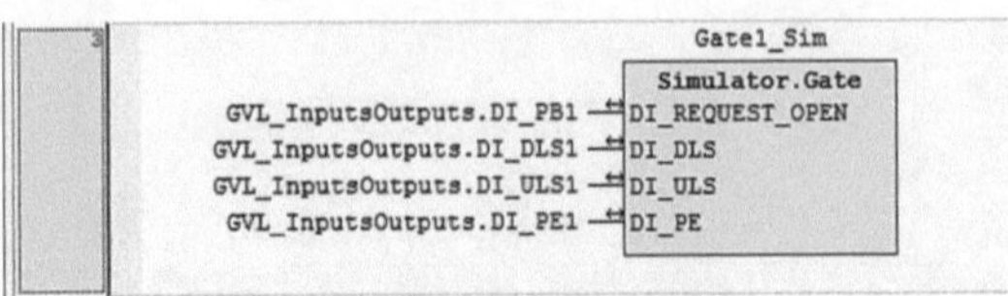

Figure 5-53. *Network 3 with simulator*

The illustration shows that all input parameters have arrows pointing both left and right. This indicates that all function block inputs, *DI_REQUEST_OPEN*, *DI_DLS*, *DI_ULS*, and *DI_PE*, function as both inputs and outputs. The *Simulator.Gate* function block can not only read the variables connected to its inputs but also modify their values and set them as outputs. This capability allows the function block to simulate the operation of a physical object, in this case, a gate.

In brief, the function block simulating the gate works as follows: when the QCS-PB1 button is pressed, a signal from the upper limit switch sensor will appear after seven seconds, indicating that the gate is fully open. Then, when the gate is fully open, the closing simulation will begin, meaning the upper limit switch sensor will deactivate after two seconds, and after another seven seconds, a simulated signal from the lower limit switch sensor will appear, indicating that the gate is fully closed.

I encourage you to test how the simulator and control logic behave, for example, when the photoelectric sensor is in the low state (FALSE). Each gate opening and closing sequence starts by setting the QCS-PB1 input to TRUE.

Let's test another scenario: What happens if the QCS-PB1 input signal is continuously set to TRUE? Suppose someone blocked the button using tape, for example. In such a situation, the gate opening sequence will continuously restart upon reaching the lower limit switch.

As you can see, our control logic still requires some improvements, which we will address in the next chapter.

Summary

In this chapter, we detailed the process of implementing control logic for an automatic gate. We started by defining the necessary sensors and signals and then discussed the key aspects of opening and closing the gate under various conditions.

We introduced the *Simulator* library, which allows for the simulation of gate operation in a controlled environment. This enabled us to test and optimize the control logic without physical access to the installation.

We analyzed different scenarios, including situations where obstacles prevent the gate from closing and the impact of changing environmental conditions on gate operation.

We emphasized the importance of optimizing and thoroughly testing the control logic during the development phase, allowing for the correction of potential errors and ensuring stable operation after deployment.

The next stage of our work will focus on further refining the control logic.

CHAPTER 6

Advanced Gate Control in the Production Facility

In this chapter, we will focus on optimizing the gate control logic. As we discovered in the previous chapter, when implementing a PLC program, it is crucial to consider various scenarios – including how a given installation or machine should behave in the event of danger or unpredictable situations.

Our current control logic still has some gaps that need to be addressed. To fix these errors, we will introduce new function blocks. We will learn about rising and falling edges, as well as the TON timer.

We will simulate the entire gate control process. These simulations will be visible in the visualization that we will create at the end of the chapter.

Implementation of the PLC Program

TON Timer

During tests with the simulator, we noticed that the gate closes immediately after reaching full openness unless the photoelectric sensor interrupts the closing. This happens because we implemented

D. Wrebiak, *Practical PLC Programming for Beginners*, Maker Innovations Series,
https://doi.org/10.1007/979-8-8688-2430-2_6

the control logic this way in Network 2. When the gate is fully open and
the photoelectric sensor does not interrupt the closing, the *AND* logic
gate immediately sets the *Gate1_RS_Close* flip-flop, setting the SET input
to TRUE.

This needs to be changed to allow time for people who pressed the gate
opening button to pass through – the gate should not close immediately
after reaching full openness. In other words, we need to implement a delay
for the gate to close when it is fully open and the photoelectric sensor
allows it to close.

There is a way to do this – we can use function blocks called timers. To
do this, let's start by declaring the local variable *Gate1_TON_Close*, which
will be of type TON. We declare this variable in the *GatesAndEntrances*
program (Figure 6-1).

```
    GatesAndEntrances  X
 1      PROGRAM GatesAndEntrances
 2      VAR
 3          Gate1_RS_Open : RS;
 4          Gate1_RS_Close : RS;
 5          Gate1_Sim : Simulator.Gate;
 6          Gate1_TON_Close : TON;
 7      END_VAR
 8
```

Figure 6-1. *Declaration of the local variable Gate1_TON_Close*

Next, we insert an additional block between the output of the *AND*
block and the SET input of the *Gate1_RS_Close* block and set its type
to TON. We assign the name *Gate1_TON_Close* to this block, which we
declared as a local variable in the *GatesAndEntrances* program. Then, we
set the delay time parameters to ten seconds by setting the PT parameter
to T#10s. We leave the ET output unassigned by removing the three
question marks. This is how the gate closing control logic should look
(Figure 6-2).

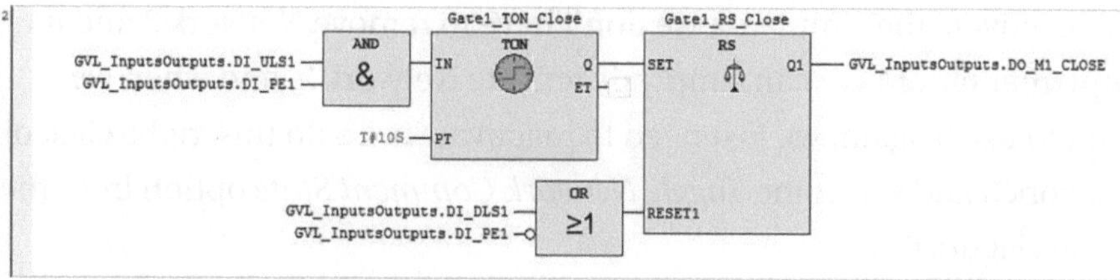

Figure 6-2. *Using the TON timer*

TON Timer (Timer On-Delay)   A function block in Programmable Logic Controllers (PLCs) used to delay the activation of an output by a specified time after the input signal is activated. When the signal at the IN input is activated (changes from FALSE to TRUE), the timer starts counting the time specified in PT. If the input signal remains active for the entire set delay time, the Q output becomes active (changes from FALSE to TRUE). If the IN input signal is deactivated before the set PT time elapses, the timer resets, and the Q output remains inactive. When the IN signal is activated again, the timer starts counting from the beginning.

Let's test our control logic. We see that the TON timer starts counting when the gate is fully open, and the photoelectric sensor does not block the closing. However, after two seconds, the timer stops counting. The *DO_M1_CLOSE* output has not been activated, although after seven seconds, the lower limit switch sensor *QCS-DLS1* signals that the gate is closed. This happens because the function block simulator is not intelligent enough to recognize the actual state of the gate. This simulator has a programmed simple sequence that does not account for the real state of the process.

So, how can we test our program without an appropriate simulator? The simplest way is to deactivate the network where the simulator function block is called and test everything manually, as we did before.

To deactivate the simulator, we don't have to remove Network 3 and its implementation. We can simply deactivate Network 3, and when we want to use it again, we just need to reactivate it. To do this, right-click on Network 3 and select the *Toggle Network Comment State* option from the menu (Figure 6-3).

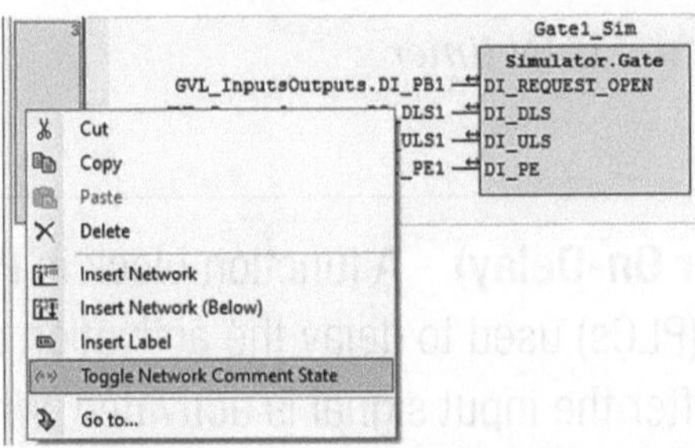

Figure 6-3. *Toggle Network Comment State*

We will then see that the entire network changes to a uniform color, indicating that after downloading this program to the controller, the *Gate1_Sim* function block will not be called. To reactivate Network 3, follow the same procedure. For now, leave the simulator deactivated and test the control logic manually (Figure 6-4).

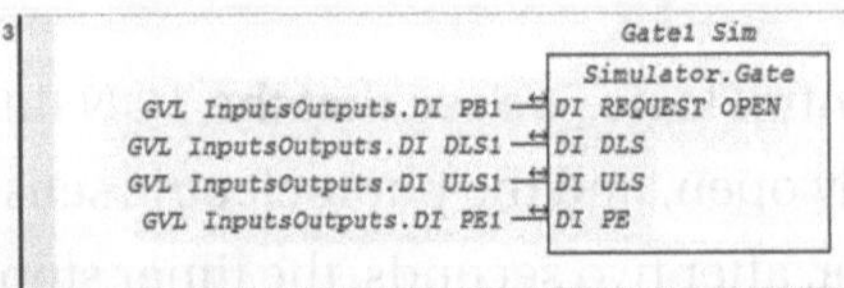

Figure 6-4. *Deactivated simulator*

After adding the TON timer, we successfully implemented a closing delay, allowing passage through the gate when it is fully open.

Defining Gate States in the PLC Program

The current control logic allows for opening and closing the gate but requires some adjustments. Primarily, we need to extend the program to clearly define the exact state of the gate we are controlling.

The gate can be in one of the following states:

- *Gate fully closed*: The state where the sensor *QCS-DLS1* indicates TRUE, with no gate opening occurring.

- *Gate opening*: The state where the gate is in the process of lifting but is not yet fully open.

- *Gate fully open*: The state where the sensor *QCS-ULS1* indicates TRUE, with no gate closing occurring.

- *Gate closing*: The state where the gate is in the process of descending but is not yet fully closed.

At any given moment, the gate can only be in one state. It cannot be both open and closed simultaneously. If an anomaly is detected, such as the gate being fully open and fully closed at the same time, the PLC program must alert the operator of the installation. Therefore, it is crucial to precisely define, recognize, and implement these states.

Another important aspect is the sequential transitions between states. The initial state of the gate is fully closed. The gate then transitions to the opening state, followed by the fully open state. From there, the gate moves to the closing state, which completes the cycle back to the fully closed state. This way, the cycle repeats (Figure 6-5).

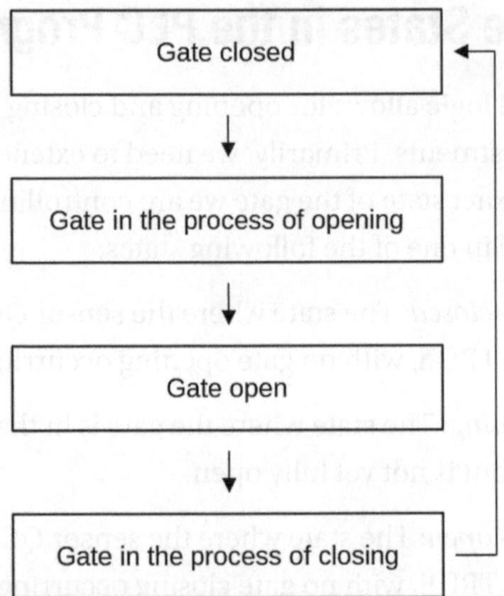

Figure 6-5. *Sequential transitions between states*

To define and determine the gate states, we will start with the *Gate closed* state. In this state, the sensor *QCS-DLS1* indicates TRUE, with no gate opening occurring. Why is it important that the gate is not in the opening state? The information provided by the *QCS-DLS1* sensor about the fully closed state is not sufficient because, when the opening process begins, the *QCS-DLS1* sensor remains active for several seconds while the *QCS-M1* motor is already lifting the gate. This means we have an active *QCS-DLS1* sensor while the *QCS-M1* motor is operating.

Similarly, the gate is considered *fully open* when the *QCS-ULS1* sensor is active and the gate is not in the closing process. This informs us that the gate is fully open.

To implement the fully closed and open states, we first need to determine when the gate is in the process of opening or closing. Whenever the *QCS-M1* motor is in motion, the gate is either in the opening or closing state. The control of opening and closing is managed through separate digital outputs *DO_M1_OPEN* and *DO_M1_CLOSE*, allowing us to precisely identify when the gate is in the opening state and when it is in the closing state.

Rising and Falling Edges

Now that we know how to define the various states of the gate, we can proceed with implementing the PLC program. Before we do that, however, we need to become familiar with new function blocks that will allow us to accurately detect the start and end of the opening and closing states.

We have established that the opening state always occurs while the *QCS-M1* motor is operating and is controlled by the *DO_M1_OPEN* signal. Below is the waveform of the digital signal that controls the gate opening (Figure 6-6).

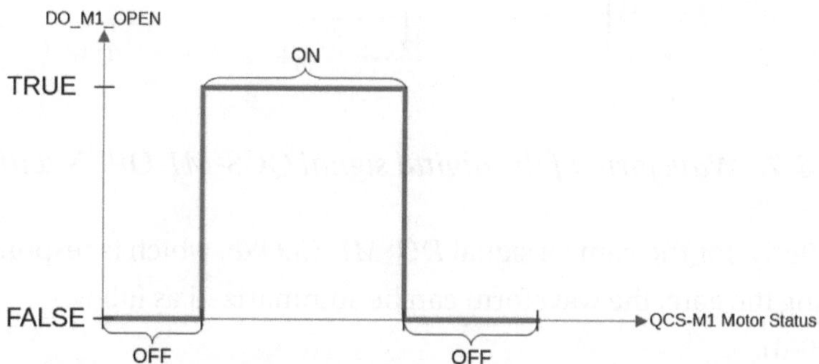

Figure 6-6. *Sequential transitions between states*

The moment when the signal is activated, meaning it changes from FALSE to TRUE, marks the start of the gate opening. This is known as the rising edge of the digital signal, as the signal transitions from a low to a high state. Similarly, when the signal changes from high to low, it indicates the end of the gate opening, as the control signal changes from TRUE to FALSE. In this case, we refer to this as the falling edge.

To summarize, we can describe the signal waveform as follows
(Figure 6-7):

- Change of the *DO_M1_OPEN* signal from FALSE to
  TRUE (*rising edge*) → Start of gate opening.

- *DO_M1_OPEN* signal is TRUE → Gate is still opening.

- Change of the *DO_M1_OPEN* signal from TRUE to
  FALSE (*falling edge*) → End of gate opening.

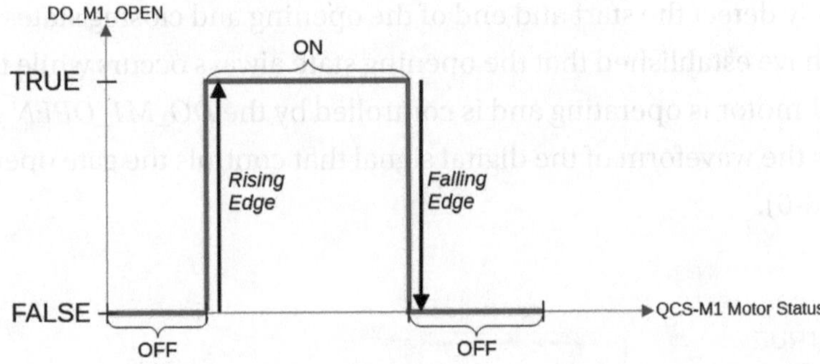

Figure 6-7. *Waveform of the digital signal QCS-M1-OPEN with edges*

Similarly, for the control signal *DO_M1_CLOSE*, which is responsible
for closing the gate, the waveform can be summarized as follows
(Figure 6-8):

- Change of the *DO_M1_CLOSE* signal from FALSE to
  TRUE (*rising edge*) → Start of gate closing.

- *DO_M1_CLOSE* signal is TRUE → Gate is still closing.

- Change of the *DO_M1_CLOSE* signal from TRUE to
  FALSE (*falling edge*) → End of gate closing.

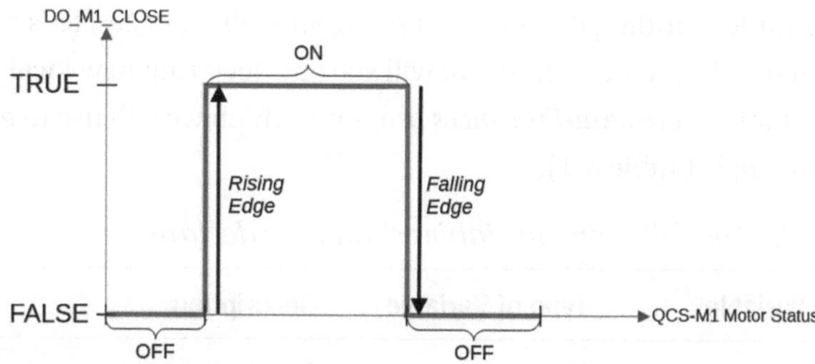

Figure 6-8. *Waveform of the digital signal QCS-M1-CLOSE with edges*

As seen, determining the start and end of the opening or closing state involves recognizing the rising and falling edges of the control signals *QCS-M1-OPEN* and *QCS-M1-CLOSE*. To detect the rising edge of a signal, we use the *R_TRIG* function block, while the falling edge is detected using the *F_TRIG* function block.

R_TRIG (Rising Edge Trigger)   This function block detects the rising edge of an input signal. It operates by producing a brief pulse (TRUE) at the output whenever the input signal changes from low (FALSE) to high (TRUE), lasting for one scan cycle of the PLC controller. It is used to trigger operations that should be executed only once when the signal transitions to the high state.

F_TRIG (Falling Edge Trigger)   This function block detects the falling edge of an input signal. It operates by producing a brief pulse (TRUE) at the output whenever the input signal changes from high (TRUE) to low (FALSE), lasting for one scan cycle of the PLC controller. It is used to trigger operations that should be executed only once when the signal transitions to the low state.

After understanding the theory of rising and falling edges, let's move on to practical implementation. We will start by declaring new local variables for the *GatesAndEntrances* program, which we will use to expand the control logic (Table 6-1).

Table 6-1. *The following variables should be declared.*

Name of Variable	Type of Variable	Description
Gate1_OPEN	BOOL	Gate is Open
Gate1_CLOSE	BOOL	Gate is Closed
Gate1_OPENING	BOOL	Gate is Opening
Gate1_CLOSING	BOOL	Gate is Closing
Gate1_RS_Opening	RS	RS Flip-Flop for Gate Opening
Gate1_RS_Closing	RS	RS Flip-Flop for Gate Closing
Gate1_R_TRIG_Open	R_TRIG	Rising Edge Detection for Gate Opening Control Signal
Gate1_F_TRIG_Open	F_TRIG	Falling Edge Detection for Gate Opening Control Signal
Gate1_R_TRIG_Close	R_TRIG	Rising Edge Detection for Gate Closing Control Signal
Gate1_F_TRIG_Close	F_TRIG	Falling Edge Detection for Gate Closing Control Signal

Below is the method for declaring local variables for the *GatesAndEntrances* program (Figure 6-9).

```
   GatesAndEntrances  X
 2   VAR
 3        Gate1_RS_Open : RS;
 4        Gate1_RS_Close : RS;
 5        Gate1_Sim : Simulator.Gate;
 6        Gate1_TON_Close : TON;
 7        Gate1_OPEN : BOOL;
 8        Gate1_CLOSE : BOOL;
 9        Gate1_OPENING : BOOL;
10        Gate1_CLOSING : BOOL;
11        Gate1_RS_Opening : RS;
12        Gate1_RS_Closing : RS;
13        Gate1_R_TRIG_Open : R_TRIG;
14        Gate1_F_TRIG_Open : F_TRIG;
15        Gate1_R_TRIG_Close : R_TRIG;
16        Gate1_F_TRIG_Close : F_TRIG;
17   END_VAR
```

Figure 6-9. *Local variables for the GatesAndEntrances program*

Once we have declared all the variables, it's time to implement the
control logic. First, we will add another network between Network 2 and
Network 3, where we will implement the gate opening state. To do this,
click on Network 2 and select from the menu *FBD/LD/IL* ➤ *Insert Network
(Below)*. This will shift the network where the function block simulator
is called down by one level, and in the newly added network, we will
implement the following control logic (Figure 6-10).

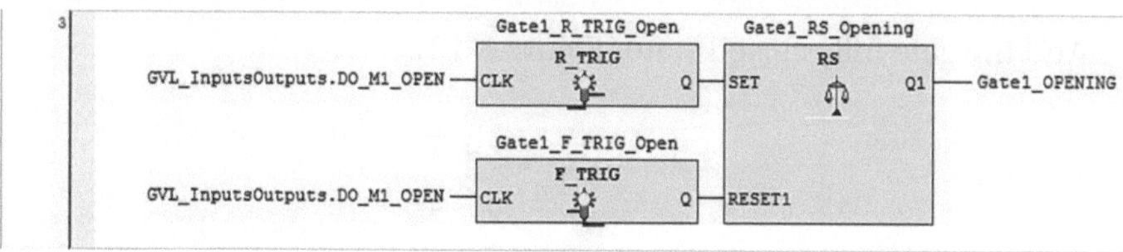

Figure 6-10. *Gate opening*

As we can see, this program will set or reset the *Gate1_OPENING*
variable depending on the state of the Q1 output of the *Gate1_RS_Opening*
flip-flop. The Q1 output will be set when the *R_TRIG* block detects the
rising edge of the control signal *DO_M1_OPEN*. The Q1 output will be
reset when the *F_TRIG* block detects the falling edge of the control signal
DO_M1_OPEN.

Similarly, we apply the same approach to detecting the edges of the gate closing control signal *DO_M1_CLOSE*. This is how the control logic is implemented (Figure 6-11).

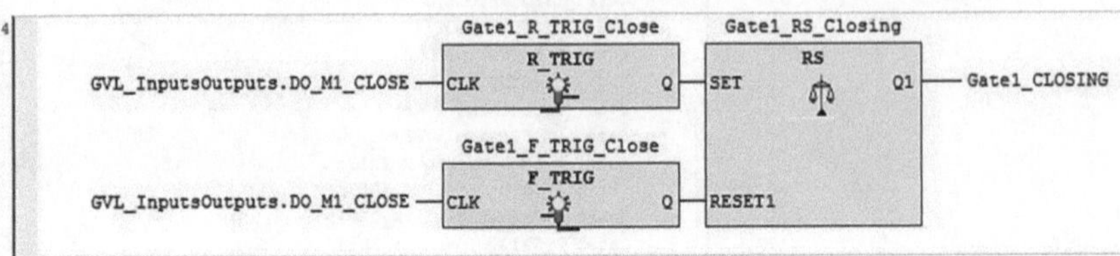

Figure 6-11. *Gate closing*

Once we have implemented the gate opening (*Gate1_OPENING*) and closing (*Gate1_CLOSING*) states, we can add two more networks to the program to implement the gate fully open state (Figure 6-12).

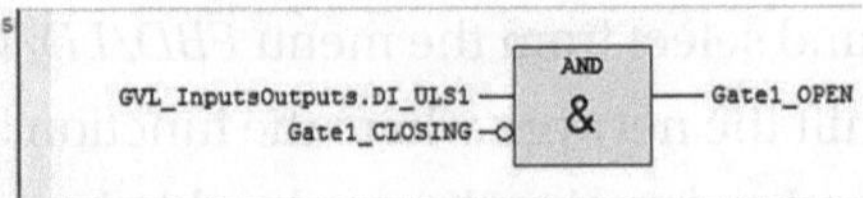

Figure 6-12. *Gate is open*

And the gate fully closed state (Figure 6-13).

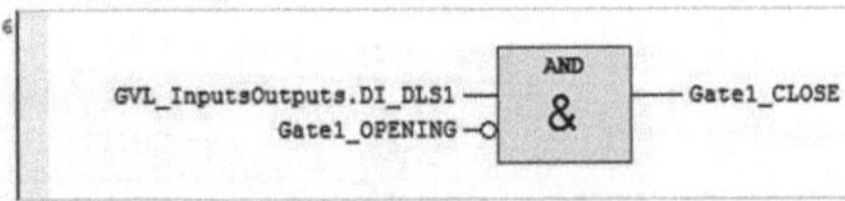

Figure 6-13. *Gate is closed*

At this point, we would like to test our application. We can manually test everything. The application will operate by changing the gate states, which can be observed in the *Watch* table. I encourage you to perform this manual test, as it helps solidify your skills in navigating the CODESYS environment. The next step we will learn is managing libraries to install a new, enhanced version of the simulator that will be able to recognize the current state of the gate.

Managing Libraries

As previously noted, the current version of the simulator has limited functionality and does not fully understand the operational context, i.e., the actual conditions and situations in which the system operates. We will now learn how to manage libraries in the repository as well as within the project itself to use a newer version of the simulator.

As we recall from the previous chapter, we installed the 1.0 version of the simulator in the repository and added it to our project. This is visible in the *Library Manager* (Figure 6-14).

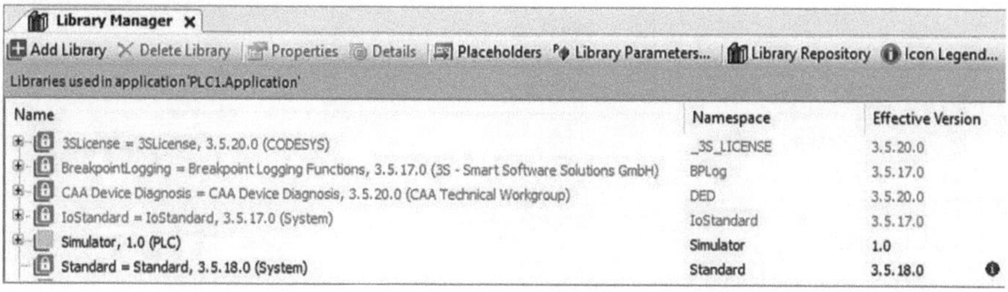

Figure 6-14. Library Manager with Simulator V1.0

Let's now open the *Library Repository*. In the libraries section *(Miscellaneous)*, we can see that the first version of the simulator is installed in the repository (Figure 6-15).

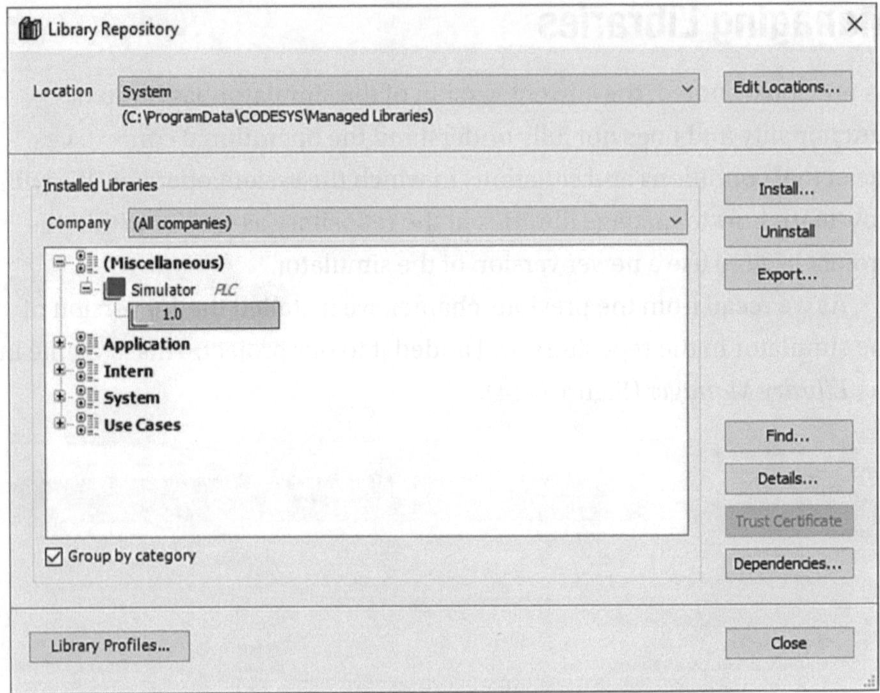

Figure 6-15. *Library Repository with Simulator V1.0*

Now, click the *Install...* button located on the right side of the *Library Repository* window, and install the compiled library *Simulator.compiled-library* found in the *Chapter_06* folder on the GitHub repository. After installing the library, you will see in the *Library Repository* window that a new, second version of the simulator has appeared in our repository (Figure 6-16).

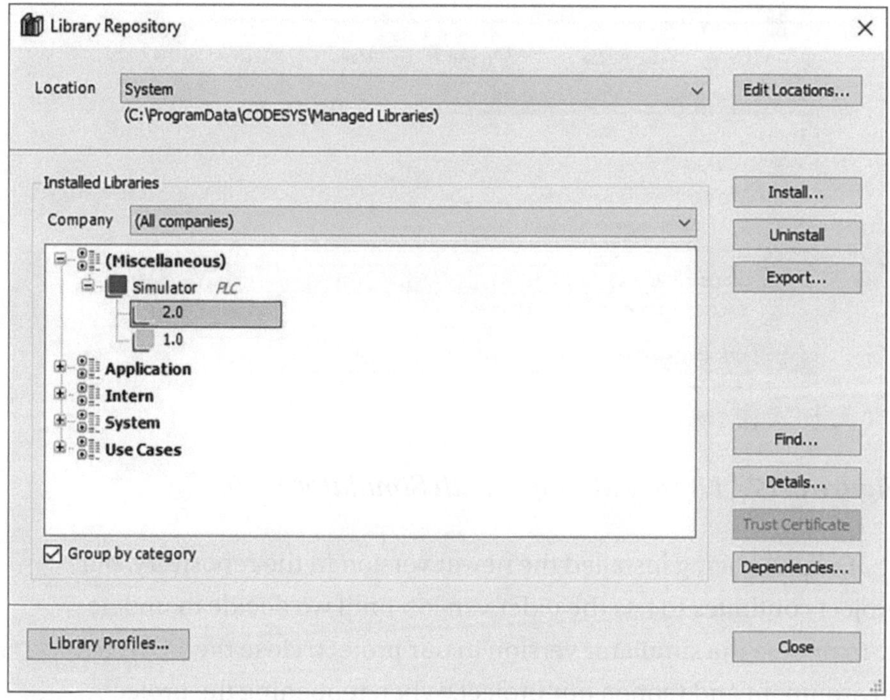

Figure 6-16. *Library Repository with Simulator V2.0*

Close the *Library Repository* window by clicking the *Close* button. In
the *Library Manager* window, you will notice that our project is still using
version 1.0 of the library, even though a new, version 2.0 of the simulator
has been installed in the repository. If you select the library in the *Library
Manager* window, you will see that only the *Gate* function block is
available, and the new version with additional functionalities has not yet
been assigned to our project (Figure 6-17).

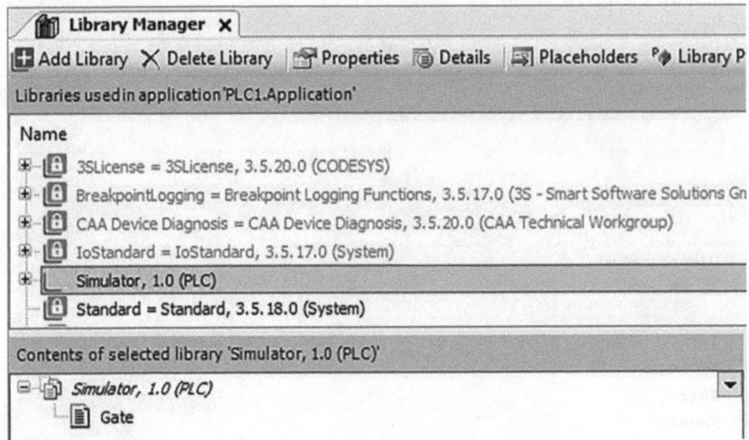

Figure 6-17. *Library Manager with Simulator V1.0*

Despite having installed the newer version in the repository, our project continues to use the older version until we decide to update it. To update the simulator version in our project, close the CODESYS environment and reopen our project. When reopening the project, CODESYS will recognize that a newer version of the *Simulator* library is available in the repository and that we are using the older version. The program will suggest an update, allowing us to apply the new version to our project (Figure 6-18).

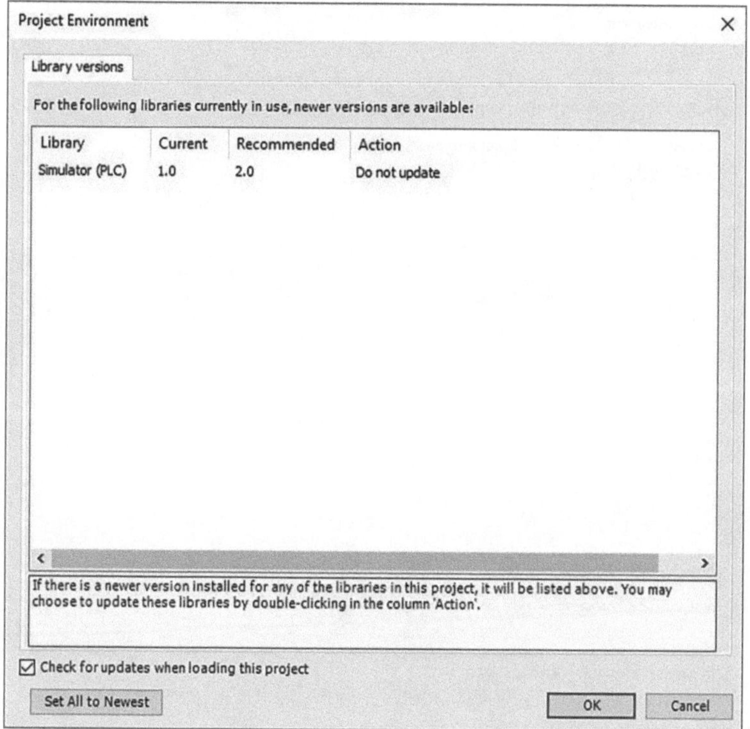

Figure 6-18. *Project Environment window*

In the *Project Environment* window, we can decide whether to update
the library. In our case, change the *Action* field from *Do not update* to
Update to 2.0. Additionally, we can deactivate the automatic project
update check by unchecking the *Check for updates when loading this
project* check box in the lower left corner of the *Project Environment*
window. However, I will leave this option activated and click *OK* to confirm
the settings (Figure 6-19).

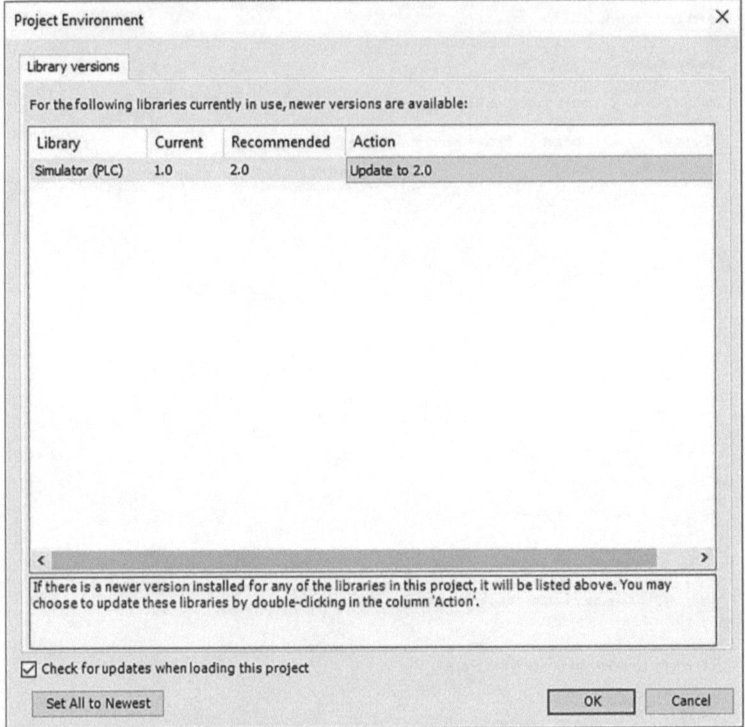

Figure 6-19. *Project Environment window with library update*

At this point, in the *Library Manager* window, we can see that our project is now using the new version of the simulator. We now have access to two function blocks: *Gate* and *GateFeedbacks* (Figure 6-20).

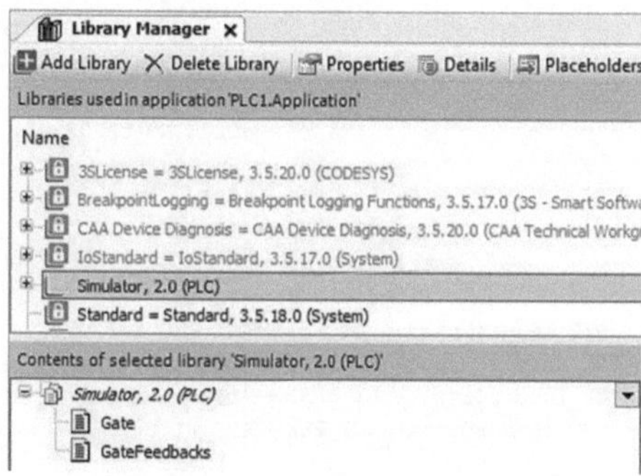

Figure 6-20. *Library Manager with Simulator V2.0*

We can always manage libraries manually from the *Library Manager*.
To do this, we can remove the *Simulator V1.0* library from the project using
the *Delete Library* function and then re-add the library to the project using
the *Add Library* option.

Now that we have the newest version of the simulator in our project,
we can use the new function block *GateFeedbacks*. First, change the
type of the local variable *Gate1_Sim* from *Simulator.Gate* to *Simulator.
GateFeedbacks* in the *GatesAndEntrances* program. Next, re-activate
Network 7, where the simulator function block is called, and change its
type from *Simulator.Gate* to *Simulator.GateFeedbacks*. The final step is to
parameterize the inputs of the function block. This is how the function
block *Simulator.GateFeedbacks* should be called (Figure 6-21).

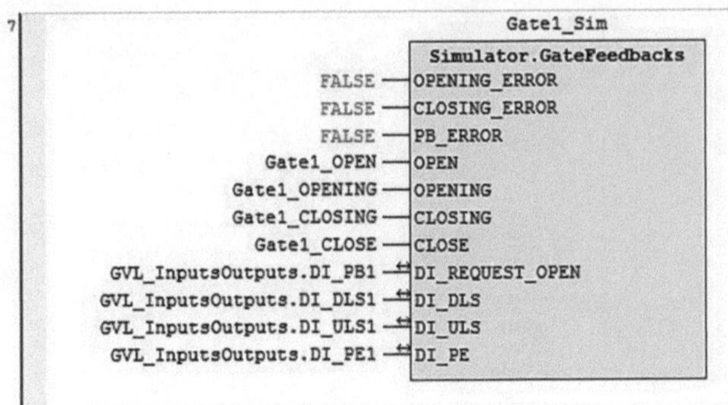

Figure 6-21. *Call of the simulator function block*

Let's download the program to the controller and observe the four states we added to the program in the *Watch* table. During the simulation of the entire process, we will see how the states of the variables transition sequentially from CLOSE → OPENING → OPEN → CLOSING, and the entire cycle ends back at the CLOSE state.

Error Handling

When creating control logic, it is crucial to anticipate various anomalies and scenarios that may occur. In the event of such an error, the control system should immediately generate an error message and notify the maintenance team responsible for the operation of the installation or machine.

In our case, we need to immediately generate an error if the gate simultaneously reports both full open and full closed states to the controller. Such a situation is unacceptable and must be accounted for in the control program. Therefore, we will declare a new local variable, *Gate1_ERROR*, of type BOOL. We will move the simulator to Network 8 and implement the error handling logic related to the gate operation in Network 7.

Consider the situation where both inputs, *DI_ULS1* and *DI_DLS1*, are in a high state, which would indicate that the gate is both open and closed simultaneously. An error should also be generated if the gate is in both opening and closing states at the same time, resulting in both outputs, *DO_M1_OPEN* and *DO_M1_CLOSE*, being high (Figure 6-22).

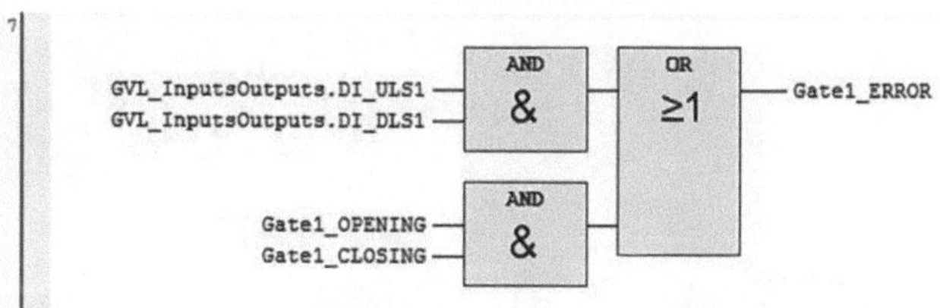

Figure 6-22. *Error handling*

To test this scenario, remember to deactivate the simulator, as it will not allow us to set both inputs *DI_DLS1* and *DI_ULS1* to a high TRUE state simultaneously. In simulation mode, the simulator takes control of the inputs and changes their values based on the gate's state.

Next, we need to account for situations where the gate is in the process of opening or closing. In these states, neither of the sensors, *QCS-ULS1* nor *QCS-DLS1*, provides feedback, meaning the gate is neither fully open nor fully closed. However, if the gate remains in such a state for too long, it indicates a problem. In this case, when the motor *QCS-M1* is operating and neither of the limit sensors is activated, a TON timer helps by delaying the error trigger.

The question arises: What should be the correct delay time for triggering an error? Since we do not know the exact time required for the gate to fully open or close, this time is usually determined during the hot commissioning of the installation. For our simulation, we can assume that the gate should fully open or close within ten seconds. After this period, an error should be immediately generated in the control logic. When implementing this logic, also remember to add a local variable *Gate1_TON_ Error* of type TON.

To add additional inputs to *AND* and *OR* logic gates, right-click on the logic gate and select *Append Input*. This is how the error handling logic should be implemented (Figure 6-23).

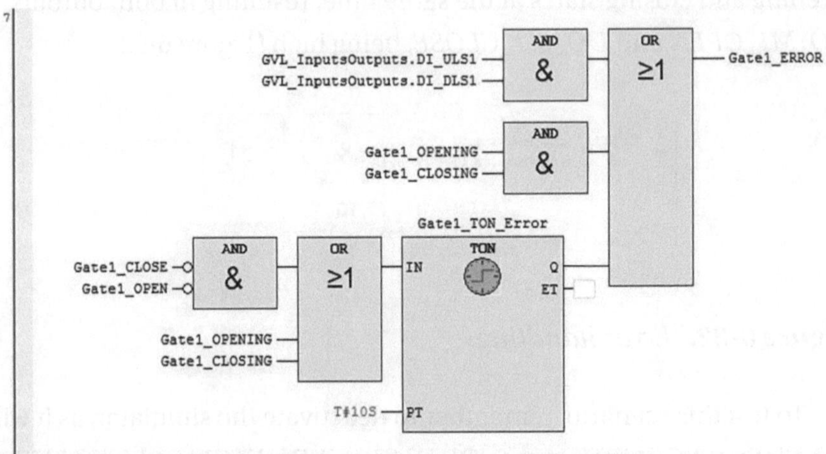

Figure 6-23. *Error handling: TON timer*

Let's download our program to the PLC and test Network 7 with the simulator running. During the gate opening and closing procedure, we'll observe how the `Gate1_TON_Error` timer starts counting, but no error will be generated since the gate states change within less than ten seconds.

Since everything is proceeding as planned, let's now check how the control logic behaves when an opening error is generated. Our simulator allows us to test such a case by setting the `OPENING_ERROR` input of the function block to TRUE. Until now, the `OPENING_ERROR`, `CLOSING_ERROR`, and `PB_ERROR` inputs were inactive. Now, activate the opening error by setting the `OPENING_ERROR` input to TRUE. This will simulate a situation where the gate started opening but did not reach the switch limit sensor, `QCS-ULS1` (Figure 6-24).

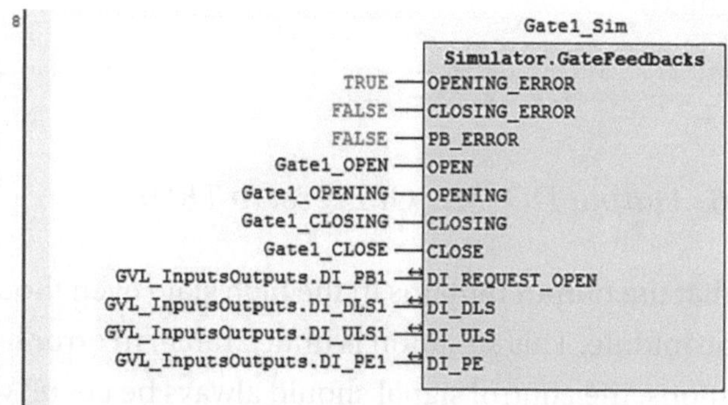

Figure 6-24. *Simulator with the opening error activated*

When we initiate the gate opening procedure, an opening error will be generated after ten seconds because the simulator did not set the digital input *DI_ULS1* to a high state. We simulated a situation where the gate got stuck somewhere between the *QCS-DLS1* sensor and the *QCS-ULS1* sensor (Figure 6-25).

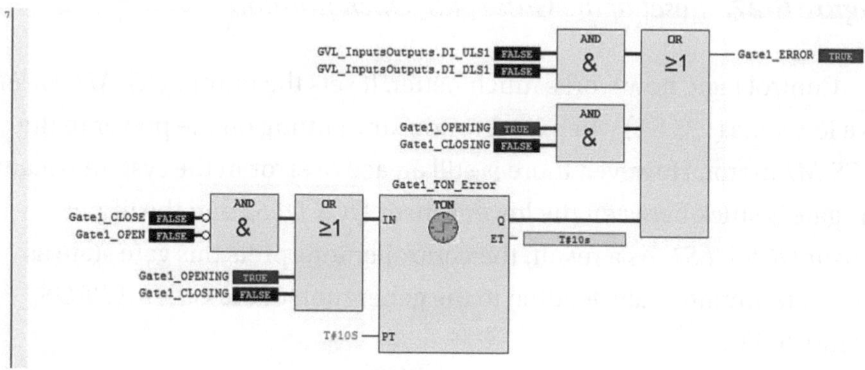

Figure 6-25. *Opening error active*

The error handling worked as expected. Now let's carefully analyze the entire control program. We see that the *Gate1_ERROR* was generated because the gate is in the opening mode, and the variable *Gate1_OPENING* is in a high state (TRUE) (Figure 6-26). Let's now check what happens to the output *DO_M1_OPEN*, which issues the command to open the gate.

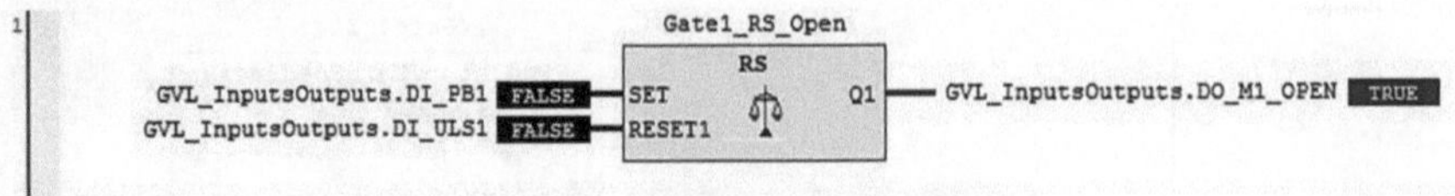

Figure 6-26. *Output DO_M1_OPEN set to TRUE*

We see that the output remains in the high state even though the gate
is stuck in the middle. This situation is undesirable. In error handling
implementations, the control signal should always be cut off when an error
occurs; in this case, the output *DO_M1_OPEN*. We need to improve the
control logic in Network 1 by adding an additional condition that will reset
the *Gate1_RS_Open* flip-flop (Figure 6-27).

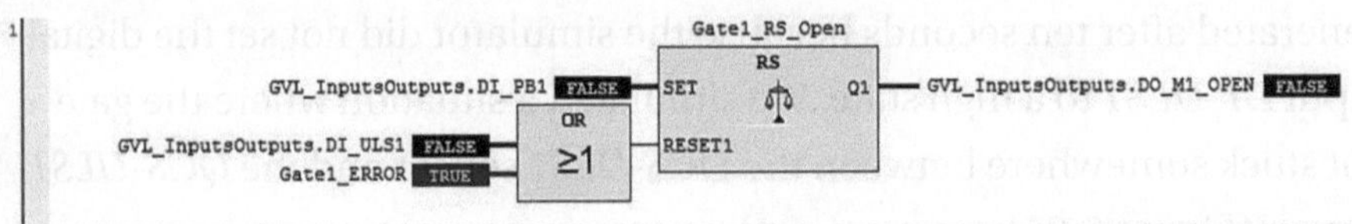

Figure 6-27. *Reset of the Gate1_RS_Open flip-flop*

Control logic now works much better. It sets the output *DO_M1_OPEN*
to a low state (FALSE) when an error occurs, cutting off the power to the
QCS-M1 motor. However, there is still an active error in the system because
the gate is stuck between the lower sensor *QCS-DLS1* and the upper
sensor *QCS-ULS1*. As a result, the controller interprets this gate state as
an indeterminate state, leading to the generation of the *Gate1_ERROR*
(Figure 6-28).

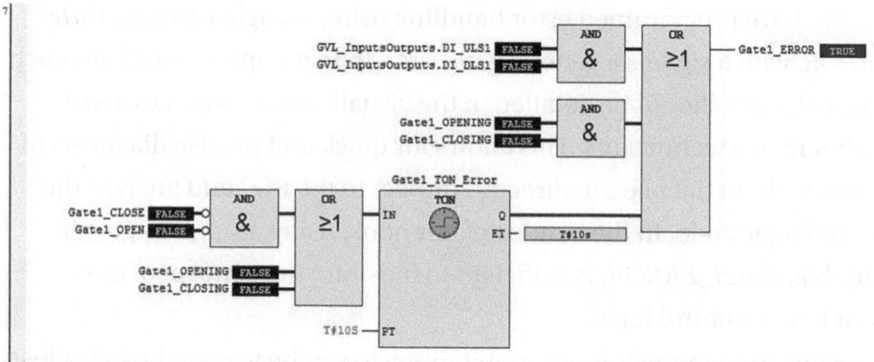

Figure 6-28. *Gate1_ERROR active*

This is a simulation of a very realistic scenario. At this point, the maintenance team would need to respond, diagnose the fault, and set the gate to its default position, which is fully closed. We can do this very quickly by setting the *DI_DLS1* input to TRUE. This will immediately deactivate the *Gate1_ERROR*.

A similar simulation should be conducted for closing the gate by setting the simulator's *CLOSING_ERROR* input to TRUE. We will observe an analogous situation to the opening error. This time, however, after ten seconds from the start of closing the gate, a closing error will be activated. Despite this error, the *DO_M1_CLOSE* output, which controls the gate closing, will remain activated. In this case, we also need to modify the logic to reset the *Gate1_RS_Close* flip-flop when the *Gate1_ERROR* occurs (Figure 6-29).

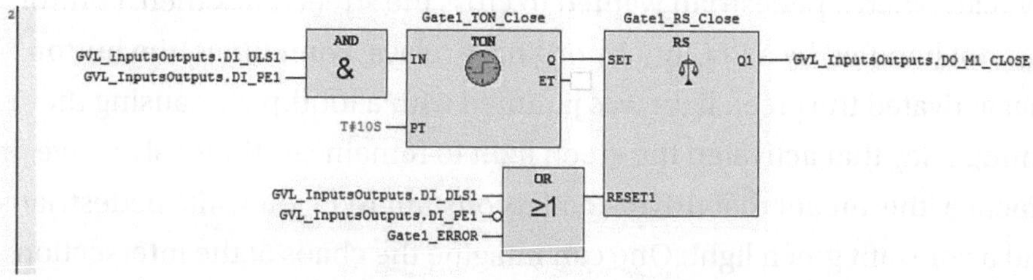

Figure 6-29. *Reset of the Gate1_RS_Close flip-flop*

We have programmed error handling using a single variable, *Gate1_ERROR*, which signals a general gate error. In real implementations, each type of failure should be detailed in the visualization system to assist maintenance technicians. This allows for quick and precise diagnosis of issues without the need to directly connect to the PLC and analyze the control logic code. In the context of our book, using a single aggregate variable, *Gate1_ERROR*, is sufficient to illustrate the concept of error handling in control logic.

After completing this test, don't forget to set the gate to the fully closed position by setting the *DI_DLS1* input to TRUE.

Final Optimization of Gate Opening and Closing

Let's now analyze another scenario related to opening the gate. Currently, when we simulate pressing the button *QCS-PB1* by setting the input *DI_PB1* to TRUE, the simulator immediately resets this variable once the gate opening procedure is activated. Let's see what would happen if this input remained continuously set to TRUE. Such a situation is quite realistic – for example, the button might get stuck, and the spring might not push it back, resulting in a continuous request for the gate to open from the controller.

In this context, I am reminded of an anecdote from my childhood. Near where I grew up, there was a traffic intersection with a button that pedestrians had to press to get the green light. The idea was simple: it should not block vehicle traffic, and drivers should only stop their vehicles when a pedestrian wanted to cross the street. Back then, control was not handled by a PLC but by ordinary relays. Sometimes, the button that activated the green light was jammed with a toothpick, causing the timing relay that activated the green light to remain continuously active. In practice, this meant that drivers had a constant red light while pedestrians had a constant green light. One can imagine the chaos at the intersection instead of a smooth traffic flow.

Let's see how our control logic behaves when the request signal for opening is continuously set to TRUE. As mentioned earlier, the simulator automatically sets the value of input *DI_PB1* to FALSE when the gate opening procedure is activated. To simulate a stuck *QCS-PB1* button in the simulator, the input *PB_ERROR* of the simulator should be set to TRUE (Figure 6-30).

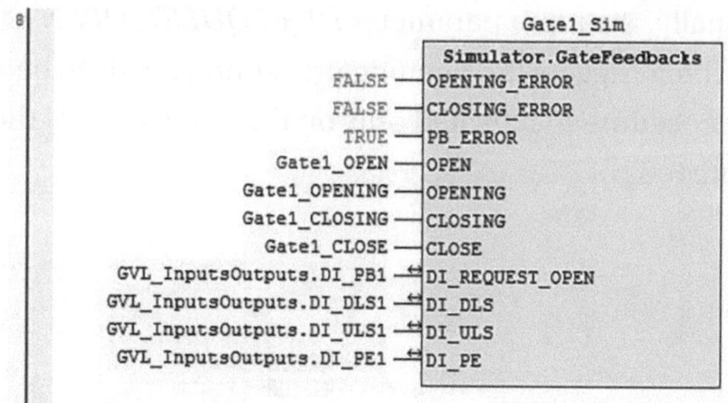

Figure 6-30. *Simulator with the push button error activated*

At this point, the input *DI_PB1* remains high. As we observe, our control logic encounters a problem when the gate is closing. When the gate moves away from the upper limit switch *QCS-ULS1*, the opening command is immediately reactivated, leading to an endless loop where the gate continuously tries to open. This situation persists as long as the input *DI_PB1* remains high (TRUE), resulting in a condition where the gate never closes.

To resolve this issue, we need to change how we handle the gate opening. Instead of reacting to a continuous signal, we should react to the rising edge of the *DI_PB1* input signal. This way, only one pulse will be generated when the button is pressed, preventing the endless opening cycle. Therefore, let's add a local variable `Gate1_R_TRIG_RequestOpen` of type `R_TRIG` and modify the control logic in Network 1 to accommodate this change (Figure 6-31).

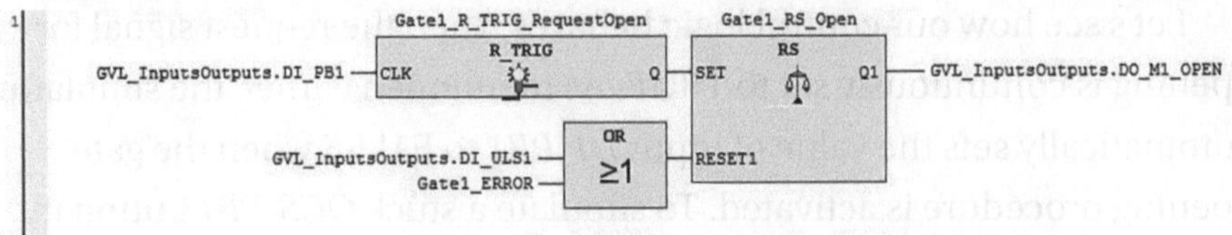

Figure 6-31. *Opening the gate based on rising edge detection*

Additionally, the input parameter *DI_REQUEST_OPEN* of the simulator, which triggers the opening procedure, needs to be adjusted so that the procedure is activated only on the rising edge of the *QCS-PB1* signal (Figure 6-32).

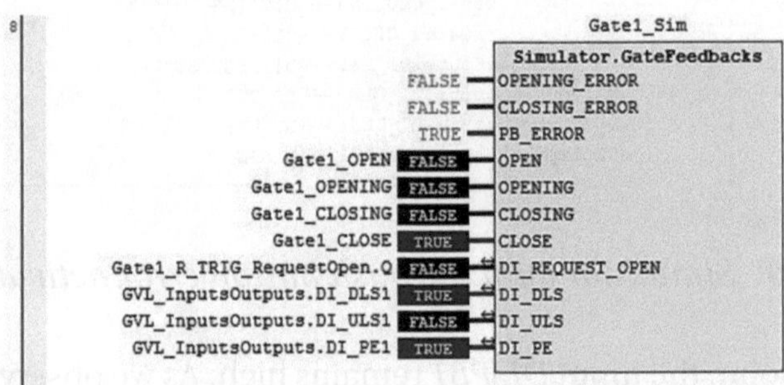

Figure 6-32. *Input parameter DI_REQUEST_OPEN of the simulator*

As our analysis shows, to reactivate the opening procedure, the *DI_PB1* input must first be set to FALSE and then back to TRUE. This approach resolves the issue and illustrates an important principle that every PLC programmer should keep in mind. The RS flip-flop with a dominant RESET input should always be set on the rising edge, while it should be reset from a continuous signal. This helps avoid problems similar to those we encountered.

To complete the implementation, let's apply a similar logic for the closing procedure of the gate. We will need a new variable, *Gate1_R_TRIG_ RequestClose* of type R_TRIG, which will allow the activation of the gate closing procedure based on the rising edge rather than a continuous signal (Figure 6-33).

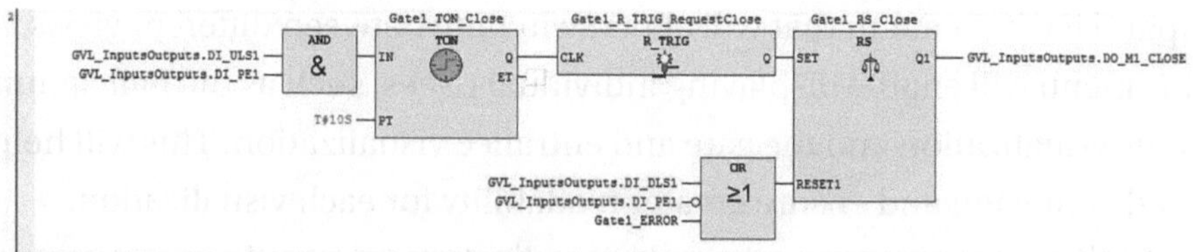

Figure 6-33. *Closing the gate based on rising edge detection*

Our gate opening and closing control logic is almost complete. There is one more scenario that should automatically open the gate. Specifically, if a photoelectric sensor detects a lack of permission to close while the gate is closing, the gate should immediately open. If we don't add this condition, the closing process will be interrupted, and the gate will only open again after pressing the button. However, we will automate this process by opening the gate from the control logic (Figure 6-34).

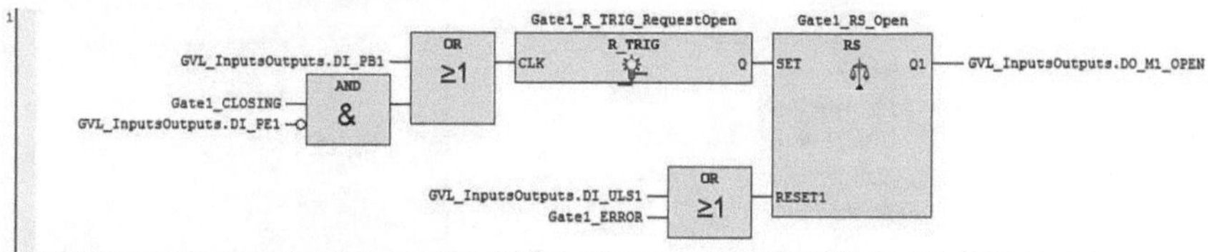

Figure 6-34. *Automatic gate opening*

This concludes the implementation of the control logic for opening and closing the gate. We will now proceed to the implementation of the visualization of the entire process.

Implementation of Visualization

Menu Structure

Currently, our visualization consists of a single page that shows the lighting status in the hall and allows for changing the lighting control mode. To enhance the clarity and functionality of the visualization, it is necessary to expand it with a menu that will allow switching between different views. This menu will enable displaying individual pages, such as the hall lighting status visualization and the gate and entrance visualization. This will help avoid confusion and ensure greater readability for each visualization.

Let's start by renaming the only visualization we have in our project to structure the project and make it more readable. To do this, right-click the *Visualization* object located in the *Application* ➤ *Visualization* ➤ *Pages* folder, and select *Refactoring* ➤ *Rename 'Visualization'...* from the menu (Figure 6-35).

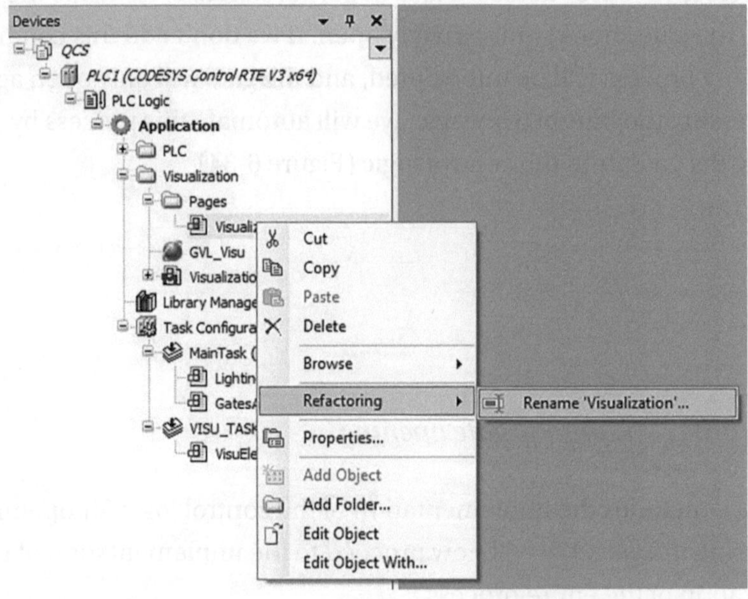

Figure 6-35. *Refactoring* ➤ *Rename 'Visualization'...*

In the *Rename* window, let's provide a new name for this visualization; let it be *P00_Lighting* (Figure 6-36).

Figure 6-36. *Rename window*

We confirm all the changes we are notified about in the *Refactoring* window by clicking the *OK* button. At this point, the name of our visualization is more descriptive. From the name alone, it can be inferred that the screen will display elements related to the lighting of the hall (Figure 6-37).

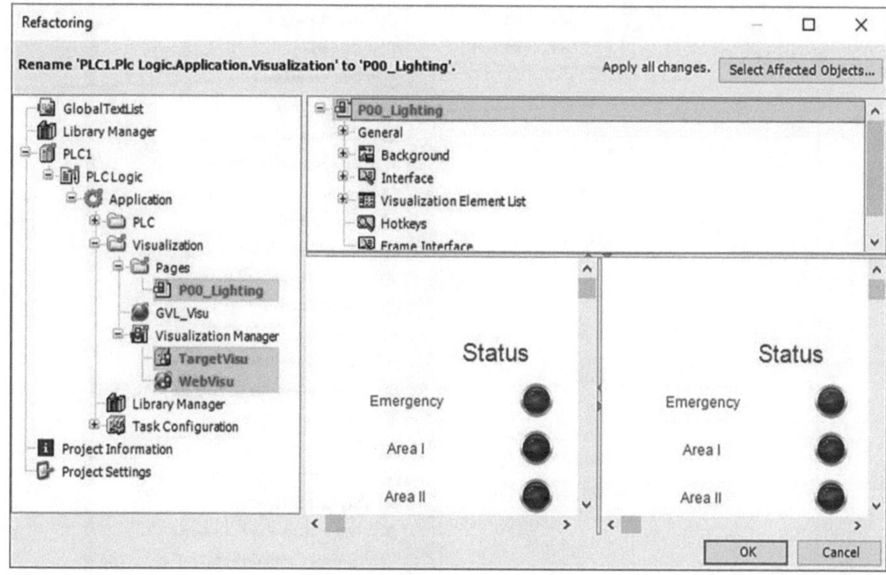

Figure 6-37. *Refactoring window*

Since we already have a visualization page for the hall lighting, let's now add another visualization page where we will later display the gates and entries in the quality control hall. To do this, right-click the folder *Application* ➤ *Visualization* ➤ *Pages*, and select *Add Object* ➤ *Visualization...* from the menu (Figure 6-38).

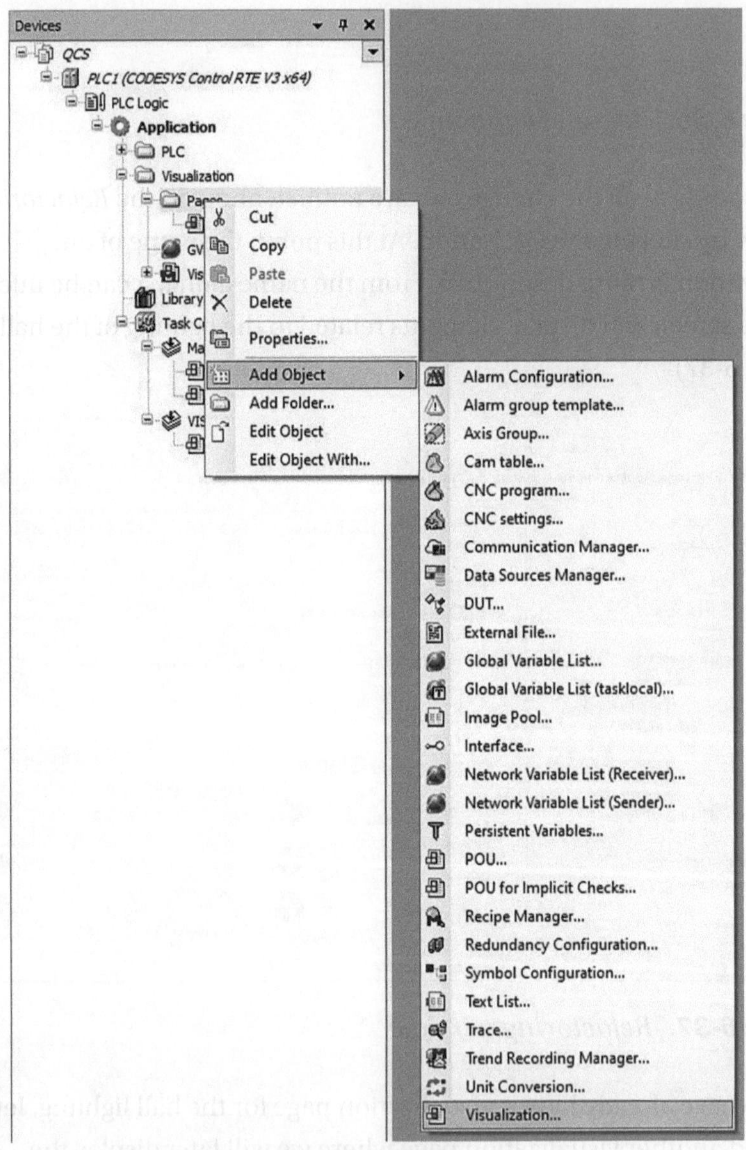

Figure 6-38.   *Add Object* ➤ *Visualization...*

In the *Add Visualization* window that appears, name the new visualization *P01_GatesAndEntrances* and confirm your choice by clicking the *OK* button (Figure 6-39).

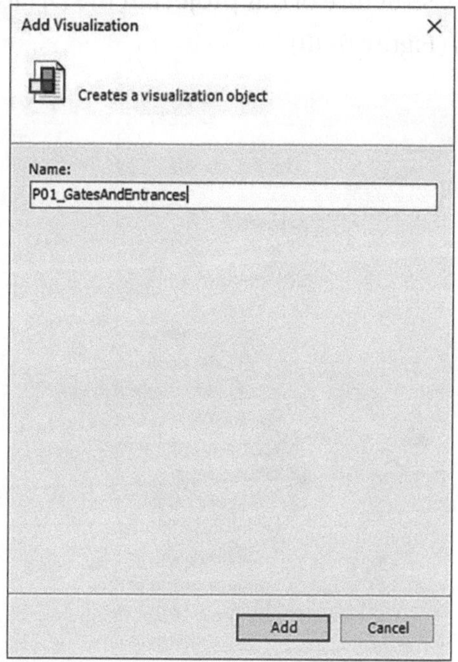

Figure 6-39. *Add Visualization window*

The newly added visualization will open in the editor. Let's add one element to this visualization – a *Label* – and set its properties as follows:

- Texts → Text: Gates & Entrances

- Position → X: 0

- Position → Y: 5

- Position → Width: 1000

- Texts properties → Font: Large Headline

This will create a page where we will visualize all the gates and entrances located in the quality control hall.

Similarly, let's add another visualization page to our project and name it *MainWindow*. The structure of our project in the *Devices* window should now look as follows (Figure 6-40).

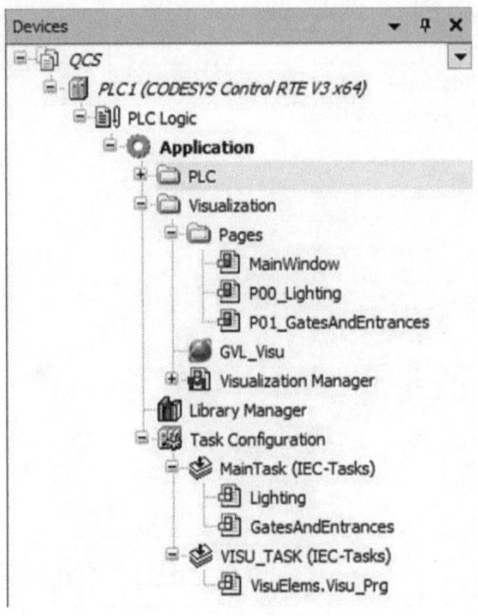

Figure 6-40. *Devices window*

As you might easily guess, on the visualization named *MainWindow*, we will create a navigation menu that allows switching between different visualization pages. For the *MainWindow* page, let's add two *Button* objects and set the following properties (Table 6-2).

Table 6-2. *Properties of Button controls*

Properties	1st Button	2nd Button
Texts → Texts	Lighting	Gates & Entrances
Position → X	20	20
Position → Y	20	75

Next, let's add a *Frame* component to the *MainWindow* visualization, which we can find under the *Basic* tab. After dragging and dropping the *Frame* control onto the *MainWindow* visualization, a configuration window will appear, which we need to set up accordingly.

The *Frame Configuration* window is divided into two sections: *Available Visualizations* on the left side and *Selected Visualizations* on the right. Our task is to select the visualizations we want to display within the *Frame* component from the available visualizations in the project. For now, we want to switch between the *Lighting* view and the *Gates & Entrances* view. To do this, select both visualizations on the left side: *P00_Lighting* and *P01_GatesAndEntrances* (Figure 6-41).

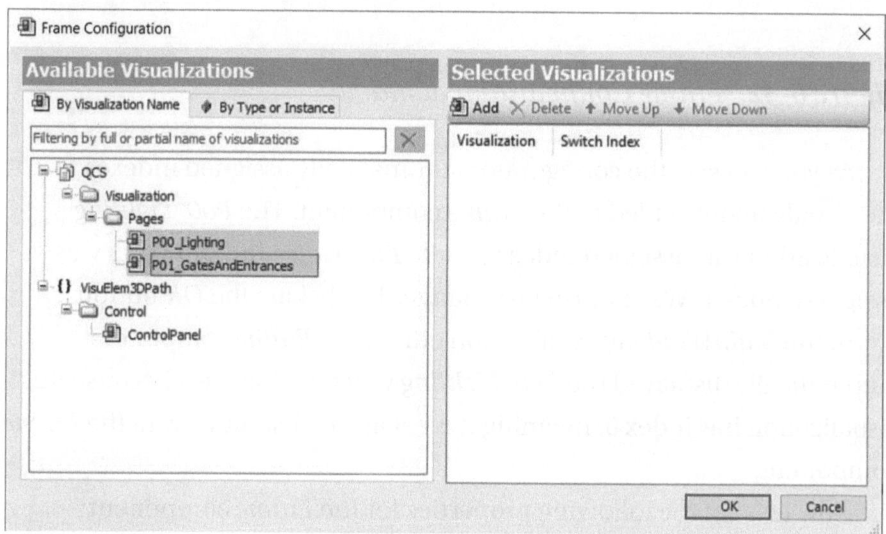

Figure 6-41. *Selected visualizations on the left side*

Next, click the *Add* button located in the top right corner of the *Selected Visualizations* window. After correctly configuring it, the *Frame Configuration* window should look like this (Figure 6-42).

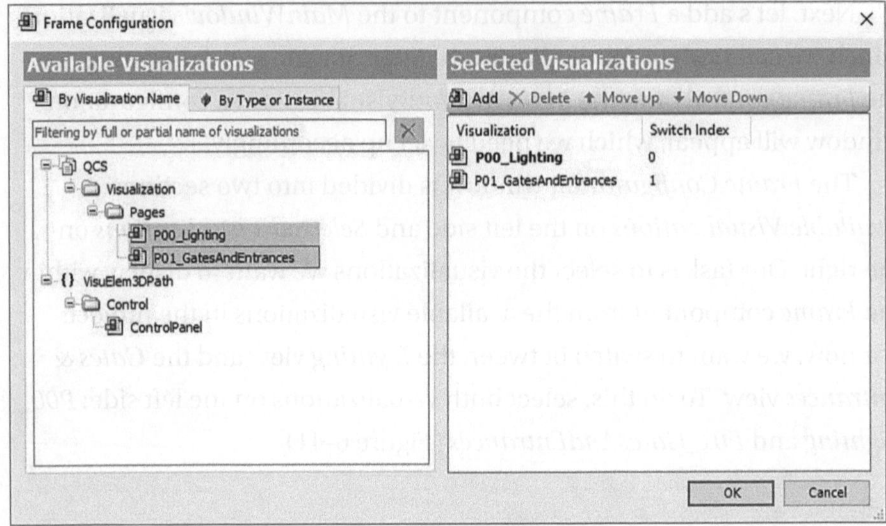

Figure 6-42. *Frame Configuration window*

As you can see, the configurator automatically assigned indexes to the visualizations added to the *Frame* component. The *P00_Lighting* visualization was assigned index 0, while *P01_GatesAndEntrances* was assigned index 1. We confirm our changes by clicking the *OK* button.

In the *MainWindow* visualization editor, the *Frame* component automatically displayed the *P00_Lighting* visualization view because this visualization has index 0, meaning it is set as the default view in the *Frame* component.

Now let's set the following properties for the *Frame* component:

- Position → X: 200

- Position → Y: 0

- Position → Width: 1000

- Position → Height: 350

Let's now download our project to the controller and open the *MainWindow* visualization. As you can see, the visualization starts with the *P00_Lighting* view in the *Frame* component. Our goal is to change the content of the *Frame* component depending on which button is clicked in the menu on the left. If the *Lighting* button is clicked, the *P00_Lighting* visualization should be displayed in the *Frame* component. If the *Gates & Entrances* button is clicked, the *P01_GatesAndEntrances* visualization should be displayed in the *Frame* component.

Let's start by configuring the *Lighting* button. In the properties window of this component, open the configuration window for the *OnMouseClick* event by selecting *Input configuration* ➤ *OnMouseClick* ➤ *Configure....*

In the *Input Configuration* window that appears, select the *Switch Frame Visualization* event on the right side, and click the arrow button pointing to the right. Then, in the window on the right side, leave the *Switch local visualization* field checked and select the *P00_Lighting* visualization. Confirm your changes by clicking the *OK* button (Figure 6-43). With this configuration, clicking the *Lighting* button will set the content of the *Frame* component to the *P00_Lighting visualization*.

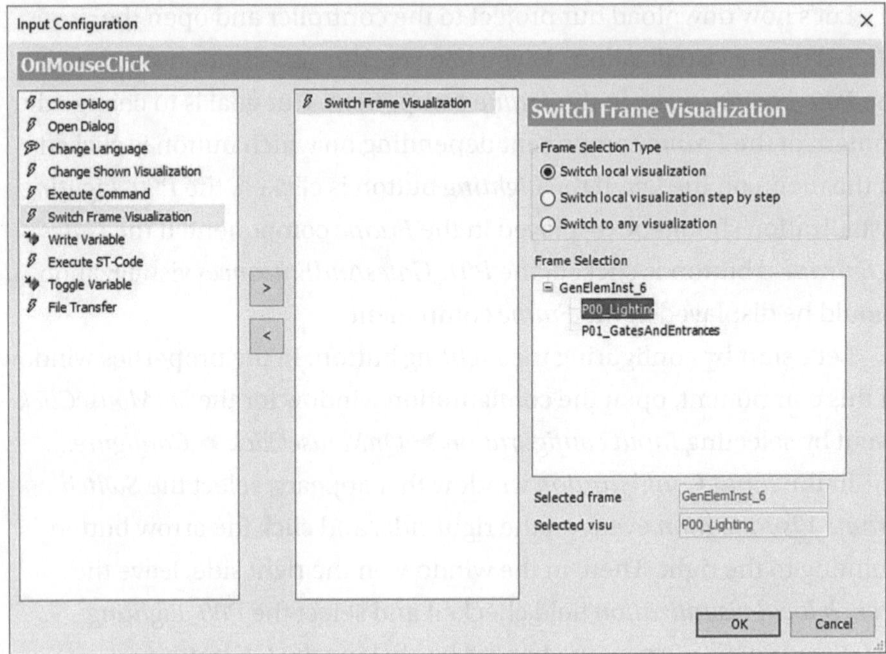

Figure 6-43. *Input Configuration window for the Lighting button*

Similarly, we proceed with the *Gates & Entrances* button, but in this case, we need to link the *OnMouseClick* event to the *P01_GatesAndEntrances* visualization (Figure 6-44).

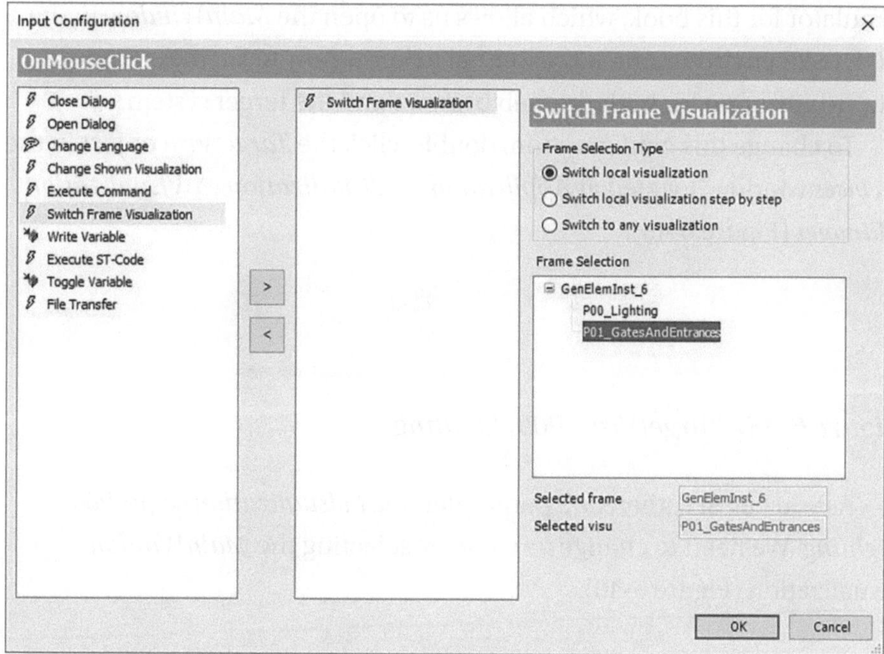

Figure 6-44. *Input Configuration window for the Gates &*
Entrances button

Let's now download our project to the controller and test the
navigation menu by clicking the *Lighting* and *Gates & Entrances* buttons.
Although the *Gates & Entrances* view still needs further refinement,
we now have the main functionality that allows us to switch between
visualizations.

Start Page of Visualization

We need to perform one more crucial step in the configuration of
our visualization. If we download our project to a controller that has,
for example, an operator panel, or if we are testing the visualization
using a web browser, the visualization currently always starts with the
P00_Lighting view instead of the *MainWindow*. Although we are using a

simulator for this book, which allows us to open the *MainWindow* in the CODESYS environment, it is essential to know how to set the start page of the visualization for both the web browser and the target system.

To change this configuration, double-click the *TargetVisu* object in the *Devices* window, located at *Application → Visualization → Visualization Manager* (Figure 6-45).

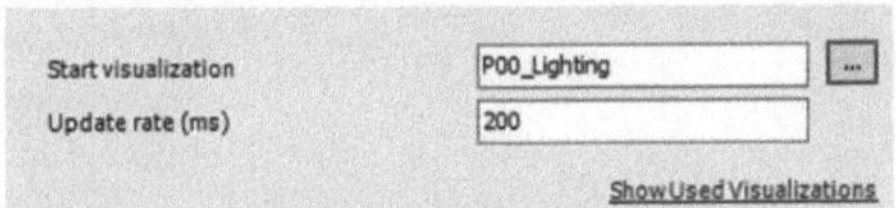

Figure 6-45. *TargetVisu: P00_Lighting*

As you can see, there is a parameter *Start visualization* set to *P00_Lighting*. We need to change its value by selecting the *MainWindow* visualization (Figure 6-46).

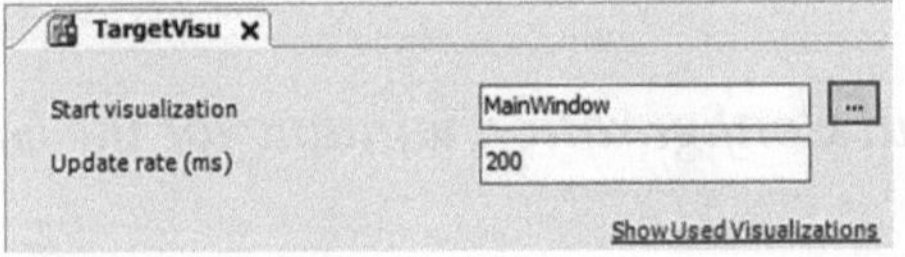

Figure 6-46. *TargetVisu: MainWindow*

Similarly, we proceed with the *WebVisu* object, located in the same place: *Application → Visualization → Visualization Manager*. Here, too, we set the *Start visualization* parameter to *MainWindow* (Figure 6-47).

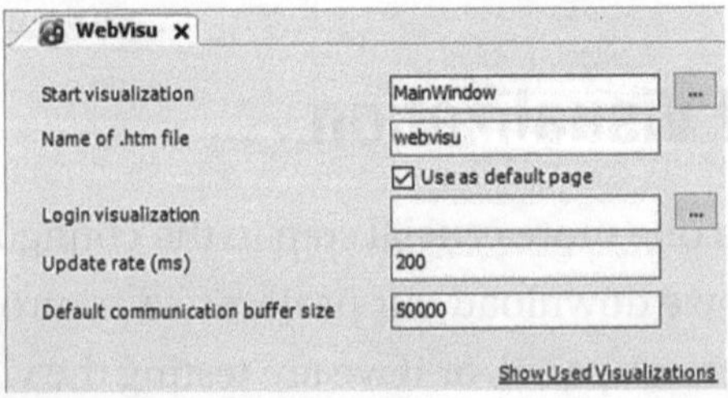

Figure 6-47. *WebVisu: MainWindow*

Visualization of *Gate1*

It's time to present the visualization of *Gate1* on the *Gates & Entrances* page. Let's start by adding five *Label* components and setting their properties according to the table below (Table 6-3).

Table 6-3. *Properties of Label controls*

Properties	1st Label	2nd Label	3rd Label	4th Label	5th Label
Texts → Text	Area I – Gate1	QCS-M1	QCS-ULS1	QCS-PE1	QCS-DLS1
Position → X	10	35	245	245	245
Position → Y	215	35	55	120	185
Position → Width	200	50	60	55	60
Position → Height	15	30	30	30	30

Next, we will add four *Lamp* controls to display the status of sensors and the *M1* motor. Set their properties according to the table below (Table 6-4).

Table 6-4. *Properties of Lamp controls*

Properties	1st Lamp	2nd Lamp	3rd Lamp	4th Lamp
Position → X	220	220	220	10
Position → Y	190	125	60	40
Position → Width	20	20	20	20
Position → Height	20	20	20	20
Variable	GVL_Inputs Outputs. DI_DLS1	GVL_Inputs Outputs. DI_PE1	GVL_Inputs Outputs. DI_ULS1	GVL_InputsOutputs. DO_M1_OPEN OR GVL_ InputsOutputs.DO_M1_ CLOSE
Background → Image	Green	Green	Green	Green

Upload the program to the controller with the simulator running. We should see the following gate visualization layout: the lower sensor *QCS-DLS1* should be active, indicating that the gate is closed. The photoelectric sensor *QCS-PE1* should show a ready state (Figure 6-48).

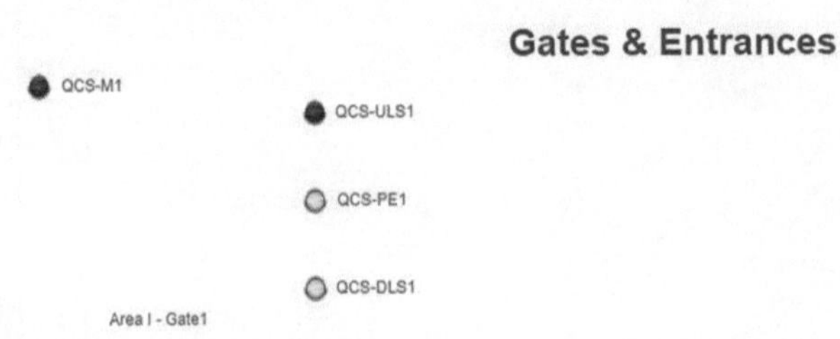

Figure 6-48. *Gates & Entrances view*

Let's now simulate the opening and closing of the gate by activating the input *DI_PB1*. We will observe changes in the sensor states on the visualization. Additionally, the operation of the *QCS-M1* motor will be visible on the visualization.

Next, add a *Rectangle* element to the visualization, which can be found under the *Basic* tab. This rectangle will be used to indicate that the gate is in an error state. Set its properties according to the following values:

- Position → X: 10

- Position → Y: 60

- Position → Width: 200

- Position → Height: 150

- Color variables → Toggle color: GatesAndEntrances. Gate1_ERROR

Download the program to the controller while deactivating the simulator, and set the sensor inputs *DI_DLS1* and *DI_ULS1* to TRUE. At this point, the gate should indicate an error, and its state will be highlighted in pink (Figure 6-49).

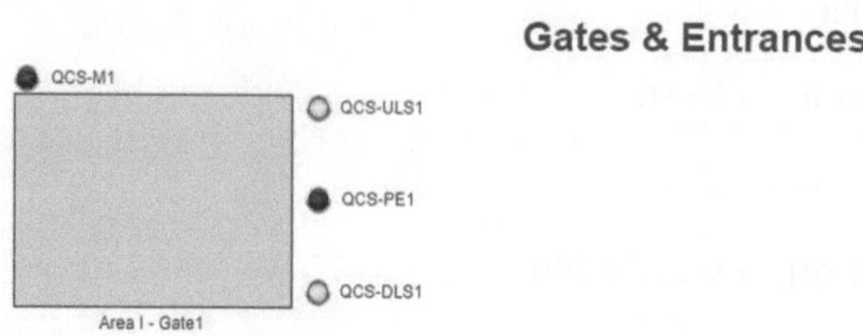

Figure 6-49. *Gates & Entrances view: gate error*

This happens because we assigned the variable *Gate1_ERROR* to the property *Color variables → Toggle color*. When this variable is TRUE, the rectangle's color changes to the one specified in the *Colors → Alarm state* properties. If *Gate1_ERROR* is FALSE, the rectangle adopts the colors defined in the *Colors → Normal state* settings (Figure 6-50). This allows for customization of the visualization elements color scheme according to your preferences.

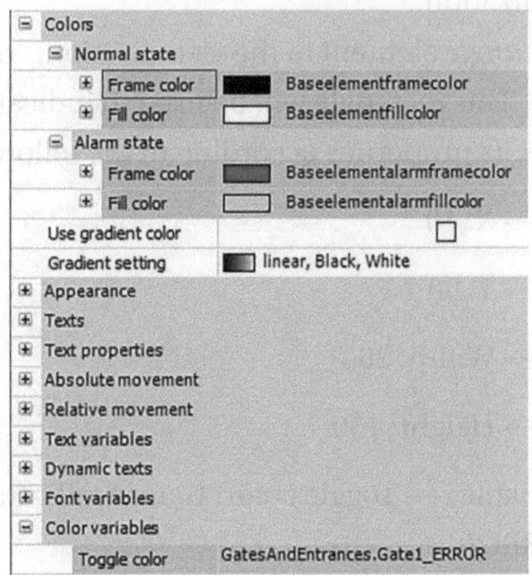

Figure 6-50. *Colors properties*

Let's now add another *Rectangle* element to the visualization, which will represent the gate in the closed position. Set its properties according to the following list:

- Position → X: 10

- Position → Y: 60

- Position → Width: 200

- Position → Height: 150

- Colors → Normal state → Fill color: Blue

- State variables – Invisible: NOT GatesAndEntrances.
  Gate1_CLOSE OR GatesAndEntrances.Gate1_ERROR

Using the *State variables* → *Invisible* properties, we can control the visibility of components on the visualization. In this case, we configured a simple condition: if the gate is not in the closed position or is in an error state, this component will be hidden on the visualization. This is how the gate appears when it is fully closed (Figure 6-51).

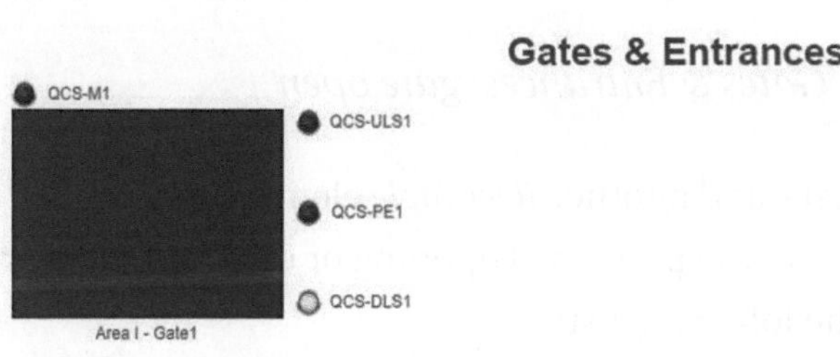

Figure 6-51. *Gates & Entrances: gate closed*

Let's now add another *Rectangle* element that will symbolize the gate in the open position. Set its properties according to the following list:

- Position → X: 10

- Position → Y: 60

- Position → Width: 200

- Position → Height: 20

- Colors → Normal state → Fill color: Blue

- State variables – Invisible: NOT GatesAndEntrances. Gate1_OPEN OR GatesAndEntrances.Gate1_ERROR

This is how the gate appears in the fully open position (Figure 6-52).

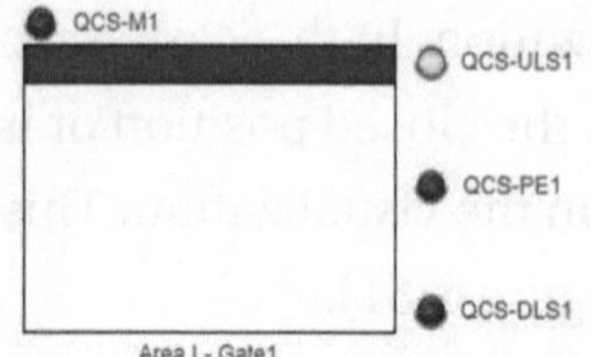

Figure 6-52. *Gates & Entrances: gate open*

Similarly, let's add another *Rectangle* element to visualize the state when the gate is in the process of opening or closing. Set its properties according to the following list:

- Position → X: 10

- Position → Y: 60

- Position → Width: 200

- Position → Height: 75

- Colors → Normal state → Fill color: Blue

- State variables – Invisible: NOT GatesAndEntrances. Gate1_CLOSING AND NOT GatesAndEntrances.Gate1_ OPENING OR GatesAndEntrances.Gate1_ERROR

Let's now download our program to the controller and run a simulation of the full gate opening and closing procedure. Currently, the visualization does not specify whether the gate is in the opening state or the closing state. To more accurately illustrate the current state of the gate, we can extend the visualization with additional elements.

Let's add three *Line* elements, which can be found in the *Basic* tab. Set the following properties for each line (Table 6-5).

Table 6-5. *Properties of Line controls*

Properties	1st Line	2nd Line	3rd Line
Position → Points → [0] → X	451	451	451
Position → Points → [0] → Y	205	205	205
Position → Points → [1] → X	451	443	459
Position → Points → [1] → Y	141	193	193
Appearance → Line width	2	2	2

We have created an arrow symbol pointing downward using these three lines. To combine them into a single cohesive element, let's group the lines to form one arrow. To do this, select all three lines, right-click on the selected lines, and choose the option *Group* (Figure 6-53).

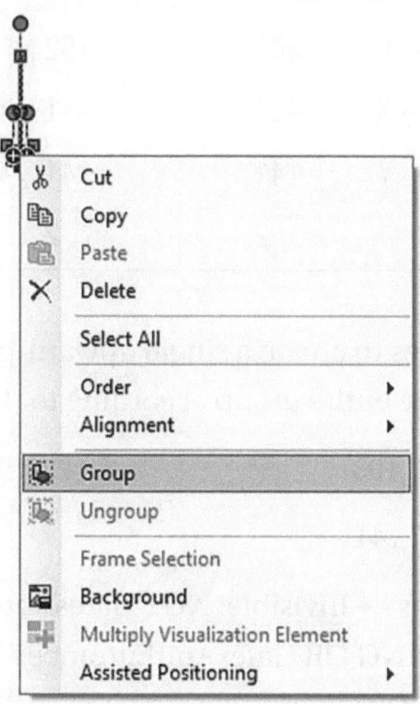

Figure 6-53. *Grouping lines*

Now, set the following properties for the entire group:

- Position → X: 103

- Position → Y: 141

- State variables → Invisible: NOT GatesAndEntrances.
  Gate1_CLOSING OR GatesAndEntrances.
  Gate1_ERROR

Similarly, create an upward-pointing arrow by setting the properties of the three lines added to the visualization according to the following table (Table 6-6).

Table 6-6. *Properties of Line controls*

Properties	1st Line	2nd Line	3rd Line
Position → Points → [0] → X	451	443	459
Position → Points → [0] → Y	205	152	152
Position → Points → [1] → X	451	451	451
Position → Points → [1] → Y	141	141	141
Appearance → Line width	2	2	2

Group the three lines to create a single upward-pointing arrow. Then set the properties for the entire group according to the following values:

- Position → X: 103

- Position → Y: 141

- State variables → Invisible: NOT GatesAndEntrances.
  Gate1_OPENING OR GatesAndEntrances.
  Gate1_ERROR

Let's test our program with the simulator. With a few simple adjustments, we have created a basic animation for opening and closing the gate. The CODESYS environment allows for the creation of more advanced animations, but the purpose of this book is to demonstrate the fundamental principles of control systems. Developing more complex visualizations could fill an entire book on its own. The key objective is to present the principles of control systems because, once you master one tool, you'll find it easy to learn programming in other engineering environments. Of course, there may be differences between manufacturers; for example, in CODESYS, we use the *Invisible* property to set an element's visibility, whereas other manufacturers might use *Visible* or another status bit. Nevertheless, the basic principles are very similar.

Organizing the Code

After completing the implementation of the control logic for gate *Gate1* and creating its visualization, it is time to expand our program and visualization to include another gate, *Gate2* in area III, and two entrances: *Entrance1* in area I and *Entrance2* in area II. This task aims to consolidate and organize the knowledge gained in previous chapters. Essentially, it involves copying the control logic created for gate *Gate1* and adapting it for the new gates and entrances.

Currently, our program contains eight networks, including the simulator. After adding the additional gate and two entrances, this number will increase to 32 networks, which may lead to suboptimal programming and confusing control logic. To improve code organization, we can introduce some enhancements.

Let's add a new subprogram to the *GatesAndEntrances* program named *Action*. Right-click the *GatesAndEntrances* program, and select the option *Add Object* ➤ *Action...* (Figure 6-54).

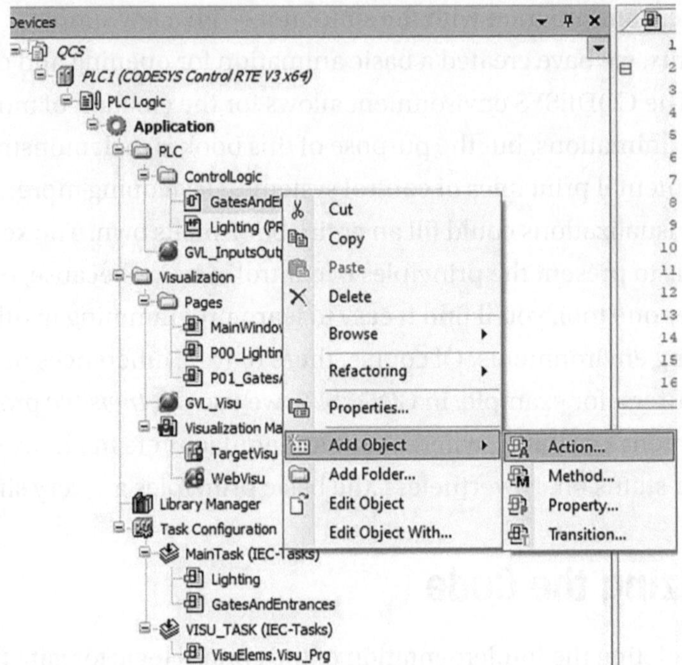

Figure 6-54. *Add Object ➤ Action...*

In the *Add Action* window, enter the subprogram name as *Gate1*, and then click the *OK* button (Figure 6-55).

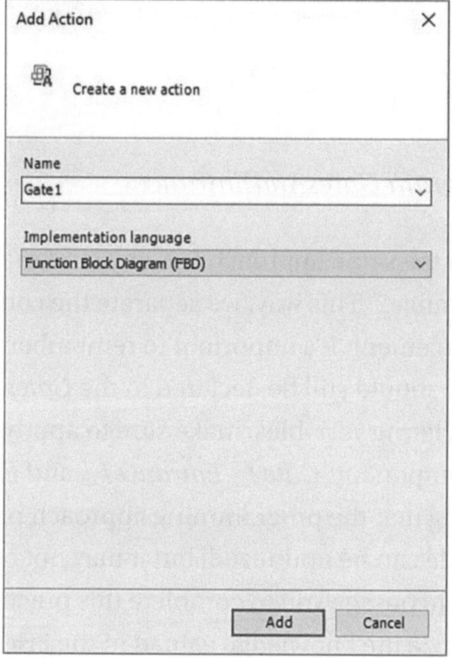

Figure 6-55. *Add Action window*

Next, move all the networks from the *GatesAndEntrances* program to the *Gate1* subprogram. To do this, select the networks in the *GatesAndEntrances* program, cut them, and then paste them into the Gate1 subprogram.

In the *GatesAndEntrances* program, we now need to call the code that was moved to the *Gate1* subprogram. In Network 1 of the *GatesAndEntrances* program, insert an empty block and name it *Gate1*. This will ensure that all the control logic for Gate1 is transferred to the *Gate1* subprogram, which will be called from the *GatesAndEntrances* program. Network 1 in the *GatesAndEntrances* program should now look like this (Figure 6-56).

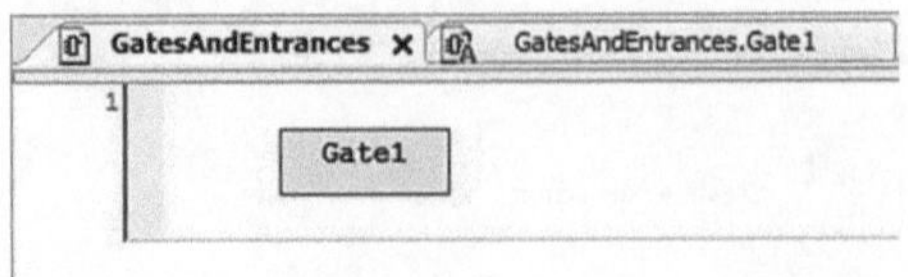

Figure 6-56. *Program GatesAndEntrances*

Similarly, apply the same approach to Gate2 and the entrances Entrance1 and Entrance2. This way, we separate the code, which enhances its clarity and management. It's important to remember that all variables required for control should still be declared in the *GatesAndEntrances* program. When declaring variables, make sure to appropriately adjust prefixes for each component: *Gate2_*, *Entrance1_*, and *Entrance2_*.

It is worth noting that the programming approach presented here is an example of how code can be optimized, but it may not be the best practice in the long term. I encourage you to complete this practical exercise to reinforce and organize the knowledge gained in the last two chapters. If you encounter any issues with implementation, the full source code is available on GitHub. In the following chapters, we will discuss better methods for code organization within the program.

Summary

In this chapter, we focused on the implementation and visualization of an industrial gate control system. We began by developing the control logic, considering various gate states and mechanisms for tracking them. We then proceeded to configure the visualization in CODESYS, creating a navigation menu and adding graphical elements to represent the gate's status.

Finally, we concentrated on code organization by transferring the control logic to subprograms, improving readability and organization. This chapter introduces fundamental skills in creating and managing visualizations and code organization, which will be further developed in the subsequent parts of the book.

CHAPTER 7

Heating and Cooling Control in the Production Facility

In this chapter, we will focus on temperature regulation in the quality control hall. After setting up lighting control and successfully managing the gates and entrances in the hall, we will move on to controlling and regulating the temperature. There are two temperature sensors installed in the hall, each of which will independently control the cooling and heating systems. When the temperature drops below the setpoint, the heating will automatically turn on. Conversely, when the temperature rises above the setpoint, the cooling system will be activated.

We will start by familiarizing ourselves with the theory of temperature measurement in control systems. We will learn how to read an analog signal in a PLC controller and scale it to engineering units. Next, we will implement a Bang-Bang controller, which we will use to regulate the temperature. Later in the chapter, we will introduce new concepts such as function and function block and explain the difference between them. Finally, we will add a new view to the visualization, where the temperature regulation will be displayed.

© Dariusz Wrebiak 2026
D. Wrebiak, *Practical PLC Programming for Beginners*, Maker Innovations Series,
https://doi.org/10.1007/979-8-8688-2430-2_7

Temperature Measurement in Control Systems

To measure temperature in control systems, it is necessary to first handle the appropriate hardware. The process works as follows: the temperature sensor is connected to the analog card of the PLC controller. The analog card in the controller functions as an analog-to-digital converter (ADC), which converts the analog signal into a digital value (Figure 7-1). This digital value is then used in the PLC application. Let's now take a closer look at each of these components.

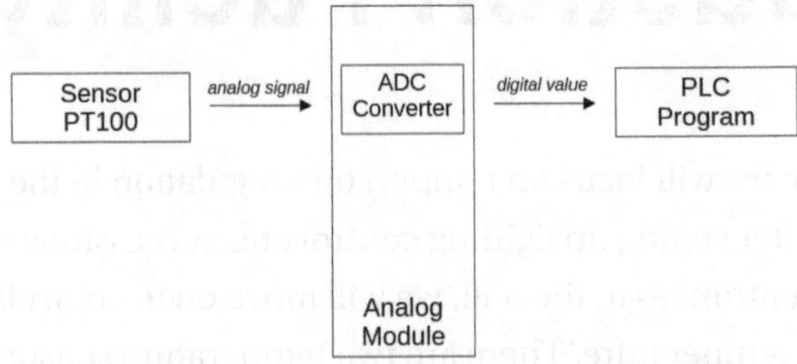

Figure 7-1. *Converting an analog signal to a digital value*

Analog-to-Digital Converter (ADC)   Is a device that converts an analog signal, which is continuous and varies over time, into a digital signal, which is discrete and consists of numerical values. ADCs are crucial in automation systems because they allow computers and PLC controllers to receive and process data from analog sensors and instruments.

PT100 Sensor: Basics

The PT100 sensor is a temperature sensor based on platinum resistance, with a resistance value of 100 ohms at 0°C. Its resistance changes linearly with temperature, allowing for accurate measurements. In PLC systems, special RTD (Resistance Temperature Detector) input modules are typically used, which are designed to work with resistive sensors like the PT100. This module measures the resistance of the PT100 sensor by passing a small measurement current through it and then converts the measured resistance into a temperature value. The typical measurement range of PT100 sensors is from -200°C to +850°C, enabling the measurement of both very low and high temperatures.

RTD Module (Resistance Temperature Detector)   Is a device used for temperature measurement. An RTD is a temperature sensor that changes its electrical resistance based on the temperature. The RTD module measures this resistance and converts it into a temperature value. RTDs are known for their high accuracy and stability in measurements.

The operation of the PT100 sensor is based on the principle that the resistance of platinum changes with temperature. Here are examples of how the resistance of a PT100 sensor varies at different temperatures (Figure 7-2).

- *-100°C*: 60.26 ohms

- *0°C*: 100 ohms

- *100°C*: 138.51 ohms

- *200°C*: 175.86 ohms

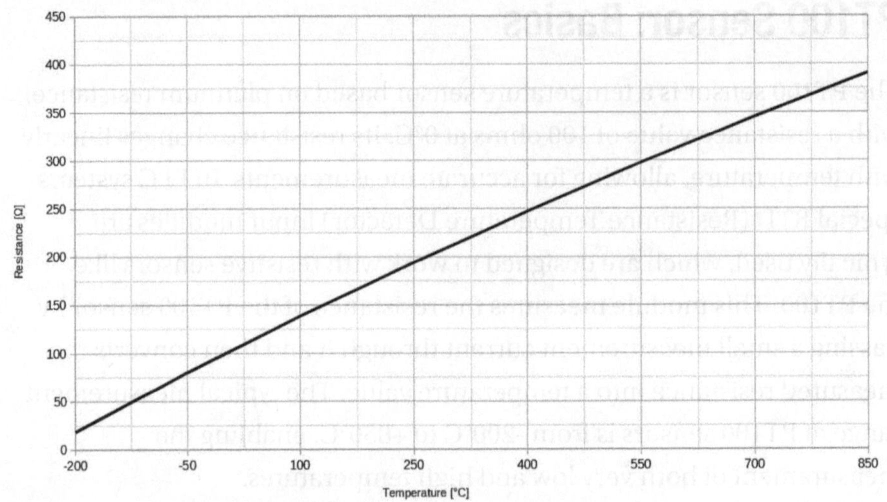

Figure 7-2. *Linear characteristics of the PT100 sensor*

PT100 Sensors: Two-Wire, Three-Wire, and Four-Wire Configurations

PT100 sensors are available in two-wire, three-wire (Figure 7-3), and four-wire configurations, each affecting the compensation of errors caused by wire resistance. Below are the differences and advantages of each configuration:

Two-Wire PT100 Sensor

- *Construction*: Consists of two wires connected to the platinum resistor

- *Advantages*: Simple design and easy installation

- *Disadvantages*: Does not compensate for errors due to wire resistance, which can lead to inaccurate measurements, especially with longer cables

- *Applications*: Best suited for short distances where wire resistance is minimal

Three-Wire PT100 Sensor

- *Construction*: Includes an additional wire that allows partial compensation for errors caused by wire resistance.

- *Advantages*: Significantly improves measurement accuracy by compensating for wire resistance. Most commonly used in industrial applications.

- *Disadvantages*: Slightly more complex installation compared to the two-wire version.

- *Applications*: Widely used in industrial applications where accuracy is important and wires may be of considerable length.

Four-Wire PT100 Sensor

- *Construction*: Equipped with two current-carrying wires and two voltage-sensing wires, enabling full compensation for wire and connection resistance.

- *Advantages*: Provides the most accurate compensation for errors, ideal for very precise measurements.

- *Disadvantages*: More complex installation and higher cost.

- *Applications*: Used in applications where the highest precision is required, such as calibration laboratories.

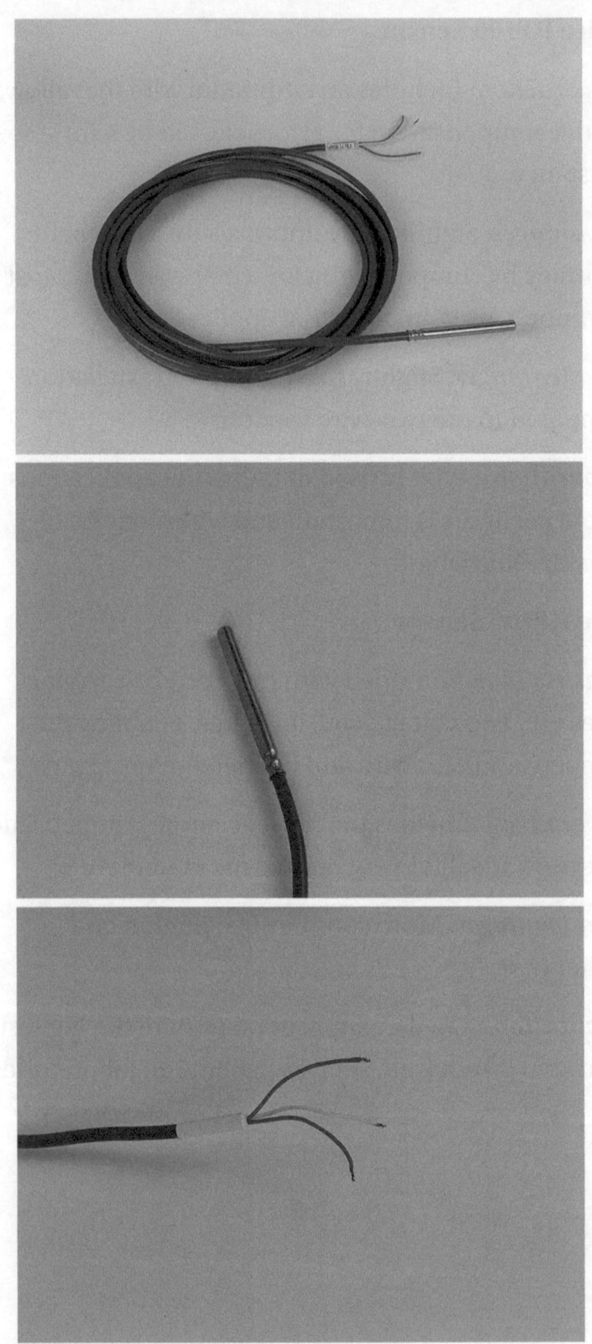

Figure 7-3. *Three-wire PT100 sensor*

Why Use Three or Four Wires?

Wire resistance: The resistance of the wires adds to the total resistance of the sensor circuit, which can affect the accuracy of the readings. With long wires, this additional resistance can be significant and lead to measurement errors.

Error Compensation

- *Three-wire sensor*: The additional wire allows for error compensation by using a measurement system that detects the potential difference between two signal wires. This setup helps eliminate the impact of wire resistance on the measurement result.

- *Four-wire sensor*: Two wires are used for carrying current through the sensor, while the other two wires measure the voltage directly across the sensor. This setup ensures that the resistance of the current-carrying wires does not affect the measurement result, providing the highest accuracy.

Summary

- *Two-wire sensors*: Simple and cost-effective, but less accurate with longer cables

- *Three-wire sensors*: A good compromise between simplicity and accuracy, most commonly used in industrial settings

- *Four-wire sensors*: The most accurate, used in applications requiring the highest precision

The choice of the appropriate PT100 sensor type depends on the accuracy requirements and installation conditions. In industrial applications where cables may be long, three-wire sensors are often preferred as they offer adequate accuracy with relatively simple installation.

PT100 vs. PT1000

In addition to the widely used PT100 sensors in industry, PT1000 sensors are also commonly employed for temperature measurement (Table 7-1).

Table 7-1. *Comparing PT100 and PT1000 sensors*

	PT100	PT1000
Resistance at 0°C	100 ohms	1000 ohms

Similarities

- Both sensors are made from platinum, which ensures a linear relationship between resistance and temperature.

- Both sensors can measure a wide temperature range, typically from -200°C to +850°C, depending on the specific model's specifications.

Differences

- The primary difference is the resistance at 0°C. With its higher resistance, the PT1000 is less affected by the resistance of the measurement wires, making it more suitable for applications with longer cables. This reduces the impact of errors related to wire resistance.

The PT1000 sensor's higher resistance makes it advantageous for minimizing the effect of lead wire resistance, especially in situations where long cable runs are necessary.

$$Temperature = \left(\frac{INPUT - INPUT_{MIN}}{INPUT_{MAX} - INPUT_{MIN}} \right)$$
$$\times \left(TEMPERATURE_{MAX} - TEMPERATURE_{MIN} \right) + TEMPERATURE_{MIN}$$

Analog Module

As PLC programmers, it is essential to thoroughly review the documentation of the analog module, as it contains crucial information about the range of resistance or voltage that the Analog-to-Digital Converter (ADC) maps to digital values. For PT100 sensors, the typical temperature range is from -200°C to 850°C, but the measurement range of the analog module may vary.

The measurement range of the analog module defines how the resistance values of the PT100 sensor are mapped to the digital value range. For instance, with a 12-bit ADC, this digital range might be from 0 to 4095. For example, if the documentation for the analog module specifies a temperature range from -50°C to 150°C for a PT100 sensor, then the digital values 0 and 4095 would correspond to -50°C and 150°C, respectively. This mapping ensures that the analog signals are accurately represented in the PLC system, allowing for precise temperature measurements and control.

Calculating Temperature from Digital Value

To convert a digital value to temperature, linear interpolation is used. Given that the analog module documentation specifies that a temperature range from -50°C to 150°C is mapped to digital values ranging from 0 to 4095, the conversion can be performed using the following formula:

Where

- INPUT is the value read from the ADC

- INPUT _ MIN=0 is the minimum value read from the ADC

- INPUT _ MAX=4095 is the maximum value read from the ADC

- TEMPERATURE_MIN=–50°C is the minimum temperature value

- TEMPERATURE_MAX=150°C is the maximum temperature value

Now that we know how to properly scale the values read from the PT100 sensor to temperature in the PLC program, let's proceed to the implementation.

Reading and Scaling Analog Signals in the PLC Program

We will start by creating two global variables to receive signals from the analog inputs. In PLC programs, analog signals are typically represented by the INT data type. Therefore, we will create two global variables of type INT, named *AI_TIC1* and *AI_TIC2*, in the global variables area for inputs and outputs *GVL_InputsOutputs* (Figure 7-4).

```
49      (* Temperature *)
50      // Analog Inputs
51      AI_TIC1 : INT;              // 1st Temperature
52      AI_TIC2 : INT;              // 2nd Temperature
```

Figure 7-4. *Global variables GVL_InputsOutputs*

Next, go to the *ControlLogic* folder, and add a new program in FBD (Function Block Diagram) language, naming it *Temperatures.* The *Temperatures* program should be called in the *MainTask.* The structure of our program in the *Devices* window should look as follows (Figure 7-5).

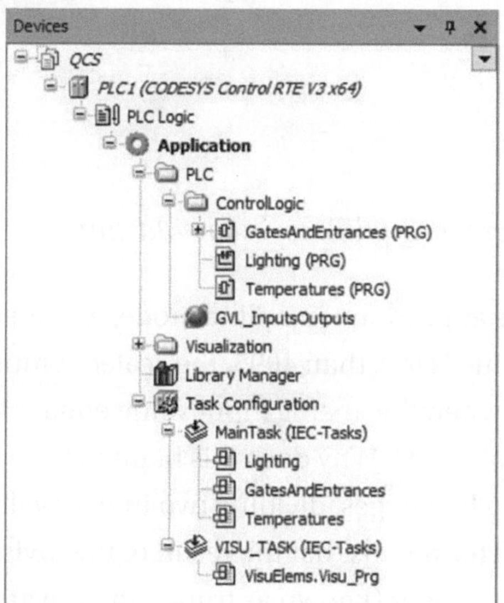

Figure 7-5. *Devices window*

In this program, we will implement linear interpolation, which we discussed in the theoretical part about calculating temperature based on the digital value read from the analog input. For this purpose, we will use the appropriate arithmetic operators.

The PT100 sensor, which measures temperature at point QCS-TIC1, is connected to an analog module with a 12-bit Analog-to-Digital Converter (ADC). This module is capable of measuring temperatures in the range from -50°C to 150°C. Consequently, a digital value of 0 will correspond to a temperature of -50°C, while a digital value of 4095 will correspond to a temperature of 150°C.

Below is how *Network* 1 should look in the *Temperatures* program (Figure 7-6).

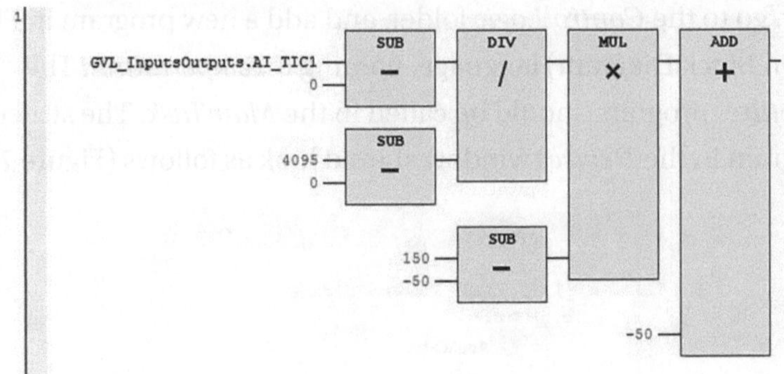

Figure 7-6. *Implementing linear interpolation*

After testing the application in online mode, we can observe that if the analog input value is less than 4095, the scaled temperature is equal –50°C. Conversely, when the analog input value equals 4095, the scaled temperature is equal 150°C. Why does this happen?

In programming languages, dividing two integer values (INT) also returns an integer. This means that the result of the division is rounded down to the nearest integer (known as truncation toward zero). When dividing two integers, if the dividend is smaller than the divisor, the division result in real numbers will be less than 1. Since integer division must return an integer, the result is rounded down to the nearest integer, which is zero (Figure 7-7).

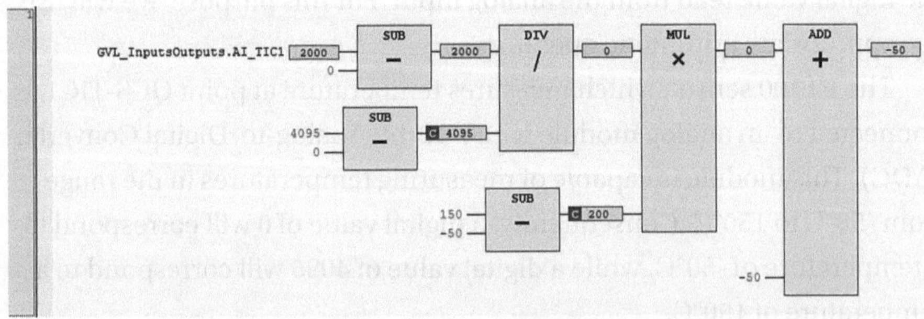

Figure 7-7. *Dividing 2000 by 4095, which results in 0*

Therefore, it is important to use appropriate data types and methods for scaling values in PLC applications to avoid such issues, for example, by using floating-point numbers (REAL) or by implementing precise rounding methods.

To obtain the result of the division as a real number, we need to ensure that at least one of the numbers in the division operation is of the floating-point type, i.e., REAL. To avoid the problem of rounding to zero when dividing two integers, one of the numbers should be converted to a floating-point type before performing the division. This ensures that the result will also be of the floating-point type, preserving the decimal value.

To achieve this, we use the *INT_TO_REAL* conversion operator, which converts an integer to a real number. Here is how the modified *Network 1* looks (Figure 7-8).

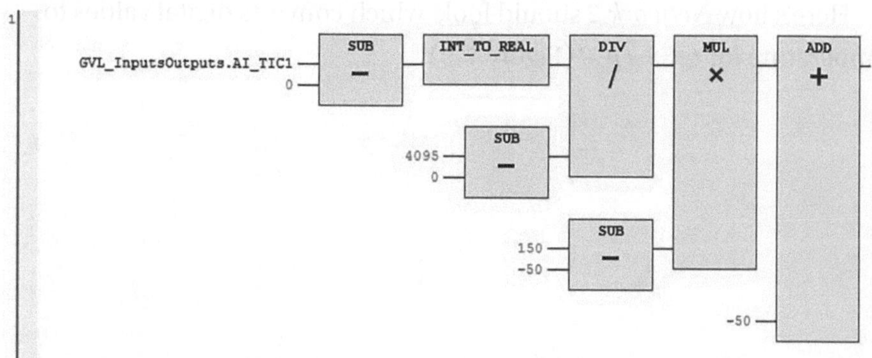

Figure 7-8. *Linear interpolation implementation with INT to REAL conversion*

When we set the analog input value *AI_TIC1* in the range from 0 to 4095 using the *Watch* table, the output of *Network 1* will show the scaled temperature ranging from -50°C to 150°C.

Now, let's add *Network 2* to the *Temperatures* program, where we will scale the temperature for *QCS-TIC2*. In this case, the PT100 sensor is connected to an analog module with a 10-bit Analog-to-Digital Converter (ADC).

This module has a 10-bit resolution, meaning its digital range is from 0 to 1023. Thus, a digital value of 0 corresponds to the lowest measured temperature, which is 0°C, and a digital value of 1023 corresponds to the highest measured temperature, which is 100°C.

To correctly scale the digital values to temperature, linear interpolation must be performed. Therefore, the digital value range is from 0 to 1023, and the temperature range is from 0°C to 100°C. Consequently, digital values will be mapped to the temperature range as follows:

- A digital value of 0 will correspond to a temperature of 0°C.

- A digital value of 1023 will correspond to a temperature of 100°C.

Here's how *Network 2* should look, which converts digital values to temperature for *QCS-TIC2* (Figure 7-9).

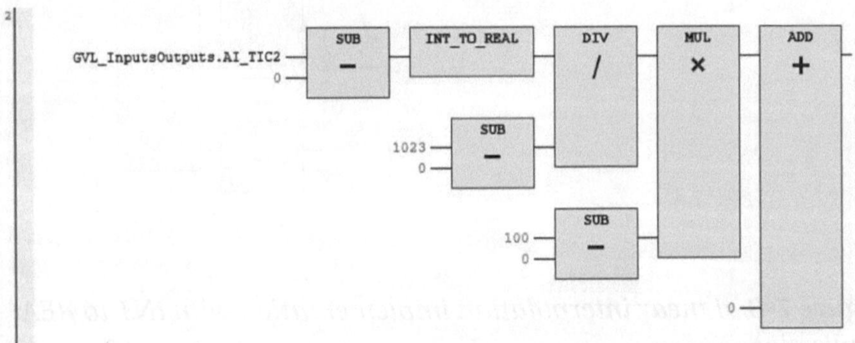

Figure 7-9. *Implementation of linear interpolation for temperature QCS-TIC2*

Everything seems easy and straightforward, but again, we're copying a lot of code and only changing the input parameters for the arithmetic operators, depending on how we want to scale the temperature measurement. With two measurements, this method can still be used, but what if we have 100 measurements in our control system? It's time to simplify things by implementing our own functions.

Let's add a new folder to our application in the *Application* ➤ *PLC* directory and name it *FunctionBlocks* (Figure 7-10).

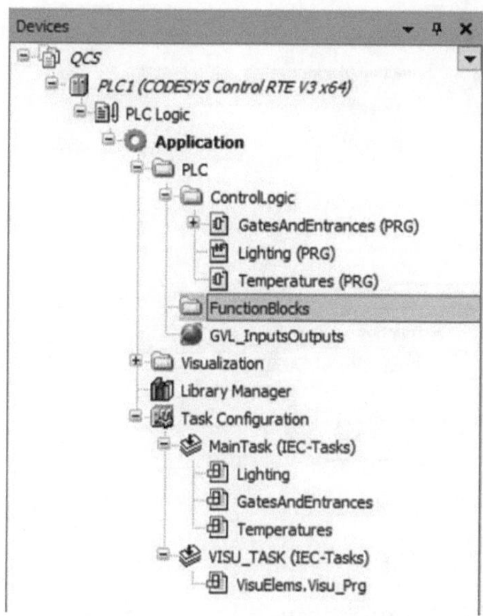

Figure 7-10. *Devices window*

Next, let's add a new object to the *FunctionBlocks* folder. Right-click on the *FunctionBlocks* folder and select the option *Add Object* ➤ *POU* from the menu. In the *Add POU* window, name the function *TemperatureScale*. Choose *Function* as the type of object, and set the return type of the function to *REAL*. The programming language should be *Structured Text (ST)*. Click the *Add* button to confirm your selection (Figure 7-11).

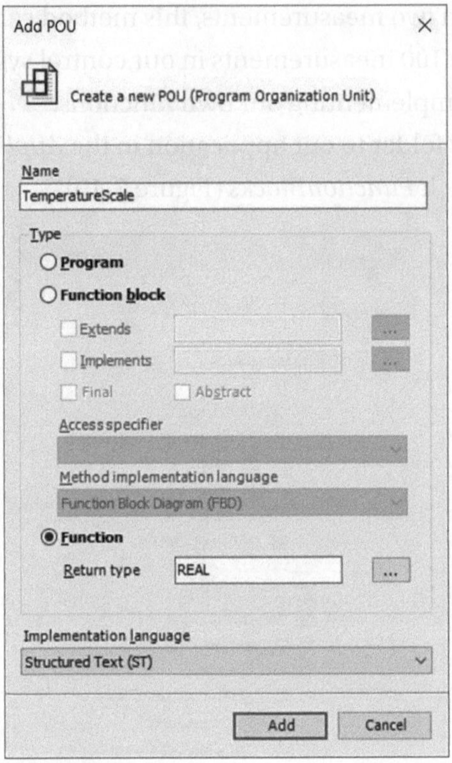

Add POU   ✕

Create a new POU (Program Organization Unit)

Name

TemperatureScale

Type

○ Program

○ Function block

☐ Extends

☐ Implements

☐ Final   ☐ Abstract

Access specifier

Method implementation language

Function Block Diagram (FBD)

◉ Function

Return type   REAL

Implementation language

Structured Text (ST)

Add   Cancel

Figure 7-11. *Add POU window*

Let's declare the inputs in the interface of our *TemperatureScale*
function, which will be used to implement the function that scales digital
values to temperature (Figure 7-12).

```
TemperatureScale  ✕
 1    FUNCTION TemperatureScale : REAL
 2    VAR_INPUT
 3        INPUT : INT;
 4        INPUT_MIN : INT;
 5        INPUT_MAX : INT;
 6        TEMPARATURE_MIN : REAL;
 7        TEMPARATURE_MAX : REAL;
 8    END_VAR
 9    VAR
10    END_VAR
```

Figure 7-12. *Declaration of inputs for the TemperatureScale function*

In the section where we implement the code, we need to use
mathematical operators to calculate the temperature value. This time,
we will use Structured Text (ST) instead of the graphical languages
FBD or LAD.

As you can see, the implementation of scaling the digital values
read from the analog input to temperature takes only one line of code
(Figure 7-13). The syntax of ST is similar to Visual Basic, which might make
it easier for those familiar with that language.

```
1  TemperatureScale := (INT_TO_REAL(INPUT - INPUT_MIN) / (INPUT_MAX - INPUT_MIN)) * (TEMPARATURE_MAX - TEMPARATURE_MIN) + TEMPARATURE_MIN;
```

Figure 7-13. *Implementation of the TemperatureScale function*

To use the *TemperatureScale* function in our PLC program, let's return
to the *Temperatures* program and call this function. To do this, expand the
POUs list in the *ToolBox* window on the right side. At the very bottom of
the list, you'll find our *TemperatureScale* function (Figure 7-14).

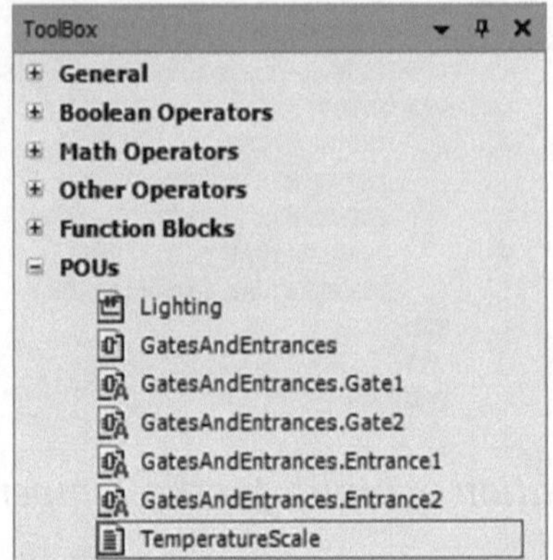

Figure 7-14. *ToolBox ➤ POUs ➤ TemperatureScale*

Using the *Drag and Drop* function, place the *TemperatureScale* function above *Network 1*. To do this, hover the cursor over the green arrow (Figure 7-15).

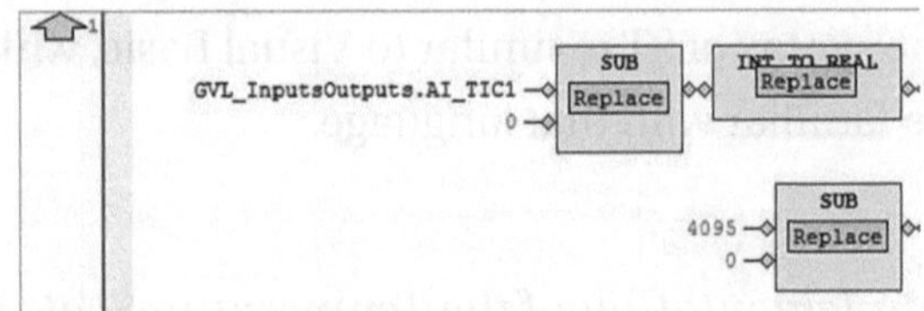

Figure 7-15. *Calling the TemperatureScale function using Drag and Drop*

This will cause the current code in *Network 1* to be moved to *Network 2*, and the *TemperatureScale* function will be placed in *Network 1*, which we will need to parameterize accordingly (Figure 7-16).

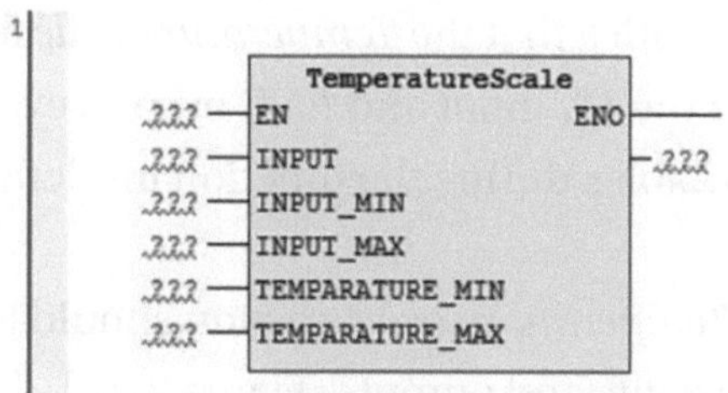

Figure 7-16. *Calling the TemperatureScale function*

The *INPUT* is the digital value read from the analog input. The values *INPUT_MIN* and *INPUT_MAX* are the ranges of digital values provided by the analog-to-digital converter. For the temperature QCS-TIC1, we use a 12-bit converter, which means a range from 0 to 4095. The values *TEMPERATURE_MIN* and *TEMPERATURE_MAX* are the minimum and maximum temperature ranges provided by the analog module, respectively. For the temperature QCS-TIC1, this range is from -50°C to 150°C.

The value returned by the function is the scaled temperature, expressed in degrees Celsius. We will store this value in the global variable *Temperature_TIC1*, which we will declare in *GVL_Visu* (Figure 7-17), as we will present these values in the visualization later in this chapter.

```
GVL_Visu  X
1    {attribute 'qualified_only'}
2    VAR_GLOBAL
3        (* Lighting *)
4        HANDMODE : BOOL;
5        AUTOMODE : BOOL;
6
7        (* Temperatures *)
8        Temperature_TIC1 : REAL;
9        Temperature_TIC2: REAL;
10   END_VAR
```

Figure 7-17. *Declaration of global variables in GVL_Visu*

Additionally, we notice that the *TemperatureScale* function interface automatically added the *EN* input and *ENO* output, even though we did not declare these variables during the function implementation. Set the *EN* input to TRUE.

This is how the *TemperatureScale* function should look after correctly parameterizing the inputs and outputs (Figure 7-18).

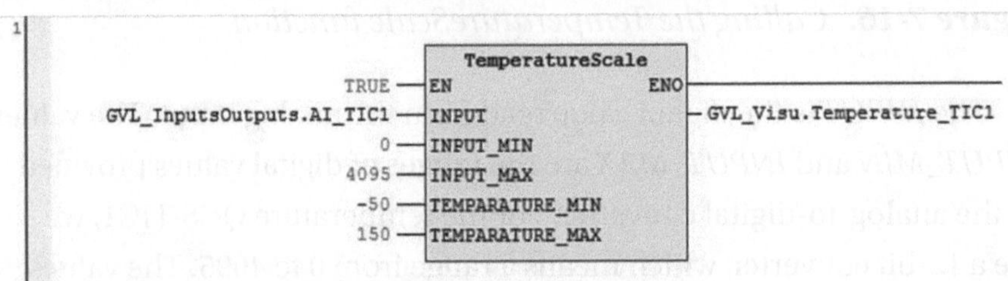

Figure 7-18. *Parameterization of the TemperatureScale function: temperature QCS-TIC1*

Let's now download our program to the controller and test the functionality of the *TemperatureScale* function by adjusting the analog input value *AI_TIC1* using the *Watch* table. Observe how the function processes the input data by performing arithmetic operations implemented within the function and returns the scaled temperature, saving it in the variable *Temperature_TIC1*.

By implementing the *TemperatureScale* function, we have created a module where we input different values through the inputs and receive processed data on the output. This approach simplifies and speeds up our work as we only need to parameterize the function appropriately. It has streamlined our work because we can create "containers" with code that frequently repeats, avoiding the need to copy and paste the same code. Imagine having a control system handling 100 temperature measurements. With such a function, our task is reduced to calling the function 100 times and parameterizing it correctly, as all the arithmetic is already contained within the function.

We will similarly process the scaling of temperature for QCS-TIC2, keeping in mind that the sensor is connected to a 10-bit analog module measuring temperature in the range of 0°C to 100°C. We should also remove the Networks responsible for scaling temperature directly in the *Temperatures* program using mathematical operators. Since we have implemented the function, this code is no longer needed. *Network 2* should now look with the function properly parameterized (Figure 7-19).

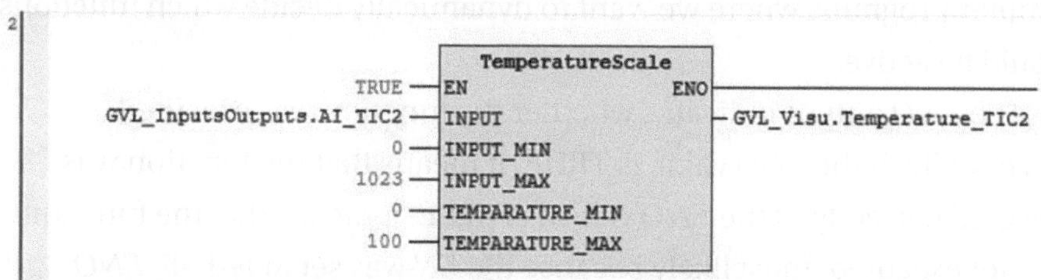

Figure 7-19. *Parameterization of the TemperatureScale function: temperature QCS-TIC2*

We still need to explain the input *EN* and the output *ENO*. Let's start by declaring a local variable *enable* of type BOOL in the *Temperatures* program. Then, assign this variable to the input *EN* of the *TemperatureScale* function, which is called in *Network 1* (Figure 7-20).

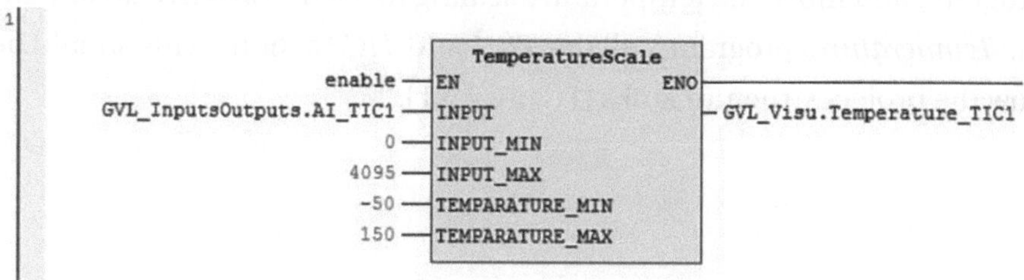

Figure 7-20. *Dynamic activation of the TemperatureScale function*

Download the program to the controller, and use the *Watch* table to manipulate the value of the *AI_TIC1* variable. You will notice that regardless of what value is set for *AI_TIC1*, the function in *Network 1* always returns the same value. Only when the *enable* variable is set to TRUE does the *TemperatureScale* function immediately start processing the input data and calculating the temperature.

As you might guess, the *EN* input is used to control whether the function should be executed. If the *EN* value is set to TRUE, the function will be executed. If the *EN* value is FALSE, the function will not be executed, and the *ENO* output will be set to FALSE. This can be useful in complex programs where we want to dynamically decide which functions should be active.

The *ENO* output indicates whether the function was executed successfully. If the *ENO* value is TRUE, it means that the function was executed correctly. If the *ENO* value is FALSE, it means that the function was not executed, most likely because the *EN* was set to FALSE. *ENO* allows informing other parts of the program about the result of the function execution. You can monitor *ENO* to check if a particular block was executed correctly.

To conclude the scaling topic, let's tidy up our PLC program by separating the two temperatures, QCS-TIC1 and QCS-TIC2, into two separate subprograms. This will allow for better structuring of the control program. To do this, add two actions *TIC1* and *TIC2* to the *Temperatures* program, and move the temperature scaling to each respective action. In the *Temperatures* program, call the *TIC1* and *TIC2* actions. This should be how the project structure looks (Figure 7-21).

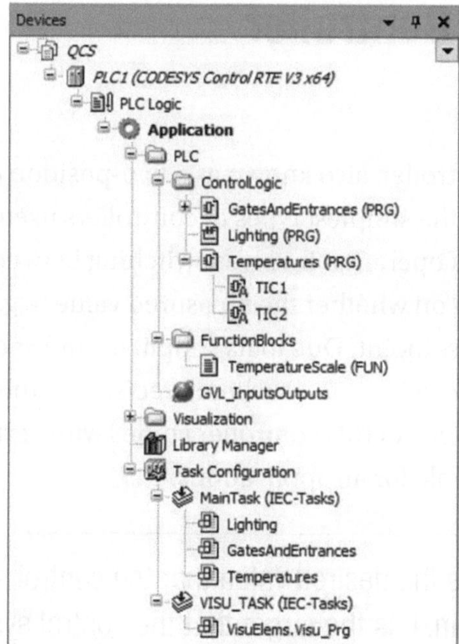

Figure 7-21. *Devices window*

Calling the individual *TIC1* and *TIC2* actions in the *Temperatures* program (Figure 7-22).

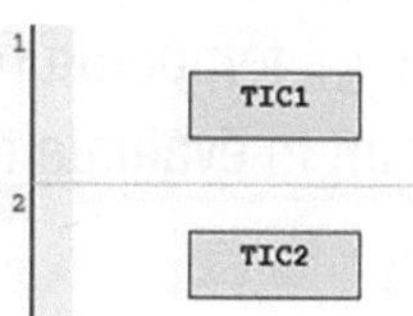

Figure 7-22. *Temperatures program*

Bang-Bang Controller

Introduction

The Bang-Bang controller, also known as a two-position or on-off controller, is one of the simplest types of controllers used in automation. Its basic principle of operation involves switching between two states – on and off – depending on whether the measured value (e.g., temperature) is below or above the setpoint. Due to its simplicity and speed, this type of controller is often used in systems where precise control is not necessary. However, the simplicity of this controller comes with certain limitations that make it unsuitable for all applications.

Setpoint (SP)   Is the desired value that the control system aims to reach and maintain. It is the target that the control system compares with the currently measured process values to adjust the operation of actuators such as valves, motors, etc.

Process Value (PV)   Is the current value that is monitored and measured in the process system. It represents the actual value of the process parameter (e.g., temperature, pressure, level) that is compared with the setpoint to evaluate the performance of the control system.

Operation Principle

The Bang-Bang controller operates on simple logic: if the process value (PV) falls below the setpoint (SP), the device is turned on. When the process value exceeds the setpoint, the device is turned off. This mode of operation is often used in household thermostats, where heating is activated when the temperature drops below a certain level and deactivated when the temperature rises above a set threshold. However, in some cases, this operation can lead to a phenomenon known as "chattering," where the device frequently switches between states, potentially causing excessive mechanical wear.

Examples of Applications

Bang-Bang controllers are commonly used in simple applications such as

- *Home thermostats*: Controlling heating and cooling in air conditioning systems. In these systems, precise temperature regulation is not required, but quick response to changes is important for user comfort.

- *Street lighting*: Managing the switching on and off of street lamps based on daylight intensity. The simplicity of the Bang-Bang controller allows for reliable operation even in harsh environmental conditions.

- *Water pumps*: Controlling pumps in irrigation systems or water tanks based on water level. Here, a quick response to changes in water level is crucial, and the simplicity of the system minimizes the risk of failure.

Hysteresis in Bang-Bang Controllers

To avoid continuous switching between states (which could lead to excessive wear on the device), hysteresis is often used in Bang-Bang controllers. Hysteresis introduces a tolerance range around the setpoint value within which the device does not change its state. For example, cooling may only be turned on when the temperature rises 1°C above the setpoint, and it is turned off only after the temperature falls back below the setpoint by 1°C (Figure 7-23).

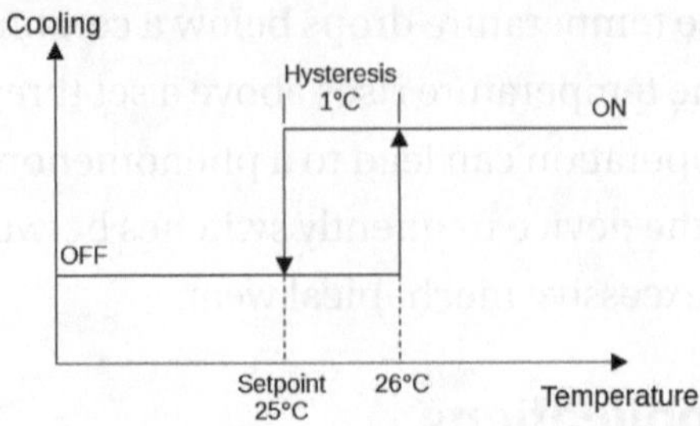

Figure 7-23. *Cooling controller with hysteresis*

Similarly, heating may only be turned on when the temperature drops 1°C below the setpoint, and it is turned off only after the temperature rises 1°C above the setpoint (Figure 7-24).

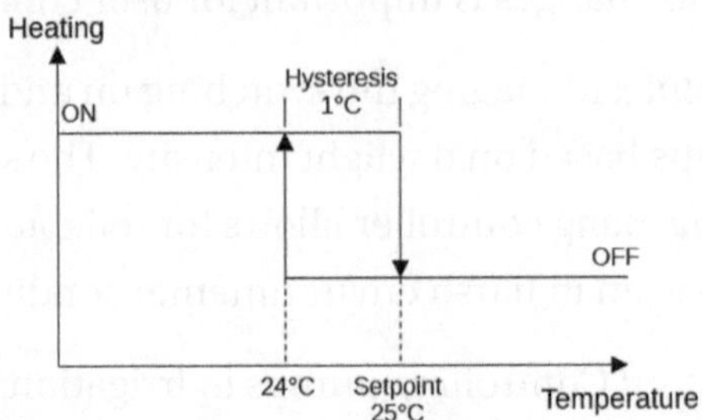

Figure 7-24. *Heating controller with hysteresis*

Hysteresis   Is a phenomenon where there is a delay in the system's response to changes in the input signal, affecting the output signal. In the context of control systems, hysteresis is used to prevent frequent switching, which can cause undesirable fluctuations in system performance. The hysteresis value is a relatively small difference between the turn-on and turn-off points, which stabilizes the system's operation and prevents excessive cyclical behavior.

Advantages and Disadvantages of Bang-Bang Controller

Advantages

- *Simplicity of design*: The Bang-Bang controller is easy to design and implement, making it an attractive choice for systems where complexity is not required.

- *Fast response*: Systems based on this type of controller react immediately to changes in the process value, which is beneficial in applications requiring instant intervention.

Disadvantages

- *Oscillations*: Since the system operates in an on/off mode, it can cause oscillations of the process value around the setpoint, which can be undesirable in certain cases. For example, in precision systems like motor control circuits, oscillations can lead to instability of the equipment.

- *Lack of precision*: The Bang-Bang controller does not offer precise regulation, which can be problematic in systems requiring accurate control of parameters. Therefore, in applications requiring high precision, more advanced controllers like PID are used.

Official Terminology and Standards

Although the term *Bang-Bang controller* is commonly used in technical literature and among engineers, it is not officially recognized in technical standards. In more formal documentation, the term *two-position controller* or *on-off controller* is often used. Regardless of the terminology, the principle of operation remains the same. For example, in technical documentation from the International Organization for Standardization (ISO), the term *on-off controller* is frequently used.

It is worth noting that there is no single, rigid international standard defining the implementation of the Bang-Bang control algorithm. However, there are recommendations and best practices widely adopted in industry and control systems engineering. For instance, the configuration of hysteresis and methods for setting the setpoint may vary depending on the specific requirements of the system and the preferences of the engineer.

Summary

The Bang-Bang controller is a simple yet effective solution for many applications where precise control is not crucial, and simplicity and speed of response are prioritized. Although its operation can lead to oscillations and does not provide precision, it is ideal for situations where these factors are not critical. Due to its simplicity, the Bang-Bang controller often serves as a starting point in control system design, and when necessary, it can be replaced with more advanced solutions, such as PID controllers, in systems that require greater precision and stability.

Implementation of the Bang-Bang Controller

After discussing the theoretical basics of the Bang-Bang controller, we will now move on to its practical implementation. First, we will add new global variables that will be presented in the visualization, which are necessary for implementing the temperature controller (Figure 7-25). These variables will be crucial for monitoring the system's state and controlling the regulation process.

```
GVL_Visu  X
 1    {attribute 'qualified_only'}
 2    VAR_GLOBAL
 3        (* Lighting *)
 4        HANDMODE : BOOL;
 5        AUTOMODE : BOOL;
 6
 7        (* Temperatures *)
 8        Enable_Controller_TIC1 : BOOL;
 9        Temperature_TIC1 : REAL;
10        Setpoint_TIC1 : REAL;
11        Hysteresis_TIC1 : REAL;
12        Enable_Controller_TIC2 : BOOL;
13        Temperature_TIC2 : REAL;
14        Setpoint_TIC2 : REAL;
15        Hysteresis_TIC2 : REAL;
16    END_VAR
```

Figure 7-25. *Global variables GVL_Visu*

Next, in the *TIC1* subroutine, we will implement the temperature controller. First, in the *Temperatures* program, we will add two local variables: *cooling* and *heating*, both of type BOOL. These variables will be crucial in implementing the controller as *cooling* will activate the cooling system, while *heating* will control the heating system.

Additionally, to simplify the code and improve its functionality, we will remove the local *enable* variable from the declaration. Instead, the temperature scaling function (*TemperatureScale*) will be called whenever the controller is in RUN mode. To achieve this, we will set the *EN* input of the *TemperatureScale* function in the *TIC1* subroutine to TRUE, ensuring continuous temperature calculations while the system is operational (Figure 7-26).

```
Temperatures  X
 1    PROGRAM Temperatures
 2    VAR
 3        cooling : BOOL;
 4        heating : BOOL;
 5        Cooling_RS_TIC1 : RS;
 6        Heating_RS_TIC1 : RS;
 7    END_VAR
```

Figure 7-26. *Local variables of the Temperatures program*

In *Network 2* of the subroutine, we will implement the cooling control logic. Cooling will be activated when the temperature exceeds the value of *Setpoint_TIC1 + Hysteresis_TIC*. When the temperature drops below the setpoint, cooling will be turned off. This control logic can be implemented using the components we have already learned about, such as arithmetic operators, comparison operators, and an RS flip-flop:

- *Arithmetic operator*: We use it to add the hysteresis value (*Hysteresis_TIC1*) to the setpoint (*Setpoint_TIC1*), which defines the threshold for turning on the cooling.

- *Comparison operator*: Used to compare the current temperature with the calculated threshold. If the temperature is higher, it activates the signal to turn on the cooling.

- *RS flip-flop*: Used to store the state of whether cooling is on or off, based on the comparison results.

With this logic, the cooling system will respond to temperature changes according to the set values and hysteresis, ensuring effective temperature management. Here's how this control logic is structured (Figure 7-27).

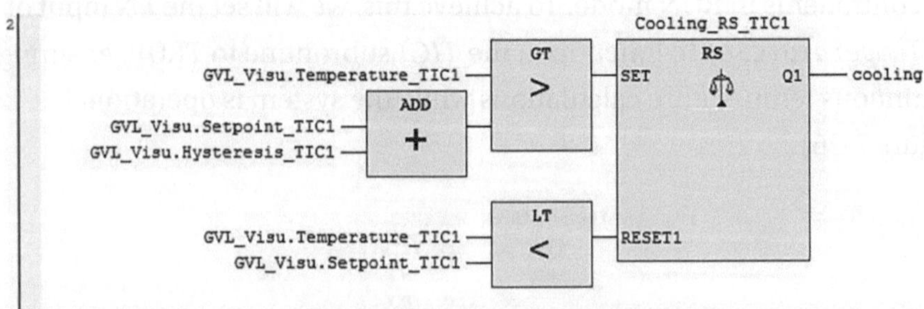

Figure 7-27. *Implementation of the cooling control logic*

To test the functionality of the program, download it to the controller and manipulate the analog input signal *AI_TIC1* using the *Watch* table. With a setpoint value of 25°C and a hysteresis of 1°C, cooling will be activated when the temperature exceeds 26°C and deactivated when the temperature drops below 25°C. For easier testing, note that an analog input value of 1557 corresponds to a temperature of 26.04°C, while an input value of 1535 corresponds to a temperature of 24.97°C.

The next step will be to implement heating in *Network 3*. In this case, if the temperature falls below the setpoint minus hysteresis (*Setpoint_TIC1 – Hysteresis_TIC1*), heating must be turned on. If the temperature rises above the setpoint (*Setpoint_TIC1*), heating should be turned off. Here is how the heating control logic is presented (Figure 7-28).

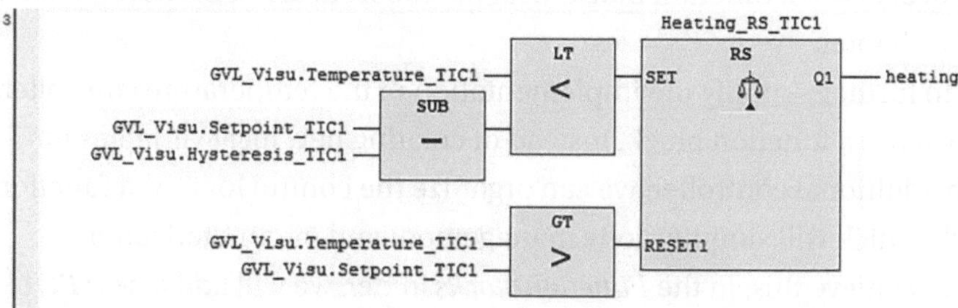

Figure 7-28. *Implementation of the heating control logic*

In the case where the setpoint is 25°C and the hysteresis is 1°C, heating will be activated when the temperature drops below 24°C. Heating will be deactivated when the temperature rises above 25°C. For easier testing, an analog input value of 1515 corresponds to a temperature of 23.99°C, while an input value of 1536 corresponds to a temperature of 25.02°C.

As seen, this control is simple but relatively imprecise, as the temperature will oscillate around the setpoint value. When the goal is to maintain the temperature within a range, such as between 18°C and 21°C, this type of controller is ideal. However, it is important to note that a smaller hysteresis leads to more frequent on-off cycles, which can be significant in terms of device wear and energy efficiency.

Function Block

In the previous steps, we implemented a temperature controller for *QCS-TIC1*. If we wanted to implement a similar solution for *QCS-TIC2*, we would need to define additional local variables and repeat many of the same steps. Instead, we can encapsulate the entire control logic in a single, efficient container, simplifying the implementation and management process. This is where a function block comes into play.

Although it might seem that a function could be used in this case, a function block is actually a better solution. It allows for a more organized and flexible implementation, with parameters that can be adjusted for different applications. In this part of the chapter, we will look at the practical use of a function block, with the theoretical details covered later in the chapter.

To further simplify the implementation of the temperature controller, we will use a function block. Instead of creating new local variables for each additional controller, we can organize the control logic as a function block, which will simplify code management and parameterization.

To achieve this, in the *FunctionBlocks* folder, we will add a new *POU* (Program Organization Unit) object named *TemperatureController*. Set its type to *Function Block*, and choose *Structured Text (ST)* as the programming language for the implementation (Figure 7-29).

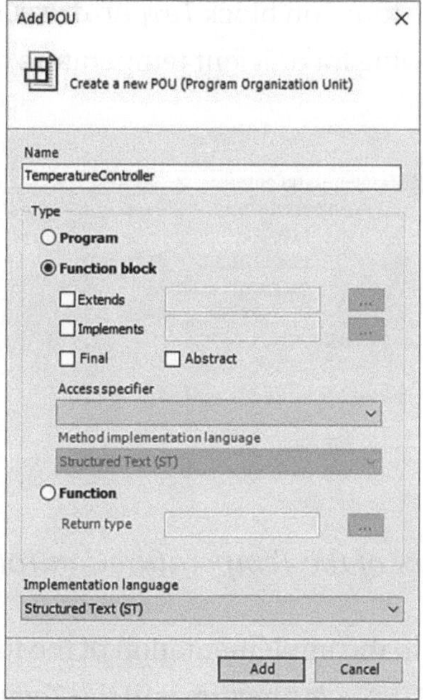

Figure 7-29. *Add POU window*

We start by implementing the function block by defining its interface, which includes the declaration of inputs and outputs. In our case, the function block *TemperatureController* will have three inputs and two outputs:

Inputs

- *TEMPERATURE*: The measured temperature value

- *SETPOINT*: The desired temperature value

- *HYSTERESIS*: The hysteresis value, which is the tolerance range around the setpoint value

Outputs

- *COOLING*: The control signal for activating cooling

- *HEATING*: The control signal for activating heating

The interface of the function block *TemperatureController* defines these parameters, allowing for efficient temperature control management (Figure 7-30).

```
TemperatureController  ×
 1     FUNCTION_BLOCK TemperatureController
 2     VAR_INPUT
 3         TEMPERATURE : REAL;
 4         SETPOINT : REAL;
 5         HYSTERESIS : REAL;
 6     END_VAR
 7     VAR_OUTPUT
 8         COOLING : BOOL;
 9         HEATING : BOOL;
10     END_VAR
11     VAR
12     END_VAR
```

Figure 7-30. *Interface of the TemperatureController function block*

Now let's proceed to the implementation of the function block itself. For both the *TemperatureScale* function and the *TemperatureController* function block, I have chosen to use the *Structured Text (ST)* programming language. Many readers might wonder if the implementation of custom function blocks and functions can only be done using this programming language. The answer is no, but *ST* is a very popular choice.

In this book, I aim to introduce new concepts and practices, so we are currently exploring the next programming language used in PLC controllers. Functions and function blocks can also be implemented in other languages, such as *Ladder Diagram (LAD)* or *Function Block Diagram (FBD)*. Typically, *ST* is used for more complex calculations, while graphical programming languages are often employed for implementing control logic. These practices are widely used, but the final decision on program structure is up to the programmer.

In this section, I would like to show how the same algorithm, which we implemented in *FBD*, can be written in *ST*. The implementation in Structured Text would look as follows (Figure 7-31).

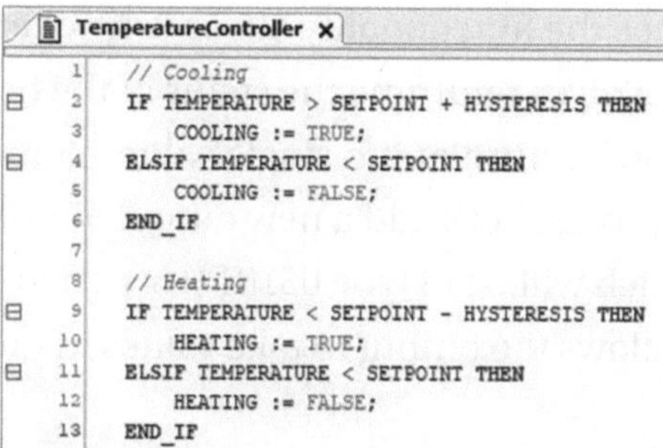

```
  1    // Cooling
  2    IF TEMPERATURE > SETPOINT + HYSTERESIS THEN
  3        COOLING := TRUE;
  4    ELSIF TEMPERATURE < SETPOINT THEN
  5        COOLING := FALSE;
  6    END_IF
  7
  8    // Heating
  9    IF TEMPERATURE < SETPOINT - HYSTERESIS THEN
 10        HEATING := TRUE;
 11    ELSIF TEMPERATURE < SETPOINT THEN
 12        HEATING := FALSE;
 13    END_IF
```

Figure 7-31. *Implementation of the TemperatureController function block*

Let's call our function block in the *TIC1* subroutine, similar to how we previously called the *TemperatureScale* functions. We will immediately notice a difference: with function blocks, we need to assign a specific instance name to the block, which was not necessary with functions.

Let's declare this function block as a local variable *TemperatureController_TIC1* in the *Temperatures* program and appropriately parameterize the inputs and outputs of the function block. In our case, we will assign the *COOLING* and *HEATING* outputs to specific digital outputs that control the heating and cooling systems (Figure 7-32). This means that the local variables *cooling, heating, Cooling_RS_TIC1,* and *Heating_RS_TIC1* will become redundant, as the entire control logic is encapsulated in the function block. Practically, this means that *Network 2* and *Network 3* in the *TIC1* subroutine can be completely removed.

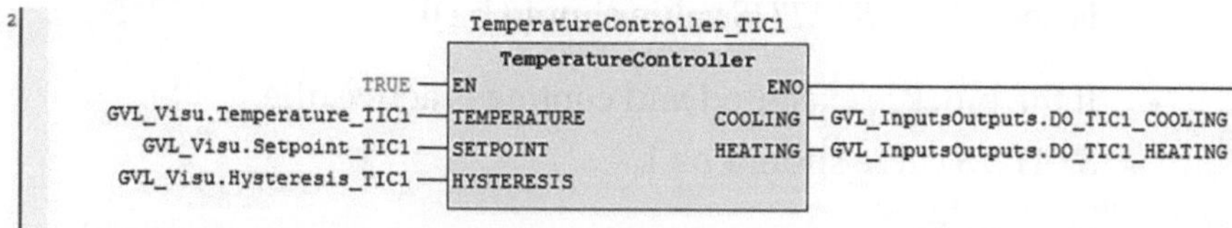

Figure 7-32. *Calling and parameterizing the TemperatureController_TIC1 function block*

We could enhance the functionality of our controller by adding a useful feature that involves returning the status of the function block. Unlike functions, which return only a single value, a function block can generate multiple outputs. Let's add a new output *STATUS* to the interface of our controller, which will be of type USINT (Unsigned Short Integer) (Figure 7-33). This allows the output to take values in the range from 0 to 255.

```
TemperatureController  ×
 1    FUNCTION_BLOCK TemperatureController
 2    VAR_INPUT
 3        EN : BOOL;
 4        TEMPERATURE : REAL;
 5        SETPOINT : REAL;
 6        HYSTERESIS : REAL;
 7    END_VAR
 8    VAR_OUTPUT
 9        ENO : BOOL;
10        COOLING : BOOL;
11        HEATING : BOOL;
12        STATUS : USINT;
13    END_VAR
14    VAR
15    END_VAR
```

Figure 7-33. *Interface of the TemperatureController function block*

We need to implement our function block so that the *STATUS* output reflects the state of the function block:

- If the block is not executed, the *STATUS* value should be set to 255.

- If the block is executed but neither cooling nor heating is active, the *STATUS* value should be 0.

- If the block is executed and cooling is active, the *STATUS* value should be 1.

- If the block is executed and heating is active, the *STATUS* value should be 2.

- To implement this logic, we also need to declare the *EN* (Enable) input and *ENO* (Enable Output) output in the interface of the function block. Here is how the interface of the function block should look, including the new *STATUS* output.

Below is the extended logic of the function block with the added STATUS output (Figure 7-34).

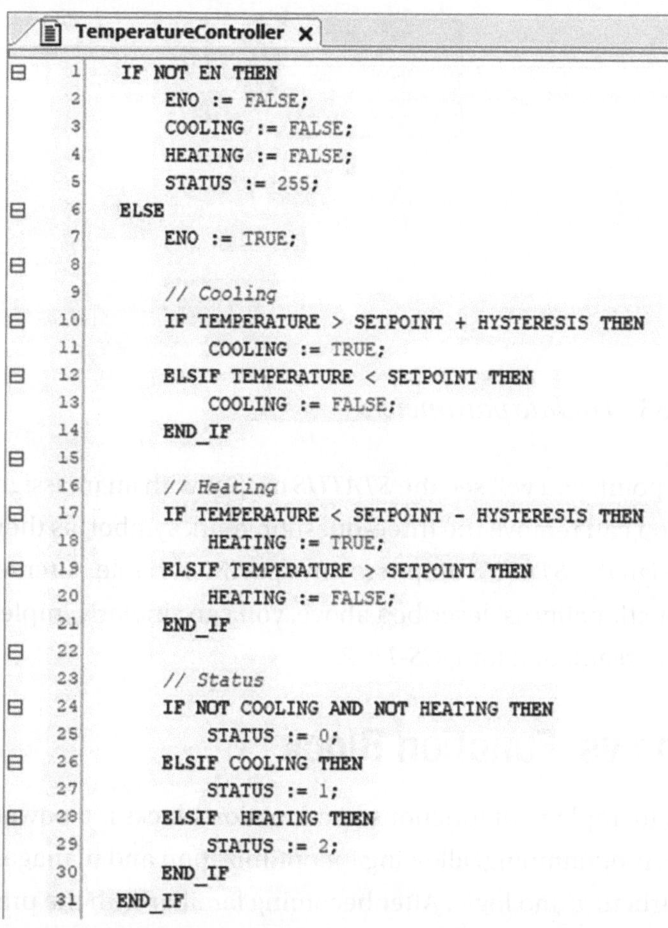

```
TemperatureController  ✕

 1    IF NOT EN THEN
 2        ENO := FALSE;
 3        COOLING := FALSE;
 4        HEATING := FALSE;
 5        STATUS := 255;
 6    ELSE
 7        ENO := TRUE;
 8
 9        // Cooling
10        IF TEMPERATURE > SETPOINT + HYSTERESIS THEN
11            COOLING := TRUE;
12        ELSIF TEMPERATURE < SETPOINT THEN
13            COOLING := FALSE;
14        END_IF
15
16        // Heating
17        IF TEMPERATURE < SETPOINT - HYSTERESIS THEN
18            HEATING := TRUE;
19        ELSIF TEMPERATURE > SETPOINT THEN
20            HEATING := FALSE;
21        END_IF
22
23        // Status
24        IF NOT COOLING AND NOT HEATING THEN
25            STATUS := 0;
26        ELSIF COOLING THEN
27            STATUS := 1;
28        ELSIF  HEATING THEN
29            STATUS := 2;
30        END_IF
31    END_IF
```

Figure 7-34. *Implementation of the TemperatureController function block*

It's time to test the new functionality of our controller. In the *TIC1* subprogram, you'll notice that despite modifying the function block interface, the CODESYS environment did not automatically update these changes. To fix this, we need to manually update the function block parameters. Right-click on the *TemperatureController* function block, and select the *Update Parameters* option from the context menu (Figure 7-35).

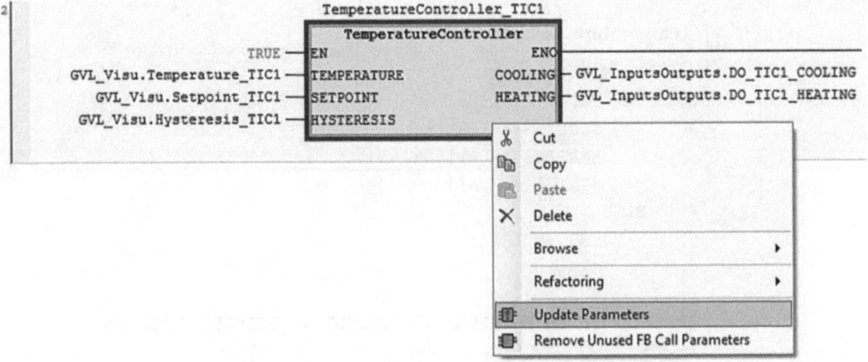

Figure 7-35. *Update parameters*

At this point, you will see the *STATUS* output with an unassigned variable. You can remove the three-question mark symbol, as there's no need to assign the *STATUS* output to any specific variable. After testing the new functionality as described above, you can similarly implement temperature regulation for *QCS-TIC2*.

Function vs. Function Block

The ability to implement functions and function blocks is a powerful tool in PLC programming, allowing for optimization and management of program structure and logic. After becoming familiar with the practical use of functions and function blocks, it is worth analyzing these two key elements (Table 7-2) theoretically to better understand their differences and applications.

Function

A function is a predefined block of code that performs a specific task and returns a single value. Functions are typically stateless, meaning they do not store data between calls.

Characteristics

- *No internal state*: Functions do not store data between calls. Each function call is independent of others.

- *Return value*: A function always returns one value, which can be used in further calculations.

- *No internal memory*: Functions lack internal memory, meaning they cannot store data between calls.

- *Static*: Functions are deterministic, meaning they always return the same value for the same inputs.

Function Block

A function block is a more complex piece of code that can maintain an internal state between calls. Function blocks have both inputs and outputs, as well as internal variables that store values.

Characteristics

- *State retention*: Function blocks can store data between calls. Each instance of a function block can have its own state.

- *Multiple outputs*: A function block can return more than one value through its outputs.

- *Internal memory*: Function blocks have internal variables that can store values and states between calls.

- *Dynamic behavior*: Function blocks can be more dynamic since their outputs can depend on the internal state, not just the inputs.

Table 7-2. *Key differences between function and function block*

Aspect	Function	Function Block
Internal State	Stateless, does not store data between calls	Stateful, can store data between calls
Return Value	Returns a single value	Can return multiple values through outputs
Memory Usage	No internal memory	Has internal memory to store variables and state
Determinism	Always returns the same results for the same inputs	Results may depend on internal state as well as inputs
Usage	Simple operations that do not require state retention	Complex operations that may require state retention between program cycles

Statelessness vs. Statefulness

- *Stateless function*: A stateless function does not store any data between calls. Each call is independent and relies solely on the provided inputs. Stateless functions are deterministic, meaning they always return the same results for the same inputs.

- *Stateful function block*: A stateful function block stores data between calls, allowing it to maintain an internal state and operational history. This means that a function block can behave differently depending on its state and inputs.

Understanding these differences is crucial because it affects how you design and implement logic in PLC systems. Functions are ideal for simple calculations and operations, while function blocks are better suited for complex tasks that require storing state and operational history.

If you're not entirely clear on the difference yet, don't worry. In the following sections of this book, we'll work through examples that will help clarify these concepts. For now, let's take a break from control logic implementation and move on to creating a visualization of our temperature control process.

Visualization

Let's start by expanding the menu to allow opening a new view named *Temperatures*. To do this, you'll need to add a new visualization object. Right-click the *Application* ➤ *Visualization* ➤ *Pages*. From the context menu, select *Add Object* ➤ *Visualization...* (Figure 7-36). This will allow you to create a new view that can be configured according to your needs.

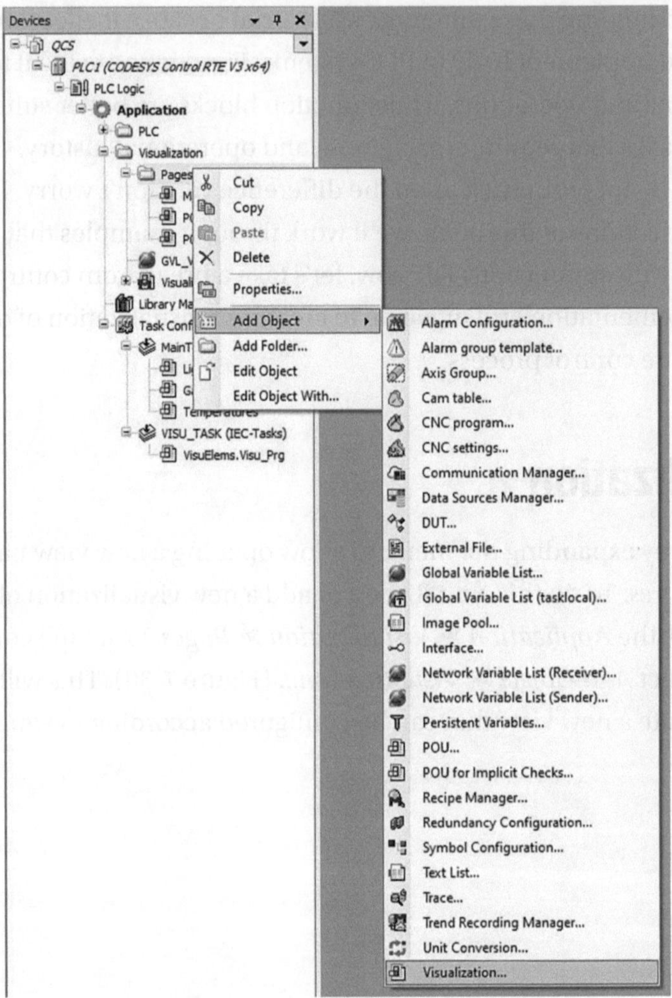

Figure 7-36. *Add Object ➤ Visualization...*

In the *Add Visualization* window, enter the name of the new view as P02_Temperatures, and then confirm by clicking the Add button (Figure 7-37).

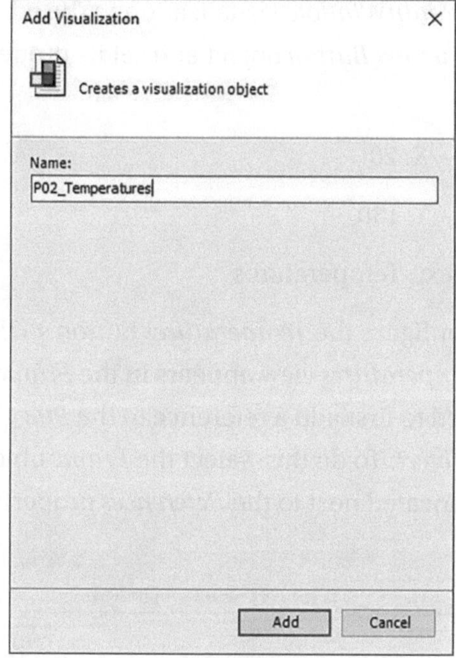

Figure 7-37. *Add Visualization window*

Next, in the newly created visualization, add a Label object and set its properties to the following values:

- Texts → Text: Temperatures

- Position → X: 0

- Position → Y: 5

- Position → Width: 1000

- Text properties → Font: Large Headline

Then, open the *MainWindow* visualization in the editor, which we created earlier. Add a new *Button* object and set its properties to the following values:

- Position → X: 20

- Position → Y: 130

- Texts → Text: Temperatures

Our goal is to configure the *Temperatures* button so that when it is clicked, the *P02_Temperatures* view appears in the *Frame* object. To achieve this, we need to first add a reference to the *P02_Temperatures* view in the *Frame object*. To do this, select the *Frame* object, and click the *Configure...* button located next to the *References* property (Figure 7-38).

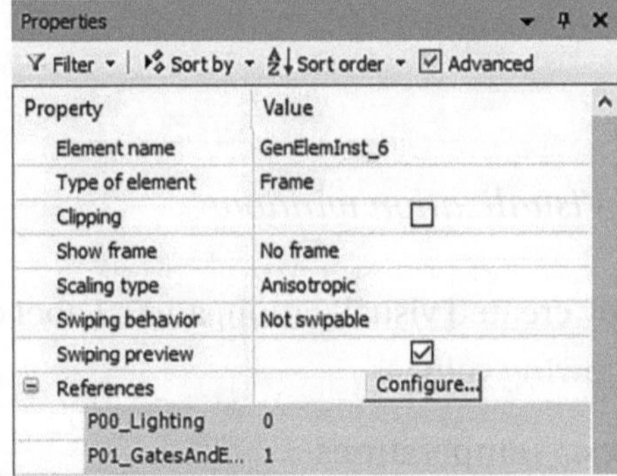

Figure 7-38. *Properties window: References* ➤ *Configure*

This will open the familiar *Frame Configuration* window. In the *Available Visualization* section on the left, select the *P02_Temperatures* view. Then, in the *Selected Visualizations* section on the right, click the *Add* button. This action adds the new *P02_Temperatures* view to the Frame object, automatically assigning it index 2. Confirm your selection by clicking the *OK* button in the lower right corner (Figure 7-39).

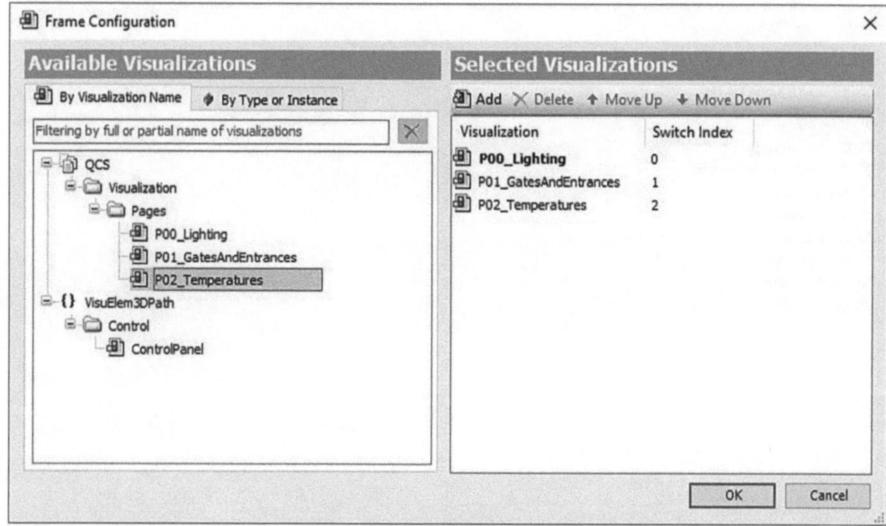

Figure 7-39. *Frame Configuration window*

When the new view is added to the *Frame* object, we can configure the *OnMouseClick* event for the *Temperatures* button. To do this, go to the Properties window of the button, and click the *Configure...* button next to the Input configuration ➤ OnMouseClick option. This will open the Input Configuration window, where you can set the appropriate action for this event (Figure 7-40).

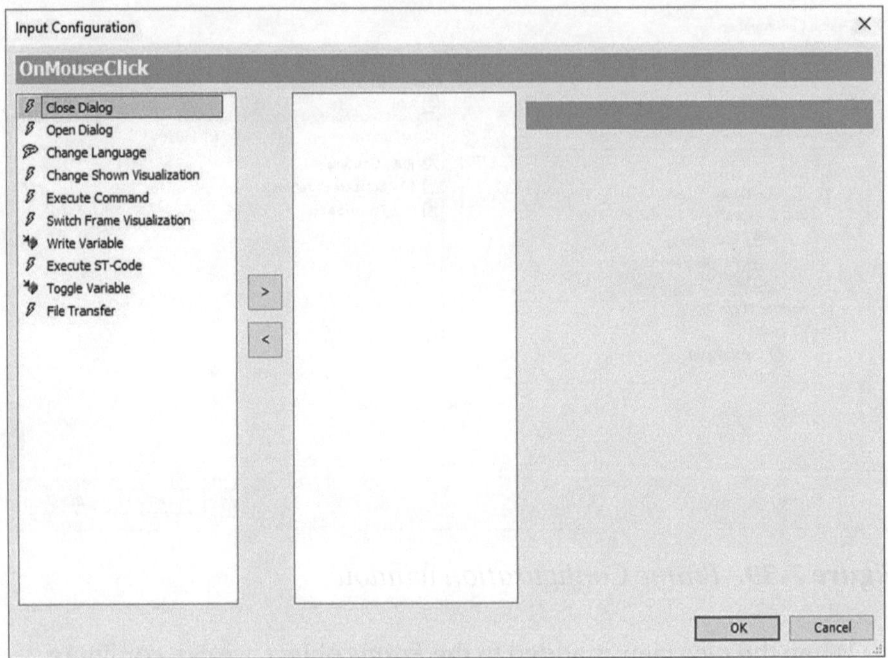

Figure 7-40. *Input Configuration window*

Next, using the previously learned methods, configure the
OnMouseClick event so that when the button is clicked, it changes the
content of the *Frame* object to the *P02_Temperatures* view. After making
these settings, confirm your choice by clicking the *OK* button in the bottom
right corner (Figure 7-41).

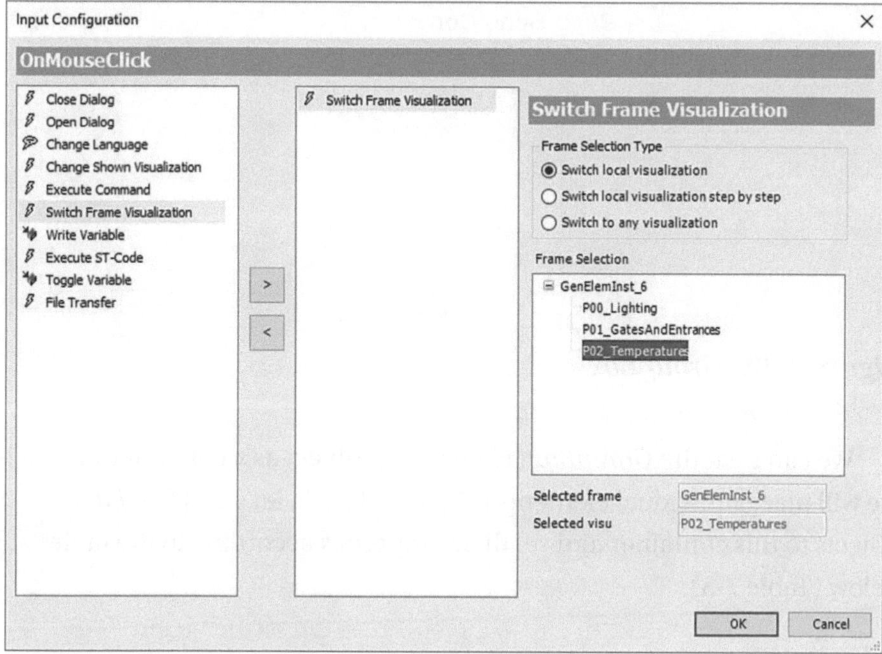

Figure 7-41. *Input Configuration window*

Let's download our program to the controller and test the functionality of switching between visualization views. We are now ready to display the temperature controllers *QCS-TIC1* and *QCS-TIC2* on the *P02_Temperatures* view.

Add an object named GroupBox from the Common Controls tab to the P02_Temperatures visualization, and set its properties as follows:

- Position → X: 50

- Position → Y: 50

- Position → Width: 410

- Position → Height: 340

- Texts → Text: Bang-Bang Controller TIC1

- Text properties → Font: Large Headline

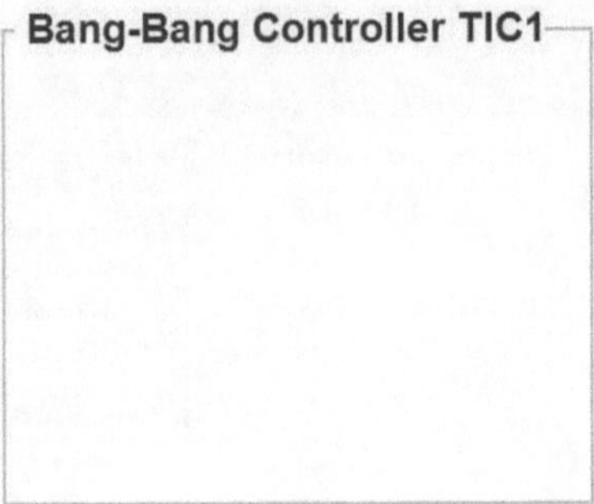

Figure 7-42. *GroupBox*

We can treat the *GroupBox* (Figure 7-42) object as a container in which
we will place individual elements (Figure 7-43). So let's add five *Label*
objects to this container and set their properties according to the table
below (Table 7-3).

Table 7-3. *Properties of Label controls*

Properties	1st Label	2nd Label	3rd Label	4th Label	5th Label
Texts → Text	Temperature	Setpoint	Hysteresis	Cooling	Heating
Position → X	10	10	10	30	200
Position → Y	40	80	120	285	285
Position → Width	150	150	150	100	100
Text properties → Font	Headline	Headline	Headline	Headline	Headline

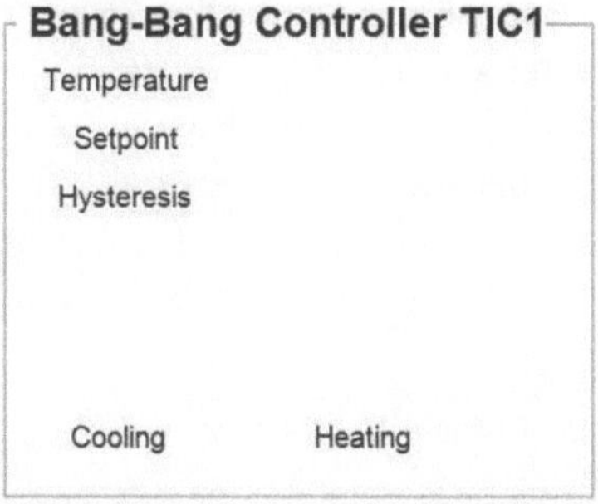

Bang-Bang Controller TIC1

Temperature

Setpoint

Hysteresis

Cooling   Heating

Figure 7-43. *GroupBox with Labels*

Next, let's add three *Text Field* elements to the *GroupBox* container, which can be found under the *Common Controls* tab (Figure 7-44). Configure their properties according to the table below (Table 7-4).

Table 7-4. *Properties of Text Field controls*

Properties	1st Text Field	2nd Text Field	3rd Text Field
Position → X	220	220	220
Position → Y	40	80	120
Texts → Text	%3.1f °C	%2.1f °C	%2.1f °C
Text properties → Font	Headline	Headline	Headline
Text variables → Text variable	GVL_Visu. Temperature_TIC1	GVL_Visu.Setpoint_ TIC1	GVL_Visu. Hysteresis_ TIC1

Figure 7-44. *GroupBox with Text Fields*

In the *Texts → Text* property, we added variable formatting, which is assigned to the *Text Field* in the *Text variables → Text variable* section. In the first *Text Field* element, we see the value "%3.1f °C." Here's what each element means:

- %: Introduces formatting

- *3.1*: Specifies the number of digits before and after the decimal point

- *f*: Indicates a floating-point number format

- *°C*: Adds the unit after the numerical value

The first *Text Field* will display the measured temperature *QCS-TIC1*. Since the analog module can measure temperatures ranging from -50°C to 150°C, we need to be able to display up to three digits before the decimal point. The other two *Text Fields* will be input by the operator, and in this case, two digits before the decimal point will suffice, as these values will also be set with limits. The setpoint ranges from 15°C to 30°C, and the hysteresis ranges from 0°C to 10°C.

To allow the operator to enter data from the visualization, we need to adjust the *OnMouseClick* event for the Setpoint and Hysteresis *Text Fields*. First, select the *Text Field* to which we assigned the variable `GVL_Visu.Setpoint_TIC1`, and click the *Configure...* button for the

Input configuration ➤ *OnMouseClick* event. A familiar *Input Configuration* window will appear. Configure the *OnMouseClick* event as described earlier. Confirm your selection by clicking the *OK* button located at the bottom right corner (Figure 7-45).

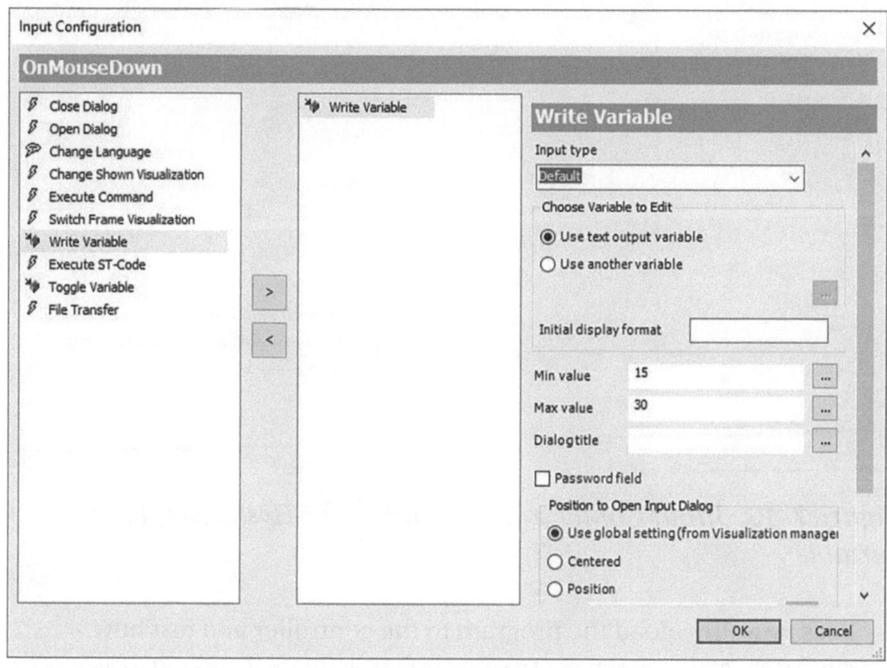

Figure 7-45. *Input Configuration window for Setpoint_TIC1 variable*

Configure the *Text Field* element to which the variable `GVL_Visu.Hysteresis_TIC1` is assigned in the exact same way. Here is the correct configuration (Figure 7-46).

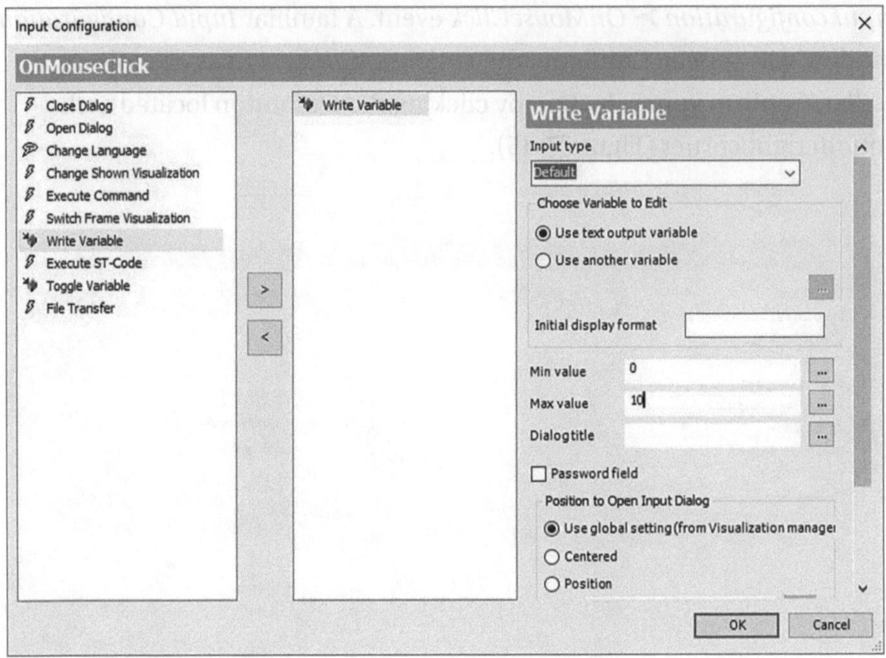

Figure 7-46. *Input Configuration window for Hysteresis_TIC1 variable*

Let's now download the program to the controller and test how the *GVL_Visu.Temperature_TIC1* variable is displayed, as well as the modifications of the *GVL_Visu.Setpoint_TIC1* and *GVL_Visu.Hysteresis_TIC1* variables. Additionally, we can monitor the values of these variables in the controller using the *Watch* table and compare them with the values displayed in the visualization (Figure 7-47).

Figure 7-47. *Visualization of the TIC1 controller and the Watch table*

Next, let's add two *Lamp* elements to the *GroupBox* container
(Figure 7-48), which we'll use to visualize the cooling and heating status.
Set the properties of each element according to the table below (Table 7-5).

Table 7-5. *Properties of Lamp controls*

Properties	1st Lamp	2nd Lamp
Position → X	140	310
Position → Y	280	280
Position → Width	40	40
Position → Height	40	40
Variable	GVL_InputsOutputs. DO_TIC1_COOLING	GVL_InputsOutputs. DO_TIC1_HEATING
Background → Image	Green	Green

Figure 7-48. *GroupBox with Lamps*

The final step will be placing a switch in the *GroupBox* container, which the operator can use to turn the temperature controller on and off. Let's add a *Rocker Switch* element to the *GroupBox*, which can be found in the *Lamps/Switches/Bitmaps* section (Figure 7-49). Then, set its properties according to the following list:

- Position → X: 180

- Position → Y: 180

- Variable: GVL_Visu.Enable_Controller_TIC1

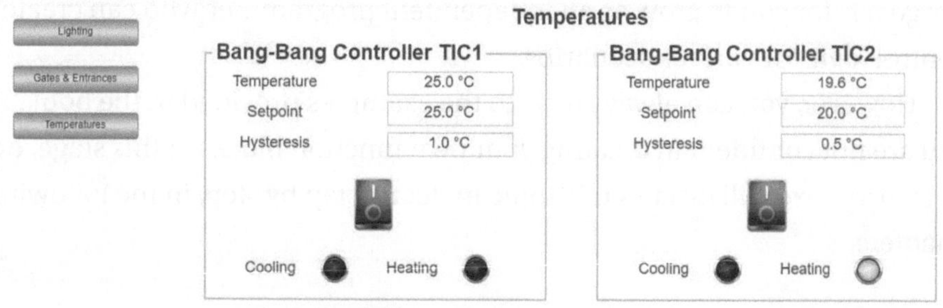

Figure 7-49. *GroupBox with Rocker Switch*

It is worth noting that the variable *GVL_Visu.Enable_Controller_TIC1* must be assigned to the *EN* input of the *TemperatureController_TIC1* function block, which will allow the activation and deactivation of the QCS-TIC1 temperature controller.

Next, download our program to the controller and test the controller's operation from the visualization. In the *Watch* table, manipulate the analog input *AI_TIC1* and observe the controller's behavior.

To visualize the QCS-TIC2 temperature controller, simply copy the entire *GroupBox*, which will give us the complete controller layout. This approach significantly simplifies and speeds up the work, as we only need to adjust the header of the *GroupBox* element and the variables attached to the individual elements. The visualization of *Temperatures* should look like this (Figure 7-50).

Figure 7-50. *Visualization of the Temperatures*

Additional Task

In this chapter, we have explored functions and function blocks. With the knowledge gained, we can now move on to modifying the program for controlling gates and entrances in a building. The goal of this task is to implement a function block for controlling gates and entrances.

Task Execution

1. *Define the function block interface*: Specify the inputs and outputs of the function block that will manage the control of gates and entrances.

2. *Reorganize existing code*: Move the current control logic into the function block to achieve better code organization.

3. *Call the function block*: Configure the function block call with the appropriate input and output parameters.

I encourage you to attempt this exercise on your own. Although a solution will be available in the GitHub repository, trying to solve it yourself will help reinforce your knowledge and develop your skills.

Remember, there are many ways to achieve the desired result. Just because I have presented one solution does not mean it is the only or the correct approach. I do not have a monopoly on writing PLC programs. My goal is for you to grow as an independent programmer who can create control logic for various scenarios.

However, you can always refer to the examples provided in the book. If you are not confident in creating your own function blocks at this stage, do not worry – we will discuss this topic in detail, step by step, in the following chapters.

Summary

In this chapter, we also learned about a very simple yet effective two-state controller, commonly known as a Bang-Bang controller. We used it to regulate temperature by controlling the cooling and heating of the quality control area. As a result, the building is automated, and soon all components responsible for automating the quality control process will be delivered.

We discovered the fundamental differences between functions and function blocks in the context of PLC programming. We understood how functions enable the execution of simple, stateless operations, while function blocks offer advanced capabilities by maintaining internal state and handling multiple outputs.

We practically applied the knowledge gained by implementing and configuring function blocks in the control system and creating visualizations that allow for effective monitoring and management of processes. Specifically, we focused on creating and customizing temperature controller visualizations, demonstrating how to integrate various program elements into a cohesive whole.

The additional task presented at the end of the chapter is an excellent opportunity for self-practice and reinforcement of knowledge. Remember that PLC programming is an art that requires both theoretical understanding and practical skills. I encourage you to experiment and tailor solutions to your needs. In the following chapters, we will continue our learning journey, developing programming skills and refining control techniques.

Trends and Alarms

In this chapter, we will focus on the key tools used for analyzing and monitoring control systems: trends and alarms. Trends allow for the visualization and analysis of real-time and long-term data, which is essential for assessing and optimizing system performance. Alarms, on the other hand, are a crucial component of any installation, enabling a quick response to irregularities and potential issues.

We will discuss how to configure and manage these features to effectively monitor and diagnose the control system.

Installation and Update of the Simulator Library

In the previous chapter, we ran the temperature controller by manually changing the value of the analog input, which was then converted to temperature. However, this method is quite cumbersome, as each value change requires manual intervention. To streamline our work, we will use the new version of the simulator library, which includes a function block called *Temperature*, automating the temperature simulation.

Following the method we learned in earlier chapters, we will install the new version of the *Simulator* library, available in the *Chapter_08* folder in the GitHub repository. After installing the library, remember to use version 3.0 in the project, as CODESYS does not automatically update this.

© Dariusz Wrebiak 2026

D. Wrebiak, *Practical PLC Programming for Beginners*, Maker Innovations Series,
https://doi.org/10.1007/979-8-8688-2430-2_8

There is also another way to update the library in the project without restarting the CODESYS environment, which I haven't mentioned before. After installing the library in the *Library Repository*, go to *Library Manager* and select the *Simulator* library version 2.0 (Figure 8-1).

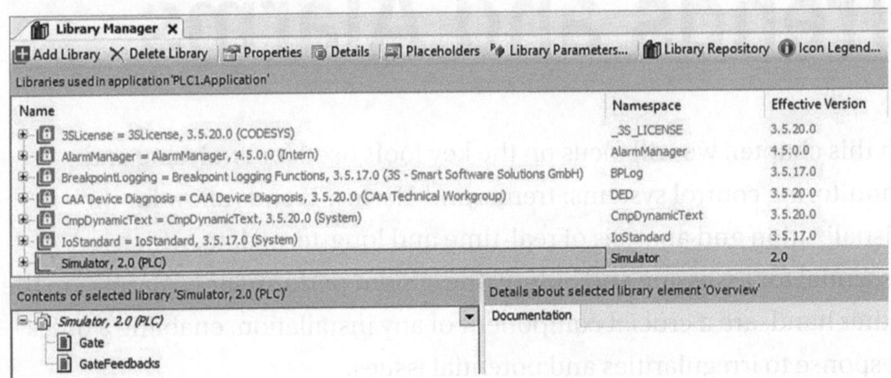

Figure 8-1. *Library Manager with version 2.0 of the Simulator library*

As we know, version 2.0 of the Simulator library contains two function blocks: *Gate* and *GateFeedbacks*. To update the library to version 3.0, we select the library and then click the *Properties* tab in the *Library Manager*. In the *Properties* window, we can manage the version of the library used in the project by selecting the appropriate version in the *Specific version* field. In our case, we are updating from version 2.0 to 3.0. It's worth noting that the same method can also be used to downgrade to earlier versions of the library. We confirm the selection by clicking *OK* (Figure 8-2).

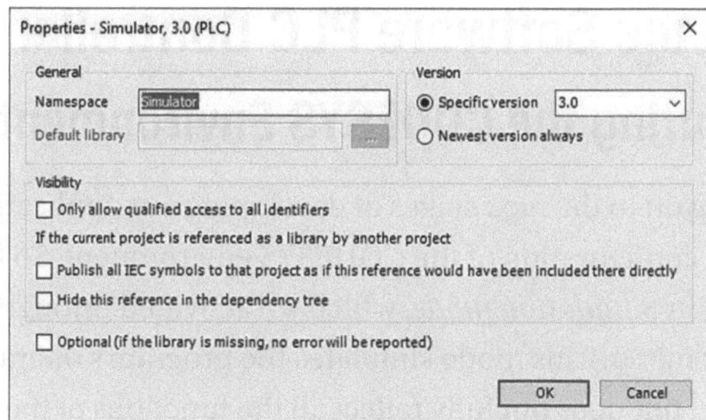

Figure 8-2. *The Properties window for managing the library*

After successfully updating the *Simulator* library to version 3.0, we can see a new function block called *Temperatures,* which will simulate the temperature in our project (Figure 8-3).

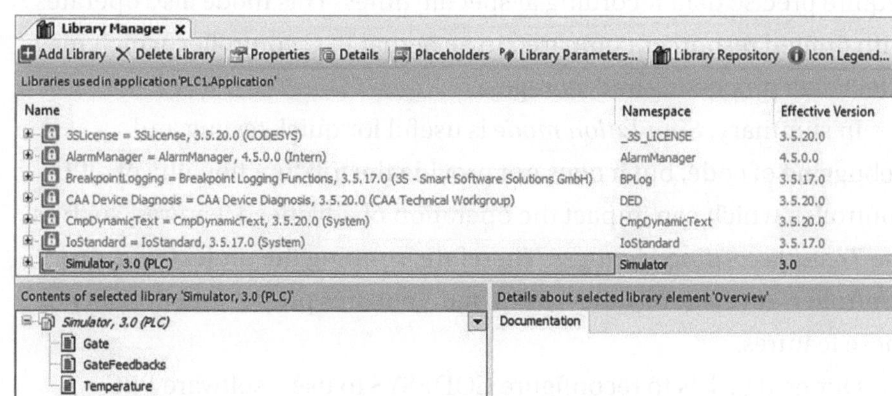

Figure 8-3. *Library Manager with version 3.0 of the Simulator library*

Starting the Software PLC Controller
Reconfiguring the CODESYS Environment

Before moving on to the next stages of developing our application, we need to change the configuration of the CODESYS environment. So far, we have been working in *Simulation mode*, which we activated through the *Online ➤ Simulation* menu. This mode simulates the program's operation at the PLC logic level but does not fully reflect all the functions of the controller. It is mainly used for testing and debugging program logic, without providing full emulation of the controller's operation, including advanced functions.

In *Simulation mode*, CODESYS does not have access to the real system clock of the PLC, which can lead to problems with accurately reading the date and time. This is crucial for features such as trend logging, which require precise data recording at specific times. This mode also operates with limited resources compared to an actual PLC controller, which may affect data processing and storage.

In summary, *Simulation mode* is useful for quick testing and debugging of code, but it does not provide the full functionality of a PLC controller, which can impact the operation of advanced features, such as the *Trend Recording Manager*. Therefore, running the project on a real controller – even a software-based one – ensures proper functionality of these features.

Our next task is to reconfigure CODESYS to use a software PLC controller running on our computer, instead of *Simulation mode*. The software PLC controller, known as *CODESYS Control Win SL*, was installed along with CODESYS, but its full functionality requires a license. However, we will use the *CODESYS Control Win V3* version, which works without a license but with some limitations. This is a demo version that operates for a limited time (usually two hours), after which the controller automatically stops. It can be restarted after the time expires.

First, we will deactivate *Simulation mode* by unchecking the option in the *Online* ➤ *Simulation* menu (Figure 8-4).

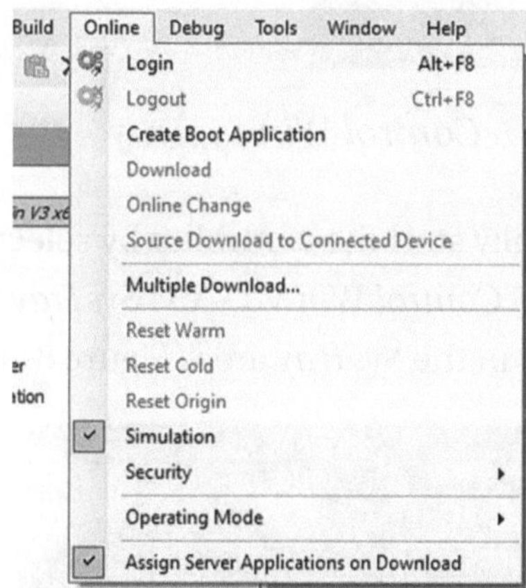

Figure 8-4. *Online* ➤ *Simulation*

If *Simulation mode* is active, a red field with the label *SIMULATION* will be visible in the lower right corner of CODESYS (Figure 8-5). If *Simulation mode* is not active, a red field with the label *SIMULATION* will be not visible in the lower right corner of CODESYS (Figure 8-6).

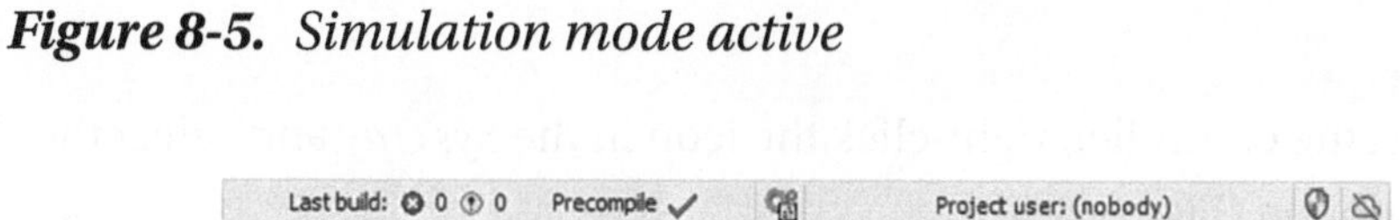

Figure 8-5. *Simulation mode active*

Figure 8-6. *Simulation mode inactive*

Before we can connect CODESYS to the software PLC controller, we need to start it. If the installation was done with the default settings, the controller icon should be located in the *SysTray* area (Figure 8-7).

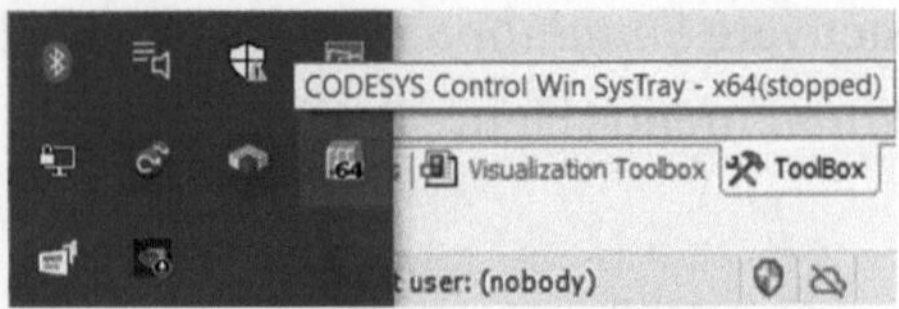

Figure 8-7. *CODESYS Control Win SysTray*

We can also manually start the controller by selecting *Start* ➤
CODESYS ➤ *CODESYS Control Win V3 – x64 SysTray* from the Start menu
if we don't see the icon in the *SysTray* area (Figure 8-8).

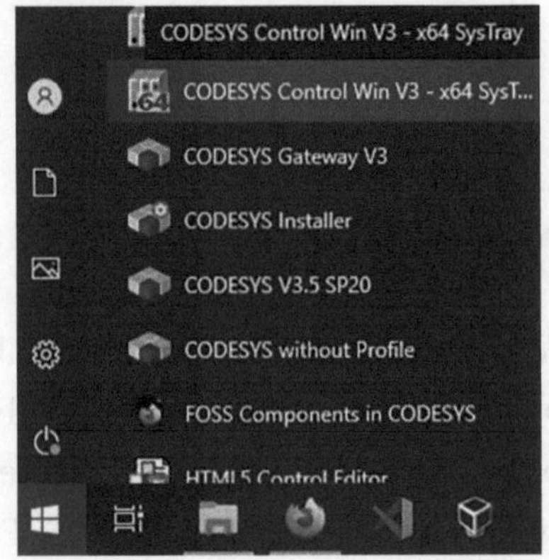

Figure 8-8. *Start* ➤ *CODESYS* ➤ *CODESYS Control Win V3 – x64
SysTray*

To start the controller, right-click the icon in the *SysTray* and select the
Start PLC option (Figure 8-9).

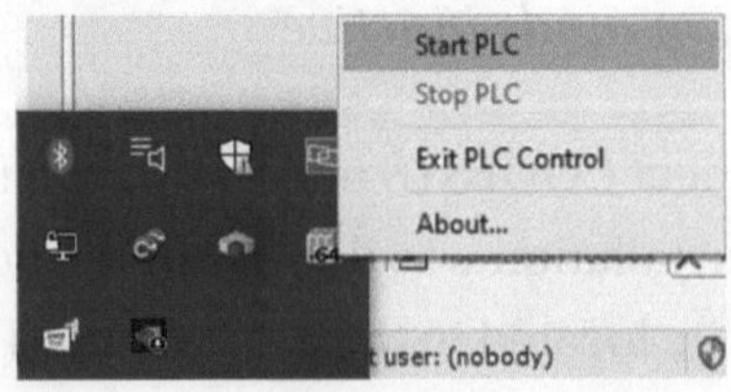

Figure 8-9. *Start software PLC controller*

During the startup of the controller, we will be informed that *CODESYS Control PLC* allows the execution of program code with system-level access on our computer. We confirm by clicking *OK* (Figure 8-10).

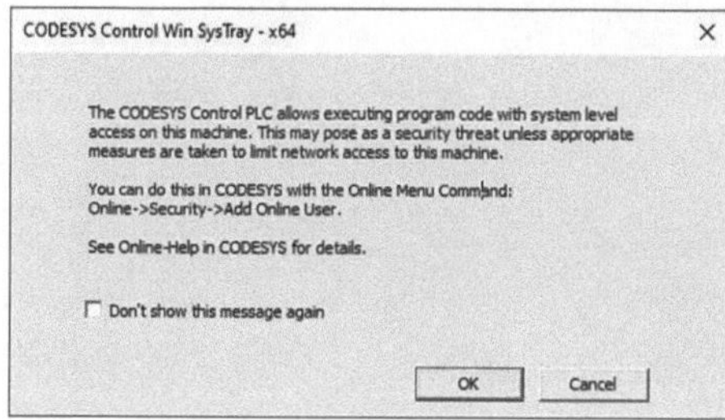

Figure 8-10. *CODESYS Control Win SysTray – x64 window*

Now we can connect the CODESYS environment to the locally running software PLC controller. In the *Devices* window, double-click the device *PLC1 (CODESYS Control Win V3 x64)* (Figure 8-11).

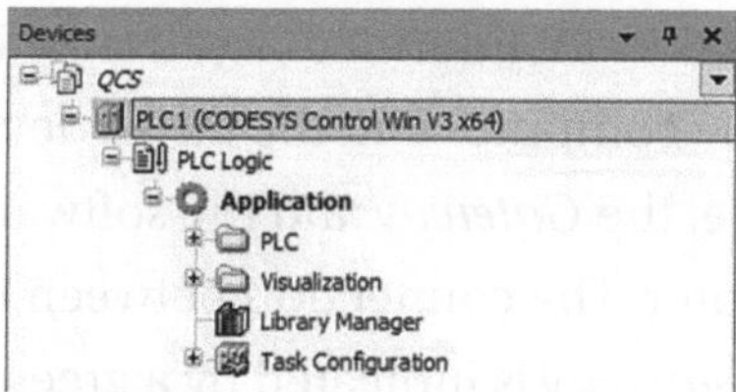

Figure 8-11. *Devices window*

In the newly opened window, we will see the network topology consisting of our computer and the PLC controller, with a *Gateway* in between (Figure 8-12).

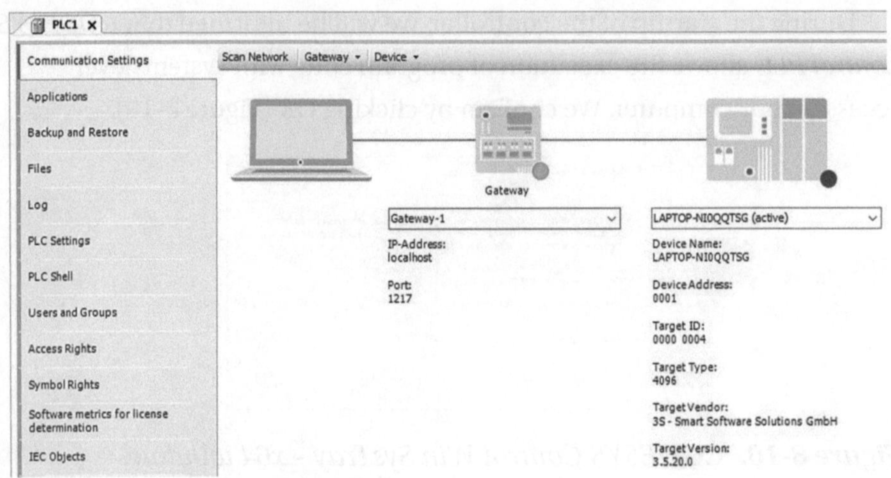

Figure 8-12. *PLC1 window*

The *Gateway* in CODESYS is a key component that enables communication between the CODESYS environment and devices such as PLC controllers. It acts as an intermediary, transmitting data and commands between the computer and the target devices where programs are running. In our case, the *Gateway* and the software PLC controller are on the same computer. The connection between the CODESYS environment and the *Gateway* is indicated by a green symbol, meaning it is established. The next step is to establish a connection between the *Gateway* and the PLC controller. To do this, click the *Scan Network* button to search the network and find available PLC controllers (Figure 8-13).

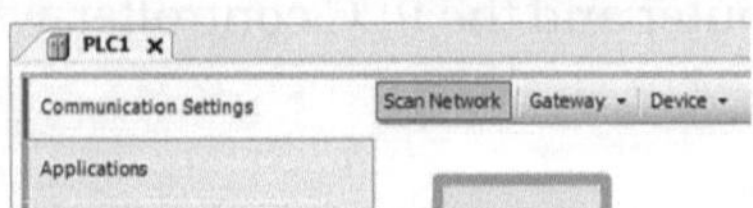

Figure 8-13. *Scan Network*

It is possible that the PLC controller may not be found during the initial network scan (Figure 8-14).

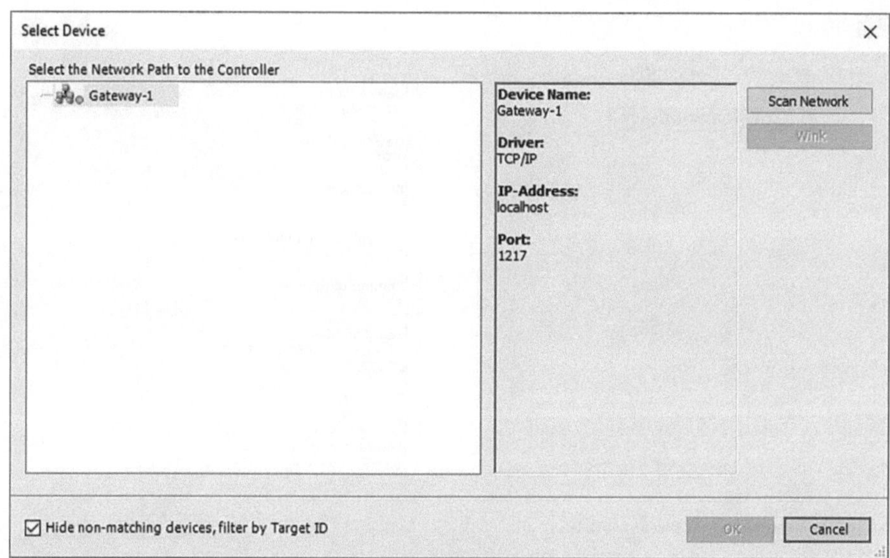

Figure 8-14. *Select Device window without PLC*

If the PLC controller is not found, in the *Select Device* window, uncheck
the *Hide non-matching devices, filter by Target ID* options, then click *Scan
Network* again. The name of the found PLC controller will match the
hostname of our computer, as the software PLC controller operates locally.
Select the found PLC controller and click *OK* (Figure 8-15).

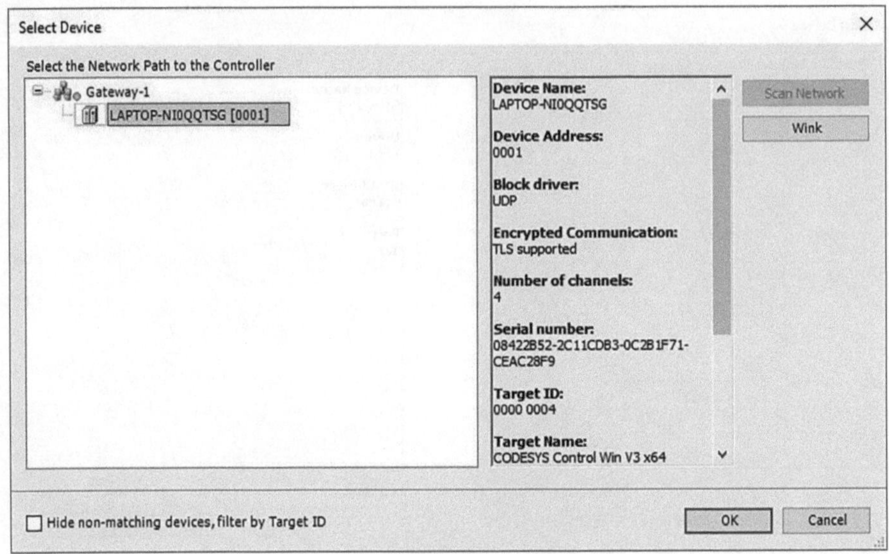

Figure 8-15. *Select Device window with PLC*

After establishing a successful connection, in the *PLC1* window, we will see a green symbol next to the PLC controller, indicating that the connection has been established (Figure 8-16).

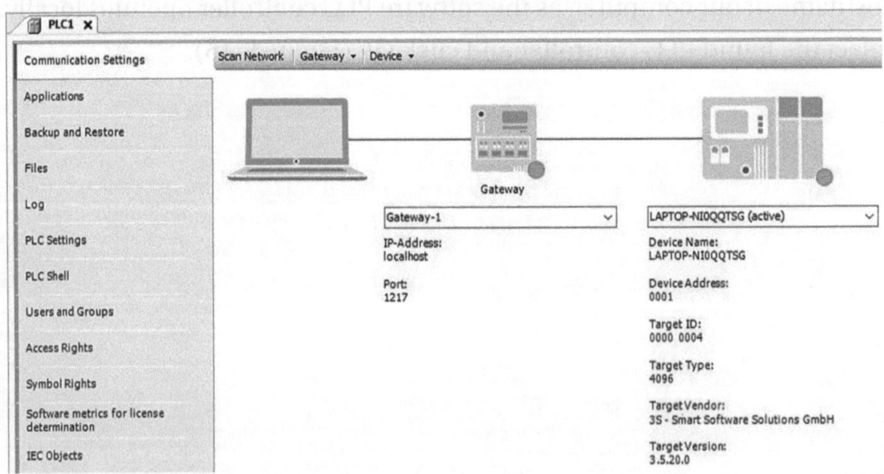

Figure 8-16. *PLC1 window*

Now, using the *Online* ➤ *Login* command, we download our project to the PLC controller. This entire process was necessary to access the real-time clock, which is essential for the proper implementation of trends and alarms that we will discuss later in the chapter.

To summarize briefly, the differences between *Simulation mode* and the *software PLC controller* running on our local computer are as follows (Table 8-1).

Table 8-1. *Differences between Simulation mode and the software PLC controller*

Aspect	Simulation Mode	Software PLC Controller
Application	Used for quick testing and debugging of program logic in CODESYS without connecting a real PLC.	Full simulation of PLC controller operation on the computer with complete support for system functions.
Functionality	Limited, lacks support for full system functions.	Full, accurately replicates the operation of a real PLC controller.
Limitations	No emulation of system clock, issues with advanced functions.	Requires a license for continuous operation; demo version has a time limit (usually two hours).

Starting the Temperature Simulator in the PLC Project

Since our software PLC is already in RUN mode and we have connected to it, we can add the function block responsible for temperature simulation to the project. In the program, navigate to *PLC* ➤ *ControlLogic* ➤ *Temperatures*, and add two new local variables that will serve as instances of the function block *Simulator.Temperature* for temperatures *QCS-TIC1* and *QCS-TIC2* (Figure 8-17).

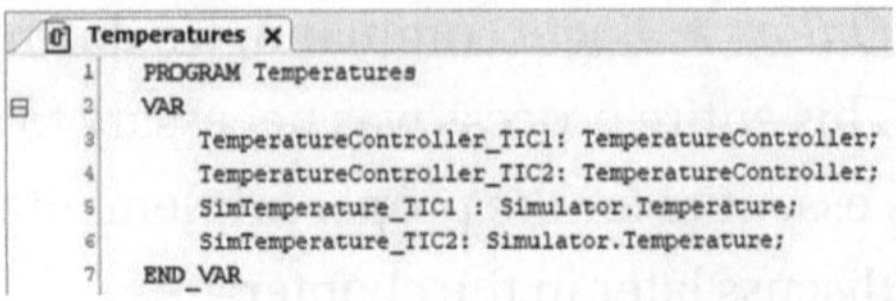

Figure 8-17. *Local variables of the Temperatures program*

In the *TIC1* subprogram, add *Network 3*, where we will call the function block *Simulator.Temperature*, assigning it the instance *SimTemperature_TIC1* (Figure 8-18).

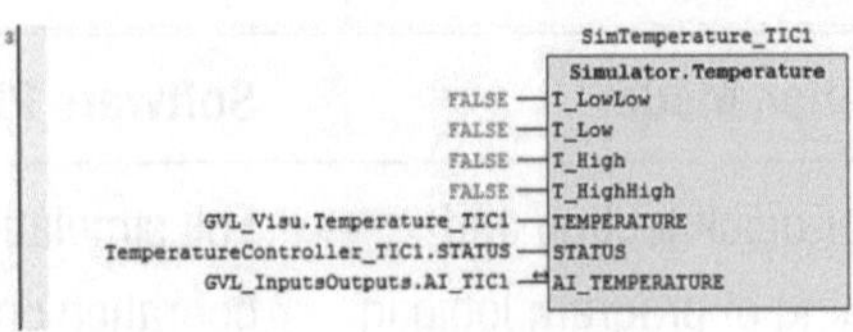

Figure 8-18. *Action TIC1 ➤ Network 3*

At this stage, we do not focus on the input functions *T_LowLow*, *T_Low*, *T_High*, and *T_HighHigh*, as their roles will be discussed later in the chapter. For now, simply set their values to *FALSE*. We assign the input *TEMPERATURE* to the currently measured temperature *QCS-TIC1*, which is obtained after scaling the analog input in *Network 1*. Based on this value, the *Simulator.Temperature* function block receives information about the current temperature. Additionally, we assign the input *STATUS* to the state of the temperature controller, which is set by the *TemperatureController* block in *Network 2*.

The simulator function block uses this information to manipulate the analog input *AI_TIC1*. This means we no longer need to manually input values into the *Watch* table – the simulator algorithm will handle that. The algorithm works as follows:

- If the controller is off, the temperature remains unchanged.

- If cooling is active, the temperature decreases.

- If heating is active, the temperature increases.

After downloading the program to the controller, set the setpoint and hysteresis values to 20°C and 2°C, respectively, turn on the controller, and observe temperature changes based on the cooling and heating states (Figure 8-19).

Figure 8-19. *Temperature controller*

With the environment running, we are ready to proceed to the next topic: Trends.

Trends

What They Are and How They Are Used

At the moment, we can continuously monitor temperature measurements on the *Temperatures* visualization mask. However, in real control systems, it is impractical to expect an operator to constantly monitor the visualization screen and track the behavior of the controlled process. The role of the operator is to supervise the control system, while the automation provided by the PLC controller reduces this workload, allowing the operator to focus on other, more productive tasks.

In the event of a system failure, it is crucial to be able to trace historical values of various parameters, such as temperatures or the states of actuators controlled by the PLC. In such cases, trends play an invaluable role, serving as a key diagnostic, analytical, and optimization tool.

Trends in control systems are tools used for monitoring, recording, and visualizing process variable values over time. They are an essential component of supervision and analysis in visualization systems, allowing engineers, operators, and analysts to gain insights into the production process, identify issues, optimize processes, and make maintenance decisions. Trends collect and record data from various measurement points, such as sensors or process variables. For example, monitoring temperature allows data to be displayed as line charts, showing changes in variable values over time. This enables operators to observe how temperature has varied over the past 24 hours.

Historical data recording enables long-term analysis, which is useful for assessing process performance, diagnosing failures, and predicting issues. Historical analysis may reveal that certain variable values regularly exceed safe limits, leading to preventive actions. Trends also support predictive models and algorithms that forecast future system behavior, aiding in the optimization of settings and operational activities. Based on historical data, the system can predict the need for a service visit to replace a control system component.

Trends   In control systems are tools for monitoring and visualizing changes in process variable values over time, enabling analysis, process optimization, and early detection of anomalies.

Trend Recording Manager

Let's now configure the temperature trend visualization for *QCS-TIC1*. Start by adding a new view named *P03_Trends* to the project, and save it under *Application* ➤ *Visualization* ➤ *Pages*. In the *P03_Trends* view, add a single *Label* element and set its properties as follows:

- *Texts* → *Text*: Trends

- *Position* → *X*: 0

- *Position* → *Y*: 5

- *Position* → *Width*: 1000

- *Text properties* → *Font*: Large Headline

Next, enhance the *MainWindow* view by adding a button named *Trends* that links to the *P03_Trends* view. After completing these steps, the visualization should appear as shown below (Figure 8-20).

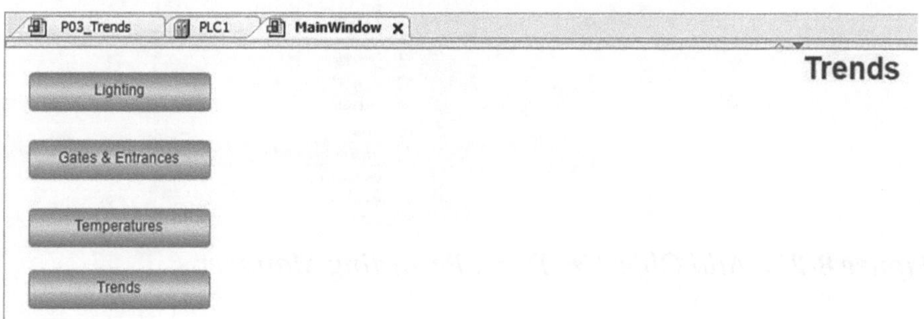

Figure 8-20. *MainWindow* ➤ *Trends*

In the next step, let's add a new object *Trend Recording Manager* to the project and save it under the folder *Application* ➤ *Visualization* (Figure 8-21).

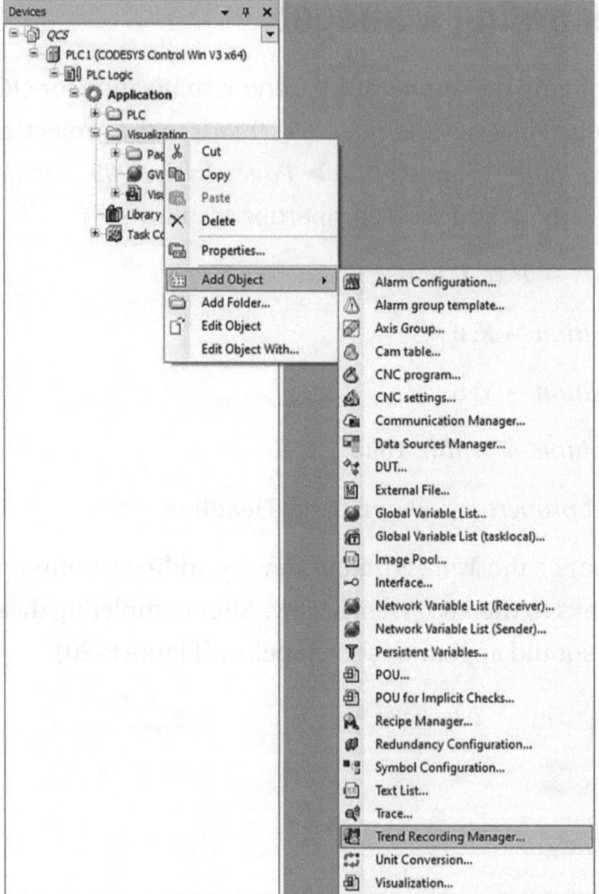

Figure 8-21. *Add Object ➤ Trend Recording Manager*

In the *Add Trend Recording Manager* window, we can assign a unique name to our Manager, but for this case, we will keep the default name (Figure 8-22).

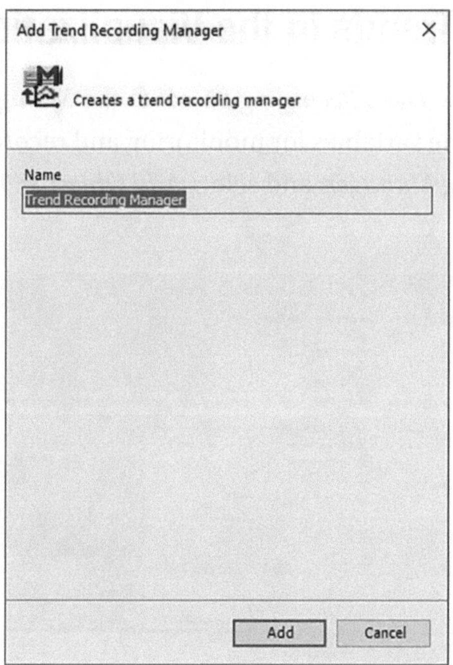

Figure 8-22. *Add Trend Recording Manager window*

Note that in addition to adding the *Trend Recording Manager* to the
project, a task named *TrendRecordingTask* has been automatically created
in the *Task Configuration*. This task handles the cyclic invocation of the
Trend Recording Manager. This is how the structure of our project should
look (Figure 8-23).

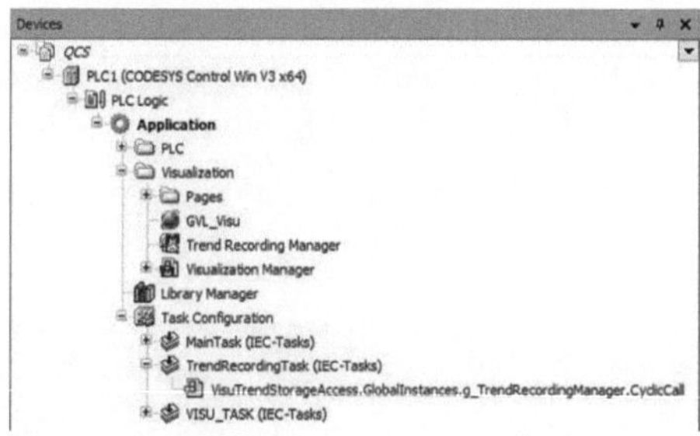

Figure 8-23. *Devices window*

Configuring Trends in the Visualization System

Next, let's add a new *TrendRecording* object to the *Manager*, which will be used to configure the variables for monitoring and recording. Right-click the *Trend Recording Manager*, and select *Add Object* ➤ *Trend Recording...* (Figure 8-24).

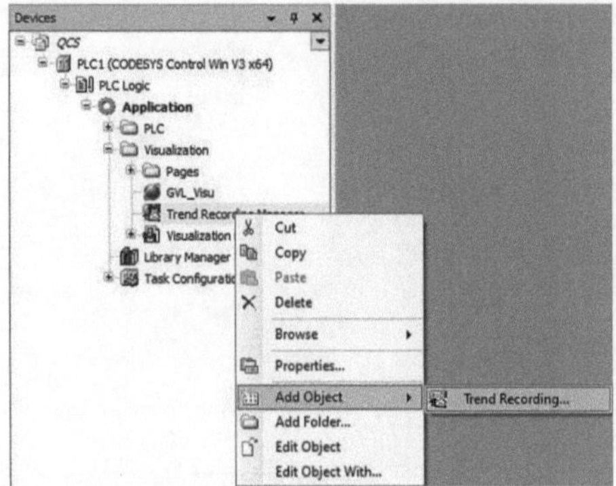

Figure 8-24. *Add Object* ➤ *Trend Recording...*

In the *Add Trend Recording* window, name the object *TrendRecording_TIC1* (Figure 8-25).

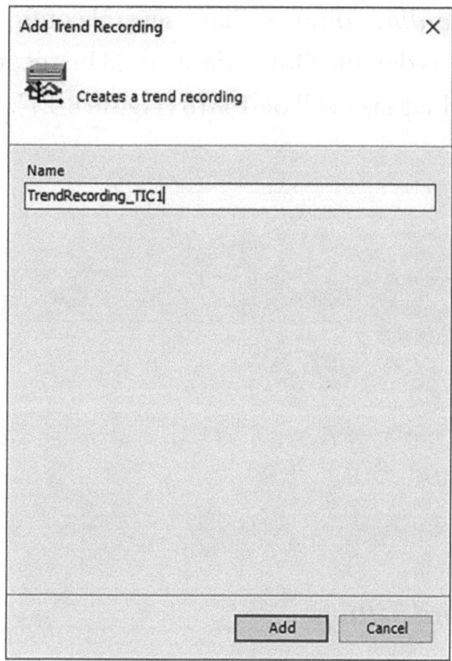

Figure 8-25. *Add Trend Recording window*

This is how the structure of our project should look (Figure 8-26).

Figure 8-26. *Devices window*

In the *TrendRecording* editor, we have several configuration options which we will leave as default. Our variables will be recorded every one second, and the archive size will be 16MB (Figure 8-27).

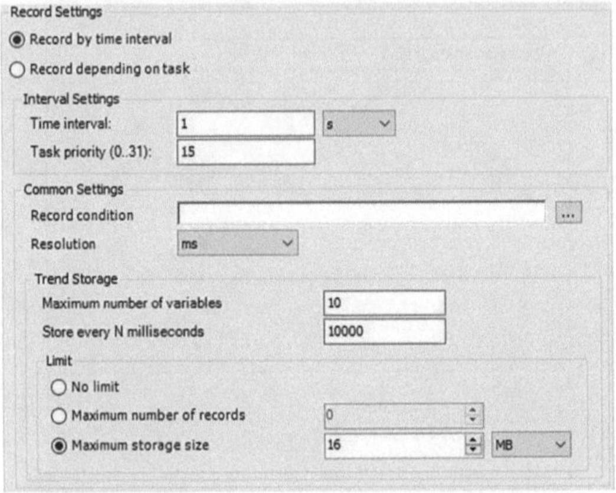

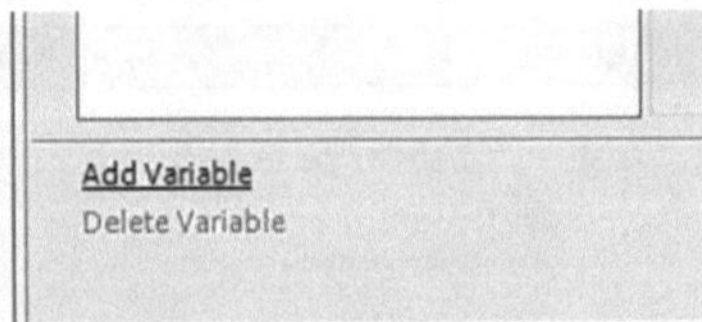

Figure 8-27. *Record Settings*

Now, let's add variables for monitoring through the *Trend Recording Manager*. In the *TrendRecording* editor, click the *Add Variable* option (Figure 8-28).

Figure 8-28. *Add Variable*

Fill in the *Variable* field with the name of the variable you want to monitor, which in our case will be the global variable *GVL_Visu. Temperature_TIC1*, storing the current temperature of *QCS-TIC1*. Set the trend color to black (*Graph color ➤ Black*). Additionally, configure the color warnings: blue for temperatures below 10°C and red for temperatures above 30°C. This is how the trend should be configured for the *QCS-TIC1* temperature variable (Figure 8-29).

Variable Settings

Variable	GVL_Visu.Temperature_TIC1
Record condition	
Attached y axis	Default y-axis: QCS-TIC1 / Q
Display variable name	☑
Description	Description of variable to display in tooltip
Curve type	Line
Graph color	Black
Line type	Line
Line width	1
Line style	Solid
Point type	None
Minimum warning	☑
Critical lower limit	10
Color	Blue
Maximum warning	☑
Critical upper limit	30
Color	Red

Figure 8-29. *TrendRecording_TIC1* ➤ *GVL_Visu.Temperature_TIC1*

Let's also add the variable that stores the setpoint for the *QCS-TIC1* temperature, so that both the setpoint and the measured temperature values are presented on the same timeline. Set the *Variable* field to *GVL_Visu.Setpoint_TIC1* and the trend color to green (*Graph color* ➤ *Green*) (Figure 8-30).

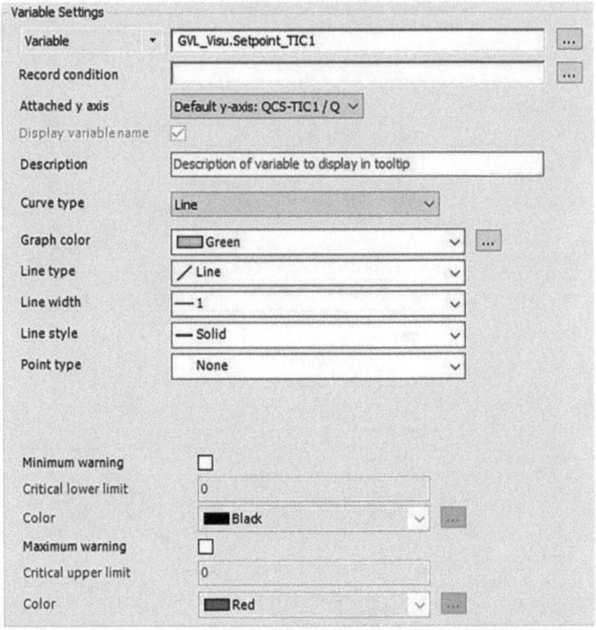

Figure 8-30. *TrendRecording_TIC1* ➤ *GVL_Visu.Setpoint_TIC1*

Configuring the Trend View

We have now configured the *TrendRecording* for temperature *TIC1*. Next, we need to display the recorded values on the visualization. Add a *Trend* object to the *P03_Trends* view, which can be found under the *Special Controls* tab. Once the *Trend* object is placed on the *P03_Trends* view, a new *TrendRecording* object will automatically be added to the *Trend Recording Manager* and the *Trend Configuration* window will open. Since we have already configured the *TrendRecording* named *TrendRecording_ TIC1*, you can close the *Trend Configuration* window by clicking *Cancel*. In the *Devices* window, also remove the newly added object *P03_Trends_ Trend1* from the *Trend Recording Manager*. Set the properties of the *Trend* object according to the following requirements (Figure 8-31).

Properties	
Filter ▾	Sort by ▾	Sort order ▾	☑ Advanced	
Property	**Value**
Element name	GenElemInst_2
Data source	⚙ <local application>
Type of element	Trend
Trend recording	TrendRecording_TIC1
Display settings	Click here to edit...
⊟ Position	
X	10
Y	50
Width	410
Height	340
Angle	0
Show cursor	☐
Show frame	☑
Number format	
Default time range	🕓 1m

Figure 8-31. *Trend* ➤ *Properties*

The most important property is *Trend recording,* which we set to *TrendRecording_TIC1.* This links the *Trend* object on the *P03_Trends* visualization to the trends configured in *TrendRecording_TIC1* (current temperature value and setpoint). Another essential property is *Default time range,* set to one minute, allowing for the observation of recorded variable values from the last minute.

Adjust the appearance of the trend window by right-clicking the *Trend* object and selecting *Configure Trend Display Settings...* (Figure 8-32).

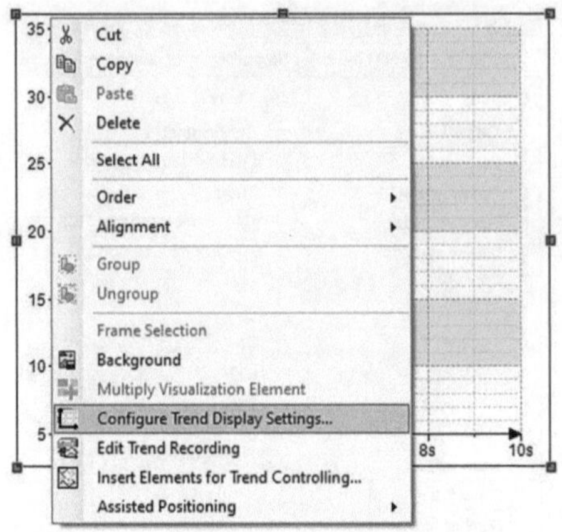

Figure 8-32. *Configure Trend Display Settings...*

In the *Display Settings* window, we can customize the appearance of the *Trend* object. In the *X Axis* tab, leave the default settings and move on to the *Y Axis* tab. Set the value axis to a fixed range from 5 to 35 (*Display mode ➤ Fixed; Minimum & Maximum*), and set the axis description to *QCS-TIC1* (*Description*) (Figure 8-33).

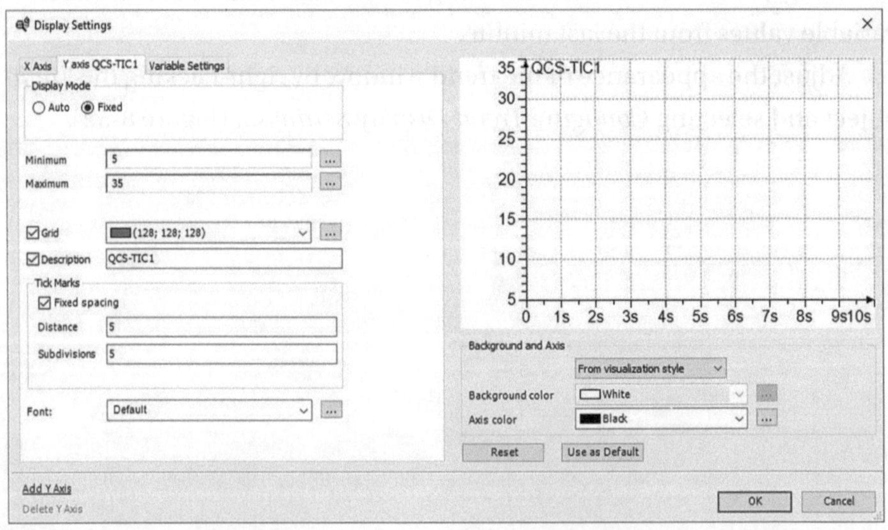

Figure 8-33. *Y axis tab*

In the *Variable Settings* tab, configure the *Trend* object so that the setpoint temperature value (*GVL_Visu.Setpoint_TIC1*) is visible only when the temperature controller is active (*GVL_Visu.Enable_Controller_TIC1*) (Figure 8-34).

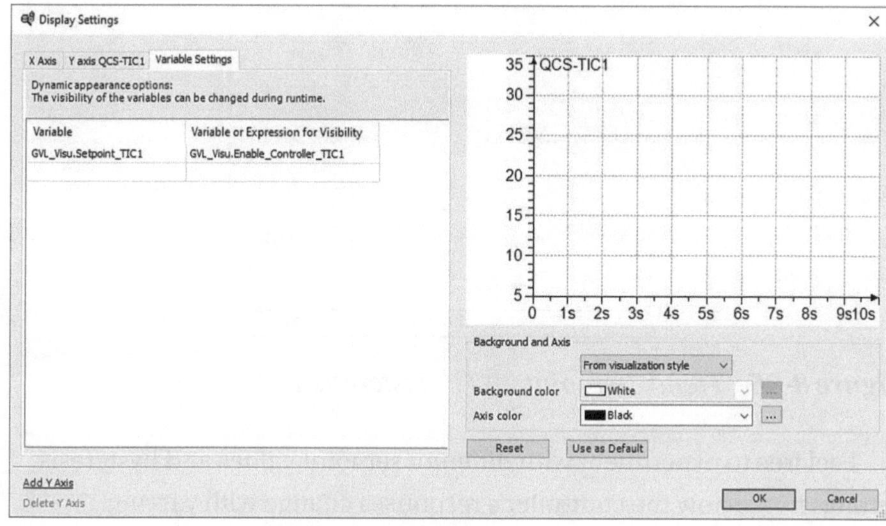

Figure 8-34. *Variable Settings tab*

Finally, test our program by downloading it to the PLC. Then, activate the temperature controller *QCS-TIC1* (Figure 8-35).

Figure 8-35. *Bang-Bang Controller TIC1*

The temperature trend for *QCS-TIC1* should look like this with the controller set to a setpoint of 20°C and a hysteresis of 1°C. Observe the trend changes when the temperature controller is active (Figure 8-36).

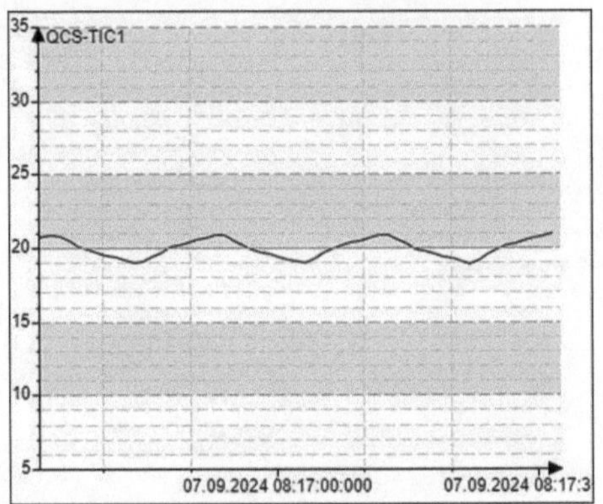

Figure 8-36. *Trend: Setpoint 20°C; Hysteresis 1°C*

Feel free to experiment with different setpoint values and hysteresis settings to see how the controller's responses change with varying parameters.

On the trends, it is clearly visible that a smaller hysteresis results in an increased number of switching cycles between heating and cooling (Figure 8-37).

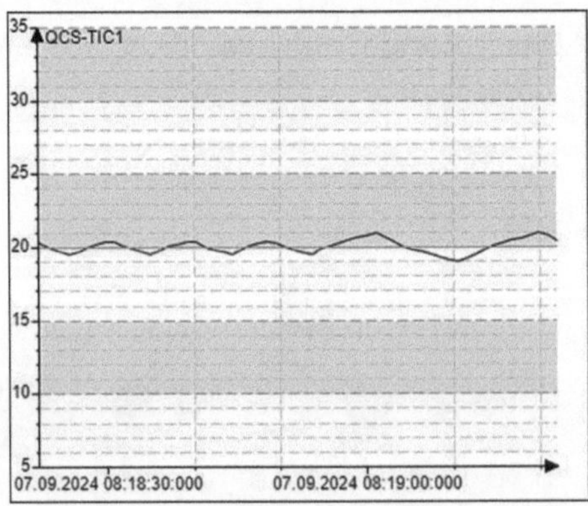

Figure 8-37. *Trend: changing Hysteresis from 0.5°C to 1°C*

On this trend, we also observe the effect of the Bang-Bang controller, which, as described in the previous chapter, does not allow for precise control of the setpoint. Instead, the measured value oscillates around the setpoint (Figure 8-38). This serves as a reminder about the Bang-Bang controller.

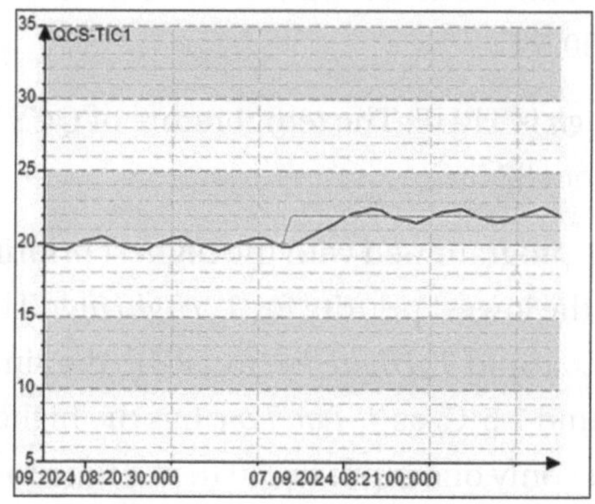

Figure 8-38. *Trend: changing Setpoint from 20°C to 22°C*

Practical Reinforcement Exercise

As part of the exercise, I encourage you to add and configure another *Trend* object in the *P03_Trends* view, which will visualize the temperature of *QCS-TIC2*, similarly to how it was done for the temperature of *QCS-TIC1*.

Additional Functions of the Temperature Simulator

Initially, we set all four inputs *T_LowLow*, *T_Low*, *T_High*, and *T_HighHigh* to *FALSE*. These inputs allow us to simulate temperature exceeding threshold values, regardless of the state of the controller. The measured temperature behaves as follows:

- *T_LowLow is TRUE*: The temperature of *QCS-TIC1* will drop to about 7.5°C.

- *T_Low is TRUE*: The temperature of *QCS-TIC1* will drop to about 9.5°C.

- *T_High is TRUE*: The temperature of *QCS-TIC1* will rise to about 30.5°C.

- *T_HighHigh* is TRUE: The temperature of *QCS-TIC1* will rise to about 32.5°C.

The simulator is programmed with the highest priority for the *T_LowLow* input and the lowest priority for *T_HighHigh*. This means that if we set both *T_LowLow* and *T_HighHigh* to TRUE, the simulator will set the temperature to around 7.5°C, as *T_LowLow* has the higher priority. It is recommended to set only one input to TRUE at a time to precisely control the simulated state.

During trend configuration, we set the trend color to blue for temperatures below 10°C (Figure 8-39). This can be simulated by setting either *T_LowLow* or *T_Low* to TRUE.

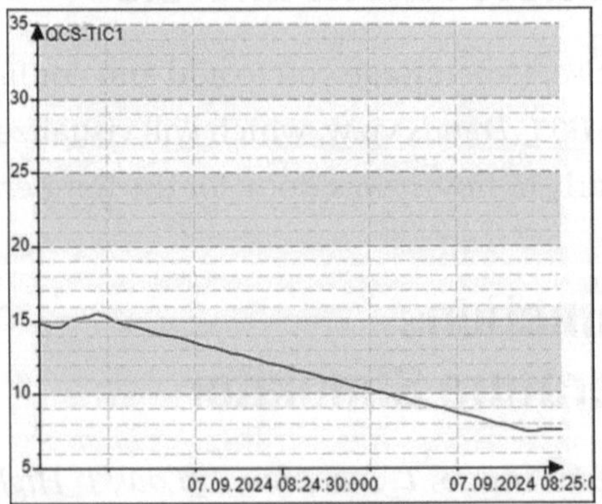

Figure 8-39. *Change the trend color from black to blue*

If the temperature rises above 30°C, the trend color should change to red (Figure 8-40). This can be simulated by setting the *T_High* or *T_HighHigh* input to TRUE.

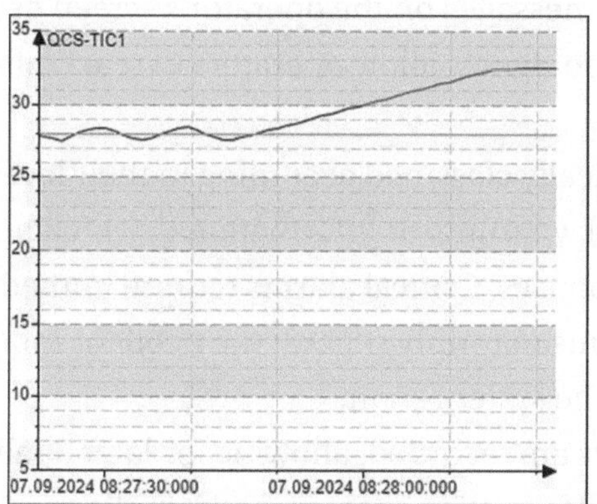

Figure 8-40. *Change the trend color from black to red*

We can see that the change in trend color effectively visualizes warnings. However, with the current configuration of the *Trend* object, we only see the last minute of recorded data. It would be beneficial to locate the exact time of anomalies, which introduces the need to use tools such as *Alarms*.

Alarms

What They Are and How They Are Used

Alarms in control systems are mechanisms designed to detect, signal, and manage undesirable states or events in industrial processes. Their primary function is to inform operators about the exceeding of certain parameters or the occurrence of an emergency situation, enabling prompt action to prevent potential equipment damage, production disruptions, or safety hazards.

Alarms are triggered when process variables exceed established limits. For instance, if the temperature in a process surpasses a safe level, the system automatically generates an alarm. Notifications can take various forms, such as text messages on the operator's screen or audible signals, such as sirens. These signals allow operators to react quickly and take appropriate action.

Alarms are typically classified according to their level of importance. They can be critical, warning, or informational, which helps operators prioritize their responses. Critical alarms require immediate intervention, while warning alarms may only suggest the need for monitoring and possibly checking the system soon.

All alarm events are recorded, allowing for later analysis. Alarm history provides valuable information that can assist in diagnosing the causes of problems, optimizing processes, and preventing future failures. Regular analysis of this data can also reveal patterns indicating the need for maintenance of specific equipment.

After taking corrective actions, operators can reset or acknowledge alarms, signaling that the problem has been resolved or is under control. For example, after restoring normal temperature, the operator acknowledges the alarm, removing it from the active list.

In industrial systems, alarms play a crucial role in protecting personnel and equipment from hazards, enabling early detection of dangerous states. Their prompt handling prevents costly downtimes and failures. Combined with analytical tools, such as process trends, alarms are invaluable for optimizing control processes.

Alarms   In control systems are a key element of process supervision in industrial settings, serving to detect, signal, and manage undesirable conditions to ensure safety, efficiency, and reliability of operations.

Alarm Configuration

After the theoretical introduction, let's move on to the practical implementation of alarms in our application. We will start by adding a new folder named *Alarms* to the *Visualization* directory. In this folder, we will store all components related to the alarm system. Below is how the structure of our project should look (Figure 8-41).

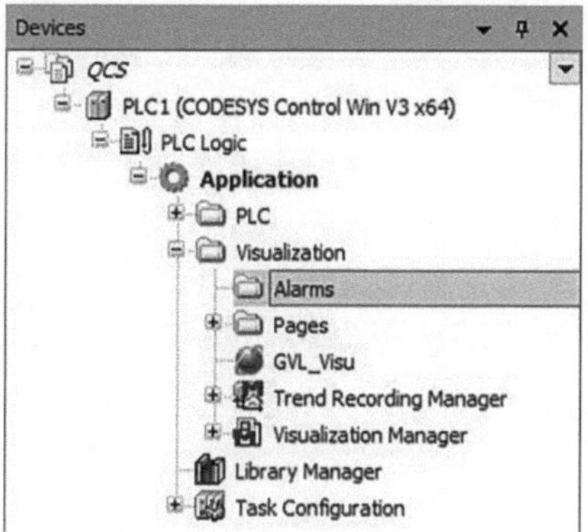

Figure 8-41. *Devices window*

The next step is to add a new object to the *Alarms* folder. Select the *Add Object* option, and click *Alarm Configuration* (Figure 8-42).

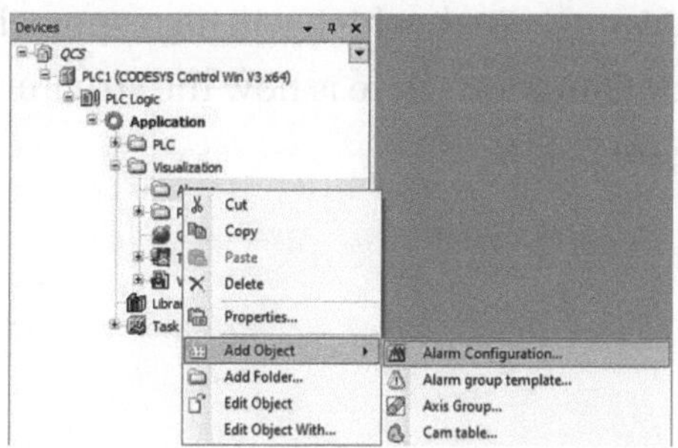

Figure 8-42. *Add Object* ➤ *Alarm Configuration…*

We leave the default name for the *Alarm Configuration* and confirm our choice by clicking the *Add* button in the *Add Alarm Configuration* window (Figure 8-43).

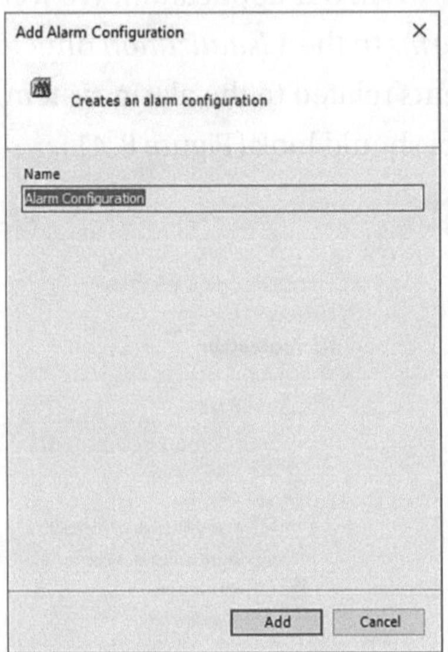

Figure 8-43. *Add Alarm Configuration window*

It's worth noting that in addition to adding the new object to the *Alarms* folder, the CODESYS environment automatically creates a new Task named *AlarmManagerTask*, which will be responsible for handling the alarm system configuration. Here is how the structure of our project currently looks (Figure 8-44).

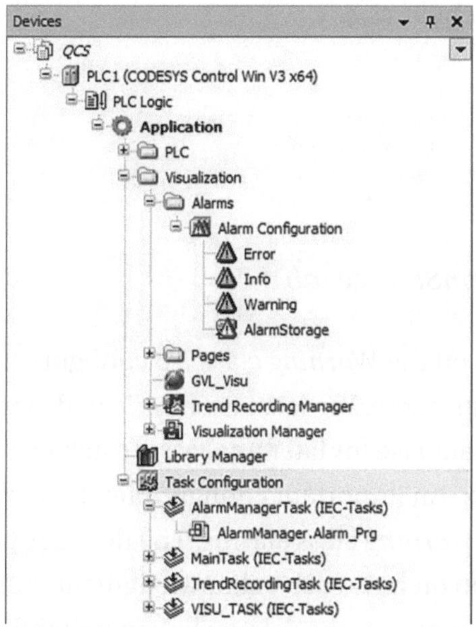

Figure 8-44. *Devices window*

Alarm Classes

In the alarm configuration system, *Alarm Configuration* typically offers
three basic alarm classes: *Error, Info,* and *Warning.* These three classes
represent the fundamental standard in control systems and are supported
by most visualization systems. As the control system evolves and
depending on individual needs, it is also possible to define custom alarm
classes.

In addition to these classes, the *Alarm Configuration* includes
an *AlarmStorage* component, which acts as a database for storing all
generated alarms. You can configure the storage limit based on the
number of records or the size of the database, but in our case, we will
stick with the default configuration without setting quantitative limits
(Figure 8-45).

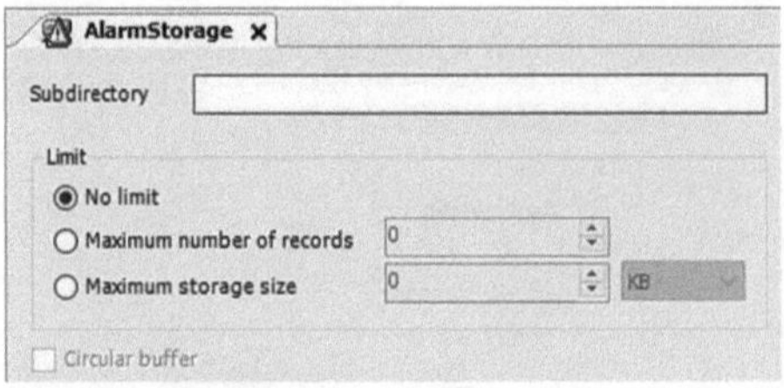

Figure 8-45. *AlarmStorage tab*

Let's now focus on the *Warning* class. To configure this class, you need
to double-click on its name. We want each activated alarm of this class
to be saved in the database for later analysis. To achieve this, check the
Archiving check box. An important configuration parameter is the method
for acknowledging *Warning* class alarms. The default option is *REP*. For
detailed information on how each acknowledgment method functions,
hover the mouse cursor over the acknowledgment method field to display
a window with descriptions of states and transitions (Figure 8-46).

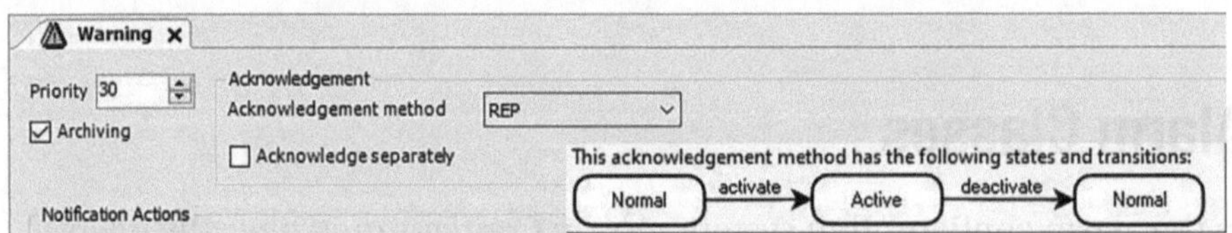

Figure 8-46. *Acknowledgment method REP*

For the *Warning* class, an alarm can be in one of two states: *Normal*
or *Active*. These states can be configured in the *Display Options for Alarm
Table/Alarm Banner* table. For the *Warning* class, I will set the background
to yellow and the font to black when the alarm is *active*. For the *Normal*
state, I will choose a background color of BlanchedAlmond and the font
color identical to that in the *Active* state (Figure 8-47).

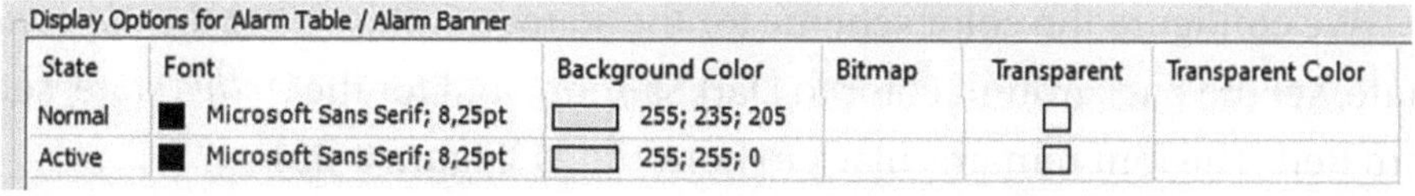

Display Options for Alarm Table / Alarm Banner					
State	Font	Background Color	Bitmap	Transparent	Transparent Color
Normal	■ Microsoft Sans Serif; 8,25pt	255; 235; 205		☐	
Active	■ Microsoft Sans Serif; 8,25pt	255; 255; 0		☐	

Figure 8-47. *Display Options for Alarm Table/Alarm Banner table*

The configuration for the *Warning* class is as follows (Figure 8-48).

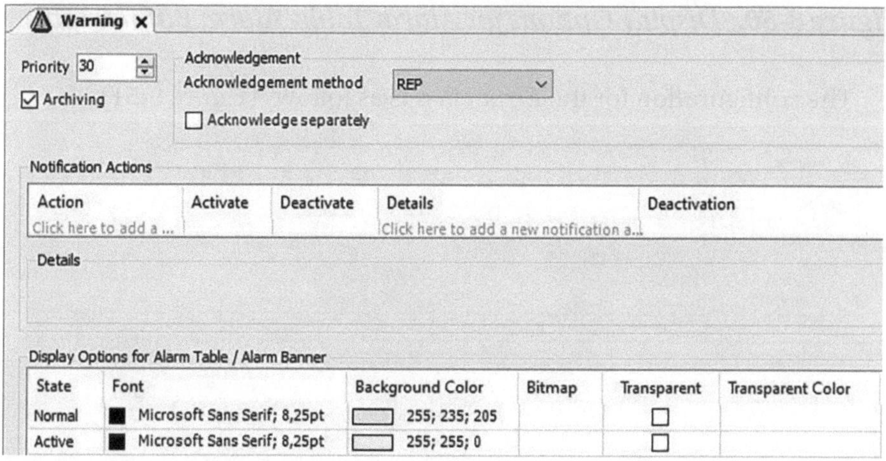

Figure 8-48. *Warning class*

Now let's take a look at the *Error* class. Alarms of this class should also be archived, so we check the *Archiving* check box. We set the acknowledgment method for the *Error* class to *ACK*, which means that each alarm of this class, in addition to the *Normal* and *Active* states, requires acknowledgment by the system operator (Figure 8-49).

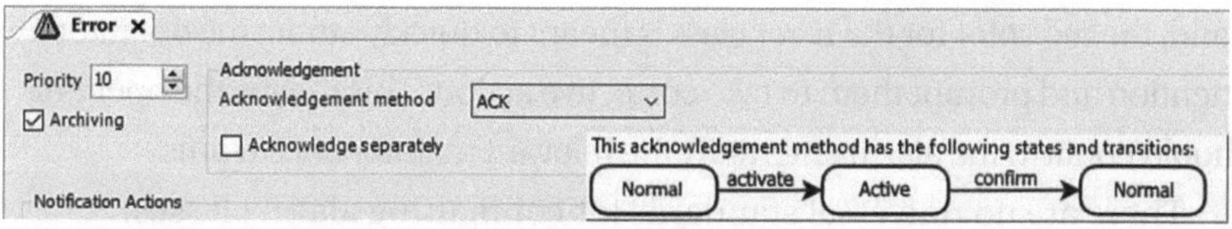

Figure 8-49. *Acknowledgment method ACK*

We configure the color scheme for the states as follows: for the *Normal* state, set the background color to DarkSalmon, and for the *Active* state, set it to Red. The font remains black in both states (Figure 8-50).

Display Options for Alarm Table / Alarm Banner

State	Font	Background Color	Bitmap	Transparent	Transparent Color
Normal	■ Microsoft Sans Serif; 8,25pt	233; 150; 122		☐	
Active	■ Microsoft Sans Serif; 8,25pt	255; 0; 0		☐	

Figure 8-50. *Display Options for Alarm Table/Alarm Banner table*

The configuration for the *Error* class is as follows (Figure 8-51).

⚠ Error ✕

Priority 10

☑ Archiving

Acknowledgement

Acknowledgement method   ACK

☐ Acknowledge separately

Notification Actions

Action	Activate	Confirm	Details	Deactivation
Click here to add a ...			Click here to add a new notification a...	

Details

Display Options for Alarm Table / Alarm Banner

State	Font	Background Color	Bitmap	Transparent	Transparent Color
Normal	■ Microsoft Sans Serif; 8,25pt	233; 150; 122		☐	
Active	■ Microsoft Sans Serif; 8,25pt	255; 0; 0		☐	

Figure 8-51. *Error class*

When designing the scenario for this chapter, I adopted a specific color logic for alarm classes. The yellow color for the *Warning* class is intended to draw the operator's attention to a non-critical anomaly in the system. On the other hand, the red color for the *Error* class is meant to quickly attract the operator's attention and prompt them to take corrective action. This means the operator should confirm the alarm and notify the relevant maintenance teams.

There are no universal standards for configuring alarm classes; different manufacturing plants may have different interpretations of colors and configuration methods. In one plant, red might indicate a critical failure, while in another, it could signify an informational status about the mode of operation. Therefore, when configuring alarm classes in a visualization system, it is crucial to adjust the settings according to the operators' requirements and preferences to ensure their comfort and effectiveness.

Ultimately, the goal is to satisfy the client who will be operating the control system on a daily basis. Our role as PLC programmers ends with the system being set up and handed over for operation.

Alarm Groups

After configuring the individual alarm classes, it's time to add specific alarms to our project that will be triggered based on the states of the installation. These alarms can be grouped according to various criteria. In our case, we will create a single alarm group where we will configure all events related to temperature measurements.

To do this, right-click the *Alarm Configurator* object and select *Add Object ➤ Alarm Group…* from the menu (Figure 8-52).

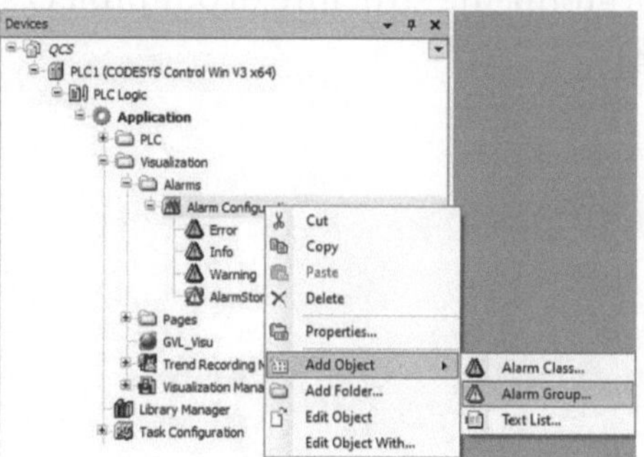

Figure 8-52. *Add Object ➤ Alarm Group…*

In the *Add Alarm Group* window, assign the name *AlarmGroupTemperatures* to our group (Figure 8-53).

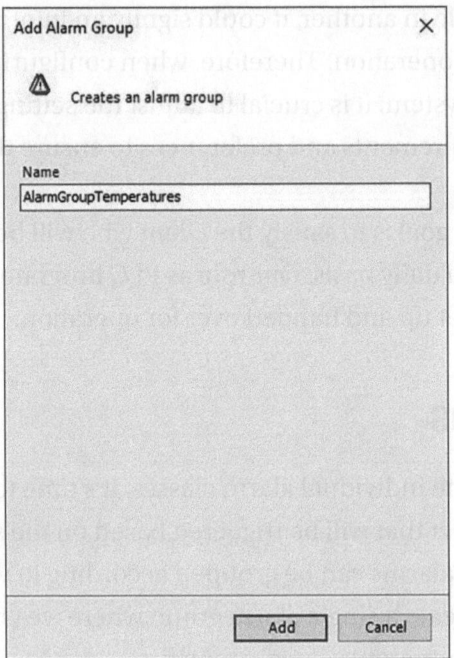

Figure 8-53. *Add Alarm Group window*

After adding the group, the structure of our project should look as follows (Figure 8-54).

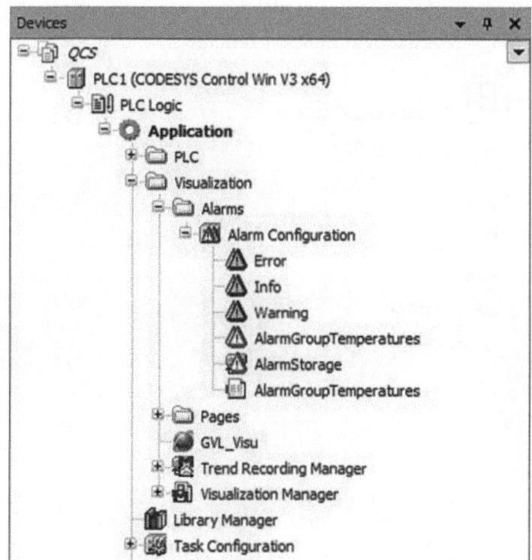

Figure 8-54. *Devices window*

Alarm Triggers

In the next step of implementing alarms in our application, we will add a *POU* object responsible for triggering alarms of different classes. To do this, right-click the *Alarms* folder, and select *Add Object* ➤ *POU*.... In the *Add POU* window, set the parameters according to the following instructions, and then confirm by clicking the *Add* button (Figure 8-55).

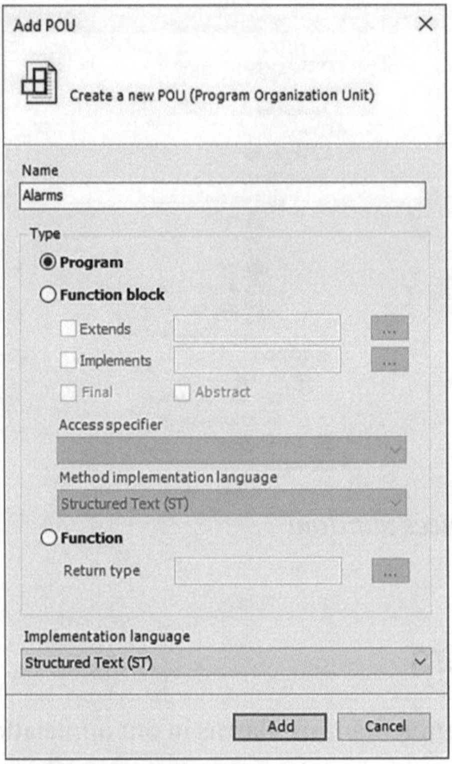

Figure 8-55. *Add POU window*

Make sure to add the *Alarms* program to one of the tasks in the
Task Configurator. Otherwise, the code within this program will not
be executed by the PLC. It is best to add the program call to the task
named *AlarmManagerTask* to maintain a consistent project structure
(Figure 8-56).

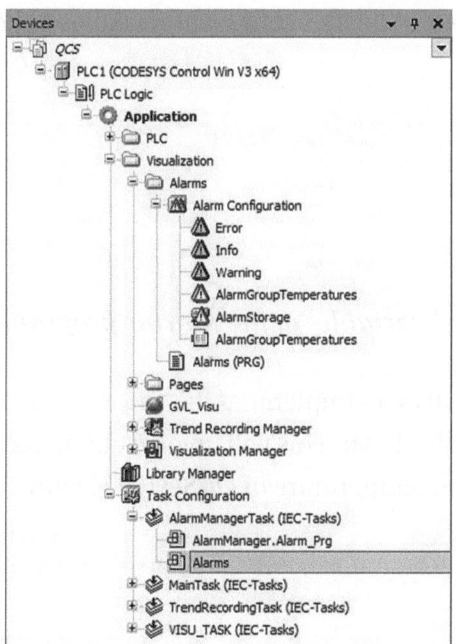

Figure 8-56. *Devices window*

We will start the implementation of alarm triggering by declaring local variables in the *Alarms* program. We assume that for the temperature *QCS-TIC1*, we will have four alarms: two of class *Warning* and two of class *Error* (Table 8-2).

Table 8-2. *List of Alarms*

Trigger	Alarm Class	Trigger Condition
Temperature_TIC1_LowLow	Error	Temperature QCS-TIC1 below 8°C
Temperature_TIC1_Low	Warning	Temperature QCS-TIC1 below 10°C
Temperature_TIC1_High	Warning	Temperature QCS-TIC1 above 30°C
Temperature_TIC1_HighHigh	Error	Temperature QCS-TIC1 above 32°C

For this task, we will declare four local variables of type BOOL
(Figure 8-57).

```
Alarms  X
  1    PROGRAM Alarms
  2    VAR
  3          Temperature_TIC1_LowLow : BOOL;
  4          Temperature_TIC1_Low : BOOL;
  5          Temperature_TIC1_High : BOOL;
  6          Temperature_TIC1_HighHigh : BOOL;
  7    END_VAR
```

Figure 8-57. *Local variables of the Alarms program*

The next step will be to implement the triggers that activate the alarms
according to the table above. This will involve changing the values of the
triggers based on the temperature of *QCS-TIC1* (Figure 8-58).

```
  1    // Warnings
  2    Temperature_TIC1_Low := GVL_Visu.Temperature_TIC1 < 10.0;
  3    Temperature_TIC1_High := GVL_Visu.Temperature_TIC1 > 30.0;
  4
  5    // Errors
  6    Temperature_TIC1_LowLow := GVL_Visu.Temperature_TIC1 < 8.0;
  7    Temperature_TIC1_HighHigh := GVL_Visu.Temperature_TIC1 > 32.0;
```

Figure 8-58. *Implementation of the Alarms program*

Next, in the *AlarmGroupTemperatures* group, assign these triggers
to specific alarms, which will be presented in the visualization as text
messages. Let's examine the alarm with ID 0. Note that this alarm has the
Observation Type set to *Digital*. In the *Details* column, we can see that the
alarm will be activated when the value of Trigger in *Alarms.Temperature_
TIC1_Low* is TRUE. As we remember, this trigger was implemented in the
Alarms program and will be active when the temperature of *QCS-TIC1* falls
below 10°C. If this condition is met, a *Warning* class alarm will be activated
(column *Class*), and the alarm message will be *"Temperature TIC1 has
fallen below 10°C"* (column *Message*). Similarly, configure the remaining
alarms, adjusting the triggers, classes, and messages accordingly
(Figure 8-59).

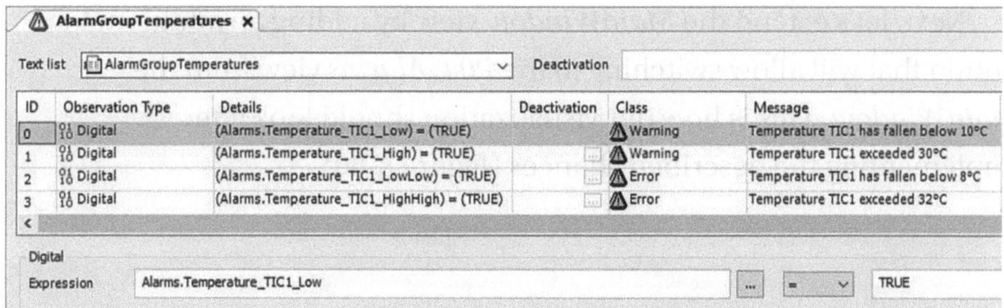

Figure 8-59. *Alarm configuration for temperature QCS-TIC1*

Alarm Table

After completing the configuration and implementation of alarms for temperature *QCS-TIC1*, it's time to test the changes made to the project. We will start by adding a new view *P04_Alarms* to the visualization. In this view, we will add two elements: *Label* and *Alarm Table*. The *Alarm Table* element can be found in the *Alarm Manager* tab. Next, set the properties of the added elements according to the table below (Table 8-3).

Table 8-3. *Properties of Label and Alarm Table controls*

Properties	Label	Alarm Table
Texts → Text	Alarms	Not available
Position → X	0	10
Position → Y	5	50
Position → Width	1000	1000
Position → Height	30	208
Text properties → Font	Large Headline	Default

Next, let's extend the *MainWindow* view by adding an additional button that will allow switching to the *P04_Alarms* view from the *MainWindow*. This is how our visualization should look after implementing the described changes (Figure 8-60).

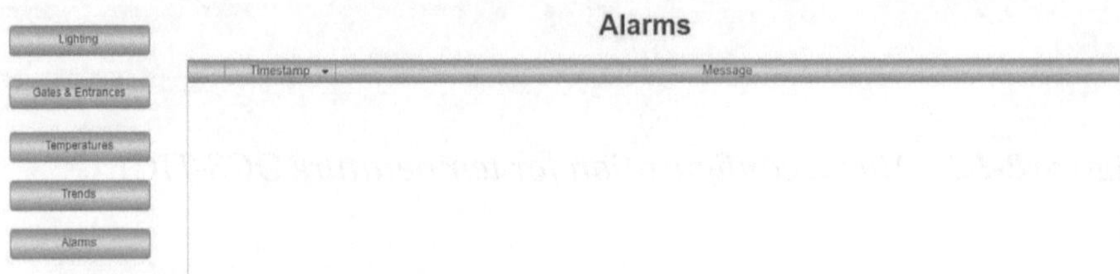

Figure 8-60. *P04_Alarms view*

Let's now download our program to the PLC controller and set the *T_HighHigh* input of the temperature simulator to a high state. This will cause the temperature to rise above 32°C, which will first trigger a *Warning* alarm indicating that the temperature has exceeded 30°C and, shortly afterward, an *Error* alarm indicating that the temperature has risen above 32°C (Figure 8-61).

	Timestamp ▼	Message
0	07.09.2024 08:34:31	Temperature TIC1 exceeded 32°C
1	07.09.2024 08:34:19	Temperature TIC1 exceeded 30°C
2	07.09.2024 08:32:29	Temperature TIC1 has fallen below 8°C

Figure 8-61. *Active alarms signaling high temperature*

Trigger Delay for Alarms

As seen in the alarm table, there is also an *Error* class alarm indicating that the temperature of TIC1 dropped below 8°C. This occurs because when the PLC controller starts, the analog input values are usually set to zero, resulting in a minimum measurement value for scaled temperatures. To handle this challenge, I use a simple trick: I always introduce a delay of about three to five seconds for triggering alarms in my applications, giving the PLC controller time to start up and execute at least one program cycle.

For this purpose, we will use a *BOOL* variable named *INIT* and a new type of timer – *TOF (Timer OFF Delay)*.

Timer TOF (Time OFF Delay)   Is a type of timer used in control systems. When it receives an activation signal (IN), it immediately switches to the ON state. After the signal is removed, the TOF timer counts down for a specified delay period before switching off. In other words, the TOF timer keeps the output (Q) in the ON state for the defined time after the input signal (IN) is turned off.

Let's declare these variables in the *Alarms* program as local variables (Figure 8-62).

```
Alarms  X
1     PROGRAM Alarms
2     VAR
3         TOF_Delay : TOF;
4         INIT : BOOL := FALSE;
5         Temperature_TIC1_LowLow : BOOL;
6         Temperature_TIC1_Low : BOOL;
7         Temperature_TIC1_High : BOOL;
8         Temperature_TIC1_HighHigh : BOOL;
9     END_VAR
```

Figure 8-62. *Local variables of the Alarms program*

At the beginning of the *Alarms* program, let's add a short piece of code to halt further execution by invoking the RETURN instruction until five seconds have passed since the PLC controller started. The *INIT* variable is set to *FALSE* in the first cycle of the PLC controller and to *TRUE* in subsequent cycles. The *TOF_Delay* timer starts counting five seconds immediately after *INIT* variable was set to *TRUE*. After this time, the remainder of the *Alarms* program, including the triggering of the Triggers, will continue. This simple trick allows us to delay alarm triggering by five seconds from the PLC start. Here is the modified *Alarms* program code (Figure 8-63).

```
 1   // Delay trigerring the alarms
 2   TOF_Delay(IN := NOT INIT, PT := T#5S);
 3   INIT := TRUE;
 4   IF TOF_Delay.Q THEN
 5      RETURN;
 6   END_IF
 7
 8   // Warnings
 9   Temperature_TIC1_Low := GVL_Visu.Temperature_TIC1 < 10.0;
10   Temperature_TIC1_High := GVL_Visu.Temperature_TIC1 > 30.0;
11
12   // Errors
13   Temperature_TIC1_LowLow := GVL_Visu.Temperature_TIC1 < 8.0;
14   Temperature_TIC1_HighHigh := GVL_Visu.Temperature_TIC1 > 32.0;
```

Figure 8-63. *Implementation of the Alarms program*

Presenting Alarms in the Visualization System

Testing our program by downloading it to the PLC controller, the alarm
table should initially be empty. Only after exceeding 30°C will a *Warning*
class alarm appear, and after exceeding 32°C, an *Error* class alarm will be
triggered. The alarm indicating a temperature drop below 8°C will not be
visible, as was the case before adding the delay for alarm triggering in the
Alarms program (Figure 8-64).

	Timestamp ▾	Message
0	07.09.2024 08:39:34	Temperature TIC1 exceeded 32°C
1	07.09.2024 08:39:22	Temperature TIC1 exceeded 30°C

Figure 8-64. *Active alarms signaling high temperature*

Similarly, we can set the *T_LowLow* input of the temperature simulator
to a high state to generate alarms indicating too low a temperature
(Figure 8-65).

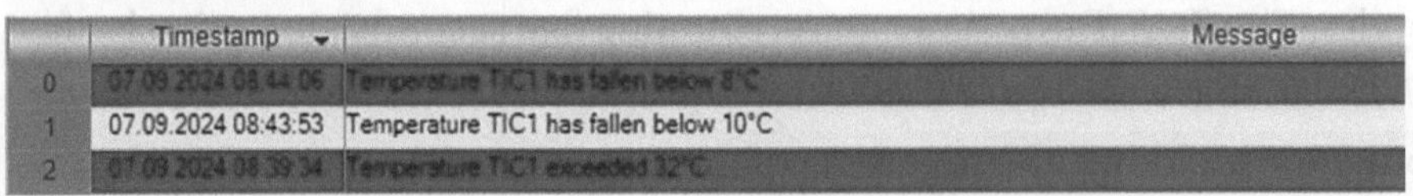

	Timestamp ▾	Message
0	07.09.2024 08:44:06	Temperature TIC1 has fallen below 8°C
1	07.09.2024 08:43:53	Temperature TIC1 has fallen below 10°C
2	07.09.2024 08:39:34	Temperature TIC1 exceeded 32°C

Figure 8-65. *Active alarms signaling low temperature*

As seen in the alarm table, first a *Warning* alarm appeared, indicating that the temperature dropped below 10°C, and then an *Error* alarm, indicating that the temperature dropped below 8°C. However, the alarm indicating that the temperature exceeded 32°C is still present in the table.

This is because the *Error* alarm requires acknowledgment from the operator. We set the acknowledgment method for this class of alarms to *ACK*, meaning that the alarm will remain visible in the table until it is acknowledged, even if it is no longer active.

Acknowledging Alarms in the Visualization System

To add the capability for operator interaction with the alarm table, right-click on the alarm table in the *P04_Alarms* view, and select the option *Insert elements for acknowledging alarms...* from the menu (Figure 8-66).

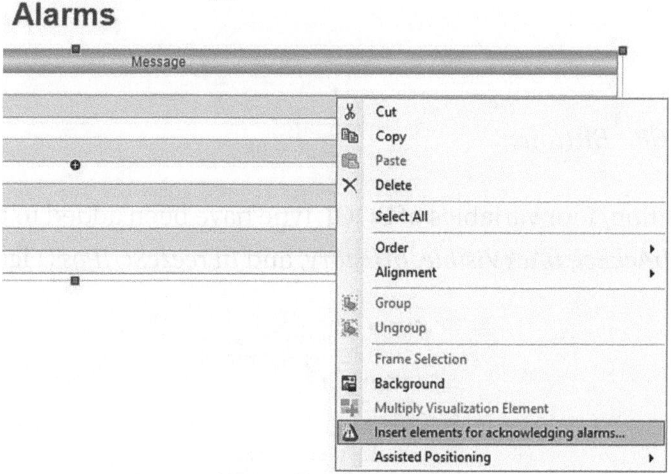

Figure 8-66. *Insert elements for acknowledging alarms...*

In the *Alarm Table Wizard* window that appears, confirm your selection without making any changes by clicking the *OK* button (Figure 8-67).

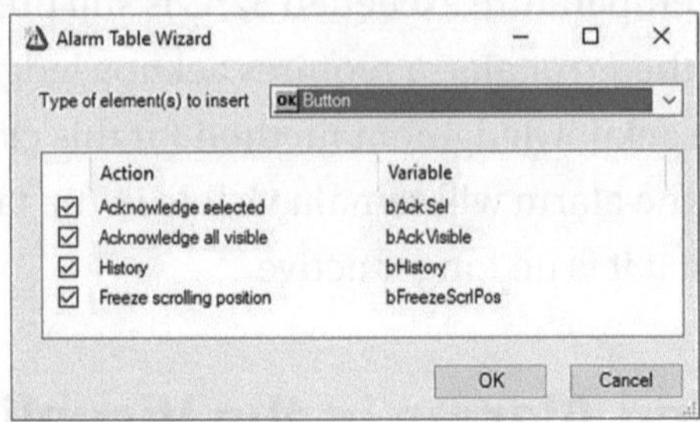

Figure 8-67. *Alarm Table Wizard window*

After making these changes, you will notice that four buttons have been added to the *P04_Alarms* view just below the alarm table: *ACK selected*, *ACK all visible*, *History*, and *Freeze Scrl Pos* (Figure 8-68).

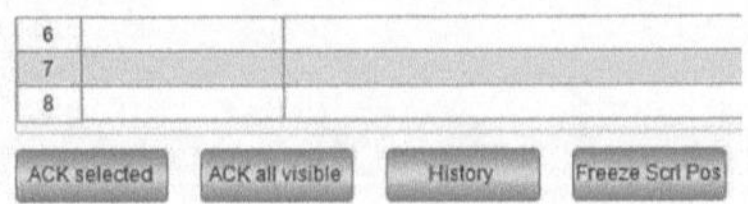

Figure 8-68. *Buttons*

In addition, four variables of BOOL type have been added to the editor interface: *bAckSel*, *bAckVisible*, *bHistory*, and *bFreezeScrlPos* (Figure 8-69).

```
1   VAR_IN_OUT
2   END_VAR
3   VAR
4       bAckSel : BOOL;
5       bAckVisible : BOOL;
6       bHistory : BOOL;
7       bFreezeScrlPos : BOOL;
8   END_VAR
```

Figure 8-69. *Interface Editor*

These variables have been automatically assigned to the *Input configuration* ➤ *Toggle* ➤ *Variable* property of each of the four buttons. This means that when the *ACK selected* button is pressed, the *bAckSel* variable will toggle between *TRUE* and *FALSE* (Figure 8-70). The same behavior will apply to the other three buttons as well.

Input configuration	
OnDialogClosed	Configure...
OnMouseClick	Configure...
OnMouseDown	Configure...
OnMouseEnter	Configure...
OnMouseLeave	Configure...
OnMouseMove	Configure...
OnMouseUp	Configure...
OnValueChanged	Configure...
Toggle	
Variable	bAckSel

Figure 8-70. *The Input configuration ➤ Toggle ➤ Variable property of the ACK selected button*

All four variables have also been linked to the *Control variables* properties of the *Alarm Table* element (Figure 8-71).

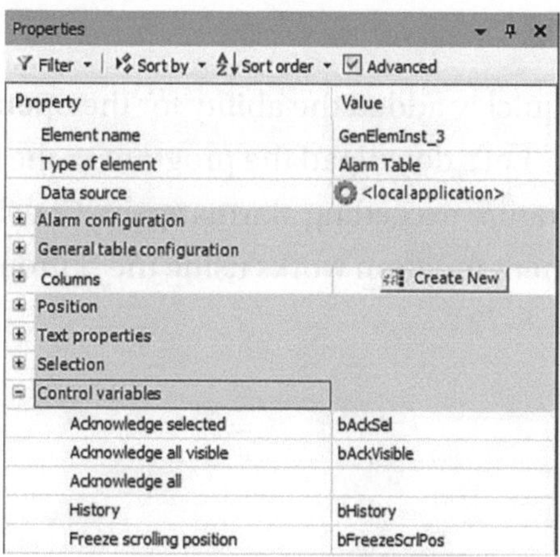

Figure 8-71. *Control variables properties of the Alarm Table element*

Thanks to these four variables, a simple interface between the *Buttons* and the *Alarm Table* has been created within the *P04_Alarms* view, without the need to declare separate variables in the PLC program logic. Everything operates at the visualization and *P04_Alarms* interface level.

Here's how the individual alarm table properties work:

- *Acknowledge selected*: The rising edge of the variable assigned to this property acknowledges a single selected alarm in the alarm table.

- *Acknowledge all visible*: The rising edge of the variable assigned to this property acknowledges all selected alarms in the alarm table.

- *History*: This property switches the alarm table to *historical mode* (if the variable is TRUE) or *normal mode* (if the variable is FALSE).

- *Freeze scrolling position*: This property freezes the scroll bar position, even if a new alarm appears in the alarm table.

In this way, we quickly added the ability for the operator to interact with the alarm table. Let's download the program to the PLC and simulate the temperature exceeding alarms again. Check how the alarm acknowledgment function works using the buttons added to the visualization (Figure 8-72).

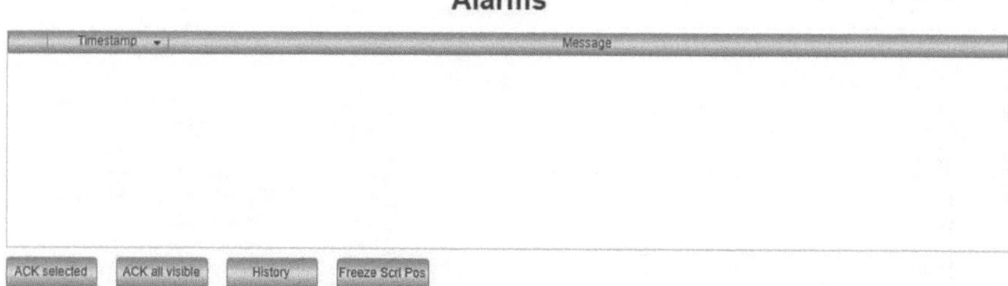

Figure 8-72. *P04_Alarms with buttons*

Triggering Alarms Using Limits

The next step in developing our alarm system is to add functionality for generating alarms for the *QCS-TIC2* temperature. This time, I want to introduce another method offered by the CODESYS environment, which is also supported by other control system manufacturers. This will allow us to use it in different programming environments in the future. Learning this functionality will enhance our skills in creating control systems.

Let's open our *AlarmGroupTemperatures* and add four new alarms. This time, instead of selecting the *Digital* type in the *Observation Type* column, we will configure the alarms using the *Upper limit* and *Lower limit* types.

The difference in triggering alarms using *Upper limit* and *Lower limit* types is that there's no need for additional logic in the PLC program, as was the case when using the *Digital* type. For *Digital*, we used the *Alarms* program to set specific triggers. With *Upper limit* and *Lower limit* types, the configuration is done graphically within the alarm group.

For example, we will configure an alarm with ID 4, which triggers a *Warning* class alarm, indicating that the TIC2 temperature has dropped below 10°C (Figure 8-73).

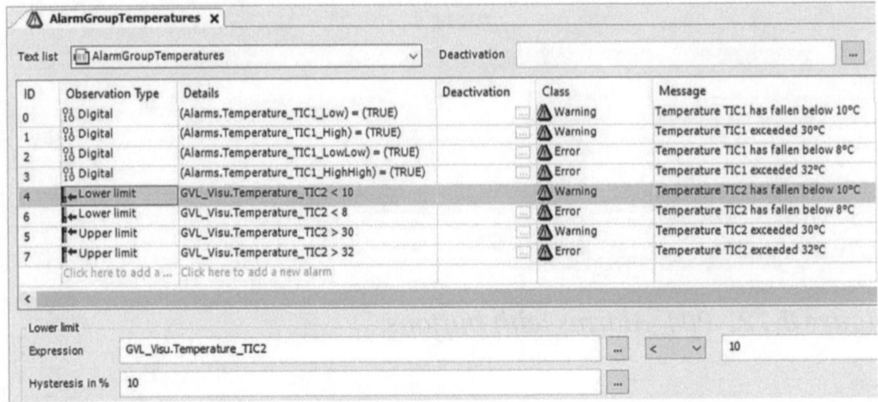

Figure 8-73. AlarmGroupTemperatures

As you can see, the condition we implemented in the *Alarms* program for *Digital* type alarms is set directly in the Alarm Configuration window for *Upper limit* and *Lower limit* types. Additionally, for these alarms, we can set a hysteresis value, expressed as a percentage. Once the hysteresis is defined, the alarm condition is met until a specified deviation from the threshold is reached. In this case, for a hysteresis of 10% from the 10°C threshold, the alarm will activate when the temperature drops below 10°C, but it will deactivate when the temperature rises above 11°C.

This is an interesting functionality that we currently don't have in our *Alarms* program responsible for triggering for the *QCS-TIC1* temperature. If the *QCS-TIC1* temperature oscillated around 10°C, the *Warning* class alarm indicating that the temperature dropped below 10°C would constantly appear and disappear from the alarm table. To avoid this, we would need to implement hysteresis or a time delay in the *Alarms* program as well.

Now, let's configure the remaining three alarms according to the following expressions (Figure 8-74, Figure 8-75, Figure 8-76).

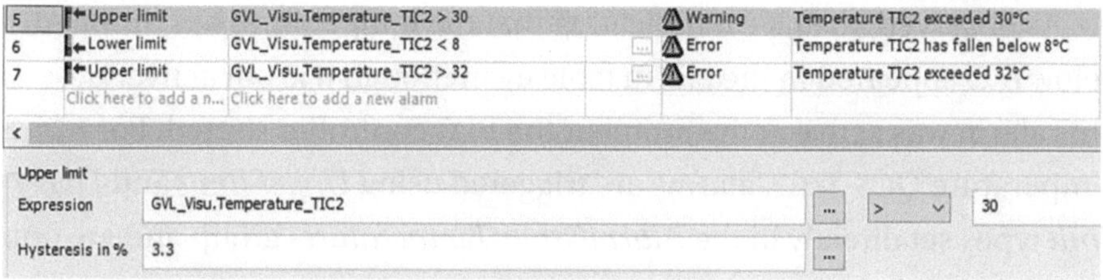

5	Upper limit	GVL_Visu.Temperature_TIC2 > 30	Warning	Temperature TIC2 exceeded 30°C
6	Lower limit	GVL_Visu.Temperature_TIC2 < 8	Error	Temperature TIC2 has fallen below 8°C
7	Upper limit	GVL_Visu.Temperature_TIC2 > 32	Error	Temperature TIC2 exceeded 32°C
	Click here to add a n...	Click here to add a new alarm		

Upper limit

| Expression | GVL_Visu.Temperature_TIC2 | ... | > | ∨ | 30 |
| Hysteresis in % | 3.3 | ... | | | |

Figure 8-74. *TIC2: Upper Limit 30°C*

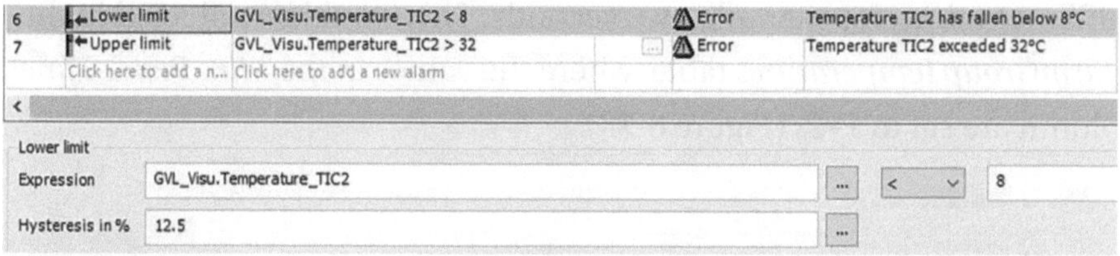

6	Lower limit	GVL_Visu.Temperature_TIC2 < 8	Error	Temperature TIC2 has fallen below 8°C
7	Upper limit	GVL_Visu.Temperature_TIC2 > 32	Error	Temperature TIC2 exceeded 32°C
	Click here to add a n...	Click here to add a new alarm		

Lower limit

| Expression | GVL_Visu.Temperature_TIC2 | ... | < | ∨ | 8 |
| Hysteresis in % | 12.5 | ... | | | |

Figure 8-75. *TIC2: Lower Limit 8°C*

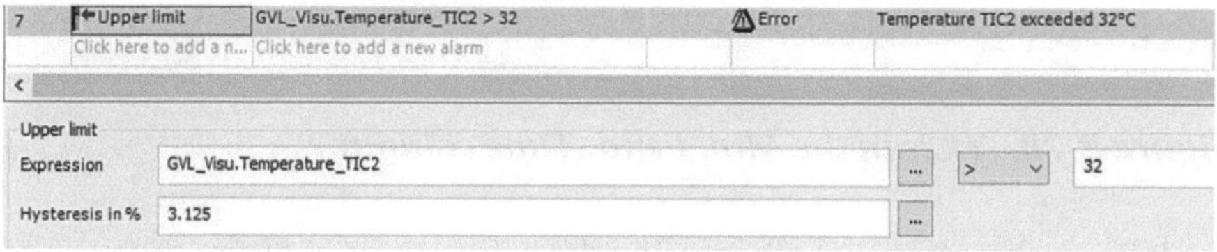

| 7 | Upper limit | GVL_Visu.Temperature_TIC2 > 32 | Error | Temperature TIC2 exceeded 32°C |
| | Click here to add a n... | Click here to add a new alarm | | |

Upper limit

| Expression | GVL_Visu.Temperature_TIC2 | ... | > | ∨ | 32 |
| Hysteresis in % | 3.125 | ... | | | |

Figure 8-76. *TIC2: Upper Limit 32°C*

Let's now download our program to the PLC controller and check what happens in the alarm table right after the control system starts (Figure 8-77).

	Timestamp	Message
0	07.09.2024 08:50:55	Temperature TIC2 has fallen below 8 C

Figure 8-77. *Visible alarm signaling low temperature TIC2*

As observed, the alarm indicating that the temperature has dropped below 8°C appeared in the alarm table even though it is not active. This alarm was active at the moment the PLC controller started. For temperature *QCS-TIC2*, alarms are triggered using *Upper limit* and *Lower limit* types set directly in the *AlarmGroupTemperatures* group and are not associated with the logic of the *Alarms* program.

To prevent this alarm from appearing during the PLC controller startup, we can use CODESYS functionality to set a minimum condition fulfillment time, for example, two seconds. This would be reflected in the *AlarmGroupTemperatures* table, where the values in the *Min. Pend. Time* column are set to *T#2s* (Figure 8-78).

ID	Observation Type	Details	Deactivation	Class	Message	Min. Pend. Time
0	Digital	(Alarms.Temperature_TIC1_Low) = (TRUE)		Warning	Temperature TIC1 has fallen below 10°C	
1	Digital	(Alarms.Temperature_TIC1_High) = (TRUE)		Warning	Temperature TIC1 exceeded 30°C	
2	Digital	(Alarms.Temperature_TIC1_LowLow) = (TRUE)		Error	Temperature TIC1 has fallen below 8°C	
3	Digital	(Alarms.Temperature_TIC1_HighHigh) = (TRUE)		Error	Temperature TIC1 exceeded 32°C	
7	Upper limit	GVL_Visu.Temperature_TIC2 > 32		Error	Temperature TIC2 exceeded 32°C	T#2s
5	Upper limit	GVL_Visu.Temperature_TIC2 > 30		Warning	Temperature TIC2 exceeded 30°C	T#2s
6	Lower limit	GVL_Visu.Temperature_TIC2 < 8		Error	Temperature TIC2 has fallen below 8°C	T#2s
4	Lower limit	GVL_Visu.Temperature_TIC2 < 10		Warning	Temperature TIC2 has fallen below 10°C	T#2s

Figure 8-78. *T#2s in the Min. Pend. Time column*

It is worth noting that when using delay functions in alarm groups, such as setting the minimum time for alarm conditions, this delay time is applied both during the PLC startup and in every subsequent cycle. This means that alarms can be delayed during each cycle.

In contrast, the delay implemented in the *Alarms* program only operates during the initial PLC startup cycle. In our case, using the *INIT* variable, alarm triggering is delayed by five seconds from the start of the PLC, but after this time, alarms are activated in normal mode, without additional delays.

The purpose of this exercise was to demonstrate that multiple approaches can achieve the same goal, and details are crucial. Personally, I prefer not to mix different types because it leads to confusion about how and where an alarm will be triggered. I always try to decide on a single solution, which helps maintain clarity in the project structure. Over time, while building additional control systems, habits will form, and you will make decisions regarding the appropriate solutions. Sometimes the solution may be dictated by the client for whom you are designing the control system. The most important thing is to be flexible and not limit yourself to one solution, as this can narrow your perspective. In this work, we must adapt to the client's expectations, especially when designing visualization systems, because it is from this application that people who are not proficient in control system construction often interact, expecting that the installation or machine they operate will be fully operational and perform its assigned tasks.

Additional Task

Expand the trend to allow for retrieving historical data, not just data from the last minute. I considered whether it is worth describing this process in detail. In reality, it would involve nothing more than copying and pasting documentation from the CODESYS environment, which would make this section too lengthy. My goal is to demonstrate the concept of trends. If someone wants to extend the functionality of this application, they should right-click the *Trend* object and select the option *Insert Elements for Trend Controlling* (Figure 8-79).

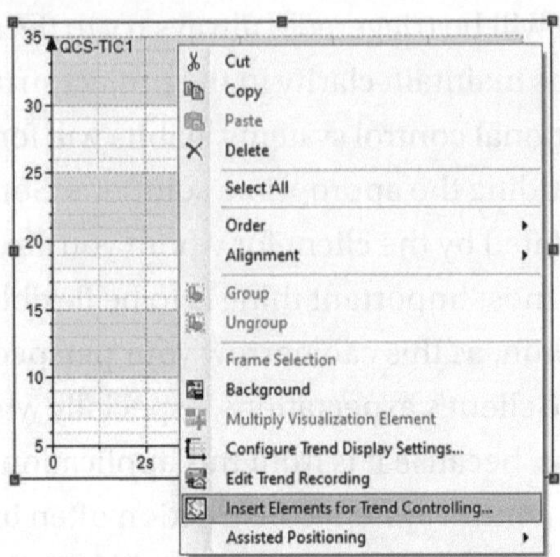

Figure 8-79.   *Insert Elements for Trend Controlling...*

Additionally, expand the *AlarmGroupTemperatures* to use custom alarm classes and experiment with different types of *Observation Type* to discover the capabilities offered by the system. These exercises will help in learning how to use the CODESYS technical documentation. In the role of a PLC programmer, the ability to read and use technical documentation is crucial. Often, while deploying systems, we work under time pressure and need to quickly find information about the operation of specific functions to promptly implement the functionalities required by the client for the efficient operation of the control system.

Summary

In this chapter, we examined two key tools in visualization systems: trends and alarms. Both elements are essential for effective monitoring and analysis of a control system's performance. Trends allow for the observation and analysis of data in real time and over longer periods, while alarms provide a rapid response to irregularities and potential issues.

Together, trends and alarms create a powerful tool that significantly enhances the ability to analyze, diagnose, and manage a control system. We became familiar with the basic functions and configurations of these tools, which provide a solid foundation for exploring their advanced capabilities. To fully harness the potential of trends and alarms, I encourage you to review additional materials and documentation that will allow you to expand the functionality of these tools according to your individual needs.

CHAPTER 9

Conveyor Control and Product Quality Assurance

In the previous chapters, we focused on building automation, implementing tasks such as automated gate and door control, as well as managing heating and cooling systems. Now, it's time to take the next step – automating production processes in the quality control hall of a factory.

The quality control line we are designing will consist of three conveyors, each playing a critical role in the product transport and inspection process:

- *First conveyor (QCS-CONV1):* Transfers products from the production hall and delivers them for analysis

- *Second conveyor (QCS-CONV2):* Equipped with an analyzer that performs product quality checks

- *Third conveyor (QCS-CONV3):* Equipped with a pusher actuator responsible for sorting products into two categories: those meeting quality standards and defective ones.

© Dariusz Wrebiak 2026
D. Wrebiak, *Practical PLC Programming for Beginners*, Maker Innovations Series,
https://doi.org/10.1007/979-8-8688-2430-2_9

In this chapter, we will focus on designing the control logic and visualization for this line, covering all process stages – from product reception to sorting at the end of the line.

Technology and Operation of Conveyors

Conveyor QCS-CONV1

The *QCS-CONV1* conveyor is powered by a drive controlled by a frequency inverter, allowing for adjustable speed operation. The speed control logic is based on the status of the analyzer on the *QCS-CONV2* conveyor:

- *Analyzer in STANDBY state:* The *QCS-CONV1* conveyor operates at 100% speed.

- *Analyzer in ANALYZING state:* The conveyor speed is reduced to 50%.

Conveyor QCS-CONV2

The *QCS-CONV2* conveyor receives products from *QCS-CONV1* and transports them through the quality analyzer. The analyzer conducts quality control tests and returns one of two possible outcomes:

- *Positive result:* The product has passed quality control.

- *Negative result:* The product has failed quality control.

The test results are stored in the PLC, enabling decisions to be made regarding the sorting of products on the *QCS-CONV3* conveyor.

Conveyor QCS-CONV3

The *QCS-CONV3* conveyor is responsible for transporting products to two separate pallets based on the quality control results:

- Products meeting quality standards are transported to a pallet designated for accepted products.

- Defective products are removed from the conveyor by the pusher actuator and placed on a pallet for rejected products.

The conveyor's operation is dependent on the number of products accumulated on each pallet. If either pallet reaches its maximum capacity (ten products), the conveyor halts, and the forklift operator receives a notification to collect the full pallet.

Pusher Actuator Process

- A defective product is identified based on data received from the analyzer and stored in the PLC.

- When the defective product reaches the actuator's position, the actuator is triggered to push the product onto the rejection pallet.

- Accepted products continue along the conveyor to the end, where they are placed on the accepted products pallet.

Implementation of the Conveyor Function Block for Conveyor Control

Introduction to the *Conveyor* Function Block

As discussed in earlier sections of this book, function blocks enable the creation of modular and manageable control logic components. Within the implementation of the quality control line, the *Conveyor* function block is a key element in the system that governs the operation of the conveyors. Its primary role is to manage the conveyor's states – starting, stopping, and holding – based on specified input signals.

Global Variable Declaration

We will begin the implementation of the quality control line by declaring global variables that will be responsible for controlling the operation of the conveyors and the devices installed on them (Table 9-1, Table 9-2, Table 9-3). Global variables provide easy access to data across different parts of the program, significantly simplifying the creation and management of control logic.

Table 9-1. *Control signals for the QCS-CONV1 conveyor*

Type of Signal	Name	Description
Digital Output	QCS-CONV1-START-CMD	Start/Stop command for the conveyor
Analog Output	QCS-CONV1-SPEED	Speed of conveyor

Table 9-2. *Control signals for the QCS-CONV2 conveyor*

Type of Signal	Name	Description
Digital Input	QCS-CONV2-ANALYZER-STANDBY	Analyzer in standby mode
Digital Input	QCS-CONV2-ANALYZER-ANALYZE	Analyzer performing product analysis
Digital Input	QCS-CONV2-ANALYZER-QUALITY-PASS	Quality control result – product passed
Digital Input	QCS-CONV2-ANALYZER-QUALITY-FAIL	Quality control result – product failed
Digital output	QCS-CONV2-START-CMD	Start/Stop command for conveyor
Analog output	QCS-CONV1-SPEED	Speed of conveyor

Table 9-3. *Control signals for the QCS-CONV3 conveyor*

Type of Signal	Name	Description
Digital Input	QCS-CONV3-PASSED_COUNT	Counting products that passed quality control
Digital Input	QCS-CONV3-FAILED-COUNT	Counting products that failed quality control
Digital Input	QCS-CONV3-PUSHER-REQUEST	Request to activate pusher for rejected products
Digital Output	QCS-CONV3-START-CMD	Start/Stop command for conveyor
Digital Output	QCS-CONV3-PUSHER-CMD	Command to activate pusher for rejected products
Digital Output	QCS-CONV3-HOLD	Conveyor in hold mode (notify for operator)

Global variables are declared in the *GVL_InputsOutputs* namespace, as outlined in the tables provided earlier (Figure 9-1).

```
59      (* Conveyors *)
60      // Digital Inputs
61      DI_ANALYZER_STANDBY : BOOL;          // CONV2-ANALYZER: Analyzer in standby mode
62      DI_ANALYZER_ANALYZE : BOOL;          // CONV2-ANALYZER: Analyzer performing product analysis
63      DI_ANALYZER_QUALITY_PASS : BOOL;     // CONV2-ANALYZER: Quality control result - product passed
64      DI_ANALYZER_QUALITY_FAIL : BOOL;     // CONV2-ANALYZER: Quality control result - product failed
65      DI_CONV3_PASSED_COUNT : BOOL;        // CONV3: Photocell counting products that passed quality control
66      DI_CONV3_FAILED_COUNT : BOOL;        // CONV3: Photocell counting products that failed quality control
67      DI_CONV3_PUSHER_REQUEST : BOOL;      // CONV3-PUSHER: Request to activate pusher for rejected products
68      // Analog Outputs
69      AO_CONV1_SPEED : INT;                // CONV1: Speed of conveyor
70      // Digital Outputs
71      DO_CONV1_START_CMD : BOOL;           // CONV1: Start/Stop command for conveyor
72      DO_CONV2_START_CMD : BOOL;           // CONV2: Start/Stop command for conveyor
73      DO_CONV3_START_CMD : BOOL;           // CONV3: Start/Stop command for conveyor
74      DO_CONV3_PUSHER_CMD : BOOL;          // CONV3: Command to activate pusher for rejected products
75      DO_CONV3_HOLD : BOOL;                // CONV3: Conveyor in hold mode, requiring forklift operator intervention
76
```

Figure 9-1. *Global variables GVL_InputsOutputs*

Creating a Function Block *Conveyor*

To begin, let's add a new function block named *Conveyor* to the folder *Application* ➤ *PLC* ➤ *FunctionBlocks* (Figure 9-2). It will be responsible for controlling the operation of conveyors in the system.

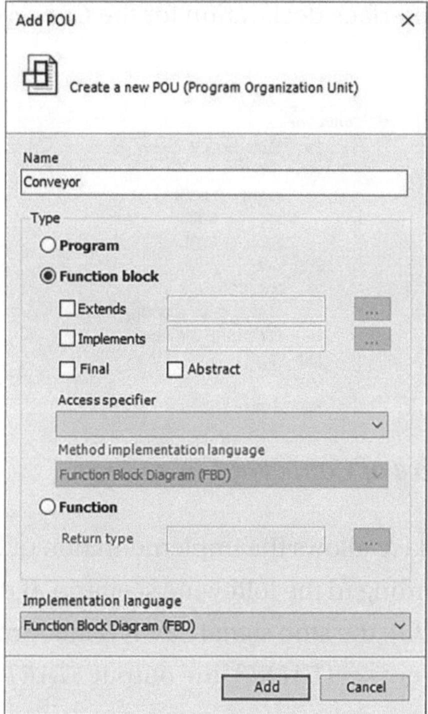

Figure 9-2. *Global variables GVL_InputsOutputs*

The first step after creating the function block is to define its interface, which consists of a set of input and output variables that will enable communication with other elements of the system (Table 9-4).

Table 9-4. *Interface of the function block*

Type of Variable	Name	Description
Input (BOOL)	START	Variable which starts the conveyor operation
Input (BOOL)	STOP	Variable which stops the conveyor operation
Input (BOOL)	HOLD	Variable which pauses the conveyor operation
Output (BOOL)	START_CMD	Variable controlling the digital output
Output (DWORD)	STATUS	Variable storing the conveyor status

This is how the interface declaration for the *Conveyor* function block looks (Figure 9-3).

```
  Conveyor  ×
 1    FUNCTION_BLOCK Conveyor
 2    VAR_INPUT
 3        START : BOOL;
 4        STOP : BOOL;
 5        HOLD : BOOL;
 6    END_VAR
 7    VAR_OUTPUT
 8        START_CMD : BOOL;
 9        STATUS : DWORD;
10    END_VAR
11    VAR
12    END_VAR
```

Figure 9-3. *Interface of Conveyor FB*

The simple interface allows the implementation of basic control logic, which operates according to the following scenario. If the start signal *START* is active (*TRUE*), the stop signal *STOP* is inactive (*FALSE*), and the hold signal *HOLD* is not set (*FALSE*), the output *START_CMD* should be activated (Figure 9-4).

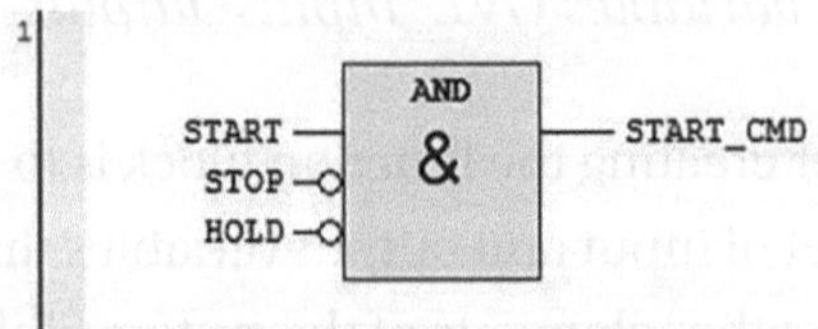

Figure 9-4. *Conveyor FB: Network 1*

To increase the reliability of the block's operation and simplify control, we will introduce a flip-flop. As we already know, this is a logical element that "remembers" its state. With its help, we can easily manage the signals for turning on (*START*) and turning off (*STOP*), eliminating potential logical conflicts.

In the variable declaration section of the function block, we need to add the variable *START_STOP_RS* for the flip-flop (Figure 9-5).

```
     Conveyor  ✕
      1      FUNCTION_BLOCK Conveyor
      2    VAR_INPUT
      3        START : BOOL;
      4        STOP : BOOL;
      5        HOLD : BOOL;
      6    END_VAR
      7    VAR_OUTPUT
      8        START_CMD : BOOL;
      9        STATUS : DWORD;
     10    END_VAR
     11    VAR
     12        START_STOP_RS : RS;
     13    END_VAR
```

Figure 9-5. *Interface of Conveyor FB: flip-flop*

After introducing the flip-flop, the control logic is expanded and operates as follows (Figure 9-6).

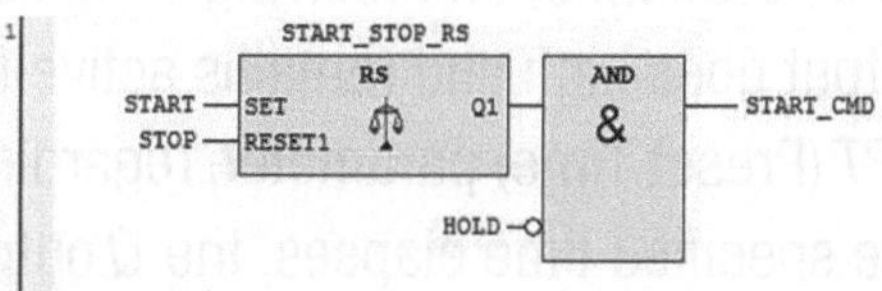

Figure 9-6. *Conveyor FB: Network 1 with flip-flop*

Using TP Timers

To implement the control logic for the *Conveyor* function block, we will use TP type timers to simplify the handling of rising edge detection. In this example, we will declare two TP timers that will be used for setting and resetting the flip-flop. To start, let's add the variables *START_TP* and *STOP_TP* to the function block, which will represent the TP timers (Figure 9-7).

```
     ┌─ Conveyor  X ──────────────────────────────
      1       FUNCTION_BLOCK Conveyor
   ⊟  2       VAR_INPUT
      3           START : BOOL;
      4           STOP : BOOL;
      5           HOLD : BOOL;
      6       END_VAR
   ⊟  7       VAR_OUTPUT
      8           START_CMD : BOOL;
      9           STATUS : DWORD;
     10       END_VAR
   ⊟ 11       VAR
     12           START_STOP_RS : RS;
     13           START_TP : TP;
     14           STOP_TP : TP;
     15       END_VAR
```

Figure 9-7. *Interface of Conveyor FB: timers*

Timer TP (Timer Pulse)   The TP function block generates a time
pulse of a specified duration. Upon receiving a high state signal at the
IN input, the *Q* output goes high and remains active for the duration
specified by the *PT* (Preset Time) parameter, regardless of the state of
the input. After the specified time elapses, the *Q* output returns to the
low state, and the *ET* (Elapsed Time) value indicates the time that has
passed since the block was activated.

Below is the implementation of the control logic using TP timers
(Figure 9-8).

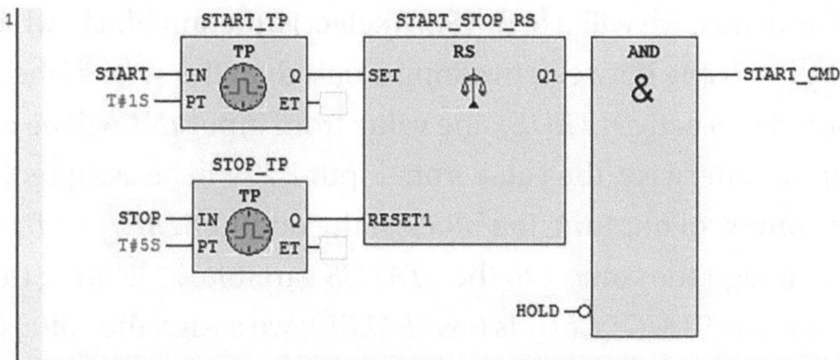

Figure 9-8. *Conveyor FB: Network 1 with timers*

The TP timer automatically detects the rising edge on the input *IN*. As soon as this input becomes active (*TRUE*), the timer begins counting the time specified at the input *PT*. Once the countdown is complete, the output *Q* is deactivated. This way, the TP timer eliminates the need to manually implement the detection of rising edges for the *START* and *STOP* signals.

Many readers may wonder why the *PT* time differs for the *START_TP* and *STOP_TP* timers. The difference in the *PT* time values results from the type of *RS* flip-flop used, where the *RESET* input is dominant. As long as the signal on the *RESET* input is active, the flip-flop's output *Q* remains low, regardless of the signal at the *SET* input.

Introducing different *PT* time settings for the TP timers ensures a minimum delay time before the conveyor can be turned on again. After deactivating the conveyor, at least five seconds must pass before it can be restarted. This is a standard practice in motor control to prevent frequent switching on and off of devices.

Implementation of Conveyor State

After implementing the logic for turning the conveyor on and off, the next step is to add functionality that will monitor the current state of the conveyor. This state will be used to display information on the visualization to indicate whether the conveyor is on or off.

To achieve this, we will use the *SEL* (select) function block, which operates by choosing between two inputs based on the state of the signal at the *G* input. If *G* is active (*TRUE*), the value from input *IN1* will be assigned to the output; otherwise, the value from input *IN0* will be assigned.

In the context of our function block, if the output *START_CMD* is high (*TRUE*), we assign the value 1 to the *STATUS* variable, indicating that the conveyor is on. If *START_CMD* is low (*FALSE*), we assign the value 0 to the *STATUS* variable, meaning the conveyor is off.

This is the logic for implementing the *Conveyor* function block in *Network 2* (Figure 9-9).

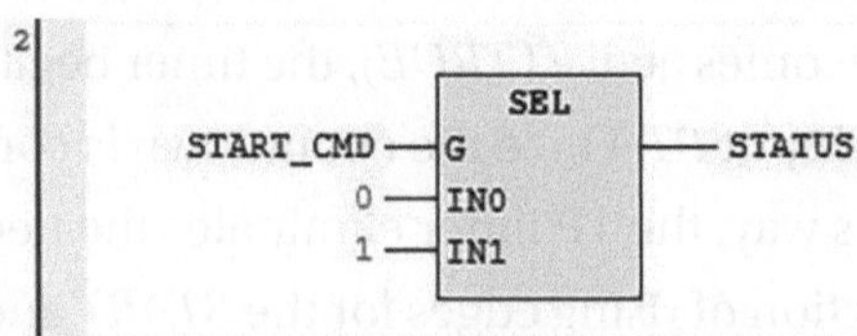

***Figure 9-9.** Conveyor FB: Network 2*

Switching Between LAD and FBD Languages

In the CODESYS environment, developers have the option to switch between different programming languages, such as LAD (Ladder Diagram) and FBD (Function Block Diagram). As mentioned, the LAD language is particularly valued by electricians because it resembles traditional electrical diagrams, making it easier to understand control logic. On the other hand, FBD is often considered more intuitive and convenient for creating more complex functions.

When creating the Conveyor function block, we declared the use of the FBD language for implementing the logic. However, CODESYS offers the ability to switch between FBD and LAD views, depending on the user's preference. To switch the view to the LAD language, simply click in the menu *FBD/LD/IL* ➤ *View* ➤ *View as Ladder Logic* (Figure 9-10).

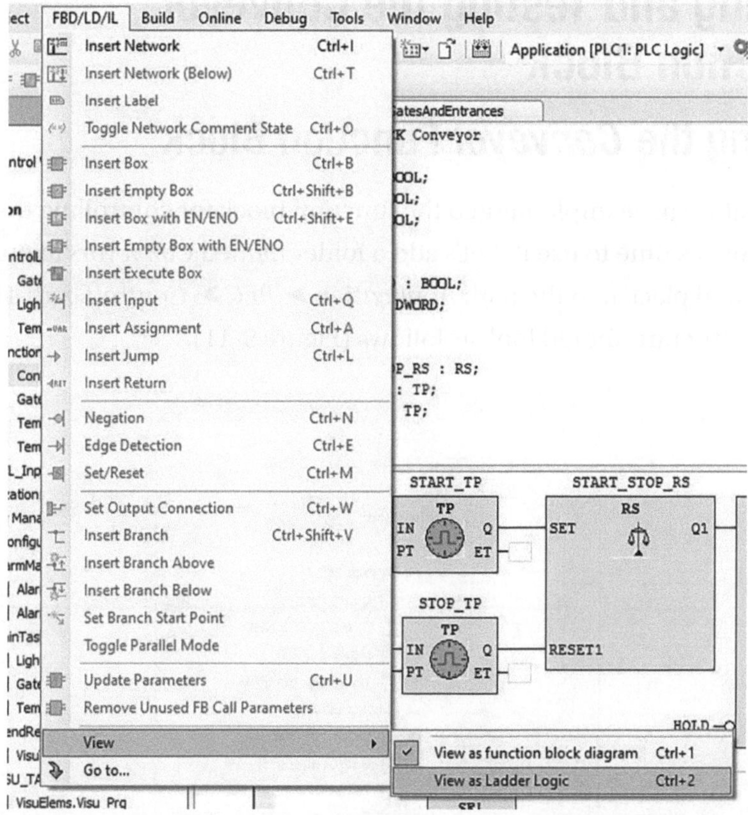

Figure 9-10. *FBD/LD/IL ➤ View ➤ View as Ladder Logic*

After switching, the CODESYS environment will change the way the program is displayed from a Function Block Diagram (FBD) to a Ladder Diagram (LAD) while retaining the entire program logic. This feature allows developers to work in a more familiar format, which can speed up the coding process, especially when the logic is complex. To return to the FBD view, simply select the option *FBD/LD/IL ➤ View ➤ View as Function Block Diagram* again.

Calling and Testing the Conveyor Function Block

Calling the *Conveyor* Function Block

Now that we have implemented the function block for controlling the conveyor, it's time to use it. Let's add a folder named *Conveyors* to our project and place it in the path *Application* ➤ *PLC* ➤ *ControlLogic*. The project structure should look as follows (Figure 9-11).

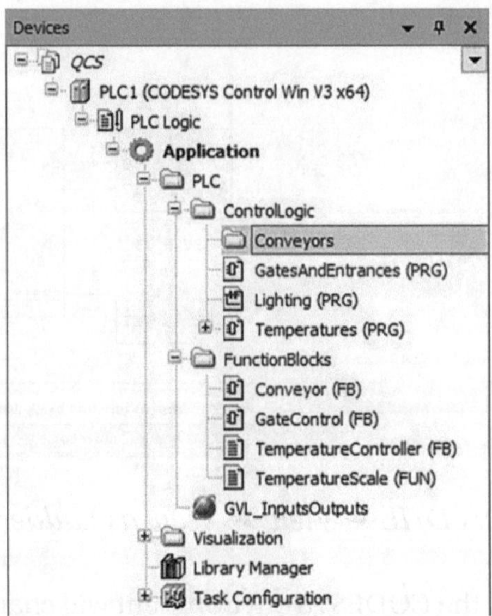

Figure 9-11. *Devices window*

In this folder, let's create a program named *CONV1*, where we will implement the control logic for the first conveyor, *QCS-CONV1*, on the product quality control line (Figure 9-12).

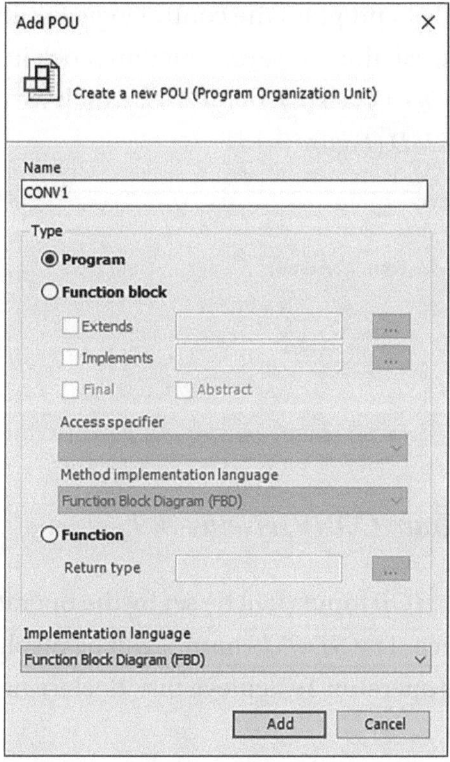

Figure 9-12. *Add POU: CONV1*

Next, add the call to the *CONV1* program in *MainTask (Figure 9-13).*

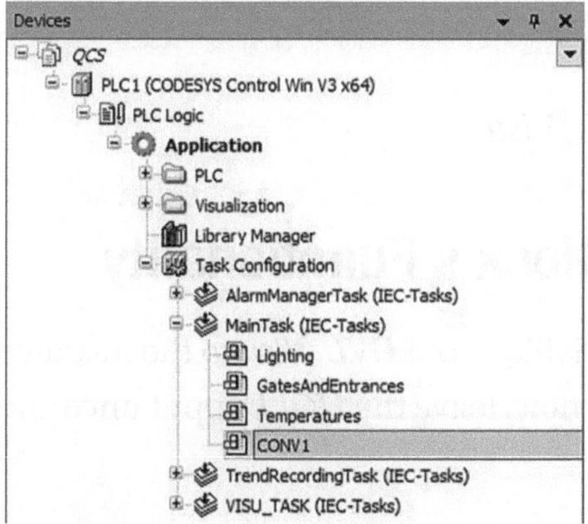

Figure 9-13. *Task Configuration*

Now we are ready to program the control logic for the *QCS-CONV1* conveyor. To do this, call the *Conveyor* function block in *Network 1*. Assign the digital output *DO_CONV1_START_CMD*, which we declared earlier, to the output *START_CMD (Figure 9-14)*.

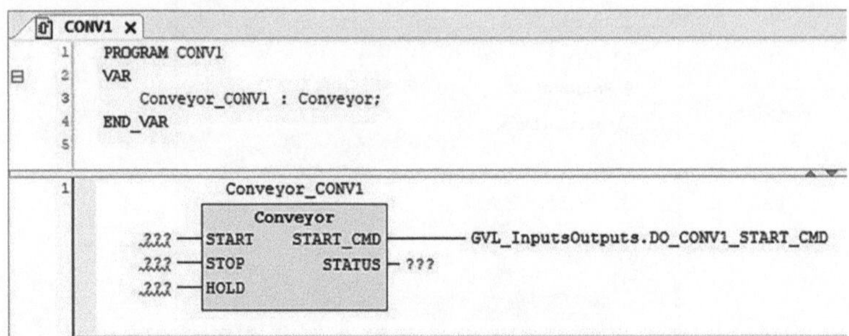

Figure 9-14. *Program CONV1: Network 1*

The *START* and *STOP* inputs will be set by the operator from the visualization interface. The *STATUS* output will be displayed on the visualization for the operator. To achieve this, declare new global variables in *GVL_Visu (Figure 9-15)*.

```
(* Conveyors *)
CONV1_START : BOOL;
CONV1_STOP : BOOL;
CONV1_STATUS : DWORD;
```

Figure 9-15. *GVL_Visu*

Testing the Block's Functionality

Next, assign the variables from *GVL_Visu* to the instance of the *Conveyor* function block. For now, leave the *HOLD* input unconnected (Figure 9-16).

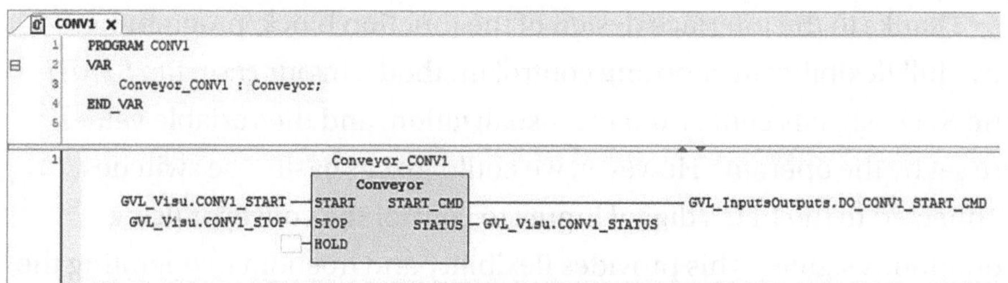

Figure 9-16. *Program CONV1: Network 1*

Now, download our program to the controller, and test the functionality of the function block using the *Watch* Table. We will manipulate the variables *GVL_Visu.CONV1_START* and *GVL_Visu. CONV1_STOP and* then observe how the values of *GVL_InputsOutputs. DO_CONV1_START_CMD* and *GVL_Visu.CONV1_STATUS* change (Figure 9-17).

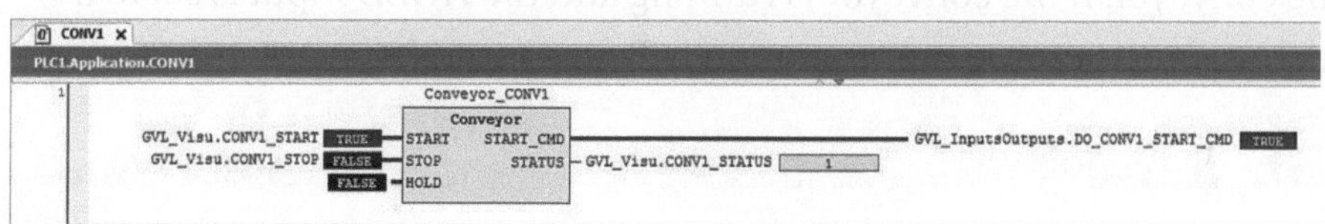

Figure 9-17. *Conveyor is on*

Remember that in the function block, we implemented a flip-flop that sets or resets the start command. This means that we do not need to keep the variable *CONV1_START* in a high state. A short pulse is enough to turn the conveyor on. The conveyor will remain on until the variable *CONV1_STOP* is set to a high state (Figure 9-18).

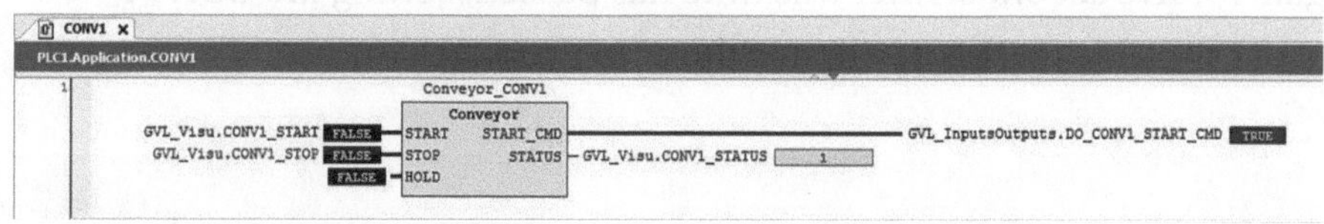

Figure 9-18. *Conveyor is on, while START is FALSE*

Thanks to the interface design of the function block, programmers have full flexibility in choosing control methods. In our case, the *START* and *STOP* signals come from the visualization, and the variable values are set by the operator. However, we could just as easily use switches connected to the PLC's digital inputs to control the conveyor using continuous signals. This provides flexibility and freedom in operating the function block.

Moreover, the code implemented once can be easily reused for additional conveyors, which we will demonstrate in the next section of this chapter.

Testing the Conveyor Hold Functionality

Now, let's test one of the implemented functionalities of the block: holding the conveyor. If the conveyor is running and the *HOLD* input is set to a high state, the conveyor's operation will be paused (Figure 9-19).

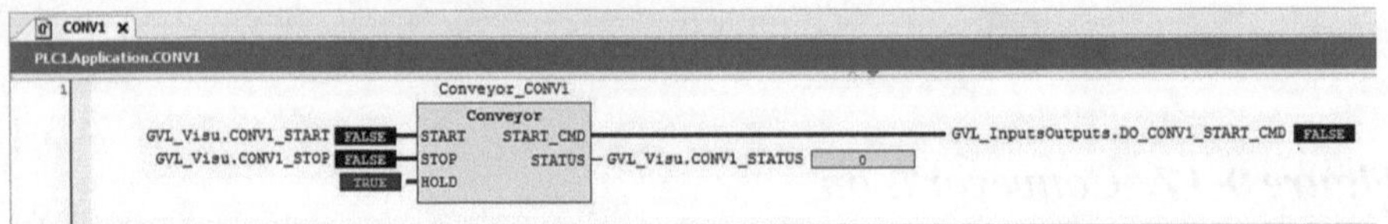

Figure 9-19. *Conveyor is hold*

Once the *HOLD* variable is set to *FALSE*, the conveyor will resume operation. We can also stop the conveyor by setting the *CONV1_STOP* variable to *TRUE*. After turning off the conveyor, it cannot be turned on again for five seconds. After this time has passed, setting the *CONV1_START* variable to *TRUE* will turn the conveyor back on.

Visualization and Conveyor Control
Creating the Conveyors View

Similar to previous chapters, let's add a view named *P05_Conveyors* to our visualization. Below is how the project structure should look (Figure 9-20).

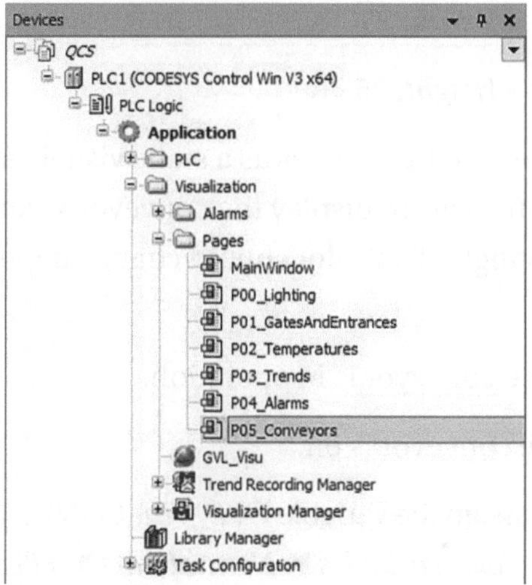

Figure 9-20. *Devices window*

Next, in *MainWindow*, let's add a navigation button that will display the *Conveyors* view. After adding the button, the visualization should look like the example below (Figure 9-21).

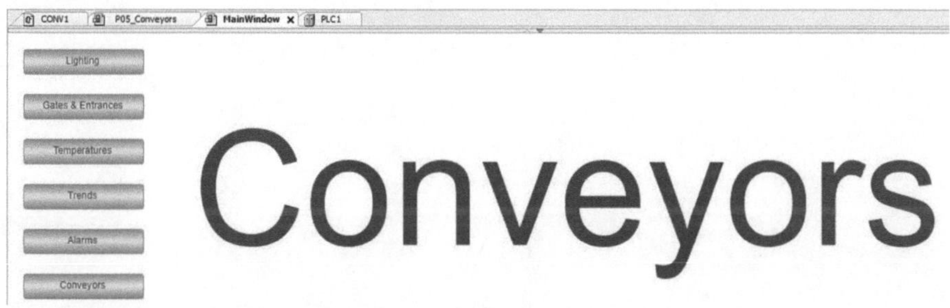

Figure 9-21. *MainWindow ➤ Conveyors*

To begin the conveyor visualization, we will place a *Rectangle* element on the *Conveyors* view. Set its properties according to the parameters below:

- *Position* → *X:* 16

- *Position* → *Y:* 195

- *Position* → *Width:* 250

- *Position* → *Height:* 35

At this stage, the rectangle serves as a static visualization element representing the conveyor. To display the conveyor's status, we will modify the color of the rectangle. The color should change depending on the conveyor's state:

- *Green:* The conveyor is in operation.

- *Gray:* The conveyor is off.

To achieve this, assign the variable *GVL_Visu.CONV1_STATUS* to the rectangle's property *Color variables* ➤ *Normal state* ➤ *Fill color (Figure 9-22)*. This will allow the color of the rectangle to change based on the conveyor's status.

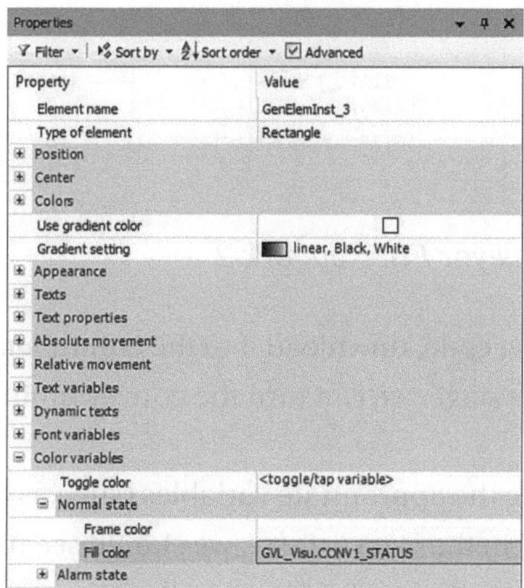

Figure 9-22. *Property Fill color*

However, for the rectangle to actually change color, it's necessary to modify the *Conveyors* function block. In *Network 2*, where the *STATUS* output is set, we currently assign:

- *0:* When the conveyor is off

- *1:* When the conveyor is on

These values are not compatible with the format required by the *Fill color* property, which uses hexadecimal encoding:

- *Gray:* 16#FF808080

- *Green:* 16#FF00FF00

According to CODESYS documentation, the *Fill color* property interprets colors in a specific format. Below is the updated code in *Network 2* of the *Conveyor* function block, which takes the correct color encoding into account. This modification ensures that the *STATUS* output now assigns the correct hexadecimal color codes for the rectangle in the visualization (Figure 9-23).

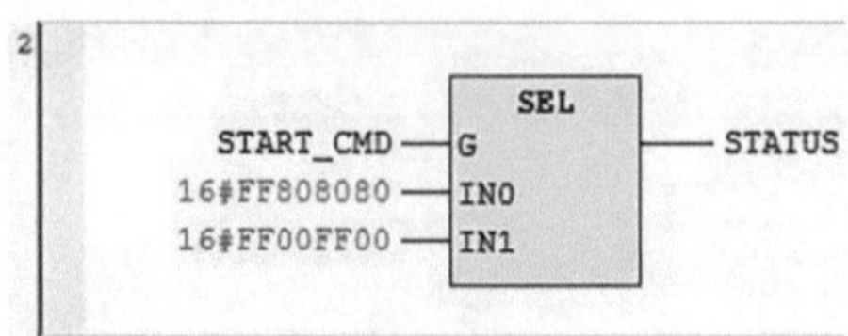

Figure 9-23. *Conveyor FB: Network 2*

Let's compile the code, download it to the controller, and test the visualization. At this stage, we can turn the conveyor on and off from the *Watch Table*.

By manipulating the appropriate variables (such as *CONV1_START* and *CONV1_STOP*) in the *Watch Table*, we should see the rectangle's color change between green (Figure 9-25) (when the conveyor is running) and gray (Figure 9-24) (when the conveyor is off) in the *Conveyors* view.

Figure 9-24. *Conveyor is off*

Figure 9-25. *Conveyor is on*

Control Panel of Conveyor

It's time to control the conveyor without using the *Watch Table*. To do this, we will create a control panel for the conveyor, which will be opened in a dialog window when clicking the button with the name of the conveyor.

First, add a *Button* element to the *Conveyors* view, and set its properties according to the following list:

- *Position → X:* 43

- *Position → Y:* 198

- *Position → Width:* 90

- *Position → Height:* 29

- *Texts → Text:* QCS-CONV1

Our task is to configure this button so that, when clicked, a control panel dialog for the conveyor will open. To do this, we need to add a new visualization component to the project and set its type to *Dialog*. We will store all control panels in the folder *Application* ➤ *Visualization* ➤ *ControlPanels*. Let's start by creating the *ControlPanels* folder. The project structure should look like this (Figure 9-26).

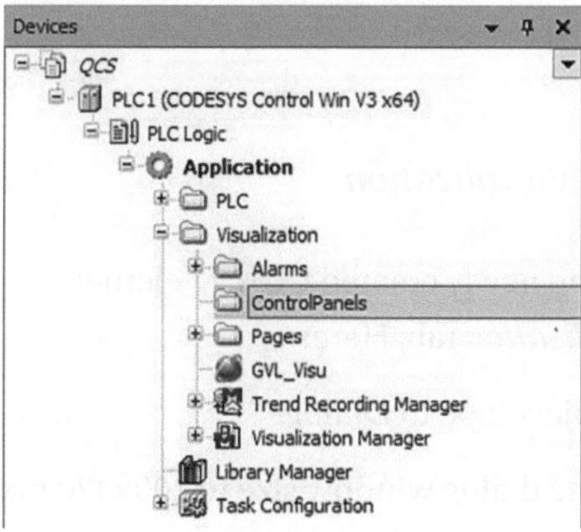

Figure 9-26. *Devices window*

Next, let's add a new element of type *Visualization* to the *ControlPanels* folder. In the *Add Visualization* window, set its name to *CONV1* *(Figure 9-27).*

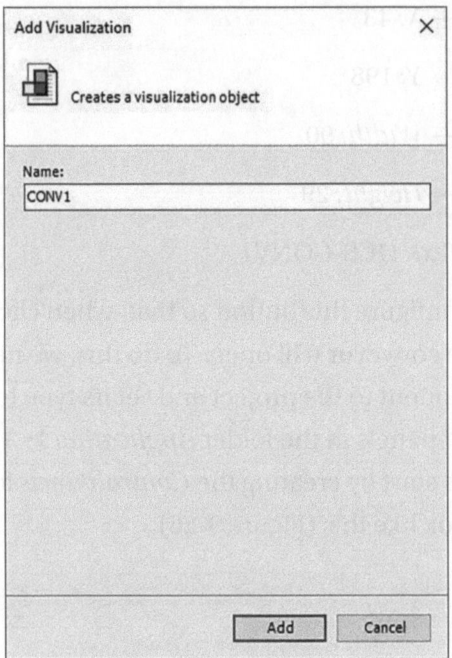

Figure 9-27. *Add Visualization*

Right-click on the newly created *CONV1* element, select *Properties...*, and go to the *Visualization* tab. Here:

- Set the object type to *Dialog*.

- Change the dialog window size to 200×420 pixels.

Confirm the changes by clicking *Apply (Figure 9-28)*.

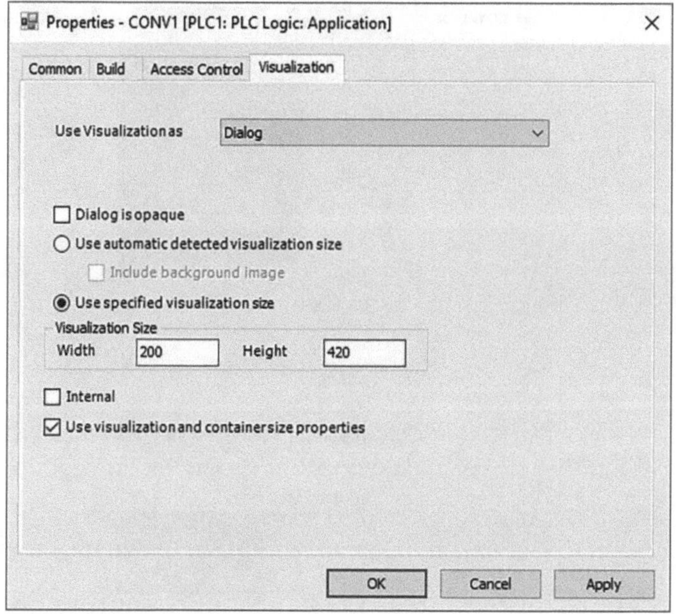

Figure 9-28. *Visualization tab*

Now, let's set the background color of the control panel to white. Right-click on the control panel, and select *Background (Figure 9-29)*.

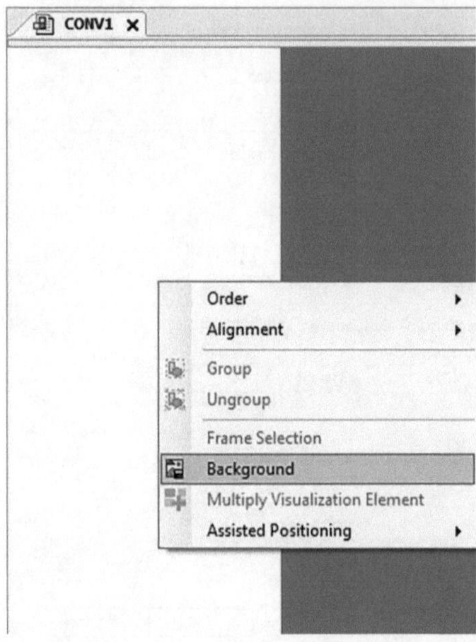

Figure 9-29. *Background*

Next, in the *Color Settings* properties, check the *Use color* check box, and select the color *White* from the drop-down list (Figure 9-30).

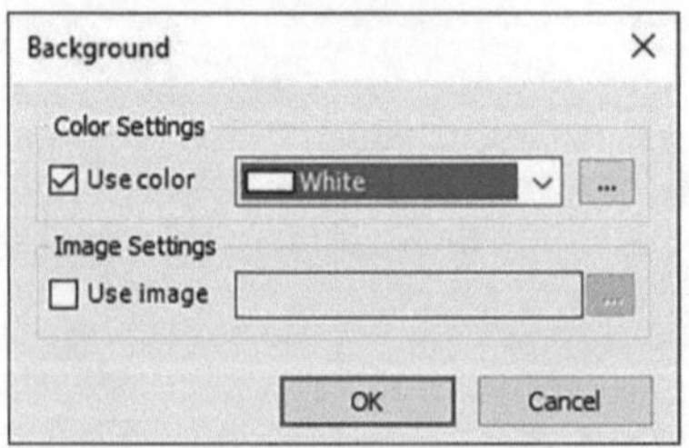

Figure 9-30. *Background* ➤ *White*

Let's start designing the conveyor control panel by adding a *Button* that will allow closing the dialog window. Set its properties according to the following list:

- *Position → X:* 25

- *Position → Y:* 375

- *Texts → Text: Close*

Next, configure the *OnMouseClick* event for this button so that it closes the currently open dialog window. This property can be found in the *Input configuration* section, which we have already configured in previous chapters. Confirm the configuration by clicking *OK (Figure 9-31).*

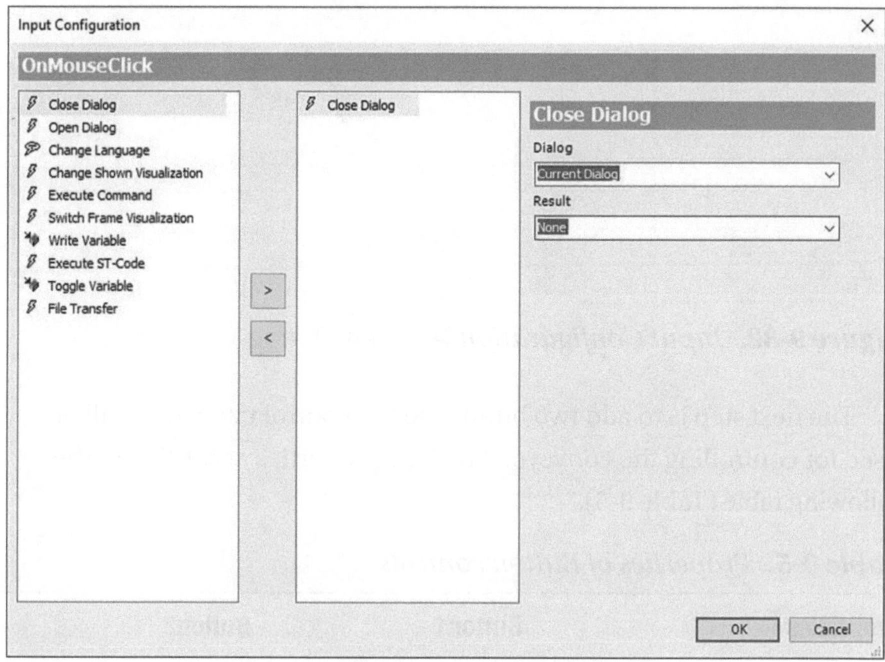

Figure 9-31. *Input Configuration* ➤ *Close Dialog*

Once we have the dialog window ready with the close option, let's configure the *QCS-CONV1* button in the *Conveyors* view. Set its *OnMouseClick* event so that, when clicked, it opens the conveyor control panel. Confirm the configuration by clicking *OK (Figure 9-32).*

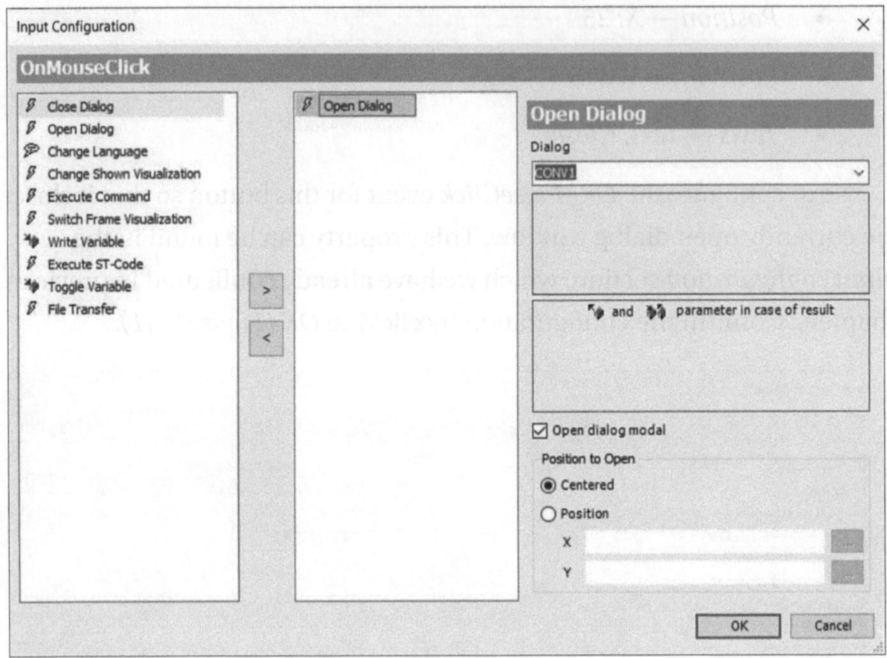

Figure 9-32. *Input Configuration* ➤ *Open Dialog*

The next step is to add two buttons to the control panel that will be used for controlling the conveyor. Set their properties according to the following table (Table 9-5).

Table 9-5. *Properties of Button controls*

Properties	Button1	Button2
Position → X	25	25
Position → Y	209	249
Texts → Text	START	STOP
Input configuration → Tap → Variable	GVL_Visu.CONV1_START	GVL_Visu.CONV1_STOP

By using the *Tap* property, the variables assigned to these buttons will take the value *TRUE* only when the button is pressed and *FALSE* when it is released.

Download the application to the controller and test its functionality. In the *MainWindow* ➤ *Conveyors* view, clicking the *QCS-CONV1* button should open the dialog window with the control panel. The *START* and *STOP* buttons allow turning the conveyor on and off. The *Close* button closes the dialog window.

Personalization of the Control Panel

After testing the functionality of the control panel by turning the conveyor on and off, let's focus on improving its readability and aesthetics. In its current form, the operator has no information about which conveyor is being controlled. To address this, let's add a label for the controlled device on the control panel.

Place a *Label (Figure 9-33)* element on the control panel, and configure its properties according to the following list. This will provide the operator with clear information about which device is being controlled by the panel.

- *Position* → *X:* 25

- *Position* → *Y:* 5

- *Texts* → *Text:* QCS-CONV1

- *Text properties* → *Font:* Headline

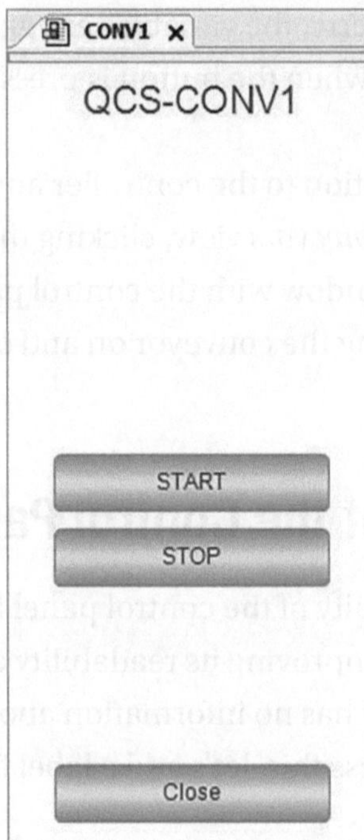

Figure 9-33. *Control panel*

A common practice when designing control panels is to place a symbol of the actuator below the device name. In the case of a conveyor, let's add a symbol for the electric drive. To do this, add an *Ellipse* element and set its properties as follows:

- *Position → X:* 70

- *Position → Y:* 50

- *Position → Width:* 60

- *Position → Height:* 60

- *Appearance → Line width:* 2

- *Texts → Text:* M

- *Text properties → Font:* Large Headline

To ensure that the electric drive symbol reflects the current state of the conveyor, let's add a dynamic background color change. Assign the variable *GVL_Visu.CONV1_STATUS* to the *Color variables* ➤ *Normal state* ➤ *Fill color* property.

With this configuration, when the conveyor is running, the background color of the symbol will change, allowing the operator to quickly recognize the device's status (Figure 9-34).

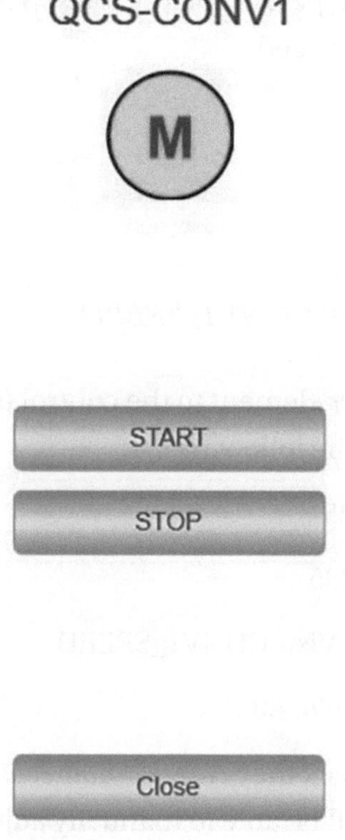

Figure 9-34. *Control panel*

Conveyor Speed Control

The *QCS-CONV1* conveyor is equipped with a frequency inverter, which allows its speed to be controlled via the analog output *AO_CONV1_SPEED*. This output operates in the range from 4 mA to 20 mA, corresponding to speeds from 0% to 100%, where 100% represents the maximum conveyor speed.

Let's start by adding a global variable to *GVL_Visu* called *CONV1_SPEED*, which will be of type *INT* (Figure 9-35). This variable will be used to control the conveyor's speed.

```
16
17        (* Conveyors *)
18        CONV1_START : BOOL;
19        CONV1_STOP : BOOL;
20        CONV1_STATUS : DWORD;
21        CONV1_SPEED : INT;
22
```

Figure 9-35. GVL_Visu: CONV1_SPEED

Next, let's add a *Slider* element to the control panel and set its properties according to the following list:

- *Position → X:* 25

- *Position → Y:* 295

- *Variable:* GVL_Visu.CONV1_SPEED

- *Position → Height:* 60

Additionally, let's check the *Scale → Show scale* check box. With this element, the operator will be able to manually adjust the conveyor's speed (Figure 9-36). The value will be stored in the variable associated with the slider.

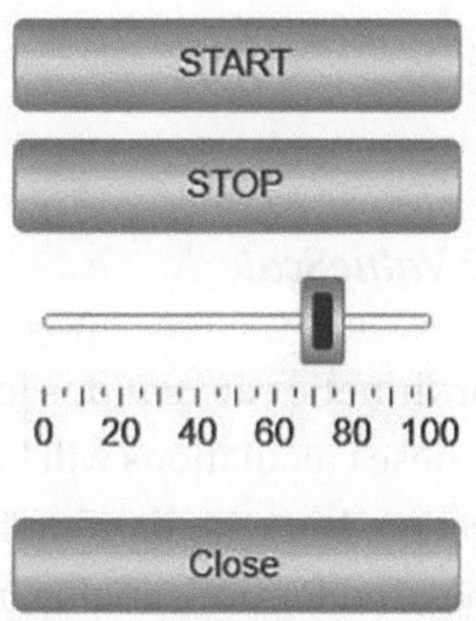

Figure 9-36.   *Control panel with slider*

Currently, the slider changes the variable's value in the range of 0% to 100%, but we need to scale this value to the current signal range of 4 mA to 20 mA, which corresponds to a digital value from 0 to 1023. To accomplish this, let's add a scaling function to the project. In the folder *Application* ➤ *PLC* ➤ *FunctionBlocks*, add a new function named *ValueScale* and confirm its creation (Figure 9-37).

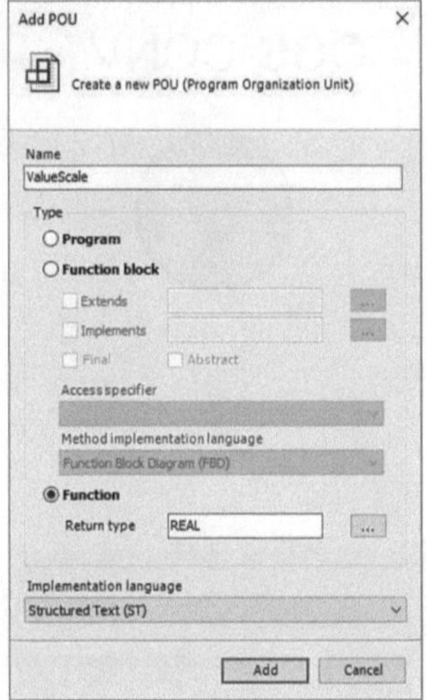

Figure 9-37. *Add POU: ValueScale*

Let's implement the arithmetic calculations for scaling the value in the *ValueScale* function. These calculations will be identical to those in the *TemperatureScale* function, but with more universal variable names, allowing the function to be used for both analog inputs and outputs, regardless of the scaled units (Figure 9-38).

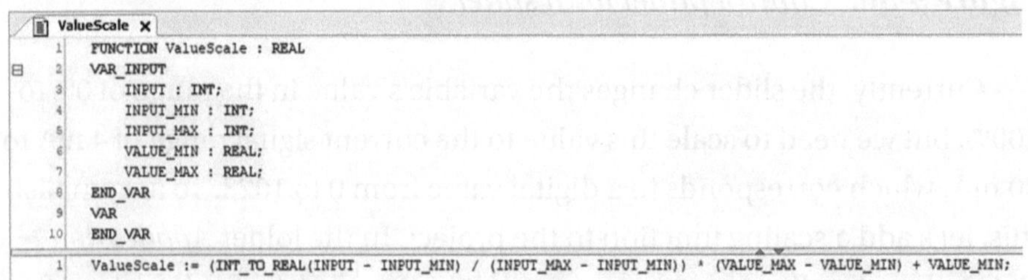

Figure 9-38. *Function ValueScale*

In the *CONV1* program, in *Network 2*, let's implement the scaling of the *CONV1_SPEED* variable from the range of 0% to 100% to a digital value in the range of 0 to 1023. It is important to remember that

- The type of the *CONV1_SPEED* variable is *REAL*.

- The type of the analog output variable is *INT*.

After using the *ValueScale* function, let's convert the data type from *REAL* to *INT* using the *REAL_TO_INT* function. Here is the code implementation in *Network 2* (Figure 9-39).

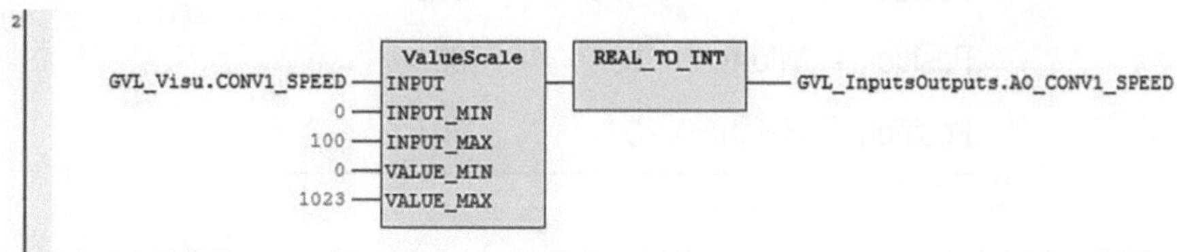

Figure 9-39. *Program CONV1: Network 2*

HAND and AUTO Mode

The last element we will add to the control panel is the ability to select the operating mode of the conveyor: manual (*HAND*) or automatic (*AUTO*). To do this, we will use a *Rotary Switch* element and set its properties according to the following list:

- *Position* → *X:* 65

- *Position* → *Y:* 135

- *Variable:* GVL_Visu.CONV1_HAND

We add the variable *CONV1_HAND* to the global variables *GVL_Visu*, setting its type to *BOOL*. When the switch is toggled, the value of this variable will be set to *TRUE* (for HAND mode) or *FALSE* (for AUTO mode).

To improve the readability of the visualization interface, let's add two *Label* elements. Set their properties according to the table below (Table 9-6).

Table 9-6. *Properties of Label controls*

Properties	Label1	Label2
Texts → Text	HAND	AUTO
Position → X	30	120
Position → Y	120	120
Position → Width	50	50
Position → Height	30	30

Next, let's configure the property *State variables* ➤ *Deactivate
inputs* for the *START* and *STOP* buttons as well as the *Slider*. Add the
condition *NOT GVL_Visu.CONV1_HAND* so that these three elements
are deactivated when the conveyor is in *AUTO* mode. This means the
operator can only use these elements in *HAND* mode (Figure 9-40).
This configuration prevents the accidental activation of the conveyor in
automatic mode, which enhances operational safety.

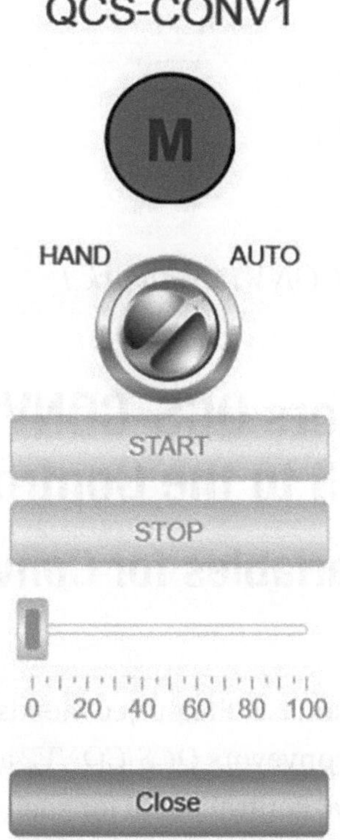

Figure 9-40. *AUTO mode*

Additionally, let's modify the control logic for the conveyor *CONV1* to allow it to be turned on and off only in *HAND* mode. If the conveyor is operating in *AUTO* mode, manual activation and deactivation of the conveyor will not be possible.

Below is the modified control logic (Figure 9-41).

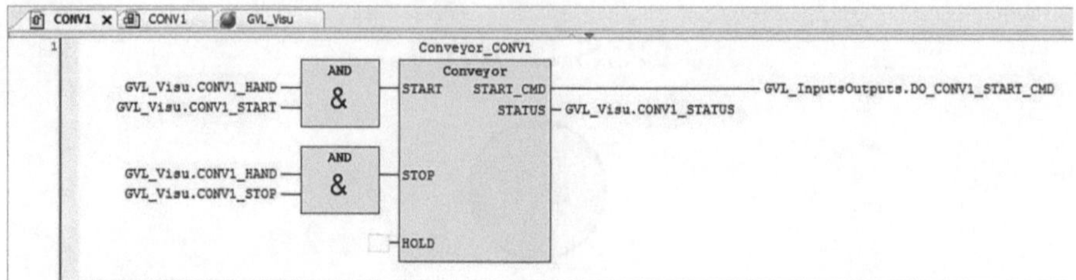

Figure 9-41. *Program CONV1: Network 1*

Adding Conveyors QCS-CONV2 and QCS-CONV3 to the Control System

Declaration of Variables for Conveyors CONV2 and CONV3

As part of this practical exercise, the project needs to be expanded to include control logic for conveyors *QCS-CONV2* and *QCS-CONV3*. Additionally, an individual control panel for each conveyor should be created to allow the operator to turn the conveyors on and off directly from the visualization interface.

Let's begin by declaring global variables. New variables will be responsible for controlling and monitoring conveyors *CONV2* and *CONV3*. Below is a summary of these variables in *GVL_Visu* (Figure 9-42).

```
16
17        (* Conveyors *)
18        CONV1_START : BOOL;
19        CONV1_STOP : BOOL;
20        CONV1_STATUS : DWORD;
21        CONV1_SPEED : INT;
22        CONV1_HAND : BOOL;
23
24        CONV2_START : BOOL;
25        CONV2_STOP : BOOL;
26        CONV2_STATUS : DWORD;
27        CONV2_SPEED : INT;
28        CONV2_HAND : BOOL;
29
30        CONV3_START : BOOL;
31        CONV3_STOP : BOOL;
32        CONV3_STATUS : DWORD;
33        CONV3_SPEED : INT;
34        CONV3_HAND : BOOL;
35
```

Figure 9-42. *GVL_Visu: CONV2 and CONV3 variables*

Adding Control Logic for Conveyors

The next step is to expand the program with the control logic for conveyors *QCS-CONV2* and *QCS-CONV3*. To streamline the process, it is best to copy the existing program for *CONV1* and then refactor the code by adjusting the variable names and labels to match the new conveyors.

It is important to note that conveyors *CONV2* and *CONV3* always operate at a fixed speed. Therefore, the logic in *Network 2* of the *CONV1* program, which is responsible for speed regulation, is not required here and can be completely removed for these conveyors.

Finally, ensure that the *CONV2* and *CONV3* programs are correctly added to the *Task Configurator*, which will allow them to function properly within the project. After these changes, the project structure should look as follows (Figure 9-43).

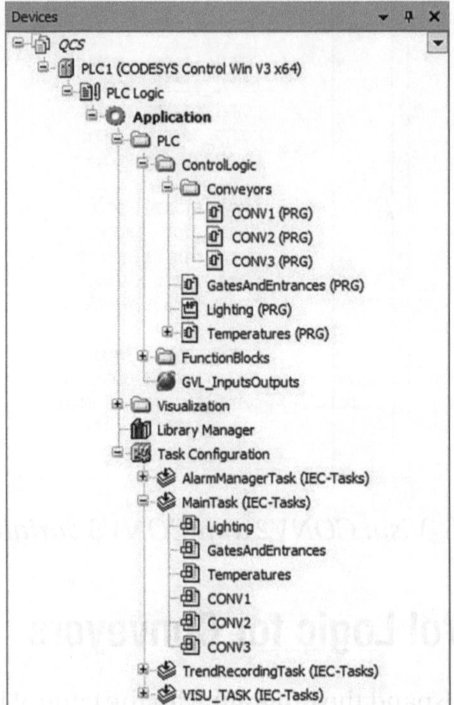

Figure 9-43. *Devices window*

Creating Control Panels for CONV2 and CONV3

The next step is to prepare the control panels for conveyors *CONV2* and *CONV3*. The easiest approach is to copy the control panel for *CONV1* and perform refactoring.

After copying the control panel for *CONV1*, an object named *CONV1_1* will appear in the *ControlPanels* folder. The project structure should look like this (Figure 9-44).

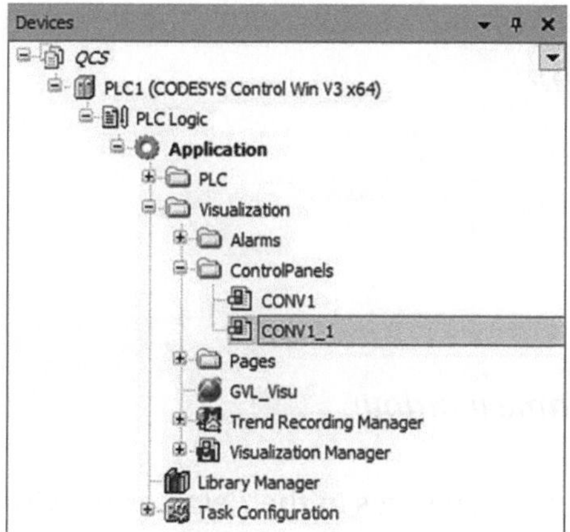

Figure 9-44. *Devices window*

Right-click the object *CONV1_1*, and from the menu, select the option *Refactoring* ➤ *Rename 'CONV1_1'...* (Figure 9-45).

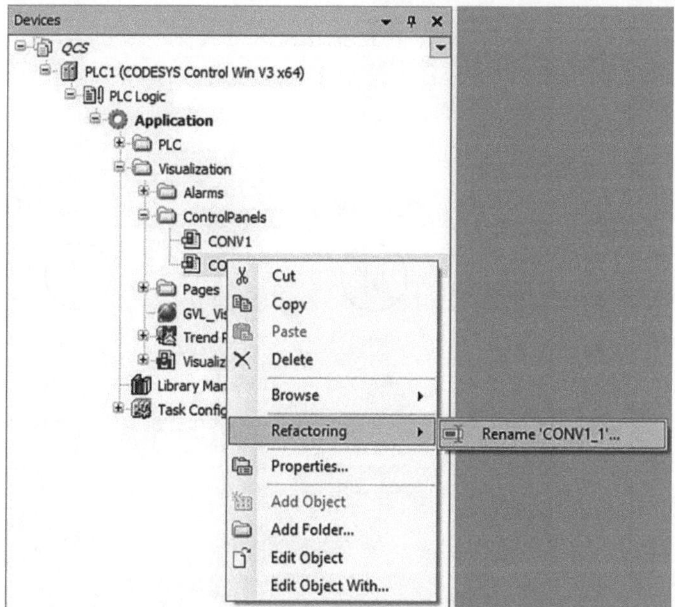

Figure 9-45. *Refactoring ➤ Rename 'CONV1_1'...*

In the displayed *Rename* window, enter the new name for the object: *CONV2* (Figure 9-46).

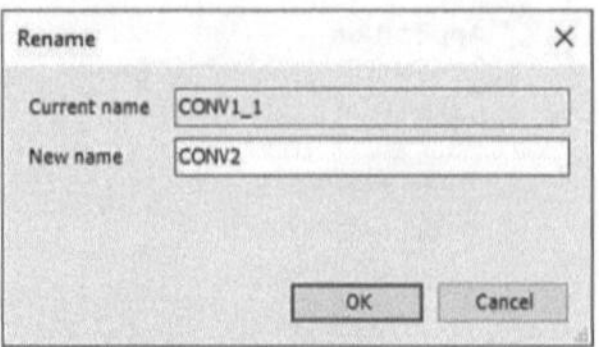

Figure 9-46. *Rename window*

After confirming the changes in the *Refactoring* window, click *OK* (Figure 9-47).

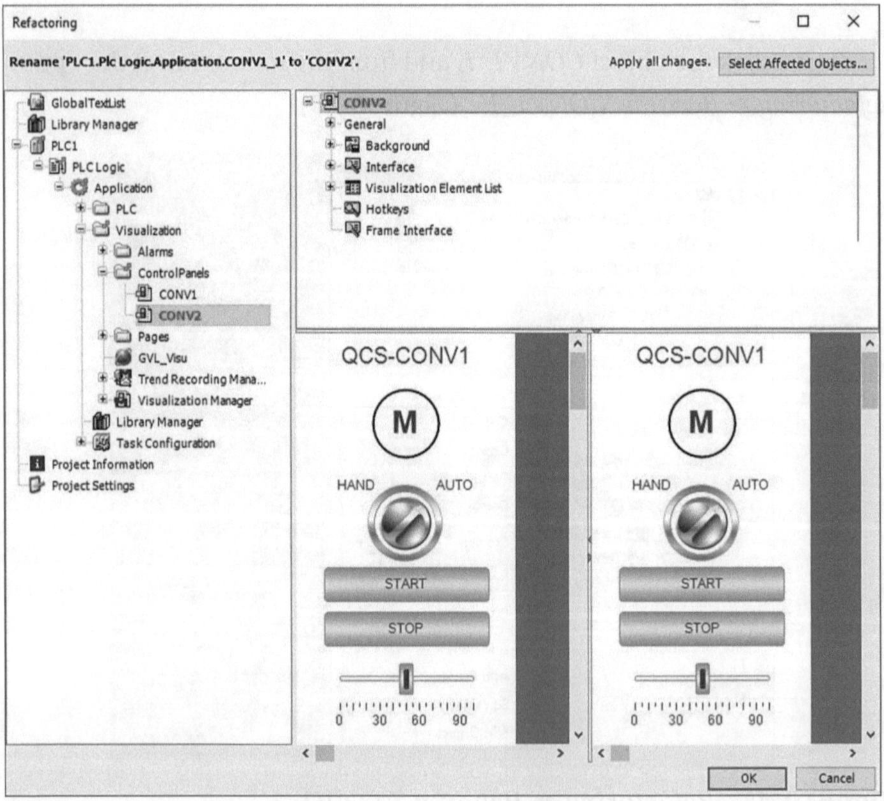

Figure 9-47. *Refactoring window*

Next, let's open the *CONV2* control panel in the editor by double-clicking on it. As we can see, all the texts and variables still refer to *CONV1* (Figure 9-48).

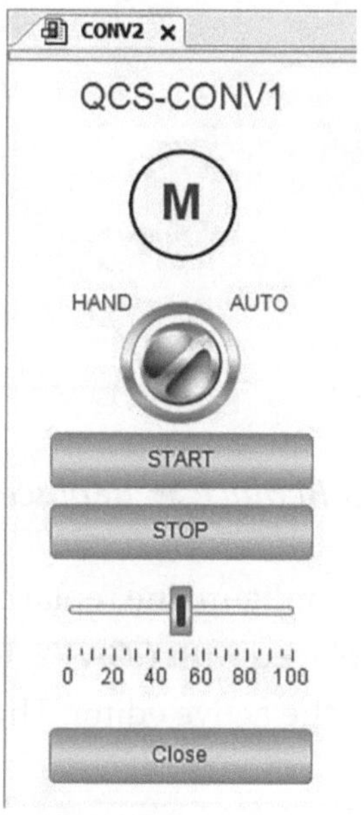

Figure 9-48. *Control panel CONV2*

To replace all references of *CONV1* with *CONV2*, in the open control panel editor, go to the menu, and select *Edit ➤ Find Replace ➤ Replace* (Figure 9-49).

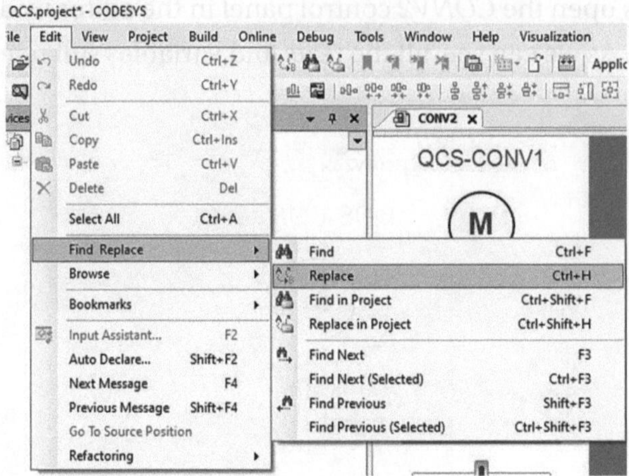

Figure 9-49. *Edit ➤ Find Replace ➤ Replace*

In the *Replace* window, configure the replacement so that every occurrence of *CONV1* is replaced with *CONV2*. Ensure that the *Search* field is set to limit the changes to the active editor. Then, click the *Replace All* button (Figure 9-50).

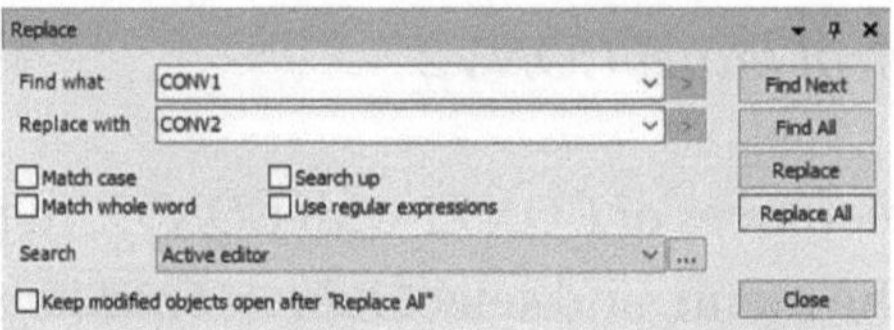

Figure 9-50. *Replace window*

In this way, all variables and texts have been adapted for the *CONV2* conveyor.

The only additional modification to make is to hide the *Slider* element, which is used for manual speed control of the conveyor. For *CONV2* and *CONV3*, the conveyors always operate at a constant speed. Hiding this element is a common programming trick – in the future, it can be enabled again if needed. For example, if the control system is modified to equip *CONV2* with a frequency inverter for speed control.

To hide the *Slider*, set the *State variables* ➤ *Invisible* property to *TRUE* (Figure 9-51).

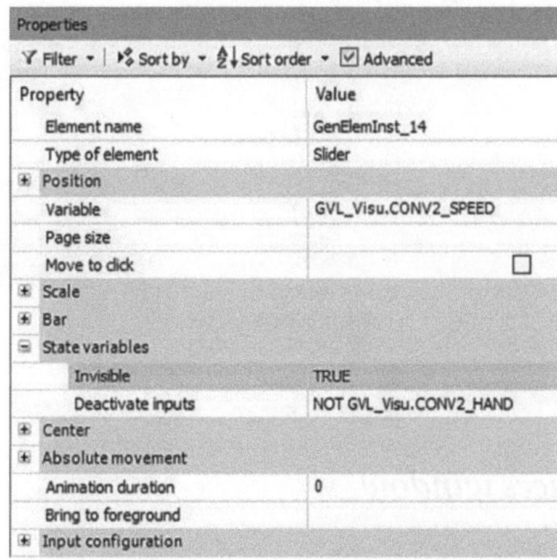

Figure 9-51. *State variables* ➤ *Invisible*

In this way, we have quickly adapted the control panel for *CONV2*. The same process should be applied to the *CONV3* conveyor.

Once the refactoring is complete, the project structure should look as follows (Figure 9-52).

Figure 9-52. *Devices window*

Expansion of the Conveyors View with New Conveyors

The next step in our project is to expand the *Conveyors* view with new conveyors. To do this, let's add two *Rectangle* elements to the view and set their properties according to the table below (Table 9-7).

Table 9-7. *Properties of Rectangle controls*

Properties	Rectangle1	Rectangle2
Position → X	266	476
Position → Y	195	195
Position → Width	210	250
Position → Height	35	35
Color variables → Normal state → Fill color	GVL_Visu.CONV2_STATUS	GVL_Visu.CONV3_STATUS

Next, let's add buttons that will allow us to open the control panels for conveyors *CONV2* and *CONV3*. Set their properties according to the table below (Table 9-8).

Table 9-8. *Properties of Button controls*

Properties	Button1	Button2
Position → X	285	483
Position → Y	198	198
Position → Width	90	90
Position → Height	29	29
Texts → Text	QCS-CONV2	QCS-CONV3

The next step will be to assign the appropriate *OnMouseClick* events to both buttons, just like with the *CONV1* conveyor. Each event should be configured to open the control panel of the respective conveyor – *CONV2* or *CONV3*.

If everything is configured correctly, after downloading the application to the controller, the operator will be able to start all three conveyors using the control panels in *HAND* mode (Figure 9-53).

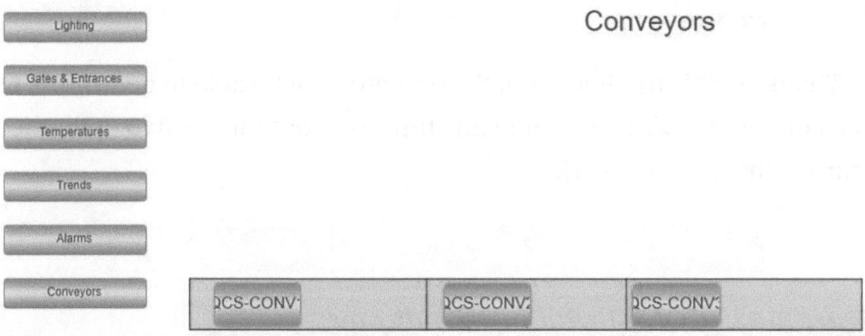

Figure 9-53. *All conveyors are on*

Adding a Speed Indicator for *CONV1* in the *Conveyors* View

As we know, the *CONV1* conveyor has the ability to regulate speed. Currently, the operator can only access information about the current conveyor speed from the control panel. To make the operator's job easier and allow for quicker assessment of the *CONV1* conveyor's status, let's add a speed indicator directly on the conveyor in the *Conveyors* view. This will allow the operator to immediately check the speed of the conveyor without having to open the control panel.

To do this, let's add a *TextField* element to the *Conveyors* view and configure its properties according to the following list:

- *Position* → *X:* 163

- *Position* → *Y:* 199

- *Position* → *Width:* 70

- *Position* → *Height:* 27

- *Texts* → *Text:* %i %%

- *Text properties* → *Font:* Headline

- *Text variables* → *Text variable:* GVL_Visu.
  CONV1_SPEED

Thanks to this modification, the operator will be able to determine the speed of the *CONV1* conveyor at any time, without the need to open the control panel (Figure 9-54).

Figure 9-54. *CONV1 with speed indicator*

Photoelectric Sensors on the QCS-CONV3 Conveyor

Introduction

Once all three conveyors are operational, a photoelectric sensor should be added at the end of the third conveyor. Its purpose is to inform the controller that a product has passed through it, triggering an increment of the counter by one.

We will begin the implementation with the PLC program and then proceed to visualization.

Global Variable Declaration

In the global variable area *GVL_Visu*, three variables should be declared according to the following table (Table 9-9).

Table 9-9. *Declaration of global variables*

Name	Type	Description
PASSED_COUNTER	WORD	Variable storing the count of items that passed the quality control
PASSED_FULL	BOOL	Variable indicating that the number of items passing quality control has reached 10
PASSED_RESET	BOOL	Variable used to reset the counter for items that passed the quality test

These are how the declared variables should appear in the *GVL_Visu* area (Figure 9-55).

```
35
36          PASSED_COUNTER : WORD;
37          PASSED_FULL : BOOL;
38          PASSED_RESET : BOOL;
39
```

Figure 9-55. *Global variables GVL_Visu*

Counting Products Using the CTU Counter

In the control logic program for the conveyor *CONV3*, the product
counting functionality will be implemented in *Network 1*. This feature
tracks the number of items that have passed quality control and been
transported to the pallet. To achieve this, the *CTU* (Count Up) function
block will be used.

Counter CTU (Count-Up)   The *CTU* function block is an up counter.
The counter increases its value *CV* (Current Value) by one each time
the *CU* (Count Up) input signal transitions from low to high (rising
edge). When the preset value *PV* (Preset Value) is reached, the *Q*
output goes high. The counter can be reset to zero using the *R*
(Reset) input.

Before implementing the counter, declare a local variable *CTU_Passed*
of type *CTU* in the *CONV3* program.

This is how the control logic for the counter should look (Figure 9-56).

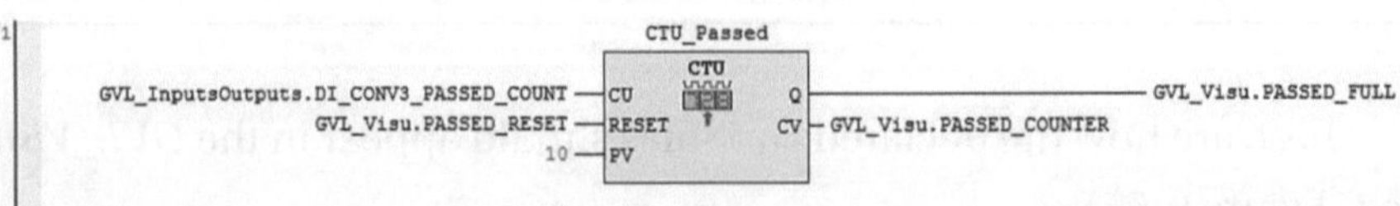

Figure 9-56. *Program CONV3, Network 1: counter CTU_Passed*

To test the functionality of the counter, download the program to the controller, and manipulate the value of the digital input *DI_CONV3_PASSED_COUNT* using the *Watch* table. Each time the input changes from *FALSE* to *TRUE*, the *CTU* counter increments its *CV* value by one (Figure 9-57).

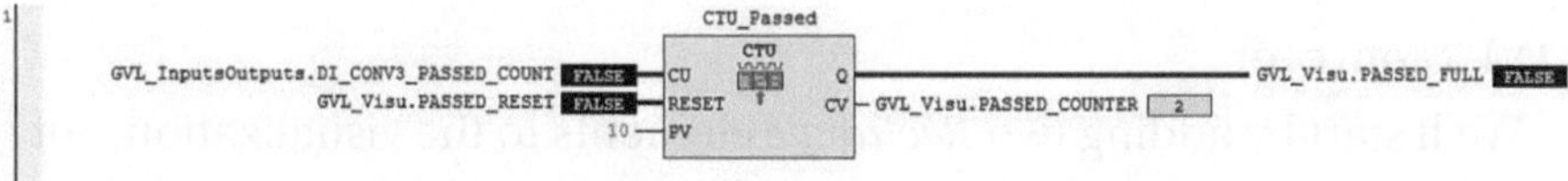

Figure 9-57. *Value of CV output*

When the output value *CV* reaches or exceeds the preset value *PV* (in this case, 10), the output *Q* will be set to *TRUE*. Additionally, the variable *PASSED_FULL* will also take the value *TRUE* (Figure 9-58).

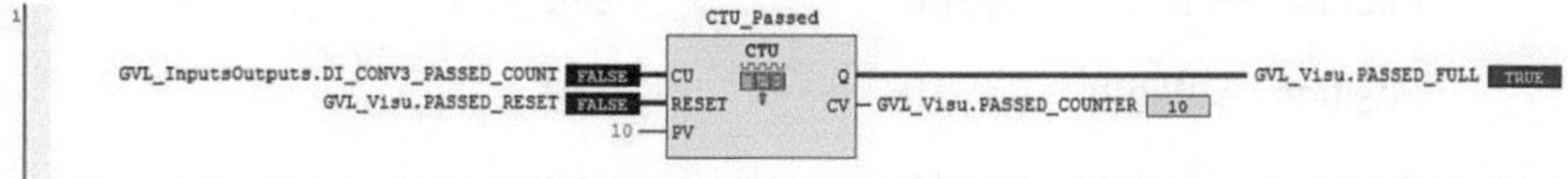

Figure 9-58. *Value of Q output*

Setting the variable *PASSED_RESET* to *TRUE* will reset the counter. At this point, the output variable *PASSED_COUNTER* will be set to 0, and the variable *PASSED_FULL* will be set to *FALSE* (Figure 9-59).

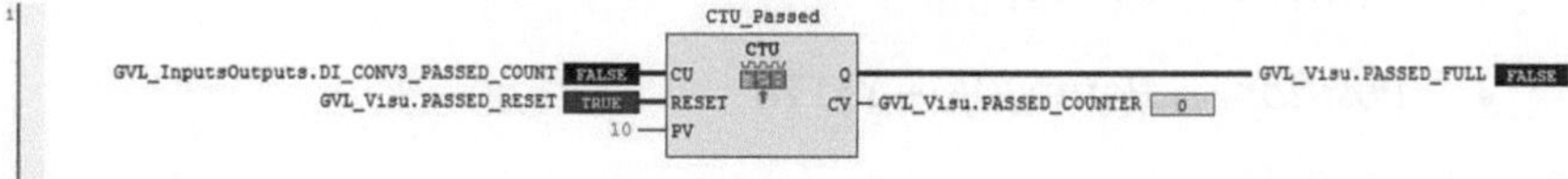

Figure 9-59. *Reset of the counter*

Visualization of the Product Counter

After implementing the counter in the PLC program, let's proceed to its visualization. The counter will tally all products that have successfully passed the quality control test. The signal incrementing the counter's value is provided by the photoelectric sensor installed at the end of the *QCS-CONV3* conveyor.

We'll start by adding two *Rectangle* elements to the visualization. Set their properties according to the table below (Table 9-10).

Table 9-10. *Properties of Rectangle control*

Properties	Rectangle1	Rectangle2
Position → X	708	708
Position → Y	168	248
Position → Width	10	10
Position → Height	10	10

To visualize the light beam emitted by the photoelectric sensor, we will use a *Line* element. This line will represent the light beam between the sensor and the reflector. We will configure its properties as follows:

- *Position → Points[0] → X:* 713

- *Position → Points[0] → Y:* 178

- *Position → Points[1] → X:* 713

- *Position → Points[1] → Y:* 248

- *State variables → Invisible:* GVL_InputsOutputs.DI_CONV3_PASSED_COUNT

- *Animation duration:* 500

422

When the product does not interrupt the light beam of the photoelectric sensor, the line representing this light beam will be visible on the visualization (Figure 9-60). This is possible by assigning a digital input to the *Invisible* property of the *Line* element. The digital input is set to a high state when the product crosses the light beam of the photoelectric sensor.

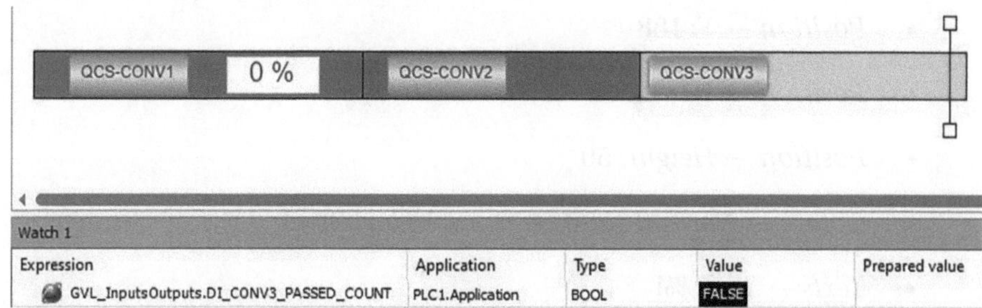

Figure 9-60. *Photoelectric sensor at the end of CONV3 conveyor*

After the product crosses the light beam, the line representing the light beam smoothly disappears. This is controlled by the *Animation duration* property, set to 500 ms, which ensures a smooth animation effect (Figure 9-61).

Figure 9-61. *Invisible light beam*

Displaying the Counter Status

Each time a product crosses the light beam, the counter increases its value by one. To allow the operator to monitor the current counter status, let's add a *TextField* element to the visualization with the following properties:

- *Position → X:* 737

- *Position → Y:* 188

- *Position → Width:* 50

- *Position → Height:* 50

- *Colors → Normal state → Frame color:* Black

- *Texts → Text:* %i

- *Text properties → Font:* Headline

- *Text properties → Font color:* Black

- T*ext variables → Text variable:* GVL_Visu.
  PASSED_COUNTER

For better readability, let's add a label indicating that the counter refers to products that have passed the quality control test. We'll use a *Label* element and configure it as follows:

- *Texts → Text:* PASSED

- *Position → X:* 737

- *Position → Y:* 230

- *Position → Width:* 50

- *Text properties → Font color:* Black

Holding the Conveyor After Reaching 10 Products

When a product crosses the photocell light beam, the counter increments by one, and the product is packed onto the pallet. When the number of products on the pallet reaches 10, the *QCS-CONV3* conveyor must stop and wait for the operator's action.

To implement this functionality, we will modify the control logic for the *QCS-CONV3* conveyor in the *CONV3* program, in *Network 2*. The variable *GVL_Visu.PASSED_FULL*, assigned to the *Q* output of the *CTU_Passed* counter, indicates that the number of products on the pallet is exactly 10.

We will assign this variable to the *HOLD* input of the function block controlling the conveyor. This way, when the number of products reaches 10, the conveyor will hold. Below is the modified control logic (Figure 9-62).

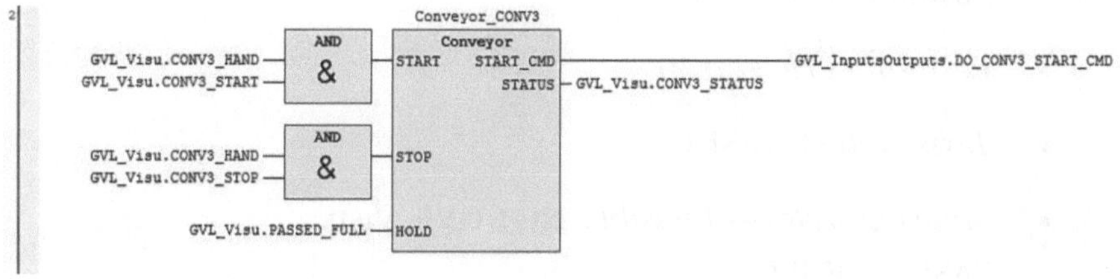

Figure 9-62. *Program CONV3: Network 2*

When the counter indicates a number of products less than 10, the *QCS-CONV3* conveyor continues its operation (Figure 9-63).

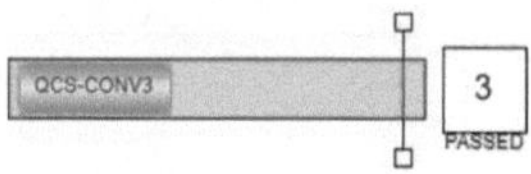

Figure 9-63. *Conveyor CONV3 is on*

When the counter reaches the value of 10, the conveyor is hold and enters a waiting state (Figure 9-64).

Figure 9-64. *Conveyor CONV3 is hold*

Resetting the Counter by the Operator

To provide the operator with the ability to reset the counter after the pallet
with products is picked up by the forklift, an appropriate visualization
element must be added. This element will allow the conveyor to restart
after reaching a standstill. To accomplish this, let's add a *Button* element to
the visualization (Figure 9-65) and configure its properties as follows:

- *Position → X:* 797

- *Position → Y:* 198

- *Position → Width:* 80

- *Position → Height:* 30

- *Texts → Text:* RESET

- *State variables → Invisible:* NOT GVL_Visu.
  PASSED_FULL

- *Input configuration → Tap → Variable:* GVL_Visu.
  PASSED_RESET

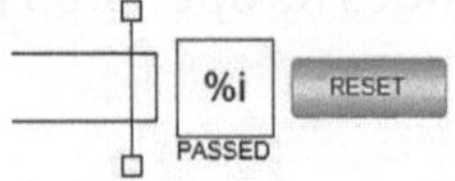

Figure 9-65. *Reset button*

When the *RESET* button is pressed, the counter will be reset to 0, and the conveyor will automatically return to operation mode. If the counter reaches the value of 10 again, the conveyor will be hold and enter a standstill state. This cycle will repeat each time the operator resets the counter to its initial value.

Implementation of a Counter for Products That Failed the Quality Control Test

We have completed the implementation of the counter for products that passed the quality control test. Now, let's focus on the counter for rejected products. In the middle of the *QCS-CONV3* conveyor, a pusher actuator will be installed, responsible for removing products that do not meet the requirements. The details of the actuator's operation will be addressed later in the chapter. In the meantime, we will create a visualization of the transport trough, which will receive the rejected products. At the end of the trough, a photoelectric sensor will be mounted to count the products that fail the quality control criteria.

The implementation process will be similar to the previous counter for accepted products. Let's start by adding new variables to the global area *GVL_Visu*, as shown in the following table (Table 9-11).

Table 9-11. *Declaration of global variables*

Name	Type	Description
FAILED_COUNTER	WORD	Variable storing the count of items that failed the quality control test
FAILED_FULL	BOOL	Variable indicating when the number of failed items reaches 10
FAILED_RESET	BOOL	Variable used to reset the counter for failed items

Below is an example of how to declare these variables in the *GVL_Visu* area (Figure 9-66).

```
39
40        FAILED_COUNTER : WORD;
41        FAILED_FULL : BOOL;
42        FAILED_RESET : BOOL;
43
```

Figure 9-66. *Global variables GVL_Visu*

Next, let's implement the counter in the *CONV3* program, in *Network 2*, similarly to the counter for accepted products. We will copy the counter logic from *Network 1* and adjust the names of the inputs and outputs related to the counters for products that failed the quality control test. Don't forget to declare the local variable *CTU_Failed* in the *CONV3* program, of type *CTU*. Here is the modified *Network 2* (Figure 9-67).

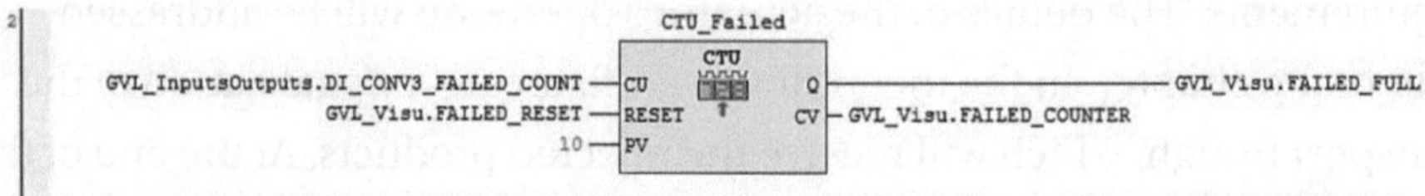

Figure 9-67. *Program CONV3: Network 2*

Visualization

Let's now add a visualization representing the conveyor trough and the counter for products that failed the test. Add a *Rectangle* element with the following properties:

- *Position → X:* 595

- *Position → Y:* 230

- *Position → Width:* 30

- *Position → Height:* 150

This element will symbolize the conveyor trough, where products that do not meet quality standards will fall (Figure 9-68).

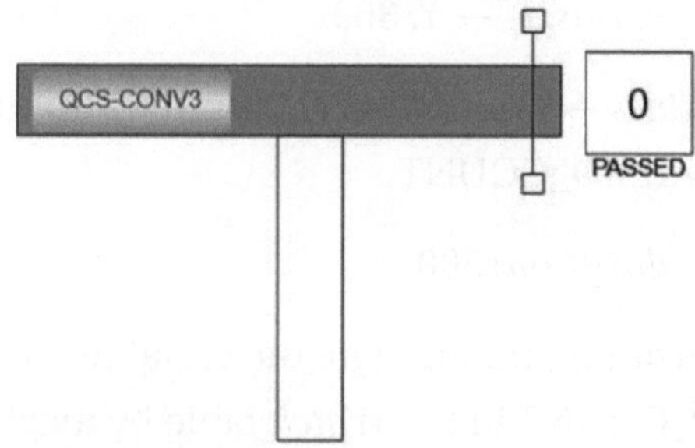

Figure 9-68. *Transport trough*

At the end of the trough, let's add a photoelectric sensor that will count the products. Let's create two *Rectangle* elements and configure their properties according to the following table (Table 9-12).

Table 9-12. *Properties of Rectangle control*

Properties	Rectangle1	Rectangle2
Position → X	566	646
Position → Y	358	358
Position → Width	10	10
Position → Height	10	10

For the visualization of the photoelectric sensor beam, we will use a *Line* element with the following properties:

- *Position → Points[0] → X:* 576
- *Position → Points[0] → Y:* 363
- *Position → Points[1] → X:* 646

- *Position → Points[1] → Y:* 363

- *State variables → Invisible:* GVL_InputsOutputs.DI_
  CONV3_FAILED_COUNT

- *Animation duration:* 500

To test the visualization, manipulate the variable *GVL_InputsOutputs. DI_CONV3_FAILED_COUNT* in the *Watch* table by toggling its state from *FALSE* to *TRUE* and observing the behavior in the visualization (Figure 9-69).

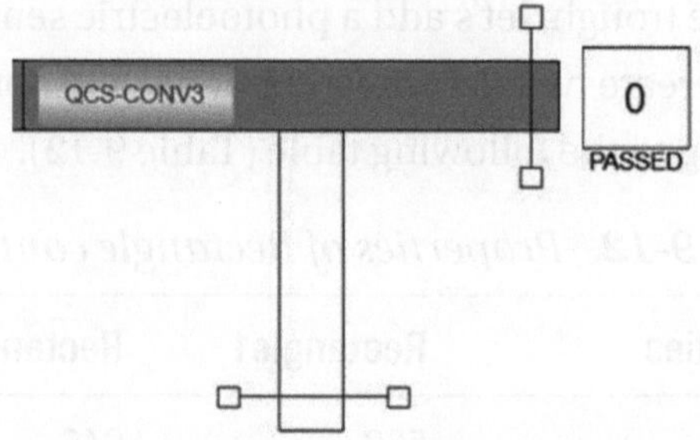

Figure 9-69. *Photoelectric sensor on transport trough*

To allow the operator to easily monitor the number of products that do not meet the requirements, add a *TextField* element with the following settings:

- *Position → X:* 585

- *Position → Y:* 390

- *Position → Width:* 50

- *Position → Height:* 50

- *Colors → Normal state → Frame color:* Black

- *Texts → Text:* %i

- *Text properties → Font:* Headline

- *Text properties* → *Font color:* Black

- *Text variables* → *Text variable:* GVL_Visu.
  FAILED_COUNTER

Let's also add a label to indicate the counter (Figure 9-70). Create a *Label* element with the following settings:

- *Texts* → *Text:* FAILED

- *Position* → *X:* 585

- *Position* → *Y:* 432

- *Position* → *Width:* 50

- *Text properties* → *Font color:* Black

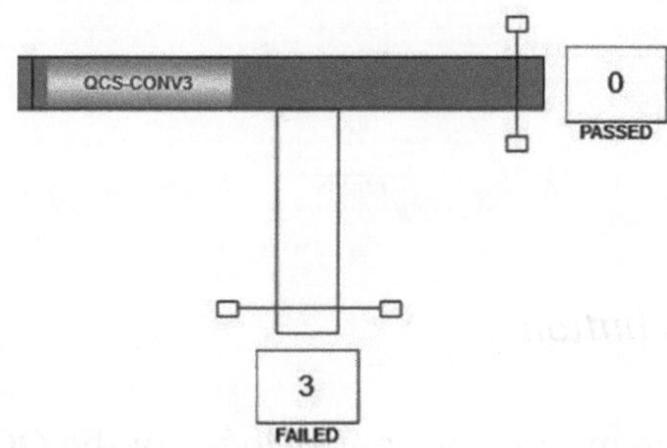

Figure 9-70. *Counter CTU_Failed*

Resetting the Counter

Similarly to the accepted product counter, let's add the ability for the operator to reset this counter. Create a *Button* element with the following properties:

- *Position* → *X:* 570

- *Position* → *Y:* 459

- *Position → Width:* 80

- *Position → Height:* 30

- *Texts → Text:* RESET

- *State variables → Invisible:* NOT GVL_Visu.
  FAILED_FULL

- *Input configuration → Tap → Variable:* GVL_Visu.
  FAILED_RESET

Let's test the reset function by increasing the counter to a value of 10, so that the *RESET* button appears (Figure 9-71). When the button is pressed, the counter should be reset to zero, and the *RESET* button should become invisible.

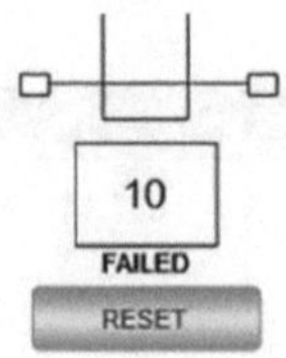

Figure 9-71. *Reset button*

The final step is to modify the control logic for the *QCS-CONV3* conveyor. The conveyor should stop when the number of products failing the quality test reaches 10. We need to make changes in *Network 3* of the *CONV3* program. Below is the modified logic (Figure 9-72).

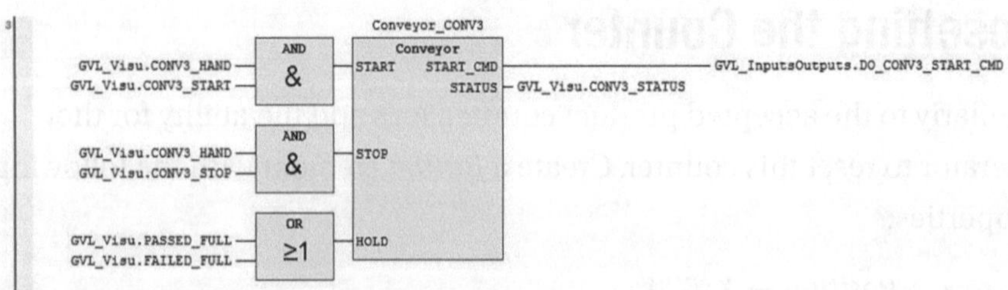

Figure 9-72. *Program CONV3: Network 2*

After making the changes, let's verify if the program works correctly: the conveyor should stop when the counter reaches a value of 10, and after resetting the counter, it should start again.

Simulation of Photoelectric Sensors

So far, to test the program, we manually changed the values of inputs such as *DI_CONV3_PASSED_COUNT* or *DI_CONV3_FAILED_COUNT* using the *Watch* table. Now, we will configure a simulator that will automatically carry out tests in a more realistic way. The simulator will operate as follows: every sixth product will be rejected as failing to meet quality standards. Additionally, when a product reaches the photoelectric sensor, its presence will be visualized.

To activate the conveyor simulator, we need to install the new version of the *Simulator* library (version 4), available in the *Chapter_09* directory of the project repository. The installation process is similar to previous chapters. After the installation is complete, we should activate the library in the project using the *Library Manager*.

After successful installation and configuration of the *Simulator* V4 library, we should see this version marked as active in the *Library Manager* window (Figure 9-73). This will give us access to the new functional block called *Conveyors*.

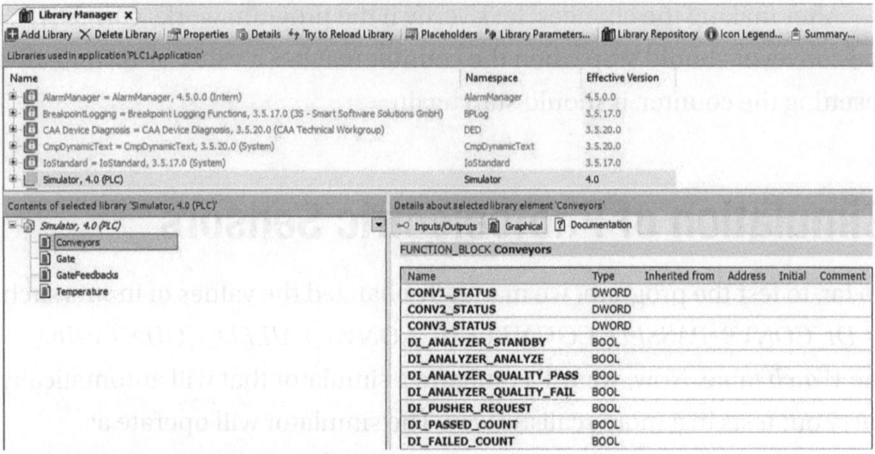

Figure 9-73. *Library Manager with version 4*

Next, in the *CONV3* program, within *Network 4*, we will call the simulator function block and configure its parameters. Before adding the block, we need to declare a local variable *ConvSim* in the *CONV3* program with the type *Simulator.Conveyors*. This is how the configuration of *Network 4* will look like (Figure 9-74).

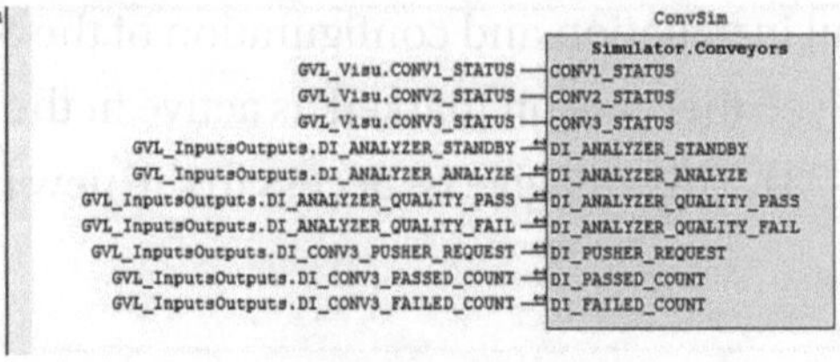

Figure 9-74. *Program CONV3: Network 4*

After configuring the simulator, download the program to the controller, and start all three conveyors. During operation, you will notice that the light beam emitted by the photoelectric sensor will disappear periodically, which corresponds to detecting a product. In response, the appropriate counter will increment its value.

If any of the counters reaches a value of 10, the *QCS-CONV3* conveyor will automatically stop. The stopped state will be maintained until the operator resets the counter using the *RESET* button (Figure 9-75).

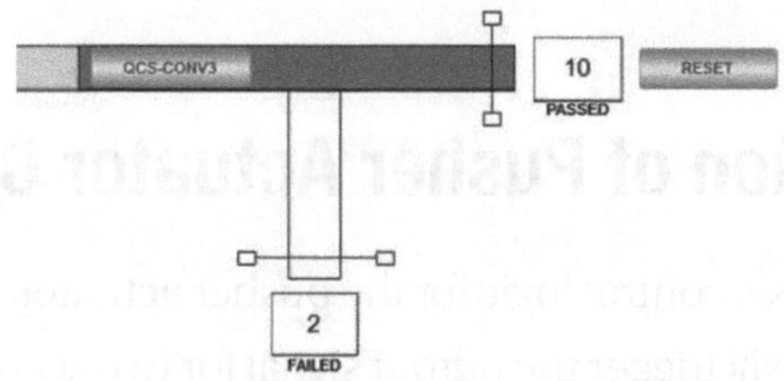

Figure 9-75. *Conveyor CONV3 in hold mode*

The simulation mode allows testing of the control logic without the need for manual manipulation of the *DI_CONV3_PASSED_COUNT* and *DI_CONV3_FAILED_COUNT* inputs. This makes the testing process more efficient and realistic while also enabling the quick detection of potential errors in the control logic.

Pusher Actuator

Description of the Pusher Actuator Function

A pusher actuator will be installed in the middle of the *QCS-CONV3* conveyor. Its purpose is to remove products that failed the quality test by pushing them off the conveyor onto a transport trough.

The actuator is controlled using two signals:

- *DI_CONV3_PUSHER_REQUEST* (digital input): Set to high when a product is within the actuator's range.

- *DO_CONV3_PUSHER_CMD* (digital output): Set to high to extend the actuator piston, which pushes the product off the *QCS-CONV3* conveyor.

When the input signal *DI_CONV3_PUSHER_REQUEST* goes high, the activation of the output signal *DO_CONV3_PUSHER_CMD* extends the actuator piston, allowing the product to be effectively removed from the conveyor.

Implementation of Pusher Actuator Control Logic

To implement the basic control logic for the pusher actuator, assume that a high (*TRUE*) input signal will trigger the output signal for two seconds. As a result, the actuator piston will extend, push the product off the *QCS-CONV3* conveyor, and then return to its initial position once the output signal is set to low.

This logic will utilize a *TP* timer block, which generates a pulse lasting a specified duration. For this purpose, declare a local variable *TP_Push* of type *TP*. The control logic should be implemented in the *CONV3* program, in *Network 4* (Figure 9-76).

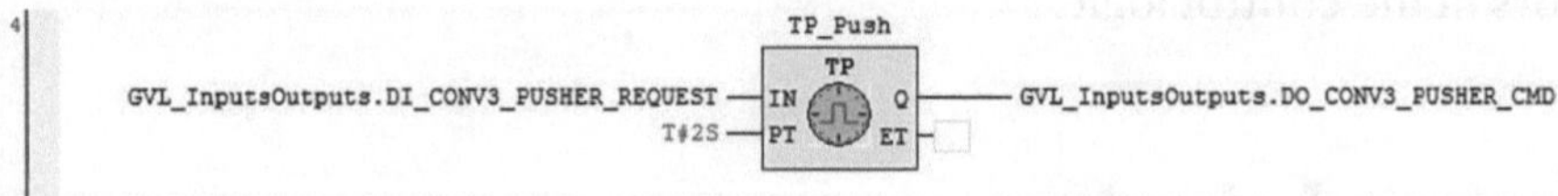

Figure 9-76. *Program CONV3, Network 4: Pusher*

To test the functionality, set the input *DI_CONV3_REQUEST_PUSHER* to high. This should cause the digital output to remain high for two seconds and then switch to low. The simulator running in the background will automatically set the input signal to low once the operation is complete.

Creating the Actuator Visualization

After implementing the control logic for the pusher actuator, we proceed to create its visualization. This visualization will not only help to understand the actuator's operation but also serve diagnostic and monitoring purposes in the control system. Additionally, during this process, we will learn how to group graphical elements, a necessary step for representing more complex system components.

We will start by creating the actuator's piston. To do this, add a *Rectangle* element to the visualization, and configure its properties as follows:

- *Element name:* Piston_Rod

- *Position* → *X:* 10

- *Position* → *Y:* 0

- *Position* → *Width:* 10

- *Position* → *Height:* 62

Next, add a *Rounded Rectangle* element to the visualization and configure its properties with the following values:

- *Element name:* Rod_End

- *Position* → *X:* 0

- *Position* → *Y:* 52

- *Position* → *Width:* 30

- *Position* → *Height:* 10

In this way, we have created the pusher actuator piston using two simple elements (Figure 9-77).

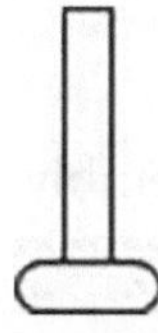

Figure 9-77. *Piston of pusher actuator*

To simplify the management of the visualization, we will group the *Piston_Rod* and *Rod_End* elements. To do this, hold down the left mouse button, and select both elements (Figure 9-78).

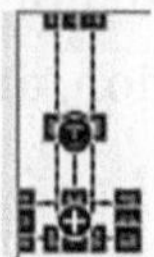

Figure 9-78. *Pusher: selected elements*

Next, right-click on the selected elements, and choose the *Group* option (Figure 9-79).

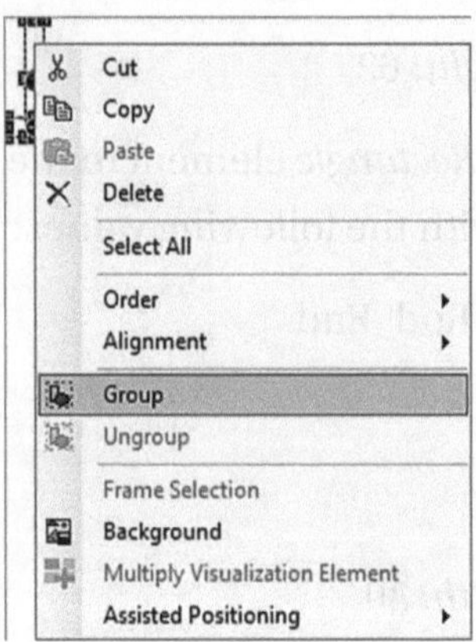

Figure 9-79. *Pusher: Group*

In the *Element List* tab, a new group will appear in the list of graphical components for the project. Rename this group to *Rod_Assembly*, and configure the following properties:

- *Element name:* Rod_Assembly

- *Position → X:* 10

- *Position → Y:* 8

After creating the piston, we will enclose it in a housing by adding a new graphical element of type *Rectangle* (Figure 9-80) and configuring its properties as follows:

- *Element name:* Piston

- *Position* → *X:* 17

- *Position* → *Y:* 8

- *Position* → *Width:* 16

- *Position* → *Height:* 50

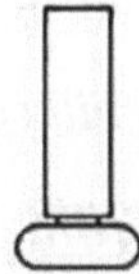

Figure 9-80. *Piston*

Let's add another enclosure to surround the entire actuator. We will use a *Rectangle* (Figure 9-81) element with the following properties:

- *Element name:* Pusher_Body

- *Position* → *X:* 0

- *Position* → *Y:* 0

- *Position* → *Width:* 50

- *Position* → *Height:* 50

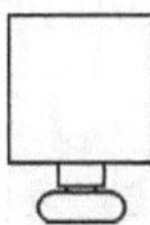

Figure 9-81. *Pusher: body*

Let's add signaling to indicate that the item on the conveyor is within the range of the pusher actuator. To do this, we will use an *Ellipse* (Figure 9-82) element with the following properties:

- *Element name:* Pusher_Request

- *Position* → *X:* 20

- *Position* → *Y:* 30

- *Position* → *Width:* 10

- *Position* → *Height:* 10

- *Colors* → *Normal state* → *Frame color:* Black

- *Colors* → *Normal state* → *Fill color:* Darkgreen

- *Colors* → *Alarm state* → *Frame color:* Black

- *Colors* → *Alarm state* → *Fill color:* Green

- *Colors variables* → *Toggle color:* GVL_InputsOutputs. DI_CONV3_PUSHER_REQUEST

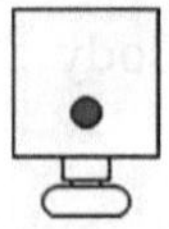

Figure 9-82. *Pusher*

At the end, let's group all elements, including the piston, enclosure, and signaling indicator (Figure 9-83). Perform the grouping in the same way as we did earlier. Then, set the properties of the group as follows:

- *Element name:* Pusher

- *Position* → *X:* 585

- *Position* → *Y:* 120

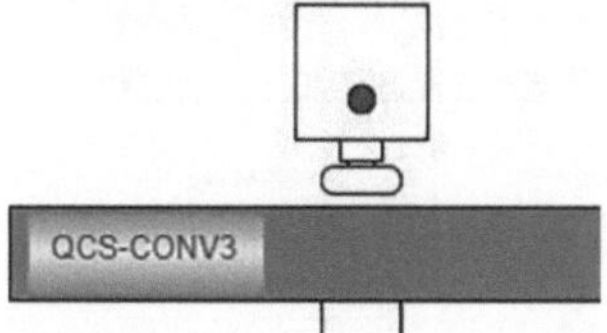

Figure 9-83. *Pusher: Group*

In this way, we have created a complete visualization of the pusher actuator. It is now ready for use in the control system and allows for intuitive monitoring of the actuator's status.

Piston Actuator Movement Animation

By using several basic graphic elements, we have successfully built the entire device. Now, we can add an animation of the piston actuator movement to enrich our visualization. When the digital input *DI_CONV3_PUSHER_REQUEST* is set to high, the signal light on the actuator should change to bright green. At the same time, the piston should extend. Let's introduce a simple animation that will enable this.

In the *GVL_Visu* space, declare a variable *PUSHER_MOVEMENT* of type *INT.* Then, assign this variable to the property *Absolute movement → Movement → Y* of the *Rod_Assembly* group, which we created earlier (Figure 9-84).

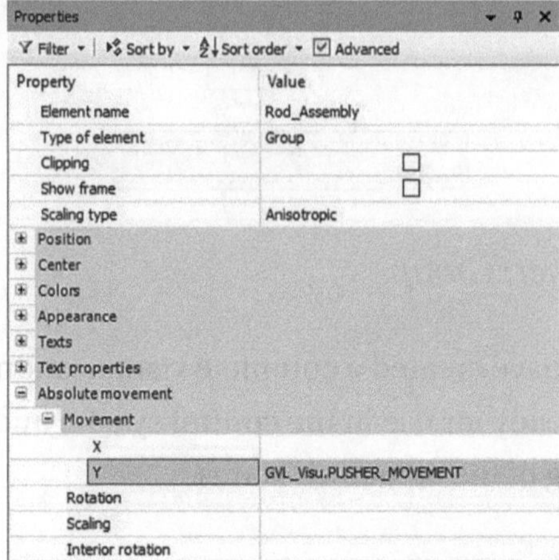

Figure 9-84. *Absolute movement ➤ Movement ➤ Y*

By assigning the variable to the *Movement* property, we can dynamically change the position of the *Rod_Assembly* group along the Y axis. To add a smooth animation transition, let's set the *Animation duration* property of the group to 200ms.

The next step is to implement the change of the *PUSHER_MOVEMENT* variable value in the actuator control logic.

- When the actuator piston is retracted, the value of the *PUSHER_MOVEMENT* variable should be 0.

- When the piston is extended, the *Rod_Assembly* group should be moved by 35 pixels along the Y axis.

To achieve this, let's modify the control logic in the *CONV3* program, in `Network 4`, using the *SEL* function block (Figure 9-85).

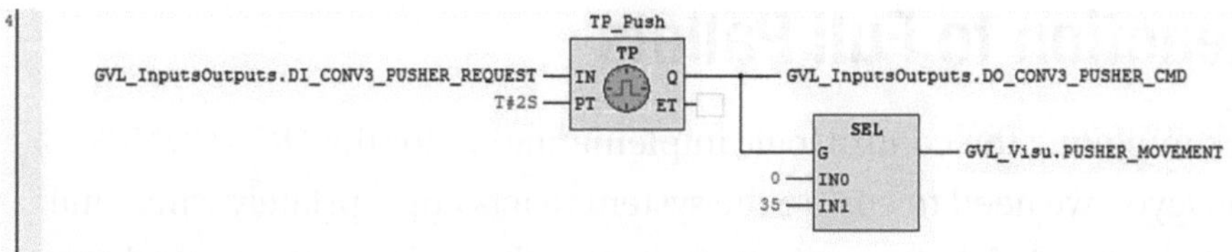

Figure 9-85. *Program CONV3: Network 4*

SEL (Select)   The *SEL* (Select) block is a selector that chooses one of two input values (IN0 or IN1) based on the state of the control signal *G*. If *G* is low, the output *OUT* reflects the value of *IN0*, and if *G* is high, the value of *IN1*.

Let's download the modified program to the controller and test the actuator visualization. Set the input *DI_CONV3_PUSHER_REQUEST* to high and observe how the actuator piston smoothly extends to push the product off the *QCS-CONV3* conveyor (Figure 9-86).

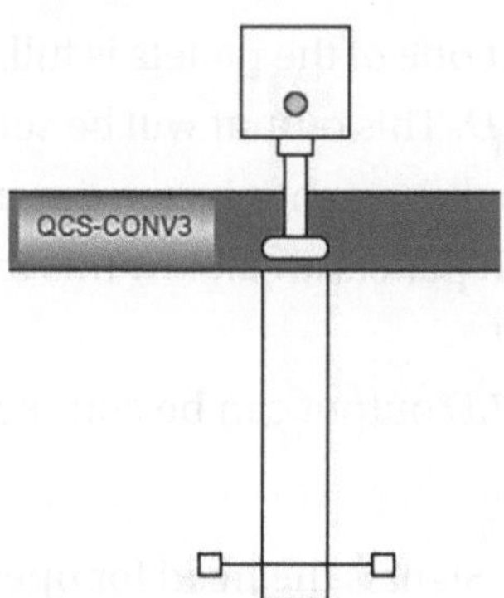

Figure 9-86. *Piston extended*

Reaction to Full Pallets

In completing the control logic implementation for the *QCS-CONV3* conveyor, we need to ensure the system reacts appropriately when one of the pallets is full. Regardless of whether the pallet contains products that passed or failed the quality control test, the system must meet the following requirements:

- *Holding the conveyor operation:* When the pallet is full, the QCS-CONV3 conveyor must be stopped.

- *Notifying the forklift operator:* The operator will be informed that the full pallet needs to be removed. After removing it, they must confirm the action by pressing the *RESET* button on the visualization, which will resume the operation of the conveyor.

Notification of Full Pallet

To notify the operator that one of the pallets is full, we will use the digital output *DO_CONV3_HOLD*. This output will be set to a high state when the product counter on any pallet reaches its maximum value – in our case, 10. If the counters for both pallets are below this threshold, the output will return to a low state.

The *DO_CONV3_HOLD* output can be connected to various signaling devices, such as

- *Light indicator:* Signals the need for operator intervention

- *Siren:* Emits a sound indicating that the conveyor operation has been stopped

- *GSM gateway:* Allows sending an SMS message to the operator

444

In real-world installations, this process is fully automated, but in our simplified example, we focus on demonstrating the basic functionality of the system.

Implementation of Notification Logic

To control the output *DO_CONV3_HOLD*, we will use an *SR* flip-flop with a dominant *SET* input. To implement this solution:

- Declare a local variable *Notification* of type *SR* in the *CONV3* program.

- Implement the control logic in *Network 5* of the *CONV3* program, using the *SR* flip-flop.

Below is an illustration of the control logic (Figure 9-87).

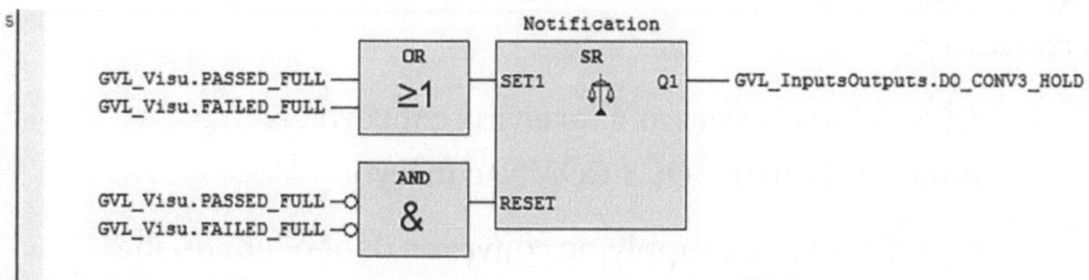

Figure 9-87. *Notification*

SR Flip-Flop (Set-Reset)   The SR flip-flop is a basic memory block in automation, used for storing a state. It has two control inputs: *S* (Set) and *R* (Reset). When the *S* input signal is active, the *Q* output goes high (TRUE) and remains in this state until the *R* input signal is activated, which sets *Q* to low (FALSE). If both inputs (S and R) are activated simultaneously, the block is dominated by the *SET* input, meaning the *Q* output will remain in the high (TRUE) state.

Analyzer

Implementation of the *HOLD* Function for the *QCS-CONV2* Conveyor

In this section, we will focus on expanding the control logic for the *QCS-CONV2* conveyor. The first step we need to take before implementing the analyzer is to add a function that holds the *QCS-CONV2* conveyor when the *QCS-CONV3* conveyor stops working.

Consider the situation where one of the pallets on the *QCS-CONV3* conveyor is full, causing it to stop. If the *QCS-CONV2* conveyor continues to operate at this moment, it could lead to an accumulation of products between the *QCS-CONV2* and *QCS-CONV3* conveyors, disrupting the entire transport process.

To prevent this, we need to understand the relationship between these two conveyors:

- *QCS-CONV3* serves as a receiving conveyor, taking products from the *QCS-CONV2* conveyor.

- *QCS-CONV2* is a supplying conveyor, dependent on the operational state of the *QCS-CONV3* conveyor.

Therefore, *QCS-CONV3* grants permission for the *QCS-CONV2* conveyor to operate. This function is implemented via the *HOLD* input in the function block controlling the *QCS-CONV2* conveyor (Figure 9-88).

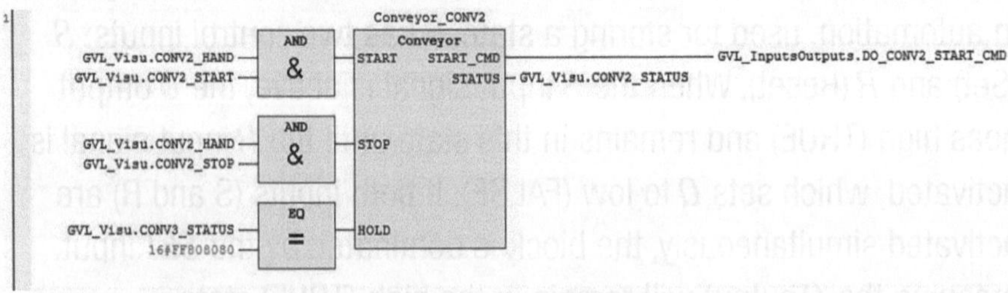

Figure 9-88. *Program CONV2: HOLD input*

The operation principle is simple. The comparison operator *EQ* checks whether the value of the variable *GVL_Visu.CONV3_STATUS* is *16#FF808080*, indicating that the *QCS-CONV3* conveyor is stopped.

- When the condition is met, the *HOLD* input of the *QCS-CONV2* conveyor is set to *TRUE*, which stops the conveyor.

- When the *QCS-CONV3* conveyor starts again, the *HOLD* input is automatically switched off, and *QCS-CONV2* resumes operation.

With this implementation, we ensure the synchronization of the two conveyors, which helps prevent potential blockages and streamlines the entire transport process.

Description of the Product Quality Analyzer

Let's now discuss the operation of the product quality analyzer, including its integration with the *QCS-CONV2* and *QCS-CONV3* conveyors. The analyzer monitors the quality of the products transported on the conveyors, providing the PLC controller with information based on the recorded parameters.

First, let's review the signals handled by the analyzer (Table 9-13).

Table 9-13. *Signal list for Analyzer*

Type of Signal	Name	Description
Digital Input	DI_ANALYZER_STANDBY	Analyzer in standby mode
Digital Input	DI_ANALYZER_ANALYZE	Analyzer checking the quality of the product
Digital Input	DI_ANALYZER_QUALITY_PASS	Product quality confirmed
Digital Input	DI_ANALYZER_QUALITY_FAIL	Product quality not confirmed

When we talk about product quality, it can refer to various parameters, such as dimensions, weight, or other physical properties. In our case, we focus on one simple criterion – the height of the object. We assume that

- Products with a height of less than 10 cm do not meet the quality requirements and should be rejected. The rejection information is sent to the PLC controller via the signal *DI_ANALYZER_QUALITY_FAIL*.

- Products that meet the height criteria receive a quality confirmation through the signal *DI_ANALYZER_QUALITY_PASS*.

The analyzer operates as a peripheral device, autonomous from the PLC controller. The controller only receives input signals from the analyzer and, based on these signals, controls the operation of the *QCS-CONV2* conveyor and other system components.

Key Signals

- *DI_ANALYZER_ANALYZE*: A signal indicating that the analyzer is checking the product. During this time, the *QCS-CONV2* conveyor should be stopped to avoid disrupting the analysis process.

- *DI_ANALYZER_STANDBY*: A signal indicating that the analyzer is ready for operation. In this state, the *QCS-CONV2* conveyor should operate normally.

When a product is in the analyzer:

1. *DI_ANALYZER_ANALYZE* becomes high, which causes the *QCS-CONV2* conveyor to stop.

2. After the analysis is complete, the analyzer sets the appropriate signal:

   - *DI_ANALYZER_QUALITY_PASS* if the product passed the quality test.

   - *DI_ANALYZER_QUALITY_FAIL* if the product does not meet the quality requirements.

The controller then makes further decisions on how to handle the product based on the received signal. For example, rejected products are directed to a side track by the pusher actuator integrated with the *QCS-CONV3* conveyor.

The product quality analyzer provides precise quality control within the transport system. By integrating signals with the PLC system, the operator has full control over the process, and products that do not meet the quality standards are effectively eliminated.

Expansion of Control Logic with Analyzer

When expanding the control logic for the conveyor, we consider the situation where the analyzer examines the product for quality. The key element in this implementation is the use of the *DI_ANALYZER_ANALYZE* signal. When this input signal is high, the *QCS-CONV2* conveyor should be stopped.

The control logic has been extended to include a function that monitors the *DI_ANALYZER_ANALYZE* signal. When this signal is activated (high state), the *QCS-CONV2* conveyor is stopped to allow the analyzer to perform the quality test. Once the analysis is completed, the signal returns to a low state, enabling the conveyor to resume operation.

Here's how the updated control logic for the conveyor looks (Figure 9-89).

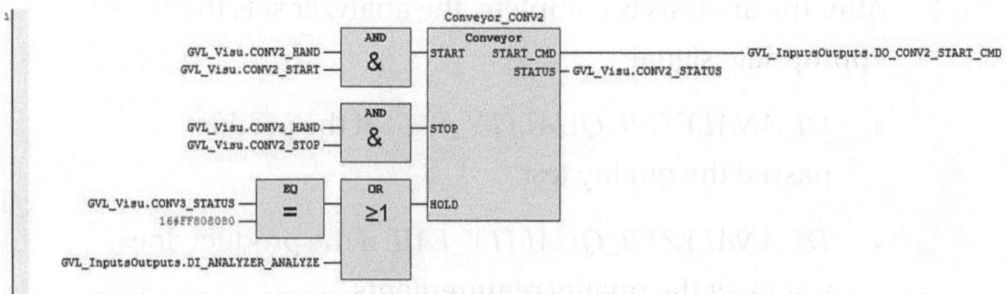

Figure 9-89. *Program CONV2: Network 1*

After downloading the program into the controller, it can be observed in the visualization that the *QCS-CONV2* conveyor stops cyclically for the analysis period. Once the test is completed, the activation of one of the photoelectric sensors indicates whether the product has passed the quality control or not (Figure 9-90).

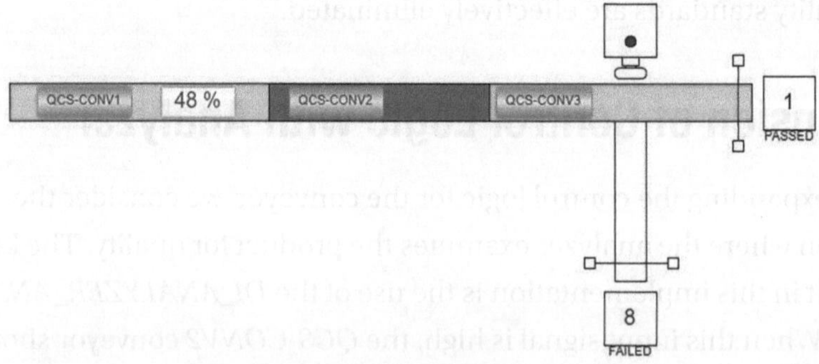

Figure 9-90. *Holding conveyor CONV2*

The simulator in the *CONV3* program has been equipped with logic responsible for simulating the operation of the analyzer. The operation cycle includes

- Activating the *DI_ANALYZER_ANALYZE* input (high state)

- Performing the analysis

- Setting the input to low state after the test is completed

Additionally, the simulator logic automatically toggles the other input signals, such as *DI_ANALYZER_QUALITY_PASS* or *DI_ANALYZER_QUALITY_FAIL*, according to the results of the analysis.

To allow visualization of the analyzer's state, we introduce a graphical representation using appropriate colors that represent the current status of the device:

- *Gray:* STANDBY (analyzer ready for operation)

- *Yellow*: Analyzer performing the product test

- *Green*: Product passed quality control

- *Red*: Product failed quality control

Implementation of Visualization

- Declare a global variable *ANALYZER_STATUS* of type *DWORD* in the *GVL_Visu* area. This variable will store the current status of the analyzer.

- In the *CONV2* program, create logic to handle the analyzer's state in *Network 1*, based on the analysis of digital inputs.

This approach ensures that the PLC controller receives the input signals from the analyzer and controls the visualization based on those signals, without directly controlling the analyzer's operation. This approach allows a clear and intuitive representation of the analyzer's state in the system's visualization (Figure 9-91).

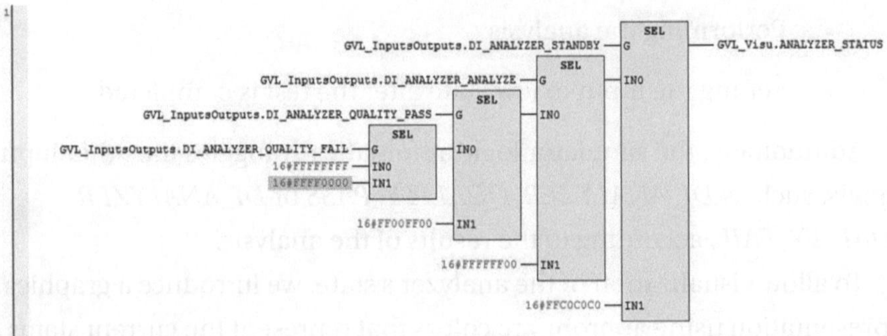

Figure 9-91. *Program CONV2: Network 1*

Visualization of the Analyzer on the *QCS-CONV2* Conveyor

The next step is to add the analyzer visualization in the user interface. To do this, let's follow these steps. Add a *Rectangle* element to the visualization and set its properties according to the values below:

- *Element name:* Analyzer_Body

- *Position → X:* 0

- *Position → Y:* 0

- *Position → Width:* 50

- *Position → Height:* 50

The next element we will place in the visualization is a *Rounded Rectangle*, and we will set its properties according to the values below:

- *Element name:* Scanner_Beam

- *Position* → *X:* 20

- *Position* → *Y:* 0

- *Position* → *Width:* 10

- *Position* → *Height:* 50

After adding the above elements, let's group them together and name the group *Analyzer*. The final appearance of the group is shown in the illustration below (Figure 9-92).

Type	X	Y	Width	Height	ID	Name
T #19 Label	585	432	50	30	27	GenElemInst_42
#20 Button	570	459	80	30	29	GenElemInst_44
⊞ #21 Group	585	120	50	70	38	Pusher
⊟ #22 Group	0	0	50	50	40	Analyzer
#0 Rectangle	0	0	50	50	18	Analyzer_Body
#1 Rounded Rectangle	20	0	10	50	20	Scanner_Beam

Figure 9-92. Analyzer: Group

Thanks to the access to individual elements in the group, we can change their properties independently. Let's take advantage of this opportunity and assign the value of the variable *GVL_Visu.ANALYZER_STATUS* to the *Fill color* property of the *Normal state* ➤ *Color* for the element *Scanner_Beam* (*Rounded Rectangle*). The visualization of this configuration is shown below (Figure 9-93).

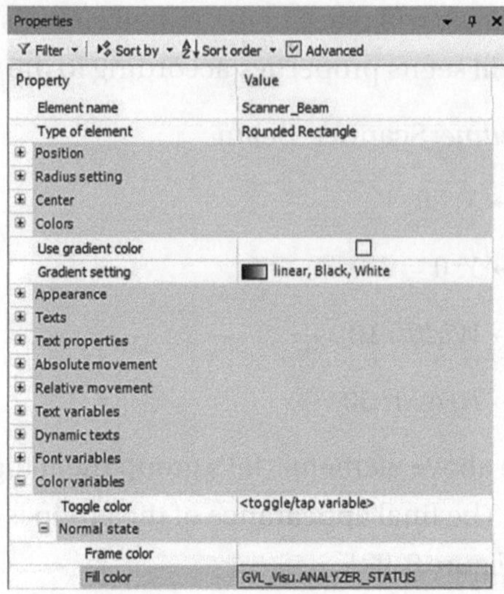

Figure 9-93. *Color variables* ➤ *Normal state* ➤ *Fill color*

To adjust the analyzer to the *QCS-CONV2* conveyor visualization, set the position of the group *Analyzer* according to the following parameters:

- Position → X: 395

- Position → Y: 187

In this way, we have added the analyzer to the *QCS-CONV2* conveyor visualization. This makes the user interface more intuitive and readable for the operator. Below is an example of the analyzer in operation (Figure 9-94).

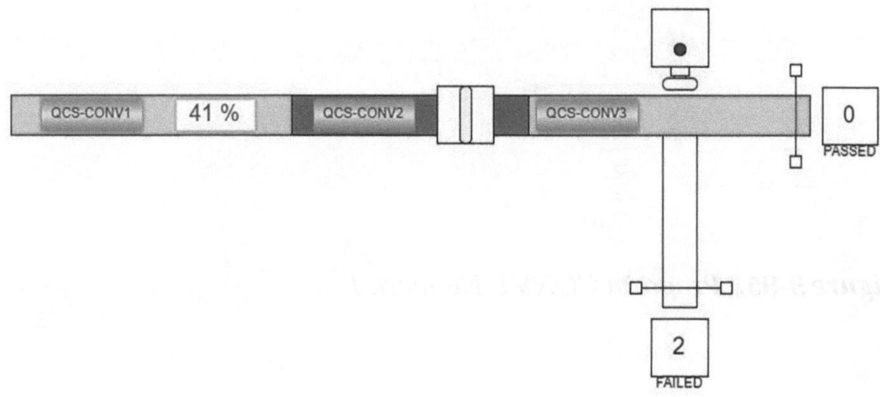

Figure 9-94. *Analyze mode*

QCS-CONV1 Conveyor

Automatic Holding of QCS-CONV1 Conveyor

The last element we need to implement in our program is automation
for the *QCS-CONV1* conveyor. Similar to the *QCS-CONV2* conveyor, it
is necessary to stop the *QCS-CONV1* conveyor when the *QCS-CONV3*
conveyor stops working. Otherwise, the products transported by *QCS-
CONV1* could block the other receiving conveyors, disrupting the
continuity of the process.

To prevent this, we implement control logic that will automatically stop
the *QCS-CONV1* conveyor when the *QCS-CONV3* conveyor stops. Below is
the modified control logic (Figure 9-95).

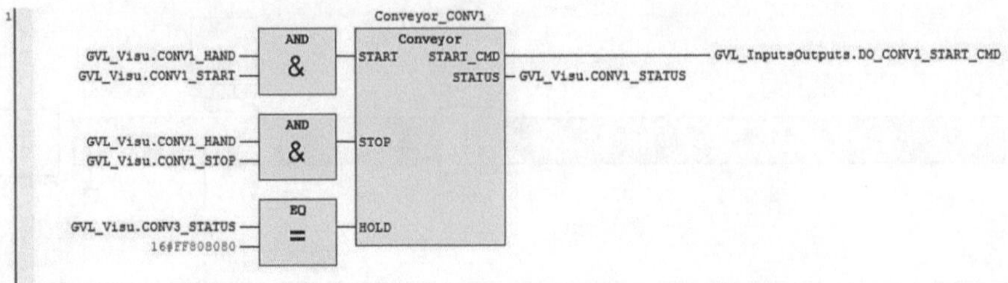

Figure 9-95. *Program CONV1: Network 1*

Dynamic Speed Control for *QCS-CONV1* Conveyor

The next step in the development of the control logic is to implement dynamic speed management for the *QCS-CONV1* conveyor, particularly in situations when the product is being analyzed. The assumptions are as follows:

- If the *QCS-CONV1* conveyor is in *HAND* mode, the operator manually sets the conveyor speed.

- If the conveyor operates in *AUTO* mode, the following applies:

  - When the analyzer is testing the product on the *QCS-CONV2* conveyor, the speed of the *QCS-CONV1* conveyor is automatically reduced to 50%.

  - In all other cases, the conveyor operates at full speed, i.e., at 100%.

To implement this logic, appropriate control elements should be added to the *CONV1* program, within *Network 1*. Below is the updated control logic (Figure 9-96).

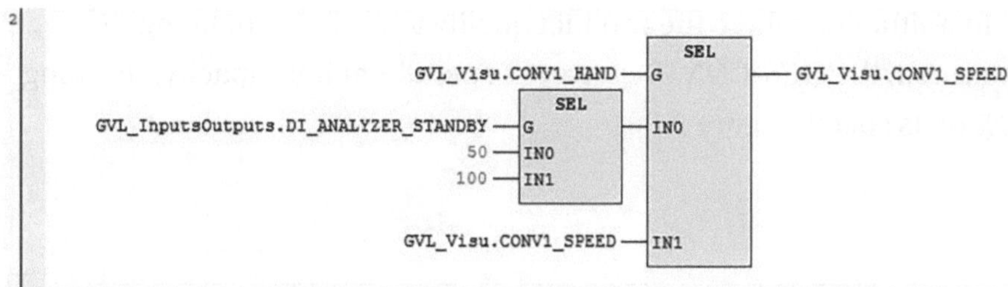

Figure 9-96. *Program CONV1: Network 2*

Testing the Application and Observing the Operation of the *QCS-CONV1* Conveyor

To test the functionality of the application, all three conveyors should be started according to the previous instructions. However, this time, on the control panel of the *QCS-CONV1* conveyor, set the control mode to *AUTO*.

While operating in automatic mode, you will notice that when the analyzer is checking the product quality, the speed of the *QCS-CONV1* conveyor is automatically reduced to 50% (Figure 9-97).

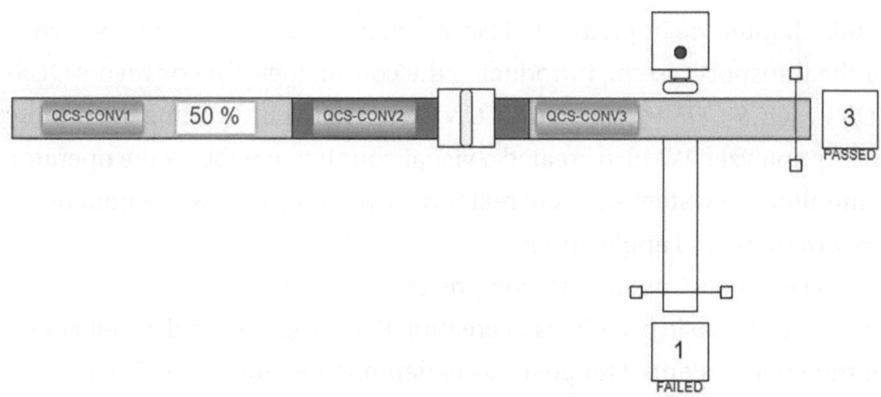

Figure 9-97. *Speed of CONV1 conveyor reduced to 50%*

In a situation where the product quality analysis is not being performed, the *QCS-CONV1* conveyor operates at full capacity, reaching 100% of its speed (Figure 9-98).

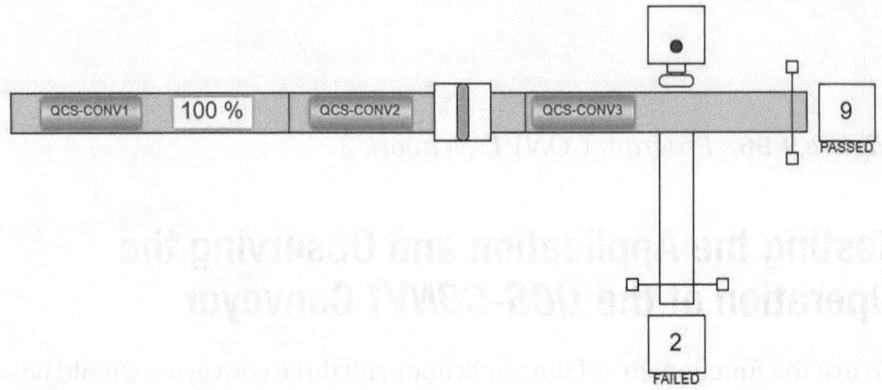

Figure 9-98. *Speed of CONV1 conveyor is 100%.*

Summary

In this chapter, we implemented key elements of the automation system for the transport system, introducing the control logic for conveyors *QCS-CONV1*, *QCS-CONV2*, and *QCS-CONV3*, as well as integrating the product quality analyzer. We also created a visualization that enables the operator to monitor the system status in real time, which is a crucial element of modern industrial applications.

The example implementation presented in this chapter aimed to introduce the basic principles of creating PLC programs and visualizations for transport systems. Our goal was to demonstrate the control logic in which the conveyors work together, and the quality analyzer plays a key role in the production process.

However, it is important to note that in reality, similar installations are much more complex. Typical transport systems in industry are equipped with sensors that provide real-time feedback on conveyor movements, as well as emergency safeguards such as emergency stop buttons and systems for detecting product jams between conveyors. Advanced diagnostics and redundancy are key elements that ensure reliability in industrial environments.

In the next chapter, we will move on to the implementation of control sequences using the Sequential Function Chart (SFC) language. We will learn the principles of building sequences and how to apply them in automation processes.

CHAPTER 10

Sequential Function Chart (SFC) Programming for Conveyor and Quality Control Automation

This chapter discusses the implementation and testing of a control sequence for a quality control line using the SFC programming language. The process begins by creating a basic sequence structure, which is then expanded with additional functionalities such as sequence control through visualization, state management, and the implementation of safety measures and emergency procedures. The chapter also includes examples of solutions to problems that may arise during emergency scenarios encountered by operators, along with methods for resolving them.

© Dariusz Wrebiak 2026
D. Wrebiak, *Practical PLC Programming for Beginners*, Maker Innovations Series,
https://doi.org/10.1007/979-8-8688-2430-2_10

Simulator Library Update

Our next step in exploring the world of PLC controllers begins with updating the simulator library to version *V5.0*. This is crucial because, up until now, all decision-making regarding whether a given product is rejected from the *QCS-CONV3* conveyor was implemented within the simulator's *Conveyors* function block. However, as PLC programmers, our task is to transfer this logic to the PLC program controlling the quality control line.

Installing the Simulator Library V5.0

Let's begin by installing the new version of the library, which can be found in the repository under the *Chapter_10* directory. After installing the library, we proceed to update it within our PLC project. This process has been described in detail in previous chapters of the book.

Upon successful completion of the update, a significant change in the interface of the *Conveyors* function block becomes apparent – a new input named *DO_PUSHER_CMD* has been introduced (Figure 10-1).

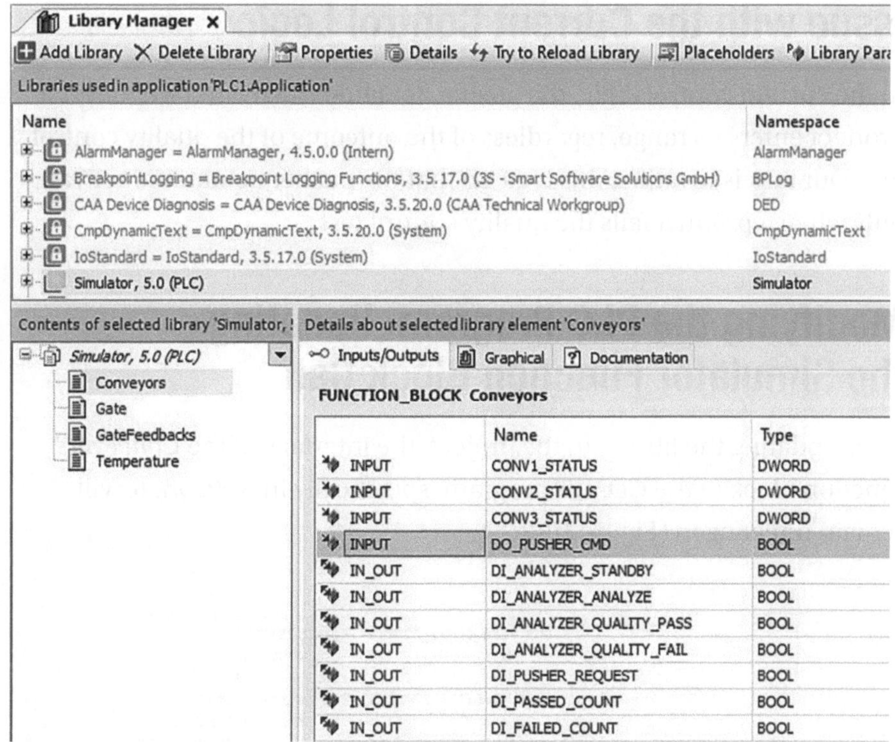

Figure 10-1. *The Library Manager view with the new entry of the
function block Conveyors – DO_PUSHER_CMD – highlighted*

New Functionality in Version V5.0

In version *V4.0* of the simulator, the *Conveyors* function block
automatically determined whether a product on the conveyor would be
rejected by the pusher. In version *V5.0*, the logic has been made more
realistic: the *DI_PUSHER_REQUEST* signal will now always be set to high
whenever a product enters the range of the pusher actuator on the *QCS-
CONV3* conveyor. However, it is up to us to inform the simulator's function
block whether the pusher actuator has been activated by using the *DO_
PUSHER_CMD* input.

Issue with the Current Control Logic

In the current control logic, the pusher actuator is activated whenever a product enters its range, regardless of the outcome of the quality control test. Our task is to adjust this logic so that the pusher actuator is activated only when a product fails the quality control test.

Modifying the PLC Program: Updating the Simulator Function Block Call

After updating the library in the project, the interface of the *Conveyors* function block in the *CONV3* program, specifically in *Network 6*, will remain unchanged (Figure 10-2).

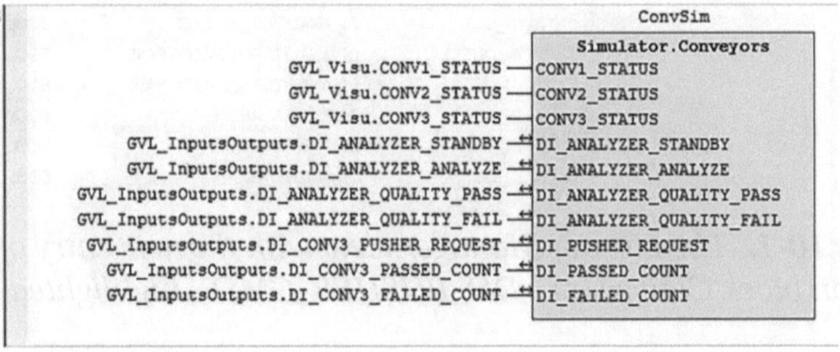

```
6                                                    ConvSim

                                                Simulator.Conveyors
                 GVL_Visu.CONV1_STATUS ──CONV1_STATUS
                 GVL_Visu.CONV2_STATUS ──CONV2_STATUS
                 GVL_Visu.CONV3_STATUS ──CONV3_STATUS
         GVL_InputsOutputs.DI_ANALYZER_STANDBY ─⏛DI_ANALYZER_STANDBY
         GVL_InputsOutputs.DI_ANALYZER_ANALYZE ─⏛DI_ANALYZER_ANALYZE
   GVL_InputsOutputs.DI_ANALYZER_QUALITY_PASS ─⏛DI_ANALYZER_QUALITY_PASS
   GVL_InputsOutputs.DI_ANALYZER_QUALITY_FAIL ─⏛DI_ANALYZER_QUALITY_FAIL
     GVL_InputsOutputs.DI_CONV3_PUSHER_REQUEST ─⏛DI_PUSHER_REQUEST
       GVL_InputsOutputs.DI_CONV3_PASSED_COUNT ─⏛DI_PASSED_COUNT
       GVL_InputsOutputs.DI_CONV3_FAILED_COUNT ─⏛DI_FAILED_COUNT
```

Figure 10-2. *The view of the CONV3 program in Network 6*

To add the new input *DO_PUSHER_CMD*, right-click on the *Conveyors* function block call, and select the *Update Parameters* option (Figure 10-3).

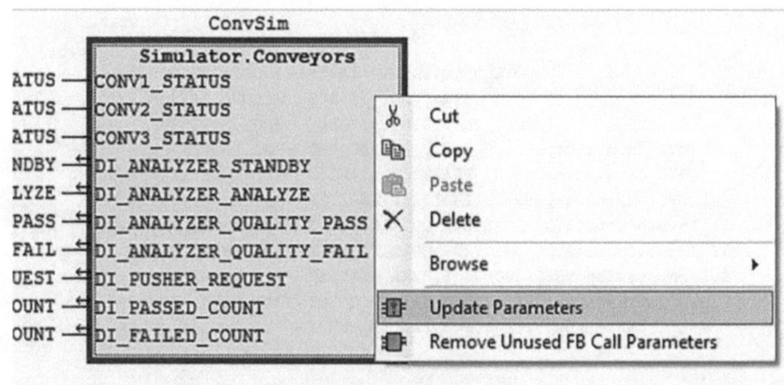

Figure 10-3. *The contextual menu of the Conveyors function block
with the "Update Parameters" option*

After refreshing the interface, you will see the new input *DO_PUSHER_
CMD*, which does not yet have an assigned variable (Figure 10-4).

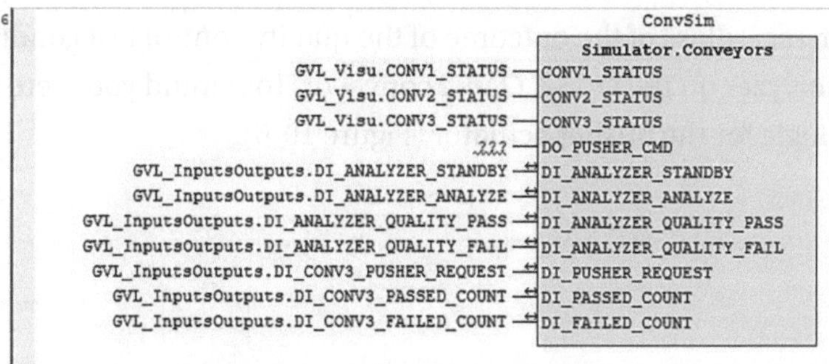

Figure 10-4. *The updated interface of the Conveyors function block
with the new input DO_PUSHER_CMD*

To integrate the new input into the control logic, assign the value of
the digital output *GVL_InputsOutputs.DO_CONV3_PUSHER_CMD* to the
DO_PUSHER_CMD input (Figure 10-5). This ensures that the simulator
function block correctly detects the activation of the pusher actuator, and
the rejected product counter is updated accordingly.

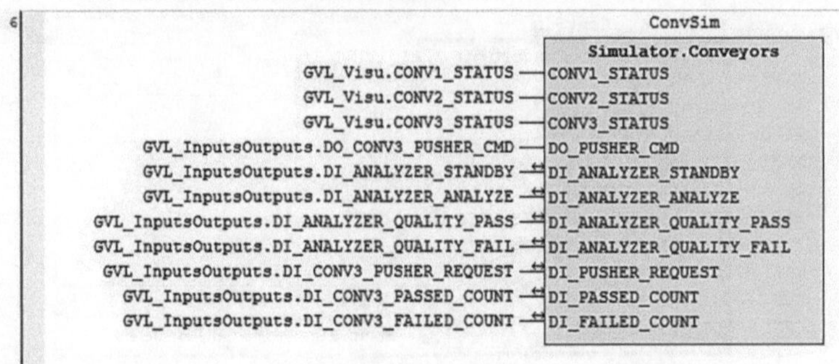

Figure 10-5. *Calling the Conveyors function block with an assignment to the input variable DO_PUSHER_CMD*

After making the modifications, let's download the PLC project to the controller and test the conveyor control logic. We will quickly notice that the reject conveyor is activated every time a product enters the range of the actuator, regardless of the outcome of the quality control test conducted by the analyzer on the *QCS-CONV2* conveyor. To remind you, here is the control logic for the pusher actuator (Figure 10-6).

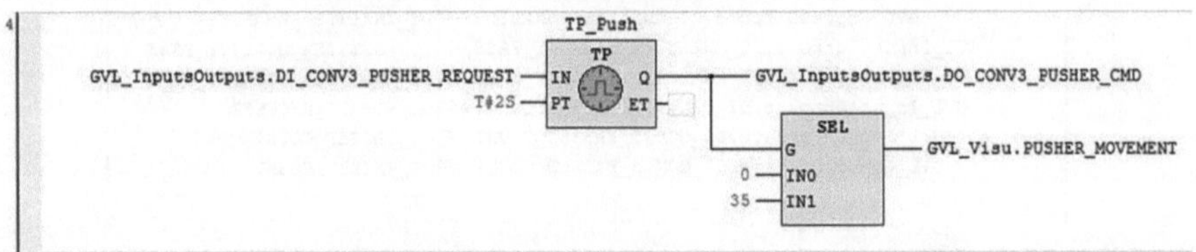

Figure 10-6. *Program CONV3 in Network 4 showing the control logic for the pusher actuator*

Expanding the Pusher Actuator Control Logic

To resolve this issue, we need to expand the pusher actuator control logic. The actuator should only be activated when the product is within its range and has also failed the quality control test, thus qualifying it as non-compliant.

We move on to modifying the logic in *Network 4* of the *CONV3* program, which is responsible for controlling the pusher actuator. In the current logic, the pusher actuator is activated whenever the *DI_CONV3_ PUSHER_REQUEST* signal is set to high. We need to add a condition so that the actuator is only activated when

- The product is within the range of the pusher actuator (DI_CONV3_PUSHER_REQUEST = TRUE).

- The product has failed the quality control test (DI_ ANALYZER_QUALITY_FAIL = TRUE).

Here is the modified control logic (Figure 10-7).

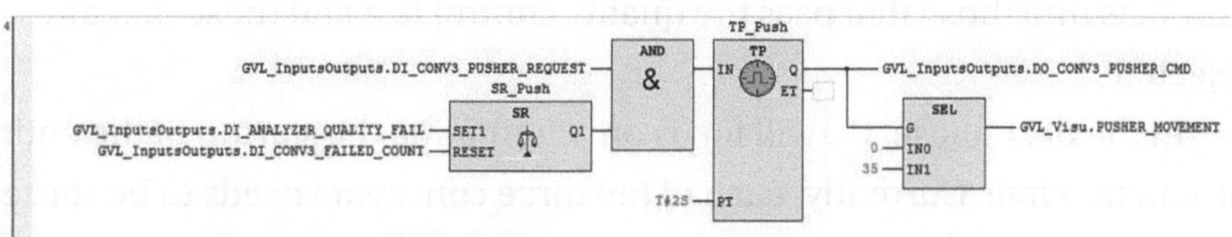

Figure 10-7. *Updated Network 4 of the CONV3 program with extended logic*

A key component of the decision logic is the *SR_Push* flip-flop. The flip-flop is set to active when the analyzer indicates a negative result of the quality control test (*DI_ANALYZER_QUALITY_FAIL = TRUE*). The flip-flop is reset when the product is rejected and the appropriate counter (*DI_CONV3_FAILED_COUNT = TRUE*) is updated.

Make sure to declare the local variable *SR_Push* as type *SR* in the *CONV3* program (Figure 10-8).

```
[ů] CONV3  ✕
    1      PROGRAM CONV3
    2      VAR
    3          Conveyor_CONV3 : Conveyor;
    4          CTU_Passed : CTU;
    5          CTU_Failed : CTU;
    6          SR_Push : SR;
    7          TP_Push : TP;
    8          Notification : SR;
    9          ConvSim : Simulator.Conveyors;
   10      END_VAR
```

Figure 10-8. *Local variables of the CONV3 program*

With the changes implemented, we have created a complete control
logic for the quality control line. The system is now capable of sorting
products into those that pass the quality control test and those that are
rejected.

In the next phase, we will focus on automating the startup of the entire
production line. Currently, each of the three conveyors needs to be started
manually. Later in the chapter, I will demonstrate how the use of the SFC
(Sequential Function Chart) programming language can simplify the
management of more complex production lines.

Creating the Auto Sequence

Let's begin by navigating to the folder *Application* ➤ *PLC* ➤ *Control Logic*
➤ *Conveyors*, where we will add a new object of type *POU*. We will name
it *Auto* and select the programming language *Sequential Function Chart
(SFC)* (*Figure 10-9*).

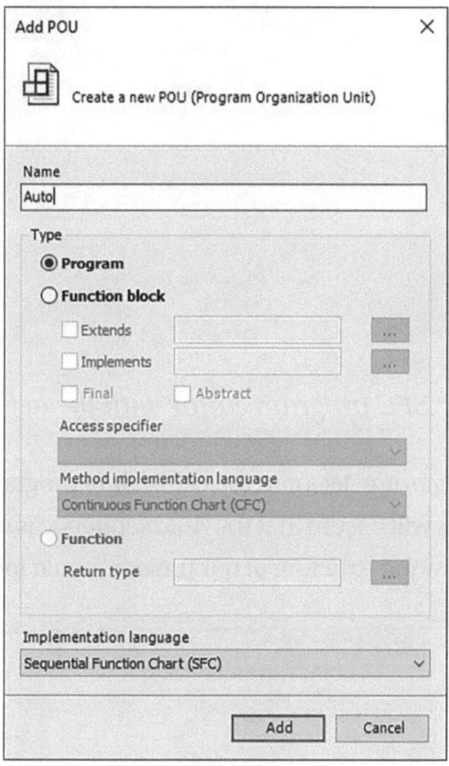

Figure 10-9. *The window for creating a new POU object named Auto*

Sequential Function Chart (SFC)   A graphical programming
language used in industrial automation systems. It allows for the
design of event sequences by defining steps, transitions, and
associated actions, which particularly facilitates the management of
sequential processes.

After clicking the *Add* button, the SFC program editor will open, where
we will define the sequence. It will contain one *Step* named *Init,* a single
Transition that will be permanently set to TRUE, and one *Jump* that will cause
the sequence to return to the *Init* step. This is how it will look (Figure 10-10).

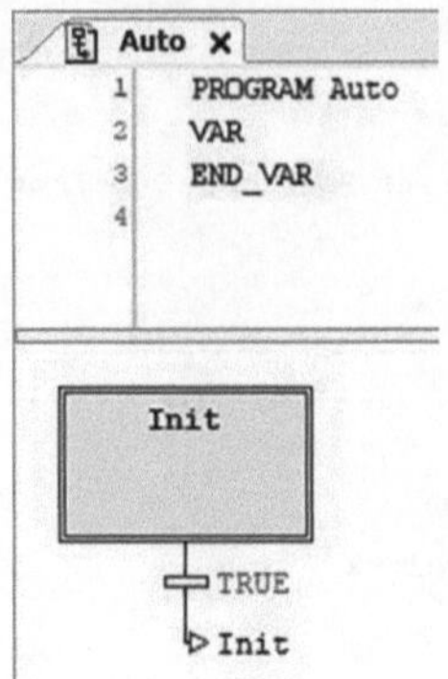

Figure 10-10. *The SFC program editor with the defined sequence*

In the *Task Configurator*, let's add the call of *Auto* program at the end of the
MainTask group. This will ensure that the *Auto* sequence is executed after the
main tasks. Here's how the structure of our project should look (Figure 10-11).

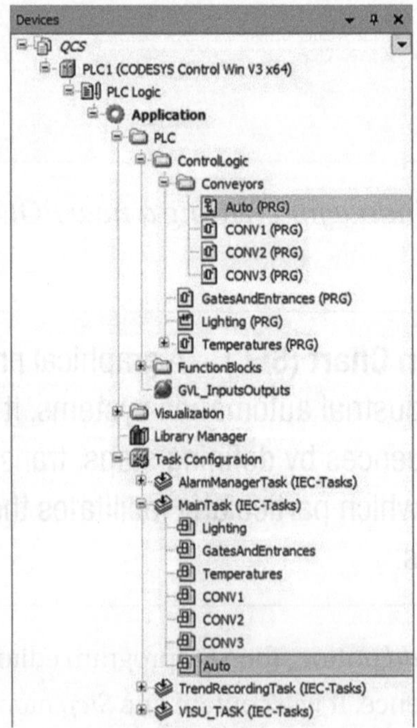

Figure 10-11. *Devices window*

Now, let's download our program to the controller and analyze what exactly is happening. As shown in the illustration (Figure 10-12), at this point, nothing spectacular occurs. The program simply loops through the *Init* step continuously due to the *TRUE* transition and the *Jump* returning to the same step. This is expected behavior for now, as we have yet to define more actions or steps in the sequence.

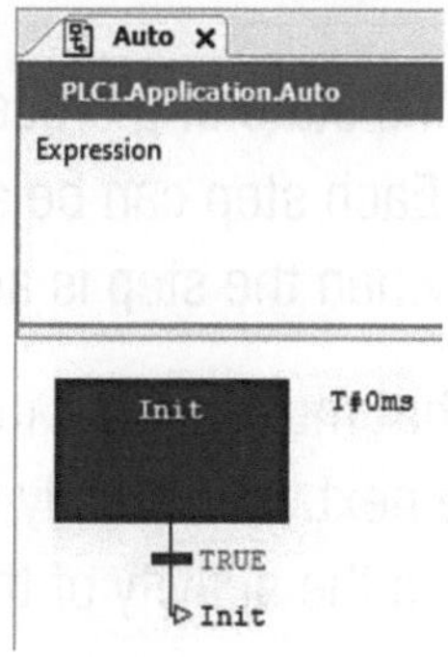

Figure 10-12. *The view of the Auto program in Online mode*

To fully understand what is happening in this case, we will introduce two fundamental concepts of SFC programming: *Step* and *Transition*.

SFC programming consists of *steps* and *transitions* that separate them. In each *Step*, we implement the control logic, i.e., the program that should be executed. This program will continue running as long as the *transition* remains low (FALSE). Once the transition condition is met and the *transition* reaches a high state (TRUE), the program will proceed to the next *Step*.

In our case, we have a single *Step* called *Init*. Currently, there is no logic implemented in this step, which means it is essentially a call to an empty block. The transition is permanently set to high (TRUE), which means that after the empty *Init* step is executed, the program will automatically proceed to the next instruction in the SFC program, which is a *Jump* back to the *Init* step. At this point, the whole process restarts: the empty *Init*

471

step is called again, as the transition condition is satisfied (TRUE), and the jump leads back to the *Init* step.

An SFC program is created by linking individual *steps* and *transitions*, which form the sequence. This allows us to expand the program so that tasks that were previously done manually can now be automated, step by step, according to our design.

Step   Represents a specific state of a process or an operation performed by the system. Each step can be associated with a specific action, which is triggered when the step is active.

Transition   A condition that must be met in order for the system to move from one step to the next. It is usually a logical expression, the fulfillment of which changes the activity of the steps in the sequence.

Creating the Sequence: First Steps

In our case, we will create a sequence that, upon activation, will set all conveyors to *AUTO* mode. The sequence will then begin starting the conveyors on the quality control line, starting with the *QCS-CONV3* conveyor. After waiting five seconds, the *QCS-CONV2* conveyor will be started, and five seconds after that, the *QCS-CONV1* conveyor will be activated.

We will organize the program in such a way that the entire sequence can be triggered from the visualization interface with a single button, instead of starting each conveyor individually as we did previously.

We will begin expanding the sequence by declaring a variable *On* in the local variable section of the *Auto* program (Figure 10-13). This *BOOL* variable will be used to activate the sequence.

```
Auto ✕
1     PROGRAM Auto
2     VAR
3         On : BOOL;
4     END_VAR
```

Figure 10-13. *Declaration of the local variable On*

The next step will be to expand the sequence. To begin, we will set up
the sequence to work in such a way that when the *On* variable is set to high
(TRUE), the program will jump to the *Init* step. If the *On* variable is in a low
state (FALSE), the *Init* step should continue to be executed.

To achieve this, we simply need to assign the *On* variable to the
condition of the transition that was previously set to TRUE. This way, the
transition will only be triggered when *On* is TRUE, causing the program to
jump to the *Init* step.

Here is the current *Auto* program code, implemented using SFC
language (Figure 10-14).

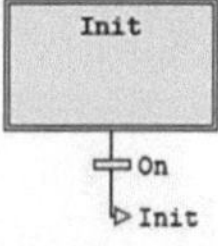

Figure 10-14. *Updated program Auto*

Now, let's download our program to the controller and switch to
Online mode to observe what difference the modifications have made
(Figure 10-15).

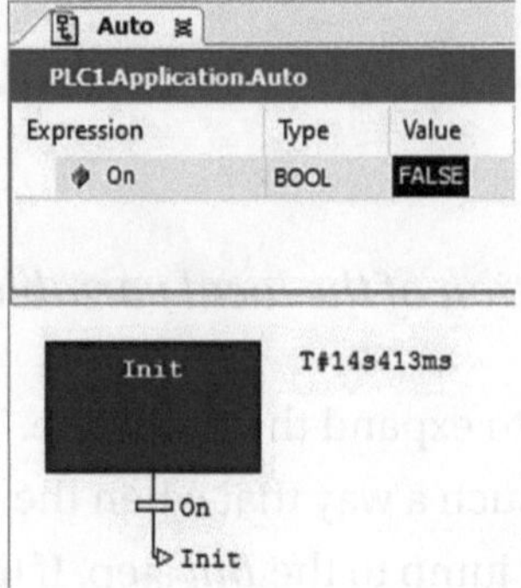

Figure 10-15. *Program Auto in Online mode*

At this point, we can observe that when the value of the *On* variable is FALSE, the transition condition is not met, which is why the *Init* step is being executed. The time displayed on the right side of the *Init* step indicates how long this step is being called.

Using the table visible above the sequence, let's set the *On* variable to TRUE. This can be done just as we did in previous chapters using the *Watch* table (Figure 10-16).

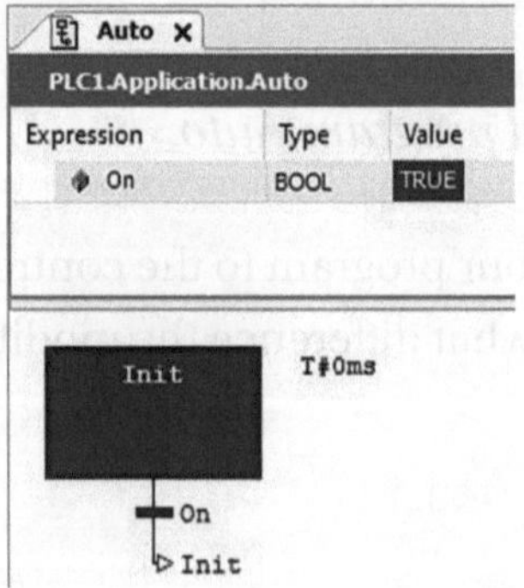

Figure 10-16. *Program Auto in Online mode with the variable On set to TRUE*

We can see that the entire sequence is repeating continuously. This means that the *Init* step is being called because the transition condition is met. Immediately after calling the *Init* step, the program jumps, and the *Init* step is called again.

Now, if we set the *On* variable to low (FALSE), the *Init* step will be called until the transition condition is met again. Note that the time, which tracks how long the *Init* step has been called, has been reset, and the countdown starts over. This behavior shows that the program is executing the *Init* step as long as the *On* variable remains FALSE and the transition condition is not met (Figure 10-17).

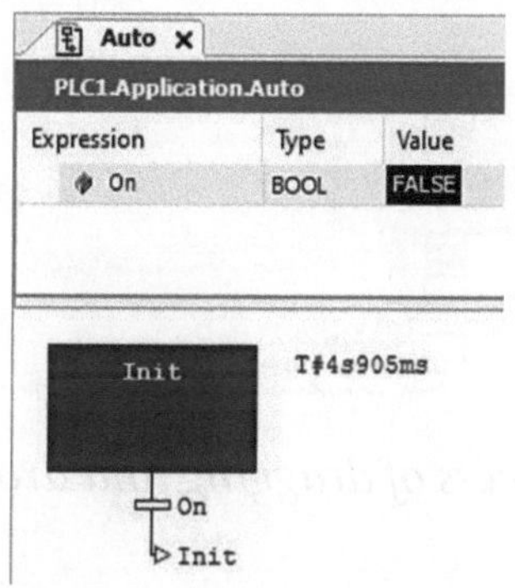

Figure 10-17. *Program Auto in Online mode with the variable On set to FALSE*

Sequence Implementation: Adding the *Run* Step

After familiarizing ourselves with the basic elements of the SFC program, let's expand our sequence by adding another step called *Run*. This step will be added immediately after the *On* transition. To do this, use the *Toolbox* and the SFC program element called *Step (Figure 10-18)*.

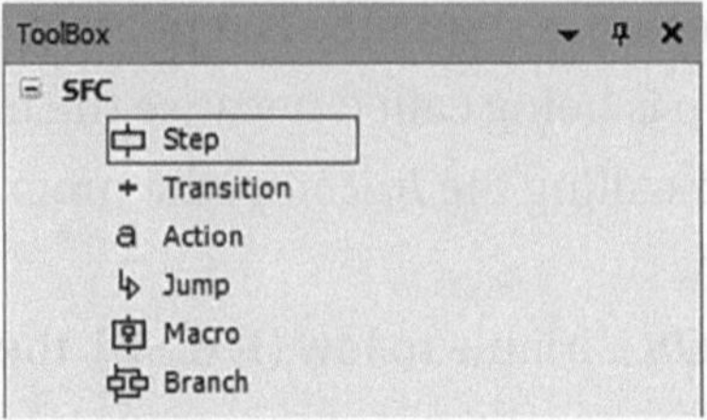

Figure 10-18. *Toolbox view with SFC language elements*

Using the *Drag'n'Drop* method, drag the *Step* element into our
Auto program, placing it between the *On* transition and the *Init* jump
(Figure 10-19).

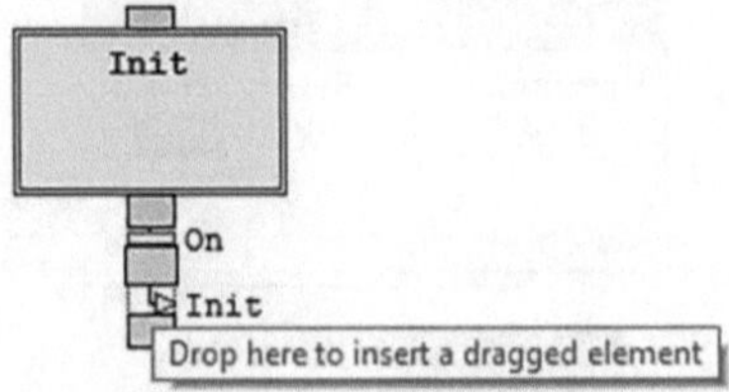

Figure 10-19. *The process of dragging and dropping the Step element
into the Auto program*

A new step will be added to our sequence, which will automatically be
named *Step0 (Figure 10-20).*

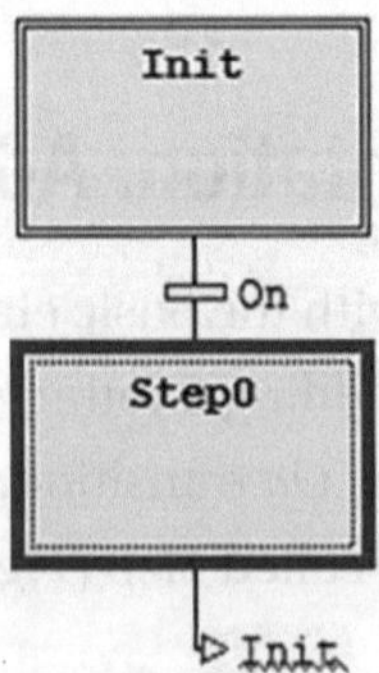

Figure 10-20. *The newly added Step element in the Auto program*

Let's rename this step to *Run* to reflect the fact that our sequence has been started (Figure 10-21).

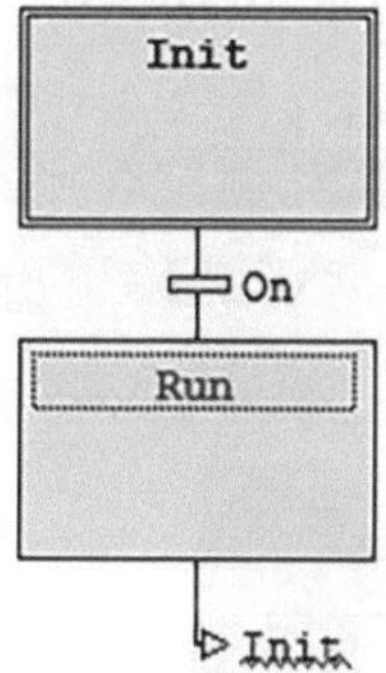

Figure 10-21. *The changed name of the step to "Run" in the Auto program*

As we already know, each step must be associated with a transition. So let's use the *Drag'n'Drop* method to add a transition between *Run step* and *Init jump*. The transition will automatically be named *Trans0*. Let's change the transition condition to the negation of the *On* variable (Figure 10-22). This means that if the *On* variable is in a low state (FALSE), the jump to the *Init* step will be executed.

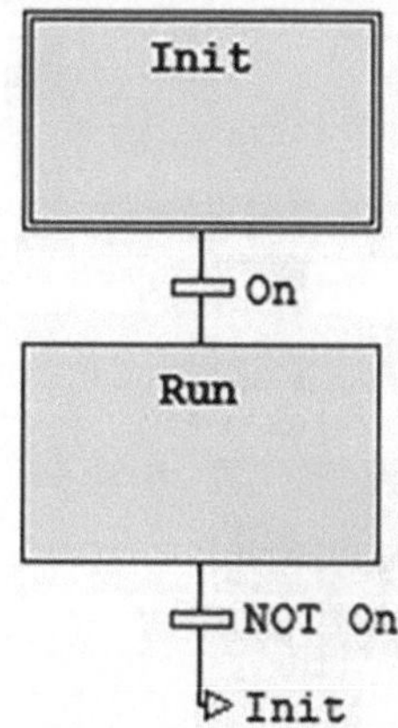

Figure 10-22. *Transition between step Run and jump Init*

With this, we have created a simple switch that ensures that when the *On* variable is in a low state (FALSE), the program code implemented in the *Init* step will be executed (Figure 10-23).

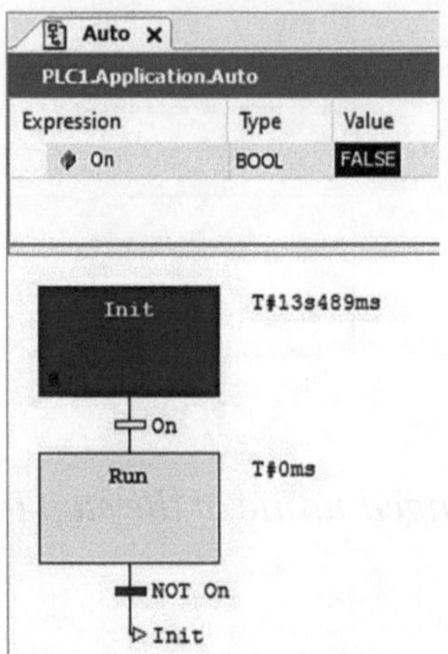

Figure 10-23. *Step Init in the Auto program*

On the other hand, if we set the *On* variable to a high state (TRUE), the *Run* step will be called (Figure 10-24).

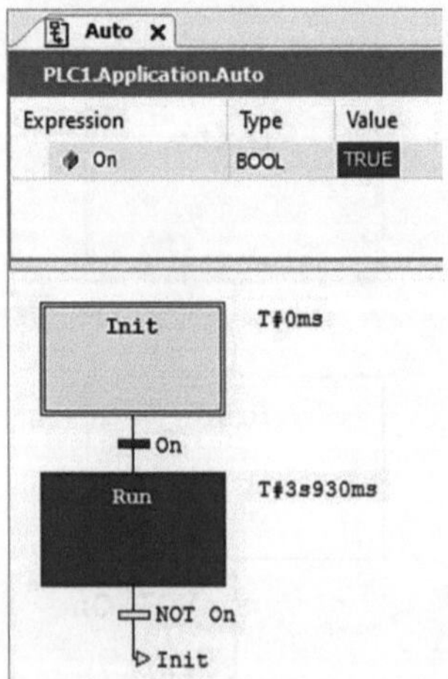

Figure 10-24. *Step Run in the Auto program, called when the variable On is set to TRUE*

Sequence Implementation: Step *SetAuto*

Our sequence already switches between two basic steps, but we haven't yet implemented any code to be executed during these steps. It's time to change that.

We'll add another step to our sequence responsible for automatically switching all three conveyors to *AUTO* mode. Additionally, we will program a transition to ensure this step runs for two seconds before moving on to the next step.

Using the *Drag'n'Drop* function from the *Toolbox*, insert a step between the *On* transition and the *Run* step, naming it *SetAuto*. Here's what our sequence should look like now (Figure 10-25).

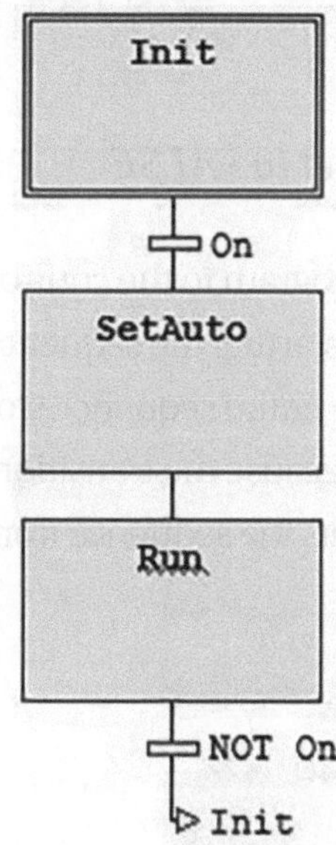

Figure 10-25. *Added step SetAuto in the Auto program*

We also need to add a transition that will handle the condition for moving to the next step. For now, let's set the condition of this transition to FALSE (Figure 10-26).

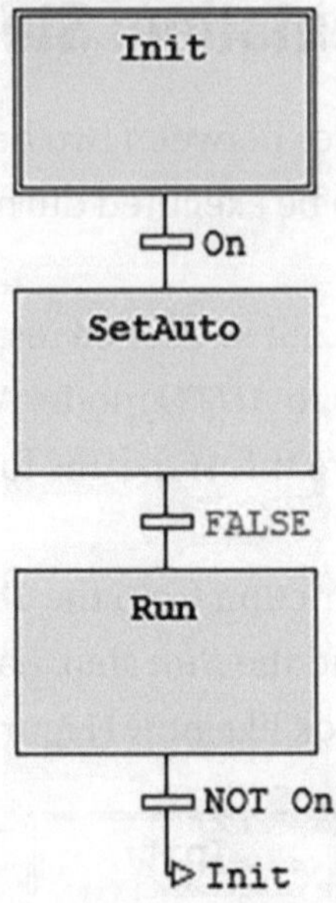

Figure 10-26. *Transition set to FALSE*

Now, let's download our program to the controller and switch to Online
mode to test its behavior. After starting the sequence by setting the *On* variable
to TRUE, we will notice that the entire sequence stops at the *SetAuto* step
(Figure 10-27). This happens because the transition is currently programmed to
a value of FALSE, which prevents the sequence from moving to the next step.

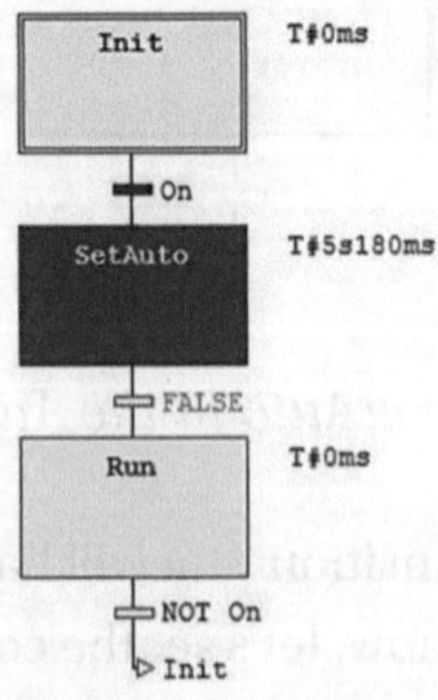

Figure 10-27. *Program Auto in Online mode*

480

It's time to make a change. According to the technological requirements, the *SetAuto* step should run for two seconds and then move to the next step. Now we will see the benefits of using the SFC programming language. When each step is called, the call time for that step is visible on the right side in Online mode. One of the advantages of SFC is that we can easily refer to this time without implementing an additional timer. All we need to do is type the name of our step, followed by a dot, and then select the *t* element from the list (Figure 10-28).

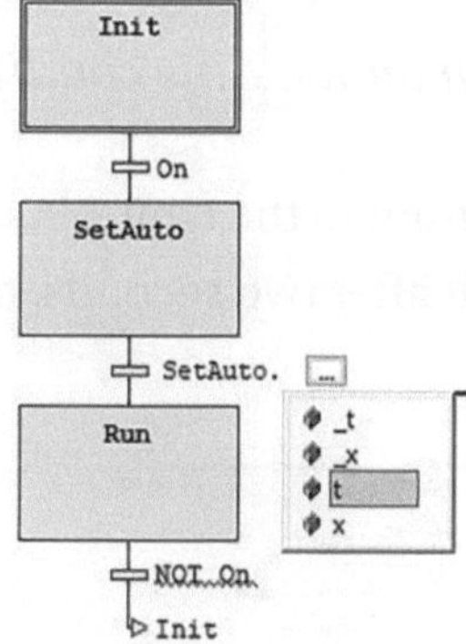

Figure 10-28.   *Use of the element SetAuto.t*

Next, we will implement the transition condition that will cause the sequence to move to the next step when the execution time of the *SetAuto* step exceeds two seconds. Here's what the code for our sequence should look like (Figure 10-29).

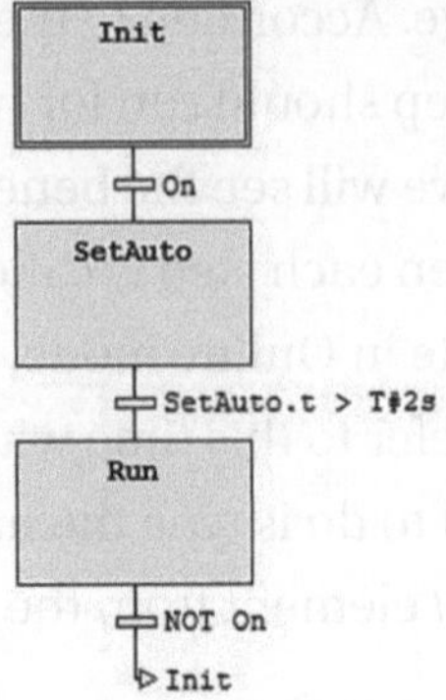

Figure 10-29. *A transition with a time condition SetAuto.t > T#2s*

Let's download our program to the controller. After starting the
sequence, we will notice that after two seconds, the sequence will go to the
Run step (Figure 10-30).

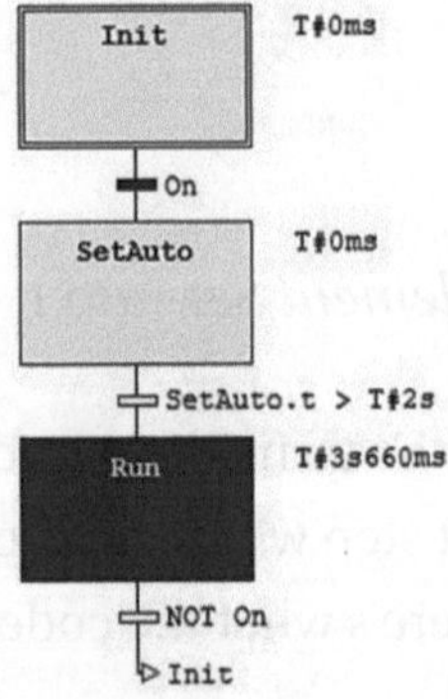

Figure 10-30. *Program Auto in Online mode*

We have already designed the next step in our sequence. Now it's time
to add the code that will be executed when a specific step is called.

We will introduce a new concept – *Action*. Our code, which will be
implemented during the execution of the steps, is organized into actions.
In this book, we will learn about three basic actions that we will use
when implementing our sequence. For the *SetAuto* step, we will add an

active action where we will implement our code. To do this, we select
the *Action* element from the *Toolbox* (on the right side) and, using the
Drag'n'Drop method, place it in the upper right corner of the *SetAuto* step
(Figure 10-31).

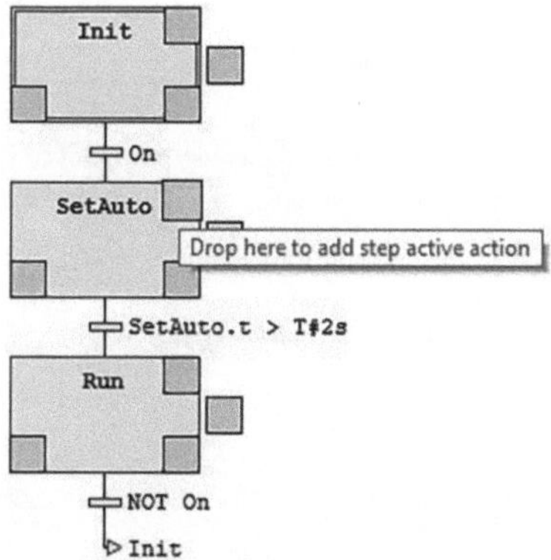

Figure 10-31. *Adding an active action to the SetAuto step*

After adding the *Action* element to the *SetAuto* step, a window will
appear asking how to copy the action. To keep the default settings, simply
click the *OK* button to confirm your choice (Figure 10-32).

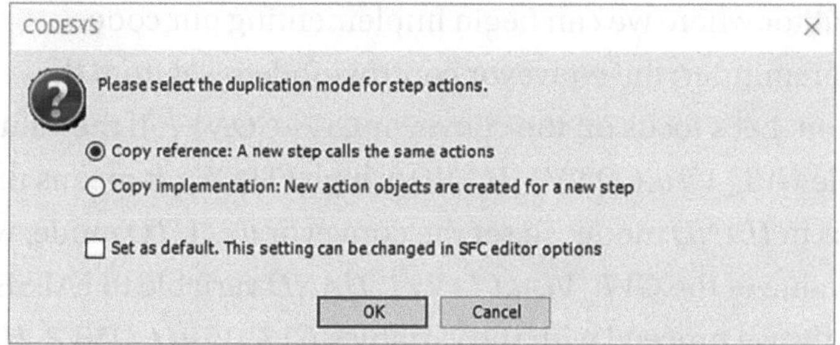

Figure 10-32. *Confirmation window for copying the action selection*

Next, in the *Add Action* window, we can assign a name to our action
where we will organize our code and select the preferred programming
language. I will leave the settings unchanged and name the action *SetAuto_*

active, as suggested by the CODESYS environment. I will also leave the programming language as LAD (Figure 10-33). It's worth mentioning the option to switch between LAD and FBD languages within the same editor.

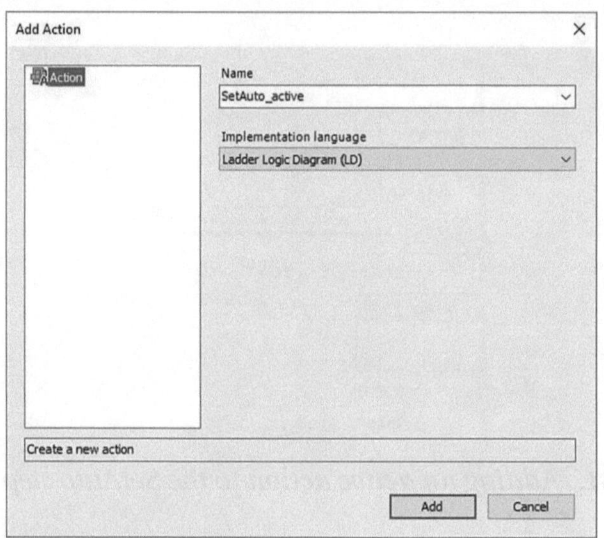

Figure 10-33. *Add Action window*

After adding the action to the *SetAuto* step, we will see an empty LAD program editor where we can begin implementing our code.

A brief reminder: the conveyor control mode is set from the visualization. Let's focus on the conveyor *QCS-CONV1*. If the value of the variable *GVL_Visu.CONV1_HAND* is high (TRUE), it means that the conveyor is in *HAND* mode. To set the conveyor to *AUTO* mode, we need to set the value of the *GVL_Visu.CONV1_HAND* variable to FALSE.

Similarly, we proceed with the variables *GVL_Visu.CONV2_HAND* and *GVL_Visu.CONV3_HAND* for conveyors *QCS-CONV2* and *QCS-CONV3*, respectively. Our task is simply to set these three variables to low (FALSE) in the *SetAuto* step.

This is how the code for our *SetAuto_active* action should look (Figure 10-34).

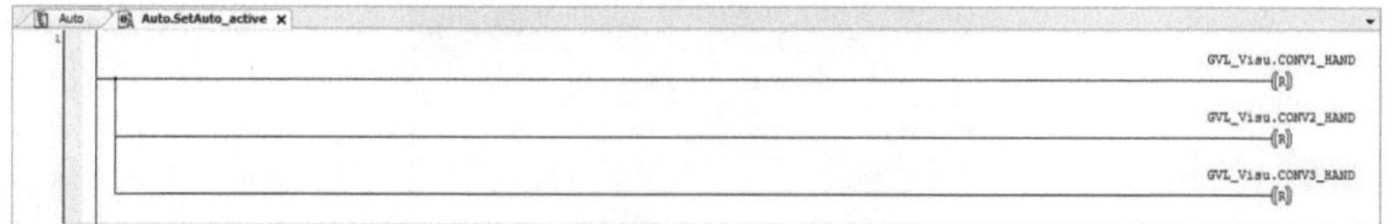

Figure 10-34. *SetAuto_active action code in the LAD editor*

After adding the *active* action to the *SetAuto* step, the small triangle
in the upper right corner of this step indicates that the step now contains
code that will be executed when it is called (Figure 10-35). This signals
that the *SetAuto* step is no longer just an empty step in our sequence but
contains logic that will be activated during its execution.

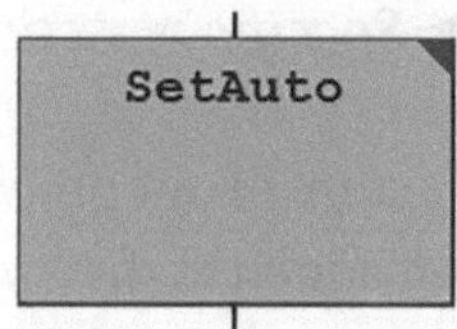

Figure 10-35. *The "SetAuto" step with a triangle in the upper
right corner*

To find out exactly which action will be executed when the *SetAuto*
step is called, click the *SetAuto* step. On the right-hand side, in the
Properties tab, under the *Specific* section ➤ *Actions* ➤ *Main action*, we
will see that the action assigned to this property is named *SetAuto_active*
(Figure 10-36).

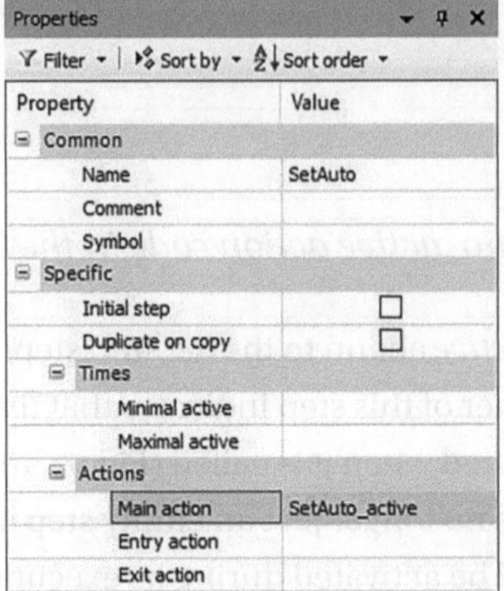

Figure 10-36. *Properties ➤ Specific ➤ Actions ➤ Main action*

Let's take a look at the structure of our project. We will notice that the
SetAuto_active action has been added to the *Auto* program (Figure 10-37).

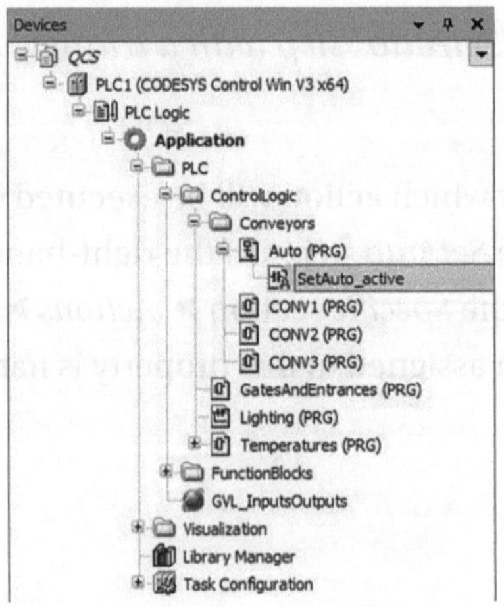

Figure 10-37. *Devices window*

It's time to test the new functionality of our sequence, specifically
the step where all conveyors will be automatically switched to *AUTO*
mode. Let's download our program to the controller, and then from the

visualization, set all three conveyors to *HAND* mode by selecting the appropriate control mode on the conveyor control panel.

Next, let's start the sequence by setting the variable *On* to TRUE and observe in the visualization how the control mode in the *SetAuto* step changes to *AUTO*.

To conclude this section, let's summarize that, in this case, the control logic that sets the conveyors to *AUTO* mode was implemented in the *active* action. The code of this action is executed whenever the corresponding sequence step is called.

Active Action   Executed as long as the step is active. It is useful in situations where specific operations need to be continuously performed during the execution of a given step.

Sequence Implementation: Step *Start_CONV3*

We are now able to set all conveyors to automatic mode from the sequence. It's time to start the conveyor from within the SFC sequence.

In such installations that transport materials, the conveyors are always started from the last one in the line. This is due to dependencies between the conveyors. To remind you, the last conveyor, *QCS-CONV3*, automatically gives permission for the operation of conveyors *QCS-CONV2* and *QCS-CONV1*.

Let's begin the implementation of starting conveyor *QCS-CONV3* from the sequence by adding another step, right after the *SetAuto* step and its transition, which we will name *Start_CONV3*. We will also implement a transition condition for this step, so that it lasts for five seconds. This is how our sequence should look (Figure 10-38).

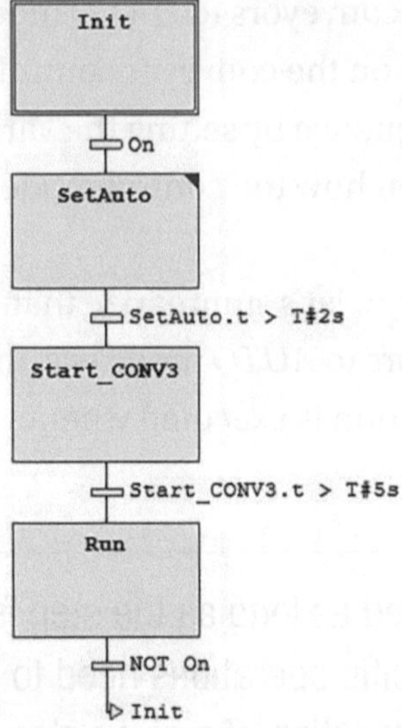

Figure 10-38. *Step Start_CONV3 added to the sequence*

As we already know, the execution of this step will last five seconds, but during this time, no program will be executed because this step has not yet been assigned any actions.

In the previous step, we learned about the *active* action, whose program is always executed when the step is called. In this step, we will learn about two new actions that can be assigned to a step: *entry* and *exit*.

The difference between the *active* action and these two is that the code implemented in the latter two actions is only executed once. As you can easily guess, the code in the *entry* action will be executed when the step is first called, i.e., when the transition preceding this step reaches the TRUE condition. On the other hand, the *exit* action will be executed when leaving the current step, i.e., when the transition assigned to this step is set to TRUE.

With the ability to implement *entry* and *exit* actions, we can generate a signal that will control the activation of the conveyor. Let's declare new variables that we will use in the programs for controlling the activation

and deactivation of the conveyors. Therefore, it is best to declare variables
for all three conveyors. These variables should be declared in the local
variable area of the *Auto* program, which is our sequence. Here is how the
declaration of these variables should look (Figure 10-39).

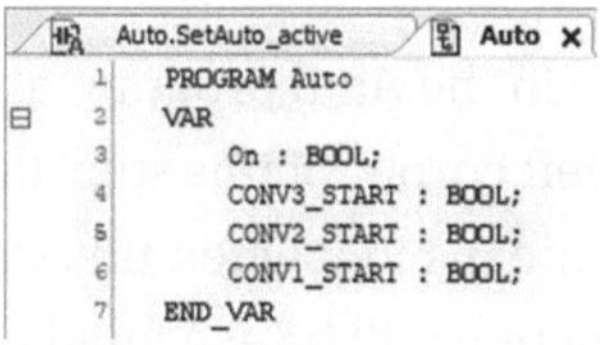

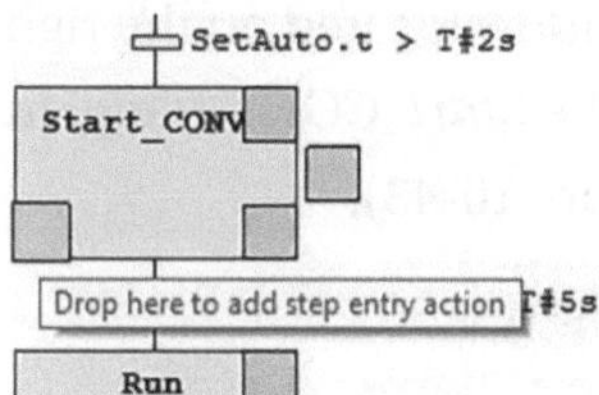

Figure 10-39. *Local variables in the Auto program*

Having declared the variables, let's move on to implementing the
control logic that will set and reset these variables. To do this, add an *entry*
action to the *Start_CONV3* step. To achieve this, in the *Toolbox*, select the
Action element, and assign it to the *Start_CONV3* step in the bottom left
corner of this step (Figure 10-40).

Figure 10-40. *Adding an entry action to the step Start_CONV3*

After adding the *entry* action to our step, the editor will automatically
open, where we will implement our control logic. As we already know,
this action will be triggered only once, during the first execution of the
Start_CONV3 step. At this point, we want to set the variable *CONV3_
START* to TRUE, which will generate a signal that can be used to turn on
the conveyor in the control logic program responsible for this conveyor.
The control logic for the *Start_CONV3_entry* action will be very simple and
looks as follows (Figure 10-41).

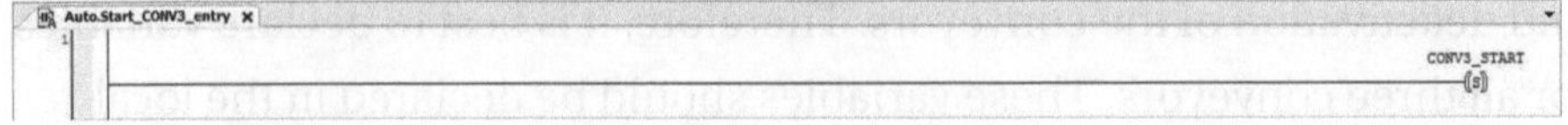

Figure 10-41. *Start_CONV3_entry: setting the variable CONV3_START to TRUE*

Our *Start_CONV3* step in the *Auto* program also changed its appearance. In the lower left corner of this step, the letter "E" appeared, standing for *Entry*, which means that when this step is executed, the program assigned to this action will be executed (Figure 10-42).

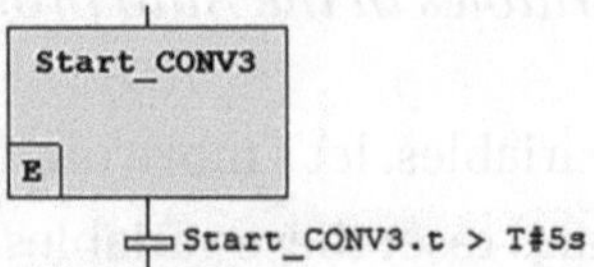

Figure 10-42. *Step Start_CONV3 with an assigned entry action*

If we want to check exactly which action is assigned to this step, we can do so in the *Properties* window located on the right side of the CODESYS environment by clicking the *Start_CONV3* step. In our case, it is the *Start_CONV3_entry* action (Figure 10-43).

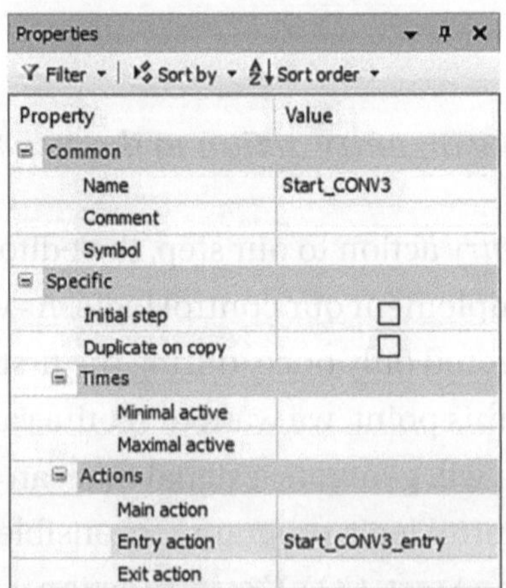

Property	Value
⊟ Common	
Name	Start_CONV3
Comment	
Symbol	
⊟ Specific	
Initial step	☐
Duplicate on copy	☐
⊟ Times	
Minimal active	
Maximal active	
⊟ Actions	
Main action	
Entry action	Start_CONV3_entry
Exit action	

Figure 10-43. *Properties window for the Start_CONV3 step*

Entry Action   Triggered once when the step is activated. It is typically used for initializing operations that need to be performed immediately upon entering the step.

Currently, when executing the *Start_CONV3* step, the variable *CONV3_START* will be set to TRUE. After five seconds, the transition condition to the next step will be met, and the value of the *CONV3_START* variable will remain TRUE. However, we need to ensure that when leaving the *Start_CONV3* step, the value of the *CONV3_START* variable is reset because only the *Start_CONV3* step is responsible for turning on the *QCS_CONV3* conveyor. Therefore, in any other step of our sequence, the value of this variable should not be TRUE.

We will implement resetting the *CONV3_START* variable in the *exit* action, which we will add to the *Start_CONV3* step by placing the *Action* element in the bottom right corner of this step (Figure 10-44).

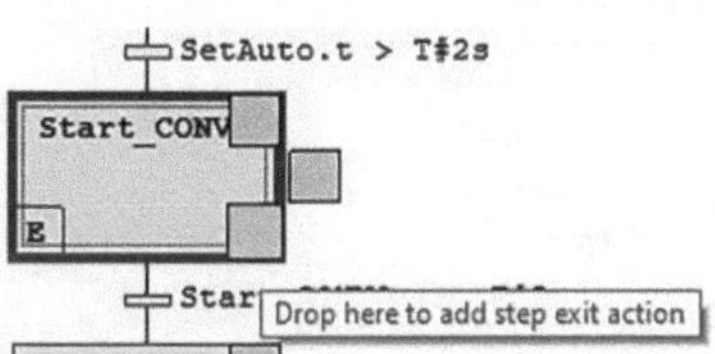

Figure 10-44. *Adding an exit action to the step Start_CONV3*

The control logic contained in this action is simple and looks as follows (Figure 10-45).

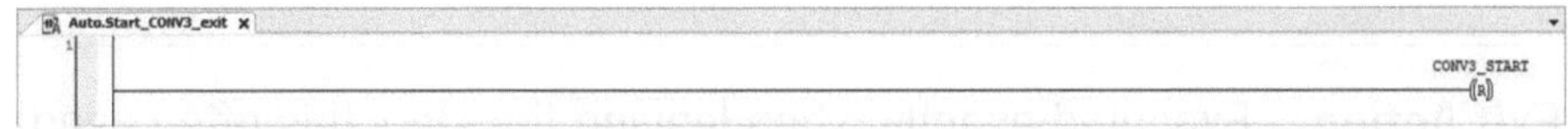

Figure 10-45. *Start_CONV3_entry: setting the variable CONV3_START to FALSE*

In the *Auto* program, our step *Start_CONV3* now has the letter "X" in the lower right corner, indicating that the *eXit* action has been added to this step (Figure 10-46).

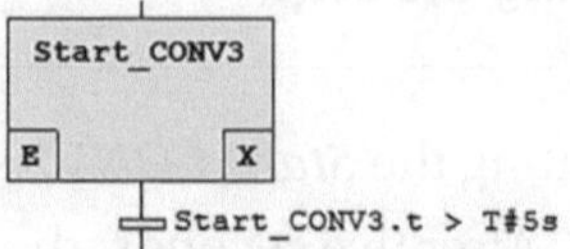

Figure 10-46. *Step Start_CONV3 with an assigned exit action*

To see exactly which actions are linked to the step, we can check the *Properties* window located on the right side of the CODESYS environment (Figure 10-47).

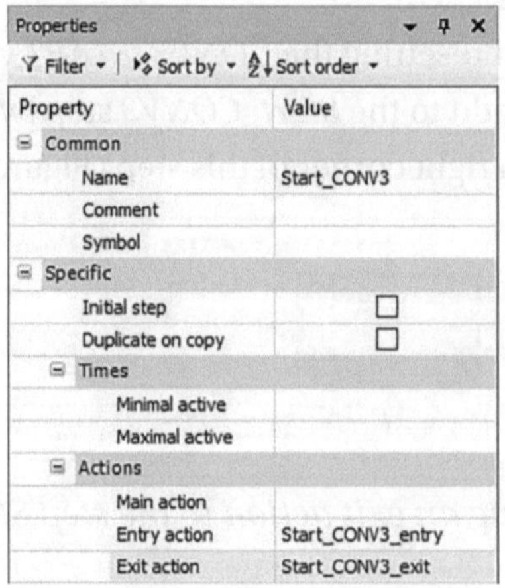

Figure 10-47. *Properties window for the Start_CONV3 step*

Exit Action   Executed exactly when leaving the step. It is often used for tidying up actions or resetting settings before transitioning to the next step.

Once we have implemented the step that activates the *QCS-CONV3*
conveyor and controls the *CONV3_START* variable, it's time to expand the
control logic for the *QCS-CONV3* conveyor itself. To do this, we will go to
the *CONV3* program and expand the logic in *Network 3* to control the *QCS-
CONV3* conveyor.

Let's start with the condition that activates the conveyor in *AUTO*
mode. To do this, we need to set the *START* input of the *Conveyor* function
block to a high state (TRUE). To achieve this, we must add a condition that
will be met when the conveyor is in *AUTO* mode and the *CONV3_START*
variable, implemented in the sequence in the *Auto* program, is set to
TRUE. This is how the control logic for the conveyor, which allows it to
start in *AUTO* mode, is structured (Figure 10-48).

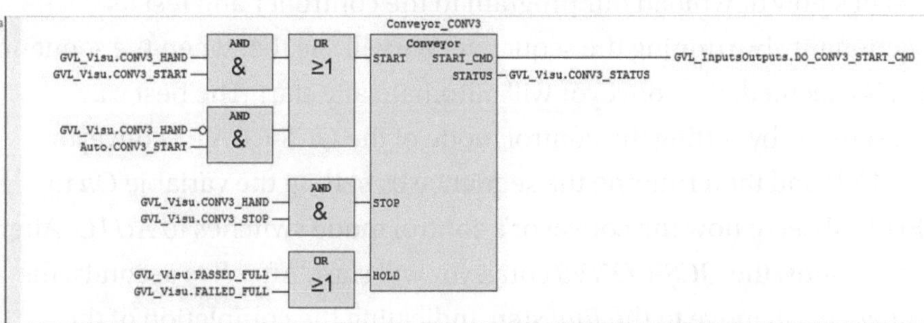

Figure 10-48. *Control logic for the QCS-CONV3 conveyor, switching
on the conveyor in AUTO mode*

When implementing the control logic for the automatic mode of the
QCS-CONV3 conveyor, we also need to ensure that the conveyor is turned
off if it is in automatic mode but the sequence is not activated. In other
words, if the conveyor is in *AUTO* mode but there is no need for it to be on
because the quality control line is off, the conveyor should also be turned
off. This is how the control logic for setting the *STOP* input of the *Conveyor*
function block to high (TRUE) is structured (Figure 10-49).

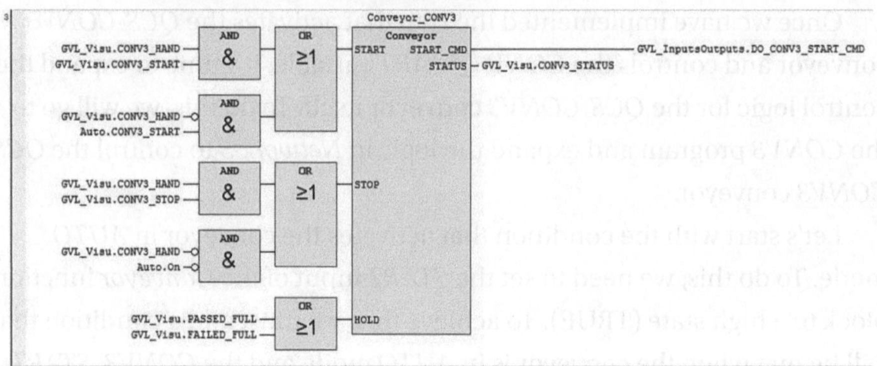

Figure 10-49. *Control logic for the QCS-CONV3 conveyor, switching off the conveyor in AUTO mode*

Let's now download our program to the controller and test its functionality by running the sequence. We will see that when the sequence step is executed, the conveyor will automatically start. The best way to test this is by setting the control mode of the *QCS-CONV3* conveyor to *HAND* and then running the sequence by setting the variable *On* to TRUE. Observe how the conveyor's control mode switches to *AUTO*. After two seconds, the *QCS-CONV3* conveyor will start. After five seconds, the sequence will move to the *Run* step, indicating the completion of the sequence startup. When we turn off the entire sequence by setting the *On* variable to FALSE, the *QCS-CONV3* conveyor will be turned off, and the sequence will return to the *Init* step.

The Essence of Implementing the Transition Condition to the Next Step

There is one very important topic that I need to address. Namely, the transition condition for the *Start_CONV3* step. Currently, we have implemented a simple condition where after five seconds the sequence moves to the next step. In real industrial automation systems, this

494

approach would be inappropriate. In such cases, when we start controlling any device, we need to make sure that what was supposed to be done by that step has been completed 100%. Only then can we proceed to the next step in the sequence.

In our case, the *Start_CONV3* step is responsible for starting conveyor *QCS-CONV3*. Therefore, we need to expand the transition condition to check whether the conveyor is actually running. How can we do that? In real industrial automation systems, we have many more signals associated with each device. In the case of conveyors, it is common to check whether the electric drive that powers the conveyor is rotating. This signal is connected to the PLC as a digital input, allowing the PLC programmer to confirm that the conveyor is operational.

For simplicity, in this application, we assume that we are using the signal *DO_CONV3_START_CMD*, which in a TRUE state indicates that the conveyor is running. If this digital output is TRUE, we can assume that the conveyor is on. Otherwise, the conveyor is off. Therefore, let's expand the transition with this condition.

Here is how the modified sequence should look (Figure 10-50): it will proceed to the next step only when the *Start_CONV3* step has been executed for five seconds and the *QCS-CONV3* conveyor is running, i.e., the digital output *DO_CONV3_START_CMD* is in a high state.

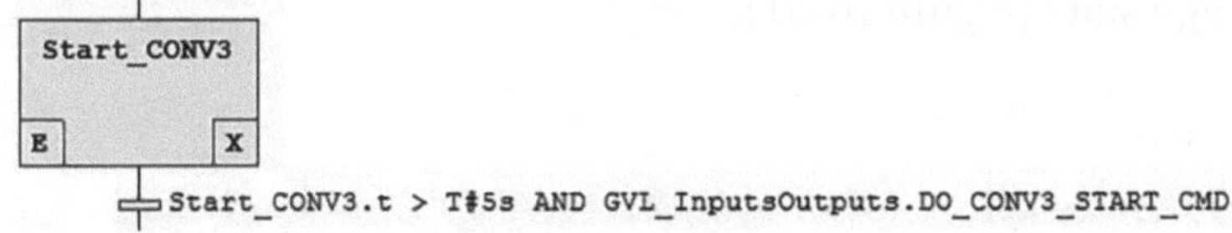

Figure 10-50. *Transition condition checking the state of the DO_
CONV3_START_CMD output*

I will emphasize once again the importance of this issue. In a real environment, if we were programming the operation of such a conveyor, we would have many more signals available for that device. Therefore, we would need to implement a condition that guarantees that the program executed in the given step has actually completed its task and that the transition condition has been met. In our case, instead of directly checking the state of the digital output *DO_CONV3_START_CMD*, we could use, for example, a digital input that informs us that the conveyor is indeed running, such as *DI_CONV3_OPERATION*.

Implementation of the Sequence: Steps *Start_CONV2, Start_CONV1*

We already know how to implement control logic in actions assigned to individual steps. When the transition condition for a given step is met, the sequence proceeds to the next step.

As a practical exercise, let's extend our sequence so that when the *Start_CONV3* step executes its action (which means it starts the *QCS-CONV3* conveyor), the sequence will transition to the next step, which we will now add. This step will be called *Start_CONV2* and will be responsible for starting the *QCS-CONV2* conveyor. Additionally, we will add a transition for this step, where the condition will be met if the *Start_CONV2* step has been executed for at least five seconds and when the digital output *DO_CONV2_START_CMD*, controlling the start of the conveyor, is set to a high state (Figure 10-51).

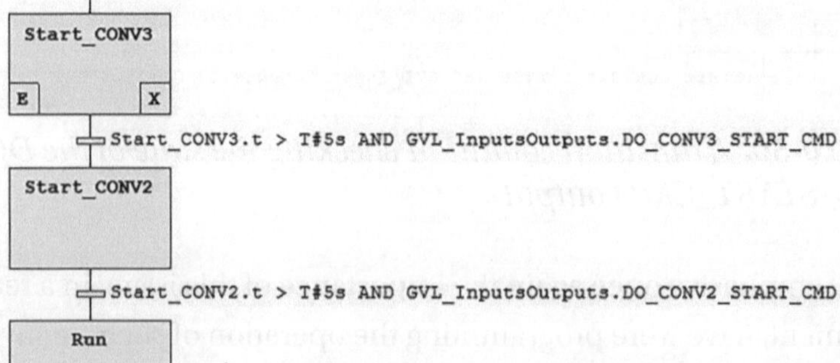

Figure 10-51. *Step Start_CONV2 with transition*

If we download the program to the controller and run the sequence, we will see that when the *Start_CONV2* step is executed, the transition will not yet meet the condition to proceed to the next step. This happens because, at this point, the digital output controlling the *QCS-CONV2* conveyor is set to FALSE. This occurs because we have not yet implemented the *entry* and *exit* actions for this step, which will set and reset the *CONV2_START* variable accordingly.

We need to carry out the same steps that we implemented for the *Start_CONV3* step, appropriately adjusting the variable names associated with the *QCS-CONV2* conveyor. I will skip the illustration with the detailed step-by-step procedure at this point. If any readers have not yet grasped this knowledge, they can easily refer to the previous pages for a clear explanation.

After adding the *entry* and *exit* actions for the *Start_CONV2* step, we must also not forget to expand the control logic for the *QCS-CONV2* conveyor, where we will implement the automatic mode for this conveyor. Below is the modified control logic (Figure 10-52).

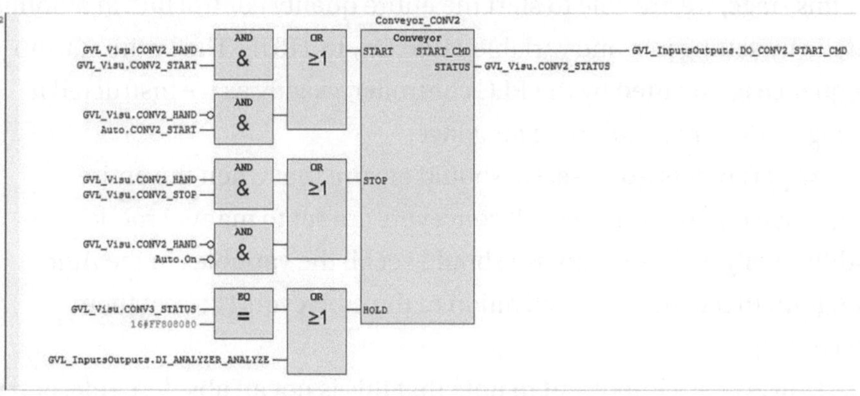

Figure 10-52. Conveyor QCS-CONV2 control logic, including automatic mode

Let's now download the program to the controller and test it. If
everything has been implemented correctly, we should be able to start the
conveyors *QCS-CONV3* and *QCS-CONV2* from the sequence, assuming
that the *QCS-CONV2* feeder conveyor will start five seconds after the *QCS-CONV3* receiving conveyor is started.

The next task will involve independently expanding the sequence and
control logic for the *QCS-CONV1* conveyor. At this point, I will refrain from
showing the exact procedure through illustrations, so this exercise can
be completed entirely on your own. We are slowly nearing the end of this
book, and I hope that if you've made it this far, the topic has piqued your
interest. This means you have the potential to continue growing in the field
of PLC programming. I believe this could be the beginning of your journey
toward becoming an expert in this area and, over time, a professional who
confidently navigates this field.

Sequence Implementation: Step *Init*

At this stage, we are able to start the entire quality control line in automatic
mode by setting just one variable, *Auto.On*, to TRUE. The entire startup
sequence is executed by the PLC controller, exactly as we instructed it
using the SFC programming language.

As part of this exercise, we should ensure that when the entire
sequence is in the *Init* step, all conveyors are set to manual mode.
Additionally, to be certain, we should set all the variables in the *Auto*
program that control the activation of the conveyors (i.e., set them
to FALSE).

However, it's important to note that this is not an absolute rule, and we
don't always have to proceed in this manner. This is simply my approach
to the application scenario I created while writing this book. In reality, it
would be the engineer or process technologist who would determine how
to program the appropriate sequence. At this stage, the goal is to practice
working with actions and implementing control logic.

So, let's add an *entry* action to the *Init* step and program its control logic as follows (Figure 10-53).

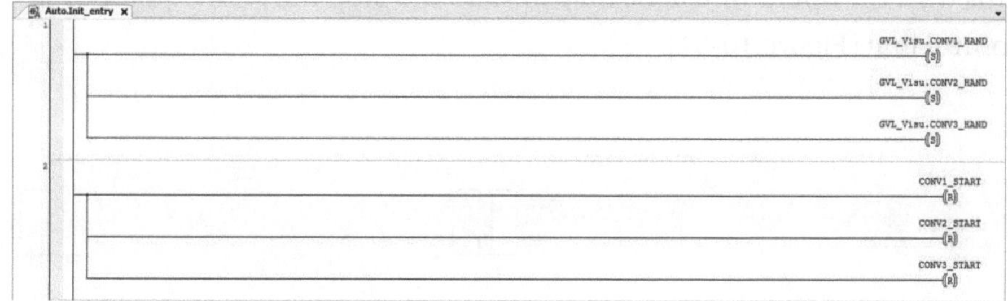

Figure 10-53. *Control logic in the entry action for the Init step*

Starting the Sequence from Visualization

In the current state, to start the entire quality control line from CODESYS, you need to set the value of the variable *Auto.On* to TRUE. The sequence is stopped by changing this value to FALSE. The entire process is controlled within the CODESYS environment.

It's time to enable the operator to start and stop the quality control line directly from the visualization using the implemented sequence created in the SFC language.

Dip Switch Button Controlling the Sequence

To allow the operator to control the sequence from the visualization, we will use a *Dip Switch* element. We will place it in the *Conveyors* view, configuring its properties according to the following parameters:

- *Position* → *X*: 285

- *Position* → *Y*: 316

- *Variable:* Auto.On

After downloading the program to the controller, we can test its operation by toggling the state of the *Dip Switch* from the visualization. This way, the operator will be able to start and stop the entire quality control line (Figure 10-54).

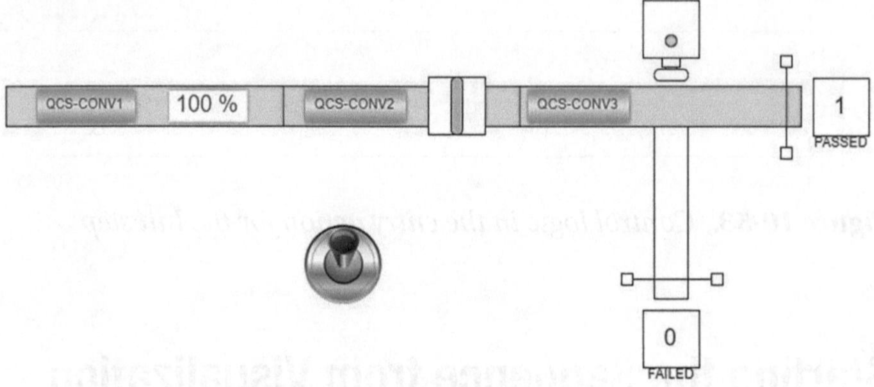

Figure 10-54. *Dip Switch on the visualization*

During automatic mode operation, simply toggling the *Dip Switch* again is enough to turn off the line. From this point on, the operator can fully manage the line from the visualization, without the need to use CODESYS.

Sequence State Visualization

In the current configuration, the operator lacks information about the current state of the sequence controlling the quality control line. Although we could visualize the entire sequence, including its steps and transitions, a simple text-based system status display will suffice for the operator. Let's adopt the following assumptions:

- *STOP*: The sequence is in the *Init* step.

- *STARTING*: The sequence is in one of the *SetAuto*, *Start_CONV3*, *Start_CONV2*, or *Start_CONV1* steps.

- *RUN*: The sequence is in the *Run* step.

We will display these states on the visualization using dynamic texts.

Sequence Status Implementation in SFC

To display the sequence status on the visualization, we first need to implement a variable representing the current state in the *Auto* program. We start by declaring a local variable *Status* of type *USINT* (Figure 10-55). This variable will act as an indicator for the sequence status.

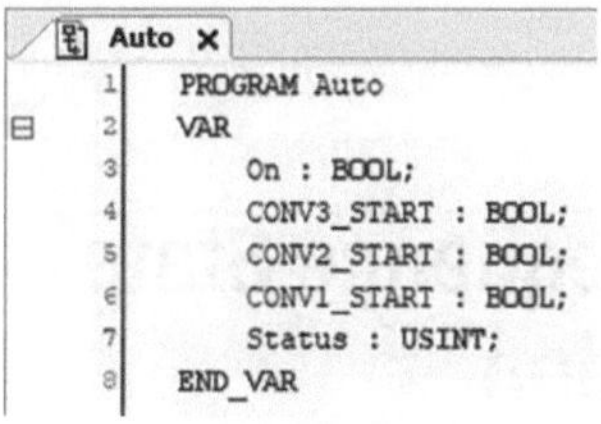

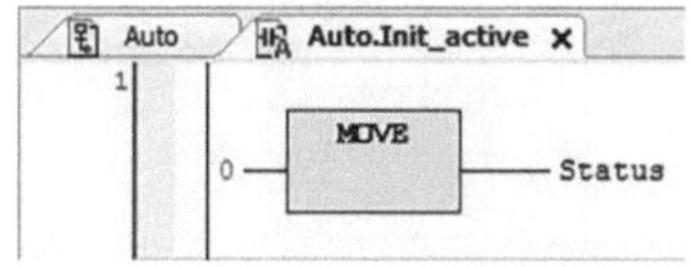

Figure 10-55. *Declaration of the local variable Status*

Next, we will assign appropriate values to the *Status* variable depending on the current step of the sequence by using *active* actions. For the *Init* step, we add the action *Init_active* and then set the *Status* variable to 0 using the *MOVE* function block (Figure 10-56).

Figure 10-56. *Control logic in the active action for the Init step*

For the *SetAuto* step, we edit the existing action *SetAuto_active*, adding the assignment Status := 1 in *Network 2* (Figure 10-57).

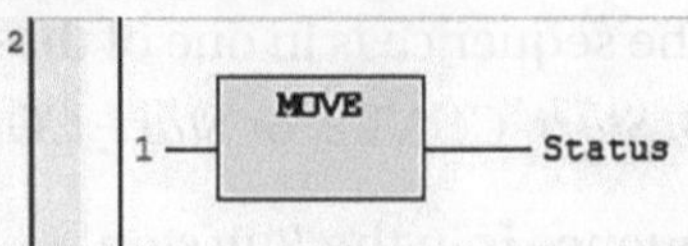

Figure 10-57. *Control logic in the active action for the SetAuto step*

We apply analogous changes for the remaining steps as follows:

- Start_CONV3, Start_CONV2, Start_CONV1: Status := 1

- Run: Status := 2

After downloading the program to the controller, we can test how the *Status* variable changes its value depending on the current step in the sequence. This way, we have implemented a mechanism that reflects the state of the sequence.

Displaying the Sequence State on the Visualization

To display the state of the sequence, we add a *Text List* object to the project in the *Application* ➤ *Visualization* folder (Figure 10-58).

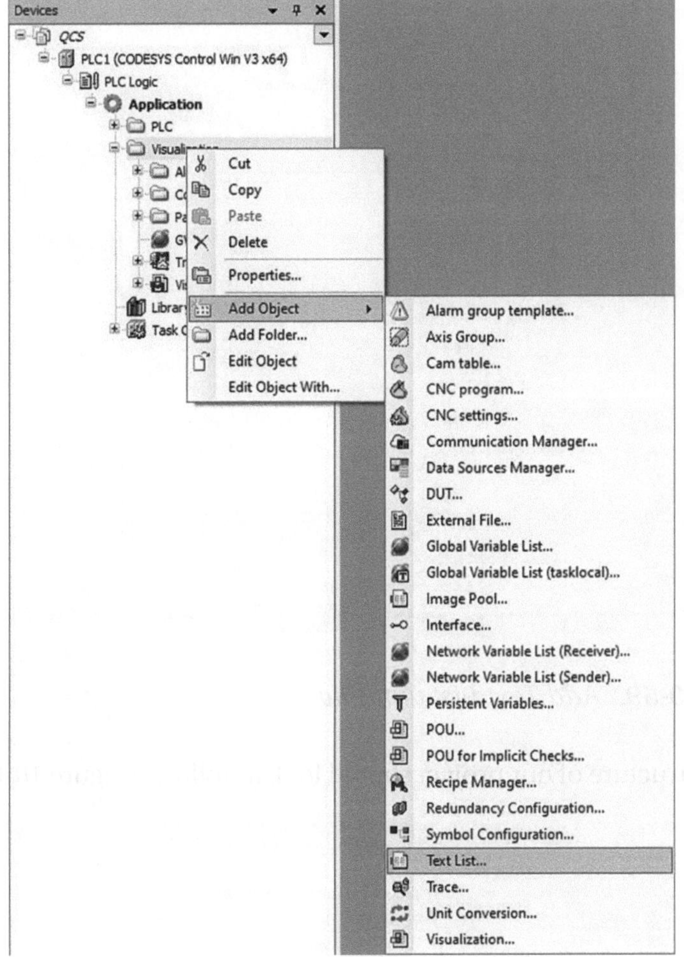

Figure 10-58. *Adding a Text List object to the project*

In the *Add Text List* window, we give it the name *StatusAuto* and confirm by clicking the *Add* button (Figure 10-59).

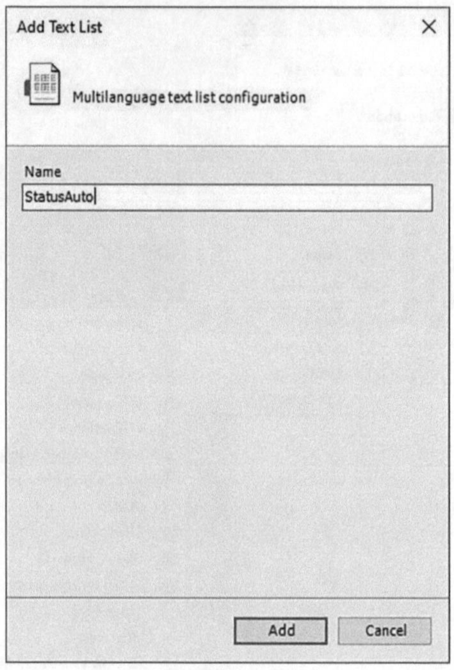

Figure 10-59. *Add Text List window*

The structure of our project should look as follows (Figure 10-60).

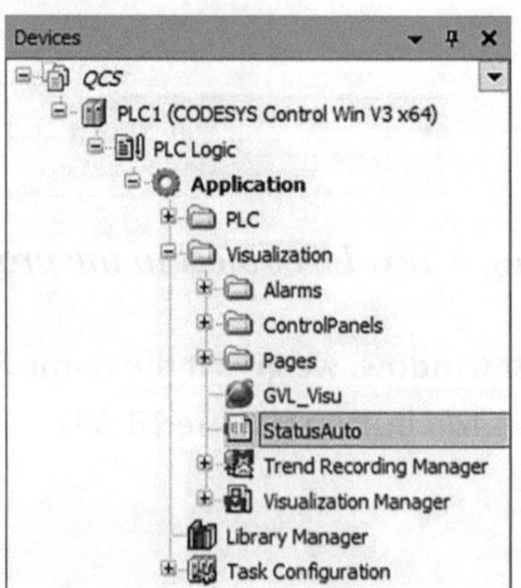

Figure 10-60. *Devices window*

In the text editor, we fill in the table according to the following description (Table 10-1).

Table 10-1. *TextList: StatusAuto*

ID	Default
0	STOP
1	STARTING
2	RUN

This is how it should look in the CODESYS environment (Figure 10-61).

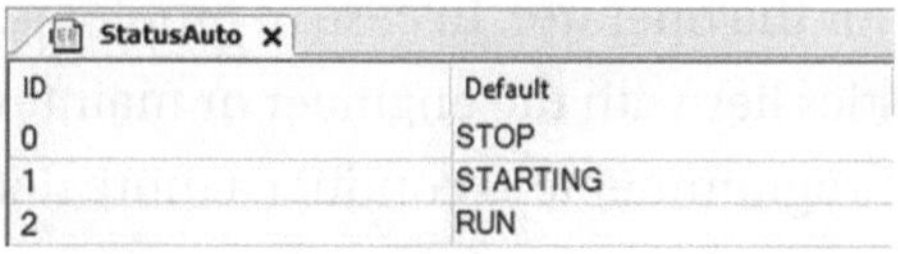

ID	Default
0	STOP
1	STARTING
2	RUN

Figure 10-61. *Text List: StatusAuto*

Next, in the *Conveyors* view, we add a *TextField* element and configure its properties as follows:

- *Position → X:* 245
- *Position → Y:* 395
- *Dynamic texts → Text list:* StatusAuto
- *Dynamic texts → Text index:* Auto.Status

The properties of *Dynamic texts* allow the dynamic display of text in the *TextField* based on the value of the *Status* variable (Figure 10-62).

Figure 10-62. *TextField element*

In this way, we have created a simple and intuitive visualization that
will make it easier for the operator to manage the system on a daily basis.
Although we do not display detailed information about the STARTING
state, it is sufficient for the operator. In case of problems, the responsibility
for detailed diagnostics lies with the engineer or maintenance technician,
who can connect a programmer and conduct a more detailed system
analysis.

Debugging and Fixing Errors

During the startup and testing of the quality control line, the programmer
knows the control logic because they implemented it themselves. However,
it is not possible to test every possible scenario in the application's usage.
When the system reaches the client's hands, operators often encounter
situations that the programmer did not anticipate. An example of such a
scenario could be when the operator starts the automation sequence, but
due to a sudden need, decides to interrupt the process by turning off the
Dip Switch before the line reaches full operation.

To understand the potential problem, let's conduct a test. Start
the sequence from the visualization and interrupt the process in the
STARTING state by turning off the switch. After this operation, we
will notice that the sequence status remains STARTING, even though

all conveyors have been turned off (Figure 10-63). Worse still, further attempts to restart the sequence are unsuccessful – the application stops responding.

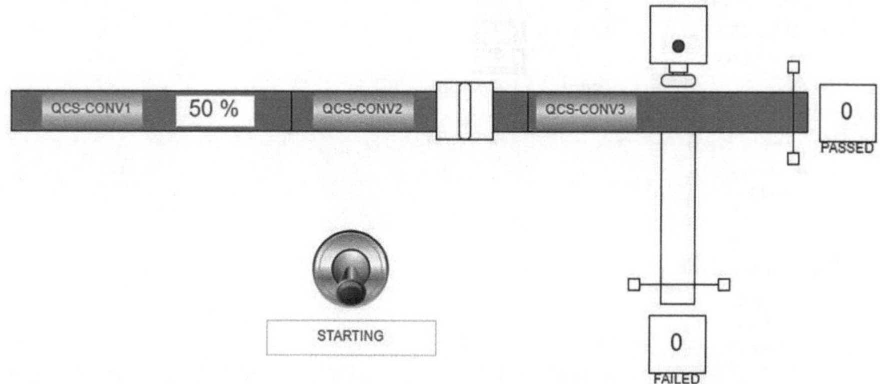

Figure 10-63. *Testing the sequence: enabling and interrupting the process in the STARTING state*

In such a situation, the operator usually asks for help from the maintenance department, and in the case of more serious issues, they may contact an engineer. By connecting a laptop with the CODESYS environment installed and going into diagnostics, the programmer may notice that the sequence has stopped at the *Start_CONV3* step. The active action in this step still sets the value of the *Status* variable to 1, which is displayed on the visualization as the STARTING state (Figure 10-64).

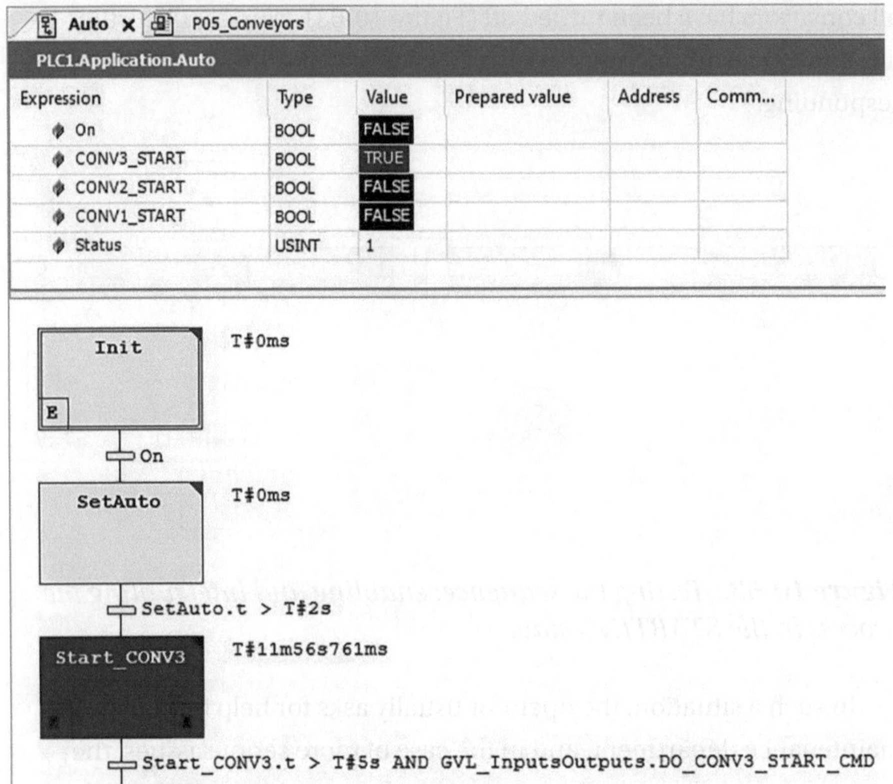

Figure 10-64. *Diagnostics: sequence stopped at the Start_
CONV3 step*

The problem lies in the lack of handling for the situation where the
operator interrupts the startup process of the line. To fix this, we need
to expand the sequence with a condition that will allow an immediate
transition to the *Init* step when the variable *Auto.On* is set to FALSE during
the execution of the current step.

The simplest approach is to add a parallel transition to each step,
generating the STARTING state that checks the value of the *Auto.On*
variable. If this variable is set to FALSE, the program will jump to the
Init step.

508

From the *ToolBox*, select the *Branch* element and insert it between the *SetAuto* step and the transition *SetAuto.t > T#2s* (Figure 10-65).

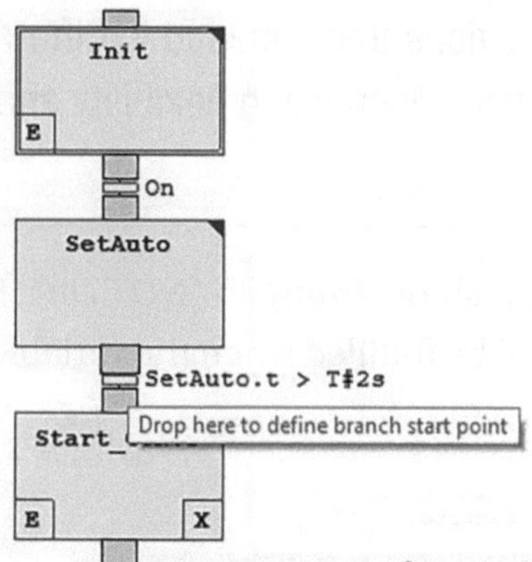

Figure 10-65. *Adding a Branch element*

After adding the branch in the sequence, new elements will appear: the *Step0* step and the transitions *Trans0* and *Trans1* (Figure 10-66).

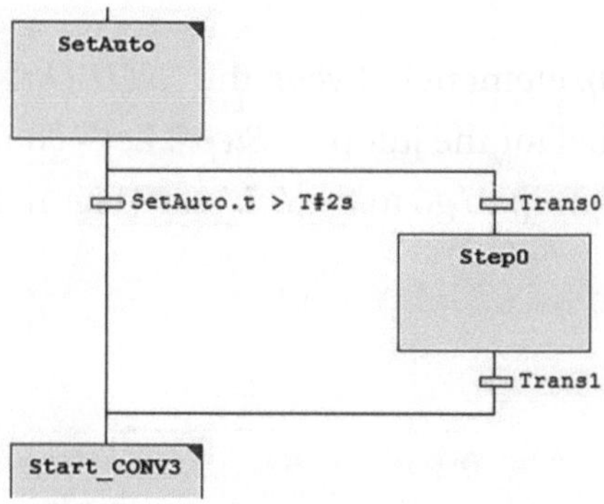

Figure 10-66. *Step0 and transitions Trans0 and Trans1*

Branch   Element in SFC programming allows for the creation of parallel transition conditions within a single step. This enables the addition of extra transitions that can lead to different steps based on the fulfilled conditions, increasing flexibility and control over the sequence flow.

Let's rename the transition *Trans0* to *"NOT On"* (Figure 10-67). The transition condition will be fulfilled when the variable *Auto.On* takes the value FALSE.

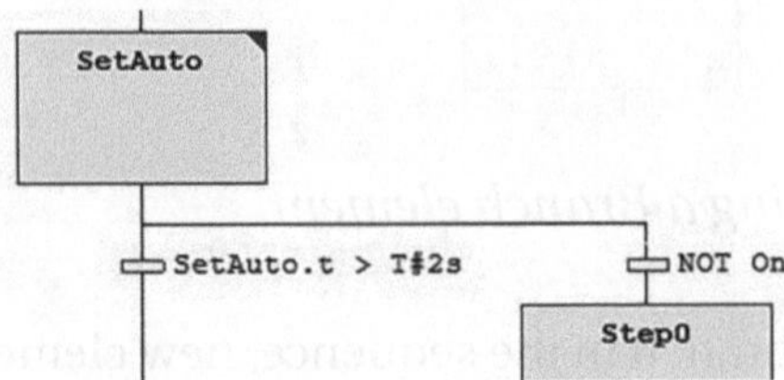

Figure 10-67. Transition "NOT On"

Let's insert a *Jump* element between the *"NOT On"* transition and the *Step0*. The default label for the jump is *"Step"*. Let's change it to *"Init"*, which will cause the jump to go to the *Init* step (Figure 10-68).

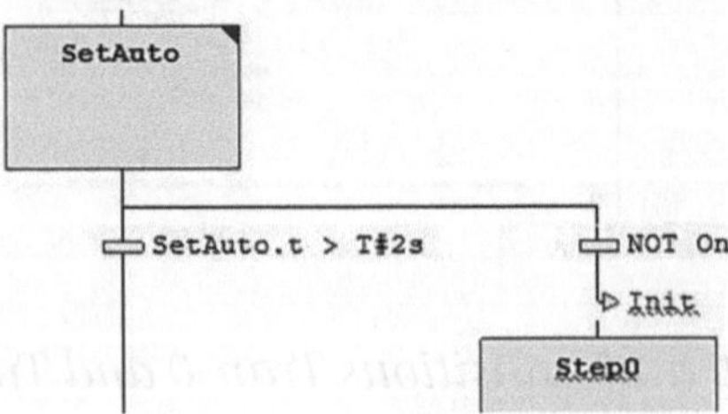

Figure 10-68. Jump to the Init step

Let's remove the unnecessary elements, such as the *Step0* and *Trans1* transitions. The corrected structure of the *SetAuto* step should look like this (Figure 10-69):

- Transition condition: NOT On.

- Jump to the *Init* step.

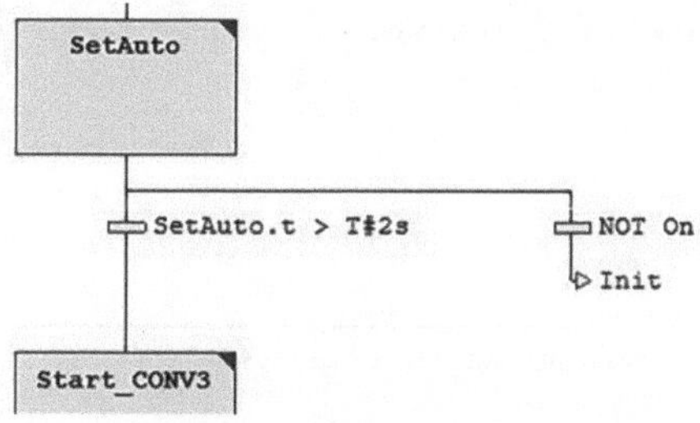

Figure 10-69. *Parallel branch with a jump to the Init step*

Jump   Allows for a direct transition to a specific step, regardless of the logical sequence. Using jumps helps simplify or optimize complex control sequences.

In a similar way, let's extend the steps for *Start_CONV3*, *Start_CONV2*, and *Start_CONV1*. This should be the complete sequence for the *Auto* program (Figure 10-70).

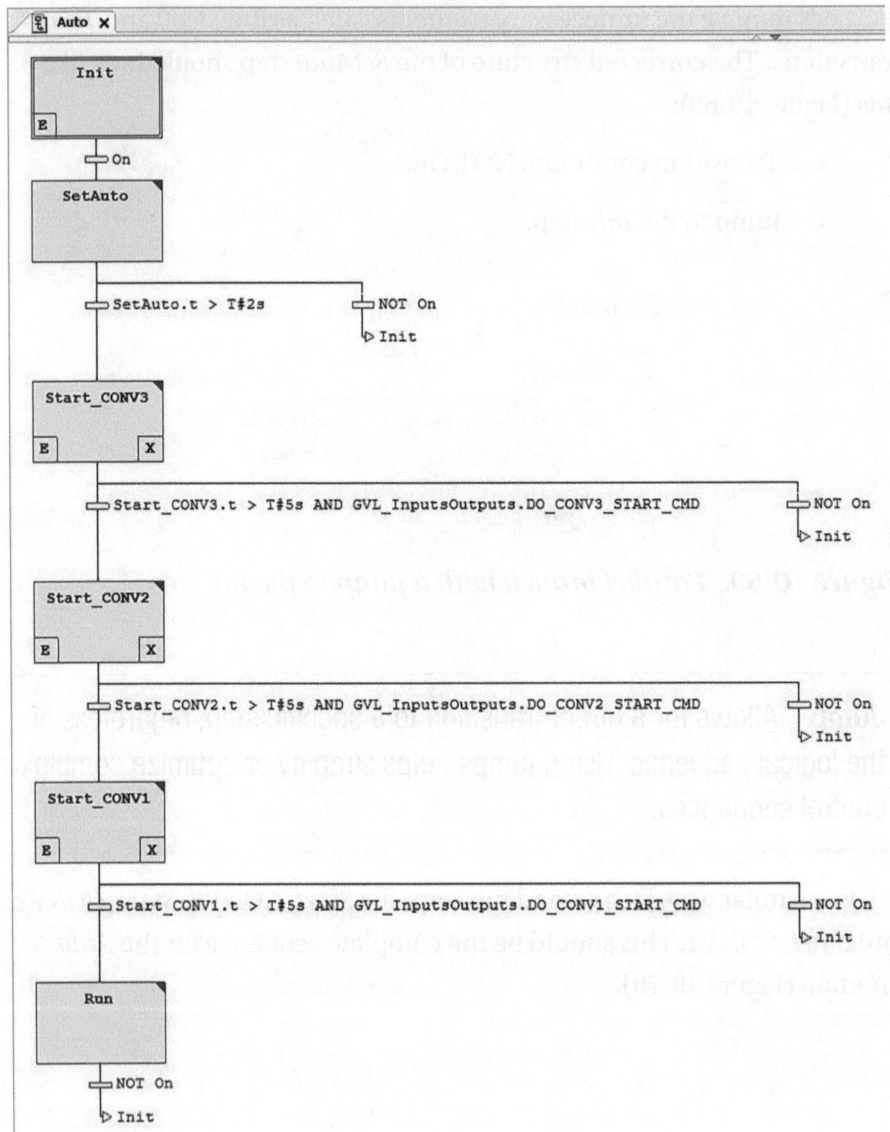

Figure 10-70. *The complete sequence of the Auto program*

By adding parallel branches and a transition condition to the *Init* step, the application gained reliability in emergency situations. Now, when the operator interrupts the process of starting the line, the sequence will automatically return to the initial state, allowing it to be restarted without the need for engineer intervention.

Such improvements are crucial for ensuring the stability of the system and efficient operation by the operators.

Final Practical Task

Our sequence is now running flawlessly – at least it seems so at first glance. To verify this, we will perform one more test. First, let's start the sequence and wait until all three conveyors are running. Then, we will stop the sequence so that all conveyors are turned off, and quickly start the sequence again.

In this situation, an unexpected problem may arise: the sequence will get stuck in the *Start_CONV3* step. Why does this happen? Well, each conveyor has been programmed in such a way that after it is turned off, it cannot be restarted earlier than five seconds after being stopped. To prevent such situations, it's useful to introduce an additional mechanism that, after stopping the sequence, will prevent it from being turned back on for a specific time, for example, ten seconds. This ensures that all conveyors will have enough time to stop completely, and the minimum required times are maintained.

There are several ways to solve this problem. For example, you can add a time condition to the transition in the *Init* step, forcing it to run for at least ten seconds. A more elegant and typical approach is to introduce a new step in the sequence – STOPPING. In this step, a procedure for gradually stopping the conveyors can be implemented. Importantly, the conveyors should not be turned off simultaneously to avoid material blockages between them.

The stopping process should proceed in the order from the *QCS-CONV1* (feeding) conveyor, through *QCS-CONV2*, to the *QCS-CONV3* (receiving) conveyor. Only after completing this procedure should the sequence transition to the *Init* step, which resets the sequence and allows it to be restarted.

I encourage you to try solving this problem on your own. On GitHub, you will find an example that shows how I decided to solve it. However, this is not the only solution nor necessarily the best one – it's worth exploring your own, creative ideas.

Summary

In this chapter, I presented the complete process of designing a control sequence, starting from setting up a basic startup sequence, all the way to adding control functionality from the visualization level. The use of status variables allowed for easy tracking of the system's state, and the addition of emergency procedures increased the application's reliability. Additionally, I described issues related to testing and debugging, including situations where operators encounter problems when starting the sequence. The conclusions drawn from the experiments and tests highlight the importance of carefully designing emergency mechanisms that ensure the safe and efficient operation of the production line by operators.

It should be noted that I only presented the basics of the SFC programming language, focusing on the three fundamental actions: *entry*, *active*, and *exit*, completely omitting more advanced topics such as *Action Qualifiers*. If I wanted to discuss the entire SFC language in detail, this topic could easily fill several separate chapters of a book. However, remember that this publication is aimed at beginner PLC programmers.

CHAPTER 11

Practical Tips and Best Practices

Programming PLC controllers requires knowledge of various techniques and tools that facilitate the design and diagnostics of industrial applications. In this chapter, we will focus on several key aspects of working with controllers. We will start by analyzing errors that occur during program compilation and methods for eliminating them. Next, we will move on to creating a custom library, enabling the reuse of developed functions and function blocks across multiple projects. In the following section, we will discuss the *CFC* programming language by developing a sample program that controls a process variable. Finally, we will explore the *Trace* tool, which allows real-time monitoring and analysis of process variables – an invaluable feature for diagnostics and process optimization.

Compilation Error

While developing a program – both its logic and visualization – it may happen that the project fails to compile. This was exactly the case for me while writing this book (Figure 11-1). I was performing code refactoring, and after completing it, errors appeared when I attempted to compile the project.

© Dariusz Wrebiak 2026

D. Wrebiak, *Practical PLC Programming for Beginners*, Maker Innovations Series, https://doi.org/10.1007/979-8-8688-2430-2_11

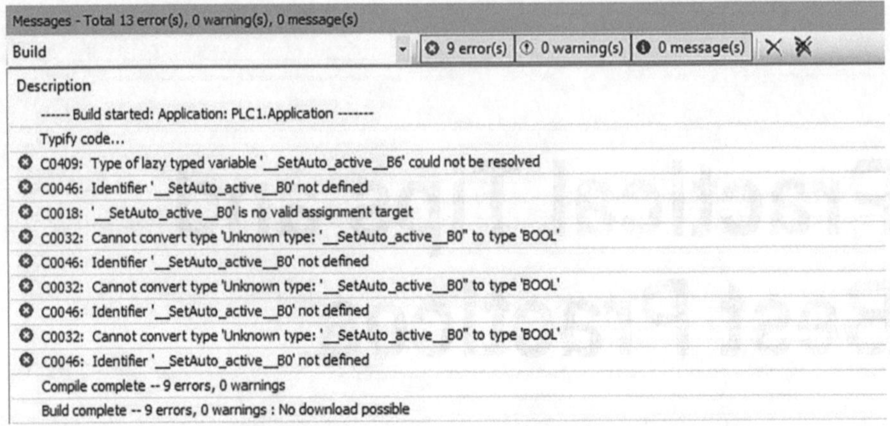

Figure 11-1. *A compilation error that occurred while writing this book*

Naturally, the first step was to analyze the cause of the problem. However, despite checking the code and ensuring that everything seemed correct, the errors persisted.

Sooner or later, every PLC programmer will encounter a similar issue – and this is not limited to the CODESYS environment. I have faced similar situations in every PLC programming system, as well as in other development tools. The reason is simple: wherever people work, mistakes happen. PLC programming software is not free from bugs either, because it is created by humans – and no one is infallible.

The solution is often simpler than it seems. In this case, all I had to do was clean the entire project and recompile it. This principle applies to other programming environments as well. In CODESYS, you can do this by selecting *Build* ➤ *Clean all* (Figure 11-2).

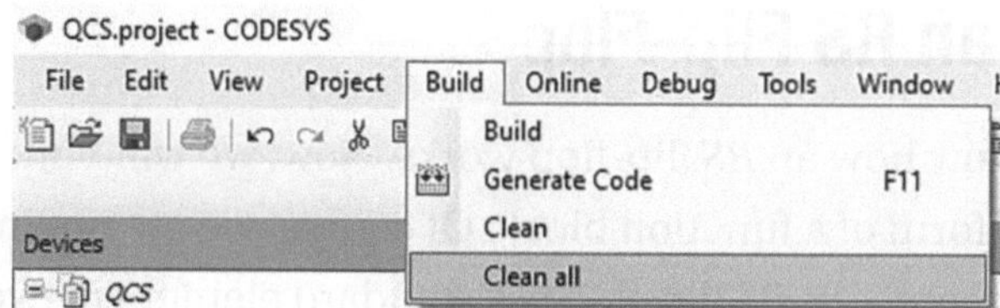

Figure 11-2. *The "Clean all" option in CODESYS, allowing the project to be cleaned before recompilation*

An additional piece of advice, which is not strictly technical but can be just as helpful: if you've spent a long time programming or commissioning an installation, fatigue can negatively impact your problem-solving ability. Sometimes, the best solution is simply to take a break – go for a walk, drink coffee or water, or step away from work for a moment.

When we are exhausted, our perception narrows, and we can get stuck in a loop, searching for a solution that seems just out of reach. That's why it's important to remember that mental recovery is just as crucial as knowing the programming environment itself.

Creating a Custom Library

When programming PLC controllers, sooner or later, you will reach a point where you start creating your own function blocks and functions to be used across multiple projects.

To optimize your workflow, you should avoid copying these elements from project to project. Instead, it's best to store them in libraries and update the source code only when necessary.

So far, we have learned how to install and manage versions of external libraries. In this book, we have worked with the *Simulator* library, whose function blocks simulated a quality control system. Now, we will learn how to create our own library, where we will store our functions and function blocks.

Creating an RS Flip-Flop

We already know how an *RS* flip-flop works. Now, we will build our own version in the form of a function block. Of course, we are not inventing anything new here – an *RS* flip-flop is a standard element in every PLC library – but this example serves as a great demonstration of how the internal mechanisms of such blocks function.

In real-world applications, it is not always practical to reimplement existing functions. However, sometimes it becomes necessary to create custom solutions when standard components do not fully meet our requirements.

To get started, let's create a new project in CODESYS by selecting *File ➤ New Project*. In the *New Project* window, select *Libraries* on the left side, and choose *Empty library* on the right. Name the library *MyFirstLib* and click *OK* (Figure 11-3).

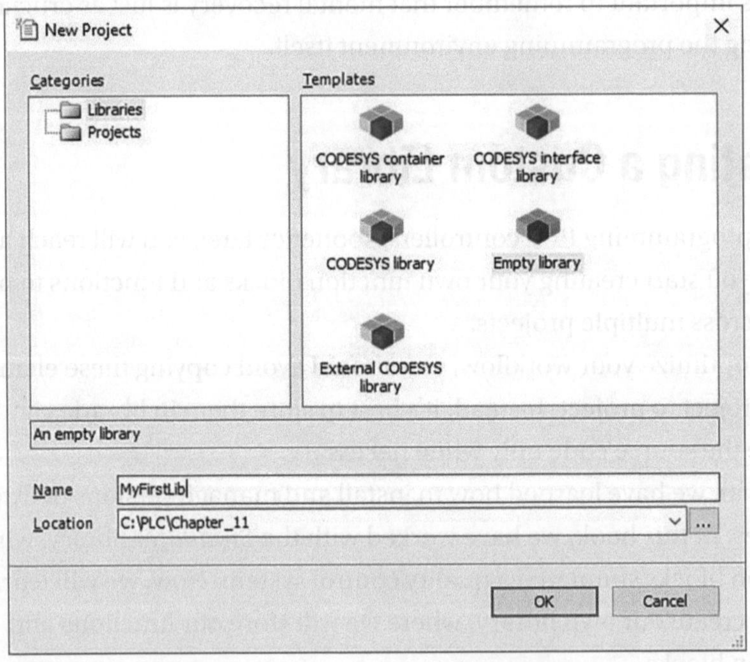

Figure 11-3. *Creating a new library in CODESYS*

Next, let's add a new *POU* to our newly created library. In the *Add POU* window, enter *RS* as the name of the object, select *Function block* as the type, and choose *LAD (Ladder Diagram)* as the programming language. Confirm your selection by clicking the *Add* button (Figure 11-4).

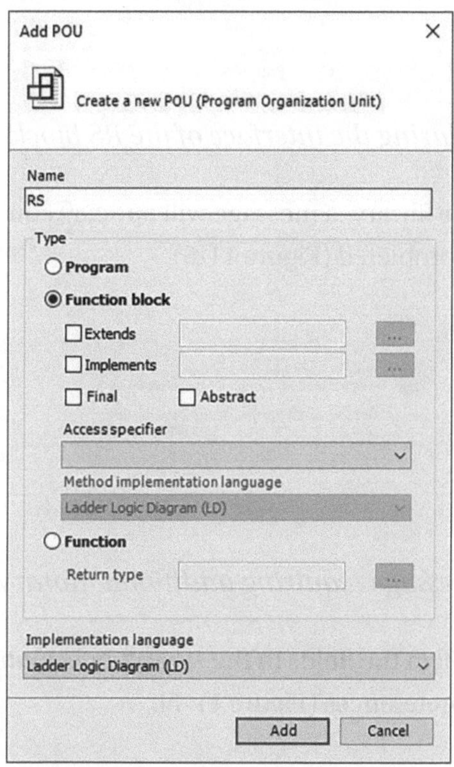

Figure 11-4. *Adding the RS function block to the library*

After completing these steps, a blank LAD program editor will open with the interface definition of our function block. This looks exactly the same as when creating a function block within a project. However, this time, we are implementing it as part of our custom library.

Let's declare two input variables: *SET* and *RESET1*, as well as an output variable *Q*. All variables should be of type *BOOL*. This way, we are recreating the existing *RS* function block, which is part of the standard PLC library (Figure 11-5).

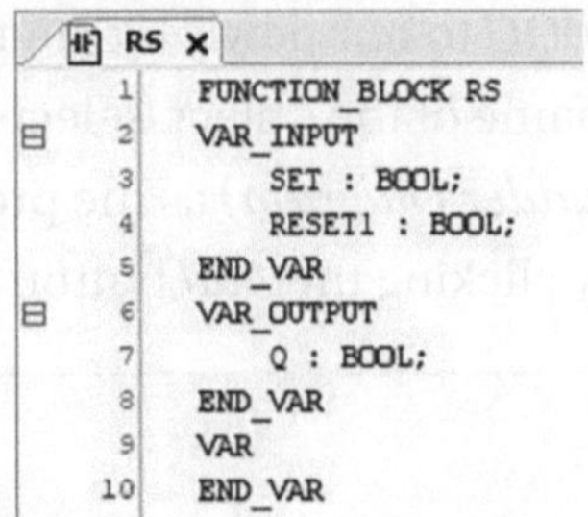

Figure 11-5. *Declaring the interface of the RS block*

When saving the library, a message will appear requiring additional information to be completed (Figure 11-6).

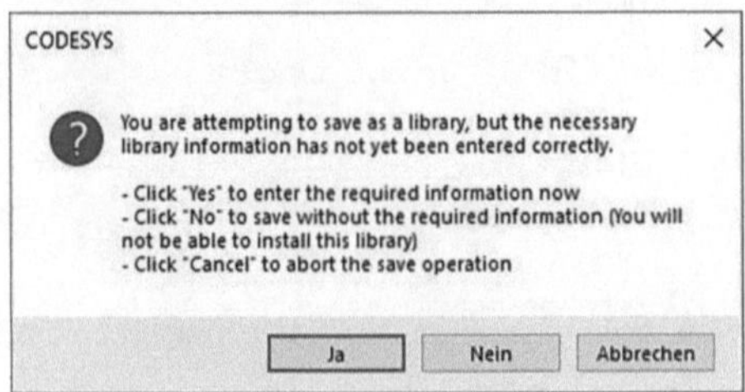

Figure 11-6. *A message requiring additional library information*

Click *Yes,* and fill in the fields in the *Project Information* window according to your preferences (Figure 11-7).

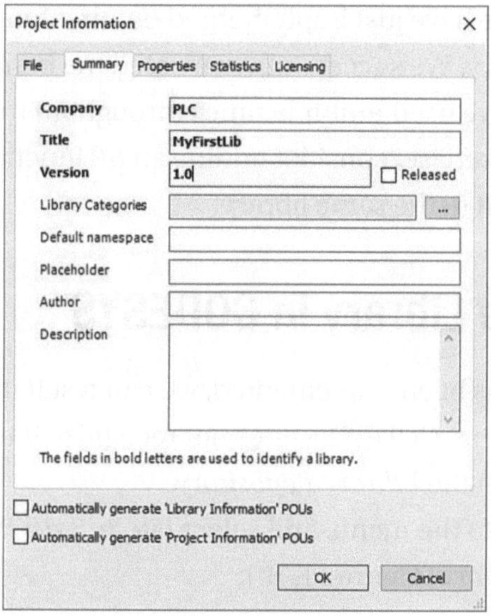

Figure 11-7. Entering library information

Implementing RS Logic

As a reminder, the *RS* function block has a dominant *RESET* input, meaning that if both inputs are set to *TRUE*, the output *Q* remains *FALSE*.

In the first *Network*, we will implement the logic that sets the *Q* output to *TRUE* when the *SET* input is active (Figure 11-8).

Figure 11-8. Logic for setting the Q output in the RS block

The next step in implementing the function block is resetting the *Q* output when the *RESET1* input is set to *TRUE* (Figure 11-9).

Figure 11-9. Logic for resetting the Q output in the RS block

And that's it! We have just implemented our first function block as part of our custom library. We successfully recreated the behavior of the *RS* block, which we have used multiple times throughout this book.

As a practical exercise, consider adding an *SR* function block with a dominant *SET* input to the same library.

Installing the Library in CODESYS

Once our library has been implemented, we can test it in a project. However, at this point, CODESYS does not recognize it because it has not yet been installed in the *Library Repository*.

To install it, go to the menu, and select *File ➤ Save Project and Install into Library Repository* (Figure 11-10).

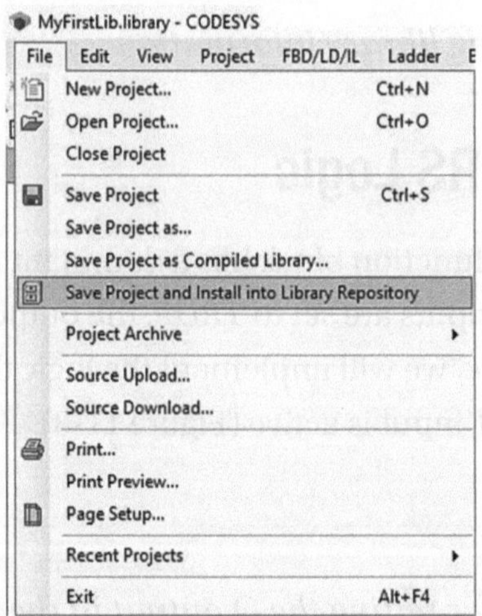

Figure 11-10. *Installing the library in the Library Repository*

Next, open a second instance of CODESYS and create a new project named *Test_MyFirstLib*, where we will test the functionality of the function blocks implemented in the *MyFirstLib* library.

In the *Library Repository,* we can now see that *MyFirstLib* is available for use (Figure 11-11).

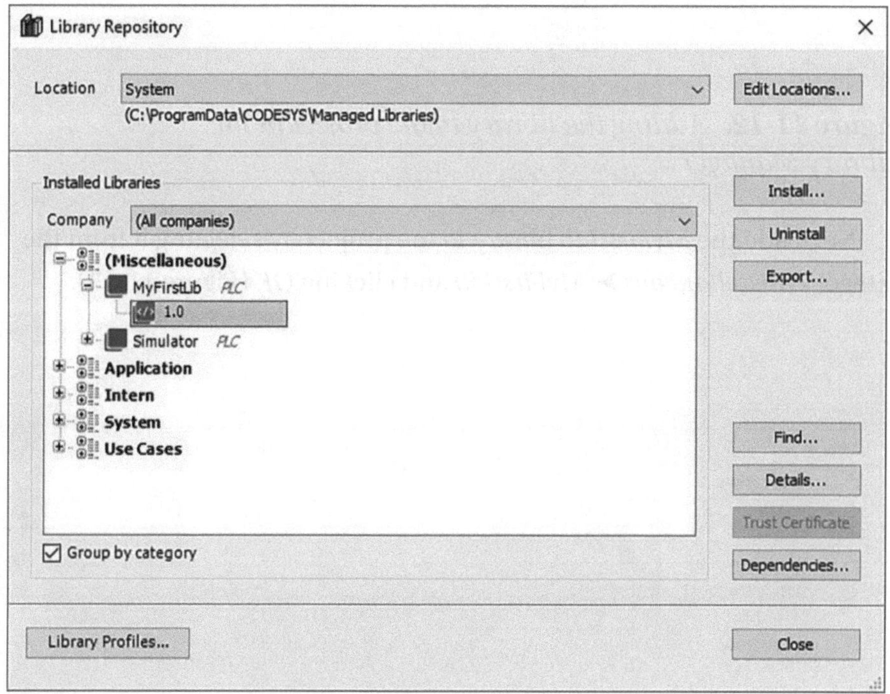

Figure 11-11. *Checking the library availability in the Library Repository*

Now, we need to add the library to our project to access the function blocks.

In the *Library Manager,* click the *Add Library* button (Figure 11-12).

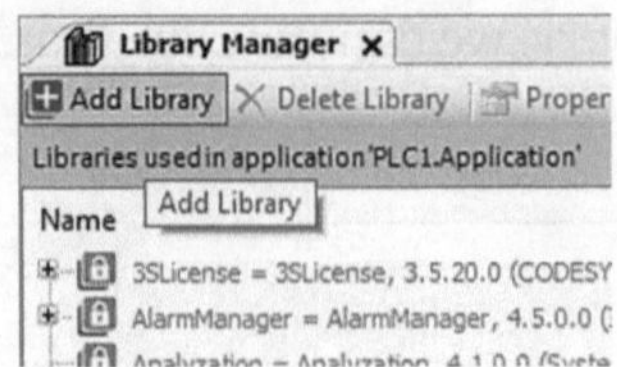

Figure 11-12. *Adding the library to the project in the Library Manager*

Next, add the *MyFirstLib* library to the project by selecting it from the category *Miscellaneous* ➤ *MyFirstLib* and clicking *OK* (Figure 11-13).

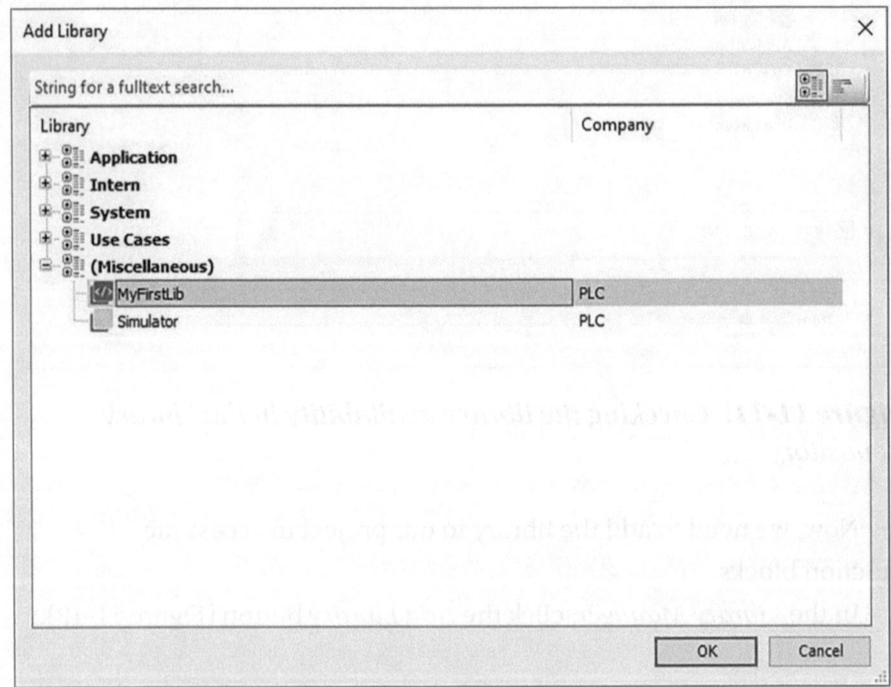

Figure 11-13. *Selecting the MyFirstLib library in the Library Manager*

Notice that the symbols for the *MyFirstLib* and *Simulator* libraries look different. It's important to understand why this happens.

We installed *MyFirstLib* directly from the CODESYS environment, which means we have access to its source code within our project. This is very useful when developing the library and testing its functionality.

However, if we have completed the implementation and want to share the library with other developers without revealing the source code, we need to save it as a compiled library. To do this, go to the menu, and select *File ➤ Save Project as Compiled Library...*, then save the library in this format (Figure 11-14).

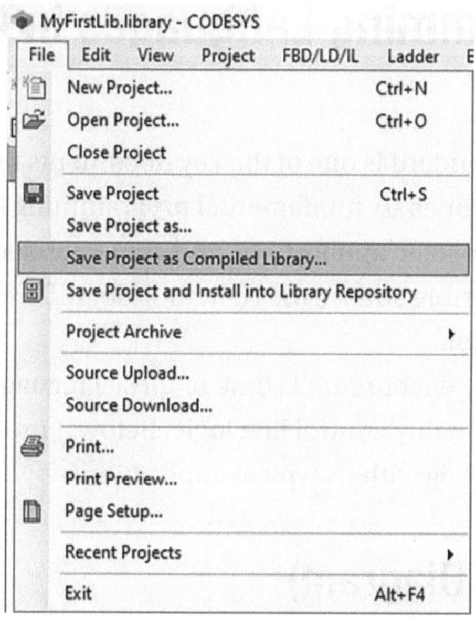

Figure 11-14. *Saving the library as a compiled file*

I shared the *Simulator* library with you in exactly the same way. However, if anyone wants to explore how it works in detail, the source code is also available in my GitHub repository.

Testing Function Blocks

Now it's time for a practical task – testing the function blocks implemented in the *MyFirstLib* library. You have complete freedom in how you implement and call them in your project.

If you'd like to see my solution, you can find it in the *Chapter_11* folder in the repository.

PLC Programming Languages in IEC 61131-3 Standard

The *IEC 61131-3* standard is one of the key documents related to PLC programming. It defines six fundamental programming languages, each with its own specific applications and characteristics. This allows programmers to flexibly choose the right tools for different tasks in industrial automation.

We have already encountered some of these languages while implementing the quality control line logic. Below, I provide an overview of each language along with its typical applications.

LAD (Ladder Diagram)

LAD, or Ladder Diagram, is the most commonly used language in PLC programming. It is a visual representation of control logic, resembling an electrical relay circuit diagram.

Characteristics

- Readable and intuitive for electricians and technicians

- Well-suited for simple control applications

- Based on ladder branches, where signals flow from left to right

Applications

- Simple machine control

- Sequential processes

- On/Off control logic

Example: Implementation of an *RS* flip-flop with *SET* and *RESET* inputs and an *Q* output, just like we implemented in our custom library.

FBD (Function Block Diagram)

FBD is a graphical programming language where the program consists of connected function blocks. Each block performs a specific logical or mathematical operation.

Characteristics

- Clear and intuitive, making it easier to develop complex applications.

- Logic is represented in a diagrammatic form, simplifying program analysis.

Applications

- Continuous processes

- Control systems with multiple input and output signals

Example: Converting LAD code into FBD in the CODESYS environment.

ST (Structured Text)

ST is a text-based programming language similar to traditional languages like Pascal or Basic. It allows for the creation of more complex control algorithms.

Characteristics

- Similar to traditional programming languages, making it easier for software developers to adapt

- Ideal for mathematical operations and conditional logic

Applications

- Computational algorithms

- Complex control operations

Example: Implementing an *SR* flip-flop using Structured Text (ST) is shown in Listing 10-1.

Listing 10-1. SR flip-flop

```
IF SET THEN
    Q := TRUE;
ELSIF RESET THEN
    Q := FALSE;
END_IF;
```

IL (Instruction List)

IL is a low-level programming language, similar to assembly language. The program consists of a sequence of instructions executed one after another.

Characteristics

- Compact but less readable than other PLC languages

- Requires a good understanding of PLC operation

Applications

- Code optimization for minimal memory usage

- Legacy PLC systems

Example: Implementing an *SR* flip-flop using Instruction List (IL) is shown in Listing 10-2.

Listing 10-2. SR flip-flop

```
LD  SET
ST  Q
LD  RESET
RST Q
```

SFC (Sequential Function Chart)

SFC allows for the design of sequential processes using step diagrams. Each step represents a specific state of the process.

Characteristics

- Ideal for processes with well-defined steps.

- Visual structure simplifies the design of complex sequences.

Applications

- Step-based machine control

- Industrial process automation

Example: Controlling the conveyor startup sequence in a quality control line.

CFC (Continuous Function Chart)

CFC is an extension of FBD, allowing free placement of function blocks on a grid without requiring a structured data flow.

Characteristics

- High flexibility in arranging blocks

- Clear design for complex systems

Applications

- Advanced industrial applications

- DCS (Distributed Control Systems)

Example: Implementation from the *Trace* section of this chapter.

The choice of the appropriate PLC programming language depends on the specifics of the project and the programmer's preferences. Visual languages allow for intuitive design of both simple and complex control systems, while text-based languages offer greater flexibility in implementing complex algorithms and computational operations. Understanding each of them provides the programmer with a solid foundation for working in the world of industrial automation.

Trace

In this section, we will explore one of the key diagnostic tools in PLC programming – *Trace*. It is used to record process variables and signals processed by the control program.

When programming industrial systems, sooner or later, we will encounter a problem whose cause is not immediately apparent. In such situations, *Trace* allows us to capture anomalies, record the relevant values, and analyze them in detail.

Simple Program in CFC Language

To configure the *Trace* tool, we first need to create process variables that we will analyze. For this purpose, we will use another graphical programming language – *CFC* – which is used for designing control logic.

Let's add a new *POU* object to our *Test_MyFirstLib* project and name it *Trace_PRG*. Set the type as *Program*, and choose *CFC* as the programming language. Then, confirm the selection by clicking the *Add* button (Figure 11-15).

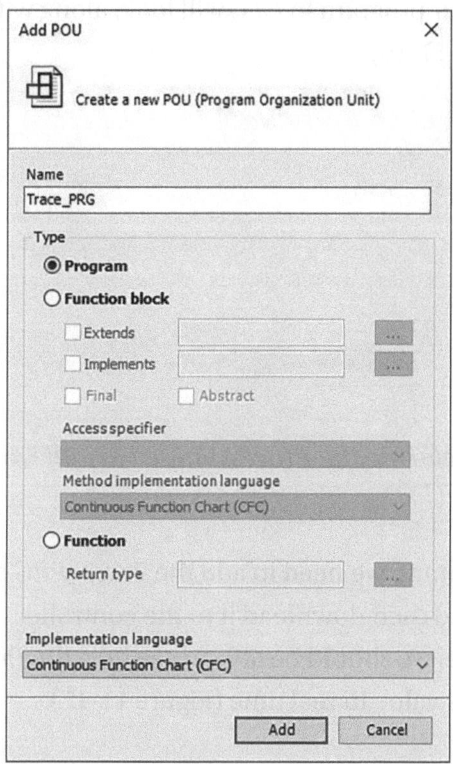

Figure 11-15. *Adding a new POU object named Trace_PRG*

Next, we will create a simple program that generates a process variable. We will start by declaring it as a local variable in the *Trace_PRG* program. The variable type will be set to *SINT*, and we will name it *ProcessValue*.

Using the *CFC* language elements available in the *ToolBox* on the right side, we will build a program that increments the *ProcessValue* variable in each new cycle. To achieve this, we will use

- Two *Input* elements

- An *ADD* block

- An *Output* element

Below is how our program in *CFC* will look, along with the variable declaration (Figure 11-16).

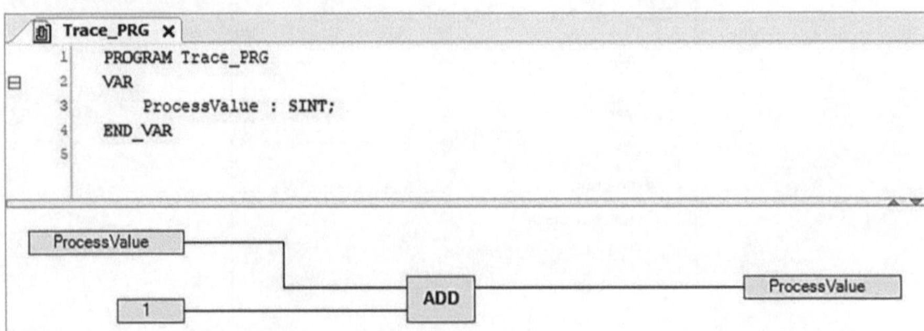

Figure 11-16. *Declaring the ProcessValue variable and implementing the program in CFC*

To run our program, we need to add the *Trace_PRG* call to the *MainTask* group and then download it to the controller.

In Online mode, we should be able to see how the *ProcessValue* variable changes its value in real time (Figure 11-17).

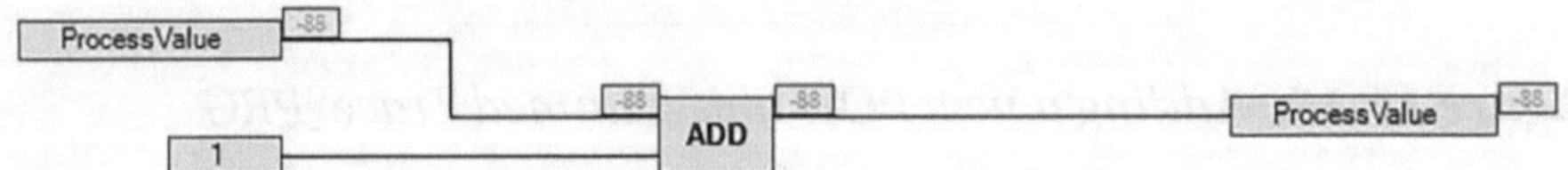

Figure 11-17. *Viewing the Trace_PRG program in Online mode*

Trace Configuration

The next step is to add a new *Trace* object to our project. To do this, right-click *Application*, and select *Add Object* ➤ *Trace* from the menu.

In the *Add Trace* window, leave the object name unchanged, and for the *Task* responsible for recording process variable values, select *MainTask*. Confirm your selection by clicking the *Add* button (Figure 11-18).

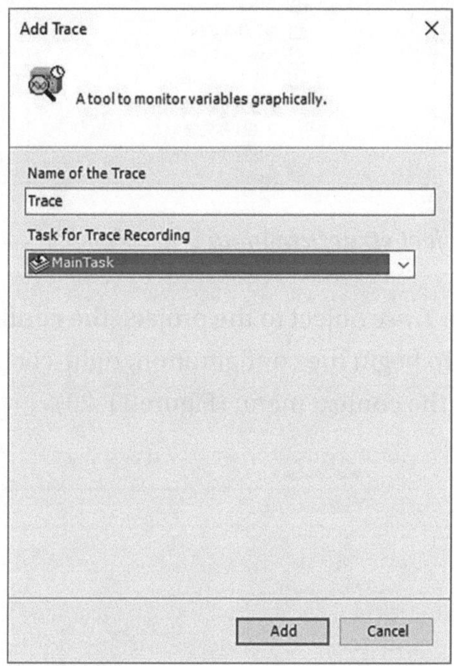

Figure 11-18. *Adding a new Trace object to the project*

A new *Trace* object has been added to our project. The project structure now looks as follows (Figure 11-19).

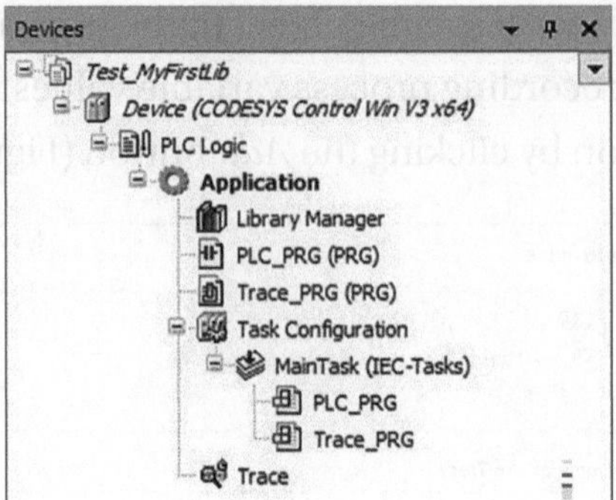

Figure 11-19. *Project structure view*

After adding the *Trace* object to the project, the configuration window will open. To begin the configuration, right-click on it, and select *Configuration* from the context menu (Figure 11-20).

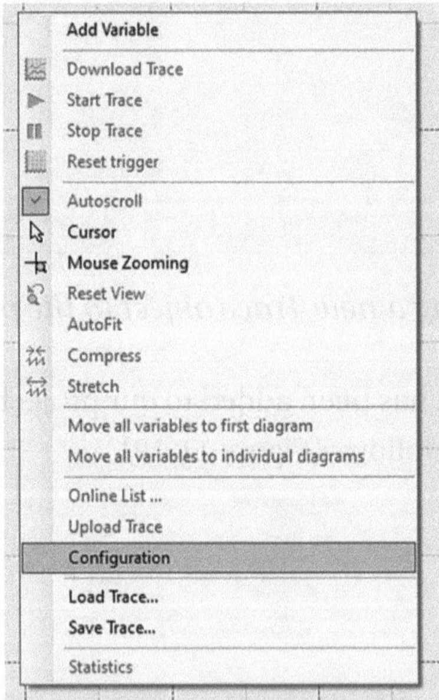

Figure 11-20. *Configuration settings via the context menu*

In the *Trace Configuration* window, click *Add Variable* in the lower left corner to add the process variable that will be recorded in the *Trace* tool (Figure 11-21).

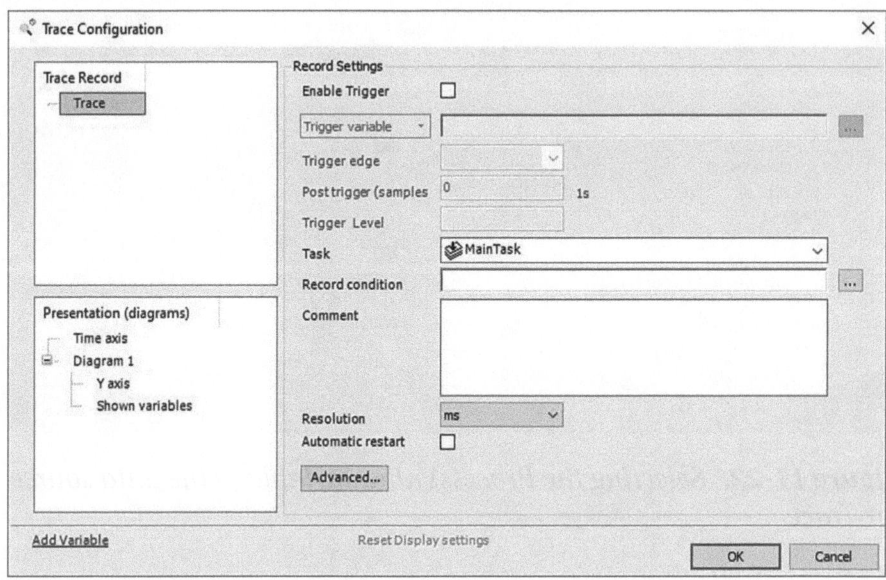

Figure 11-21. *Adding a process variable to the Trace tool*

In the *Variable* field, select the *ProcessValue* variable from the *Trace_ PRG* program. Additionally, we have the option to configure several other settings, which resemble the *Trends* configuration from previous chapters of the book. Confirm everything by clicking the *OK* button (Figure 11-22).

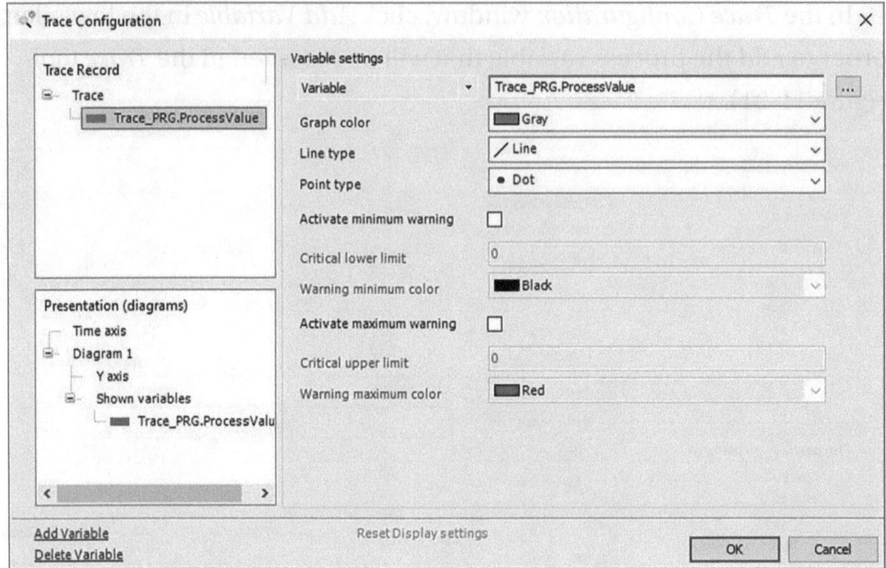

Figure 11-22. *Selecting the ProcessValue variable as the data source for Trace*

Testing Trace

After configuring the *Trace* object, we can proceed with testing it. Note that our PLC is still in *RUN* mode. When we configure *Trace* and switch to *Online* mode, the *Trace* object displays the message "*No samples have been recorded*." This means that *Trace* has been configured in CODESYS, but it has not yet been downloaded to the PLC.

It is crucial to understand that this step can be performed even while the PLC is in *RUN* mode. This is what makes *Trace* such a powerful diagnostic tool – it allows debugging without the need to stop the installation or the machine controlled by the PLC.

To download *Trace* to the PLC, right-click on it, and select *Download Trace* from the menu (Figure 11-23).

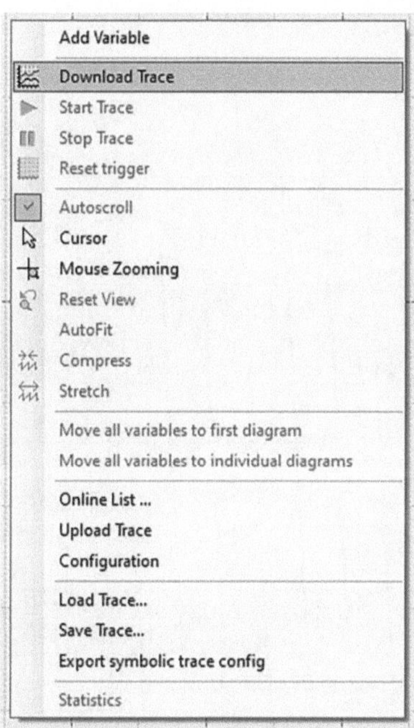

Figure 11-23. *Downloading the Trace configuration to the controller*

After downloading *Trace* to the PLC, we can observe in real time how the value of the *ProcessValue* variable changes in the *Trace_PRG* program.

The configuration looks similar to setting up *Trends* in visualization; however, there are several key differences. With *Trace*, we don't need to create any visualization in the project – everything is handled directly in the CODESYS environment. Moreover, at any time, we can stop recording *Trace* and reconfigure it, for example, by adding new process variables or removing existing ones.

This allows us to monitor variable changes in real time and display them on a graph (Figure 11-24). This feature is extremely useful, especially when diagnosing issues in a control system.

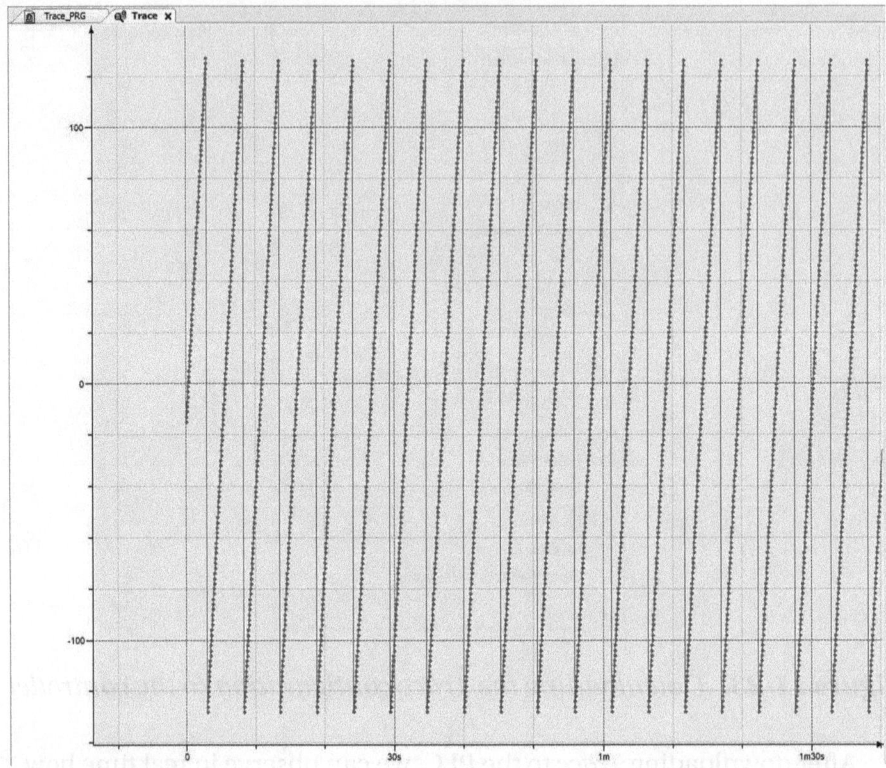

Figure 11-24. *Viewing the ProcessValue variable on the Trace graph in real time*

Trigger Trace

It often happens that during the operation of an installation or machine, an issue arises that we want to analyze by checking the values of specific process variables at the moment it occurs. In such cases, we can configure a *Trigger*, which will automatically stop *Trace* recording when a specified event happens.

Before adding a *Trigger* in the *Trace* configuration window, we will expand our *Trace_PRG* program with a simple code that generates a pulse

538

every minute. This will allow us to demonstrate how a *CFC* program looks when all function blocks are placed on a single plane.

To achieve this, we will add a *TON* timer to the program, which will generate a pulse at one-minute intervals (Figure 11-25).

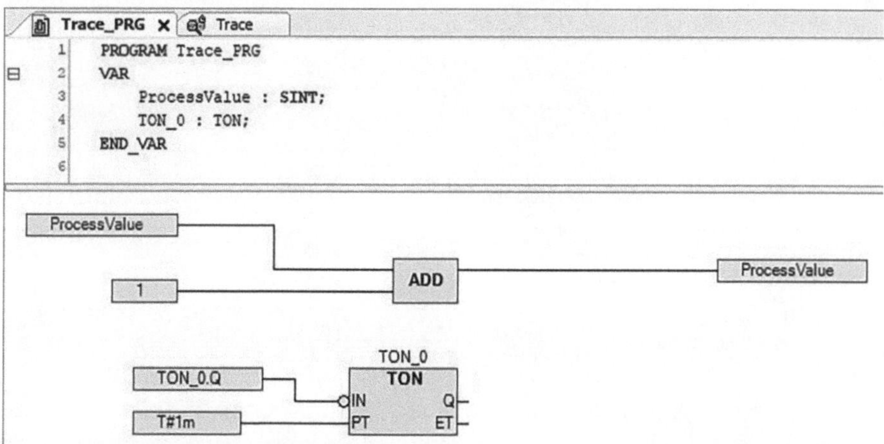

Figure 11-25. *Extending the Trace_PRG program with a TON timer generating a pulse every minute*

Next, we will use the moment when the Q output of the *TON_0* timer is set to a high state and use it as a *Trigger* in our *Trace* tool.

To activate the *Trigger*, in the *Trace Configuration* window, check the *Enable Trigger* check box, and then assign a variable to the *Trigger variable*. In our case, this will be the Q output of the *TON_0* timer implemented in the *Trace_PRG* program.

Additionally, we can specify

- *Trigger edge*: The signal edge that will activate the *Trigger*

- *Post trigger*: The number of samples we want to record after activation

Let's leave these options at their default values and test the newly configured *Trace* (Figure 11-26).

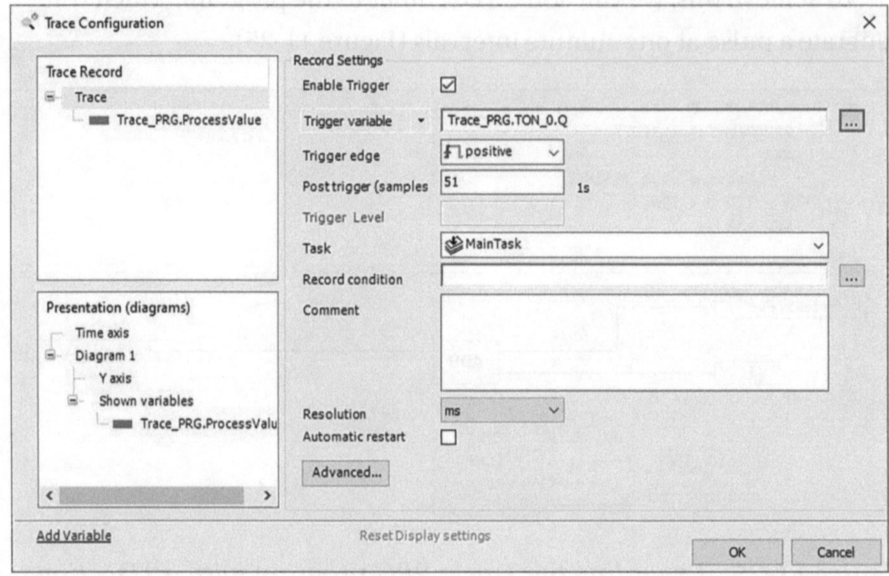

***Figure 11-26.** Configuring the Trigger in the Trace tool*

Remember that after each update to the *Trace* configuration, we must reload it to the controller along with the applied changes.

At the moment when the *Q* output of the *TON_0* timer is set to high, a black vertical line will appear on the *Trace* object, indicating that the *Trigger* has been activated. From that moment on, an additional 51 samples of the process variable will be recorded, according to our *Trace* configuration (Figure 11-27).

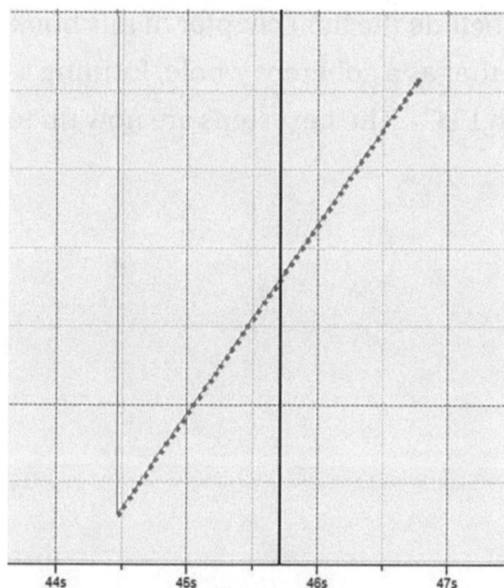

Figure 11-27. *Activating the Trigger and recording process variable samples upon event detection*

Trace is an extremely useful diagnostic tool that allows for real-time analysis of process variables without the need to stop the controller. Thanks to the ability to configure triggers and flexibly adjust parameters, it simplifies the detection and analysis of issues in control processes.

Moreover, similar functionalities can also be found in systems from other manufacturers, such as SIEMENS, making it a standard solution in industrial automation.

Summary

We are reaching the end of our journey through the world of PLC programming. In this chapter, we explored tools and methods that assist in error diagnosis, creating custom libraries, and real-time process monitoring. Each of these topics is a crucial aspect of working with automation systems, and mastering them allows for more efficient design and implementation of control applications.

With this, we conclude the final chapter of this book. All the discussed concepts come together as a coherent whole, forming a solid foundation for further work with PLCs. The next steps are now up to you – the world of automation awaits!

Epilogue

We have reached the end of our journey into PLC programming.

Have you become an expert in this field after reading this book? Of course not. But before we can run, we must first learn to walk, and before we can walk, we must always take that first step. I hope this book has been that first step for you – a solid foundation for further exploration of industrial automation.

You may be someone standing at a crossroads, considering a career in automation. Or perhaps you have an idea for an invention that could change the world and need the knowledge to create a working prototype. Regardless of your motivation, one thing is certain – today, almost every machine and every production line requires intelligent control. PLCs are the heart of these systems, and understanding them opens the door to vast opportunities.

Industrial automation is undergoing rapid transformation. The Fourth Industrial Revolution, the rise of artificial intelligence, the integration of IT and OT systems, the Internet of Things (IoT), and the growing importance of cybersecurity in industrial environments are just some of the factors shaping the future of this field. Technologies that enable data processing directly at the control device level (edge computing), new communication standards, and the increasing integration of PLCs with industrial robots and data analysis systems are playing an ever-growing role. The industry is also placing greater emphasis on energy efficiency and process optimization. All these changes mean that automation is constantly evolving, requiring continuous learning and adaptation to new realities.

© Dariusz Wrebiak 2026

D. Wrebiak, *Practical PLC Programming for Beginners*, Maker Innovations Series,

https://doi.org/10.1007/979-8-8688-2430-2

Writing this book was not only an opportunity to summarize my years of experience in PLC programming but also a great pleasure, as it allowed me to revisit the early days of my career. I wanted to create something that I would have enjoyed reading at the start of my professional journey – a guide to help you take your first steps in the world of automation. I hope I have managed to present the knowledge in an accessible and inspiring way. If this book has encouraged you to continue learning, experimenting, and developing your passion, then I have achieved my goal.

Now, it's all up to you. Automation is a field full of challenges and endless possibilities. You now have a solid foundation – it's time to take the next step.

Good luck!

Index

A

ADC, *see* Analog-to-digital
converter (ADC)

Advanced Planning and
Scheduling (APS), 85

Alarms
acknowledging alarms,
359–361, 363
classes, 345–348
configuration, 343–345
groups, 349–351
limits, 363–367
table, 355, 356
TOF, 357
trend controlling, 367, 368
triggers, 351–354
usage, 341, 342
visualization system, 358

American Petroleum Institute
(API), 158

Analog-to-digital converter (ADC),
256, 263

API, *see* American Petroleum
Institute (API)

APS, *see* Advanced Planning and
Scheduling (APS)

Automation pyramid
control level, 59–62, 64, 65, 67,
72, 73, 75, 76
field level, 59–62, 64, 65, 67,
72, 75, 76
HMI, 76, 77, 79
management level, 59, 87, 89
planning level, 59, 85–87
SCADA, 79–85
supervisory level, 89

Automation Studio, 41

B

Bang-Bang controller
function *vs.* function
block, 292–294
function block, 286, 287,
289–292, 311
implementation, 282, 284, 285
operation principle, 278–282
task execution, 310
visualization, 295,
297–304, 306–309

C

CFC, *see* Continuous Function
Chart (CFC)

D. Wrebiak, *Practical PLC Programming for Beginners*, Maker Innovations Series,
https://doi.org/10.1007/979-8-8688-2430-2

D, E